Annual Review of
BEHAVIOR THERAPY
THEORY AND PRACTICE
1977

ANNUAL REVIEW OF
BEHAVIOR THERAPY THEORY & PRACTICE
1977

Edited with Commentaries by

CYRIL M. FRANKS, Ph.D.
Professor, Graduate School of Applied and Professional Psychology, Rutgers University (New Brunswick)

and

G. TERENCE WILSON, Ph.D.
Professor, Graduate School of Applied and Professional Psychology, Rutgers University (New Brunswick)

BRUNNER/MAZEL, *Publishers* • New York

Published by
BRUNNER/MAZEL, Inc.
19 Union Square, New York, N. Y. 10003

Library of Congress Catalog Card No. 76-126864
SBN 87630-156-1

MANUFACTURED IN THE UNITED STATES OF AMERICA

It could be argued that the essence of the scientific approach is not the validity and precision of the procedures that are used; these are the results *of the application of scientific method. The essence lies elsewhere: in the ability to differentiate between interpretation and observation, in the practice of Claude Bernard's "philosophical doubt," in the ability to harness all that is known in a particular science to the solution of a particular problem, in the willingness to admit ignorance and to insist that a particular procedure is not well enough validated to go into general use.*

M. B. Shapiro

PREFACE

This year's Annual Review contains more pages of commentary and fewer reprinted articles—a trade-off that offers certain advantages with respect to the scope of the series. The first section, an overview of behavior therapy, consists entirely of Commentary. While many pertinent and even significant articles appeared during 1976, we felt that none merited reprinting in full. As is our custom, the articles we do reprint encompass the calendar year 1976, with the commentaries extending to the following mid-summer, that is, to the middle of 1977.

In last year's Preface, we designated 1975 as the Year of the Paradigm for the theoretician, and the Year of Assertion for the practitioner. 1976 could well be designated the Year of Cognition for both theoretician and practitioner. Like the activities of Superman and the Scarlet Pimpernel, cognition is in the air, it is here, there and everywhere. Newly established cognitive therapy journals, organizations, conferences and newsletters abound. Cognitive techniques and do-it-yourself cognitive change manuals are sprouting like mushrooms in the forest. To some, this flurry of activity portends a conceptual renaissance, a paradigm shift leading to a new era. Less happily, others view this "cognitive connection" as a regressive passage back to some form of mentalistic psychotherapy, heralding not a glorious new era but the demise of behavior therapy. Yet others—and we fall into this category—welcome the incorporation of cognition into the behavior therapy structure as long as it is predicated upon operational definition and firmly anchored to performance and data. We address ourselves to such issues throughout the present volume, and particularly in the first section.

Twenty years ago, Professor Joseph Wolpe completed his landmark text, *Psychotherapy by Reciprocal Inhibition,* at the Center for Advanced Study in the Behavioral Sciences, Stanford, California. The publication of the present volume, the fifth in a series devoted exclusively to an annual review of developments in behavior therapy, bears testimony to the remarkable growth of the field in a relatively short span. It is thus with considerable satisfaction that we report what should be evident to all—that behavior therapy, with its imperfections and problems, is alive and well and living in the real world.

We are grateful to the numerous authors, editors and publishers involved for permission to make these articles available here. We are indebted to Prentice-Hall and the authors concerned for permission to reproduce the table which appears on page 425 of this volume. It originally appeared in Seligman, Klein and Miller's chapter on Depression in Leitenberg's *Handbook of Behavior Modification and Behavior Therapy*.

We acknowledge our gratitude to the Center for Advanced Study in the Behavioral Sciences where one of us (GTW) was a Fellow during the 1976-77 academic year. This Fellowship was made possible by the financial support of the Foundations Fund for Research in Psychiatry, the National Institute of Mental Health, and Rutgers University. The kindness and comaraderie of the Center staff and its director, Dr. Gardner Lindzey, contributed in no small measure to making the Center an idyllic intellectual and social environment. Special thanks are due to Margaret Amara and Christine Hoth for their library assistance, to Carol Treanor for computer services and to Kay Jenks for her secretarial skills and general support throughout the year. Numerous discussions with members of the "behavior therapy group" at the Center (Stewart Agras, Nate Azrin, Alex George, Alan Kazdin, Walter Mischel and Jack Rachman), and Albert Bandura at Stanford, contributed both directly and indirectly to this volume. The unique contributions of other Center Fellows, not the least of which was that of Henry Bienen, cannot pass unnoticed.

We express appreciation to our colleagues at the Graduate School of Applied and Professional Psychology of Rutgers University and the Carrier Clinic, in particular Drs. Peter Nathan, Arnold Lazarus, Violet Franks, Ralph Tarter and Arthur Sugerman, for the many stimulating discussions which likewise contibuted to the making of this volume. But, of course, the final responsibility for its contents, including any errors or other deficits, remains ours and ours alone. As always, we invite our readers to draw our attention both to any such limitations and to new articles of significance for future consideration. Last year, we inadvertently failed to acknowledge the creative contribution of Steven Weitz to the preparation of one of our Commentaries.

Sometimes inspiration and factual information are found in the strangest places. For example, while sitting in a Nairobi cafe and writing the rough draft of part of the Commentaries, one of us (CMF) had a chance meeting with Dr. Paul Bronstein, who turned out to be a fellow psychologist living the proverbial stone's throw from us in the United States! This encounter led to the introduction of a new word into our vocabulary, and hence into this volume, to describe a concept with which we were long familiar but quite unable to label (thereomorphism: the attribution of infrahuman, animal characteristics to man).

We (the Editorial "we"—in this case CMF) are also indebted to Peter and Nicola Wallace for the good natured manner in which they permitted their small London flat to serve not only as hotel, but also as general office and summer study center during the preparation of this volume. Finally, we thank Hanna Fox for her graciously extended editorial acumen, and Karen Peterson of Rutgers University and Daryl Gross of the Carrier Clinic for secretarial assistance at short notice.

Cyril M. Franks
G. Terence Wilson

Graduate School of Applied and Professional Psychology
Rutgers University
September 1977

CONTENTS

Annual Review of

BEHAVIOR THERAPY THEORY AND PRACTICE 1977

Section 1

BEHAVIOR THERAPY: AN OVERVIEW

Commentary

In this Section of last year's Annual Review we focused on the nature of the conditioning process, the changing concept of reinforcement, the emergence of "cognitivism" and certain legal and ethical developments. This year we are reprinting no paper in these areas. Instead, we will use the space to review pertinent key articles which we feel warrant comment. We will also focus upon certain criticisms of behavior therapy from within and from without.

THE NATURE OF BEHAVIOR THERAPY

This year has seen a provocative paper by Biglan and Kass (1977) on "the empirical nature of behavior therapies" (note the use of the plural form—a point to which we will return shortly). In essence, they take issue with two kinds of behavior therapists: those who reject the study of private events entirely, and those whose attempts to incorporate such events pivot upon ambiguous concepts and mentalistic explanations. It is their contention that any psychological problem can be construed in terms of specific organismic events, the independent variables which effect these events and the empirical evidence that these variables actually do effect the behavior in question. Both the "beyondism" of Lazarus and, to a much lesser extent, the arguments of such writers as Bandura (1974) —reprinted and discussed in last year's Annual Review—and Mahoney (1974) that many behaviorists place too much emphasis on behavioral and environmental variables to the neglect of "cognition" are indicted. Biglan and Kass suggest that these developments represent a drift towards earlier, less effective conceptual practices.

A closely related issue raised by Biglan and Kass is that of the proposed rapprochement between behavior therapy and other therapeutic approaches. This is a popular road which has been travelled by many (e.g., London, 1972; Feather & Rhoads, 1973; Rhoads & Feather, 1974; and, now, Wachtel, 1977). Wachtel presents by far the most comprehensive, but still fundamentally unconvincing, argument that we have seen in support of the position that the psychodynamic and behavioral approaches are essentially compatible and that integration would be mutually advantageous. Correctly, he points out that most contemporary behavior therapists view neither man nor psychology in terms of passive reactions to environmental events. Most behavior therapists reject the sterile implication that all stimuli can best be understood as physical quanta of energy impinging upon receptors, regardless of motives, feelings and cognitions. But the leap from this reasonable statement to his justification for philosophical and technical integration is totally unacceptable.

The call for rapprochement has many sounds. Garfield and Kurtz (1976) suggest that contemporary clinical psychology is becoming increasingly eclectic (a trend analyzed as long ago as 1974 in the Annual Review by Mahoney, Kazdin and Lesswing), and many psychiatrists would probably resonate sympathetically to this point of view within their own discipline. The call for rapprochement of the American Psychiatric Task Force on Behavior Therapy (1973) has not gone unheeded. For example, Chandra (1976), offers the curious argument that, since both Freud and Skinner performed *functional* analyses of behavior, it should be possible to compare the two models if—and this is an "if" which would almost certainly be unacceptable to most psychoanalysts—the superfluous notion of the intrapsychic in Freud's account were ignored!

Of more interest are the attempts to reconstitute the hoary old issue of "symptom substitution." Gale and Carlsson (1976) draw attention to the fact that, if only the exploration of all pertinent parameters is thorough enough, the so-called examples of symptom substitution can much more usefully be conceptualized in terms of environmental changes rather than failure to treat an underlying pathology. Blanchard and Hersen (1976) adopt a somewhat different tack in their attempt to resolve the apparent contradiction between those who say that symptom substitution does occur and those who say that it does not. The argument is made, with case illustration, that symptom substitution and/or symptom return will frequently occur when a mere symptomatic treatment approach is applied to certain hysterical neuroses. For the effective treatment of such neuroses, they recommend a three-pronged behavioral intervention program: an extinction period during hospitalization to decrease the symptoms; programming the natural environment so that positive behaviors are reinforced and presenting symptoms ignored; teaching new methods of obtaining attention from the environment by way of appropriate social skill training. The maintaining conditions for hysteric behavior are the social reinforcers received contingent upon evidencing particular symptoms. Thus, the so-called symptoms function as sources of secondary gain and such patients experience little subjective discomfort or stress. By contrast, the dysthymic type of neurotic (phobic, obsessive-compulsive, anxiety state and certain depressives) feels generally uncomfortable and engages in neurotic behavior to help alleviate or avoid such situations. Thus, whether "symptoms" return or not depends very much on the type of disorder and the way it is treated.

Wolpe (1976a) takes us to task for our 1974 Annual Review comment that behavior therapy is a fuzzy entity whose definition is a matter of debate. According to Wolpe, a man-made construct like "behavior therapy" means whatever it has been laid down to mean and it is senseless to investigate its properties. It is Wolpe who stipulates what behavior therapy is, and any deviation is the work of a malcontent—a point to which we shall return shortly. For Wolpe, there is a clear-cut label already in use for his concept of behavior therapy and those who wish to investigate psychotherapy in a different fashion should use a different name.

If Wolpe takes strong and unswerving issue with anyone who does not accept his clear-cut formulation of behavior therapy, London (1972) assails behavior therapy from the quite different stance that it is a "myth" that behavior therapy arose out of principles of learning in the first place. Apart from the devastating critique of London's position by Dunlap and Lieberman (1973), we have taken up London's challenge on a variety of occasions in previous Annual Reviews, and we will doubtless have occasion to refer to it again.

Krasner (1976) mourns the death of behavior modification and, since we use this term synonymously with behavior therapy, one may raise a question whether the term "behavior therapy" is dead too. Biglan and Kass, it will be recalled, revert to the earlier term "behavior therapies." Originally conceived as the *Association for the Advancement of the Behavior Therapies,* in 1966 the name was changed to the *Association for Advancement of Behavior Therapy* (a reflection of Eysenck's position that, though there are many behavioral techniques, they are all derived from a common core of learning principles if not learning theory; see

Franks, 1969 for further discussion of this thesis). Many more or less related terms have arisen since those early days: behavioral engineering; behavioral shaping, behavioral programming; contingency management; broad-spectrum behavior therapy; cognitive behavior therapy; multimodal behavior therapy; clinical behavior therapy; comprehensive behavior therapy. And the integrationists have come up with such horrendous hybrids as psychobehavioral therapy and psychodynamic behavior therapy. The observation noted almost a decade ago that there is both diversity and complexity of meaning to the phrase "behavior therapist" and to the concept of behavior therapy is perhaps even more appropriate now than when it was first written (Franks, 1969). There is no official behavior therapy and no one has exclusive rights to the term. And while the many suggested alternative names have their respective merits, as far as brand names go, behavior therapy has much to recommend it (Wilson, in press d).

THE EFFICACY OF BEHAVIOR THERAPY

In 1952, Eysenck questioned the efficacy of psychotherapy. The many allegations to the contrary not withstanding, he did not say that psychotherapy is not effective; he did say that there is no evidence that psychotherapy is effective. Despite a quarter of a century of debate and accumulating data, the issue is still alive and very much with us. But it is not the purpose of the present discussion to focus upon the question of whether psychotherapy is superior to no therapy. Comprehensive reviews yielding conflicting interpretations depending on the theoretical positions adopted are readily available in the literature (e.g. Bergin, 1971; Rachman, 1971). Our concern here is with the treatment outcome problem as it pertains to a comparison of behavior therapy with other forms of psychotherapy. Among the more important recent reviews of the treatment outcome literature are the following: Luborsky, Singer & Luborsky, 1975; Sloane, Staples, Cristol, Yorkston & Whipple, 1975; Glass & Smith, 1976; Chesser, 1976; Marks, 1976b; Shapiro, 1976a.

Before discussing these surveys in some detail, it is well to point out a noticeable social change that has taken place during the past few years. We are living in an era where more is expected out of life than the absence of malfunction. It is no longer sufficient for sexual relationships not to be actually unpleasant or for physical performance not to be inadequate (see Franks & Wilson, 1976). Similarly, it is no longer sufficient to stay out of a psychiatric facility. Successful therapy must bring with it positive feelings of joy, well-being and joie de vivre, just as successful sex therapy must bring with it a positive delight in sexual intimacies at every level.

According to Strupp (1973), most outcome research to that date had involved unknown therapists with little experience, primarily because they were the ones most available to the researcher. Studies such as that of Becker and Rosenfeld (1976), which make a direct analysis of some leading therapist (in this instance, Albert Ellis) are unfortunately rare. However, psychotherapy being what a therapist does and not necessarily what he says he does, it is important to observe the activities of leaders in the field during their sessions. There may well be a tendency for all therapists to function at times in ways that are broader than those described in their publications (cf. Goldfried & Davison, 1976). This consideration may well be one of the limiting factors in the outcome studies that we are about to discuss. Equally important is the bias of the reviewer. It is possible to confirm any preconceived notion if one is sufficiently selective, deliberately or otherwise, in the selection of data from the vast pool of accumulated information. For example, Burton (1976) has recently edited a book dedicated to the search for *What Makes Behavior Change Possible?* Although, as Burton points out, everyone subscribes to the idea of behavior change, we do not all subscribe to the same information service. Thus, Burton begins his intended objective presentation of 16 position papers by eminent leaders in the field—ranging from Joseph Wolpe to Jerome Frank—with the fiat that "psychoanalysis is the beginning and end of all current healing theories"!

It is with such caveats in mind that we approach current surveys of the efficacy of behavior therapy. As one might expect, the staid *British Medical Journal* adopts a cautiously favorable position, the title of its modestly anonymous leading article characterizing its point of view: "Behaviourism: A framework for common sense therapy" (Oct. 2, 1976). The unknown writer points out that the practice of behavior therapy is supported by an enormous amount of "subtle theorizing and ingenious research" and that it has led to a variety of viable therapeutic strategies.

However, even in this favorable climate, there is one observation that is particularly unfortunate, namely that when behavior therapists require treatment for themselves, they turn to non-behavioral therapists. This very damaging statement is based on a misleading paper by Lazarus (1971b) reporting the self-referral practices of 23 so-called "behavior therapists." Since his sample was extremely small and since, in any event, he supplied no information whatsoever about the individual behavior therapists who consulted other therapists, it is not possible to draw any meaningful conclusion from his study. In a much better study by Foa (1976) it was found that, unlike eclectic users of behavior therapy, some 90% of those who actually practice behavior therapy exclusively use behavior therapy for themselves. Thus, the general contention that, regardless of ilk, clinicians evaluate their own orientations as superior to others and prefer to be treated by methods used in their own practices is borne out by Foa's study.

However, the patient's point of view seems to be somewhat different. A very recent survey by Sloane, Staples, Whipple and Criston (1977) of 50 patients treated either by behavior therapy or short-term analytically-oriented psychotherapy shows that both patient groups place a high value on insight, the patient-therapist relationship, and trust. Many of the factors that patients consider important, regardless of treatment label, are nonspecific, such as "helping you to understand your problems" (the item most frequently endorsed by both groups). While the type of explanatory model provided by each type of therapy and the kinds of insight achieved are different, both serve the same therapeutic purpose in the eyes of the patient. It is important that behavior therapists stress these "nonspecific" factors—which, given sufficient attention to a behavioral analysis, can be specified (see Wilson & Evans, 1976).

Writing in the *British Journal of Psychiatry,* Chesser (1976) reaffirms the fact that there is no agreed definition of behavior therapy nor even agreement with respect to its name. Recognizing the many faces of behavior therapy, he is willing to include under its rubric those who are strictly Skinnerian, those who accept a dimensional view of personality, those who focus entirely upon the environment, those who stress neurophysiological foundations, those who emphasize cognition and those who give it a minimal role. In his own words, the behavioral approach is "wide based, grounded in experimental psychology principles, ready to take cognizance of organismic variables, individual differences, organic pathology, the developmental history of the patient, the factors initiating and maintaining undesirable behaviour, the existing behavioural repertoire of the patient (potential assets) and the social environment of the patient" (p. 292). His considered conclusion with respect to efficacy is that comparative control group studies "have not shown behavioural treatment to be inferior" and that "behaviour therapy now has a well-established place in psychiatric practice . . . and that it seems unlikely that it will not have a lasting influence." The evidence cited to substantiate these statements cannot be readily dismissed.

Writing in the *American Journal of Psychiatry,* Marks (1976b) concludes that behavior therapy is a vigorous, growing part of psychiatric treatment which is best regarded as the treatment of choice for perhaps 10% of all adult psychiatric patients. According to Marks, some 90% of all adult cases require other approaches as the main form of treatment. He rightly points out that behavior therapy is of little value in the treatment of acute schizophrenia, severe depression and hypomania. What he does not go on to say is that no form of psychotherapy is of much value under such circumstances. In similar fashion, he notes that much of the evidence for behavior therapy falls short of the ideal, but he neglects to point out that, by the same token, the evidence against behavior therapy also falls into this category.

Marks makes his position quite explicit: "Like psychopharmacology, it is a therapeutic technology that can aid in general clinical management and has its indications and contraindications." Behavior therapy is not useful with adult neurotic patients for whom clearly definable goals cannot be worked out. But, as Wolpe (1977b) points out, clearly definable goals can always be worked out when an adequate behavior analysis is carried out.

In a well-known Japanese film (*Rashomon*), we are shown how the same events are seen by different observers and the discrepancies are extraordinarily wide. In 1973, a Task Force of the American Psychiatric Association issued a report on behavior therapy and psychiatry. When reviewing this report (Franks & Bien, 1974) we were encouraged by what we thought to be an essentially fair, albeit favorable, evaluation. It was our impression that this book would do much to allay the fears of the psychiatric profession and to correct the misinformation that abounds. How wrong we were, if the diatribe of Shapiro (1976a) is any indication. Fortunately, we believe that it is not. Shapiro begins his attack with a clear statement: If the theory is correct, either psychiatrists will have to spend considerable time and energy in mastering the theory and practice of behavior therapy, or this therapy will increasingly be conducted by psychologists! He adumbrates nine points of criticism, to which we shall return shortly, and then arrives at the following conclusions: "The therapeutic claims for behavior therapy are excessive and have outdistanced the controlled clinical evidence. Behavioral procedures are being used in an indisciplined way, too extensively and by inadequately trained clinicians. In this sense, behavior therapy may be the latest fad" (p. 158).

In his restrained rebuttal of Shapiro's intemperate article, Brady

(1976) suggests that it fails to deal adequately with any of the issues and that it will not add to the reader's understanding. He illustrates this with but one example. Shapiro's third point takes issue with the Task Force's conclusion that behavior therapy is applicable to both psychological and organic illnesses, pointing out that behavior therapy techniques have been used to treat patients with Gilles de la Tourette's syndrome who probably would have been better treated with haloperidol. As Brady points out, this may well be true, but patients with this symptom are also sometimes treated by psychoanalytic psychotherapy and a variety of inappropriate drugs. This is no basis for Shapiro's sweeping statement that behavior therapy is not applicable to patients with organic illness ("adherence to it may be harmful and occasionally is lethal and it is often pragmatically irrelevant"). Brady then goes on to cite evidence to the contrary, including some of the by now traditional behavioral treatments for such disorders as bronchial asthma and migraine headache, and the whole area of biofeedback literature. As Brady concludes, Shapiro's statements are "far more oversimplified and polemical than anything in the Task Force report"—to which Shapiro's (1976b) reply, in part, is that, even if effective, the application of behavior therapy in managing and improving the functioning of mentally retarded, schizophrenic and other patients may well not be classifiable as clinical therapies at all!

Shapiro draws an analogy with the harmful effects of over-elaborate theoretical formulations in medicine which have, in the past, led to erroneous theory and to treatment by charletons being more "correct" than that of physicians. He also draws attention to the facts that placebo effects occur less frequently in laboratory experiments than in clinical situations, that generalization from laboratory data is hazardous and that convincing demonstrations of the success of applied behavior modification in the natural environment are limited. With all of this we concur, and it is the very readiness of behavior therapy researchers to recognize these limitations that contributes to the strength of behavior therapy as a methodological approach. Ultimately, it is the rigor of behavior therapy as a methodology that will contribute to its viability rather than any specific therapeutic success, no matter how spectacular. What Shapiro fails to recognize is that, while the selection of a particular technique may best be engendered within a particular theoretical model or arising out of some laboratory experiment, the validation of that technique in terms of direct, controlled clinical evidence is a sine qua non of good behavior therapy research.

Shapiro's second point is that clinical behavior therapy is based primarily on unverified supposition, that supporting data such as reliability and validity are generally absent. Anyone who has been a consistent reader of these Annual Reviews or the behavior therapy literature over the past decade would know that this is not so. While the deficits of behavior therapy case studies and clinical research are major, these are readily acknowledged by investigators in the field who strive, in the tradition of behavior therapy, to bring about necessary improvements in subsequent investigations. And his claim that such deficits are as marked for behavior therapy investigations as they are for those couched in psychodynamic formulations would seem too questionable to warrant refutation here.

Shapiro himself, it should be noted, is not above involving his own favorite explanatory concept, the placebo effect, to account across the board for any successes that might occur in behavior therapy. But it is his fifth point that is most extraordinary: The claim of the Task Report that evaluation of utcome is more common in behavior therapy than any other kind of psychotherapy is "without substance, since most clinicians claim that they continually evaluate outcome, reformulate hypotheses and reevaluate outcome." We can think of few individuals of substance, other than Shapiro, who believe that behavioral scientists are not more prone to rigorous outcome evaluation than psychodynamically oriented clinical investigators. His contention that the efficacy of the $N = 1$ design has been shown primarily in a few selected studies of changes in ward milieu and social behavior of psychotic patients is patently false, as referral to past issues of this Annual Review series will indicate (see also Hersen & Barlow, 1976).

One could go on at length to take point by point issue with Shapiro, but it would be merely repetitious. As further evidence of Shapiro's profound misunderstanding of what behavior therapy is all about, we note his reference to the famed medical historian, Garrison, who observed that "whenever many different remedies are proposed for a disease, it usually means that we know very little about the disease, which is also true of a . . . (remedy) when it is vaunted as a panacea or cure-all for many diseases." Behavior therapy can in no way be regarded as a remedy for anything. It is an approach, a methodology and little more. The methodology is not exclusive to behavior therapy and is indeed that which any good behavioral scientist would apply in investigating social phenomena. Unfortunately, it is an all too common mistake among the uninformed and the misinformed alike to conclude that behavior therapy is a series of specific techniques which are claimed to cure a vast array of disorders.

We do not, of course, belittle the importance of outcome studies or the need to demonstrate the validity of specific techniques for specific disorders. Kazdin and Wilson (in press) review in detail the available evidence with respect to these matters and it will suffice here to note briefly their general conclusions and offer a few examples by way of illustration.

As far as disorders involving institutionalized psychotic patients are concerned, a relatively large number of comparative studies have been conducted. In general, these studies are of two kinds: comparisons of a behavior therapy technique with a specific alternative or comparisons of reinforcement programs with routine ward care. Both indicate consistent patterns. Reinforcement programs lead to improvements on measures of cognitive, affective and social aspects of psychotic behavior, in specific interview and ward behavior, and also on global measures of adjustment or discharge from the hospital. Patient improvements in most of these areas are far greater for reinforcement than routine ward care. While studies comparing reinforcement programs with another single technique are few, once again the general conclusion seems to be that reinforcement techniques are more effective than a comparative treatment.

As far as childhood disorders are concerned, the bell and pad method for the treatment of psychogenic enuresis seems to be consistently more effective than supportive or psychodynamically-oriented verbal psychotherapy, medication or fluid intake control. When reinforcement and drug treatments for children and mentally retarded adults are compared, reinforcement of adaptive behaviors tends to be more effective in suppressing conduct problem behaviors and in developing specific adaptive behaviors than alternative drug treatments (a notable exception is reported by Gittelman-Klein, Klein, Abikoff, Katz, Gloisten & Kates, 1976).

Recent evidence across a variety of diverse areas is likewise cautiously encouraging. For example, Rush, Beck, Kovacs and Hollon (1977) report that cognitive behavior therapy results in significantly greater reductions in depression and patient attrition rates than do other forms of treatment. Taylor, Farquhar, Nelson and Agras (1977) provide a well-controlled demonstration of the efficacy of relaxation as an adjunct to medical treatment in the management of hypertension. Finally, Ritchie (1976) found that a token reinforcement program produced a marginal increase in activity level in chronic pain patients in comparison to a control group following a routine hospital activity management schedule (see Section X).

In not a single comparison among the studies reviewed by Kazdin and Wilson was behavior therapy found to be significantly inferior to the alternative treatment (usually some form of verbal psychotherapy). In most studies, behavior therapy was even marginally or significantly more effective than the alternative.

This is no trivial pronouncement. During the late 1950s and early 1960s, behavior therapy was widely rejected as ineffective at best, dangerous at worst. Attention has now shifted to how effective behavior therapy is and when it should be applied rather than whether it should ever be employed. This is considerably at variance with the extraordinary conclusions of Shapiro. Furthermore, Shapiro notwithstanding, there is no evidence to suggest that behavior therapy is any less broadly applicable to complex disorders than psychotherapy. There is also no evidence that behavior therapy produces fewer changes in either specific target behaviors or more general measures of adjustment than psychotherapy, a claim offered by the critics of behavior therapy. Behavior therapy cannot be viewed as a limited and relatively superficial form of treatment to be used as an occasional adjunct to traditional psychotherapy (see Kazdin & Wilson, in press).

THE MALCONTENTS

Modern behavior therapy, as we view this term, is susceptible to criticism from within as well as without. For Wolpe, no debate about the nature or definition of behavior therapy is possible. This is expressed most clearly and typically, for example, in the title of his contribution to Burton's (1976) series of discourses on what makes behavior change possible. The title of Wolpe's (1976c) chapter is boldly stated as "Conditioning is the Basis of All Psychotherapeutic Change." Wolpe makes it quite explicit that, even though "conditioning" and "learning" are used synonymously in behavioral parlance, he prefers conditioning because it refers "quite precisely to the establishment or disestablishment of stimulus-response relationships." (See Franks & Wilson, 1976, Commentary to Section I for a detailed discussion of this and related issues; see also Kantor, 1976, who makes it clear that "behaviorism" and "conditioning" are complex and not necessarily synonymous terms—a position with which we concur.)

Be the above as it may, Wolpe's discussion of "behavior therapy and its malcontents" (Wolpe, 1976a, 1976b) is significant. Wolpe defines a malcontent as one who does not fully understand the basic premises of the field, yet takes up the cudgels against them. Malcontents, says Wolpe, do not understand what they are talking about—at least not entirely. Their dominant theme is that experimentally established principles of learning are not very often relevant to the treatment of neuroses. There are five classes of malcontentedness: 1) denial of experimental bases; 2) psychodynamic fusionism; 3) multi-modal ecclecticism; 4) cognitive exclusivism; and 5 one-way empiricism. The prime example of his first category is Perry London (1972), with his assertion that it is a myth that the practices of behavior therapy are based on principles of learning. We concur with Wolpe that London is wrong, that he has misread the data and that he has misconstrued the conceptual relationships between theory construction and scientific investigation. We are also in total agreement with Wolpe's rejection of what he terms "psychodynamic fusionism." Apart from problems of conceptual consistency, there is no evidence that adding psychoanalytic procedures to behavior therapy produces any demonstrable increment of therapeutic benefit.

The multimodal eclecticism of A. A. Lazarus, Wolpe's third target, has evolved sequentially through various overlapping stages: technical eclecticism, personalistic psychotherapy; broad spectrum behavior therapy, and now multimodal behavior therapy. We have commented in some detail upon these developments in preceding Annual Reviews and we also take up this matter in Section X this year. Let it suffice here, therefore, to reaffirm our unswerving commitment to a behavior therapy firmly anchored to a data based, outcome oriented, social learning theory, linked closely to the methodology of the behavioral scientist. It is by these standards, in our opinion, that all current and new developments in this area must be judged. It may well be that, by these criteria, multimodal behavior therapy is not behavior therapy at all and that, regardless of its merits and demerits, it should not be evaluated as such.

Wolpe's fourth malcontent, the "cognitive exclusivist," is personified by Albert Ellis ("neurosis is really a matter of wrong thinking"). In rebutting those who see behavior therapy as based entirely on cognitive change, particular issue is taken with Meichenbaum's (1975) conclusion that appropriate verbalizations can produce significant beneficial changes even if the individual concerned realizes that his fear is irrational. Change in an autonomic response habit, contends Meichenbaum, occurs entirely as a function of cognitive change, and without involvement of the autonomic system. But for Wolpe, cognitive events can change autonomic habits only if they have autonomic effects, and cognitive behavior is a subclass of behavior which unquestionably obeys the same rules of conditioning, no matter how complex or subtle the context may be. Cognitive therapy is thus a subclass of behavior therapy—a point to which we shall return shortly. Wolpe's final candidate for his "malcontentineering" campaign is Marks, whom Wolpe not unreasonably describes as a fellow traveller of Perry London's. This matter has already been discussed.

THE COGNITIVE CONNECTION

Cognitive behavior therapy, for want of a better term, encompasses Ellis' rational-emotive therapy, Meichenbaum's cognitive behavior modification (1977), Beck's (1976) cognitive therapy, covert modeling (Kazdin, 1974a), modified systematic desensitization (Goldfried, 1971), anxiety management training (Suinn & Richardson, 1971), stress innoculation (Meichenbaum, 1977) and a variety of therapeutic problem solving procedures (e.g. D'Zurilla & Goldfried, 1971; Mahoney, 1977b; Spivack, Platt & Shure, 1976).

According to Mahoney and Arnkoff (in press) all forms of cognitive behavior therapy share the following three components:

a) That humans develop adaptive and maladaptive behavior and affective patterns via cognitive processes (e.g., selective attention, symbolic coding).
b) These cognitive *processes* are functionally activated by *procedures* which are generally isomorphic to those of the human learning laboratory.
c) The resultant task of the therapist is that of a diagnostician-educator who assesses maladaptive cognitive processes and subsequently arranges learning experiences which will alter cognitions and, in turn, the behavior affect patterns with which they correlate.

Cognitive therapy is neither passive fad nor indicative of a paradigm shift, and it is to be viewed neither as an independent third force nor as a putative link between the behavioral and psychodynamic enclaves. Firmly (for the most part) rooted in experimental psychology (see this Section in last year's Annual Review), we do know that cognitions exert causal influences on behavior (Mahoney, 1974) and that behavior is more a function of its environmental consequences for anticipated than for actual consequences (Bandura, 1977b). And Moore, Mischel, and Zeiss (1976) show convincingly that the manner in which children cognitively represent rewards is a significantly more potent determinant of self-control than the actual reward stimulus to which the child is physically exposed. Nevertheless, there is really no more reason for uncritically accepting cognitive behavior therapy today than there was for rejecting or ignoring it in the late 1960s (see Wilson, in press c). Even such stalwart enthusiasts as Ellis (1977) himself, in reviewing Beck's new book (1976), concludes that many different modes of cognitive behavior therapy exist and that we have much to learn about their relative effectiveness.

One of the clearest summaries of those who staunchly advocate a cognitive-learning position in psychotherapy is that of Mahoney (1977a). Mahoney is not so much an integrationist as a proponent of a third-force which is consonant neither with behavioral nor traditional perspectives (a "compromising hybrid that endorses interactive 'or reciprocal' determinism—that is, the interaction between organismic and environmental influences").

This perspective is dependent upon four general assumptions:

1. The human organism responds primarily to cognitive representations of its environments rather than to those environments per se.
2. These cognitive representations are functionally related to the processes and parameters of learning.
3. Most human learning is cognitively mediated.
4. Thoughts, feelings and behaviors are causally interactive. (Mahoney, 1977a, p. 7)

From these generalities, Mahoney makes several inferences. From the first, if the model is valid, such constructs as beliefs or expectancies should be better predictors of human behavior than external variables. From the second, such beliefs, attitudes and other cognitive representations are modifiable by procedures that parallel those of the learning laboratory. In this respect, Mahoney—like a variety of writers excluding Wolpe—is convinced that, despite certain close parallels, the principles of learning are not synonymous with the principles of conditioning (see this Section in last year's Annual Review). The third assertion makes cognition both the process and the product of learning, and it is when this is combined with the fourth contention that complications arise. On the one hand, cognitive representations are said to have a causal influence on feelings and actions; on the other hand, it is also argued that actions—and particularly their consequences—help to shape our cognitive representations. This circularity, argues Mahoney, is not tautological. It is a causal circularity, an interactive (or reciprocal) determinism.

In his understandable enthusiasm for his advocacy, Mahoney proclaims that we are on the verge of a "new and challenging era in clinical psychology." This remains to be seen. Certainly, the picture of the cognitive-learning therapist that Mahoney portrays is an enticing one. Such an individual appreciates and evaluates the possible relevance of the client's physiology and biochemistry and also recognizes the roles of significant factors in the physical, cognitive and social environments. She or he must be a good listener, an accurate observer, and an effective problem-solver, with skills that will need to range from the theatrical to the rhetorical. Mahoney goes on, perhaps in somewhat grandiose fashion, to suggest that there is hardly a field that is not relevant to optimal therapist training—sociology, logic, neuropathy, nutrition, philosophy, cybernetics, pharmacology, medicine, communication and so forth. To us, Mahoney's "compleat therapist" sounds strikingly like the all-encompassing model to which every brave new therapist has always aspired.

There are, of course, many critics of cognitive behavior therapy. We have already discussed Wolpe's (1976b) exposure of "cognitive exclusivism." But Wolpe's somewhat outmoded defense of simple S-R theory, in which cognitive therapy is merely a subclass of behavior therapy, fails to do justice to the contributions of cognitive therapists or even to come to grips with recent developments in learning theory (e.g., Bandura, 1977b). Eysenck (1976b) has himself acknowledged the importance of cognitive factors in conditioning and its clinical applications, invoking Pavlov's second signal system to provide the basis for his model. Eysenck's suggestion that conditioning and cognitive therapies have few differential experimental consequences is somewhat negated by Bandura's (1977a) findings that the social learning analysis of self-efficacy is a significantly better predictor of behavior change than traditional conditioning theory (see Wilson, in press c).

Those who espouse an operant conditioning model firmly reject any form of meditational process whatsoever and translate virtually all cognitive concepts into strictly behavioral terms (e.g. Catania, 1975). Observer (1977), the anonymous but clearly radical behaviorist commentator in *The Psychological Record,* will have no truck whatsoever with what he or she believes to be a resurgence of mentalism. Like sex in a bygone era, Observer sees mentalism rearing its ugly head everywhere. Observer even goes so far as to accuse the *Journal of the Experimental Analysis of Behavior* of being guilty of "current reversionary thinking," citing an article by Shimp (1976) in which it is argued that experiments on memory can serve to illustrate the concinnity of cognitive and behavioral viewpoints, with the ultimate goal of reconciliation between the structuralist and functional traditions. As Observer sadly remarks:

"What makes this backtracking movement so damaging is that it is propagated at a time when psychology is capable of becoming genuinely observational and experimental, and therefore genuinely progressive."

As they advance into the vast unknown of cognitive competencies, behavior therapists would do well to heed the note of caution sounded by McKeachie (1976) in his presidential address to the American Psychological Association. We conclude this portion of our Commentary in McKeachie's own words:

> One of the strengths of the cognitive approaches is the recognition that the links between situation and behavior are often tortuously and tridirectionally affected by cognitions; one of the dangers is that, just as Skinner's disciples often too easily assumed simple stimulus-response connections, disciples of cognitive psychology may too easily assume simple connections between thought and action. . . . We *remain* behaviorists in the sense that behavior is still the ultimate criterion of our theories; we still accept the goal of objectivity that has characterized behaviorism. There remains a real danger, I think, that we will be too easily satisfied with the glow of general understanding and not specify as carefully and precisely as we can how cognitions are formed and regulated and how they influence, and are influenced by, behavior" (p. 831).

ETHICAL AND LEGAL ISSUES

Throughout this Series, we have endeavored to be particularly sensitive to the complex and changing societal implications of developments in our field. The ethical and legal aspects of what behavior modifiers do have been, and are, of increasing concern. And as more extensively documented elsewhere (Franks, 1977b), some of the responsibility for this type of not always welcome attention can be directly attributed to the utterances of certain behavior modifiers themselves. For example, Koocher (1976) draws attention to an American Psychological Association Convention sanctioned publicizing of a "Remote Shocker" which is proudly proclaimed to deliver "a painful shock from up to 300 feet away" for the treatment of such behaviors as "spitting, projectile vomitting and public toiletting." With Koocher, we wonder whether such activities ought to be put on a par with self-destructive behavior (for which a good case can be made for the use of aversion therapy) and on what basis the decision is made to apply such techniques.

Some concern has been expressed concerning the Food and Drug Administration medical device legislation recently passed by Congress

(Butterfield & Schwitzgebel, 1976). While, at first glance, there may be reason for feeling uneasy about the new law and its effects on practice, it is likely that the long-term effects are going to be positive. Certainly, if nothing else, it will force those who manufacture and use such instruments to be more cautious in their claims and recommended usage.

As noted in previous Annual Reviews, behavior modification can be used and has been used—sometimes deliberately and sometimes unwittingly—as a means of domineering helpless people. Civil libertarians have brought at least two charges against behavior modification prisoner rehabilitation programs, and the complex legal and ethical issues involved are still under scrutiny. In this respect, the establishment by the Institute for Behavioral Research in Bethesda, Maryland, of the Behavioral Law Center as a forum for behavioral psychologists and lawyers working in concert to devise therapeutic practices which are maximally effective without violation of individual rights is a step forward.

Redd and Sleator (1976) point out that it is difficult but necessary to devise some effective strategy for weighing such issues as pain and discomfort for the patient against the potential benefit of the procedure. That is, what is the cost-benefit ratio of the technique or program? Only under circumstances of maximum individual and group accountability, plus public availability of information, is a meaningful and socially responsive decision likely to be generated. Even with the implementation of elaborate safeguards and review committees, it is possible—as former Senator Ervin has noted in his preface to the report on the Federal Government's role in behavior modification (see Franks & Wilson, 1976)—for the power of behavior modification to be abused. To exert control, it is necessary that we understand what is being done to us and it is significant that, upon admission, leading psychiatric facilities now give each new entrant a pamphlet outlining in clear detail exactly what his or her rights as a patient are.

Regardless of the product, the educated consumer is at an advantage. However, ensuring that the consumer is informed does not relieve those who are offering the service or product of responsibility. For example, Stolz, Wienckowski, and Brown (1975—see also Franks & Wilson, 1976) deal with a variety of ethical issues and their resolution, including the need for client participation in the formulation of therapeutic objectives. As far as aversive control procedures are concerned, they advocate its use only for behaviors that are life-threatening.

Feshbach (1976) makes the important point that the varied procedures utilized by behavior therapists do not necessarily involve the same order of ethical dilemma. Thus, desensitization and modeling techniques are basically informative or experiential, whereas reinforcement methods depend much more on the direct manipulation of behavior through controlling rewards or punishment contingencies. And the ability to control reinforcers to determine when a reward is to be provided or withheld, is one of the fundamental defining properties of social power. Thus, a reinforcement strategy poses an ethical dilemma which is of a different order of magnitude to that presented by the utilization of perhaps less powerful techniques such as desensitization. In the use of desensitization in the clinical situation, it is reasonable to proclaim that both parties are engaged in a more or less mutually reinforcing, contractual relationship. By contrast, when hospitalized patients or prisoners are subjected to such procedures, the relative powers of the two parties is virtually always in favor of the establishment.

In philosophy, ethics is not a matter of right and wrong, it is a study of values. Nowhere is this more evident than in the still highly debated controversy with respect to the treatment of homosexuality (see last year's Annual Review and previous volumes). The now generally recognized ruling that homosexuality in and of itself is not necessarily cause for treatment does not resolve the ethical dilemma presented to the therapist by the homosexual who seeks such treatment. Davison (1977) draws attention to the fact that behavior therapists have not attended sufficiently to the factors influencing the desire for some homosexuals to change their sexual orientation. The prevailing social climate still views homosexuality as an undesirable deviation and therapists themselves generally regard homosexuality as undesirable even if it is not pathological. Thus, the very existence of individual and collective change-of-orientation programs strengthens societal prejudice against homosexuality and reinforces the "voluntary" desire of certain homosexuals to become heterosexual. It is for this reason that Davison proposes that, regardless of firmly expressed desires for therapeutic intervention aimed at altering the direction of their sexuality, we stop offering therapy to homosexuals and focus instead on improving the quality of their personal relationships.

Begelman (1977) strengthens this argument by drawing attention to a question which he views as misleading: On what ethical basis are we obliged to desert a client in need in favor of allegiance to an abstract set of societally determined considerations? Begelman recommends not that we desert clients in distress, but that we address ourselves to all aspects of their behavioral plights. In so doing, we must avoid reinforcing the prevailing social belief system about homosexuality. And to provide any sort of re-orientation service whatsoever would be to do just that.

In sharp contrast. Money (1977) points out that present day prognoses of the outcome of any form of psychosexual therapy are so uncertain that it may well be ethically unjust either to force an individual into therapy or to deny it. Each individual, argues Money—and experts such as Bancroft (1976) would seem to concur—needs to have his or her individual case evaluated and a conjoint decision made with respect to the most appropriate course of action. Money further argues that society's ideal should be to endorse neither heterosexuality, bisexuality, nor homosexuality, but to accept all three as viable options, each with its own acceptable time, place and person. Freund (1977) adopts a somewhat intermediary position: Sexual reorientation therapy for homosexuals is a second-best choice and should be advocated only when counseling towards self-acceptance is no longer viable or appropriate.

Feldman (1977) spells out the options available to the therapist who is presented with the problem of what to do about the homosexual client who comes expecting sexual reorientation. There are four possibilities: a) Persuade the client to "accept" his or her sexuality; b) refuse to help the client change; c) refer the client to another therapist; or d) carry out the treatment despite distaste. The first two alternatives are tantamount to a reduction of client rights. For most of us, the last requires too much in the way of self-abnegation. For Feldman, the third is the least satisfactory.

Feldman's position, that helping a homosexual achieve therapeutic reorientation be included in the list of viable alternatives, rests upon an important and perhaps hitherto unstated point. It is an as yet unsubstantiated assertion that the existence of therapists prepared to help homosexuals reorient their sexual behavior must inevitably increase the social disabilities of homosexuals in general. And Begelman notwithstanding, even if such evidence did exist, we would still have to think very carefully indeed before sacrificing the individual client to the long-term victory of the general cause.

TRAINING

Training programs in behavior therapy are proliferating at all levels and this brings with it a new order of ethical issues. Well-thought out training programs for highly professional groups such as graduate students in clinical psychology (e.g. Evans, 1976), present few or no ethical problems. Ethical problems begin to present themselves when innovative strategies are attempted. For example, Armstrong and Bakker (1976) were concerned with the criticisms offered by both students and faculty in an undergraduate medical training curriculum with respect to the lack of relevance of many of their courses. Medical students in a first-year behavioral course were required to conduct a behavior change project to alter their own behaviors, such as smoking, eating, studying, or exercise patterns. And it was also suggested that similar projects involving the behavior of another person would be equally appropriate. This involves a number of obvious ethical issues with respect to accountability, follow-up, skills of first-year medical students and so forth. And if carried through to its logical conclusions, an ingenious pilot study by Geller, Chaffee and Farris (1975) involving the use of a feedback procedure to teachers by students to increase the probability of student understanding and maintain an optimal lecture pace could also present a variety of professional, if not ethical, dilemmas.

In our commentary to Section IX, we briefly discuss some of the problems involved in cross-cultural behavior modification. When training programs designed for implementation in one program are implemented in another, ethical as well as technical and methodological issues present themselves. A training program, like a therapy program, cannot be divorced from the cultural and societal setting in which it is implemented. Goals, aspirations and values are an integral part of setting, and it is unlikely that any program can be transferred en bloc. It is thus gratifying to see Queiroz, Guilhardi and Martin (1976) set up a systematic evaluation program in Brazil to assess their first group of graduates embarking upon a university program, modelled directly upon similar programs in North America, designed to license psychologists specializing in behavior modification.

In Section X we discuss in some detail the proliferation of self-help programs and we touch briefly upon some of the ethical implications implicit in the advocacy of unvalidated or inadequately validated programs for the layperson. The ethics of self-help programs is likely to receive increasing attention in the coming years and it is important that some objective criteria be established for their validation. One might even question the ethical advisability, quite apart from the question of validity, of a self-help program for widespread general use which is couched in phraseology unclear or inappropriate for the category of individuals concerned. To this end, the recent interest in programs and self-help text readability and the development of readily applied objective methods for the assessment of this readability is encouraging (e.g. Andrasik, Klare &

Murphy, 1976; Arkell, Kubo & Meunier, 1976; Kendall, Finch & Gillen, 1976).

Self-help programs without adequate follow-up or consistent programs of reinforcement may be ineffective at best, and harmful at worst. As behavior modification training programs proliferate, so it becomes necessary to establish standards and models applicable to both professional and nonprofessional situations. A recent edited volume by Yen and McIntire (1976) is devoted entirely to the development of such models and programs. While commending much of its content, Leon (1977) draws needed attention to certain important questions yet to be faced. A number of the projects described in this book focus upon the placement of undergraduate students in practice for the expressed purpose of practicing the techniques of behavior therapy. This is disquieting: Apart from the questionable attitude (implicitly conveyed in this volume) that, somehow, knowledge and application of behavior modification are a good thing for the world at large, it would seem important to establish guidelines for the level of training of the student and the treatment settings in which the techniques are taught. With Leon, we fail to see the virtue of teaching students how to do systematic desensitization or assertion training merely as part of an undergraduate course, even with the establishment of such guidelines. Teaching behavior therapy techniques with no specific purpose other than as a course requirement does not seem to be an appropriate use for these procedures.

When it comes to the training of nonprofessional staff to be competent behavioral engineers, the importance of adequate staff training is all too often de-emphasized. Training alone does not necessarily ensure that behavioral skills are going to be utilized on the job and it is important to develop consistent programs of reinforcement for the maintenance of these skills. To this end, a recently reported study of Patterson, Griffin and Panyan (1976) exploring various strategies for increasing the effectiveness with which the skills learned in training are then applied is noteworthy. Sometimes, careful investigation can reveal unexpected bonus benefits. Thus, Smith, Milan, Wood and McKee (1976) found not only that the training of correctional officers met its primary objective, but that, by the inmates' own report, officers who had received training appear to have improved in their general caliber, becoming less punitive and more concerned with inmate welfare. As these authors note, such findings—described as a desirable by-product of their training program in behavioral principles—are often cited as primary objectives in other programs (see also Commentary, Section VII).

Ethical and legal issues are inextricably interwoven. Unfortunately, meaning, intent and principle are sometimes at variance, even when the language used is virtually identical. Statements referring to rights and ethics are particularly susceptible to this difficulty (cf. Vargas, 1975). Budd (1974) points to certain closely related difficulties. His analysis of court opinions suggests that they are based on principles or language which may at times be in conflict with the established principles of behavior or with deductions which may be made from these principles. For example, he draws attention to the legal doctrine known as the "Least Restrictive Alternative" (see Franks & Wilson, 1976). Staff workers are enjoined to employ the mildest treatment program commensurate with being effective in achieving desired changes in behavior. In principle, this approach seems reasonable, but in practice, it encounters problems. Individual differences make it difficult to predict in advance the relative effectiveness of various techniques, and there are at least two parameters to be considered in judging the restrictiveness of a treatment technique. How severe is the technique? How long does it take to work? The courts seem to ignore the second. And how does one compare a mild procedure which takes a long time to work with a strong procedure that works very quickly? It is not possible to assume that the severity of a procedure has inevitably to be primary in consideration for use.

Such issues are increasingly likely to arise not only in the case of the institutionalized patient but also with respect to the risk of malpractice suits encountered by the individual practitioner. Behavior therapists who (rightly) emphasize accountability tend to foster in their litigious-minded clients the proposition that, if he or she has not improved as a result of therapy and has paid out large sums of money, then the therapist is now accountable for the lack of progress (Tryon, 1976b).

BEHAVIOR THERAPY AND SOCIETY

Budd and Baer (1976) remind us that recent public concern about the rights of clients in behavior modification programs is only one issue within a larger social movement. In so doing, they make the implicit assumption that behavior modifiers and civil libertarians alike strive for the same ultimate goal, the independent functioning in society of deviant individuals. Holland (1976), a responsible scientist in his own right, is one of the first behaviorally committed individuals to question this assumption seriously. It may perhaps be of significance that his probing article appears in the *Journal of Humanistic Psychology*.

To illustrate his thesis, Holland draws attention to a 1969 article by Miller and Miller showing how a contingency program could be adapted to serve a radical cause. A token system was used to reinforce welfare recipients for a variety of organizational activities geared towards maximizing their rights. Obviously, such an anomalous situation is unlikely to be supported by any agency of the establishment or corporate political system as we know it.

In similar fashion, Holland notes a proposal to deploy behavioral control of mass populations as a major weapons system by the Rand Corporation, and poses the question: Are we unwittingly and unwillingly contributing to such a development? The well-known "Achievement Place" project, rightly praised time after time in this Series, is also taken to task by Holland. Certainly, the Achievement Place model of democracy outstrips other—and perhaps less democratic—models in contingency management. Electing peers, assigning tasks and evaluating performance all meet the criteria of being effective, practical and preferred procedures. But, even in the circumscribed matter of bathroom cleaning, they resemble the less democratic systems in the determination of objectives or criteria for reinforcement—the inmates cannot vote to receive reinforcement for a dirty bathroom, should they so choose.

Thus, the behavioral psychologist is challenged by a contingency management system which serves the goals of the prevailing political organization, be it of the left or right. Good intentions may be necessary, but they can never be sufficient. As with science, the myth that behavior modification is neutral is just that—a myth. Like every other form of therapeutic intervention, it contains inherent values and implicit tendencies. Furthermore, as Matson (1976) warns us in his comments on Holland's article, if we have always to be on guard against the abuse of a good thing, there are also times that we must be on guard against the use of a bad thing.

In his onslaught against behavior modification, Lindsey (1975) shows a remarkable lack of understanding of contemporary behavior therapy and its sensitivity to social issues. Sweeping and wildly inaccurate generalizations are made to contrast sociology, with its emphasis on the social milieu, with a behavior therapy which looks only to the individual's immediate behavior. The sociologist is concerned with social issues and strives to deal with causes outside the individual and not just the symptoms of personal problems alone. The behavioral psychologist, according to Lindsey, ignores all such issues and develops treatment procedures which permit disabled individuals to reenter the existing community and so retain the status quo. Thus, the purpose of behavior modification is the creation of cooperative and conforming individuals, whereas the desire for a tolerant, democratic and just community requires a concern with much more than just this.

We agree with Lindsey that those who are a minority, without power, or different with respect to racial, sexual or physical attributes, are subject to discrimination by powerful groups and their agents. We also agree that behavioral technology could be used to strengthen the prevailing order in its negotiations with such isolated and weak individuals. As Shiverick (1976) notes in his spirited reply to Lindsey, while there is the danger that behavior therapists could misapply the technology of behavior modification and achieve only arrid conformity, this need not be. Behavior therapists focus quite explicitly upon development of a greater sense of freedom, maximizing options, accountability, self-directed programs and so forth. And Shiverick raises the point that, while society should certainly facilitate an individual's growth and strivings, it is also a function of society to provide the necessary controls for the facilitation of growth. If society is to survive, it must protect its members. Lindsey engages in a spurious dichotomy: there is no necessary schism between behavior modification and a recognition of the social causes which bring about deviant behavior. If anything, behavior therapists focus far more on socially relevant variables than do psychoanalysts, who dwell on the individual's past, or experientalists who concentrate on the phenomenological present and the development of individual awareness.

Thus, behavior control involves far more than the relationship between patient and practitioner (cf. Klerman, 1975). Somehow, we have to face and resolve fundamental problems pertaining to the relationship of the behavior therapist to society. Kazdin (1975a) has articulated clearly three main issues related to the fear that behavior control procedures may be used for freedom-limiting ends: "The *purpose* for which behavior is to be controlled, *who* will decide the ultimate purpose and exert control, and whether the behavioral control entails an abridgment of individual *freedom*." As already noted, there can be no value-free intervention.

Behavior modification offers a certain advantage over other systems with respect to its objectivity, data based orientation and accountability. It should surely not be beyond our resources to develop some form of explicit guidelines for helping to decide ethical and social issues while still leaving room for intuition and freedom of choice—even to be irrational or wrong—to the individual. For example, Tryon (1976a, 1976b), perhaps prematurely (cf. Bixenstine, 1977), has developed a formal analysis system based on Woods' taxonomy of instrumental conditioning which could conceivably be used for helping to decide ethical issues as well as matters of behavioral diagnosis and treatment selection.

CONCLUSION

The last two decades since Wolpe (1958) developed the first viable alternative to psychodynamically-based procedures for coping with neurotic problems have witnessed unprecedented research activity and the beginnings of a science of therapeutic behavior change. Clinical developments, the growth of professionalism and responsible informed concern with societal issues by behavior therapists have been equally impressive. As behavior therapy approaches maturity, so the age of polemics and strident oversimplification begins to recede in favor of a cautious optimism and concern with what has yet to be accomplished. More effective therapeutic procedures, more compelling empirical support and more adequate theories are still needed. As yet, Eysenck's (1976a) recent attempt notwithstanding, Mowrer's (1950) neurotic paradox still remains unresolved: the paradox of behavior which is at one and the same time self-perpetuating and self-defeating. Neither the models of Freud, Skinner, Watson, nor Mowrer are adequate to account for what is one of the most basic problems in any form of psychotherapy. We are but at the beginning.

Nevertheless, two decades later, behavior therapy is alive and well and living very much in the real world of the mid-seventies. We can do little better than conclude this overview with a quotation from Eysenck (1976b):

> Behaviour therapy is an applied science, not a dogma; it is those who criticize it for being like all other applied sciences who follow a dogma of idealizing science out of existence altogether. Critics would no doubt be justified in arguing that there are many psychologists and psychiatrists who call themselves behaviour therapists but who know little of the underlying theories and experiments on which these methods are based. This is unfortunately true, but it does not enable us to argue that the methods themselves have not been derived from general theories at least partially true, by methods at least very partially rigorous. Behaviour therapy as a psychological discipline is very young, dating back only to the last years of the 1950s, and learning theory itself is not very old. To expect general,

unified theories in these fields when physics and chemistry fail to possess such theories after two thousand years of study seems unreasonable. There are many deficiencies, anomalies and problems in the theories themselves and in their application; this is the fate of all progressive research programmes. It is only when the *programme* fails to predict and unearth new and important facts, when the *protective belt* safeguarding the hard core of principles becomes overburdened by fatty tissue that threatens to stifle new research and when the *heuristic* fails to integrate apparent anomalies and instead has recourse to purely verbal *post hoc* arguments trying to explain away the contradictory finding, that the programme degenerates and becomes of purely historical interest. We have witnessed the sad fate of the Freudian programme. Life for behaviour therapy has only just begun, and to date at least there are no indications that it will follow the same course. In that spirit, we ought to welcome all factual criticism and reject all purely ideological comments on the programme as irrelevant (p. 339f).

Section II

RELAXATION TRAINING, SYSTEMATIC DESENSITIZATION, FLOODING, MODELING, COGNITIVE RESTRUCTURING AND ASSERTION TRAINING

Commentary

From its inception, clinical behavior therapy with adults has been oriented towards the treatment of neurotic reactions through the use of techniques such as systematic desensitization and its different variants. Behavior therapy today is applied to a remarkably diverse range of disorders, of which the neurotic reactions are only one category. However, the assessment of the neurotic disorders continues to be a major focus of behavioral research and therapy. In addition to Wolpe's (1958) technique of systematic desensitization, newer and more effective methods have been applied successfully to these problems.

RELAXATION TRAINING

In a study reprinted in an earlier volume in this series (Franks & Wilson, 1975), Steinmark and Borkovec (1974) demonstrated the efficacy of relaxation training in the treatment of moderate insomnia (see also our Commentary to Section X). The second paper reprinted in the current Section, by Borkovec and Weerts, is part of Borkovec's continuing program of investigation of the modification of psychophysiological disorders such as sleep disturbance. The results of this study provide further support for the effectiveness of relaxation training as a treatment for moderate insomnia. Particularly encouraging in this respect is the maintenance of treatment gains from relaxation training at the one year follow-up evaluation. While there will be those who question the clinical relevance of only four treatment sessions with less than severely disturbed insomniacs, this research program, with its well-controlled studies, comprehensive and conservative analysis of outcome data, and careful comparison with and replication of previous findings under similar circumstances, constitutes an important advance toward the more effective treatment of sleep disorders.

Knapp, Downs, and Alperson (1976) review the literature on the behavioral treatment of insomnia and find only five controlled experimental studies, excluding Borkovec and Weerts. They conclude that "almost any variant of relaxation training produces statistically significant reductions in latency to sleep onset and a reduction in the number of nocturnal awakenings, so long as the relaxation involves actual tension and release of muscles [Borkovec, Kaloupek, & Slama, 1975]. Stimulus control techniques may provide even greater reductions in insomnia than relaxation techniques. A combination of the two is likely the most effective, though never tested" (p. 623). Woolfolk, Carr-Kaffashan, and McNulty (1976) compared relaxation training with a set of attention-focusing techniques in the treatment of insomnia. Although both methods were significantly more effective than no treatment in reducing sleep latency of sleep onset, they did not differ from each other. A six-month follow-up indicated maintenance of improvement.

Relaxation training was employed as a self-control coping method in the treatment of test anxiety (Deffenbacher, 1976). A limited A-B design indicated that the self-control strategy was effective in decreasing test and other non-targeted anxieties. However, the sole use of self-report as an outcome measure, the confounding of relaxation training per se with self-instructional training, and the lack of more appropriate experimental controls seriously call into question the value of such research. A potentially important clinical application of relaxation training is described by Alban and Nay (1976). A compulsive client with a life-long history of ritual re-checking was treated by delay therapy in which increasingly lengthy periods of relaxation practice were interpolated just prior to the rituals. The compulsive checking behavior was completely eliminated in 12 weeks of treatment and showed no recurrence over the course of a seven month follow-up. The use of relaxation as a means of facilitating what can be construed as graded self-administered response delay has also been discussed by Wilson (1976).

SYSTEMATIC DESENSITIZATION

The volume of research on systematic desensitization is enormous. In 1973 Paul and Bernstein noted that selective reviews of the literature prior to 1971 revealed "over 150 separate reports on the work of hundreds of therapists with thousands of clients." In the most recent review of the field, Kazdin and Wilcoxon (1976) observe that a "cursory count" of *controlled group outcome studies* published in only five journals from 1970 through 1974 produced a total of 74 studies! The quality of this research is the subject of the following analysis.

Process Studies

In our commentary on systematic desensitization in last year's volume we discussed Lick and Bootzin's (1975) review of expectancy factors in desensitization (Franks & Wilson, 1976). Kazdin and Wilcoxon (1976) have followed with a similar but more recent methodological evaluation of "nonspecific"* treatment effects in systematic desensitization. Through detailed sifting of a welter of experimental evidence, Kazdin and Wilcoxon show that the vast majority of studies on systematic desensitization have not determined empirically whether the various control conditions employed were successful in controlling for credibility and expectancy for improvement. Recent research—discussed in our commentary on systematic desensitization in last year's volume—has shown that the desensitization procedure usually generates greater credibility and expectancies of therapeutic gain in subjects than the attention-placebo control conditions that have been commonly used. Out of all the studies reviewed, Kazdin and Wilcoxon identified only *five* studies with control treatments that had been empirically demonstrated to foster comparable subject expectancies for behavior change as assessed by self-report estimates.

In two of these studies—D'Zurilla, Wilson, and Nelson (1973) and Wilson (1973)—systematic desensitization did not differ significantly from equally credible placebo controls. However, systematic desensitization also was not much superior to no treatment controls in these studies, a finding which complicates the interpretation of the role of "nonspecific" factors. The third study, by McReynolds, Barnes, Brooks, and

---

* It is more accurate to talk of treatment factors that have yet to be specified. The processes subsumed by the accommodating rubric of "nonspecifics" are neither qualitatively different from other social learning influences nor are they unspecifiable (for further discussion of this issue see Wilson & Evans, 1976).

Rehagen (1973)—discussed in our commentaries to this Section in previous years—indicates that systematic desensitization is not superior to highly credible controls. The remaining two studies are Steinmark and Borkovec's (1974) and Gelder, Bancroft, Gath, Johnston, Mathews, and Shaw's (1973). The former clearly indicates the superiority of systematic desensitization during the counterdemand control phase of the study and at follow-up. (We might add that the Borkovec and Weerts paper reprinted here similarly shows that relaxation training, a component of systematic desensitization, is more effective on some measures such as long-term follow-up, but not on others, such as EEG measures at post-treatment.) The latter found that systematic desensitization was consistently superior to a control treatment ("associative psychotherapy") across a broad range of measures, although the difference on the behavioral avoidance tests was not statistically significant.

Kazdin and Wilcoxon's conclusion is a provocative one: "Overall, the five studies do not support the proposition that desensitization includes a specific therapy ingredient beyond expectancies for improvement. The relative paucity of studies showing that desensitization is superior to an equally credible control group would seem to weaken the usual statements made about desensitization as a technique with specific therapeutic ingredients. The alternative explanation, that the therapeutic effects are due to nonspecific treatment effects, at least at the present time, cannot be ruled out" (p. 745).

Of course, it could be argued that, of the five studies referred to by Kazdin and Wilcoxon, not all are equally important. Thus the Gelder et al. study seems particularly relevant since it was conducted with severely phobic clients, including agoraphobics, in a clinical treatment setting with multiple measurements. Nonetheless, even if greater weight is given this study, Kazdin and Wilcoxon's point about the relative *paucity* of data demonstrating the specific active ingredients of systematic desensitization is well taken. One further point should be borne in mind in evaluating Kazdin and Wilcoxon's verdict. We have previously argued the case that Paul's (1966) classic study provides evidence for specific active treatment effects in systematic desensitization. This analysis is based not on the comparison between his desensitization and attention-placebo control condition (the latter having been called into question by subsequent research), but between desensitization and the psychotherapy treatment. While the latter does not constitute a fair test of psychotherapy, in our opinion it is stretching credibility of another sort to maintain that this treatment did not equate for expectancies of therapeutic improvement. Only the technicality that Paul did not conduct a specific empirical evaluation of this treatment allows it to be excluded from an analysis such as Kazdin and Wilcoxon have undertaken.

In an attempt to isolate the effective ingredients of systematic desensitization, McGlynn and McClaren (1975) assigned subjects who had been identified as highly fearful of snakes to the following groups: relevant snake imagery with and without relaxation training; irrelevant imagery with and without relaxation training; and no treatment. Neither the full desensitization procedure nor either of the components proved to be more effective than the placebo group (irrelevant imagery with no relaxation training). McGlynn and McClaren attribute this apparent ineffectiveness of a semi-automated desensitization procedure to the fact that highly fearful subjects were used. However, other explanations are at least as plausible.

In still another detailed analysis of the role of subject expectancies in systematic desensitization, Rosen (1976b) accepts that providing subjects with a therapy set consistently results in greater improvement than subjects receiving treatment without this set. He then provides a discussion of the possible mechanism that might account for this effect. His conclusion is that expectancies might interact with other social learning influences to facilitate nonreinforced exposure or habituation to critical elements of the fear-arousing stimuli (see Franks & Wilson, 1976).

In addition to proving to be an effective therapeutic technique, systematic desensitization has provided the means for studying the nature of fear in a controlled laboratory context (cf. Lang, 1969). Thus Rachman and Hodgson (1974) have discussed the "desynchrony" among the different dimensions of fear—behavioral, physiological, and self verbal self-report—and Rachman (1976b) has re-evaluated the two-factor theory of avoidance learning, leaning heavily on experimental evidence derived from laboratory investigations of systematic desensitization. Although it has served a useful heuristic function, two-factor theory is unable to account for several experimental findings, and Rachman provides a scholarly analysis of alternative theoretical formulations that are consistent with the new data.

Schroeder and Rich (1976) sampled behavioral, physiological, and subjective measures from snake phobic subjects at the end of each of eight therapy sessions in order to explore further the relationships among these three response systems. Replicating the results of previous research Schroeder and Rich found a desynchrony among measures—change in one response system was not primary in initiating change in one of the others. Linear reductions were obtained on the behavioral and subjective measures of fear, while heart rate showed a cubic trend over therapy sessions. Also consonant with previous findings is the finding that real-life exposure plays an important role in the fear reduction process. In essence, Schroeder and Rich propose a cognitive explanation of the effects of systematic desensitization. As a result of the treatment, they suggest that "One may tentatively conclude that there is less danger or that one is no longer strongly affected autonomically. Performance and autonomic feedback in real life may then validate or invalidate these belief inferences. Such a process would account for the facilitating effect of behavior change on attitudinal, threat appraisal, and subjective arousal changes. The additional quadratic trends for these measures might be explained by the invalidation of belief inferences through real-life exposure. That is, failure to change behaviorally may have led to a reevaluation of subjective estimates toward pretreatment levels. This view is also consistent with the improved correlations between measures later in the fear reduction process as subjects achieved greater consistency among fear systems" (p. 198).

This notion of overt performance affecting "belief inferences" is not dissimilar from Bandura's (1977a) new self-efficacy theory of behavior change, in which he argues that alterations in an individual's sense of self-efficacy explain all fear reduction techniques. Self-efficacy expectations are influenced by different sources of information, including performance-based, vicarious (e.g., modeling), autonomic (e.g., systematic desensitization), and verbal (e.g., traditional psychotherapy) feedback. The details of this major new theory will be presented in next year's volume.

In their review, Kazdin and Wilcoxon deal briefly with several different interpretations of systematic desensitization. One alternative not covered in the review is Silverman, Frank, and Dachinger's (1974) view that systematic desensitization works because it activates unconscious, symbiotic fantasies in which the client merges with his mother. Unlike other psychodynamic post hoc interpretations of systematic desensitization, Silverman et al., to their credit, reported the findings of a study in which subjects fearful of insects exposed to a subliminal stimulus MOMMY AND I ARE ONE showed greater fear reduction than subjects exposed to a neutral stimulus PEOPLE WALKING. Emmelkamp and Straatman (1976) suggested that the results of this study can be explained more parsimoniously in terms of demand characteristics. Accordingly, they compared two groups of snake fearful subjects. One group was exposed to the stimulus MOMMY AND I ARE ONE while the other was exposed to the stimulus THE SNAKE AND I ARE ONE. Confirming Emmelkamp and Straatman's prediction, no difference between the two groups was obtained. The authors account for this failure to replicate Silverman et al.'s results by suggesting that the stimulus THE SNAKE AND I ARE ONE was as *relevant* to the subjects as the symbiotic gratification stimulus. This then equated for the experimental demand characteristics to approach the formerly feared object. In the Silverman et al. study, the stimulus PEOPLE WALKING could be viewed as *irrelevant* rather than psychodynamically neutral and thus created a situation in which the demand characteristics favored the group viewing the supposed symbiotic stimulus. Moreover, subjects with a therapy set showed more approach behavior than subjects with a research set, a now well-documented finding (see also Rosen, 1976b).

In more clinical papers on systematic desensitization, Braff, Raskin, and Geisinger (1976) discuss the management of various interpersonal issues in the conduct of desensitization in the clinical setting, and Deffenbacher (1976) suggests ways in which desensitization can be most efficiently used in a group context in mental health settings. Finally, Koulack, LeBow, and Church (1976) report the effects of desensitization treatment on the sleep and dreams of a patient successfully treated by desensitization. Sleep laboratory measures provided evidence of generalized anxiety reduction during sleep and dreaming. Research such as this suggests how a reliable treatment procedure might be used to study the influence of anxiety on sleep and dreaming (see also Bandura, Jeffery, & Gajdos, 1975—reprinted in Franks & Wilson, 1976).

Outcome Studies

While disputing the identification of specific behavior change mechanisms in systematic desensitization, Kazdin and Wilcoxon emphasize that, as a treatment package, it has demonstrable efficacy. Similarly, in his evaluation of the behavioral treatment of neurotic disorders, Leitenberg (1976a) states that "it seems safe to conclude that systematic desensitization is demonstrably more effective than both no treatment and every psychotherapy variant with which it has so far been compared" (p. 131). Once a method has been shown to be effective, applied research can be conducted to improve its efficiency and disseminability (see Kazdin & Wilson, 1977). The first paper reprinted in this Section—by Rosen, Glasgow, and Barrera—is important because it demonstrates that an effective treatment can be self-administered. With March 1977 ushering in the year of the Snake, according to the Chinese Calendar, it seems only proper to include a study on this intensively researched reptile.

There are several notable features about this study. First, Rosen et al. were careful to use highly fearful subjects, thus obviating criticisms about clinically irrelevant "analogue" research. Second, the authors provide a clear discussion of the magnitude of change. Although statistically significant, the degree of behavior change is relatively unimpressive. Third, a two month follow-up was reported. The fact that subject attrition occurred makes it difficult to interpret these findings unequivocally. Yet the tendency for the self-administered desensitization group to show continued improvement is sufficiently important to be analyzed more systematically in subsequent studies. Rosen, Glasgow, and Barrera (1977) have subsequently reported a two year follow-up of their findings. All subjects were sent a questionnaire evaluating specific fear of snakes and general rating of improvement. Twenty-three of the 26 desensitization subjects and 11 of the 17 controls returned the questionnaire. Desensitization subjects were significantly more improved than controls, with no significant difference among the desensitization groups. Interestingly, Rosen et al. found that posttreatment behavior avoidance test scores were not related to the performance of specific target behaviors (e.g., gardening or camping) in the natural environment. Posttreatment self-report ratings, however, were related to target behaviors. To the extent that these self-ratings reflected changes in subjects' efficacy expectations, these findings would be consistent with Bandura's (1977a) self-efficacy theory.

Beyond the demonstration of the efficacy of self-administered desensitization, Rosen et al.'s study is important in providing one of the few well-controlled empirical evaluations of what Rosen (1976a) has called non-prescription therapies (see Section X of this volume). Far too many self-help books are being published that have no empirical support.

An experimental investigation of self-administered desensitization was also conducted by Marshall, Presse, and Andrews (1976). Subjects who complained of public speaking anxiety were assigned to one of the following groups: therapist administered desensitization; self-administered desensitization without any therapist contact; self-administered desensitization with minimal therapist contact; self-administered desensitization plus a pseudotherapy component; pseudotherapy; and no treatment. Therapist-administered desensitization consisted of five 45 minute sessions over a three week period; self-administered desensitization with minimal therapist contact consisted of five 15 minute meetings with the therapist.

Assessment included behavioral ratings of anxiety during the presentation of a speech and self-report measures.

The results were that none of the varied treatment groups showed greater improvement on the behavioral ratings than the no treatment control group. However, all treatment groups were superior to no treatment on self-report measures. Consistent with Rosen et al.'s findings, Marshall et al. found greater subject attrition in the self-administered desensitization group with no therapist contact. Five out of 11 subjects dropped out of this treatment, only two from each of the others. In addition, at least three of the remaining six subjects in the completely self-administered treatment reported that they had not completed the program. These data not only indicate a disturbingly low adherence rate in totally self-administered desensitization, but they also call into question the adequacy of the other desensitization treatments. In short, only three subjects in the totally self-administered treatment appeared to have engaged in anything therapeutic. Yet this group was no worse than the therapist-administered treatment. Marshall et al. suggest that their failure to replicate Paul's (1966) results is attributable to the fact that his subjects were concurrently involved in making speeches as part of the undergraduate curriculum whereas subjects in their study were not. According to Marshall et al., this involvement might have provided practice in developing the skills of making public speeches and that it is this skill learning that is reflected on the behavioral measure.

The effect of systematic desensitization on a dependent measure that is rarely given much attention in the behavioral literature is reported by Ryan, Krall, and Hodges (1976). Desensitization was compared with relaxation training and no treatment in the modification of test anxiety. The two active treatment methods produced greater reduction in test anxiety than the no treatment control, but did not differ from one another. (The absence of a credible placebo condition makes interpretation of this result well-nigh impossible.) However, systematic desensitization was significantly more effective than relaxation training on a single measure of self-concept. The authors discuss the results in terms of the experience of coping with aversive events that desensitization provides, and—more controversially—suggest that this line of research might "hasten an understanding of the relationship between the effects of behavioral and psychodynamic psychotherapies" (p. 644). The treatment of test anxiety was also the focus of a comparison between a self-control versus a counterconditioning formulation of systematic desensitization (Spiegler, Cooley, Marshall, Prince, Puckett, & Skenazy, 1976). The self-control procedural modification of the technique appeared to be more effective than the original counterconditioning format, although the only statistically significant difference was on a self-report measure.

FLOODING

In comparisons with systematic desensitization using extremely anxious clients, flooding seems to be superior to systematic desensitization (e.g., Crowe, Marks, Agras, & Leitenberg, 1972; Marks, Boulougouris, & Marset, 1971). The efficacy of flooding seems to hinge on two particularly important parameters. The first is whether flooding is conducted in imagination or in vivo; the other concerns the duration of individual sessions. The evidence thus far shows that flooding administered in vivo and over sessions of sufficiently protracted duration is most effective (Emmelkamp & Wessels, 1975; Stern & Marks, 1973—reprinted in Franks & Wilson, 1974).

Flooding in imagination was compared to flooding in vivo in the treatment of agoraphobic patients by Mathews, Johnston, Lancashire, Munby, Shaw, and Gelder (1976). The three treatment groups were as follows: a) eight sessions of imaginal flooding followed by eight sessions of flooding in vivo; b) 16 sessions of combined flooding in imagination and real-life exposure to the feared situation; and c) 16 sessions of in vivo exposure alone. The dependent measures were similar to those used by Gelder et al. (reprinted in Franks & Wilson, 1975), including behavioral avoidance tests, clinical ratings of symptoms, psychometric tests, and psychophysiological recording. There was no significant difference among treatments at eight weeks, 16 weeks, or a at a six month follow-up. Although it had not been anticipated, there was evidence of a therapist effect on some outcome measures. As Mathews et al. (1976) note, this finding may have implications for clinical practice, even in highly standardized, effective methods such as flooding. At follow-up, patients' ranked eight components of their therapy in terms of their perceived therapeutic value. To a significant degree, patients ranked the therapists' encouragement and sympathy, followed closely by the in vivo practice component, as the most helpful. Increased understanding, imaginal representation of anxiety-eliciting material, and diary keeping were perceived to be of little value.

The failure to find differences among the three treatments could be due to the fact that they were all equally effective. Alternatively, this outcome could merely reflect the operation of "nonspecific" treatment factors common to all methods. However, Mathews et al. reject the latter explanation on the grounds that the improvement observed in these agoraphobic patients was comparable to that obtained by Gelder et al. and significantly better than the minimal improvement shown by the highly credible placebo control or "associative psychotherapy" condition in the Gelder et al. study. A more plausible interpretation of the results bears on the nature of the patients' activities *between* rather than *during* treatment sessions. Considerable emphasis was placed on the patients' self-directed practice attempts at in vivo exposure in their home settings. This is all the more likely since treatment spanned a relatively long time—16 weeks—whereas previous studies demonstrating the superiority of in vivo over imaginal methods were much briefer in duration. This longer period provides more time to practice. Mathews et al. conclude that "it is possible that the anxiety experienced while thinking about phobic situations eventually declines after any treatment involving exposure in reality or imagination, so that patients are less anxious before or during later practice at home. Alternatively, it may be that if a patient repeatedly thinks about phobic situations, regardless of anxiety, this is sufficient to increase the probability that the patients will eventually attempt to practise" (p. 371).

Johnston, Lancashire, Mathews, Munby, Shaw, and Gelder (1976) conducted an analysis of the weekly measures of change in the study just described and related these within treatment measures to outcome at follow-up. Aside from confirming the presence of a therapist effect, Johnston et al.'s analyses show that the immediate effects of the treatment were different. Thus, in vivo exposure had immediate positive effects, whereas imaginal flooding had no obvious short-term effect. The authors suggest that both methods facilitate self-directed practice between sessions and that this is the effective agent of therapeutic change.

The importance of *continuous* as opposed to intermittent in vivo exposure to the feared object receives support from a study by Girodo and Henry (1976). Snake phobic subjects who were given either continuous or intermittent exposure (equating for overall amount of exposure time to the snake) were compared to bibliotherapy or no treatment control groups. Behavioral outcome measures showed that continuous exposure was significantly more effective than alternative treatments in increasing approach toward the snake. Cognitive and physiological measures of anxiety were correlated with behavioral approach scores if the subject had experienced cognitions of self-perceived lowered physiological arousal.

As we reported in last year's volume, the use of a modified flooding or in vivo exposure method appears to be an effective means of treating compulsive rituals (cf. Marks, Rachman, & Hodgson, 1975). More recently, Boersma, Den Hengst, Dekker, and Emmelkamp (1976) compared the following four methods in the treatment of obsessive-compulsive patients: a) gradual in vivo exposure with gradual response prevention; b) flooding plus total response prevention; c) flooding plus modeling; and d) gradual in vivo exposure and response prevention plus modeling. A novel feature of this study is that patients were treated in their home environments. All four methods produced substantial improvement in compulsive behavior across a number of different measures. There was no difference among the four treatments. The authors underscore the practical point that, if the gradual method is as effective as flooding, and is less emotionally taxing on the client, then it is probably the preferred method by virtue of the fact that clients are more likely to comply with therapists' requests.

Objections to behavior therapy on account of the danger of symptom substitution seem to have become a thing of the past, even psychodynamic critics bowing to the overwhelming evidence against this objection and claiming that the substitution of symptoms is not necessarily predicted by psychodynamic theory (e.g., Weitzman, 1967). Lest we forget the past, however, Hafner (1976) reports "fresh symptom emergence after intensive behaviour therapy" with agoraphobic patients. Forty-one agoraphobics were treated using an in vivo exposure procedure. Some were administered diazepam, others a placebo. Evaluation of outcome was conducted three days, one, three, six, and 12 months after treatment.

On the basis of scores on the Fear Survey Schedule (FSS) and the Middlesex Hospital Questionnaire (MHQ), a 48-item questionnaire measure of symptoms on five scales of generalized anxiety, phobic anxiety, obsessionality, depression, and somatic complaints, Hafner divided the patients into three groups: Group 1, those who showed little new symptom emergence; Group 2, those who showed a moderate amount of symptor emergence; and Group 3, those who showed a moderate to large amount. Free symptom emergence was defined as an increase over pretreatment scores on any scale of the MHQ or FSS on more than one of the posttreatment evaluations. Hafner asserts that the group that showed a large increase in new symptoms one year after treatment were inescapably worse off than they had been, and that behavior therapy was the cause. Hafner also notes that 16 individually treated agoraphobics showed no signs of fresh symptom emergence. Seven of these 16 patients dropped out during treatment, whereas there was zero attrition among the 39 patients treated in a group. He suggests that group pressure caused patients to continue in therapy who were the ones whose problems worsened.

Hafner's observations have not gone unchallenged. Stern (1977) draws attention to the specific details of Hafner's published results, pointing out that Group 3 seemed to get worse on only one measure—spouse dissatisfaction—and that this was probably within chance levels. "On what criteria, therefore," Stern asks, "were Group 3 worsened, apart from a non-significant change on a rating scale of spouse dissatisfaction whose reliability and validity has not been presented, and despite improvement in 4 other measures? To proceed from a non-significant change on 1 out of 5 measures which is in the opposite direction to all other measures given, and then to draw conclusions about 'worsening' seems illogical" (p. 418). In addition Stern notes that fluctuations in the severity of agoraphobic patients' symptoms are well documented and that before any "deterioration" in their status could be attributed to a specific form of therapeutic intervention, natural fluctuation would have to be ruled out. Finally, Stern emphasizes the results of other behavioral treatment programs for agoraphobics in which patients showed general improvement at long-term follow-up in addition to specific improvement in the target behavior progress in those areas specifically treated by behavior therapy. Meyer and Reich (1977) similarly criticize Hafner, who enters a brief rejoinder (Hafner, 1977).

MODELING

Two major reviews of the application of modeling principles and procedures as therapeutic methods were published last year (Rachman, 1976a; Rosenthal, 1976) and this remains an active area of current research. In recent years covert modeling has been shown to be an effective procedure in the treatment of fears and unassertive behavior. As part of a program of research on covert modeling (e.g., Kazdin, 1975—reprinted in Franks & Wilson, 1976), Kazdin (1976) found that multiple models are more effective than a single model, and that asking the subject to imagine the model's behavior being reinforced results in greater improvement in the development of assertive behavior.

Thase and Moss (1976) compared two forms of covert modeling to participant modeling (a performance-based method) and a waiting list control condition in the treatment of snake fearful subjects. In the one covert modeling procedure, the subject imagined someone else engaging in coping behavior towards the snake; in the second condition, subjects imagined themselves approaching the snake in a coping manner. Symbolic representation of a coping model was deliberately chosen since it has been shown to be the most effective form of covert and symbolic modeling.

Participant modeling was significantly more effective in reducing avoidance behavior. Covert modeling was marginally more effective in reducing avoidance behavior. Covert modeling was marginally more effective than in the control group. Subjects who had failed to improve with covert modeling were then treated with participant modeling and showed significant improvement comparable to that of the original participant modeling group. These findings demonstrate that performance-based methods are more effective than techniques that rely upon symbolic induction processes. Thase and Moss comment that there is no clinical justification for using covert modeling unless participant modeling is impractical for one or another reason. As they conclude, "the utility of covert modeling as a powerful *primary* treatment modality remains to be demonstrated" (p. 11) (emphasis added).

Variations of the modeling procedure were compared with systematic desensitization in a study on the treatment of spider phobics (Denney & Sullivan, 1976). Three forms of therapy were compared: systematic desensitization; symbolic modeling with narrative and relaxation training; and symbolic modeling alone. Each therapy was administered using either scenes in which the subject interacted with the spider or scenes depicting only spiders. The seventh group was a no treatment control condition. With the single exception of the symbolic modeling group that viewed pictures of spiders alone without any human interaction with the spider, all treatment groups showed significantly greater improvement on the behavioral avoidance test than the control condition. These results show that modeling is more effective than mere exposure to the phobic object.

The fact that desensitization was as effective with the spider only scenes as with the scenes depicting the subject interacting with the spider (i.e., a covert modeling treatment) raises questions about viewing systematic desensitization as a form of covert modeling. However, the authors note that subjects spontaneously reported projecting themselves into the scenes even when instructed to imagine viewing only the spider. This finding emphasizes that the way therapy methods are described and presented is not always the way in which they get implemented and are experienced by the subject. Careful questioning of subjects is necessary to ascertain the actual nature of the independent variable in studies that deal with covert processes. The fact that the same person in the Denney and Sullivan study administered all the treatments to all groups and carried out both the pre- and posttest assessments raises the possibility of unintentional bias having affected the outcome.

Covert modeling was compared to symbolic modeling in the development of assertive behavior among unassertive college women (Rosenthal & Reese, 1976). Two forms of covert sensitization were investigated, the one using a standardized hierarchy of scenes, the other employing hierarchies tailor-made to the individual subject. Significant within-group improvement was obtained on several self-report measures, although there was no difference among the groups. An attempt to use a surreptitious phone call to assess subjects' posttreatment ability to refuse unreasonable requests proved to be unsuccessful.

COGNITIVE RESTRUCTURING

The emergence of cognitive behavior therapy (the term "behavior" is occasionally omitted) appears to be one of the most prominent developments in the field today (see Commentary, Section I). Among the major sources of this approach, which has received an enthusiastic clinical reception, are Beck's (1976) book on *Cognitive Therapy,* Meichenbaum's (1977) book on *Cognitive Behavior Modification,* and several review articles by Mahoney (e.g., Mahoney & Arnkoff, in press). Wilson (in press, c) has argued that while these cognitive developments include important technical innovations and clinically relevant applications, they do not represent a major conceptual shift. Rather, they are most appropriately placed within the context of social theory as developed by Bandura (1977b). Whereas applied behavior analysis focuses almost exclusively on overt behavior, and Wolpe's counterconditioning approach emphasizes conditioned autonomic or emotional habits, cognitive (behavior) therapy assumes that the road to behavioral hell lies not in good intentions, overt behavior or autonomic habits, but in maladaptive thought patterns. One of the advantages of social learning theory is that it integrates these three regulatory systems of antecedent, consequent, and mediational influence in a comprehensive yet testable framework.

A basic tenet of social learning theory is that while cognitive mechanisms are increasingly used to explain the acquisition and regulation of abnormal behavior, the most powerful methods of behavior change are increasingly shown to be those that are performance-based. It would be difficult to exaggerate the importance of this distinction between treatment *procedure* and theoretical *process;* its relevance to the cognitive therapies is particularly great. Both Beck (1976) and Mahoney and Arnkoff (in press) state that behavioral procedures are employed to alter cognitive processes in what they call cognitive therapy. This crucial distinction is far from evident in Ellis' (1970) rational emotive therapy (RET), however. In his formulation, most abnormal behavior is viewed as nothing but a question of irrational, disordered cognitions. Moreover, the treatment methods emphasized most heavily in RET are cognitive—verbal persuasion, rational argument, and logical reasoning. A lop-sided preoccupation with cognitive processes carries with it the hazards of returning to an interview-based mode of clinical intervention in which the verbal interchange between therapist and client is over-emphasized to the neglect of specific instigative attempts to alter client behavior in the natural environment.

The question really reduces to whether behavioral treatment methods are more effective than their cognitive counterparts in facilitating therapeutic change. In this the evidence, thus far, has been unmistakably clear. Behaviorally-based treatment methods are significantly more effective in producing change on multiple subjective and objective measures of psychological functioning than methods that rely on verbal, imaginal, or even vicarious procedures (Bandura, 1977a). Participant modeling is a performance-based method that has been shown to be significantly more effective in eliminating phobic behavior than either symbolic modeling or imaginal systematic desensitization (Bandura, Blanchard, & Ritter, 1969). Similarly, participant modeling has been demonstrated to have greater efficacy than covert modeling in the reduction of phobic behavior, as indicated in the discussion of the Thase and Moss (1976) study in the preceding section. Other studies have shown the superiority of performance-based treatment over imaginal desensitization (Crowe et al., 1972) and imaginal flooding (Emmelkamp & Wessels, 1975; Stern & Marks, 1973). Even in the case of Mathews et al.'s (1976) study discussed in the section on flooding above, imaginal flooding seemed to be effective by virtue of producing self-directed in vivo practice *between* therapy sessions. There was no immediate discernible positive effect of the specific imaginal flooding sessions per se. Furthermore, as discussed more fully in Section VII of this volume, both Kockott, Dittmar and Nusselt (1975) and Mathews, Bancroft, Whitehead, Hackmann, Julier, Bancroft, Gath, and Shaw report that sexual dysfunction was most effectively treated by a Masters and Johnson-type program that relied on directed practice in vivo as opposed to imaginal systematic desensitization.

The foregoing studies indicate the greater efficacy of a performance-based treatment method over *imaginal* techniques such as systematic desensitization, flooding, symbolic and covert modeling. There is no a priori reason to expect that cognitive methods such as RET that rely on covert verbal operations should be any more effective than those that involve mental imagery. This is borne out by the available evidence. Self-instructional training was no more effective than imaginal systematic desensitization in the treatment of either public speaking anxiety (Meichenbaum, Gilmore, & Fedoravicius, 1971) or under-assertive clients (Thorpe, 1975). Meichenbaum (1972) reported that a stress inoculation treatment that combined cognitive self-instructional training with a modified desensitization procedure resulted in greater generalization of therapeutic improvement than imaginal systematic desensitization. However, the complex nature of his cognitive modification procedure makes it impossible to sort out what the effective agents of change were.

In other studies, neither D'Zurilla, Wilson, and Nelson (1973) nor Wein, Nelson, and Odom (1975) found cognitive restructuring—a technique designed to teach clients to relabel anxiety-eliciting thoughts in a more rational manner—to be superior to systematic desensitization in the treatment of fears of small animals. Lastly, in a well-controlled comparative outcome study of interpersonal anxiety, DiLoreto (1971) found that systematic desensitization resulted in significantly greater improvement on clients' self-rating and objective behavioral ratings of interpersonal anxiety than RET at posttreatment and at a three month follow-up. RET was superior in terms of subjects' estimates of their interpersonal activity in the natural environment. Systematic desensitization was equally effective with both introverted and extroverted subjects, whereas RET differed from the attention-placebo control treatment only with respect to introverts. In the absence of additional evidence it is impossible to know whether this sort of person variable is a useful predictor of the outcome of cognitive therapies like RET.

An exception to the studies reviewed above has been reported by Holroyd (1976). In a well-controlled study, Holroyd randomly assigned test anxious students to one of four treatment groups: a) cognitive therapy, which was based upon Ellis' RET; b) systematic desensitization; c) a combination of cognitive therapy and systematic desensitization; and d) a credible pseudotherapy control procedure. Commendably, Holroyd had independently shown this pseudotherapy procedure to be effective in controlling for subject's therapeutic expectancies of improvement, thereby satisfying one of the requirements laid down by Kazdin and Wilcoxon for unambiguous demonstration of specific treatment effects.

Cognitive therapy was significantly more effective than the other treatments in reducing test anxiety in an analogue testing situation and in improving subjects' grade point average. The other methods did not differ among each other. It is possible that the specific nature of the target response—test anxiety—favored a cognitive method that focused on attentional and interpretive mechanisms rather than emotional arousal. As Holroyd points out, Wine (1971) found that the former, but not the latter, arousal process was related to test performance. In addition to emphasizing the apparent superiority of cognitive therapy in this instance, Holroyd observes that the lack of difference between the systematic desensitization and pseudotherapy treatments is further evidence that desensitization is not more effective than a highly credible attention-placebo control group. This supports Kazdin and Wilcoxon's conclusion, discussed above.

One other feature of Holroyd's findings deserves mention. The combined cognitive therapy plus systematic desensitization group was no more effective than the systematic desensitization group alone, despite the greater efficacy of cognitive therapy as a single treatment. This outcome is consistent with Meichenbaum et al.'s findings, and shows that multimodal treatment approaches do not guarantee improved results. Holroyd concludes that ". . . it appears likely that the results obtained with combined treatments will be influenced by procedural variables such as the order in which treatment techniques are administered and the length of treatment, as well as by the specific treatment techniques that are combined. Thus, an accurate assessment of such complex treatment packages will probably require further research on these and other procedural variables that have been given little attention to date" (p. 1000).

Novaco (1976) extended self-instructional training to the treatment of excessive anger. Four treatments were compared: a) self-instructional training combined with relaxation training; b) self-instructional training alone; c) relaxation training alone; and d) a placebo control treatment. The results indicate that the combined treatment was more effective relative to either self-instructional or relaxation training alone. The significance of this sort of finding with respect to multimodal treatments is discussed further in the commentary to Section V.

SOCIAL SKILLS AND ASSERTIVENESS TRAINING

In the noble tradition of the Chinese calendar, we dubbed last year's volume of the *Annual Review of Behavior Therapy* as the Year of Assertion. Reading the behavior therapy literature and evaluating papers submitted for the annual convention of the Association for Advancement of Behavior Therapy, as one of us has recently done, it is clear that the furious research activity and literary outpouring show no sign of abating. However, we reiterate the caveat we sounded last year about the hyperbolic advocacy of assertion training in some quarters and the relative lack of systematic outcome research on the procedures that are being so widely prescribed.

Social skills training is closely related to assertion training, and it is in this domain that most serious research has been conducted. (Research on social skills training is also discussed in Section VIII of this volume). Curran, Gilbert, and Little (1976) compared a social skills training program with a sensitivity training approach in the treatment of heterosexual dating anxiety. The specific social skills that were the focus of the program included the following: "a) the giving and receiving of compliments, b) nonverbal methods of communication, c) assertion training, d) feeling talk, e) handling periods of silence, f) training in planning and asking for dates, g) ways of enhancing physical attractiveness, and h) approaches to physical intimacy problems" (p. 192). The goals of the sensitivity program, modeled after an established small group program, were "to increase the participants' openness to honest expression of feelings, to increase their awareness of others, and to provide a 'safe atmosphere' in which the participants could experiment with new behavioral styles that would lead to more satisfactory heterosexual relations" (p. 192). The behavioral social skills treatment was significantly more effective than sensitivity training in reducing heterosexual anxiety as assessed by specific self-report and simulated interaction measures.

Social skills training was compared to systematic desensitization and no treatment in order to assist undergraduates participate more comfortably in classroom discussions (Wright, 1976). Although treatments were equally superior to no treatment on self-report measures and on a simulated behavioral task, neither treatment produced improvement in the natural environment. Since most experimental studies utilize only laboratory measures of outcome, Wright points out that these results strongly encourage the inclusion of measures of generalization of change in laboratory-based studies.

As with much of the fear reduction research in behavior therapy, social skills procedures have often been tested in subjects with relatively minor interpersonal deficits. In this regard, Marzillier, Lambert, and Kellett (1976) report an important controlled outcome study of social skills training with more severely inadequate subjects. Their subjects were outpatients (except for one who was hospitalized) who complained of interpersonal difficulties, reported anxiety in a wide range of social situations, and showed obvious deficits in social skills. Individuals who met these criteria, showed no other disorder, and were between 16 and 45 years of age were randomly assigned to one of three groups: systematic desensitization, social skills training, and a waiting list control group. Assessment consisted of measures of social anxiety, social skills (an actual behavioral interaction), and range and frequency of subjects' social contacts (assessed by means of a social diary and standardized interview), and clinical rating scales.

The results are discouraging. Neither treatment produced a greater improvement in social anxiety, social skills, or clinical ratings than the no treatment control group. The social skills training, however, resulted in a significantly increased range of social activities compared to the control group, even at a six months follow-up. Yet even these data must be interpreted with caution. Six subjects dropped out of the desensitization group and one dropped out of the social skills training group during treatment. At follow-up, three of the eight social skills subjects were not contacted. If these subjects are counted as failures, then the results at follow-up are less impressive. Marzillier et al. provide an informative discussion of the results, as well as the practical difficulties encountered in implementing the behavioral treatment procedures.

Arkowitz, Levine, Grosscup, O'Neil, Youngren, Royce, and Largay (1976) have similarly addressed themselves to the clinical applications of social skills training. Their preliminary findings are no more encouraging than those of Marzillier et al. Arkowitz et al. emphasize that most studies have obtained statistically significant results that frequently fall far short of applied, substantive importance. Now that a treatment prototype has been developed in the laboratory using subjects with relatively simple problems, more complex and severe interpersonal deficiencies require attention.

Assertion training was shown to be more effective than attention-placebo control groups in studies by Kirschner (1976) and Winship and Kelley (1976). An attempt to develop generalized improvement in the former study was largely unsuccessful. Limited generalization occurred only to situations that were very similar to the situations employed during training, and even this generalization was not evident at the three week follow-up. Rimm, Snyder, Depue, Haanstad, and Armstrong (1976) compared the full assertion training treatment package with simple rehearsal of the target behavior. In addition to rehearsal of the target behavior by the client, the full assertion training program included modeling of the appropriate behavior by the therapist, feedback about the adequacy of the subject's rehearsal of the behavior, and reinforcement for approximations to improved assertiveness. Male college students who complained of a problem with authority figures showed marked improvement following the full assertion training program but minimal change as a result of the rehearsal component alone. These data are consistent with Hersen, Eisler, and Miller's (1974) finding that practice alone does not necessarily produce an increase in assertive behavior.

In other applications, assertion training has been discussed as a "rape prevention measure" by Mastria and Hosford (1976). In essence, these authors suggest that the typical rape prevention, self-defense programs may be unsuccessful with unassertive women. The reason, they propose, is that the unassertive woman who is consistently passive in interpersonal interactions is unlikely to become assertive and implement self-defense and aggressive behavior during the crisis brought on by a sexual assault. Assertion training might prepare the woman for implementing the various measures she is taught in rape prevention classes. The speculation that unassertive women particularly attract rapists is simply that—speculation. The determinants of rape, while imperfectly understood at the present time, are certain to involve multiple factors.

Predictably, attempts are being made to link assertiveness to personality traits and to measure the effect of assertion training on such traits. Whitley and Poulsen (1975) gathered information on the assertiveness and sexual satisfaction of professional women and conducted a factor analysis of the data. The results indicate that assertiveness and reported sexual satisfaction are positively correlated, and that, as assertiveness increases, the women's reported sexual behavior became more diverse. Hartsook, Olch, and de Wolf (1976) examined the scores on the Edwards Personal Preference Schedule of women in assertiveness training groups. They concluded, perhaps not surprisingly, that these women are concerned with approval from others and that they are moderately inhibited in expressing their feelings. In other respects, the woman who enters an assertion training group is said to be "integrated and autonomous." Behavioral researchers and therapists will be more interested in the assessment of specific behaviors that relate to treatment outcome.

SECTION II: RELAXATION TRAINING, SYSTEMATIC DESENSITIZATION, FLOODING, MODELING, COGNITIVE RESTRUCTURING AND ASSERTION TRAINING

1

A CONTROLLED STUDY TO ASSESS THE CLINICAL EFFICACY OF TOTALLY SELF-ADMINISTERED SYSTEMATIC DESENSITIZATION

Gerald M. Rosen, Russell E. Glasgow, and Manuel Barrera, Jr.

University of Oregon

Highly anxious self-referred snake phobics received either (a) therapist-administered desensitization, (b) self-administered desensitization with weekly therapist phone calls, (c) totally self-administered desensitization, (d) a self-administered double-blind placebo control, or (e) no treatment. Pretreatment to posttreatment and follow-up assessments of subjects' reactions and attitudes toward snakes included behavioral approach, self-report, and heart period data. The latter two measures revealed significant differences between desensitization and control subjects. It was

---

This study was supported by Grant MH25657-01 awarded by the National Institute of Mental Health to the first author.

The authors thank J. Glasgow, J. Nyland, and K. Orton who served as research assistants. Therapists in the study were M. Barrera, G. Foss, R. Glasgow, K. Johnson, and R. Warren. Their efforts and commitment to the project are greatly appreciated. Thanks also to Gwen Kingsley for her persistent help in the preparation of this manuscript.

concluded that within the context of moderate treatment effects the present study provides support for the clinical efficacy of totally self-administered desensitization. Implications of these findings for the clinical management of specific fears are discussed.

A number of clinical case reports and partially controlled studies have had clients self-administer systematic desensitization with only minimal therapist contact (Baker, Cohen, & Saunders, 1973; Clark, 1973; Dawley, Guildry, & Curtis, 1973; Kahn & Baker, 1968; Migler & Wolpe, 1967; Morris & Thomas, 1973). The possibility of totally self-administered desensitization has also been evaluated (Phillips, Johnson, & Geyer, 1972). In self-administered desensitization, clients use instructional materials to teach themselves procedural details and conduct their own treatment. These procedures are to be distinguished from automated desensitization programs that use equipment that mechanically presents treatment to a client (e.g., Lang, Melamed, & Hart, 1970).

Current findings on self-administered desensitization are only suggestive. Uncontrolled case reports are insufficient for drawing firm conclusions, and most outcome studies in the area have methodological problems. Clients' self-reported change is frequently relied on as the sole index of treatment outcome (Kahn & Baker, 1968; Morris & Thomas, 1973; Phillips et al., 1972). Even when tied to specific behavioral situations (Baker et al., 1973), reliance on self-reported change without confirmation from a second observer is not totally satisfactory. In addition to assessment problems, most studies have failed to include adequate controls. Comparisons with untreated subjects are often absent (Clark, 1973; Kahn & Baker, 1968; Morris & Thomas, 1973). Studies have consistently failed to include appropriate placebo controls.

Despite shortcomings in available data, the suggestion that individuals with specific phobias can treat themselves is an important one. Empirically validated self-help programs can extend the availability of effective clinical procedures to greater numbers of individuals. Once developed, these treatments can usefully serve as a standard against which more costly forms of treatment might be compared. The significant implications that self-help programs have for clinical practice necessitates the adequate development and assessment of these programs (Rosen, 1976).

The present study evaluates the clinical efficacy of self-administered desensitization in the context of a controlled outcome study. Highly anxious snake phobics were assigned to receive either (a) therapist-administered desensitization, (b) self-administered desensitization with weekly therapist phone calls, (c) totally self-administered desensitization, (d) a self-administered double-blind placebo control, or (e) no treatment. Pretreatment to posttreatment and follow-up assessments of subjects' reactions and attitudes toward snakes included behavioral approach, self-report, and heart period data.

The literature of recent years has been filled with analogue studies employing mildly fearful "college student" snake phobics. For valid reasons, these studies have recently come under attack (Bernstein & Paul, 1971). It is important for researchers to remember that the rejection of studies on snake phobia has been justified by the analogue nature of these investigations and not by the nature of the phobia per se. The study of *highly* anxious snake phobics can still be a clinically justifiable endeavor with implications for the treatment of specific phobia. The term "specific phobia" is used in this context to refer to single-item phobias that remain isolated from other problems of adjustment (Marks, 1969).

The present investigation took care to exclude mildly anxious analogue subjects by employing stringent selection criteria (Rosen, 1975). To further demonstrate the high level of anxiety experienced by experimental subjects, a group of nonfearful controls was assessed. Efforts were also made to avoid analogue treatment procedures. The procedural guidelines of clinical desensitization as first reported by Wolpe (1958) and later tested by Lang, Lazovik, and Reynolds (1965) and Paul (1966) were closely followed.

METHOD

Subjects

Subjects were self-referred snake phobics who (a) responded to a local newspaper announcement that offered treatment for individuals "truly terrified of snakes"; (b) refused to touch a snake during a behavior approach test; (c) scored 19 or above on the Snake Attitude Questionnaire (SNAQ; Klorman, Hastings, Weerts, Melamed, & Lang, 1974); (d) rated "very much fear" or "terror" on the snake item of Geer's (1965) Fear Survey Schedule (FSS); (e) specified a target situation such as gardening or camping that was significantly affected by fear of snakes; and (f) were not currently receiving treatment for their phobia. As discussed by Rosen (1975), 55 subjects initially met the above criteria. Because of subject loss during the study, a final N of 43 was obtained. Mean age of subjects was 33.5. The mean number of years subjects reported fearing snakes was 25.9. All but 4 of the subjects were female.

Procedure

Pretreatment to posttreatment and follow-up assessments of subjects' attitudes and reactions toward snakes were conducted by assistants blind to subjects' group assignment.* During pretreatment assessments, subjects were initially met by the first author and presented with a general time schedule for the project (e.g., assessments before and after an 8-week treatment program). Subjects then filled out several questionnaires including the SNAQ and Geer's FSS. A research assistant next met with the subjects and asked if they would view a series of 10 slides containing randomly intermixed pictures of snakes and neutral scenery. After each 15-sec slide presentation, subjects rated how anxious they had felt by using a 10-point fear thermometer (Lang et al., 1965). This was accomplished by projecting the thermometer's scale on the viewing screen and having the subjects call out their ratings. An 8-sec period was provided for subjects to make their ratings. This was followed by a 20-sec rest interval. The sequence of slide presentation/anxiety rating/rest period was repeated until 5 neutral slides (Numbers 1, 3, 4, 7, and 9) and 5 snake slides (Numbers 2, 5, 6, 8, and 10) had been shown.

Apparatus similar to that reported by Rosen, Rosen, and Reid (1972) was employed to provide simultaneous monitoring of slide presentations and subjects' heart rate reactions. With the use of a Carousel-Calvalcade programmer, signals recorded on audiotape assured the automatic changing of a Carousel slide projector at appropriate intervals. These changes were recorded on one channel of a Grass Model 7 polygraph through the use of a photocell positioned in front of the slide projector's lens. A Grass PTTI-6 finger plethysmograph was used to monitor subjects' heart reactions on a second channel of the polygraph.

Following slide presentations, subjects participated in a behavior approach test that employed a tame 4-foot Columbian boa securely enclosed in a covered glass cage. A progression of 16 requests began by asking whether the assistant could bring the caged snake into the subject's room. The final request asked the subjects to sit in a chair with the snake loose in their lap. The test was terminated whenever the subjects indicated an unwillingness to complete a request. Instructions were tape recorded and moderately high in demand for approach. After completing a request, the subjects rated how anxious they had felt. Ratings were made on a 10-point scale similar to that employed during slide presenta-

* Copies of assessment instruments and/or instructional materials associated with these assessments are available on request.

tions. Except for when the snake had to be moved into the subject's room, the research assistant remained in an adjacent room and observed the subject's performance through a one-way mirror.

After pretreatment assessments had been completed, the subjects were matched on behavior approach scores and assigned by block randomization to one of four treatment groups or a no-treatment control. Treatment programs began approximately 6 weeks after pretesting. Within 4 days after completing treatment or at the end of 8 weeks (whichever came first), subjects received a posttreatment assessment of their reactions and attitudes toward snakes. Posttreatment assessments followed the same procedural sequence already discussed, with the exception that subjects met with the first author at the end of the assessment period rather than at the beginning. In addition, subjects were asked to rate perceived changes in their fear. A 6-point scale whose answer choices ranged from "increased" to "substantially decreased" was employed for these general treatment ratings.

A 2-month follow-up was conducted in the same manner as posttreatment assessments.

*Treatment Conditions**

Therapist-administered desensitization. Subjects in this group met twice a week with one of five graduate student therapists. All therapists had at least 1 semester of supervised work in general clinical practicum. Therapists were trained in desensitization techniques during weekly group meetings that were held over a 3-month period prior to treatment. A common set of instructional materials was used as part of the training program. Articles by Lazarus (1964) and Wolpe (1973) were included as well as procedural manuals by Marquis, Morgan, and Piaget (1974), Paul (1966), and Bernstein and Borkovec (1973). Between regular training sessions, therapists met with each other and role played each step in the program. Treatment was highly standardized across therapists through the use of procedural outlines. In addition, the procedures for relaxation training and hierarchy construction were modeled by the first author with a client who served as a training case. Finally, the first author

* Copies of the manuals for self-administered desensitization, systematic relearning, and the instructional packet used for training therapists are available on request. A program for self-administered progressive relaxation may also be obtained from the first author. Minimum charges for reproducing these programs may be necessary depending on the availability of reprint funds.

reviewed audiorecordings of treatment sessions and held weekly review meetings with therapists.

Efforts were made to avoid the use of analogue procedures (Bernstein & Paul, 1971). Treatment procedures were similar to those of earlier outcome studies (Lang et al., 1965; Paul, 1966). Subjects generally met twice a week and had up to 8 weeks to complete treatment. From two to four sessions were spent teaching progressive relaxation skills. Recorded training materials were not employed since they may be less effective than therapist instructions (Paul & Trimble, 1970). During relaxation training, procedures outlined by Bernstein and Borkovec (1973) were followed. Individual hierarchies consisting of 16 to 20 items were constructed with the aid of subjective units of disturbance ratings as discussed by Wolpe (1973). Rules governing subjects' progress through hierarchy items closely paralleled those of Lang et al. (1965).

Self-administered desensitization. A manual for totally self-administered systematic desensitization was developed as part of this study (Rosen, Note 1). *The manual was written so as to closely parallel all procedures used by therapists in the clinic.* A log sheet accompanied the program so that subjects could record each session and chart their rate of progress in the program.

In addition to written materials, subjects were given a record of relaxation instructions (Kahn, cited in Kahn & Baker, 1968, p. 198) to help them learn varied instructional phrases. Subjects were instructed to always conduct practice sessions on their own and to not rely on recorded procedures. In this way, completion of individual muscle groups was contingent on the subjects' own rate of progress (Paul & Trimble, 1970).

Treatment materials were mailed to the subjects so that the programs were totally self-administered at home. The project staff had no contact with the subjects until the subjects had completed their program or until the 8-week treatment period ended.

Minimal contact desensitization. Subjects in this group were sent the same written and recorded materials for self-administered desensitization as previously described. In addition, subjects received weekly phone calls from the same therapists who worked with clients in the clinic group. During these phone calls, therapists served as consultants who answered questions and made procedural suggestions. Calls ranged from 4 to 49 minutes with an average time per call of 11.4 minutes.

Placebo control. To control for initial therapeutic expectancies and other nonspecific treatment factors (Paul, 1969), a totally self-administered bibliotherapy placebo called *systematic relearning* was included in the present study. The basic rationale of the treatment program was that people could substantially reduce their fears by replacing inaccurate perceptions with more accurate information about the feared object. To accomplish this goal, each individual studies a manual that organizes factual information about snakes into 10 chapters. Each chapter contains questions at the end to help subjects assess their mastery of the materials. As subjects work on the program they construct an "information hierarchy" from the relevant information in each chapter.

Because of recent findings that question the adequacy of many placebo procedures (Borkovec & Nau, 1972; McGlynn & McDonnell, 1974), a number of steps were taken to assure adequate experimental control over subjects' expectancies.* In addition, possible therapist expectancy effects were avoided by sending all self-instructional materials through the mail. In effect, systematic relearning and self-administered desensitization as previously described were administered under *double-blind* conditions.

No-treatment control. Subjects in this group were informed that the large number of clients in the project necessitated a delay in treatment for some individuals. After posttesting, untreated controls were offered treatment.

Nonfearful controls. A group of volunteer undergraduates ($n = 9$) reporting "little" or "no" fear of snakes participated in the assessment procedures previously described. These subjects received course credit for research participation.

---

* The rationale for systematic relearning was initially piloted on undergraduate analogue subjects and compared to descriptions of therapist and self-administered desensitization. To control for possible effects resulting from differential familiarity with rationale titles, self-administered desensitization and relearning titles were crossed with rationales in a 2×2 factorial design. Additionally, the desensitization rationale used by Paul (1966) was included to provide comparisons with earlier work on therapeutic expectancies (Borkovec & Nau, 1972). Subjects ($N = 173$) received one of these rationales and indicated their expectancy for improvement on the same 6-point scale that subjects in the present study used for general ratings of treatment outcome (answer choices ranged from increased to substantially decreased).

In the present study, subjects were sent a rationale of their treatment program in the mail after group assignments had been completed. The treatment rationales were identical to those used with the analogue investigation (the self-administered desensitization group with phone calls received the rationale for self-administered desensitization with an additional paragraph explaining the calls). Subjects rated their initial therapeutic expectancies using the same scale previously described. Their responses were returned to the project in preaddressed envelopes to avoid personal contact.

RESULTS

Subject Loss

Two subjects in each of the therapist-aided treatment groups dropped out of their programs during the first week of therapy. Three self-administered desensitization subjects, 1 placebo control, and 4 untreated controls could not be reached at time of posttesting primarily because of address changes. Accordingly, a final N of 43 was achieved, and group sizes were not equal (see Table 1). Analyses of data relating to slide presentations involved further subject reductions since 8 (18%) of the subjects refused to view the slides during pretreatment and posttreatment assessments. Also, 18 (42%) of the subjects refused during pretreatment assessment to allow the caged snake in their room. This resulted in fear thermometer data being so limited that analyses of subjects' responses to this measure were not attempted.

Interpretation of follow-up data was made difficult by substantial subject losses. Of the original 26 desensitization subjects, only 15 (58%) were available for follow-up assessments. Problems of interpretation were still greater for placebo and untreated controls. These subjects had been offered self-administered desensitization programs at the end of posttreatment assessments. Even though all untreated subjects accepted the program, only 6 of 10 placebo subjects remained interested in pursuing additional treatment. At follow-up, a few control subjects had finished self-administered desensitization ($n = 2$), others had completed only portions of their program ($n = 7$), and almost one third had never really looked at the self-instructional materials ($n = 4$). Considering the small number of these subjects and their heterogeneous experiences, analyses of follow-up data were performed on desensitization subjects alone.

Analyses

Many reports on evoked cardiac responses convert heart periods (the time between R waves of an electrocardiogram) into heart rate data. Recent studies that argue against this nonlinear transformation have demonstrated that heart period data are statistically preferred because they conform more closely than heart rate data to a normal distribution (Jennings, Stringfellow, & Graham, 1974; Khachaturian, Kerr, Kruger, & Schachter, 1972). Interpretation of heart period data is straightforward —the longer a particular period, the slower the subject's heartbeat. In the present study, subjects' heart reactions were calculated by measuring the number of millimeters between the first and fifth heartbeats that

TABLE 1

SUBJECTS' PRETEST AND POSTTEST PERFORMANCE ON THE BEHAVIOR APPROACH TEST AND QUESTIONNAIRES

Group	BAT		SNAQ		FSS item		Initial expectancies (pre only), General rating (post only)	
	M	*SD*	*M*	*SD*	*M*	*SD*	*M*	*SD*
Desensitization therapist[a]								
Pre	2.44	2.83	25.67	2.65	6.56	.53	1.89	1.10
Post	5.33	3.61	17.44	5.08	5.00	1.22	1.89	1.05
Desensitization calls[a]								
Pre	1.33	1.73	24.67	1.80	6.89	.33	1.78	1.13
Post	4.33	4.58	18.44	6.60	5.78	1.39	1.22	1.09
Desensitization manual[b]								
Pre	2.62	2.67	24.25	2.38	6.75	.46	2.38	.86
Post	5.62	4.21	15.50	7.23	5.12	1.46	1.62	1.19
Placebo[c]								
Pre	2.50	2.72	25.90	2.56	7.00	.00	1.90	1.04
Post	4.50	4.55	20.40	5.12	6.00	1.56	1.20	1.40
No treatment[d]								
Pre	1.71	2.43	25.00	3.11	6.86	.38	—	—
Post	2.86	2.80	23.00	3.42	6.71	.49	.00	.58

[a] $n = 9$.
[b] $n = 8$.
[c] $n = 10$.
[d] $n = 7$.

followed each slide presentation. Heart periods for five beats immediately preceding slide presentations were used to determine comparable rest periods. Analyses of heart period data were performed on slide presentation scores corrected for resting level. This was accomplished by following the "lability score" conversion recommended by Lacey (1956) and recently used by Paul and Trimble (1970).

One-way analyses of variance were performed on subjects' pretest scores to assess initial comparability of groups. Significant between-group differences on subjects' rated expectancies of therapeutic improvement were not observed. Analyses also failed to reveal significant between-group differences on any assessment measure relevant to snakes. Group means and standard deviations for each measure are reported in Table 1.*

Within-group changes (pre to post and post to follow-up) were evaluated with two-tailed t tests for paired observations. Between-group comparisons of subjects' posttest performance were obtained using analyses of covariance with pretest scores serving as the covariate. When appropriate assumptions are met, these analyses are preferable to analyses of change scores (Cronbach & Furby, 1970; Harris, 1963). In the one case in which the required assumption of equality of slope was not met (heart period data), a standard analysis of variance was performed on subjects' posttreatment scores. Subjects' general ratings of treatment outcome were also subjected to an analysis of variance since these ratings were made posttreatment only.

Comparison with Nonfearful Controls

The following comparisons between phobic subjects' pretreatment performance and the performance of nonfearful controls were all highly significant ($p < .01$ or greater). Phobic subjects showed significantly less approach behavior, $F(1, 50) = 190.34$, significantly higher scores on the SNAQ, $F(2, 50) = 687.30$, significantly higher scores on the FSS snake item, $F(1, 50) = 960.22$, and significantly greater heart reactions, $F(1, 41) = 8.79$, and higher ratings of anxiety, $F(1, 41) = 39.62$, while viewing

* Behavioral approach tests vary from study to study. To help the reader assess the magnitude of change observed for subjects in the present study, specific behaviors associated with various points in the test are clarified. Average mean pretest performance for all subjects was between 1 (letting the snake in the room) and 2 (letting the experimenter take a cloth cover off of the cage). Posttest performance for all treated subjects was generally between 4 (approaching the snake) and 6 (looking at the snake). A mean of 8.38 observed for self-administered subjects who completed at least half of their hierarchy items indicates that most of these subjects were able to lift the cover off the cage (8) or place their hand in the cage and touch the inside glass (9).

snake slides. Phobic subjects and nonfearful controls did not significantly differ in their ratings and heart reactions to neutral slides.

Posttreatment Assessment of Phobic Subjects

Within-group comparisons. Two-tailed correlated t tests performed on subjects' pretreatment and posttreatment scores revealed a consistent pattern. Subjects in the therapist-administered desensitization group showed significant change on the behavioral avoidance test, $t(8) = 3.25$, $p < .001$, the SNAQ, $t(8) = 5.82$, $p < .001$, the FSS snake item, $t(8) = 3.50$, $p < .01$, and anxiety ratings for snake slides, $t(6) = 4.74$, $p < .01$. Subjects who totally self-administered desensitization evidenced significant changes on these same measures: behavioral avoidance test, $t(7) = 3.17$, $p < .05$, SNAQ, $t(7) = 3.90$, $p < .001$, FSS snake item, $t(7) = 3.05$, $p < .05$, and the slide ratings, $t(6) = 8.68$, $p < .001$. With the exception of the FSS item, significant changes on these measures were also observed for subjects receiving self-administered desensitization with weekly phone calls: behavioral avoidance test, $t(8) = 2.85$, $p < .05$, the SNAQ, $t(8) = 2.55$, $p < .05$, the FSS snake item, $t(8) = 2.29$, *ns*, and the slide ratings, $t(5) = 3.27$, $p < .05$. General ratings of treatment outcome were significantly greater than zero (no change) for all desensitization groups: therapist administered, $t(8) = 5.38$, $p < .001$, totally self-administered, $t(7) = 3.87$, $p < .01$, and self-administered with calls, $t(8) = 3.36$, $p < .01$.

In contrast to the findings for desensitization subjects, the only significant change observed for untreated controls was an increase in heart reactions to snake slides, $t(4) = 4.35$, $p < .05$. Subjects receiving the placebo control evidenced significant changes on self-report measures only: SNAQ, $t(9) = 3.41$, $p < .01$, and general ratings, $t(9) = 2.71$, $p < .01$. The finding that 13 of 18 comparisons indicated significant improvement for desensitization subjects while only 2 of 12 comparisons did so for controls is not likely to be due to chance, $\chi^2(1) = 6.80$, $p < .01$.

Between-group comparisons. Analyses of covariance failed to reveal significant between-group differences at time of posttesting on the behavioral avoidance test, $F(4, 37) = .55$, the SNAQ, $F(4, 37) = 1.86$, or the FSS snake item, $F(4, 37) = 1.88$. However, significant between-group differences were observed on the following three measures: general treatment ratings, $F(4, 38) = 2.84$, $p < .05$, heart reactions to snake slides,*

* As previously noted, the between-group comparison for posttreatment heart period data is based on a one-way analysis of variance. As with other assessment measures, an analysis of covariance was first performed on these data with pretreatment scores serving as the covariate. This analysis was also significant, $F(4, 28) = 3.96$, $p < .025$, but the assumption of equality of slope was not met, $F(4, 24) = 3.96$, $p < .025$.

TABLE 2

SUBJECTS' POSTTREATMENT REACTIONS TO SNAKE SLIDES

	Heart period							
	Rest		Slide		Lability score		Anxiety ratings	
Group	*M*	*SD*	*M*	*SD*	*M*	*SD*	*M*	*SD*
Desensitization therapist[a]	27.66	2.36	27.68	2.75	48.17	8.06	4.83	2.20
Desensitization calls[b]	30.07	2.33	31.20	2.44	60.63	7.04	4.80	2.05
Desensitization manual[a]	28.00	3.13	28.66	2.57	53.73	3.14	4.20	2.01
Placebo[c]	28.76	2.87	28.26	2.67	45.65	8.31	6.86	2.02
No treatment[d]	31.72	2.92	30.28	1.39	42.43	10.81	8.28	1.91

Note. Means presented in this table were not adjusted for subjects' pretreatment performance. Heart period scores are based on the number of millimeters between the five heartbeats preceeding (rest) and the five beats following (slide) stimulus presentations. Lability scores are based on a conversion of the slide presentation scores that takes into account rest levels (Lacey, 1956).

[a] $n = 7$.
[b] $n = 6$.
[c] $n = 9$.
[d] $n = 5$.

$F(4, 29) = 4.49$, $p < .01$, and anxiety ratings to snake slides, $F(4, 28) = 4.23$, $p < .01$. Subjects' heart reactions and anxiety ratings in response to posttreatment presentations of snake slides are presented in Table 2.

Scheffé post hoc comparisons were performed when significant *F*s were obtained. Pair-wise comparisons between desensitization groups did not reveal significant differences on any measure. Significant differences were not obtained between the two controls. When pair-wise comparisons were conducted between desensitization groups and untreated controls, one of the desensitization groups always differed significantly: (a) the self-administered desensitization group with phone calls differed on heart period data; (b) the self-administered desensitization group differed on anxiety ratings during slide presentations; and (c) the therapist-administered desensitization group differed on general ratings. In addition, comparisons between combined desensitization groups and combined controls on heart data and anxiety ratings to snake slides revealed significant differences. When the two self-administered desensitization groups were compared to combined controls, significant differences were again obtained. For general ratings of treatment outcome, comparisons revealed significantly greater improvement for combined desensitization groups as compared to untreated controls.

Progress in Treatment

Data from earlier studies suggest a relation between treatment outcome and subjects' progress in their program (Kennedy & Kimura, 1974; Lang et al., 1965). These findings may have important implications for self-administered programs. In the present study only 8 of 17 subjects in the two self-administered desensitization groups completed at least half of their hierarchy items. Six self-administered subjects failed to progress past the relaxation phase of their program. These findings contrast with progress made by therapist-trained subjects. Six of 9 subjects who received desensitization from therapists completed their entire program within an average of 10 sessions. The remaining 3 subjects successfully completed at least 17 hierarchy items before the posttest.

Correlations between self-administered subjects' *pretest* performance and whether or not subjects completed at least half of their hierarchy items failed to approach significance with the exception of behavioral avoidance test scores, $r = .46$, $p < .10$. Correlations between posttest performance (with pretest partialed out) and whether self-administered subjects completed half of their hierarchy were significant on the behavioral avoidance test, $r_{12.3} = .76$, $p < .01$, the SNAQ, $r_{12.3} = -.78$, $p < .01$, the FSS snake item, $r_{12.3} = -.68$, $p < .01$, anxiety ratings to snake slides, $r_{12.3} = -.83$, $p < .01$, and anxiety ratings to neutral slides, $r_{12.3} = -.52$, $p < .05$. Nonsignificant correlations were obtained for heart reactions to snake slides, $r_{12.3} = .21$, and heart reactions to neutral slides, $r_{12.3} = .05$.

As revealed by analyses of covariance, subjects from the two self-administered desensitization groups who completed half of their hierarchy showed significantly greater posttest improvement on all relevant measures ($p < .01$ or better) as compared to combined controls. The means for these self-administered subjects (behavioral avoidance test = 8.38; SNAQ = 11.63; FSS snake item = 4.50; general rating = 2.38; snake slide ratings = 3.38; snake slide lability scores = 58.14) can be compared to reported group means in Tables 1 and 2 to illustrate the magnitude of change that was observed. Although a posteriori subject divisions are difficult to interpret, the present findings suggest impressive treatment effects for subjects who successfully complete self-administered desensitization.

Follow-up

Substantial subject losses make interpretation of follow-up findings difficult. Nevertheless, an interesting pattern of results emerged. Correlated *t* tests performed on posttreatment and follow-up scores were consistently nonsignificant for subjects who received therapist-administered desensitization ($n = 4$). Similar tests for subjects whose self-administered programs were supplemented with therapist calls revealed significant improvement only on the FSS snake item, $t(4) = 3.16$, $p < .05$. In contrast to these findings that suggest simple maintenance of initial treatment gains, subjects who totally self-administered desensitization ($n = 6$) showed significant improvement from posttest to follow-up on the behavioral avoidance test, $t(5) = 2.67$, $p < .05$, and the SNAQ, $t(5) = 3.31$, $p < .05$. Continued gains for these subjects were also evidenced on anxiety ratings of snake slides, $t(5) = 2.29$, and general treatment ratings, $t(5) = 2.24$. These latter changes attained marginal levels of significance ($p < .10$) when alpha levels for two-tailed tests were used. The only measure on which these subjects failed to show further improvement over posttesting levels was heart period data, $t(5) = -.49$.

DISCUSSION

Within the context of generally moderate treatment effects, the present investigation provides support for the use of totally self-administered desensitization in the treatment of specific animal phobia. Highly fearful snake phobics who self-administered desensitization did not differ significantly on any index of treatment outcome from similar subjects who met with a therapist. In addition, weekly therapist phone calls did not augment the effects obtained by a totally self-administered program. As compared to controls, desensitization subjects had significantly longer heart periods (slower heart rate) and lower anxiety ratings in response to posttest presentations of snake slides. General ratings of treatment outcome also indicated significantly greater improvement for desensitization subjects. Finally, within-group comparisons of pretest-posttest scores showed a trend that strongly favored desensitization groups over controls. Inspection of Tables 1 and 2 reveals a consistent pattern among group means that distinguishes desensitization groups from the controls.

Additional findings of possible importance in evaluating self-administered programs were obtained at follow-up. The follow-up data suggested that subjects who totally self-administered desensitization continued to improve after posttesting, whereas subjects treated by therapists simply maintained earlier treatment gains. These findings are only suggestive because of substantial subject losses. Nevertheless, they are consistent with data reported by Baker et al. (1973), who found that self-directed subjects at time of follow-up showed additional gains on self-reported behavioral improvement while therapist-directed subjects only maintained posttest levels of performance. Future studies on self-administered programs should continue to include follow-up evaluations to assess the extent to which self-help programs facilitate generalization and maintenance of treatment effects.

Whereas the present study suggests that totally self-administered desensitization is clinically useful, it is also clear that treatment effects were often unimpressive. Limited treatment effects were particularly apparent on the behavioral approach test that failed to reveal significant between-group differences. In this context, it is interesting to note that many desensitization studies commonly employ anxiety hierarchies whose items exactly parallel the behavior test on which subjects are to be evaluated (e.g., Bandura, Blanchard, & Ritter, 1969; Davison, 1968; Leitenberg, Agras, Barlow, & Oliveau, 1969). This type of hierarchy probably maximizes differential treatment effects when desensitization subjects and controls are compared. Following the procedures employed by Lang et al. (1965), subjects in the present study constructed hierarchies based on relevant situations in their natural environment. It remains unclear which method of hierarchy construction is preferred when the goal is to maximize change in the subjects' relevant environment. The method used in the present study could have had a limiting effect on the magnitude of change in approach behavior observed for desensitization subjects.

Even when procedural variations are taken into account, the magnitude of treatment effects observed in the present study was at times disappointing. It is important to note that the findings are not dissimilar from those obtained by other studies in the area. Lang et al. (1965) reported statistically significant effects only for those comparisons involving combined control groups. In other investigations, desensitization has not always been significantly more effective than control conditions (e.g., McReynolds, Barnes, Brooks, & Rehagen, 1973; Sherman, 1972; Wilson, 1973). Desensitization may be generally more adequate than no-treatment or expectancy controls, but the magnitude of this effect is at times unimpressive (Marks, 1969).

Of possible significance to the development of self-help treatments was the finding that over 50% of the subjects assigned to self-administer desensitization failed to progress past the relaxation portions of their programs. This is in line with other investigations that report a large percentage of subjects dropping out of studies (Clark, 1973) or failing to complete their programs (Phillips et al., 1972). The issue of subject maintenance in self-administered programs is especially important in light of the significant and clinically relevant reductions in anxiety that were consistently experienced by subjects who successfully completed a majority of the items in their hierarchies.

In the present study, subjects who failed to complete their treatment generally blamed environmental factors such as illness, job changes, or general lack of available time. In this respect, self-administered treatments may be similar to weight reduction programs, exercise regimens, or other procedures that require sustained self-directed efforts. It is always possible, however, that failure to complete a self-administered treatment relates to specific effects that the program has with a particular client. Future research might look more closely at subject characteristics associated with successful completion of self-administered treatments (Baker et al., 1973). It may also be useful to consider alternative instructional formats, the use of money deposits, programmed reinforcers, and/or other manipulations specifically designed to help maintain subjects' involvements.

In consideration of current findings, clinicians might want to inform clients who complain of specific phobias about the relative merits of self-administered and therapist-aided programs. Clients could then consider the relative efficacies and costs of these various programs, their own financial situations, their motivation to conduct a self-help program, and other factors relevant to the individual. Within this framework, both client and clinician could come to a decision regarding treatment procedures that are mutually acceptable and clinically prudent.

REFERENCE NOTE

1. ROSEN, G. M. *A Manual for Self-Administering Systematic Desensitization in Your Home*. Unpublished manuscript, University of Oregon, Eugene, 1974.

REFERENCES

BAKER, B. L., COHEN, D. C., & SAUNDERS, J. T. Self-directed desensitization for acrophobia. *Behaviour Research and Therapy,* 11:79-89, 1973.

BANDURA, A., BLANCHARD, E. B., & RITTER, B. Relative efficacy of desensitization and modeling approaches for inducing behavioral, affective, and attitudinal changes. *Journal of Personality and Social Psychology,* 13:173-199, 1969.

BERNSTEIN, D. A., & BORKOVEC, T. D. *Progressive Relaxation Training: A Manual for the Helping Professions*. Champaign, Ill.: Research Press, 1973.

BERNSTEIN, D. A., & PAUL, G. L. Some comments on therapy analogue research with small animal "phobias." *Journal of Behavior Therapy and Experimental Psychiatry,* 2:225-237, 1971.

BORKOVEC, T. D., & NAU, S. D. Credibility of analogue therapy rationales. *Journal of Behavior Therapy and Experimental Psychiatry,* 3:257-260, 1972.

CLARK, F. Self-administered desensitization. *Behaviour Research and Therapy,* 11:335-338, 1973.

CRONBACH, L., & FURBY, L. How should we measure "change"—Or should we? *Psychological Bulletin,* 74:68-80, 1970.

DAVISON, G. C. Systematic desensitization as a counterconditioning process. *Journal of Abnormal Psychology,* 73:91-99, 1968.

DAWLEY, H. H., GUIDRY, L. S., & CURTIS, E. Self-administered desensitization on a psychiatric ward: A case report. *Journal of Behavior Therapy and Experimental Psychiatry,* 4:301-303, 1973.

GEER, J. H. The development of a scale to measure fear. *Behaviour Research and Therapy,* 3:45-53, 1965.

HARRIS, C. W. *Problems in Measuring Change.* Madison: University of Wisconsin Press, 1963.

JENNINGS, J. R., STRINGFELLOW, J. C., & GRAHAM, M. A comparison of the statistical distributions of beat-by-beat heart rate and heart period. *Psychophysiology,* 11:207-210, 1974.

KAHN, M., & BAKER, B. Desensitization with minimal therapist contact. *Journal of Abnormal Psychology,* 73:198-200, 1968.

KENNEDY, T. D., & KIMURA, H. K. Transfer, behavioral improvement, and anxiety reduction in systematic desensitization. *Journal of Consulting and Clinical Psychology,* 42:720-728, 1974.

KHACHATURIAN, Z. S., KERR, J., KRUGER, R., & SCHACHTER, J. A methodological note: Comparison between period and rate data in studies of cardiac function. *Psychophysiology,* 9:539-545, 1972.

KLORMAN, R., HASTINGS, J. F., WEERTS, T. C., MELAMED, B. G., & LANG, P. J. Psychometric description of some specific fear questionnaires. *Behavior Therapy,* 5:401-409, 1974.

LACEY, J. I. The evaluation of autonomic responses: Toward a general solution. *Annals of the New York Academy of Science,* 67:123-163, 1956.

LANG, P. J., LAZOVIK, A. D., & REYNOLDS, D. J. Desensitization, suggestibility, and pseudotherapy. *Journal of Abnormal Psychology,* 70:395-402, 1965.

LANG, P. J., MELAMED, B. G., & HART, J. A psychophysiological analysis of fear modification using an automated desensitization procedure. *Journal of Abnormal Psychology,* 76:220-234, 1970.

LAZARUS, A. A. Crucial procedural factors in desensitization therapy. *Behaviour Research and Therapy,* 2:65-70, 1964.

LEITENBERG, H., AGRAS, W. S., BARLOW, D. H., & OLIVEAU, D. C. Contribution of selective positive reinforcement and therapeutic instructions to systematic desensitization therapy. *Journal of Abnormal Psychology,* 74:113-118, 1969.

MARKS, F. M. *Fears and Phobias.* New York: Academic Press, 1969.

MARQUIS, J. N., MORGAN, W. G., & PIAGET, G. W. *A Guidebook for Systematic Desensitization* (3rd ed.). Palo Alto, Calif.: Veterans' Workshop, Veterans Administration Hospital, 1974.

MCGLYNN, F. D., & MCDONNELL, R. M. Subjective ratings of credibility following brief exposure to desensitization and pseudotherapy. *Behaviour Research and Therapy,* 12:141-146, 1974.

MCREYNOLDS, W. T., BARNES, A. R., BROOKS, S., & REHAGEN, J. J. The role of attention placebo influences in the efficacy of systematic desensitization. *Journal of Consulting and Clinical Psychology,* 41:86-92, 1973.

MIGLER, B., & WOLPE, J. Automated desensitization: A case report. *Behaviour Research and Therapy,* 5:133, 1967.

MORRIS, L. W., & THOMAS, C. R. Treatment of phobias by a self-administered desensitization technique. *Journal of Behavior Therapy and Experimental Psychiatry,* 4: 397-399, 1973.

PAUL, G. L. *Insight vs. Desensitization in Psychotherapy.* Stanford, Calif.: Stanford University Press, 1966.

PAUL, G. L. Behavior modification research: Design and tactics. In C. M. Franks (Ed.), *Behavior Therapy: Appraisal and Status.* New York: McGraw-Hill, 1969.

PAUL, G. L., & TRIMBLE, R. W. Recorded vs. "live" relaxation training and hypnotic suggestion: Comparative effectiveness for reducing physiological arousal and inhibiting stress response. *Behavior Therapy,* 1:285-302, 1970.

PHILLIPS, R. E., JOHNSON, G. D., & GEYER, A. Self-administered systematic desensitization. *Behaviour Research and Therapy,* 10:93-96, 1972.

ROSEN, G. M. Is it really necessary to use mildly phobic analogue subjects? *Behavior Therapy,* 6:68-71, 1975.

ROSEN, G. M. The development and use of nonprescription behavior therapies. *American Psychologist,* 31:139-141, 1976.

ROSEN, G. M., ROSEN, E., & REID, J. Cognitive desensitization and avoidance behavior: A re-evaluation. *Journal of Abnormal Psychology,* 80:176-182, 1972.

SHERMAN, A. R. Real-life exposure as a primary therapeutic factor in the desensitization treatment of fear. *Journal of Abnormal Psychology,* 79:19-28, 1972.

WILSON, G. T. Effects of false feedback on avoidance behavior: "Cognitive" desensitization revisited. *Journal of Personality and Social Psychology,* 28:115-122, 1973.

WOLPE, J. *Psychotherapy by Reciprocal Inhibition.* Stanford, Calif.: Stanford University Press, 1958.

WOLPE, J. *The Practice of Behavior Therapy* (2nd ed.). New York: Pergamon Press, 1973.

SECTION II: RELAXATION TRAINING, SYSTEMATIC DESENSITIZATION, FLOODING, MODELING, COGNITIVE RESTRUCTURING AND ASSERTION TRAINING

2

EFFECTS OF PROGRESSIVE RELAXATION ON SLEEP DISTURBANCE: AN ELECTROENCEPHALOGRAPHIC EVALUATION

Thomas D. Borkovec and Theodore C. Weerts

University of Iowa

Subjects with reported sleep-onset disturbance were given progressive relaxation training, placebo, or no-treatment. All three conditions showed significant improvement in daily reported sleep onset over the duration of the study. Between-condition effects were limited to relaxation superiority over no-treatment on Stage I sleep, and over placebo on postquestionnaire items and sleep-latency reports at 1-year follow-up.

INTRODUCTION

Recent evidence from several investigations suggests that relaxation training may be an effective, brief therapy for reducing reported latency to sleep onset among sleep disturbed individuals (1-7). Unfortunately, the designs of these studies have failed to provide cause and effect evidence for the efficacy of relaxation training per se. Each study depended on self-report outcome measures of questionable validity, due to their susceptibility to demand characteristic effects (8), and several investiga-

---

Reprinted with permission from *Psychosomatic Medicine,* 38, 3, May-June, 1976.

tions failed to include essential placebo or no-treatment comparison conditions.

A therapy procedure demonstrated to produce improvement greater than a placebo condition regardless of whether the treatment is administered under therapeutic or nontherapeutic instructions is indeed a powerful modification technique and includes active ingredients separate from demand and placebo effects (9). Extrapolation from this conclusion resulted in the development of counterdemand instructional manipulations in which all treated subjects are told not to expect improvement in sleep disturbance during the first three sessions of treatment (counterdemand period) and to expect improvement only after the fourth session (positive demand period). Critical statistical comparisons of the self-reported outcome among therapy and control conditions are then made at the end of the counterdemand week prior to the positive demand week.

The counterdemand strategy has been employed in two subsequent investigations (10, 11). In both studies, progressive relaxation was found to produce significantly greater reduction in reported latency to sleep onset than placebo and no-treatment conditions during the counterdemand period. The replicated occurrence of the effect, despite an instructional demand set in opposition to reports of improvement, suggests that demand characteristics do not account for the reported gains of subjects receiving relaxation training and supports the presence of an active ingredient independent of placebo effects in that technique. Additionally, the second study (11) demonstrated that the tension release of muscle groups inherent in Jacobson's (12) relaxation procedures was a critical element in producing that improvement.

Despite these demonstrations, the issues of placebo, demand, and relaxation effects on self-reported sleep latency, phenomenological sleep improvement, and objective sleep-staging improvement remain unsettled. In addition, Monroe (13) has found that poor sleepers exaggerate their estimates of sleep latency, further complicating the relationship between reported and objective measurement of sleep improvement. The purpose of the present study was to replicate the basic aspects of the earlier investigations (10, 11) using objective sleep measures. Sleep disturbed subjects were randomly assigned to one of three treatment conditions (progressive relaxation, placebo, and no-treatment) and underwent all-night sleep evaluations for two consecutive nights at three points in the study (pre-therapy, end of counterdemand, and end of positvie demand periods).

METHOD

Subjects

A brief questionnaire on sleep behavior was given to introductory psychology students at the University of Iowa as a part of a group testing program early in the semester. Subjects indicating 31 min or greater in average latency to sleep onset and that they considered this duration to represent a problem were contacted by phone by a female graduate student and scheduled for an individual pretherapy interview. Any subject reporting 30 min or less average sleep-onset latency, current use of drugs, or current contact with other professional services during the interview was excluded from the study. Retained subjects ($N=36$) were told by the interviewer that treatment would involve four weekly sessions of group therapy designed to eliminate sleep disturbance and that all-night sleep recording would take place on six nights during the study. At this point, the counterdemand and positive demand statements were presented: "We estimate that after the fourth session you will begin to experience dramatic improvement. However, during the first few weeks, we do not expect improvement so do not get discouraged. It is only after four sessions and careful practice on your own that the real improvement will occur." The subjects were given a supply of sleep questionnaires requesting them to record daily, upon awakening, the number of minutes required to fall asleep during the previous night. Finally, after commitment to take part in the study, they were informed that they would receive course credit for their participation in therapy and $5.00 per night for sleep evaluations.

Therapists

Three male graduate students in clinical psychology served as therapists. Each therapist received extensive training in the treatment procedures from the senior author, followed detailed manuals of procedure during the treatment sessions, and treated one-third of the subjects in each therapy condition.

Procedure

The study required two 10-week periods for completion. Half of the subjects were treated during the fall semester of 1973; the remaining half during the spring semester of 1974. At the beginning of each semester, subjects were ranked on latency to sleep onset obtained in the pretherapy interview and randomly assigned within severity blocks to one of the three treatment conditions. Within each therapy condition, subjects were assigned to a therapist's group (N = 2 per group) on the basis of mutual time availability. No-treatment subjects were told that current treatment groups were filled but that new groups would be formed in 6 weeks and that they would receive priority if they continued to fill out the daily sleep questionnaires and attended the sleep evaluation nights. One subject in each treatment group terminated the study before its completion, leaving 11 subjects in each condition.

Treatment Conditions

The initial period of the first session for all treated groups was devoted to rationale presentation, treatment procedure description, and a restatement of the counterdemand instructions. The relaxation groups were then given Jacobson's progressive relaxation training (14) during the remainder of Session 1 and throughout Sessions 2, 3, and 4. The subjects were instructed to practice the relaxation technique twice a day, the last practice just prior to retiring. The placebo condition involved a quasi-desensitization procedure. During Session 1, each subject constructed an 18-item hierarchy of chronological bedtime activities and chose six neutral images to be paired with the hierarchy items and to be used as substitutes for relaxation. Viewing sleep disturbance as a problem in which bedtime stimuli elicit responses (physiological and/or cognitive) incompatible with sleep (15), then the imaginal pairing of such stimuli with varied, neutral images should not theoretically change that functional relationship. In Sessions 2, 3, and 4, each item was presented six times with intervening presentations of neutral images. The subjects in this condition were told to practice hierarchy and neutral image visualizations twice a day, the last practice at least 2 hr prior to retiring. The latter instruction was included to insure that practice would not increase sleep disturbance. Amount of time spent in therapy was equated between the two treatment conditions. To control for possible differential expectations between treatment conditions and to assess the relationship between subject expectancy and outcome improvement, subjects in both therapy conditions rated the credibility of, and expectation for improvement generated by, their respective conditions on four 10-point scales (16) after the first session.

All treated subjects returned daily sleep questionnaires from the previous week at the time of each treatment session. At the beginning of Session 4, a restatement of the positive demand instruction was presented. One week after the final session, subjects returned the last week of daily questionnaires and completed a postquestionnaire assessing their satisfaction with the program. The no-treatment subjects returned all daily questionnaires from the previous weeks during this last-week period and were immediately scheduled for therapy; no counterdemand or positive demand instructions were presented to these subjects during the study.

One year after the conclusion of the study, subjects were phoned by a research assistant, "blind" to the subject's treatment status, for a follow-up assessment and were asked to estimate their current, typical latency to sleep onset.

All-Night Sleep Evaluation

Each subject was scheduled for a total of six nights of recording during the study. The first two consecutive nights (Monday-Tuesday or Wednesday-Thursday) occurred prior to the first therapy session (pretherapy); the second two nights during the week intervening between Session 3 and 4 (counterdemand); and the third two nights during the week after the fourth session (positive demand).

Since the sleep facilities allowed recording of three subjects per night, six subjects were tested per week, with therapy for treated subjects beginning during the subsequent week. No-treatment subjects were tested on the same nights as the treated subjects without intervening therapy sessions. Subjects were run in triplets on the basis of common, typical bedtime. Each night the three subjects (one from each treatment condition) arrived together one-half hour before their typical bedtime. After electrode attachment and preparation for retiring, subjects entered separate bedrooms and lights were turned off at exactly the same time, beginning the recording period. Subjects were awakened at their usual time in the morning.

Dependent Measures

Monopolar EEG was recorded from C3 relative to a right mastoid neutral site (left mastoid being ground) using Grass gold cup electrodes. Sites were abraded with Hewlett-Packard Redux abrasive gel to insure low resistance (below 5000 ohms), and electrodes filled with EKG sol were firmly secured to the scalp by a gauze covering saturated in collodion. Recordings were made by a Beckman Type RM Dynograph with 0.05 mV/cm sensitivity and a time constant of 0.3 sec. Chart speed was set at 10 mm/sec.

First night sessions served primarily to acclimate subjects to the recording procedures, and data acquisition was of only secondary interest. Because of both numerous recording distortions of the first-night records and the possibility of first-night effects (17), only the second-night data allowed for analysis. Three research assistants, independent of each other and "blind" to the experimental condition and evaluation night of the subjects, scored the EEG records of the three evaluation nights (pretherapy, counterdemand, and positive demand). Two scores were taken, as defined by Rechtschaffen and Kales' (18) epoch method: (a) first occurrence of Stage I sleep and (b) first occurrence of Stage II sleep. All three raters independently scored 15% of the records; average interrater reliability was 0.928.

As in previous studies, all subjects filled out daily sleep questionnaires throughout the duration of the study. Mean latency scores for each subject during each week of the study were calculated and used as the basic data for subsequent analyses. Finally, each subject completed a sleep questionnaire for each lab night upon awakening in the morning. These second-night latency reports were analyzed separately.

RESULTS

Table 1 presents means and standard deviations on latencies (in minutes) for Stage 1 EEG, Stage II EEG, the second-night lab questionnaire, and daily sleep questionnaire scores for the three treatment conditions at each evaluation period. One-way analyses of variance indicated that the treatment conditions did not differ on any of the pretherapy measures.

EEG Measures

Inspection of Table 1 standard deviations indicates a large variance associated with Stage I and II means during the pretherapy evaluation week. Sleep onset was thus delayed for some subjects in each condition, while other subjects showed normal sleep latencies. Means and variances surprisingly decreased at Therapy Week 3 (counterdemand period) for all conditions, while only the progressive relaxation condition displayed a further decrease at Therapy Week 4 (positive demand period).

Planned comparisons between progressive relaxation and no-treatment conditions and tests of residual variance (19) were performed on Stage I and Stage II sleep latency scores during the counterdemand and positive demand periods.* Possibly due to large variance, only one significant

* Data on two subjects in relaxation and two subjects in placebo are absent due to missed lab sessions.

effect emerged from these analyses: improvement displayed by the progressive relaxation condition in Stage I latency from pretherapy to the positive demand period was found by planned comparison to be significantly superior to that of the no-treatment condition (one-tailed $t = 1.98$, $df = 18$, $p < 0.05$).

In addition, a test of Stage I variance differences at Week 4 (20) revealed a significant condition effect ($V = 7.83$, $df = 2$, $p < 0.02$).** Post-hoc variance comparisons (20) indicated significantly less variance at Week 4 for progressive relaxation as compared with both placebo ($F = 10.55$, $df = 7, 8$, $p < 0.01$) and no-treatment ($F = 6.31$, $df = 7, 8$, $p < 0.01$). Variance tests at other evaluation weeks and on Stage II measures were nonsignificant. Finally, although no main effect of evaluation periods emerged from a repeated measures analysis of variance on the total group, one-way analyses of variance on each treatment condition demonstrated significant Stage I improvement over evaluation periods only for progressive relaxation subjects ($F = 4.01$, $df = 2, 16$, $p < 0.05$).

Second-Night Lab Questionnaire

Planned comparisons and residual tests of self-reported sleep latency data from the corresponding lab nights revealed no between-condition differences. Repeated measures analysis of variance indicated a significant main effect of evaluation periods ($F = 4.55$, $df = 2, 52$, $p < 0.025$). One-way analyses of variance on each condition indicated that only the progressive relaxation group reported significant improvement in lab sleep latency over evaluation periods ($F = 5.60$, $df = 2, 26$, $p < 0.01$).

Daily Sleep Questionnaire

Similar analyses performed on the daily self-report latency revealed no between-condition differences, in contrast to two earlier studies (10, 11). Repeated measures analysis of variance revealed a significant main effect of evaluation periods for the total group ($F = 9.32$, $df = 4, 120$, $p < 0.01$). One-way analyses of variance on each condition found significant improvement over the duration of the study for each treatment group. Similar to earlier studies, progressive relaxation produced continuous, steady improvement over weeks, while the placebo condition displayed

** Due to these variance differences, a nonparametric Mann-Whitney *U* test was conducted between progressive relaxation and no-treatment Stage I improvement during positive demand, in order to verify the difference found by planned comparison. Improvement difference between these two conditions was found to be significant ($z = 1.69$, $p < .05$).

TABLE 1

Mean Latencies to Sleep Onset (in Minutes) and Standard Deviations as Measured by Stage I EEG, Stage II EEG, Lab-Night Questionnaire, and Daily Sleep Questionnaire for Each Treatment Condition at Each Evaluation Week

Measure of latency to sleep onset			Pretherapy week	Therapy week 1	Therapy week 2	Therapy week 3	Therapy week 4
First occurrence of Stage I EEG	Progressive relaxation	Mean	28.8			22.0	11.8
		SD	(20.7)			(17.3)	(9.0)
	Placebo	Mean	25.1			12.2	20.9
		SD	(25.3)			(10.8)	(29.3)
	No-treatment	Mean	23.0			18.3	27.6
		SD	(23.7)			(12.5)	(22.6)
First occurrence of Stage II EEG	Progressive relaxation	Mean	40.9			35.8	33.6
		SD	(19.5)			(21.4)	(20.8)
	Placebo	Mean	31.2			15.7	27.7
		SD	(23.4)			(10.9)	(28.6)
	No-treatment	Mean	40.6			26.6	33.0
		SD	(22.3)			(11.8)	(21.9)
Lab-night questionnaire	Progressive relaxation	Mean	40.0			37.0	23.5
		SD	(16.3)			(16.7)	(7.5)
	Placebo	Mean	26.2			24.2	24.4
		SD	(14.9)			(16.9)	(15.3)
	No-treatment	Mean	48.0			31.5	35.5
		SD	(28.3)			(14.5)	(25.9)
Daily sleep questionnaire	Progressive relaxation	Mean	40.0	37.7	32.3	30.7	27.5
		SD	(10.1)	(9.7)	(16.8)	(9.4)	(10.8)
	Placebo	Mean	53.1	55.6	55.1	43.2	38.7
		SD	(20.1)	(27.5)	(19.3)	(17.7)	(21.0)
	No-treatment	Mean	46.8	39.7	34.7	35.3	36.8
		SD	(12.0)	(12.0)	(14.8)	(10.2)	(8.6)

nonlinear change. Indeed, trend analyses over the counterdemand period yielded a significant quadratic difference between placebo and both relaxation ($F = 5.85$, $df = 1, 20$, $p < 0.05$) and no-treatment ($F = 9.94$, $df = 1, 20$, $p. < 0.01$); placebo subjects reported no improvement until the last week of the counterdemand period.

Credibility Questionnaire and Postquestionnaire Measures

As was the case in two previous studies employing the present treatment conditions, no significant differences were found between relaxation and placebo subjects on the credibility of, and expectation for improvement generated by, their respective treatments. The assumption that the placebo condition was controlling for subject expectation therefore appears warranted. Contrary to other psychotherapy research (21-23), ratings were not significantly correlated with any outcome improvement measure, either within each treatment condition or across all treated subjects.

Progressive relaxation subjects did obtain postquestionnaire ratings significantly greater than placebo subjects on (a) how pleased they were with their current sleep latency ($t = 2.23$, $df = 20$, $p < 0.05$), (b) the probability of their taking part in the study if they had to do it over again ($t = 2.90$, $df = 20$, $p < 0.01$), and (c) their estimation of how much improvement had occurred for other members of their group ($t = 2.59$, $df = 20$, $p < 0.02$).

Follow-up

Eleven subjects who had received progressive relaxation training and five who had received placebo were located for telephone follow-up assessment 1 year after the conclusion of the study. Relaxation subjects reported maintenance of their sleep-onset improvement (mean = 27.09 min), while placebo subjects displayed a return to pretherapy latency difficulties (mean = 58.00 min). The difference between groups was significant (one-tailed $t = 1.83$, $df = 14$, $p < 0.05$). Of the nine contacted subjects who had served in the no-treatment conditions, seven received progressive relaxation training immediately after the last week of the study. One year later, reported sleep latency for these subjects (mean = 27.86 min) was nearly identical to that for the relaxation group. The two no-treatment subjects who had declined treatment reported near-baseline latencies (40 and 45 min).

DISCUSSION

In general, the results of the present study provide modest support for the efficacy of progressive relaxation in the treatment of sleep-onset disturbance. Relaxation was the only condition to produce significant improvement in Stage I onset and in reports of sleep onset during lab evaluation nights. The gains of this group increased steadily for all measures over the duration of the study, in contrast to the variable outcome changes of the two control conditions. Between-condition differences, however, were limited. Relaxation was significantly superior only to no-treatment on Stage I onset improvement at the positive demand period, to placebo only on self-report postquestionnaire items, and to placebo and no-treatment on Stage I variance reduction at the positive demand period. Differences on EEG measures during counterdemand were precluded by the inexplicable temporary improvement displayed by the control conditions. While the trend of improvement on daily sleep questionnaires significantly favored relaxation over placebo, the same outcome was true for the no-treatment/placebo comparison, and all three conditions reported significant and equivalent improvement by the end of both the counterdemand and positive demand periods. Results from the 1-year follow-up assessment suggested that gains produced by relaxation may maintain for some time, in contrast to the long-term effects of placebo; in the absence of a true no-treatment group for follow-up, this conclusion must be regarded as tenuous. Finally, the absence of effects on Stage II sleep further limits conclusions regarding the impact of relaxation on sleep disturbance.

Relaxation was expected to be superior to the control conditions on the daily sleep questionnaire measure at the end of the counterdemand period; that outcome had been found in the earlier studies (10, 11). While neither control condition has shown improvement in previous investigations, significant gains occurred for both groups in the present study. Sleep lab evaluation represents the only substantial difference in procedure between these studies. Since moderate insomniacs have been found to be susceptible to both active and placebo manipulations (24), it is possible that the elaborate lab setting and measurement procedures themselves may have been sufficient placeboes to induce reported daily improvement in each condition, making impossible the separate identification of active treatment effects produced by relaxation training. The counterdemand instructions apparently mitigated this influence in the case of placebo subjects, but only for the first 2 weeks of the counter-demand period.

The results of the present study are sufficiently encouraging to suggest replication. Future studies will involve (a) more severely sleep disturbed subjects to preclude significant placebo effects, (b) 10 therapy sessions, rather than four, to provide a greater level of relaxation skill, and (c) four consecutive evaluation nights, rather than two, to obtain a more adequate assessment of typical sleep onset and the influence of treatment on its amelioration.

SUMMARY

Subjects reporting sleep-onset disturbance were randomly assigned to one of three conditions: progressive relaxation training, quasi-desensitization placebo, or no-treatment. Three therapists, treating one-third of the subjects in each therapy condition, administered four sessions of treatment to groups of two subjects. Treated subjects were told that improvement would not occur during the first three therapy sessions (counterdemand period) but would occur after the fourth session (positive demand period). All subjects slept in a laboratory facility for two consecutive nights at pretherapy, end of the counterdemand period, and end of the positive demand period. Dependent measures included first occurrence of Stage I and Stage II EEG on the second night of each evaluation period, corresponding self-reports of sleep-onset latency, and daily questionnaires completed during the entire duration of the study. Progressive relaxation training produced significant improvement in Stage I latency and lab self-report latency from pretherapy to the end of the positive demand period, while the control conditions failed to display improvement on these measures. The difference between relaxation and no-treatment was significant only for the Stage I data. All three conditions reported improvement on daily questionnaires, while relaxation was superior to placebo on postquestionnaire items and on reports of sleep latency obtained 1 year after the termination of the study.

This research was supported by Grant MH24603-01 from the National Institute of Mental Health awarded to the first author.

REFERENCES

1. Borkovec, T. D., & Fowles, D. C. A controlled investigation of the effects of progressive and hypnotic relaxation on insomnia. *J. Abnorm. Psychol.*, 82:153-158, 1973.
2. Borkovec, T. D., Steinmark, S. W., & Nau, S. D. Relaxation training and single-

item desensitization in the group treatment of insomnia. *J. Behav. Ther. Exp. Psychiatr.*, 4:401-403, 1973.

3. Gershman, L., & Clouser, R. Treating insomnia with relaxation and desensitization in a group setting by an automated approach. *J. Behav. Ther. Exp. Psychiatr.*, 5:31-35, 1974
4. Haynes, S., Woodward, S., Moran, R., & Alexander, D.: Relaxation treatment of insomnia. *Behav. Ther.*, 5:555-558, 1974.
5. Hinkle, J. E., & Lutker, E. R. Insomnia: A new approach. *Psychother. Theory Res. Prac.*, 9:236-237, 1972.
6. Kahn, M., Baker, B. L., & Weiss, J. M.: Treatment of insomnia by relaxation training. *J. Abnorm. Psychol.*, 73:556-558, 1968.
7. Nicassio, P., & Bootzin, R. A comparison of progressive relaxation and autogenic training as treatments for insomnia. *J. Abnorm. Psychol.*, 83:253-260, 1974.
8. Eisenman, R. Critique of "Treatment of insomnia by relaxation training": Relaxation training, Rogerian therapy, or demand characteristics. *J. Abnorm. Psychol.*, 75:315-316, 1970.
9. Borkovec, T. D. The role of expectancy and physiological feedback in fear research: A review with special reference to subject characteristics. *Behav. Ther.*, 4:491-505, 1973.
10. Borkovec, T. D., Kaloupek, D. G., & Slama, K. The facilitative effect of muscle tension-release in the relaxation treatment of sleep disturbance. *Behav. Ther.*, 6:301-309, 1975.
11. Steinmark, S. W., & Borkovec, T. D. Active and placebo treatment effects on moderate insomnia under counterdemand and positive demand instructions. *J. Abnorm. Psychol.*, 83:157-163, 1974.
12. Jacobson, E. *Progressive Relaxation.* Chicago: University of Chicago Press, 1938.
13. Monroe, L. J. Psychological and physiological differences between good and poor sleepers. *J. Abnorm. Psychol.*, 72:255-264, 1967.
14. Bernstein, D. A., & Borkovec, T. D. *Progressive Relaxation Training.* Champaign, Ill.: Research Press, 1973.
15. Bootzin, R. A stimulus control treatment for insomnia. *Proc. Am. Psychol. Assoc.*, 1:395-396, 1972.
16. Borkovec, T. D., & Nau, S. D. Credibility of analogue therapy rationales. *J. Behav. Ther. Exp. Psychiatr.*, 3:257-260, 1972.
17. Agnew, H. W., Webb, W. B., & Williams, R. L. The first night effect: An EEG study of sleep. *Psychophysiology*, 2:263-266, 1966.
18. Rechtschaffen, A., & Kales, A. (Eds.). *A Manual of Standardized Terminology, Techniques and Scoring System for Sleep Stages of Human Subjects.* National Institutes of Health Publication 204, Washington, D.C.: U.S. Government Printing Office, 1968.
19. Hays, W. L. *Statistics for Psychologists.* New York: Holt, Rinehart and Winston, 1963.
20. McNemar, Q. *Psychological Statistics.* New York: Wiley & Sons, 1969.
21. Friedman, H. J. Patient-expectancy and symptom reduction. *Arch. Gen. Psychiatry*, 8:61-67, 1963.
22. Goldstein, A. P.: Patient's expectancies and nonspecific therapy as a basis for (un)spontaneous remission. *J. Clin. Psychol.*, 16:399-403, 1960.
23. Goldstein, A. P., & Shipman, W. G. Patient expectancies, symptom reduction, and aspects of the initial psychotherapeutic interview. *J. Clin. Psychol.*, 17:129-133, 1961.
24. Nicolis, F. B., & Silvestri, L. C. Hypnotic activity of placebo in relation to severity of insomnia: A quantitative evaluation. *Clin. Pharm. Ther.*, 8:841-848, 1967.

Section III

BIOFEEDBACK AND OTHER STRATEGIES IN SELF-MANAGEMENT

Commentary

BIOFEEDBACK

Research on biofeedback and its application to a variety of clinical, predominantly psychosomatic, disorders, continues apace. The widespread interest in biofeedback has resulted in the publication of a new journal —*Biofeedback and Self-Regulation*—and, as Shapiro and Surwit (1976) note in a scholarly review of the literature on the learned control of physiological function and disease, a growth in membership of the Biofeedback Research Society to the point where there are more than 400 members. Many of these members "are in the hot pursuit of clinical goals" (p. 113). However, there appears to be a general consensus that many of the hopes—often wildly exaggerated*—that accompanied Miller's (1969) early descriptions of the phenomenon have not been realized and are not likely to be realized in the near future.

The failures to replicate the original ground-breaking findings with curarized rats—the experimental preparation that enabled Miller and his associates to rule out skeletal mediation of autonomic change—is damaging to the theoretical basis of Miller's (1969) notions of direct instrumental conditioning of autonomic functioning. Human studies, on the other hand, have consistently shown clear-cut data attesting to the efficacy of biofeedback procedures. But there are many unanswered questions and problems with this literature, too. Most of the studies have been demonstrative in nature—the persistence and practical efficacy of the effects of biofeedback have yet to be shown. Many of the studies have

* Witness the hyperbolic title of Brown's (1974) book — *New Mind, New Body: Biofeedback; New Directions for the Mind.*

reported results that are statistically significant but lacking in substantive or practical importance. Adequate controls for so-called "nonspecific" factors such as demand characteristics and placebo influences have been few and far between. Moreover, comparative studies of the utility of biofeedback have thus far failed to demonstrate convincingly that it is superior to simpler methods, such as progressive relaxation training, that do not require expensive equipment (that the Federal Drug Administration Agency might designate as medical devices which are beyond the easy application of non-medical practitioners). These various difficulties with the biofeedback literature have been thoroughly evaluated by Blanchard and Young (1974—reprinted in Franks & Wilson, 1975).

The initial interest in theoretical mechanisms of behavior change that the biofeedback findings engendered was soon surpassed by enthusiasm over their clinical potential. This resulted in a rush to find therapeutic effects, with consequent inattention to conservative, effortful, and time-consuming long-term clinical trials. The state of the art with respect to the clinical applications of biofeedback is summarized well by Shapiro and Surwit (1976) as follows: ". . . there is *not* one well controlled scientific study of the effectiveness of biofeedback and operant conditioning in treating a particular physiological disorder. The clinical data and case studies described are convincing in some instances, not at all in others. The most substantial work has been done where medical and physiological factors in the illness are given precise definition, where symptoms are shown to vary as the treatment conditions are varied, and where long-term and follow-up data are reported. As yet, the lack of controls for placebo and other nonspecific effects leaves open the question of what is unique in biofeedback training methods and what is not. Carefully controlled and evaluated clinical trials are obviously difficult, but they are vital before biofeedback methods will take their place along side other established practices in medicine" (p. 113).

The clinical applications of biofeedback are also addressed by Marcus and Levin (1977). Among other points, they caution that there is little evidence indicating the superiority of biofeedback as a method of inducing relaxation over other commonly employed procedures such as progressive relaxation training. In a practical, clinical vein they note that some clients may react negatively to biofeedback. Specifically, they cite the example of a very tense client who, upon receiving EMG-assisted relaxation training, experienced massive anxiety. Of course, this relatively rare phenomenon, not restricted to biofeedback, has been observed with other forms of relaxation training and with other techniques.

Conceptual Issues

The assumption that biofeedback can be conceptualized simply as the direct operant conditioning of autonomic responses has recently been challenged. In last year's volume, we reprinted R. Lazarus' (1975) cognitive view of biofeedback, a theoretical position that departs drastically from the extreme behavioristic analysis of the phenomenon and which carried some interesting clinical implications with it (Franks & Wilson, 1976). In similar fashion, Meichenbaum (1976) argues that cognitive factors in biofeedback have been overlooked. In line with Lazarus' (1975) thesis, Meichenbaum suggests that the modification of a specific psychophysiological function has to be viewed in the wider psychological context of how the client interprets the response, its alteration, and its consequences. Specifically, Meichenbaum urges that the client's images and self-statements before, during, and after biofeedback training need to be analyzed and incorporated into the overall therapeutic program.

On a highly speculative note, Meichenbaum predicts that a consideration of the client's "internal dialogue" about the biofeedback process will increase motivation for treatment and help to reduce the drop-out rate from treatment. While the general argument that cognitive processes influence motivation and persistence of behavior is difficult to gainsay (cf. Bandura, 1977b), there is no evidence to support the claim that motivation is increased in the manner outlined by Meichenbaum. Moreover, the specific mechanisms by which self-instructions and/or appropriate images might beneficially influence treatment motivation are not spelled out. According to Meichenbaum, another function of incorporating self-instructional analysis and training into the biofeedback treatment program is to facilitate generalization of therapy-produced changes. As several reviewers have concluded,the transfer of treatment gains from the laboratory to the real-life situation has been one of the greatest difficulties with biofeedback. Essentially, Meichenbaum's argument rests on making the client conscious or aware of previously automatic (unconscious) cognitive activities that govern the behaviors of therapeutic interest. Once these controlling variables are identified by clients, they are said to be more likely to react to problematic situations with coping behavior that defuses the emotion-producing nature of the target situation. Procedures that are advocated to sharpen this awareness and develop these coping skills are cognitive rehearsal, role-playing, and symbolic modeling as means of enhancing transfer effects. The case study reported by Reeves (1976) and reprinted in Section X of this volume is put forward by Meichenbaum as an example of how biofeedback methods should be supplemented by the modification of a client's self-talk.

The details of Meichenbaum's theory of self-control and his assertions about cognitive factors in biofeedback are sometimes too general and speculative in nature. Nonetheless, his emphasis on placing the conceptualization and practice of biofeedback within the context of a broader understanding of psychological functioning is timely. His observation that the biofeedback literature can be likened to that on verbal conditioning in the heyday of strict operant analysis of the automatic reinforcement of verbal behavior is intriguing. Then came the research on the role of awareness in the conditioning procedure (e.g., Spielberger & DeNike, 1966). As Meichenbaum points out, "the research on awareness . . . questioned whether the experimenter's reinforcement acted in an automatic fashion, and it highlighted the important role of the client's knowledge of the reinforcement contingencies and his motivation to comply. The biofeedback literature requires as much similar attention to the client's cognitive processes" (p. 214).

Empirical Findings

Modification of the Cardiovascular System. The first paper reprinted in this Section is by Friar and Beatty. The investigation at the Menninger Clinic of the manipulation of vasomotor control as a means of reducing migraine has been discussed in previous volumes of this series (Sargent, Green, & Walters, 1973—reprinted in Franks & Wilson, 1974). Friar and Beatty's study is significant on several counts. Most important is the fact that they controlled for "nonspecific" effects by training vasoconstriction at an irrelevant site. As the authors point out, given the history of biofeedback methods, this procedure would seem to have considerable face validity. Indeed, the impressive adherence of subjects to experimental instructions seems to bear out the claim that this was a credible control group that equated for therapeutic factors such as expectancies of success and demand characteristics. Moreover, one might suggest that the control group's decrease in analgesic medication following treatment indicated a response to the motivational properties of the therapy setting. The fact that migraine headaches themselves did not change is further evidence that the results were due to a treatment-specific effect. A second feature is that the results show a clear, substantive improvement in subjects suffering from severe migraine. Accordingly, the Friar and Beatty study represents a major advance over the state of the art of biofeedback applications as presented by Blanchard and Young (1974) and Shapiro and Surwit (1976).

The treatment of migraine headaches using biofeedback methods is also reported by Turin and Johnson (1976). Seven patients, all of whom were taking medication for migraine headaches that they had suffered from for considerable lengths of time, were treated by increasing peripheral temperature of the finger through biofeedback training. Autogenic relaxation training, a component of the Sargent et al. (1973) procedure referred to above, was excluded. In an attempt to control placebo-expectancy factors, three subjects received training in decreasing the temperature in their finger prior to receiving finger warming treatment.

The results showed that all seven subjects successfully learned to increase temperature in their finger over 10 treatment sessions. Of the subjects who received finger cooling training only two were able to decrease temperature. All subjects showed significant improvement following finger warming training on all three measures of migraine headaches: number of headaches, the duration of headaches, and amount of medication taken to control headaches that were experienced. Suggesting that these results were due to a treatment-specific effect, the three subjects who initially received finger cooling training with positive expectancies improved only after training in finger warming activity. Many of the subjects reported using this procedure *in vivo* situations, implementing hand warming at the first sign of a headache and often being able to forestall headaches. It is unclear why Turin and Johnson obtained such favorable results with alteration of hand temperature whereas Friar and Beatty found that training vasomotor control in the hand produced no change in migraine headaches. This discrepancy indicates that the variables involved in successful outcome have yet to be fully specified.

Finally, Turin and Johnson note that their subjects employed idiosyncratic methods in order to produce changes in peripheral temperature, such as imagery or self-verbalization. Taken in conjunction with Friar and Beatty's findings, these results suggest that biofeedback methods are a useful means of treating migraine headaches.

Behavioral treatment strategies such as systematic desensitization are based on the assumption that a reduction in autonomic nervous system arousal will result in lowered anxiety and decreased avoidance behavior. Indeed, Wolpe (1958, 1976c) has always explicitly defined anxiety in terms of conditioned autonomic responses. The procedural components of systematic desensitization, namely relaxation training, a hierarchy of graded anxiety-eliciting stimuli, and instructions to the client to terminate anxiety-elicting scenes whenever anxiety is evoked are all designed to reduce autonomic arousal to the point where it is reciprocally inhibited or counterconditioned by nonfearful approach responses. Gatchel and Proctor (1976) have suggested that, instead of using relaxation to reduce autonomic responses (an indirect influence), autonomic responses (e.g., heart rate) might be modified *directly* through the use of biofeedback methods.

College students who were anxious about public-speaking and who received course credit for their participation were recruited for a study on the effects of voluntary heart rate control on speech anxiety. Half of the subjects received two sessions of heart rate control training; half engaged in a visual tracking task. Half of each of these two groups received instructions inducing a high expectancy for improvement, the other half received instructions designed to present neutral expectancies about improvement. Thus, the four experimental groups were a) biofeedback/high expectancy; b) biofeedback/neutral expectancy; c) tracking/high expectancy; and d) tracking/neutral expectancy. Assessment procedures were similar to those used by Paul (1966) in his classic study.

Biofeedback training resulted in a significant reduction in heart rate during training. More important, this learned heart rate control was significantly more effective than the visual tracking in producing decreases in behavioral, physiological (heart rate and skin conductance level), and self-report measures of speech anxiety. The high therapeutic expectancy condition was marginally ($p < .10$) more significant than the neutral expectancy condition in reducing speech anxiety. However, Gatchel and Proctor conclude that the critical agent of change was clearly learned control of heart rate and that expectancy instructions play a secondary role in effecting improvement. Although these data indicate that biofeedback training might be effective in assisting clients to manage anxiety, it is not clear that the visual tracking control condition was a stringent comparison group for excluding "nonspecific" factors (cf. Kazdin & Wilcoxon, 1976).

Increases in heart rate as a result of learned instrumental control seems to be associated with a rise in plasma renin activity (Young, Langford, & Blanchard, 1976). Young et al. speculate that increases in heart rate triggered by emotional stimuli may lead to an increase in renin secretion which may be linked to hypertension: "Increased renin secretion produced by vasoconstriction. In addition, neurogenic activation of the renin-angiotensin-aldosterone axis would open up an important loop controlling sodium excretion. Therefore, more sodium retention would occur than would otherwise be found, and the individual would be more prone to develop hypertension" (p. 281).

The effects of biofeedback training on the blood pressure and cognitive functioning of hypertensive patients were investigated by Goldman, Kleinman, Snow, Bidus, and Korol (1975). Seven hypertensive patients received biofeedback training to decrease systolic blood pressure, while four control hypertensive patients had their blood pressure monitored without being provided any feedback. All subjects were administered a sub-test of the Halstead-Reitan Neuropsychological Test Battery before and after biofeedback training. Biofeedback produced significant decreases in systolic pressure within treatment sessions and diastolic pressure between sessions. No change in blood pressure was observed in the control subjects. Moreover, a significant correlation was obtained between reductions in blood pressure and improvement on the sub-test of the Halstead-Reitan Battery which is said to be an indicator of cerebral impairment. While the authors note the association between biofeedback-induced improvement in blood pressure and improvement in cognitive functioning as measured by the test, they prudently explore alternative explanations of what is only a correlational finding.

The treatment of a rape-induced cardiovascular disorder using biofeedback is described by Blanchard and Abel (1976) in a paper reprinted in Section X of this volume.

Evidence has been presented that psychopaths differ from non-psychopaths in terms of autonomic and central nervous system responsivity (Hare, 1970). Specifically, it has been suggested that psychopaths show different patterns of skin resistance responses but do not differ from normals in terms of heart rate responses. In a comparison of 10 clinically defined psychopaths with 12 normal control subjects, Steinberg and Schwartz (1976) required subjects to increase and decrease their frequency of spontaneous skin resistance responses (SSRRs) first with instructions alone, then with feedback, and finally without feedback. The control subjects proved to be significantly superior to the psychopaths in increasing their SSRRs during the instructions alone phase of the study. Psychopaths showed no SSRR control with instructions. However, both groups were equally effective in raising and lowering their SSRRs during biofeedback training sessions. The heart rate data showed the opposite pattern. Both groups were able to increase heart rate in accordance with instructions, but in the post-feedback phase only the normal subjects retained control over cardiovascular activity. Steinberg and Schwartz conclude that these data "highlight the value in examining the interaction of person and stimulus conditions in research on psychopathy and illustrate how examining the pattern of electrodermal and cardiovascular responses can help elucidate the underlying psychobiological differences between psychopaths and normals" (p. 414).

The instrumental control shown by psychopaths during biofeedback training indicates that observed physiological differences between psychopaths and normals are not unalterable. In contrast to an all-inclusive physiological deficit, specific situational determinants need to be taken into account in explaining the physiological responsiveness of psychopaths. Steinberg and Schwartz suggest ways of investigating the self-regulatory capacity of psychopaths but caution that "it would be premature at this time to suppose that physiological changes brought about through biofeedback training would have any substantial clinical effects on these complex personality variables" (p. 415).

Given sufficiently sensitive and sophisticated electronic equipment, there is virtually no limit on what biological function can be converted into feedback of some sort. Thus Shapiro and Surwit (1976) summarize a report by French, Leeb, and Fahrion on the use of biofeedback as a means of contraception! Male subjects, after training in controlling their hand temperature, were given training in learning to produce scrotal hyperthermia. Apparently, this resulted in a marked reduction in "viable sperm production." Scrotal training without prior hand training was unsuccessful. Not unreasonably, Shapiro and Surwit note that "the data available to date are preliminary and cannot be used as a basis for application as a means of contraception" (p. 101).

EMG Biofeedback. Ranging still farther afield in the application of biofeedback procedures, Letourneau (1976) has discussed the application of biofeedback methods to optometry. He describes two sets of apparatus that rely upon sensitive EMG feedback, and reviews the technical difficulties involved in visual training along these lines. The EMG is connected to a Schmitt trigger that is adjusted for each patient. Innovative sources of reinforcement include, for adults, music in which patients start the record player with their eyes, and, for children, an electric train in which subjects run the trains with their eyes when they reach a predetermined threshold. Letourneau does not present any data, but suggests that this approach could be applied to many specific problems, including convergence insufficiency and excess, esotropia and exotropia, ptosis and a blind eye.

The application of EMG biofeedback to problems of neuromuscular rehabilitation is discussed in an evaluative review by Inglis, Campbell, and Donald (1976). The authors provide a history of the application of EMG procedures to different types of neuromuscular injuries, tracing its use first as a dependent measure, and then as a source of feedback to which the patient was deliberately exposed. Inglis, Campbell, and Donald point out that the notion of feedback and the consideration of its role in the control of the musculature was well-established in neurophysiology by the late 1940s, and that patients had first been provided feedback (audio signals) of their muscle activity as early as 1960 by Marinnacci and Horande. Nonetheless, the interest in applying these methods only developed after Miller's (1969) publication of his results on instrumental conditioning of autonomic functioning. Most of the scientific and clinical reports reviewed by Inglis, Campbell, and Donald were published after 1970. This is all the more interesting since EMG activity has traditionally been viewed as behavior that is under voluntary control (unlike responses of the autonomic nervous system that, before Miller's demonstrations, were confidently considered to be involuntary in nature and unresponsive to instrumental conditioning). According to Inglis, Campbell, and Donald, this sudden burst of interest in a phenomenon that had failed to attract serious research attention for close to a decade illustrates Kuhn's (1962) notion of "normal" science.

EMG biofeedback has been used in the treatment of a variety of neuromuscular disorders, including peripheral nerve-muscle damage, spasmodic torticollis, the stroke hemiplegias, and cerebral palsy. Unfortunately, as is so typical of the biofeedback literature in general, almost all the data are based upon uncontrolled clinical reports that often fail to provide basic descriptive information crucial to the proper evaluation of the treatment methods. For example, treatment procedures themselves are frequently not specified in sufficient detail to permit ready replication. Inglis, Campbell, and Donald also note that indispensable information such as the degree of sensory deficits due to central nervous system damage in the case of stroke patients, or loss of function of muscles and joints as a result of disuse, is often not reported. As in other areas, the failure to include controls for the many "nonspecific" influences that accompany the use of biofeedback methods—with all the "scientific" jargon, impressive electronic equipment, and current cultural enthusiasm that attaches to them—makes it impossible to arrive at unequivocal conclusions about the results. These methodological shortcomings notwithstanding, Inglis, Campbell, and Donald conclude as follows: "At first sight the method appears to be remarkably promising. In every trial reported so far most of the patients improved; in several cases the improvement took place in patients who had been disabled for a period of years; the treatments took very little time to have their effect (in one case five minutes only) and, given standard equipment, they were relatively inexpensive when compared with supervised exercise and physiotherapy. The method seems to work equally well with spastic and with flaccid muscles. In addition, the benefits of treatment in many cases were lasting and they generalized to everyday life" (p. 319).

Alpha Biofeedback. The tension reduction hypothesis is one of the classic explanations of alcohol use and abuse. In short, this hypothesis states that a) alcohol reliably reduces tension and b) problem drinkers consume alcohol in order to reduce tension. The finding that alcoholics seem to display less alpha activity in their EEGs than non-alcoholics has been interpreted as further support for the tension reduction hypothesis. The low level of alpha in alcoholics, it is said, indicates that they are in a high state of arousal and that they consume alcohol in order reduce or "normalize" this arousal. There is a chain of related assumptions in this reasoning which is rather typical of the alcoholism literature. In the first place, one has to ask whether it is a well-established fact that alcoholics do have significantly less alpha than non-alcoholics. Jones and Holmes (1976) maintain that the data on this topic are difficult to interpret because of methodological problems. However, in a well-controlled study with 20 alcoholics and matched non-alcoholic controls respectively, Jones and Holmes demonstrated that alcoholics did in fact show less alpha activity.

Even if it is accepted that alcoholics differ from non-alcoholics in terms of alpha, it is still difficult to interpret these findings. For example, research of this sort on subjects who are already alcoholics does not permit any jugment as to whether the differences observed are the cause or the effect of excessive, prolonged alcohol consumption. Nonetheless, assuming that this low level of alpha activity is related to drinking, Jones and Holmes applied biofeedback in an attempt to increase the level of alpha activity in alcoholics on the assumption that this might remove the desire (need?) to drink. Interestingly, they failed to produce an increase in alpha in either alcoholics or their non-alcoholic control subjects. Jones and Holmes attribute their lack of success in training an increase in alpha levels to the specific subject population they used. In contrast to the typical subject of most biofeedback laboratory investigations—young, educated, sophisticated, and a "believer" in biofeedback—

their subjects were older, less well-educated, less sophisticated, and therefore less motivated about treatment outcome. If this motivational difference is actually present, and many reviewers caution that it might be, the implications are profound. At the very least, these findings suggest that practitioners show appropriate caution before too readily adopting biofeedback methods in the treatment of chronic patient populations.

SELF-MONITORING

As we reiterate in this Series year after year, the importance of the diverse set of research and clinical activities that is referred to as "behavior therapy," lies not in a collection of effective therapeutic techniques but in the way of approaching the assessment and treatment of behavior disorders. Ideally, as an applied science that remains broadly responsive to the method and substance of scientific psychology, behavior therapy will be progressively refined and modified. Thus, as Bandura (1977a) and Kazdin and Wilson (in press) indicate, some behavioral methods have been shown to be more effective than others. Systematic desensitization, for example, seems less effective than performance-based techniques such as in vivo flooding and participant modeling (Bandura, 1977a; Leitenberg, 1976a). By its very nature—operationally specified and clearly replicable—systematic desensitization encouraged subsequent research that helped establish more effective methods. Similarly exemplifying the increasing development and increasingly specific nature of behavior therapy is the case of self-monitoring.

As Wilson (1977d) points out, self-monitoring was once regarded as one of the "nonspecifics" of behavior therapy, that grab-bag category to which therapeutic influences that were viewed as being of secondary importance were relegated. As behavior therapy has matured both conceptually and methodologically, many of these "nonspecific" influences have been increasingly recognized as important elements of behavior change and have been investigated as specific procedures in their own right. An example of the analysis of the specific nature of self-monitoring and the determinants of its effects is provided by Sieck and McFall's (1976) recent evaluation. These authors start off by emphasizing that to ask whether self-monitoring is reactive or not (a topic of fairly wide research interest over the past few years) may be as unproductive as asking whether behavior therapy "works" or not. The more appropriate question to pose is "What effects occur, under what conditions, in what behaviors, with what subjects, as a function of what specific self-monitoring procedures?" (Sieck & McFall, 1976, p. 958). As has been said many times before, specificity is the hallmark of behavior therapy.

Kazdin (1974b) conducted a series of three experiments on self-monitoring using a sentence-construction task under controlled laboratory conditions. By varying the perceived social desirability of the target behavior, Kazdin found that the behavior being self-monitored increased when a positive valence was attached to it, and decreased when a negative valence was associated with it. When no particular value attached to the target behavior, little or no change was observed. Another significant finding was that providing subjects with a performance standard enhanced the effects of self-monitoring. Using a laboratory methodology not dissimilar from Kazdin's, but with the eye-blink response as the target behavior, Sieck and McFall evaluated five hypotheses: 1) that the direction of self-monitoring effects depends upon the perceived value of the target behavior; 2) that both value and self-monitoring are necessary for reactivity to occur; 3) that self-monitoring would result in greater change in the target behavior than experimenter-monitoring; 4) that multiple reports of self-monitoring would be associated with greater change than a single report; and 5) that the effects of self-monitoring are specific to the self-monitoring act itself and not the result of subjects simply attending to the target behavior.

The results support the first three hypotheses. Neither the perceived value of the target behavior nor self-monitoring alone produced a significant reactive effect. The combination of these two factors, however, was reactive, the direction of the effects being a function of the value attached to the target behavior. While the latter finding is consistent with Kazdin's data, the fact that value alone was not reactive differs from Kazdin's findings. The explanation of this discrepancy, Sieck and McFall suggest, is that Kazdin's methodology did not allow him to isolate the effects of value instructions adequately. Sieck and McFall's results show that the value of the target behavior was differentially related to the magnitude of the effects that were obtained. The positive value instructions resulted in greater change than the negative value instructions. On the basis of these findings, Sieck and McFall conclude that two general principles can be distilled from the research on self-monitoring. "First, the subject's perceived value of the target response seems to determine the direction of change produced by self-monitoring procedures. Second, there is growing evidence that it is easier for self-monitoring procedures to produce increases than decreases in target behaviors. In combination, these findings suggest that the therapist interested in using self-monitoring procedures to effect behavioral changes should make certain that the target behavior being monitored has highly positive value to the client" (Sieck & McFall, 1976, p. 965).

Unquestionably, analytic laboratory research of the sort reported by Kazdin and by Sieck and McFall is important in teasing out the specific determinants of self-monitoring effects. However, the nature of the target behaviors used in these investigations has to be borne in mind when evaluating the therapeutic implications of their results. Neither the construction of sentences nor the monitoring of eye-blinks is of intrinsic significance to most subjects—or clients. The value factor that was investigated in these studies had to be artificially—and cleverly—created by experimental instructions. There are obvious differences between this situation and the motivated obese client who is asked to self-monitor caloric intake or the cigarette smoker who is asked to monitor number of cigarettes smoked. The exact nature of these differences, and their implications for our understanding and therapeutic application of self-monitoring, needs to be determined. For the time being, it is possible to question Sieck and McFall's strong recommendation that the therapist should "make certain" that the target behavior being monitored "has highly positive value to the client."

For example, there is evidence that monitoring of daily caloric intake is effective in reducing weight (e.g., Green, 1976; Romanczyk, Tracey, Wilson, & Thorpe, 1973). Similarly, self-monitoring of estimated nicotine content per cigarette smoked seems to reduce cigarette smoking more than simple self-monitoring of cigarettes smoked per se (Abrams & Wilson, 1977). In both instances the behavior being monitored is, by definition, in some sense reinforcing to the client. However, the client is attempting to reduce the behavior, which has negative consequences, with a specific standard of evaluation in mind. Success in adhering to this performance standard presumably results in self-reinforcement (Kanfer, 1970). This situation appears to be more complex than that represented in the laboratory investigations of Kazdin or Sieck and McFall. However, these clinical findings indicate that self-monitoring of at least some negative behaviors can have very reactive effects. Theoretically, it is difficult to see why self-monitoring of positively evaluated behavior should be more reactive than self-monitoring of negatively evaluated behavior (Kanfer, 1970). Again, drawing general principles at this stage of our knowledge is not without difficulties.

The systematic investigation of the effects of self-monitoring has been the subject of a research program of Nelson and her colleagues (Nelson, Lipinski, & Black, 1976a, 1976b). In one study, Nelson et al. (1976b) obtained results that provide further support for hypothesis three of Sieck and McFall as described above. Self-monitoring was significantly more reactive than external observation in reducing frequency of face-touching in college students in a classroom situation. Nelson et al. attribute the reactivity of self-monitoring to a heightened awareness of the target behavior. In a second study, Nelson et al. (1976a) evaluated self-monitoring of three different target behaviors—talking, face-touching, and object touching—in adult retarded subjects. Marginal support for Sieck and McFall's conclusion about the importance of subjects' self-monitoring a behavior of positive value was obtained. Self-monitoring of talking (a positively evaluated behavior) was more consistently reactive than self-monitoring of face-touching (a negatively evaluated behavior). Specifically, the finding was that self-monitoring increased the frequency of talking in all five subjects and decreased the frequency of face-touching in three of the five subjects to whom it was applied. Unlike the Kazdin or Sieck and McFall findings, self-monitoring also reduced the frequency of the neutral behavior—object touching. Nelson et al. (1976a) suggest that the act of self-recording may have interfered with the behavior of touching objects. Lastly, the self-monitoring produced greater behavioral change than token reinforcement procedures, a highly unusual finding.

Another laboratory study of self-monitoring by Epstein, Miller, and Webster (1976) draws attention to a potential influence on self-monitoring and its effects—concurrent environmental events and contingencies. Subjects self-monitored their respiration rates with and without concurrent responding on a lever pressing task maintained by a multiple reinforcement schedule. Self-monitoring errors more than doubled during concurrent responding on the operant task. However, self-monitoring proved to be as reactive during concurrent reinforcement as in its absence. Thus, even though self-monitoring was not reliable, this failed to weaken its reactive effects on behavior, a phenomenon noticed in clinical studies of self-control (e.g., Thoresen & Mahoney, 1974). In contrast to Kazdin's and Sieck and McFall's results, but consistent with Nelson et al.'s (1976a) data, self-monitoring of a neutral behavior—respiration rate—proved to be very reactive. This highlights the specificity of self-monitoring effects and emphasizes the caution that needs to be had in generalizing from laboratory studies on target behaviors chosen for their suitability for experimental investigation rather than problem behaviors that clients wish to do something about.

In contrast to the focus on arbitrarily chosen responses, Katz, Thomas, and Williamson (1976) compared four conditions in the treatment of nailbiters who requested help for their problem: a) self-monitoring alone; b) self-monitoring plus an expectancy of therapeutic improvement; c) self-monitoring plus the positive expectancy plus training in an incompatible response; and d) a waiting list control. The results showed that only when coupled with expectancies of therapeutic improvement was self-monitoring effective. The addition of the incompatible response did little to increase the effects of self-monitoring. These results are at odds with those reported by Nelson, Lipinski, and Black (1975). Aside from contributing to the analysis of the reactivity of self-monitoring, Katz et al.'s study describes what appears to be a useful method for the treatment of nailbiting—at least in the short-term.

Documenting the not unexpected, Layne, Rickard, Jones, and Lyman (1976) found that self-monitoring of clean-up behavior by behaviorally disturbed 10, 11, and 12 year old boys was not reactive. Obviously, the target behavior of self-monitoring has to have some perceived value if it is to change. Also unsurprising is the finding that reinforcement of accurate self-monitoring and clean-up behavior resulted in an increase in both. This effect could be safely predicted on the basis of an abundance of evidence on the positive reinforcement of relatively simple behaviors. Of greater interest in this study is that a variable reinforcement schedule maintained high levels of both target behaviors, an indication of how self-monitoring might be used in practical situations calling for long-term maintenance.

SELF-REINFORCEMENT

Self-reinforcement procedures have been among the most actively researched areas of behavioral self-control, as reference to earlier volumes in this Series will indicate. Self-reinforcement continues to be an important concept in social learning theory (Bandura, 1977b). Much of the pioneering research on self-reinforcement was conducted by Bandura and his colleagues (cf. Bandura, 1969, 1977b), emphasizing the role of modeling in the acquisition of self-reinforcement patterns and the influence of the adoption of different performance standards for self-reinforcement. The finding that subjects will often adopt stringent and effortful performance standards even though rewards are freely available and not contingent on special performance is of particular theoretical and applied significance. This finding can not be explained away on the grounds that subjects were unaware of the external reinforcement contingencies, i.e., that they did not believe that reinforcement would be forthcoming if they failed to adhere to stringent performance standards —see our discussion of the Turkewitz, O'Leary, and Ironsmith (1975) paper reprinted in last year's volume (Franks & Wilson, 1976). This finding that subjects' behavior does not seem to be totally under the control of the prevailing external reinforcement contingencies is both intuitively obvious and interpretable as theoretically damaging to blanket accounts of human behavior in strict operant terms.

The second paper reprinted in this Section is Bandura's review of self-reinforcement from a social learning perspective, in essence a response to an earlier article in the same journal by Catania (1975). The final paper in this Section—by Goldiamond—provides an alternative perspective on self-reinforcement that is similar to Catania's (1975) position. These two papers are reprinted together because they provide the reader with a clear exposition not only of different views on self-reinforcement, but also of the two major, contrasting conceptual frameworks in behavior therapy today. Bandura's paper can be read as a statement of social learning theory, Goldiamond's as the position held by operant conditioners and most applied behavior analysts. Readers should also be aware that there is a response to the Bandura paper by Catania (1976), and that Mahoney (1976) and Thoresen and Wilbur (1976) have replied to the Goldiamond paper reprinted here. The latter interchange of views is completed by Goldiamond's (1976a) rejoinder to Mahoney (1976) and Thoresen and Wilbur (1976).

There are numerous issues deriving from the different perspectives that could well command discussion here. Suffice it to seize upon a few issues that reflect our own views about behavior change in general and self-reinforcement in particular. The question of the relative merits of between-group statistical designs and single-case experimental designs that is raised by Bandura is considered in greater detail in the following Section of this volume.

Like Rachlin (1974) before them, both Goldiamond and Catania argue that self-reinforcement does not *cause* the behavior it is made contingent upon to change. In the example of the student who rewards himself or herself with a coffee break, Catania stresses that this is not likely to lead to an increase in the completion of assignments unless such scholarly diligence is important for other reasons. But what are these "other reasons"? Inevitably, operant theorists appeal, as Bandura points out, "to ultimate benefits of prospective behavior." The student's ability to behave in accordance with the delayed reward is attributed to a previous reinforcement history. In summoning up this sort of analysis (which seems impossible to refute) the immediate influences on behavior are de-emphasized. Simply labeling self-reinforcement procedures as discriminative stimuli, or conditioned reinforcers, does little to detail how they might be best deployed to facilitate behavior change. Goldiamond agrees that procedures labeled as self-reinforcement appear to have "evident success." However, he argues that these procedures are mislabeled as "self-reinforcement" and that this mislabeling will deflect attention away from the search for the existence of the natural contingencies that account for the observed effects.

In the ultimate analysis, Catania's (1975, 1976) arguments amount to a post hoc reinterpretation of certain procedures. As Bandura (1977b) has noted elsewhere, the concept of stimulus control, allied to the notion that behavior is controlled not by its immediate consequences but by an aggregate effect of consequences over unspecified time delays, permits a reinforcement interpretation of virtually any behavioral procedure. Eysenck (1976b) has similarly concluded that reinforcement theory is difficult, if not impossible, to submit to a critical test. Be this as it may, the important issue is which conceptual framework will best facilitate the investigation of the procedures addressed by Bandura, Catania, and Goldiamond. The fact that post hoc explanations, however plausible, can be developed to accommodate self-reinforcement and other self-control procedures within a strict operant framework is less important than the utility of this conceptual scheme in generating such methods. The significance of a concept such as self-reinforcement is to be found in its heuristic function. To the extent that this purpose is served, the focus to self-reinforcement will be amply rewarded.

Catania's (1976) concluding comments are worthy of note. His statement that "many aspects of human behavior cannot be dealt with adequately solely in terms of the concept of reinforcement" is a non-trivial pronouncement.* Readers of some operant conditioning accounts of behavior modification, including Skinner's (1971) of course, may be readily excused from concluding that the principle of reinforcement is taken to be all powerful in accounting for behavior! However, Catania fails to do anything like justice to the evidence that clearly establishes the powerful but limited influence of external reinforcement contingen-

---

* Interestingly, Azrin (1977) similarly indicates that reinforcement principles are insufficient to account for the modification of human behavior. He discusses the necessity for "emergent principles" of behavior change, a view to be taken up in greater detail in next year's volume.

cies on human behavior. To acknowledge that instructions will often override the natural contingencies of reinforcement is just the beginning. As mentioned in Sections I and II of this volume and detailed elsewhere (Bandura, 1977b; Mahoney, 1974; Mischel, 1974), cognitions exert causal influence on behavior and the effects of external events on behavior are mediated largely by cognitive events. The evidence that it is the manner in which rewards are cognitively represented that is the significant determinant of behavior, rather than the actual reward stimulus the individual is physically exposed to, emphasizes the inherent limitations of Catania's argument. To take but one current example, Moore, Mischel, and Zeiss (1976) demonstrate that it is not necessarily the objective reality of what children look at but how they perceive the reward that governs their behavior. Catania finds fault with the argument that reinforcement can be effective only if the organism is aware of the contingencies. Not all learning might require an awareness of the contingencies, but this evades the fact that it usually facilitates learning and that at least in some important areas, such as verbal conditioning, it does appear necessary for behavior change (cf. Bandura, 1977b; Page, 1972).

Catania struggles to contain the burgeoning evidence on self-reinforcement procedures within the traditional framework of reinforcement. But as Bandura points out, it is not the concept of self-reinforcement but more fundamentally the concept of reinforcement itself that may be in need of reconceptualization. Finally, Catania's concern over the use and misuse of reinforcement terminology is viewed in a different perspective by Wilson and Evans (1976).

Mahoney's (1976) and Thoresen and Wilbur's (1976) responses to Goldiamond's paper once again reflect the different theoretical perspectives of workers within the general field of behavior therapy. Mahoney stresses that the "use of the term 'self' to describe [behavioral patterns that are culturally deemed 'selfy'] need not connote acceptance of free will or 'self-determination'; and need not be problematic so long as clear operational definitions are provided" (p. 516). Mahoney also emphasizes the reciprocal determinism of behavior (cf. Bandura, 1977b) rather than unidirectional control by environmental forces. "Total environmental control," he states, "is as much an explanatory fiction as is self-reinforcement."

In his rejoinder, Goldiamond (1976) disclaims all knowledge of those believers in "total environmental control" to whom Mahoney is referring. This argument, declares Goldiamond, is an "exhortatory fiction" or "e.f.". An e.f. is said to be created for "demolitional rhetoric." Apparently, the statement that there are believers in "total environmental control" is an e.f. because "behavior can be changed by drugs, by surgery, by environmental manipulations, by genetic means, among others. The description of one type of relation *does not preclude the existence of others*" (Goldiamond, 1976, p. 523). Yet this is rhetoric of another sort. For a believer in "total environmental control" one need look no further than Skinner (1971) who puts it thus: "A person does not act upon the world, the world acts upon him" (p. 211). It is not good enough to discount the charge of "total environmental control" by pointing out the obvious that surgery can alter behavior. (As Goldiamond himself remarks in another connection, "so what else is new?") What is at issue, and what Mahoney was calling into question, is whether the person is allowed any self-directive causal influence in modifying his or her behavior. The operant answer, as indicated by Skinner's comment, has been very clear.

Ruing the alleged misinterpretation of what he meant, Goldiamond offers the following reflection: "Apparently, the second academic generation of radical behaviorists is now undergoing some of the treatment accorded to the first. Those of us who have followed the reception accorded positions formulated earlier are familiar with the misinterpretations and attributions of unheld positions that characterized too many reviews (e.g., attributed denial of thinking, of emotions, of experiences), which parallel earlier charges against Darwin" (p. 524). Fittingly, Goldiamond concludes with the comment that "Readers may judge for themselves."

Returning to the pragmatic consideration of the effects of self-reinforcement *procedures,* Stumphauzer (1976) describes the apparently successful use of self-reinforcement in the elimination of stealing in a 12 year old girl. Locurto and Walsh (1976) demonstrate that reinforcement of college students for uncommon word associations produces an increase in this activity. Those students who additionally received training in self-reinforcement showed greater transfer to a dissimilar task than students who had not received such training. This finding assumes importance in view of the difficulty encountered with most behavioral methods in facilitating generalization of treatment-induced change to different situations.

Greiner and Karoly (1976) evaluated the effect of self-monitoring, self-reinforcement, and planning as components of a self-control strategy in the modification of study activity and academic performance. Neither self-monitoring nor self-monitoring plus self-reinforcement was superior to training in study methods alone. However, the full package of self-monitoring and self-reinforcement plus planning resulted in greater improvement than all other conditions across different dependent measures. The lack of reactivity of self-monitoring is noteworthy. Greiner and Karoly offer the interesting suggestion that one of the determinants of the effects of self-monitoring is the complexity of the target behavior: "If self-monitoring influences behavior in a therapeutic fashion, perhaps it occurs primarily when it is possible to self-evaluate current performance relative to a discrete and well-specified performance criterion. In the case of study activities, the long- and short-range goals are nebulous and frequently nonexistent" (p. 501). This view dove-tails with Romanczyk et al.'s (1973) and Abrams and Wilson's (1977) emphasis on the specificity of the target behavior being self-monitored.

Anderson, Fodor, and Alpert (1976) conducted a comparative investigation of self-control procedures in the treatment of disruptive adolescents. A token reinforcement condition in which self-evaluation skills, self-monitoring, and prediction of reward consequences were rewarded was compared to a behavior rehearsal condition in which subjects received feedback of emotional control during role playing of stressful situations and a traditional therapy condition. The token fading condition resulted in improved performance in the training classroom and in other classrooms, indicating generalization of change. The behavior rehearsal method produced more effective functioning of specific cognitive tasks, whereas the traditional therapy condition effected no change. Anderson et al. emphasize that self-control is not a unitary concept and discuss the importance of specifying treatment methods for particular self-control goals.

SELF-INSTRUCTIONAL TRAINING

In his response to Bandura, Catania states that we know little as yet about the interaction between verbal and nonverbal behavior. To a large extent, this may be attributable to the tendency to cling to operant analyses developed with infrahuman subjects and the behavior of those radical behaviorists within behavior modification who disdain all dalliance with covert, symbolic processes, protestations about being misunderstood, fables, and armadyllics notwithstanding. Meichenbaum's (1977) research on self-instruction is a prominent exception to this reluctance to investigate, let alone embrace, concepts of verbally mediated, cognitive self-control (see our commentary on cognitive restructuring in Section II and on biofeedback in this Section).

Using a multiple baseline across subjects design, Bornstein, and Quevillon (1976) evaluated the effects of a self-instructional training program in the treatment of overactive preschool boys. Training resulted in a major improvement in task behavior, improvement that appeared to generalize to the classroom setting. Treatment effects were maintained at a follow-up more than 22 weeks after baseline recording was started. Moreover, the behavior change obtained can be attributed to the self-instructional training package since improvement occurred only after the target behavior had been treated directly. The authors point out that their treatment package contained numerous components, and that the specific agents of change cannot be determined. Thus, the treatment method included verbal instructions, self-instruction, modeling, prompts, reinforcement, and fading. However, the success of this treatment package in producing initial behavior change, and the impressive generalization to other settings and maintenance over time clearly indicate the apparent value of this approach to behavior change.

An attempt to disentangle some of the specific treatment components of the self-instructional training procedure was reported by Thorpe, Amatu, Blakey, and Burns (1976). High school pupils who were fearful about public speaking were assigned to one of four groups: general insight, specific insight, instructional rehearsal, and insight plus rehearsal. The insight conditions consisted of an emphasis on rational-emotive therapy and its focus on irrational assumptions that people purportedly hold. The rehearsal component addressed the specific practice of repeating more constructive, coping self-statements. The results indicate that the insight component was the effective agent of change in reducing public speaking anxiety as measured by several self-report measures. The behavioral rating measure did not discriminate among the four treatment groups. The authors themselves note some of the limitations of this study, including the absence of a suitable control group.

SECTION III: BIOFEEDBACK AND OTHER STRATEGIES IN SELF-MANAGEMENT

3

MIGRAINE: MANAGEMENT BY TRAINED CONTROL OF VASOCONSTRICTION

Linda R. Friar

University of Connecticut

and

Jackson Beatty

University of California, Los Angeles

This experiment investigated the effect of operant training of vasoconstriction in the extracranial arteries involved in migraine headache in a group of nine experimental subjects. Training of vasoconstriction in an irrelevant site, the hand, served as a control in nine other subjects. Fourteen females and four males participated, ranging in age from 10 to 54. All experienced frequent and severe migraine. Arterial pulse waves were recorded from the surface of the skin with pressure of plethysmographs. Training sessions included continuous visual feedback of the reinforced pulse waveform presented on a storage oscilloscope and intermittent auditory feedback determined by a digital computer. Following eight training sessions, in a final no-feedback session

---

Reprinted with permission from *Journal of Consulting and Clinical Psychology*, 44, 1, 46-53, 1976.

This research was partially supported by the Advanced Research Projects Agency of the Department of Defense and was monitored by the Office of Naval Research under Contract N0001-70-C-0350.

the experimental group demonstrated vasoconstriction in the extracranial arteries ($p < .0005$, one-tailed), but the control group did not ($p < .50$). Subjects were instructed to apply training at the onset of migraine. Comparison of the 30-day pretraining and posttraining records shows that the experimental group experienced improvement in headache symptomatology as measured by incidence of major headache attacks ($p < .05$, one-tailed). Headache symptomatology was relatively stable in the control group ($p < .50$).

Migraine is a unilateral, extracranial headache often involving a number of other symptoms. It is one of the most common psychosomatic disorders, with an estimated incidence of at least 5% (e.g., Childes & Sweetman, 161; Lennox, 1941; Lyght, 196). The severity, length, and frequency of attacks vary widely between and within patients.

A number of the physiological aspects of migraine are well understood. In both of the major forms of migraine, classical and common, migraine pain appears to be the direct result of an unusual series of vascular events. In classical migraine prior to the onset of headache, there is a period of intense intracranial and extracranial vasoconstriction, occasionally producing ischemia; sensory prodramata may result (Skinhoj & Paulson, 1969). In common migraine the initial vasoconstriction may not be present. In both forms of migraine, headache is the product of profound dilatation of the extracranial vasculature.

At the onset of headache, pulsatory head pain results from increased amplitude of hydraulic pulsations of the extracranial vasculature, which in turn distends surrounding pain sensitive fibers. As the attack progresses, the pain becomes steady rather than pulsatory, and concurrently, a sterile inflammation and edema are produced in the extracranial arteries, rendering them thickened and rigidified. Although abnormal changes in the vasculature are directly involved in migraine, the vasculature itself does not appear to be unhealthy, and evidence points to a disorder in the neurological pathways governing the vasomotor response (Dalessio, 1972).

A wide range of substances that produce vasoconstriction, including ergotamine tartrate, pituitrin, ephedrine, benzidrine, ephinephrine, and caffeine, have been shown to be more or less effective in relieving migraine, if administered prior to the establishment of edema (Dalessio, 1972). Despite its often severe side effects, ergotamine tartrate is the most common medication for relief of migraine and its effects are so reliable that a positive response to the drug is a major sign in the diagnosis. Relief from headache pain can also be gained temporarily by pressure on the carotid artery or its external branches, application of an icecap, breathing a mixture of 10% carbon dioxide and 90% oxygen, and other means of reducing pulse amplitude. The responsiveness of migraine pain to any method of pulse amplitude attenuation, pharmacological, physical, or neuronal, suggests that operant control of extracranial pulse amplitude should be an effective treatment for migraine.

Operantly trained control of local vasomotor responses has already been demonstrated in animals (DiCara & Miller, 1968a, 1968b, 1968c; Miller, 1966). In each study, curarized rats demonstrated specific and localized control in a single training session. Although Miller (Miller & Dworkin, 1974) has recently acknowledged difficulty with the curarized preparation, the literature still suggests that only the localized vasomotor response changes during training, whereas other areas of vasculature and other autonomic responses remain unaltered.

Operantly trained vasomotor control in humans has also been demonstrated (Snyder & Noble, 1967; Stern & Pavlovski, 1974). In a single session, Snyder and Noble (1967) successfully trained subjects to produce vasoconstrictions in the finger. When reinforcement contingency was reversed for some of the subjects so that vasomotor stability was reinforced, vasomotor response changed appropriately. Stern and Pavlovski (1974) replicated the training of vasoconstriction in humans using truly and partially yoked controls.

The hypothesis that learned vasomotor control could be an effective migraine treatment has been considered in recent reports from the Menninger Clinic (Sargent, Green, & Walters, 1973). Unfortunately, the absence of quantified data, experimental uncertainties, and the lack of necessary control procedures are serious difficulties. Ostfeld (1961) presents convincing data that a large placebo effect is often observed in headache patients, and any new treatment must be evaluated with strict controls.

The utility of operant techniques in treating pathological responses other than migraine has been suggested by several investigators. Benson, Shapiro, Tursky, and Schwartz (1971) reported decreases in blood pressure in hypertensive patients; Weiss and Engel (1971) trained patients to reduce the occurrence of preventricular contractions; and Budzynski, Stoyva, and Adler (1970) observed decreases in tension headaches in patients trained to reduce electromyogram activity.

In this study an experiment is reported that investigates the application of operant techniques to the control of migraine. One group of migraine patients was trained to decrease pulse amplitude in the forehead (experimental group), a manipulation that should act specifically to relieve migraine. A control group was trained to decrease pulse amplitude in a peripheral site, the hand, a treatment that should produce only nonspecific placebo effects. Using a technique established as successful in producing vasomotor control in normal subjects (Friar & Beatty, Note 1), the present study explicitly tests the clinical utility of learned vasomotor control in migraine patients.

Based on the published literature, the following results were expected: (a) specificity of control at the reinforced site (i.e., pulse amplitude decreases in the reinforced site should be significant and greater than in the non-reinforced site) and (b) differential reduction in headache symptomatology. (Subjects in the forehead group should exhibit a greater reduction in symptomatology than subjects in the hand group.)

METHOD

Subjects

Nineteen patients, 16 females and 3 males, positively diagnosed as suffering from migraine headache, served as subjects. They were recruited from an advertisement in the school newspaper and ranged in age from 19 to 54, with an average age of 30.42. They expected an average of 8.63 migraine attacks per month.

Equipment

Pulse waves were recorded from the surface of the skin with two pressure-transducing plethysmographs (Biocom 1010). Pulse waves from the forehead were recorded from a plethysmograph held in place with an elastic headband directly above the temporal artery or one of its main ramifications. Pulse waves from the hand were recorded from a plethysmograph taped onto the ventral side of the index finger, with care being taken not to occlude blood flow. Electrocardiogram (EKG) was recorded with plate electrodes between the right arm and left leg with the right leg grounded. Skin temperature was measured adjacent to the plethysmographs with the use of two surface thermistors. Pulse wave and EKG data were digitized in a general purpose digital computer controlling the experiment and monitored by a conventional oscilloscope. The pulse wave from the reinforced site was continuously displayed on a storage oscilloscope as a temporally stable waveform triggered on the ORS complex of the EKG, indicating ventricular contraction.

The subject was seated in a padded reclining chair in the shielded subject room, which was adjacent to the computer room and connected to it with an intercom system. Under reinforcement conditions both visual and auditory feedback were delivered to the subject room. Visual feedback was provided by a videosystem that monitored the storage oscilloscope. Binary auditory feedback was generated by the computer.

Procedure

Patient selection. A migraine questionnaire, which obtained extensive information about headache characteristics, history, and medication, was completed by 74 headache patients. The questionnaires were reviewed by a physician specializing in the diagnosis and treatment of headache who rated each patient by the certainty of a migraine diagnosis. Only applicants who received a maximum certainty rating were selected. The success of ergotamine tartrate served as important evidence of true migraine and provided pharmacological evidence that induced decreases in pulse amplitude relieved headache. Of the 19 participants, 18 had found the drug effective. (The 1 exception had found the side effects prohibitive.)

Subjects receiving a maximum certainty rating were then selected for high frequency and regularity of attacks. (Applicants whose headache occurred in cycles were rejected.) The smallest number of attacks experienced by any subject during the 30-day pretraining record-keeping period was 5, and the maximum, 28.

Record keeping. Selected subjects were instructed in keeping a careful record of their pretraining headache symptoms for the 30 days preceding training. The record included the date, time of onset and offset, location and intensity of attack, and an account of all medication taken. Similar records were kept during training and for the 30 days following the final training session. The intensity of each attack was rated on a scale from 1 to 10, with a rating of 1 corresponding to the mildest headache ever experienced by the subject and 10 the most severe.

Assignment of training condition. Subjects were divided into two groups matched on the basis of the migraine questionnaire for frequency of attacks, age, and sex. After the two groups were formed, they were randomly assigned to the experimental or control group.* All sub-

* Originally 20 persons were selected to serve as subjects. Immediately before the beginning of the study, one of these persons was examined by a neurologist who questioned the diagnosis of migraine. For this reason, the original group of subjects consisted of 19 persons.

jects were trained on the side in which their headache had been most frequent during the 30-day pretraining period. For subjects in the experimental group the reinforced site was directly over the extracranial artery most affected during attacks, whereas for subjects in the control group the reinforced site was the index finger of the side most affected.

Training. Each subject was run for a total of eight training sessions and a final ninth no-feedback session, which estimated the subject's ability to exert control in the absence of feedback. An effort was made to have each subject complete training within a 3-week period. Each session was divided into a series of baseline trials followed by eight training trials. During each trial, the computer calculated pulse amplitude, skin temperature, and pulse propagation time separately for the extracranial and peripheral site. Pulse amplitude was determined by subtracting the value at a fixed time after the R wave (usually 50 msec) from the maximum value of that wave. Pulse propagation time was calculated as the time in milliseconds from the R wave to the peak of the pulse wave at the recording site. Heart period was also computed. Data from the several measures were separately averaged over 20 heartbeat periods. At the end of each 200-heartbeat trial a trial mean and the 10 20-beat submeans for each measure were printed.

The computer also detected and eliminated muscle activity artifact from the pulse-wave forms. At the beginning of each session an initial pulse wave template was obtained for each recording site by averaging 20 pulse waves judged artifact free by visual inspection. Subsequently, a pulse wave was accepted as artifact free if its correlation with the current template met or exceeded .70. The template was updated each time 20 pulse waves were accepted, and the new correlations were based on the most recent group of 20 pulse waves. This correlation criterion accepted natural variance but rejected muscle artifact. If the current pulse wave did not match the template, the data were rejected and a low volume, high frequency pitch was delivered to the subject. When two plethysmographic recordings were taken simultaneously, both were matched to criterion for their respective sites.

In addition to calculating and tabulating data and monitoring muscle artifact, the computer also determined auditory feedback, which was used to shape the subject's response. For the first 20 heartbeats of a training trial, pulse amplitudes were averaged and auditory feedback was not presented. During the second 20 heartbeats, any pulse amplitude that was less than the average of the pulse amplitudes from the first 20 resulted in the feedback tone. With each successive 20 heartbeats, only amplitudes below the lowest preceding average of 20 would allow the tone to be generated. In this way, as performance improved, the criterion for auditory feedback became more stringent. With the beginning of each training trial a new criterion was established.

Once the recording devices were attached and the initial parameters entered into the computer, the training procedure was essentially automated. Trials were separated by approximate 1½ minutes while the computer printed tabulated data.

At the beginning of each session pulse amplitude was monitored but not reinforced until stability was achieved. In these baseline trials, stability was defined as either a series of baseline trials in which the pulse amplitude means alternated up and down with no linear trend or as two consecutive trials in which the means differed no more than 5% on the reinforced pulse amplitude, at which point training began. Training trials differed from the baseline trials in that the feedback systems were operative. Pulse waves on the storage oscilloscope were transmitted to a videoscreen in front of the subject. They were stored for the duration of the trial unless movement created extraneous traces on the screen, in which case they were erased. Auditory feedback was also available during the training trials. Both signals were generated only by the reinforced site.

For all sessions but one, plethysmographic recordings were taken from both the forehead and hand. Usually during the seventh session, recordings contralateral to the reinforced site were taken rather than recordings of ipsilateral forehead and hand. In other words, forehead left and right were recorded for the experimental and hand left and right were recorded for the control subjects. The reinforced site for this contralateral session was the same as it had been throughout training. In all sessions, skin temperature was recorded from a site immediately adjacent to the two plethysmographs.

Instructions to the subjects. Prior to the first training session, detailed instructions were read to each subject. Even though they were told this was an experimental treatment and success was not guaranteed, they were given a positive set toward the outcome. Instructions for both groups were identical except for one paragraph. Subjects in the experimental group were told,

> We will train you to decrease pulse amplitude in the extracranial artery most frequently affected during your attacks. We expect the training will be generalized to other parts of your vasculature.

Subjects in the control group were told,

> Some of our research shows that learning to decrease pulse amplitude in the hand is easier than in the forehead. Training effects are generalized, and training in the hand is expected to affect your extracranial arteries.

All subjects were informed of the previous success in training normals (Friar & Beatty, Note 1) and the rationale involved in the training. They were instructed to produce vasoconstriction as they had learned in the laboratory whenever they became aware of a developing migraine.

The experimenter encouraged all subjects throughout training. At the end of Session 9, the no-feedback session, all subjects were told regardless of their performance that they had demonstrated a sizable training effect and were ready to try the training as a headache intervention.

RESULTS

To evaluate the specific therapeutic effects of learned vasomotor control on migraine two types of data are necessary. First, physiological data are needed to show that subjects can induce specific vascular changes in the absence of feedback. Second, objective clinical data are needed to demonstrate changes in headache symptomatology after intervention.

In this article only the analyses that are relevant to testing the therapeutic effects of training are presented. A detailed analysis of other aspects of the experiment appear elsewhere (Friar & Beatty, Note 1). All comparisons for which a clear prediction was made were evaluated with one-tailed significance tests.

The pulse amplitude data from the ninth experimental session in which no feedback was presented provides a test of the subjects' ability to regulate vasomotor response independent of feedback. An examinaton of these data reveal that migraine subjects were able to control vasomotor activity at the trained site.

Patients in the control group who had been reinforced for vasomotor changes in the hand were able without feedback to reduce pulse amplitude at that site to .67 of the stabilized pretraining baseline level in the last four of the eight testing trials of the no-reinforcement session, $t(8) = 4.819$, $p < .0005$, one tailed. However, these control group patients showed no significant reduction in pulse amplitude at the forehead. (Mean forehead pulse amplitude in last four testing trials was .95 of

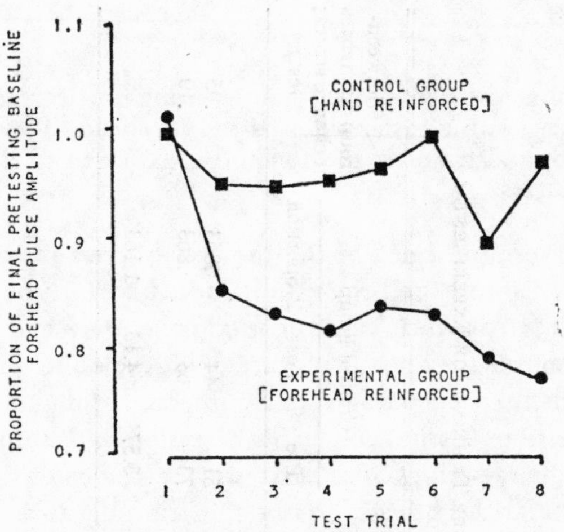

FIGURE 1. Altered incidence of migraine following vasoconstriction training.

baseline, t (8) = 1.06, p < .50.) Patients in the experimental group showed significant reductions in pulse amplitude in the final four no-reinforcement testing trials to .80 baseline in the forehead, t (8) = 3.275, p < .005, one tailed, and to .69 baseline in the hand, t (8) = 3.92, p < .005, one tailed. The two groups differed significantly from each other in their ability to reduce pulse amplitude at the critical extracranial forehead site without reinforcement, t (17) = 1.96, p < .05, one tailed, suggesting that specific effects of vasomotor training on the incidence of migraine headache should be observed only for the experimental group and not for the control patients.

Figure 1 presents the mean pulse amplitude at the forehead site on each of the eight no-reinforcement testing trials expressed as a proportion of stabilized pretesting baselines for the experimental and control groups separately. The figure shows that only subjects in the experimental group produced a systematic reduction in pulse amplitude at the forehead site.

Pretraining and posttraining headache logs provide the objective clinical data needed to evaluate the effect of training on migraine symptomatology. An examination of the subjects' headache logs in the posttraining period indicated that most subjects conscientiously followed their instructions to exert control at the previously reinforced site. (One

TABLE 1

HEADACHE SYMPTOMATOLOGY BEFORE AND AFTER TRAINING FOR EXPERIMENTAL AND CONTROL SUBJECTS

Symptom	Experimental group			Control group			$p <$ (Between-group differences in change scores; t test)
	Pre	Post	Proportion	Pre	Post	Proportion	
No. major attacks (over 3 hours)	57	31	.543**	51	44	.863	.05
No. total episodes	80	51	.638*	73	63	.863	.10
Mean intensity of pain (1–10 rating scale)	4.53	4.26	.964	3.57	4.15	1.163	

* $p < .10$.
** $p < .05$.

subject in the experimental group failed to maintain a posttraining log, and her headache data were omitted from all analyses.)

The predictions concerning the effects of training on headache symptomatology were supported. Training in the extracranial arteries in the experimental group was associated with a sizable reduction of symptoms in the 30-day posttraining period, whereas training in the peripheral vasculature of the control group had very limited effect. Table 1 presents pretaining and posttraining symptomatology for the two groups. The two groups are statistically comparable before training on number of major attacks, total number of migraine episodes, and intensity of attacks.

Comparing the reported incidence of all migraine episodes in the months preceding and following training, subjects in the experimental group who received training at the forehead site reported a mean reduction of 3.11 episodes per month. Thus, the incidence of episodes in the posttraining period is .64 of the pretraining period, $t(8) = 1.82$, $p < 10$, one tailed. Subjects in the control group reported a smaller reduction of 1.11 episodes per month to .86 of the pretraining level, $t(8) = 1.04$, ns.

A count of the total number of migraine episodes may not clearly reveal the effects of vasomotor training. Subjects were instructed to record as episodes any instance in which they felt a headache attack might be developing. Based on present understanding of the physiology of migraine, the effect of any induced vasoconstriction, whether pharmacological, mechanical or, as in the present case, operant in origin, is to abbreviate the headache attack rather than prevent its onset. Since the labile, pulsatile phase is generally of less than 3 hours in duration, the occurrence of headaches of more than 3 hours can be taken as a measure of major, unrelieved headaches. This measure of major attacks provides a better test of the effects of training than the measure of total episodes.

Both groups reported a comparable incidence of major migraine attacks in the pretraining month. Following training, the incidence of major migraine headaches was reduced to .54 of the pretraining level in the experimental group from 57 to 31 major attacks per month, $t(8) = 2.52$, $p < .05$, one tailed. In comparison, the incidence in the control group was relatively unchanged. Control subjects reported a reduction of major attacks to .86 of pretraining level from 51 to 44 per month, $a(8) = 1.17$, $p < .50$. The degree of change in major headache incidence differed significantly between groups, $t(17) = 1.97$, $p < .05$, one tailed.

For both groups there is no trend for the average intensity of headache pain to change as a result of training (experimental group: $t(8) = .77$, ns, and control group: $t(8) = 1.15$, ns). Following training, headache pain, when it occurred, was neither more or less intense than it had been prior to training.

In the experimental group there was a large reduction in the use of all categories of medication taken for the immediate relief of headache attack. In each of the three major categories—vasoconstrictors, moderate to strong analgesics and sedatives (addictive), and mild analgesics—there was a decrease to .55 or less of baseline levels in the posttraining period.

In the control group there was an unexpected decrease in the use of two of the three major categories of medication taken for relief of attacks. In the posttraining periods, the use of both mild analgesics and vasoconstrictors decreased to less than 55% of the pretraining level. The use of moderate to strong analgesics and sedatives (addictive), however, was slightly increased to 102% of the pretraining level. The decreased use of mild analgesics and vasoconstrictors was not expected on the basis of reported headache symptomatology, and the most obvious interpretation is that the use of medication is, at least in part, determined by additional factors, such as patient motivation.

As mentioned above, the information on medication does not lend itself to statistical analyses. Although it is possible to categorize drugs in terms of general mode of action or addictive qualities, it is not possible to accurately equate or compare drugs within a category. Furthermore, subjects used a wide variety of drugs and frequently substituted one for another, so analysis of individual change scores in medication would be most difficult to interpret. The data on medication is therefore presented without analyses to be taken as further corroboration of the other indices of improvement.

To summarize the results, the measures of headache symptomatology present a picture consistent with the results on training effects on pulse amplitude. Only the experimental group, which demonstrated control of the effected extracranial arteries, showed a clear reduction in migraine episodes and major attacks after training. On all indices of headache, except intensity, and in all categories of medication, the experimental group showed a decrease in symptoms. Although subjects in the control group reported applying training procedures in the posttraining period at least as consistently as subjects in the experimental group, they showed no significant improvement in symptomatology.

DISCUSSION

It appears that operant procedures may result in moderate alterations in vasomotor tone at the site of reinforcement following repeated training sessions. Learned vasomotor control may be clinically meaningful for migraine when the site reinforced is the extracranial vasculature.

In this study subjects in both the experimental and control groups seemed equally convinced at the end of training that they would be able to control their headaches. Although it is impossible to rule out the fact that forehead training was more convincing than hand training, there is reason to reject this explanation of the results. Subjects in the control group were as diligent as subjects in the experimental group in attending training and keeping logs. There was not a single instance in which a control subject expressed doubt about training procedures. The fact that as a group the subjects were familiar with reports of temperature training in the hand as a supposedly successful intervention for migraine may have made the control even more credible.

The decrease in two of the three major categories of medication in the hand-trained group cannot be explained in view of the unchanged headache symptomalogy. Apparently the use of medication is determined in part by factors other than reported headache pain. In general, the record keeping and training seemed to focus all subjects on their symptoms and use of medication. During the course of training many subjects spontaneously expressed their dissatisfaction with the amount of medication they took, and they frequently said they preferred to avoid medication, especially the ergotamine-based vasoconstrictors. Possibly, although training and record keeping did not affect reported headache for subjects trained in periphery, the procedures had an impact on their attitude or resolve regarding medication.

These initial clinically positive results with migraine patients are encouraging both for migraine treatment and for the use of biofeedback in the treatment of cardiovascular disorders. In a review of the biofeedback literature, Blanchard and Young (1973) concluded that at that time there was little evidence that learned control could bring about improvement in cardiovascular disorders. They focused on several persistent problems in the relevant research. They pointed to the relatively small physiological effects of training in most studies and suggested that successful clinical application might necessarily involve repeated training sessions. They also noted the absence of proper experimental controls in the current clinical studies.

The present study shows that using a strict experimental control and repeated training sessions seem to bring about clinical improvement in the case of migraine headaches in a group of subjects who suffered from extremely severe and frequent headaches. A final conclusion regarding the usefulness of such treatment must await replication and further study. The operantly induced improvement of migraine adds credence to the argument that regardless of etiology at least some disorders classed as psychosomatic are modifiable by techniques proved potent in altering overt behavior. The present study leaves unresolved a number of important issues, however, including the evaluation of training parameters, the duration of treatment effects, subject variables, and the applicability of operant methods to actual clinical practice.

REFERENCE NOTE

1. FRIAR, L. R., & BEATTY, J. *Learned Control of Vasomotor Activity.* Manuscript submitted for publication, 1975.

REFERENCES

BENSON, H., SHAPIRO, D., TURSKY, B., & SCHWARTZ, G. Decreased systolic blood pressure through operant conditioning techniques in patients with essential hypertension. *Science,* 173:740-742, 1971.

BLANCHARD, E. B., & YOUNG, L. D. Self-control of cardiac functioning: A promise as yet unfulfilled. *Psychological Bulletin,* 79:145-163, 1973.

BUDZYNSKI, T., SOYVA, J., & ADLER, C. Feedback-induced muscle relaxation: Application to tension headaches. *Behavior Therapy and Experimental Psychiatry,* 1:205-221, 1970.

CHILDES, A., & SWEETNAM, M. Study of 104 cases of migraine. *British Journal of Industrial Medicine,* 18:243, 1961.

DALESSIO, D. *Wolff's Headache and Other Head Pain* (3rd ed.). New York: Oxford University Press, 1972.

DICARA, L., & MILLER, N. Instrumental learning of peripheral vasomotor responses in the curarized rat. *Communication in Behavioral Biology,* 1:209, 1968 (a).

DICARA, L., & MILLER, N. Instrumental learning of urine formation by rats: Changes in ural blood flow. *American Journal of Physiology,* 215:677-686, 1968 (b).

DICARA, L., & MILLER, N. Instrumental learning of vasomotor responses by rats: Learning to respond differentially in the two ears. *Science,* 159:1485-1486, 1968 (c).

LENNOX, W. *Science and Seizures.* New York: Harper, 1941.

LYGHT, C. *The Merck Manual.* Rahway, N.J.: Merck, Sharp & Dohme, 1966.

MILLER, N. Learning of visceral and glandular responses. *Science,* 163:434-445, 1969.

MILLER, N., & DWORKIN, B. R. Visceral learning: Recent difficulties with curarized rats and significant problems for human research. In P. A. Obrist, A. H. Slack, J. Brenner, & L. V. DiCara (Eds.), *Cardiovascular Psychophysiology.* Chicago: Aldine, 1974.

OSTFELD, Z. A study of migraine pharmacotherapy. *American Journal of Science and Medicine,* 241:192, 1961.

SARGENT, J., GREEN, E., & WALTERS, E. Preliminary report on the use of autogenic feedback techniques in the treatment of migraine and tension headaches. *Psychosomatic Medicine,* 35:129-135, 1973.

SKINHOJ, E., & PAULSON, O. Regional blood flow in internal carotid distribution during migraine attack. *British Medical Journal,* 3:569, 1969.

SNYDER, C., & NOBLE, M. Operant conditioning of vasoconstriction. *Journal of Experimental Psychology,* 77:262-268, 1967.

STERN, R. M., & PAVLOVSKI, R. P. Operant conditioning of vasoconstriction: A verification. *Journal of Experimental Psychology,* 102:330-332, 1974.

WEISS, T., & ENGEL, B. Operant conditioning of heart rate in patients with premature ventricular contractions. *Psychosomatic Medicine,* 3:1-25, 1971.

SECTION III: BIOFEEDBACK AND OTHER STRATEGIES IN SELF-MANAGEMENT

4

SELF-REINFORCEMENT: THEORETICAL AND METHODOLOGICAL CONSIDERATIONS

Albert Bandura

Stanford University

How behavior is viewed determines which facets of human functioning are studied most thoroughly and which are ignored or disavowed. Conceptions thus delimit research and are, in turn, shaped by findings from paradigms embodying that particular view. Theorists who exclude self-regulatory functions from their concept of human potentialities restrict the scope of their research to external influences on behavior. Detailed analysis of behavior as a function of external consequences provides confirmatory evidence that behavior is indeed subject to external control. However, limiting the scope of scientific inquiry not only yields redundant results but, by disregarding other significant determinants and processes, it can reinforce a truncated image of human nature.

From the perspective of social learning theory (Bandura, 1976), people are seen as capable of exercising some control over their own behavior. Among the various self-regulatory phenomena that have been investigated within this framework, self-reinforcement occupies a prominent position. In this process, individuals regulate their behavior by making self-reward

---

Reprinted with permission from *Behaviorism*, 4, 2, Fall, 1976, 135-155.

Preparation of this article was facilitated by research grant M-5162 from the National Institutes of Health, U.S. Public Health Service.

conditional upon matching self-prescribed standards of performance. Acknowledgement of self-regulatory processes has added a new dimension to experimental analyses of reinforcement. Results of such studies have provided the impetus for extending the range of reinforcement practices in programs designed to effect personal change. Interest was shifted from managing behavior through imposition of contingencies to developing skills in self-regulation. In the latter approach, control is vested to a large extent in the hands of individuals themselves: They set their own goals, they monitor and evaluate their own performances, and they serve as their own reinforcing agents (Goldfried and Merbaum, 1973; Mahoney and Thoresen, 1974). The present paper discusses some major substantive issues in the conceptualization of self-reinforcement.

MULTIFACETED CRITERIA OF SELF-REINFORCEMENT

A self-reinforcement event has several defining properties.

Control of Reinforcers. One important feature is that the organism exercises full control over the reinforcers so that they are freely available for the taking. In studies of self-reinforcement, subjects have at their disposal a generous supply of tangible rewards which they are free to administer to themselves at any time in whatever quantities they choose (Bandura and Kupers, 1964; Bandura and Perloff, 1967; Mahoney and Bandura, 1972). Symbolic and evaluative reinforcers have received less study, but, here too, people can produce self-approving and self-critical reactions most anytime.

Conditional Self-Administration of Reinforcers. Although reinforcers are freely available, their self-administration is made conditional upon performing requisite behaviors. Therefore, a second critical feature of self-reinforcement is the self-prescription of a performance requirement. This entails self-denial of rewards until the appropriate or conditional behavior has been achieved. The regulated use of incentives may involve not only performance requirements but also exercise of control over the amount of self-reward (Bandura and Kupers, 1964; Bandura and Mahoney, 1974).

Adoption of Performance Standards. Self-reinforcement requires adoption of performance standards for determining the occasions on which a given behavior warrants self-reward. Performances that match or exceed the minimum criterion serve as discriminative cues for self-reward, whereas reinforcers are withheld for substandard performances. The standards by which the adequacy of behavior is judged vary in complexity ranging from simple qualitative discernments of behavior to relational rules.

For most human activities there are no absolute measures of adequacy. The speed with which distances are run or the scores obtained on tests, in themselves, convey insufficient information for self-appraisal. When adequacy is defined relationally, performances are evaluated by comparing them with the attainments of others. A student, who achieves a score of 115 points on an examination and whose personal standard is to be in the upper ten percent of the group, will have no basis for making either a positive or negative self-assessment, without knowing the accomplishments of others. In performances gauged by social criteria, self-appraisals require relational comparisons of at least three sources of information to judge a given performance: absolute performance level, one's own personal standards, and a social referent. The referential comparisons may take different forms for different tasks. For some regular activities, standardized norms based on representative groups are used to determine one's relative standing. For other endeavors, people compare themselves to particular associates in similar situations. In most activities, individuals use their previous behavior as the reference against which to judge their ongoing performances apart from any social comparison.

In brief, the criteria that together constitute a self-reinforcement event include self-administration of freely available rewards contingent upon performances that meet adopted standards.

DISTINCTION BETWEEN OPERATION AND PROCESS OF SELF-REINFORCEMENT

Theorizing and research in the area of self-reinforcement distinguish between the *operation* and the *process* of self-reinforcement. The operation is defined by the self-administration of freely accessible reinforcers contingent upon requisite performances; the process refers to the resulting increase in the conditional performances. Social learning theory views the process by which consequences affect behavior as similar regardless of whether reinforcers are administered by oneself or by others. It is before rewards are administered that the main differences between externally- and self-regulated reinforcement arise. As we have previously seen, the latter practice entails at least three component processes: adoption of, and adherence to, reference standards; comparison of performance against standards to determine when it is appropriate to engage in self-reward; and self-privation of reinforcers for insufficient performances.

A complete understanding of self-reinforcement requires two separate lines of research for which the methodologies necessarily differ (Bandura, 1974). One line of investigation is designed to explain how referential standards for determining the occasions for self-reward are acquired, maintained, and modified. In experiments conducted for this purpose, influences likely to affect establishment of standards are the independent variables, and the performance attainments, which individuals self-reward and self-punish, constitute the dependent events.

The second line of research is designed to measure whether self-administered consequences do, in fact, enhance performance. In testing for enhancement effects, self-administered consequences represent the independent variables and performances levels the dependent ones.

The issue of when individuals choose to reward themselves and whether the self-administered rewards influence their behavior are separable; both must be investigated for a full understanding of self-reinforcement. The different methodologies are emphasized here because some writers (Premack and Anglin, 1973) have failed to distinguish studies investigating induction of self-reward standards from those measuring performance enhancement through self-reward. Such misconstruals can be read as inventive post-mortems for mistaken dependent variables (Bandura, 1974).

ACQUISITION OF PERFORMANCE STANDARDS

Behavioral standards for determining self-reinforcing responses can be established either by tuition or by modeling. In the former process, adults prescribe standards that define the behavior worthy of reward. They generally respond positively when children achieve or exceed the standards and negatively when their behavior falls short of the valued levels. As a result of such differential reactions, children eventually come to respond to their own behavior in self-rewarding or self-punishing ways, depending on how it departs from the evaluative standards set by others.

Transmitting performance standards by means of differential consequences has not been analyzed experimentally with humans, but the process is illustrated in studies with infrahuman subjects (Bandura and Mahoney, 1974; Mahoney and Bandura, 1972). Standards are established by instituting performance requirements for self-reward and by administering negative consequences when animals reward themselves for insufficient performances. By progressively raising response requirements animals adopt increasingly higher performance standards for each self-reward. Once established, the performance requirements continue to be self-imposed on both familiar and novel tasks long after negative consequences for unmerited self-reward have been discontinued.

The influence of modeling in the transmission of differential standards of self-reward has received substantial attention. In the paradigm typically used to study this process (Bandura and Kupers, 1964), children observe models performing a task in which the models adopt either high or low performance standards for self-reward. When models attain or exceed their performance requirements, the models reward themselves tangibly and voice self-praise, but when they fall short of their self-prescribed requirements, they deny themselves freely available rewards and react self-critically. Observers later perform the task alone, and the performance attainments for which they reward themselves with freely available reinforcers are recorded.

The findings show that children tend to adopt standards modeled by others, judge their own performances relative to those standards, and reinforce themselves accordingly (Bandura and Kupers, 1964). Children exposed to models who set high standards reward themselves only when they achieve superior performances, whereas children exposed to models who regard low achievements as sufficient reinforce themselves for minimal performances. The behavioral standards of adults are affected by modeling influences as are those of children (Marston, 1965). Modeling has proved to be a highly efficacious way of instituting not only performance standards, but even the generosity with which differential attainments are self-rewarded (Bandura, 1971).

Having established the influential role of modeling in the acquisition of performance standards, experimentation then focused on theoretically relevant variables that affect the adoption process. Competence disparity between model and observer is one such factor (Bandura and Whalen, 1966). Ordinarily people favor reference models with ability similar to theirs over highly divergent ones whose attainments can be matched only occasionally through great effort. However, when exposed to uniformly high standards, a conducive relationship between models and observers, and bestowal of public recognition on models for upholding excellence, observers adopt, and adhere to, stringent standards of self-reward though they seldom attain the lofty performances (Bandura, Grusec, and Menlove, 1967).

Learning performance standards is complicated by the multiplicity of social influences, many of which conflict. The disparities involve inconsistencies in the standards exemplified by different models or by the same models on different occasions (Bandura, Grusec, and Menlove, 1967; Allen and Liebert, 1969; Hildebrandt, Feldman, and Ditrichs, 1973), or contradictions between the standards that are prescribed and those that are modeled (McMains and Liebert, 1968; Mischel and Liebert, 1966; Ormiston, 1972; Rosenhan, Frederick, and Burrowes, 1968). Observers must therefore process the conflicting information and eventually arrive at a personal standard against which to measure their own performances. Opposing influences that include lenient alternatives tend to reduce adoption of high standards, but the relative power of the influences is determined by a number of interacting variables. Some of these include characteristics of the observers, such as their achievement orientation, and their predilection to perceive events as being either personally or externally determined (Soule and Firestone, 1975; Stouwie, Hetherington, and Parke, 1970).

GENERALIZATION OF PERFORMANCE STANDARDS OF SELF-REWARD

Development of self-regulatory functions would have limited value if they never generalized beyond the specific activity on which they were established. Indeed, the principal goal of social development is to transmit general standards of conduct that can serve as guides for self-regulation of behavior across a variety of activities.

Generic standards are best transmitted by varying the nature of the activities while requiring a similar level of performance for self-reward. The development of achievement standards typifies this process. Adults who subscribe to high standards of accomplishment expect children to excel in whatever academic subjects they are pursuing. After children adopt the criterion that only superior performances deserve self-reward, they tend to apply similar standards to their performance in new academic activities.

Self-regulated reinforcement generally involves not only adherence to performance requirements but also control over the magnitude of self-reward on each appropriate occasion. Findings of the program of research examining self-reinforcement processes with infrahuman subjects provide some evidence for the generalizability of both aspects of self-control. After animals learn to self-reward their own performances on different tasks in limited amounts, they transfer this dual self-regulation of reinforcement to new activities in which reinforcers are freely available independently of responding (Bandura and Mahoney, 1974). Adherence to performance requirements is more stringent, however, than adherence to self-limitation in amount of reward for conditional performances. To interrupt rewarding activities repeatedly for less preferred work when the rewards are under one's own control is both a taxing order and an impressive demonstration of self-regulation.

Standards of self-reward will generalize to some extent even when acquired on a single task. Children who, through modeling, adopt high performance standards of self-reward tend to apply similar standards on later occasions to somewhat different activities in dissimilar situations (Lepper, Sagotsky, and Mailer, 1975; Sagotsky and Lepper, 1976).

DISCRIMINATIVE ACTIVATION OF SELF-REINFORCEMENT

Development of self-reinforcement functions does not create an unvarying control mechanism within the organism, as implied by theories of internalization that portray incorporated entities as continuous internal overseers of conduct. Self-reinforcing influences operate only if activated, and there are many factors that selectively control their activation. Hence, the same behavior is not uniformly self-rewarded or self-punished irrespective of the circumstances under which it is performed.

Self-reinforcement contingencies that are customarily applied to certain classes of behavior can be temporarily suspended by relabeling the activities and by environmental arrangements that obscure or distort the relationship between actions and the effects they produce (Bandura, 1973). Moreover, people learn to discriminate between situations in which self-reward is contingent upon performance and those in which it is appropriate to reward one-self noncontingently.

The way in which contextual influences operate in discriminative activation of self-reinforcement is graphically revealed in experimentation with infrahuman subjects (Bandura, Mahoney, and Dirks, 1976). During acquisition, animals were required to work before rewarding themselves in certain environmental contexts, but not in others. As a result of such differential experiences, animals consistently self-imposed performance requirements for self-reward in the appropriate settings, but they rarely made self-reward contingent upon performance in settings where rewarding themselves without working beforehand was permissible.

In humans, the activation of self-reinforcing and self-punishing responses is regulated by more complex environmental cues, and by how one construes one's conduct, its links to social effects, and the effects themselves (Bandura, 1973). The cognitive and situational operations by which customary self-generated consequences can be disengaged from censurable conduct have only recently received systematic study under controlled conditions (Bandura, Underwood, and Fromson, 1975; Diener, 1974; Zimbardo, 1969). The discriminative disengagement of internal control is achieved by moral justifications of the conduct, by obscuring or distorting the relationship between actions and the effects they cause, by dehumanizing the people toward whom the actions are directed, and by ignoring, or misrepresenting the social consequences of the actions. Because self-control through self-administered consequences can be discriminatively disengaged in these numerous ways, marked changes in people's conduct can occur without altering their moral standards and self-reinforcement systems. The extreme increase in violent conduct in military as compared to peacetime conditions is a notable example of this process.

DETERMINANTS OF SELF-DENIAL

In analyzing regulation of behavior through self-reinforcement, it is important to distinguish between two sources of incentives that operate in the process. First, there is the arrangement of self-reward contingent upon designated performances to create incentives for oneself to engage in the activities. Second, there are the incentives for adhering to the contingency. One of the significant, but insufficiently explored, issues in self-reinforcement is why people adhere to contingencies requiring difficult performances, thereby temporarily denying themselves rewards over which they exercise full control.

Adherence to performance standards is partly sustained by periodic environmental influences which take a variety of forms. When standards for self-reinforcing reactions are being acquired or when they are later applied inconsistently, unmerited self-reward often results in negative consequences. Rewarding oneself for inadequate or undeserving performances is more likely than not to evoke critical reactions from others. And lowering one's performance standards is rarely considered praiseworthy.

The role of negative sanctions in the acquisition and maintenance of contingent self-reward has been investigated in several studies with animals. Caplan (1976) found that punishment for noncontingent self-reward during acquisition increased later adherence to performance requirements for self-reward. Prior experiences, in which animals consumed rewards freely without having to work for them, did not affect the rate with which they learned to work before rewarding themselves. However, it did reduce their subsequent willingness to withhold rewards contingent upon performance when negative sanctions were no longer in effect.

When environmental supports are removed, animals continue to maintain their behavior by self-reward for some time but eventually discard self-imposed contingencies, especially if they entail onerous performances. However, periodic punishment for unmerited self-reward serves to maintain contingent self-reinforcement. The higher the certainty of negative sanctions for unmerited self-reward, the greater is their sustaining capacity (Bandura and Mahoney, 1974).

Contextual influences, which signify past environmental prescripts that self-reward should be made dependent upon performance, provide additional supports. Animals are thus inclined to adhere to self-imposed contingencies in environmental settings in which performance has been previously required for self-reward, even though negative sanctions for rewarding themselves noncontingently no longer exist (Bandura, Mahoney, and Dirks, 1976).

Findings of the preceding studies suggest that organisms continue to withhold rewards from themselves until performance standards have been met because they fail to discriminate between conditions in which they have been required to do so and subsequent periods wherein rewards are freely available for the taking without negative consequences. In the case of behaviors that are nonproblematic or useless to the organisms, the threat of occasional negative sanctions may indeed be the main restraining influence against noncontingent self-reward. However, there are some findings, even with neutral behaviors, that might not be fully explainable solely in terms of discrimination processes. In one experiment, monkeys were tested for their relative preference for externally- and self-managed systems of reinforcement (Mahoney, Bandura, Dirks, and Wright, 1974). Over a long series of sessions, the animals engaged from time to time in unmerited self-reward without any adverse consequences, but, nevertheless, they continued to self-impose a work requirement for longer periods and at higher levels than one would expect from the usual course of extinction. High transgression sessions were characteristically followed by increased, rather than less, adherence to performance requirements for self-reward. In this study the animals periodically chose the external reward system so that some of their performances were also intermittently reinforced on an external basis. These findings are sufficiently interesting to warrant further investigation of the maintenance of self-imposed performance contingencies under multiple reinforcement conditions containing varying proportions of external and self-regulated reinforcement.

Threat of negative sanctions is not the most reliable basis upon which to rest a system of self-regulation. Fortunately, there are more advantageous reasons for exercising some influence over one's own behavior through self-arranged incentives. In most instances of self-regulation, effects associated with the conditional behavior provide incentives for maintaining the contingency. People are motivated to impose upon themselves requirements for self-reward when the effects of the behavior they seek to change are aversive. To those burdened with excessive weight, for example, the discomforts, maladies, and social costs of obesity create inducements to control overeating. Heavy smokers are motivated to reduce their consumption of cigarettes by physiological dysfunctions and fear of cancer. Students are prompted to alter avoidant study habits when failures in completing assignments make academic pursuits sufficiently aversive.

By making self-reward conditional upon performance attainments, individuals can reduce the aversive effects of their behavior thereby creating a natural source of reinforcement for their efforts. They lose weight, they curtail or cease smoking, and they improve their course grades by increasing study activities. When people procrastinate about required tasks, thoughts about what they are putting off continuously intrude on, and detract from, enjoyment of their other activities. By setting themselves a given accomplishment for self-reward, they mobilize their efforts to complete what needs to be done and are thus spared intrusive self-reminders.

The benefits of self-regulated change may provide natural incentives for continued self-imposition of contingencies in the case of valued behaviors as well as for aversive ones. People commonly motivate themselves by arranging contingent self-reward to improve their skills in activities they aspire to master and to enhance their competencies in dealing with the demands of everyday life. Here the personal gains accruing from improved proficiency can strengthen self-prescription of contingencies.

As indicated in the foregoing discussion, because self-regulated reinforcement involves brief periods of self-denial it does not necessarily create an adverse state of affairs. Singling out self-privation from the total effects accompanying self-directed change overemphasizes the negative aspects of the process. Let us compare the aggregate rather than only the momentary consequences of behavior with and without the aid of conditional self-reward. Under noncontingent arrangements, rewards are available for the taking but the likelihood of engaging in potentially advantageous behavior is reduced for lack of self-motivation. In contrast, self-directed change provides both the rewards that were temporarily withheld as well as the benefits accruing from increased proficiency. For activities that have some potential value, self-regulated reinforcement can provide the more favorable aggregate consequences. Thus, on closer analysis, the exercise of momentary self-denial becomes less perplexing than it might originally appear. However, there are no particular advantages for self-regulation of behavior that is devoid of any value. It is in the latter instances that continued extraneous supports for adherence to self-reward contingencies assume special importance.

Modeling has been shown to be a powerful means of inducing behavior, but it has rarely been studied as a maintainer. In view of evidence that human behavior is extensively under modeling stimulus control (Bandura, 1976), there is every reason to expect that seeing others successfully regulate their own behavior by holding to contingent self-reward would increase the likelihood of adherence to self-prescribed contingencies in observers.

Upholding high standards is actively promoted by a vast system of rewards including praise, social recognition, and awards, whereas few accolades are bestowed on people for self-rewarding mediocre performances. Praise fosters adherence to high performance standards as does occasional admonishment for undeserved self-reward (Brownell et al., 1976; Drabman, Spitalnik, and O'Leary, 1973). Moreover, seeing others publicly recognized for upholding excellence promotes emulation of high standards (Bandura, Grusec, and Menlove, 1967). Vicarious reinforcement can therefore supplement periodic direct consequences as another source of support for abiding by self-prescribed contingencies.

In social learning theory, self-regulated reinforcement is conceptualized not as an autonomous regulator of behavior but as a personal source of influence that operates in conjunction with environmental factors. Because self-reinforcing functions are created and occasionally supported by external influences does not negate the fact that exercise of that function partly determines how people behave. In the case of refractory habits, environmental inducements alone often fail to produce change, whereas the same inducements with contingent self-incentives prove successful. Thus, for example, social pressures for and future benefits of shedding excess weight usually do not help the obese control their overeating, but exercising self-influence while actually eating effects change.

In other instances, the behavior developed through the aid of self-reward activates environmental influences that would otherwise remain in abeyance. Here the potential benefits cannot occur until self-motivated improvements in performance produce them. In still other instances, the behavior fashioned through contingent self-reward transforms the environment. Formerly passive individuals who facilitate development of assertive behavior through self-reward will alter their social environment by their firm actions.

Because personal and environmental influences affect each other in a reciprocal fashion, it is just as important to analyze the self-reinforcement determinants of environments as it is to study the environmental determinants of self-reinforcement. After all, environmental contingencies have determinants as do behaviors. Searching for the ultimate environmental contingency for activities regulated by self-reward is a regressive exercise that in no way resolves the issue under discussion because, for every ultimate environmental contingency that is invoked, one can find prior actions that created it. Promotion systems for occupational pursuits, grading schemes for academic activities, and reverence of slimness are human creations, not decrees of an autonomous impersonal environment. In the regress of prior causes, for every chicken discovered by a unidirectional environmentalist, a social learning theorist can identify a prior egg.

Operant theorists have always argued against attributing behavior to causes that extend far into the future. However, in explaining increases in self-reinforced behavior, some adherents of this view appeal to ultimate benefits of prospective behavior but neglect self-reactive determinants of behavior that operate in the here and now (Catania, 1975; Rachlin, 1974). Although anticipated benefits of future accomplishment undoubtedly provide some incentive for pursuing self-directed change, the self-regulated incentives serve as continual immediate inducements for change. We will consider later attempts to redefine the phenomenon of self-reinforcement out of existence by relabeling it or by finding some external source of reinforcement for it. In the final analysis, it is not the legitimacy of self-reinforcement but the nature of reinforcement itself that is in question.

The discussion thus far has been concerned mainly with tangible self-rewards. By initially studying operations that are fully observable, investigators were able to confirm different aspects of the phenomenon of self-reinforcement. The more complex and fascinating process concerns the self-regulation of behavior through evaluative self-reinforcement. In the social learning analysis, the process operates in the following manner: the standards people adopt for activities they invest with evaluative significance specify the conditioning requirements for positive self-evaluation. By making self-satisfactions contingent upon goal attainment, individuals persist in their efforts until their performances match what they are seeking to achieve. Both the anticipated satisfactions of desired accomplishments and the negative appraisals of insufficient performances provide incentives for action. Most successes do not bring lasting satisfaction; having accomplished a given level of performance, individuals ordinarily are no longer satisfied with it and make positive self-evaluation contingent upon higher attainments.

Writing provides a familiar example of behavior that is continuously self-regulated through evaluative self-reactions. Authors do not require someone sitting at their sides selectively reinforcing each written statement until a satisfactory manuscript is produced. Rather, they possess a standard of what constitutes an acceptable piece of work. Ideas are generated and phrased in thought several times before anything is committed to paper. Initial attempts are successively revised until authors are satisfied with what they have written. Self-editing often exceeds what would be acceptable to others.

Although covert evaluative operations are not directly measurable, they can be studied through indirect observational evidence. At this point it might be appropriate to distinguish between theorizing about unobservable events and about indirectly observable ones. Self-evaluative reactions are directly observable to the person generating and experiencing them. Although investigators cannot measure their operation directly, they can elucidate the role of evaluative self-regulation by instating the evaluative standards and testing the verifiable behavioral consequences. This is a different matter from positing unobservable events that have neither any experiential referents nor any explicitly definable effects.

In the social learning view, self-evaluative consequences enhance performance not because self-praise automatically strengthens preceding responses, but because negative discrepancies between performance and standards create dissatisfactions that serve as motivational inducements to do better. Self-satisfaction is withheld until a suitable level of performance is attained. This perspective predicts that the higher the standards upon which self-satisfaction is made conditional, the more frequent are the corrective improvements and the higher are the performance attainments likely to be. There are other performance implications of adherence to self-evaluative contingencies that permit empirical verification of the operation of this covert regulatory process.

In experiments in which children are at liberty to select the performance level they consider deserves self-reward, some impose upon themselves surprisingly difficult performance requirements. For example, in one study (Bandura and Perloff, 1967), although children worked alone and were free to select any goal, not a single child chose the lowest standard, which required the least effort. Many selected the highest level of achievement as the minimal performance deserving self-reward. Still others raised their initial standard to a higher level without commensurate increase in amount of self-reward, thereby demanding of themselves considerably more work for the same recompense. Many children do, of course, select easy performance standards, but those who adhere steadfastly to, and even raise, stringent standards for self-reward on their own provide the more challenging findings.

The social learning analysis of evaluative reinforcement predicts that, under low external constraints, standards necessitating much effort at minimum material recompense are most likely to be self-imposed in activities invested with self-evaluative significance. Performing well on such tasks becomes an index of personal merit. Conflicts therefore arise when material gains can be increased by resorting to behavior that elicits negative self-evaluative reactions. Individuals are tempted to maximize rewards for minimum effort by lowering their standards. However, rewarding mediocre performances incurs negative self-evaluative consequences. The behavioral effects will be determined by the relative strength of material and evaluative rewards. When people hold their self-evaluation above material things, they do not act in accordance with utility theories that explain behavior in terms of optimal reward-cost balances, unless such formulations include the self-evaluative costs of rewarding oneself for devalued behavior.

SOME MISCONCEPTIONS

In a recent article in this journal, Catania (1975) raises a number of issues concerning self-reinforcement. It deserves comment because the misconceptions contained in the article are a potential source of confusion regarding a phenomenon of some importance. Indeed, in many instances the characterization of theory and research on self-reinforcement bears only a superficial resemblance to what, in fact, is the case.

Self-Reinforcement of Conditional Responses. Most of the hypothetical problems posed by Catania in the designation of self-reinforcement arise only because he disregards the multifaceted criteria that define the phenomenon. Consider first the prescript that "one must speak not of reinforcing oneself but of reinforcing one's own responses." This statement conveys the impression that previous designations of self-reinforcement have not specified a conditional response. In point of fact, they always do. As evident from the defining criteria, organisms make the self-administration of rewards conditional upon performance of a selected behavior. The pseudo issue is created by singling out the self-delivery feature but ignoring the performance requirement for self-reinforcement.

Distinction Between Conditional Responses and Self-Reinforcing Responses. Catania compounds the confusion by overlooking another critical criterion of self-reinforcement. Continuing with the hypothetical problem, he reasons that "If the reinforced response is not specified, it becomes impossible to distinguish the self-delivery of a reinforcer from the delivery of a reinforcer through some other agency." The hungry rat that produces food by pressing a lever, he argues, could be said to reinforce itself with food. Hence, "All instances of reinforcement then would become instances of self-reinforcement as well." Here again, the alleged problem arises only because no account is taken of the distinguishing feature, that in self-reinforcement the organism has free access to the rewards but withholds them until requisite performances are attained. In externally regulated reinforcement, an external agent sets the performance requirement and controls the reinforcers so they cannot be obtained without working for them. Although the difference in the agency of delivery, itself, is not insignificant, self-reinforcement entails several complex functions that are carried out by external agents in externally monitored forms. To self-reinforce one's own performances contingently requires adoption of a performance standard, evaluation of ongoing performance relative to the standard, and self-privation of freely available reinforcers when performances do not warrant self-reward.

One cannot dismiss the operational differences between externally- and self-regulated reinforcement with the counterexample of a limitless supply of reinforcers that can be gained simply by performing a response. In such a situation the conditional (requisite) response and the self-delivery response become one and the same. By contrast, in self-reinforcement the self-delivery response is different from, and can be performed independently of, the conditional response. Thus, for example, in testing the response maintenance capacity of self-reinforcement, children perform effortful manual responses until they reach their preselected goal, whereupon they reward themselves by pressing a button that delivers tokens exchangeable for valued items (Bandura and Perloff, 1967). The manual activity is the conditional response; the button press that produces the reinforcers is the self-delivery response.

In other investigations, the rewards are presented with equally free access but in full view as well (Bandura and Kupers, 1964; Bandura and Mahoney, 1974; Mahoney and Bandura, 1972). In each case, the conditional response does not produce the rewards because they are already present; rather, it sets the occasion for self-delivery of rewards. Subjects, of course, are at liberty to consume the rewards noncontingently at any time, should they choose to do so.

In the most stringent test of self-regulated reinforcement, animals not only impose performance requirements for self-reward, but they even control how many reinforcers they consume on each appropriate occasion from the continually available supply (Bandura and Mahoney, 1974). Let us return now briefly to the rat at the bar. Pressing a lever to produce reinforcers is not in itself an instance of self-reinforcement, but performing requisite responses and then pressing a lever to secure reinforcers, which are continually and freely available for the taking, does qualify as a self-reinforcement operation.

Catania eventually resolves the problem of his own creation in the example of the lever-pressing rat by recognizing that, "Self-reinforcement, then, cannot involve only one response. An instance of self-reinforcement must include not only a response that is reinforced, but also the same organism's response of reinforcing the first response." These are precisely the conditions that are routinely instituted in analyses of self-reinforcement. No one, to this writer's knowledge, has ever defined self-reinforcement solely in terms of the self-delivery response. Self-administration of consequences is but one of several criteria of self-reinforcement.

Disembodied Responses and Dispossessed Organisms. Catania's dichotomization of responses and organisms brings to the fore a fundamental issue that is rarely discussed in the conceptual analysis of reinforcement. Consider a few common examples of reinforcement. An animal presses a lever whereupon food appears after a momentary delay. In the verbal conditioning paradigm, subjects emit verbal responses and, after judging them to fall within a reinforcible class, the experimenter dispenses social rewards. In applications of reinforcement practices using tangible reinforcers, tokens or preferred activities are presented minutes, hours, or even days after the requisite performances have been completed. As these examples illustrate, reinforcers are almost invariably delivered after the response has ceased to exist. How can something that is no longer in existence be reinforced? In actuality, one can only reinforce an organism for having selected and performed particular classes of responses. Theorists who adopt the position that it is responses not organisms that are reinforced are faced with a dilemma that can be resolved only by postulating some kind of enduring residue of the spent response.

One could argue that responses leave either enduring cognitive representations or lasting neural traces that get reinforced by the succeeding consequences. Reinforcement of neural traces of responses has received little study, but there is growing evidence that cognitions can partly determine how consequences affect behavior. It has been shown that behavior is not much influenced by its consequences until the point at which contingencies are discerned (Dawson and Furedy, 1976; Dulany, 1968); misinformation conveyed about the prevailing schedules of reinforcement can outweigh the influence of actual consequences in the regulation of behavior (Kaufman, Baron, and Kopp, 1966); behavior that is positively reinforced does not increase if individuals believe from other information that the same actions will not be rewarded on future occasions (Estes, 1972); and the same reinforcing consequences can increase, reduce, or have no effect on behavior depending upon whether individuals are led to believe that the consequences signify correct responses, incorrect responses, or occur noncontingently (Dulany, 1968). If cognitive determinants are disavowed or simply relegated to an epiphenomenal status, the question remains as to how functional relationships are created through juxtaposition of consequences and nonexistent events.

Control of Reinforcers. Conceptualizations of self-reinforcement have always stated explicitly that organisms have free access to reinforcers because they exercise control over them. Catania needlessly raises alleged problems with this criterion as well, by failing to distinguish between availability and free access. There are large sums of money available in local banks, but individuals are not granted free access to the supply. Consider, with this distinction in mind, Catania's example of the shopper surveying shelves of commodities: "The shopper may take the commodity and leave the store with it (perhaps changing an arrest for shoplifting), or the shopper may leave the store with the commodity only after paying the teller. Because the commodity is available for the taking at all times, is it not appropriate to say that the paying is a response that is self-reinforced by the taking of the commodity?" Certainly not. Store mangers make goods continually available, but they control them; shoppers are at liberty to take the commodities whenever, and in whatever quantities, they choose provided they negotiate transfer of control through payment. In many of the material rewards of everyday life, money provides the open access. Thus, for example, individuals do not own theaters but they are free to purchase their way into them anytime they wish.

Once again the predicament posed by Catania arises from equating the multifaceted operation of self-reinforcement solely with the self-delivery response. Shoppers paying to gain commodities constitute the self-delivery responses. In self-reinforcement individuals either already possess the reinforcers or are free to get them when they so choose, but they do not reward themselves until they achieve conditional performances. The shopping activity would qualify as an instance of self-reinforcement if individuals withheld treating themselves to appetizing foods, movies, or prized goods until they completed activities they assigned to themselves.

After citing the shoplifting case and other examples in which rewards are consumed noncontingently, Catania asks rhetorically, "What then is the essence of the concept of self-reinforcement?" The essence is easily captured by reflecting upon the defining criteria of the phenomenon.

Distinction between Induction and Testing Conditions. In analyzing paradigms for investigating self-regulated reinforcement, it is essential to distinguish training from testing conditions. Mahoney and Bandura (1972) devised a self-reward procedure for animals to examine more definitively some of the rudimentary processes in self-reinforcement that cannot be easily elucidated with humans who have undergone years of social learning. In this paradigm, animals are taught to self-reward their own performances by presenting them with food in advance, but if they help themselves to it before performing appropriate responses at a designated level, the food is temporarily withdrawn. Eventually, animals learn to make the food reinforcers contingent upon appropriate behaviors even though the reinforcers are continually present.

After animals learn to adhere to performance requirements for self-reward, punishment by loss of reinforcers for self-feeding without prior working is discontinued. Thus, during this testing phase, animals are free to consume the food reinforcers, which are continually present, without any punishment even if they treat themselves to the food before performing appropriate responses. Measures are obtained of how long animals continue to impose performance requirements for self-reward.

In speculating about the process by which self-administered rewards affect behavior, Catania presents a schematic diagram comparing the temporal relationships among requisite behavior, access to reinforcers, and consummatory responses for externally- and self-regulated reinforcement. The presentation is potentially misleading because it fails to distinguish between training and testing conditions. For example, Catania reports that the relationship between behavior and access to reinforcers is similar in external and self-reinforcement, and that in both instances there is a higher likelihood of reinforcers being present if a response has occurred than if it has not. This statement describes the training conditions, but it does not accurately represent the response-reinforcer dependencies during tests of self-reinforcement. Under testing conditions, reinforcers are continually present, there is free access to them at all times, and they can be consumed independently of responding without loss of rewards, or any other negative consequences for that matter.

PROCESS OF SELF-REINFORCEMENT

We turn now to the issue of whether people can exercise some influence over their own behavior by arranging incentives for themselves in response-contingent relationships. In recent years enhancement and maintenance of behavior through contingent self-reward has been studied extensively under both laboratory and natural conditions. These investigations differ considerably in choice of self-rewards, self-reinforced behavior, and experimental methodologies. Among the self-rewards are included such diverse incentives as food, tokens redeemable for valued objects, money, televised material, preferred activities, and self-praise. An equally diverse range of behavior, comprising manual activities, academic performances, social behavior, and refractory personal habits, has been modified through self-reinforcement.

Results of these numerous studies demonstrate that effortful performances can be effectively increased and maintained over long periods by contingent self-reward. In experiments using intergroup comparisons, subjects who reward their own behavior exhibit significantly higher levels of responding than those who perform the same activities but receive no reinforcement, are rewarded noncontingently, or monitor their own behavior and set goals but do not reinforce their own performances (Bandura and Perloff, 1967; Bellack, 1976; Felixbrod and O'Leary, 1973; Bolstad and Johnson, 1972; Glynn, 1970; Jeffrey, 1974; Johnson, 1970; Litrownik, Franzini, and Skenderian, 1976; Mahoney, 1974; Montgomery and Parton, 1970; Speidel, 1974; Switzky and Haywood, 1974).

Other studies, which measure level of performance under baseline and different reinforcement conditions, reveal substantial increases in self-reinforced behavior when subjects reward their own attainments (Drabman, Spitalnik, and O'Leary, 1973; Glynn, Thomas, and Shee, 1973; Kaufman and O'Leary, 1972; McLaughlin and Malaby, 1974). Findings based on intergroup comparisons are further corroborated by results of intrasubject reversal designs measuring performance across successive baseline and self-reinforcement conditions without any confounding effects of prior external reinforcement. All children enhance their level of performance when they self-reward their own efforts, and they reduce their productivity when they no longer arrange incentives for themselves (Glynn and Thomas, 1974). As the latter findings reveal, self-reinforcement contingencies can be suspended and the behavioral effects measured just as changes in responding can be assessed after external contingencies have been discontinued or after reinforcers are administered independently of performance.

Most of the experiments cited above also compare level of performance under externally- and self-regulated reinforcement. People who engage in contingent self-reward perform as well or better than do their counterparts whose behavior is reinforced by others. Although both procedures alter behavior, the practice of self-reinforcement can have the advantage of developing a generalizable skill in self-regulation that will be continually available. It is perhaps for this reason that self-reinforced behavior is sometimes maintained more effectively than if it has been externally regulated (Jeffrey, 1974).

Researchers favoring intrasubject designs are inclined to discount empirical evidence from intergroup comparisons on the grounds that it is presented in the form of group performances and statistical evaluations of significance (Catania, 1975). In the case of self-reinforcement, facts are not easily discounted when they are replicated by intergroup, intragroup, and intrasubject reversal designs. However, because the methodological issue is often raised in the study of other phenomena as well, the criteria used for making inferences from data deserve some comment. Preference for subjective judgments of variations in individual performance over statistical evaluations of multiple data does not necessarily establish the former approach as the more stringent one for identifying causal relationships. Advocates of intrasubject designs often argue that visual appraisal of individual data yields better evidence concerning functional relationships than does statistical analysis of group data. The claim is debatable.

Interpreting intrasubject changes poses no problems when behavior is highly stable during baseline assessment and when treatments are so powerful that performances during baseline and treatment conditions never overlap. But most factors are not that powerful when manipulated separately because behavior is typically regulated by multiple interacting variables and not every potential determinant can be controlled. Consequently, results are usually not that orderly. When researchers are asked to judge variability in the behavior of an individual across successive conditions, they do not always agree among themselves as to whether or not interventions have produced an appreciable change in level of performance (Jones, Weinrott, and Vaught, 1975). They tend to be better at detecting nonsignificant changes than in detecting significant ones. Eventually statistical analysis may replace visual inspection in the evaluation of intrasubject variability. But gaining consensus on intrasubject change is only part of the interpretative reliability problem.

Eventually researchers must move beyond inspecting individual cases to generalizing about whether a given variable influences behavior. The single-case methodology provides no criteria for determining what generalizations are warranted, given the commonly observed heterogeneous results from different individuals. Typically, procedures are applied only to a few cases; the successes are attributed to the procedures, but when effects do not obtain, the procedures are assumed not to have exercised their usual control in the negative cases. The possibility that the observed changes in behavior resulted from unrecognized factors that happen to covary with the manipulated one is rarely considered. The irreversibility of learning processes and the confounding of successive operations by previous influences hardly justifies sole allegiance to intrasubject replication designs. Without objective criteria for evaluation, investigators are likely to differ in how they interpret the same data on the basis of visual inspection of fluctuating baselines, mixed effects of initial treatments on different individuals, and confounded results from successive reversals of baseline and treatment conditions.

Investigators using intergroup designs not only collect more data for gauging the generality of lawful relationships, but they typically require a higher level of replicability before ascribing causal significance to a variable. For example, in quantitative evaluation by the Sign Test of differences between matched groups of five subjects each, all the treated subjects would have to out-perform the baseline controls before the variable will be said to have influenced the behavior. It is safe to say that, whenever statistical analyses yield significant intergroup differences, one can find more than ample evidence of lawful relationships by inspection of the individual cases.

Statistical evaluation of data from numerous subjects can indicate a causal relationship even though the effects do not occur in every case. Some writers have therefore concluded that group data obscure individual behavioral processes. But the same problem of abstraction from particular instances arises in drawing generalizations on the basis of visual appraisal of variable results from individual cases—here, too, lawful relations are claimed although the effects are not demonstrated in every single case. Hence, disputes about the methodologies for identifying the determinants of behavior ultimately reduce to whether one prefers inspectional or quantitative evaluation of generality.

It should be noted in passing that intrasubject and intergroup designs are not incompatible. One can examine how each individual is affected by experimental procedures during induction or successive phases, and also compare statistically whether the individual demonstrations of the phenomenon occur more frequently among subjects who receive the procedures than among those who do not. Adding baseline comparison groups and quantitative evaluation of data in no way detracts from inspection of individual variability. Rather, it encourages studying more cases and requires a higher proportion of individual demonstrations of effects before causal relationships are claimed. Intrasubject replication combined with intergroup quantitative evaluation provides the most rigorous method for identifying the determinants of behavior.

ALTERNATIVE EXPLANATIONS OF THE PROCESS OF SELF-REINFORCEMENT

Several alternative explanations have been proposed for why contingent self-reward enhances performance. These various interpretations are considered next.

Self-Awareness. Catania (1975) attributes the behavioral effects of self-reward to the development of "self-awareness." Self-reinforcement increases behavior because the behavior provides a discriminative stimulus for self-reward. In this view, the process of self-reinforcement becomes a matter of "self-discrimination," "self-awareness," or "self-monitoring." This type of analysis essentially amounts to explanation by description of one of the component processes operating in the phenomenon.

It is true that behavior that matches or exceeds referential standards signifies the occasions for self-reward. However, enhancement of self-reinforced behavior cannot be ascribed simply to awareness of when it is appropriate to reward oneself. An explanation contending that individuals engage in behavior over a period because they later notice that they have met a performance standard places the cause after the effect. People enhance their behavior by contingent self-reward, not because of self-awareness, but because they withhold from themselves desired incentives until they achieve self-prescribed standards. It is the subjects' *regulation* rather than *awareness* of the response-reinforcer dependency that is the critical factor. In the case of students who increase their study activities by making coffee breaks contingent on completing ten pages of a reading assignment, discriminating when it is appropriate to tap the coffee pot is of secondary interest in explaining how self-reinforcement augments behavior.

Theorists working within the operant framework subscribe to the view that awareness is a by-product rather than a determinant of performance. Being aware of aspects of one's behavior does not cause the behavior of which one is aware. Thus, in positing that self-awareness causes behavioral changes, Catania appears to be abandoning the very theory he is embracing.

The weight of the evidence is heavily against attributing effects of conditional self-incentives solely to self-monitoring. As a rule, simply observing and recording one's own behavior has no consistent behavioral effects (Kazdin, 1974). When self-monitoring does produce change, it is likely to be under circumstances that activate covert goal-setting and self-evaluative consequences. Moreover, many of the investigations of self-reinforcement explicitly include controls for the effects not only of self-monitoring but of goal-setting as well. Both children and adults who monitor their performances and goal attainments and reward themselves for goal achievement typically surpass their counterparts who also monitor their own performances and goal attainments but never engage in overt self-reinforcement (Bandura and Perloff, 1967; Bellack, 1975; Flaxman and Solnick, 1975; Mahoney, 1974; Switzky and Haywood, 1974). Those who self-monitor and receive feedback on goal attainments often do not perform any better than do baseline control groups.

Stimulus Salience. According to Rachlin (1974), performance is increased by contingent self-rewards, not because of their incentive properties, but because they are distinctive stimuli. Results of studies cited above, that include control conditions in which subjects receive distinctive feedback on goal attainments, also have bearing on this conceptualization. Neither vivid stimuli signaling goal attainments nor contingent self-administration of tokens lacking material value have demonstrable effects on behavior, whereas valued self-rewards augment performance (Bandura and Perloff, 1967; Flaxman and Solnick, 1975). It would be further predicted from social learning theory that the greater the value of the self-reward, the higher the level of performance.

There is a general observation concerning the process of self-reinforcement that should be offered in this context. Because external and self-regulated reinforcement in all probability change behavior through similar mechanisms, whatever interpretations are proposed for self-reinforcement would apply equally to external reinforcement.

Social Demand. Another explanation that is routinely invoked, whatever the phenomenon might be, is that of "demand characteristics." This is a descriptive term used as though it were explanatory. To designate changes as demand effects does not explain them. All forms of social influence (e.g., comments, environmental displays, instructions, persuasive appeals, conditioning, modeling, reinforcement) represent demands in the sense that they function as prompts for behavior. Social influences are therefore better analyzed in terms of their explicitness, coerciveness, and whether they change behavior directly or through cognitive processing, rather than whether they involve demand properties.

Characterizing the effects of self-reward as manifestations of social demand receives little support from findings of control conditions. As was previously noted, control subjects perform under identical circumstances except they do not reward themselves. In studies in which social demands and contingent self-rewards are varied factorially, performances that are difficult to maintain are enhanced by self-reward but are unaffected by increasing social pressure to engage in the activities (Flaxman and Solnick, 1975). Evidence that self-reinforcement functions established under specific modeling conditions operate over a long intervening period in dissimilar situations with different persons, and on different tasks (Lepper, Sagotsky, and Mailer, 1975; Sagotsky and Lepper, 1976) is not easily explainable in terms of situational demands.

Self-motivation. Reinforcement operations can affect behavior in several different ways. Explanation of reinforcement originally assumed that consequences increase behavior automatically without conscious involvement. This view emphasizes the automatic *strengthening function* of response consequences. Although the empirical issue is not yet fully resolved, evidence that human behavior is not much affected by consequences until the point at which the reinforcement contingencies are discerned raises serious questions concerning the automaticity of reinforcement. Therefore, if reinforcement is equated with automatic response enhancement, then most external regulation of human behavior through consequences would not qualify as "reinforcement." The notion of "response strengthening" is, at best, a metaphor. After responses are acquired the likelihood that they will be used in any given situation can be readily altered by varying the effects they produce, but the responses cannot be strengthened any further. Thus, for example, people will drive automobiles for the resulting benefits, but the benefits do not add increments of strength to the driving responses.

It is fortunate that consequences do not automatically enhance every response they follow. If behavior were reinforced by every momentary effect it produced, people would be overburdened with so many competing response tendencies that they would become immobilized. Limiting behavioral effects to events that are sufficiently salient to gain recognition has adaptive value. However, for lower organisms possessing limited symbolizing capacities there are evolutionary advantages to being biologically structured so that response consequences produce lasting effects mechanically without requiring symbolic processing of ongoing experiences.

Consequences can alter behavior through their *informative function.* By observing the differential outcomes of their actions, individuals eventually discern which responses are appropriate in which settings. Reinforcing consequences thus serve as an unarticulated way of informing performers what they must do to gain beneficial outcomes or to avoid punishing ones. Findings of research cited earlier show that people regulate their performances in accordance with contingency and schedule information even though it may not accurately reflect prevailing conditions of reinforcement.

The informative function of reinforcement is not involved in self-reinforcement because, in setting their own standards and rewarding their own attainments, participants know full well from the outset what performances they require of themselves for self-reward. In studies of self-reinforcement, control subjects, who monitor and set goals for the same activities, are likewise fully informed of the requisite behavior.

In the third mode of operation, consequences enhance behavior through their incentive *motivational function.* If valued rewards can be secured by performing certain activities, then individuals are motivated by the incentives to engage in those activities. A vast amount of evidence lends validity to the view that reinforcement serves principally as a motivational operation rather than as a mechanical response strengthener.

According to social learning theory (Bandura, 1976), self-regulated reinforcement augments performance mainly through its motivational function. By making self-reward conditional upon attaining a certain level of performance, individuals create self-inducements to persist in their efforts until their performances match self-prescribed standards. The level of self-motivation generated by this means will vary as a function of the type and value of the incentives and the nature of the performance standards. In analyzing changes resulting from reinforcement operations, whether they be externally- or self-regulated, the robust motivational functions should be given priority over the elusive strengthening function.

The dubious status of both automaticity and response strengthening, and the vestigial connotations of the term reinforcement make it more fitting to speak of *regulation* than *reinforcement* of behavior by its consequences.

REFERENCES

ALLEN, M. K., & LIEBERT, R. M. Effects of live and symbolic deviant-modeling cues on adoption of a previously learned standard. *Journal of Personality and Social Psychology,* 11:253-260, 1969.

BANDURA, A. Vicarious and self-reinforcement processes. In R. Glaser (Ed.), *The Nature of Reinforcement.* New York: Academic Press, 1971, pp. 228-278.

BANDURA, A. *Aggression: A Social Learning Analysis.* Englewood Cliffs, N.J.: Prentice-Hall, 1973.

BANDURA, A. The case of the mistaken dependent variable. *Journal of Abnormal Psychology,* 83:301-303, 1974.

BANDURA, A. *Social Learning Theory.* Englewood Cliffs, N.J.: Prentice-Hall, 1976.

BANDURA, A., GRUSEC, J. E., & MENLOVE, F. L. Some social determinants of self-monitoring reinforcement systems. *Journal of Personality and Social Psychology,* 5:449-455, 1967.

BANDURA, A., & KUPERS, C. J. Transmission of patterns of self-reinforcement through modeling. *Journal of Abnormal and Social Psychology,* 69:1-9, 1964.

BANDURA, A., & MAHONEY, M. J. Maintenance and transfer of self-reinforcement functions. *Behaviour Research and Therapy,* 12:89-97, 1974.

BANDURA, A., MAHONEY, M. J., & DIRKS, S. J. Discriminative activation and maintenance of contingent self-reinforcement. *Behaviour Research and Therapy,* 14:1-6, 1976.

BANDURA, A., & PERLOFF, B. Relative efficacy of self-monitored and externally-imposed reinforcement systems. *Journal of Personality and Social Psychology,* 7:111-116, 1967.

BANDURA, A., UNDERWOOD, B., & FROMSON, M. E. Disinhibition of aggression through diffusion of responsibility and dehumanization of victims. *Journal of Research in Personality,* 9:253-269, 1975.

BANDURA, A., & WHALEN, C. K. The influence of antecedent reinforcement and divergent modeling cues on patterns of self-reward. *Journal of Personality and Social Psychology,* 3:373-382, 1966.

BELLACK, A. S. A comparison of self-reinforcement and self-monitoring in a weight reduction program. *Behavior Therapy,* 7:68-75, 1976.

BOLSTAD, O. D., & JOHNSON, S. M. Self-regulation in the modification of disruptive classroom behavior. *Journal of Applied Behavior Analysis,* 5:443-454, 1972.

BROWNELL, K., COLLETTI, G., ERSNER-HERSHFIELD, R., HERSHFIELD, S. M., & WILSON, G. T. Stringency and leniency in self-determined and externally imposed performance standards. *Behavior Therapy,* 1976 (in press).

CATANIA, C. A. The myth of self-reinforcement. *Behaviorism,* 3:192-199, 1975.

DAWSON, M. E., & FUREDY, J. J. The role of awareness in human differential autonomic classical conditioning: The necessary-gate hypothesis. *Psychophysiology,* 1976 (in press).

DIENER, E. Deindividuation: Causes and characteristics. Unpublished manuscript. University of Washington, 1974.

DRABMAN, R. S., SPITALNIK, R., & O'LEARY, K. D. Teaching self-control to disruptive children. *Journal of Abnormal Psychology,* 82:10-16, 1973.

DULANY, D. E. Awareness, rules, and propositional control: A confrontation with S-R behavior theory. In T. R. Dixon & D. L. Horton (Eds.), *Verbal Behavior and General Behavior Theory.* Englewood Cliffs, N.J.: Prentice-Hall, 1968, pp. 340-387.

ESTES, W. K. Reinforcement in human behavior. *American Scientist,* 60:723-729, 1972.

FELIXBROD, J. J., & O'LEARY, K. D. Effects of reinforcement on children's academic behavior as a function of self-determined and externally imposed contingencies. *Journal of Applied Behavior Analysis,* 6:241-250, 1973.

FLAXMAN, J., & SOLNICK, J. V. Self-reinforcement and self-monitoring under conditions of low and high demand. Unpublished manuscript, University of North Carolina, 1975.

GLYNN, E. L. Classroom applications of self-determined reinforcement. *Journal of Applied Behavior Analysis,* 3:123-132, 1970.

GLYNN, E. L., & THOMAS, J. D. Effect of cueing on self-control of classroom behavior. *Journal of Applied Behavior Analysis,* 7:299-306, 1974,

GLYNN, E. L., THOMAS, J. D., & SHEE, S. M. Behavioral self-control of on-task behavior in an elementary classroom. *Journal of Applied Behavior Analysis,* 6:105-113, 1973.

GOLDFRIED, M. R., & MERBAUM, M. (Eds.), *Behavior Change Through Self-Control.* New York: Holt, Rinehart & Winston, 1973.

HILDEBRANDT, D. E., FELDMAN, S. E., DITRICHS, R. A. Rules, models, and self-reinforcement in children. *Journal of Personality and Social Psychology,* 25:1-5, 1972.

JEFFREY, D. B. A comparison of the effects of external control and self-control on the modification and maintenance of weight. *Journal of Abnormal Psychology,* 83:404-410, 1974.

JOHNSON, S. M. Self-reinforcement in behavior modification with children. *Developmental Psychology,* 3:147-148, 1970.

JONES, R. R., WEINROTT, M., & VAUGHT, R. S. Visual vs. statistical inference in operant research. Paper presented at the American Psychological Association Annual Convention, Chicago, September, 1975.

KAUFMAN, A., BARON, A., & KOPP, R. E. Some effects of instructions on human operant behavior. *Psychonomic Monograph Supplements,* 1:243-250, 1966.

KAUFMAN, K. F., & O'LEARY, K. D. Reward, cost, and self-evaluation procedures for disruptive adolescents in a psychiatric hospital school. *Journal of Applied Behavior Analysis,* 5:293-309, 1972.

KAZDIN, A. E. Self-monitoring and behavior change. In M. J. Mahoney and C. E. Thoresen (Eds.), *Self-control: Power to the Person.* Monterey, Calif.: Brooks/Cole, 1974, pp. 218-246.

LEPPER, M. R., SAGOTSKY, G., & MAILER, J. Generalization and persistence of effects of exposure to self-reinforcement models. *Child Development,* 46:618-630, 1975

LITROWNIK, A. J., FRANZINI, L. R., & SKENDERIAN, D. The effect of locus of reinforcement control on a concept identification task. *Psychological Reports,* 1976 (in press).

MAHONEY, M. J. Self-reward and self-monitoring techniques for weight control. *Behavior Therapy,* 5:48-57, 1974.

MAHONEY, M. J., & BANDURA, A. Self-reinforcement in pigeons. *Learning and Motivation,* 3:293-303, 1972.

MAHONEY, M. J., BANDURA, A., DIRKS, S. J., & WRIGHT, C. L. Relative preference for external and self-controlled reinforcement in monkeys. *Behaviour Research and Therapy,* 12:157-164, 1974.

MAHONEY, M. J., & THORESEN, C. E. *Self-control: Power to the Person.* Monterey, Calif.: Brooks/Cole, 1974.

MARSTON, A. R. Imitation, self-reinforcement, and reinforcement of another person. *Journal of Personality and Social Psychology,* 2:255-261, 1965.

MCLAUGHLIN, T. F., & MALABY, J. E. Increasing and maintaining assignment completion with teacher and pupil controlled individual contingency programs: Three case studies. *Psychology,* 2:1-7, 1974.

MCMAINS, M. J., & LIEBERT, R. M. Influence of discrepancies between successively modeled self-reward criteria on the adoption of a self-imposed standard. *Journal of Personality and Social Psychology,* 8:166-171, 1968.

MISCHEL, W. & LIEBERT, R. M. Effects of discrepancies between observed and imposed reward criteria on their acquisition and transmission. *Journal of Personality and Social Psychology,* 3:45-53, 1966.

MONTGOMERY, G. T., & PARTON, D. A. Reinforcing effect of self-reward. *Journal of Experimental Psychology,* 84:273-276, 1970.

ORMISTON, L. H. Factors determining response to modeled hypocrisy. Unpublished doctoral dissertation, Stanford University, 1972.

PREMACK, D., & ANGLIN, B. On the possibilities of self-control in man and animals. *Journal of Abnormal Psychology,* 81:137-151, 1973.

RACHLIN, H. Self-control. *Behaviorism,* 2:94-107, 1974.

ROSENHAN, D., FREDERICK, F., & BURROWES, A. Preaching and practicing: Effects of channel discrepancy on norm internalization. *Child Development,* 39:291-301, 1968.

SAGOTSKY, G., & LEPPER, M. R. Generalization of changes in children's preferences for easy or difficult goals induced by observational learning. Unpublished manuscript, Stanford University, 1976.

SOULE, J. C., & FIRESTONE, E. J. Model choice and achievement standards: Effects of similarity in locus of control. Unpublished manuscript, University of Wisconsin-Milwaukee, 1975.

SPEIDEL, G. E. Motivating effect of contingent self-reward. *Journal of Experimental Psychology,* 102:528-530, 1974.

STOUWIE, R. J., HETHERINGTON, E., & PARKE, R. D. Some determinants of children's self-reward behavior after exposure to discrepant reward criteria. *Developmental Psychology,* 3:313-319, 1970.

SWITZKY, H. N., & HAYWOOD, H. C. Motivational orientation and the relative efficacy of self-monitored and externally imposed reinforcement systems in children. *Journal of Personality and Social Psychology,* 30:360-366, 1974.

ZIMBARDO, P. G. The human choice: Individuation, reason, and order versus deindividuation, impulse, and chaos. *Nebraska Symposium on Motivation,* 1969. Lincoln, Neb.: University of Nebraska, 1969, pp. 237-309.

SECTION III: BIOFEEDBACK AND OTHER STRATEGIES IN SELF-MANAGEMENT

5

SELF-REINFORCEMENT

Israel Goldiamond

University of Chicago

Self-reinforcement in operant situations generally refers to those arrangements in which the subject delivers to himself a consequence, contingent on his behavior. However, it is noted that the definition of all other types of reinforcement make its delivery contingent on the subject's behavior. What is actually at issue is the agent who defines whether or not the response required for reinforcement has been met. In self-reinforcement, the subject himself defines this. In the laboratory, this requirement is machine-defined; in school examinations, it is teacher-defined; and in many clinical self-control situations, it is also independently defined. A reinforcement contingency presupposes such independence, absent in self-reinforcement. Implications for research and practice are discussed and alternative formulations are offered.

DESCRIPTORS: reinforcement, self-reinforcement, self-control, defining agency, response requirements.

Self-reinforcement and its decremental equivalent, self-punishment, are terms that seemingly designate the self-delivery of a consequence by a subject, contingent on the occurrence of his own behavior. The terms

Reprinted with permission from the *Journal of Applied Behavior Analysis*, 9, 509-514, No. 4 (Winter 1976). Copyright 1976 by the Society for the Experimental Analysis of Behavior, Inc.

This article was written with partial support from a grant by the Illinois Department of Mental Health on self-control procedures. Views presented are those of the author.

(either or both) are to be found in the literature of all three major branches of behavior modification, especially as these are applied to self-control (e.g., Goldfried and Merbaum, 1973). Since this area is an expanding one, any problems associated with the use of these terms are also likely to expand.

The present discussion briefly notes some problems associated with the use of self-reinforcement and self-punishment as they apply to operant or instrumental behavior. Among these problems is a definitional one. Since the language we use can influence our classification of events, the issue is not trivial. A misnomer can categorize as similar, events that in terms of the referent system of discourse used, are not similar. Conversely, it can categorize as dissimilar, events that are similar. Accordingly, yet another problem is created by the effects that misclassification may have on research, application, and explanation. Finally, an alternative formulation is offered that suggests other possibilities, and is consonant with the consequential system of discourse to which self-reinforcement belongs.

Self-reinforcement as a misnomer. When a term is used that designates one procedure as different from another, that term should presumably not be equally applicable to both procedures. Self-reinforcement (the same statements apply to self-punishment, hence this term will not be considered separately) presumably differentiates procedures in which the *agent* who provides the consequence is the person himself, rather than an outsider, such as the investigator or spouse.

Indeed, this use of the term is attributed to Skinner (1953), and it is of interest to examine his discussion. The particular use of the term is evident in his statement that an individual whose behavior has been strengthened may have "arranged a sequence of events in which certain behavior has been followed by a reinforcing event" (p. 238). However, the fact that such arrangement is of a very special kind is evident in statements leading to this supposition, on the same page and the one preceding:

> The place of operant reinforcement in self-control is not clear. In one sense, all reinforcements are self-administered since a response may be regarded as "producing" its reinforcement. . . . (p. 237)

Self-reinforcement or self-administration of reinforcement is considered to be, at the very least, nondiscriminative from other forms of reinforcement. This is so because it is the lever depression by the monkey, or the key peck by the pigeon, or the turning of a door knob by a human that "produces" the consequence. Self-reinforcement, as used in the self-control literature, presumably does not apply here, but the term describes these excluded relations as well as those it includes. In each of the foregoing cases, it should be noted that it is some agent other than the behaving subject who has made the arrangements. However, the consequence is self-produced. Skinner concludes the statement quoted by noting that what is meant by "'reinforcing one's own behavior' is more than this." The term is, accordingly, inadequate.

The term is also misleading, since it suggests similarities with laboratory usage. It may not refer to operant reinforcement:

> Self-reinforcement of operant behavior presupposes that the individual has it in his power to obtain reinforcement but does not do so until a particular response has been emitted. This might be the case if a man denied himself all social contacts until he had finished a particular job. Something of this sort unquestionably happens, *but is it operant reinforcement?* It is certainly *roughly parallel* to the procedure in conditioning the behavior of another person. But it must be remembered that the individual may at any moment *drop the work in hand and obtain the reinforcement.* (pp. 237-239, emphasis mine—I. G.)

Stated otherwise, he can cheat. This opportunity may at times be found in the laboratory, but the effort is to arrange things otherwise. That the individual does not do so, Skinner then suggests, may derive (in the example he gives) from consequential control by *others.** Accordingly, the fact that the person does not cheat, but engages in the task, cannot be explained simply by resort to *his* self-reinforcement by social contact, which he makes available contingent on his finishing the job.

Some effects on research and practice. Such explanation may divert an investigator from examining the contingencies that actually operate. It may serve all other functions served by what Skinner calls an *explanatory fiction,* or what semanticists designate as a *panchreston,* a much earlier term they have redefined to serve exactly this purpose. In application, the term self-reinforcement has often led to the counselling of clients to give themselves some "goodie" only after they have finished certain tasks, or have engaged in other behaviors. When this works, the efficacy of the procedure, as described, recommends it further. Since, after all, this is merely an applied instance of a well-known laboratory pro-

* If such consequential control is punitive, the cheating may then be accompanied by the experience of guilt (p. 188).

cedure called reinforcement, no further inquiry or explanation of the procedure *qua* procedure is needed. The critic who then says, maybe he's doing it to please you, maybe you and he have developed a good relation, maybe you are serving as a father surrogate (transference), is then shunted aside (but notice Skinner's reference to external agents). The bewilderment of the critic who doesn't understand why the client should set up such a silly arrangement when he can get the goodie in simpler ways (Goldiamond, 1975) provokes amazement that, in this day and age, literate people exist who have to be convinced of all the impressive laboratory work in reinforcement. How insular can they be?

Assigning the efficacy of self-reinforcement simply to the appropriate application of a well-known laboratory procedure, has yet another effect. Since the clinical procedure is clearly *not* a simple application, something else is at work. And if the procedure is effective, that something else which we do not quite understand at present may be quite powerful. By ignoring it through misnaming it, we are not simply overlooking relevant variables. We may be overlooking variables of considerable importance and pervasiveness. Further, the ingenuity of the investigator in harnessing exactly what he does, and what part of the subject's repertoire he taps, is also overlooked by denigrating his procedures to the simple application of the already-known.

What is involved in self-reinforcement? The actual procedures that the term refers to may be exemplified by comparing two cases involving exactly the same stimuli, the same behavioral requirements, and the same reinforcing consequences. One case is a programmed textbook, in which the appropriate answers are written and students then turn the page to see if they are correct, and should advance to the next frame.* The other case is of identical material placed in a teaching machine, in one of whose panels students write the same appropriate answers. If correct, as scanned and defined by the machine, the machine will advance the program by presenting the next frame. We shall assume that conditions have been established whereby presentation of the next advanced frame reinforces program participation. A difference between the two cases seems to be that in the former case, the student provided himself with a consequence, whereas in the latter, the machine provided it. The critical dimension of difference *appears* to be self-provision, as opposed to other-provision. The fact that the author of the program created the consequence is irrelevant. For example, if a student says, I shall allow myself to go to the theater

* I am indebted to Professor Susan M. Markle for this example. (*cf.* Markle, 1969).

only when I finish my assignment, he or she is still engaging in self-reinforcement as defined. If a friend withholds the ticket until the student has turned in the assignment, this is not self-reinforcement, even if the student asked the friend to do this. The fact that neither was involved in production of the movie or printing of the ticket is irrelevant to this distinction. However, the term, reinforcement, as used in the laboratory, whence it derives, would clearly be applicable to the cases of the teaching machine and the friend. Self-reinforcement, as typically used, is exemplified by the text and the self-admission, "but is it operant reinforcement?", to requote Skinner.

The difference is not in the agency that provides the reinforcer, as the term, self-reinforcement, implies. Rather, it lies in who *evaluates* whether or not the *response requirement* for delivery of the consequence has been met.* In the laboratory, the tension in the microswitch (or some other arrangement the investigator can adjust) defines the minimal force necessary to activate it, thereby to record a response, to activate consequence-related equipment, and so on. Upper as well as lower limits may be set. This gate need not be defined by force, but by location, as in the definition of a strike in baseball: "above the knee and below the shoulder."* The requirement may also be defined by which of the multiple manipulandum choices is effective. And so on. All of these laboratory definitions of the response required to activate reinforcement are independent of any other definitions the subject may make. Where the response does not meet these requirements, it is simply not defined as a response. The equipment, so to speak, evaluates the response. It is this *independent* definition of a response as a requirement for delivery of a consequence, in a specifiable relation, that *defines an operant contingency*. And *operant reinforcement* is a contingency. A reinforcer is the consequence component of a (positive) reinforcement contingency. This definition of reinforcement is met by the arrangements in the animal chamber, the classroom examination, and the teaching machine, among others. It is not met by the programmed text or the first theater case, or the other examples given, and designated as "self-reinforcement." There is no contingency relation, as the term is usually defined, between target be-

* Bandura and Perloff (1967) note that such "self-evaluation (s) . . . often involves a *social comparison process*" (italics in original). However, with reference to the present discussion, such influence by other agents is not germane to the role of other agents in defining a reinforcement contingency as the term is used in the laboratory.

* It may be of interest to younger readers that an even narrower gate once defined the respectability of young woman: a "respectable girl" did not permit petting above the knee and below the waist. *O tempera, O mores!*

havior and specified consequence, since the contingency is not independently defined.

To replicate the contingencies actually involved in self-reinforcement, it is not necessary for the subject to reinforce himself directly, rather than through mediation of a machine or other outsider. For example, if the subject is permitted to rewire the apparatus so that any of the four keys in a multiple-choice or oddity situation governs the consequence, the reinforcing component in the contingency shifts from coming under the control of the discriminative stimulus (or abstraction), to control by the force required to activate the apparatus. However, *the equipment* provides the consequence, not the subject of self-reinforcement. (See Goldiamond, 1975, for a more extended discussion.) One can imagine how readily appropriate control would then be established! The situation described is not far-fetched. It is a limiting example of cases in which the subject sets his own evaluation for defining adequacy of his own efforts. Any teacher who has allowed students to discuss their examination papers with him is acquainted with the arguments he may get: the answer graded as inadequate *was* adequate, the answer was responsive to the question as the student understood it, the grader was arbitrary in his criterion (so, too, is the machine definition of the force of a peck), and so on. The student appears to be asking for self-reinforcement (as usually defined), rather than teacher-reinforcement. What he is actually asking for is self-definition of the response requirement (for the grade). The social contingency in which a person is allowed to obtain a socially important consequence (*e.g.*, a medical license) on his recognizance of his own adequacy is not generally sanctioned (but this describes the contingencies in self-reinforcement"). Hanging up a "shingle" without the socially requisite (target) behaviors represents such an alternative contingency. The behavioral components of this contingency include those entering into use of a hammer, nail, and chutzpah, rather than those entering into professional training. Its social condemnation is attested by the pejorative labels attached, *e.g.*, fraud, deception, sociopathy.

If, under conditions of self-definition of the response requirement, target behavior is maintained, as it often is in humans, at least, the task becomes one of explaining *why*, that is, *how come*, in the literal sense of the words. What are the necessary present conditions and the relevant past contingencies? Although there are no *a priori* grounds to assume that use of the misnomer, self-reinforcement, leads one to overlook such explanatory requirements, the misnomer has often had this effect.

Alternative contingencies. Finding a concise contingency-referent term that is in better accord with the actual contingencies than is self-reinforcement seems to be difficult. *Self-congratulation* is such a term, but is limited to a particular type of consequence. Other terms raise other problems.* The issue is simply, *upon whose evaluation of the behavior* is the consequence delivered? A contingency of reinforcement requires that such evaluation be independent of the subject. The conditions under which a contingency is not met (the case in self-reinforcement) are more variable by far than the conditions under which they are. The set of all such conditions must, accordingly, be defined only by negation of the other set, that is, by exclusion of its elements from it. Accordingly, it would seem that, in applied situations, the conditions that at present come under "self-reinforcement" should be stated precisely, according to the situation. For example, "it was suggested to the client that he take a ten-minute break after each fifty minutes of reading. He was lent a pocket timer for this purpose." The procedure is *not* referred to as self-reinforcement, nor is the timer a discriminative stimulus. What the contingencies actually are is not known. Research in "self-reinforcement" might try to specify these in such situations and in contrived laboratory experiments.

The increased attention to this area derives its impetus mainly from those applied situations described as self-control (*cf.* Skinner, 1953). It is of interest that such situations often describe training in setting up genuine contingencies of reinforcement. Indeed, the target behavior is shaped in accord with such contingencies. Two disparate examples will be given. In one case, the patient learned to control her own hitherto-pervasive scratching from 180 min a week to less than 30 sec. One consequence was a reduction in skin lesions from over 80 lesions of different sizes to fewer than 10 small lesions. This was a *genuine* self-reinforcement situation. The evaluation of whether or not her handling of her skin constituted scratching was *independent* of her own assessment of the target behavior. Her sensitive skin evaluated her behavior, so to speak, and her behavior came under its control. In a vastly different case, the clients were the parents of a schizophrenic adult whom they chose to keep at home. Sessions were devoted to analyzing their logs about home events to ascertain what behavioral changes (including insights) they might make, which might occasion behavior by their son different from

* Self-definition of the response requirement (for consequence-delivery) is in accord with what goes on. However, *self-definition, self-assessment,* or *self-evaluation* as concise terms have other connotations. Rewards and awards are usually contingent on behavior, but *the former* is often considered a nontechnical synonym of reinforcement.

his more typical patterns at home. This, too, represents a *genuine* target contingency. The evaluation of whether or not their behaviors toward him were appropriate in this context was *independent* of their assessment of the adequacy of their behavior in "reaching" him. His differential progress, so to speak, evaluated the adequacy of their behavior. In the common language, both parties became more considerate of each other.

The two situations, one involving self-management of behaviors whose adequacy is assessed by one's own body, and the other involving assessment of adequacy by other people, bracket a considerable part of clinical practice. Such self-control situations describe genuine operant contingencies and maintenance of the relevant behaviors is explainable in such terms.

The term, self-reinforcement, can have adverse effects, as was noted. It can function as an explanatory fiction. It can also divert investigative effort away from study of the actual contingencies. An effect of possibly greater importance is suggested by the evident success that has accompanied the deployment of these and related procedures, and the economy by which such success can be obtained. As Skinner notes, "something of this sort undoubtedly happens." What these suggest is the existence of contingencies of considerable power and prevalence, which are already being tapped and deployed. By dislabeling them, through a term classifying them with phenomena that are fairly well understood, we tend to overlook the importance of these phenomena and their novel contributions to research as well as application.

Self-reinforcement does not refer to self-reinforcement, and this is precisely where its contribution lies.

REFERENCES

BANDURA, A., & PERLOFF, B. Relative efficacy of self-monitored and externally imposed reinforcement systems. *Journal of Personality and Social Psychology*, 7:111-116, 1967.

GOLDFRIED, M. R., & MERBAUM, M. (Eds.). *Behavior Change through Self-Control*. New York: Holt, Rinehart, & Winston, 1973.

GOLDIAMOND, I. Toward a constructional approach to social problems: Ethical and constitutional issues raised by applied behavior analysis. Behaviorism, 2:2-84, 1974.

GOLDIAMOND, I. Alternative sets as a framework for behavioral formulations and research. *Behaviorism*, 3:49-86, 1975.

MARKLE, S. M. *Good Frames and Bad: A Grammar of Frame Writing*. 2nd ed. New York: Wiley, 1969.

SKINNER, B. F. *Science and Human Behavior*. New York: Macmillan, 1953.

Section IV

ASSESSMENT AND EVALUATION

Commentary

Assessment is in the air, if not the curriculum, of the leading universities (Tryon, 1976). Two major texts have recently appeared (Ciminero, Calhoun & Adams, 1976; Mash & Terdal, 1976), others are in press, several edited volumes contain assessment chapters (e.g., Cautela & Upper, 1977; Goldfried, 1976) and there is one assessment oriented text which focuses entirely upon children (Gelfand & Hartmann, 1975). In this Section last year we reviewed the pros and cons of the single-case experimental design and its implications for the assessment process. This year, a new text by Hersen and Barlow (1976) offers one of the clearest statements about such designs that we know. At the end of this Section we append further discussion of single-case experimental designs (see also Wilson, 1977c).

Ciminero (1977) categorizes the assessment process according to the purpose served; description of the problem; selection of the treatment strategy; and evaluation of outcome. Description ranges from the early model of Kanfer and Saslow (1969) through Goldfried and Sprafkin's (1974) more complex formulation to the BASIC ID of Lazarus. Selection of a treatment strategy is still handicapped by lack of a generally applicable model. And evaluation is becoming increasingly a matter of sophistication of design (cf. this Section in Franks & Wilson, 1976).

Methods of behavioral assessment, as contrasted with process, fall into three categories: self-report, direct behavioral observation, physiological recording. But no single measure can provide a comprehensive picture of the multiple parameters of behavior and, to be fully effective, assessment has to tap three response channels—cognitive, motoric and physiological. It might also be noted that behavioral and traditional assessments face similar problems and that differences tend to be more conceptual than methodological. (The measurement of reliability and validity, much neglected in behavioral assessment with the exception of the self-report, illustrates this point well, cf. Cone, 1977; Nelson, Rudin-Hay & Hay, 1977.)

COGNITION IN ASSESSMENT

The cognitive movement in behavior therapy is paralleled by a similar, albeit less well advanced, trend in behavioral assessment (cf. Meichenbaum, 1976). The Schwartz and Gottman paper, reprinted first in this section, is of intrinsic interest not only with respect to their findings but also because of the methodology employed—the utilization of assessment to focus on the nature of the client's behavioral competencies and the accompanying cognitive processes. Cognition provides the means for the integration of self-report with behavioral observation and the elimination of what Meichenbaum (1975; 1977) views as an artificial differentiation between the two. It is, says Meichenbaum, the major function of a total assessment procedure not only to analyze the nature of the client's deficits in terms of discrete, situation-specific responses and problem-specific procedures but also to evolve with the client a cognitive conceptualization of his problems. In this way cognition forges methodological as well as conceptual links between assessment and intervention.

According to Meichenbaum, cognitive influences upon the assessment process are inescapable (see also Peterson's 1968 text, *The Clinical Study of Social Behavior*). From the very start, cognitions begin to change what the client says to himself about his problems and his behavior. Throughout a variety of cognitive assessment techniques, Meichenbaum's clients are given the opportunity to focus on the irrational, self-defeating and self-fulfilling aspects of their thinking styles and to develop the appropriate modifications. The instrument developed by Schwartz and Gottman offers an interesting example of such a device used to tap the client's cognitions.

What the client fails to say to himself, the failure to respond to the task-relevant conditions that could aid performance, may be as important as what the client actually says to himself. Equally important and equally neglected is the need to base treatment goals upon logical and realistic expectations. Goals, like any other facet of behavior therapy and assessment, must be data based (cf. Curran & Gilbert, 1975). For example, to get some measure of normal dating habits prior to planning a program for change Klaus, Hersen, and Bellack (1977) surveyed dating behavior and problems in a large sample of student males and females.

Marholin and Bijou's (1977) model similarly stresses the precise, detailed delineation of problem areas and the careful monitoring of behavior before as well as during and after treatment.

It is necessary to specify not only those areas in which behavior change should take place, but also the conditions that will probably lead to new behaviors or to the reduction of problem behaviors. Since the emphasis is upon current conditions responsible for the undesirable behaviors and the conditions necessary for new learning, it is rarely necessary to engage in the traditional detailed history taking process. Neither diagnostic categories, nor speculations about previous historical interactions, nor a groping for underlying hypothetical mechanisms are of relevance (see Bijou & Grimm, 1975). Goldfried and Linehan (1977) highlight a number of unresolved issues: Comparisons of behavioral with traditional assessment methods are rare. There is little standardization in behavioral assessment. Clinical behavioral assessment seems to be based largely upon the notions of the particular assessor and, even in research, assessment procedures focusing upon identical target behaviors differ from study to study. And failure to specify assessment procedures in adequate detail often makes meaningful replication or cross study comparison impossible. Whether and under what circumstances seemingly minor procedural variations do make a difference remains largely unknown. (Consider, for example, a recent study of Jeger and Goldfried, 1976, comparing situational tests of speech anxiety.)

Finally, Goldfried and Linehan draw attention to the ethics of behavioral assessment. Review committees rightly focus on outcome and the welfare of the participating subject. No one pays much attention to the ethical decisions implicit in the selection or rejection of specific targets for change. For example, utilizing role-playing to assess what is "appropriately assertive" involves several value judgments. Having decided what is appropriate, the therapist is obligated to employ valid assessment procedures. It is not good enough to rely on traditional psychometric procedures merely because they are convenient and economical. In the long run, the cost of the more time consuming behavioral assessment procedures might well be less than the cost of inappropriate therapy done on the basis of inaccurate assessment measures.

Description of the problem has advanced a long way from the simple S-R models expounded by Lindsley in 1966. However, while the more complex approaches of Lazarus and Meichenbaum may reflect a more sophisticated appreciation of the problem behavior, there is still no validated general model for the selection of an appropriate treatment strategy. Despite certain deficits, Lazarus' BASIC ID probably comes near to a model which is both useful in describing or identifying problem behaviors and helpful to the therapist in the selection of a treatment plan.

The selection of treatment techniques would seem to be closely related to the systems selected for therapeutic intervention. For example, biofeedback might be preferred when the disturbances are predominantly physiological, Ellis' rational emotive therapy or Meichenbaum's cognitive restructuring if the problem is verbal-cognitive, and if overt behaviors need modification, then operant techniques might be more appropriate. While this method of appraisal is not yet well developed, there are several beginnings with respect to specific problem areas (e.g. sexual behavior—Barlow, 1977; social skills—Hersen & Bellack, 1977).

Without data, or a way of obtaining these data, the clinician cannot logically decide which program to employ in any specific situation. For example, the clinician should not arbitrarily decide to use a self-control program. A pretreatment assessment is essential to determine whether self-control is the treatment of choice and, if so, how to apply it. It is easier to generate faulty than effective programs. Familiarity with available techniques is not sufficient; programs must be tailored to individual patients. Unfortunately, there are few guidelines to help the behavioral clinician make such an assessment and he is forced to rely upon a combination of intuition and his clinical experience.

Even Bellack and Schwartz, data-oriented as they are, are forced to offer an assessment schema that is based, at least in part, upon clinical experience. Writing about self-control, they conceptualize the assessment process as a series of questions to be answered in essentially sequential fashion. The two major questions asked are: 1) Is the target behavior amenable to a self-control strategy? and 2) Is self-control applicable for the individual patient? The second question is then subdivided into several component questions including: 1) Can the patient apply the procedure? 2) Are the procedures applied effectively? Unfortunately, in the present stage of our knowledge, when all is said but not done the clinician has to lean heavily upon his or her clinical experience (some would call it intuition) to provide working answers to these questions.

SELF-REPORT MEASURES

Self-report measures can be applied to overt-motor, physiological-emotional or verbal-cognitive modalities. However, most self-report measures are used to assess the verbal-cognitive response system. These range from the relatively unstructured behavioral interview through the written behavioral survey inventory to the self-monitoring of various aspects of behavior by the client in the daily living situation. Regardless of its nature, self-reporting has to cope with similar issues and problems to those faced by traditional psychometric methods (reliability, validity, norms, standardization and statistical analysis). Self-monitoring has to cope with the additional problems of unreliability and reactivity but offers the advantage that it can be an ongoing component of the treatment process if this is so desired (Ciminero, Nelson & Lipinski, 1977).

With one or two exceptions, research into assertive behavior suffers conspicuously from the absence of adequate self-report inventories. The much researched Rathus Assertiveness Scale (RAS) (1973) possesses good reliability and a certain amount of accrued validation data. But, on the debit side, the RAS appears to measure a nonspecific attitude or trait rather than a response to specific situations. The stimulus referents tend to be vague, at best: The questions asked go far beyond direct observation or recall of behavior, requiring the respondent to supply subjective inferences about the psychological meaning of the behavior. Furthermore, the validation procedure of using a question-and-answer session fails to provide an adequate external measure of the behavior. All that has been demonstrated is that self-report as assessed by the RAS is consistent with self-report as assessed by the question-and-answer session (Rich & Schroeder, 1976).

More recently, Rathus and Nevid (1977) gave the scale to a large group of psychiatric patients. Concurrent validity of the RAS scores was established by a correlation of 0.80 with the therapists' ratings of patients' assertiveness on semantic differential scales defining a general assertiveness factor. Thus, with the probable exception of schizophrenics, the RAS seems to be a valid measure of assertiveness and social aggressiveness in psychiatric patients in terms of ratings by therapists who come to know them well during clinical sessions. One interesting development, despite possible limitations in applying this procedure (cf. L .C. Miller, 1976) is the use of factor analysis to improve an existing scale or develop a new one. The 100 item factorially derived social anxiety inventory of Richardson and Tasto, reprinted next in this Section, is likely to be of considerable utility in behavioral research, assessment and therapy.

Galassi's College Self-Expression Scale (CSES), a 50-item inventory that employs a 5-point Likert format, measures three different response classes of assertiveness: positive assertive expression, negative assertive expression and self-denial behavior. Test-retest reliability is high, but concurrent validity, determined by correlating CSES scores with ratings of overall assertiveness made by independent judges, is less impressive. And no external behavior measure has ever been used to determine the predictive validity of the scale. Nor has the CSES been subjected to an item or factor analysis to determine whether more than face validity is present. And the stimulus referants, characteristically vague, seem to reflect nonspecific attitudes more than anything else.

More recently Galassi, Hollandsworth, Radecki, Gay, Howe, and Evans (1976) attempted to validate the CSES against behavioral performance criteria. Low, moderate and high scorers role played five short situations requiring assertive behaviors. Subjects identified by the CSES as low assertives were differentiated from both high assertives and a combined group of moderate and high assertives by the behavioral performance test. Assertiveness as measured by the CSES seems to reflect a combination of verbal and nonverbal behaviors such as eye contact, assertive content of verbal responses and subjectively experienced anxiety. It would seem important to subject this scale to either item or factor analysis. Alternatively, or perhaps additionally, a more systematic approach to test construction might be considered. McFall and Lillesand (1971) validated their Conflict Resolution Inventory by comparing scores on this test with behavior in an automated role-playing assessment procedure.

Gambrill and Richey's Assertion Inventory, reprinted in Franks and Wilson (1976), is still probably one of the most useful measures to appear in that it can be used with a broad range of populations. But, as yet, no comparison of scores of this test with a behavioral measure of assertiveness has been reported. It is this failure to correlate with external behavioral criteria which is characteristic of most assertion measures to date.

The 40-item scale developed and reported by Callner and Ross (1976) for use with drug addicts is interesting in that it was subsequently validated using behavioral performance and self-report measures in a multitrait-multimethod matrix (cf. Campbell & Fiske, 1959). The general concept of assertion is broken down into five subareas: authority, drugs, positive feedback, negative feedback, and heterosexual interaction. Reliability and validity data were obtained using judge's ratings and self-ratings of videotaped performance. The age-matched group of young male addicts and nonaddicts differed significantly in assertiveness in the areas of drugs, authority and positive feedback. Hopefully, the next step could be the application of factor analytic procedures to each of the subscale areas. It would also be of interest to evaluate these findings with respect to sex differences. According to Appelbaum (1976), sex is not a relevant variable with respect to RAS scores, at least not in college populations. Parenthetically, it might be noted that, as part of the same study, Appelbaum failed to find any correlation between assertiveness and social desirability. The desire to respond in a socially appropriate or acceptable manner does not seem to covary with social boldness, a finding construed by Appelbaum as providing support for the discriminant validity of this instrument.

Eisler (1976) summarizes the advantages and disadvantages of self-report measures in the behavioral assessment of social skills. Most of his observations apply to all behavioral self-report measures. First, Appelbaum notwithstanding, the individual may well be presenting himself on the questionnaire in the way he or she would like to be seen. Second, while correlations between self-report measures may be high, the ability to predict individual behavior in any specific situation can be extremely low. Respondents may or may not be able to identify accurately the relevant aspects of their social behavior. And it is sometimes questionable to what extent respondents can accurately assess the behavior of the other persons to whom they are responding. To the extent that they can not accurately assess their own behavior or the behavior of others in relation to themselves, it is difficult to evaluate the validity of their reports. Third, in addition to the failure to differentiate the effects of sex or—until recently—to extend the norms of others besides sophomoric college students, external validity in terms of behaviorally-specific criteria is rare.

On the positive side, self-report inventories are economical with respect to time, they can be scored objectively and they are ideal for preliminary screening. They are also excellent research instruments in that they lend themselves to repeated administration. Cautela (1977) has developed a useful compendium of behavior analysis forms for clinical intervention which are essentially standardized self-report interviews. Finally, it is encouraging to note that self-report studies are no longer confined to students or traditional psychiatric populations (cf. Miller, 1977—drug and alcohol addiction; Steers & Braunstein, 1976—various work settings. See Tasto, 1977, for a review of additional areas).

Self-monitoring is an even more complicated technique for assessing interpersonal behavior in that it requires the individual to record his behavior at specified intervals in a highly systematic manner which requires much training. Its major advantage is that it permits access to data which might otherwise not be readily available. Self-monitoring is also a basis for treatment activities based upon the ability to identify the frequency of engagement in undesirable behaviors and instigate self initiated behavior changes. This "reactivity" is a mixed blessing since it brings with it methodological complications as well as the potential for clinical benefit (see our Commentaries in previous volumes in this Series). Most studies of self-monitoring deal with relatively unambiguous responses such as obsessional thinking or cigarette smoking. Little attention has been paid to the use of self-monitoring procedures in assessing changes in frequency of interpersonal behavior. Eisler offers a number of innovative self-monitoring procedures for assessing specific aspects of individual social behavior which may be combined with other assessment techniques.

Direct behavioral observation by independent observers, until recently used primarily in the assessment of specific, overt responses, is now employed in a variety of naturalistic and clinic settings. But despite obvious conceptual advantages over self-report procedures, serious methodological difficulties remain, particularly with respect to the need for adequate samples of behavior.

As far as assertiveness is concerned, Rich and Schroeder (1976) suggest two main approaches to the problem: self recording by means of an interpersonal diary (Hedquist & Weinhold, 1970) and the by now common strategy of the contrived behavioral task in which a confederate behaves in an agreed manner with all subjects. For example, Weinman, Gelbart, Wallace and Post (1972) devised the Behavior in Critical Situations Scale to tap four different response classes of assertiveness. For use outside the laboratory, the contrived behavioral tasks devised by McFall and his associates (see Franks & Wilson, 1974) involve arbitrary situations such as a telephone call by a confederate for some expressed purpose such as selling subscriptions, soliciting volunteers, or requesting help. These are presumed to be unreasonable request situations and the measures (sometimes difficult to score) include time of total call, time before first refusal, rate of resistance, verbal activity, social skill and acceptance or refusal.

BEHAVIORAL MEASURES

Behavioral measures present a number of unique problems in addition to those of reliability and validity. Observational measures are often biased when the subjects know that they are being observed. The demand characteristics of the experimental situation, especially in contrived and role-playing tasks, can bring about considerable distortion in both the data themselves and their interpretation. Role-playing does not come too easily to many subjects and one can rarely guarantee that the subject is actually "in role." Finally, there is the problem of the observers themselves in direct behavioral observation (see Goldfried & Sprafkin, 1974). Often, raters are shaped to record observations that confirm the experimenter's expectancies. There also seems to be a halo effect when a rater attempts to evaluate the behavior of someone he or she has previously rated. Rich and Schroeder suggest making the raters blind to experimental hypotheses and unaware if the behavior is derived from a pre- or posttest situation. Alternatively, different raters may be used to rate pre- and postdata.

Behavior rating skills have most commonly been applied to children. When working with hyperactive children, direct behavioral rating procedures assume particular importance since this is one of the primary ways of obtaining information about the efficacy or otherwise of various drugs (Werry & Sprague, 1970). One neglected factor affecting the validity of behavioral observation is that of observer bias, the classic if much criticized study in this area being Rosenthal and Jacobson's *Pygmalion in the Classroom* (1968).

To study the effects of biasing information on behavioral observations and rating scales, Siegel, Dragovich and Marholin (1976) trained 41 undergraduate students in making reliable behavioral observations. Each was given differential expectations concerning the activity level of the target child. Then they viewed video recordings of that child and tallied frequency counts of six behavioral characteristics simultaneously. In addition, subjects completed postexperiment rating scales composed of specific identifying behaviors. Contrary to other investigations, neither the behavioral observations nor the rating scales were significantly affected by biasing information. The explanation offered for this discrepancy is that prior studies confounded "specific" and "global" behavioral definitions with behavioral codes and rating scales, respectively. In other words, since rating scales employ global definitions, they are more likely to be biased by information concerning the target subject than are more specific, operationally defined behaviors. Attempts should therefore be made to develop rating scales constructed of as specific and readily identifiable items as possible (as in the scale used by Siegel et al.).

It is tempting to submit data derived from such scales, whether they be self-report questionnaires or various behavior checklists for use by teachers and parents and others, to factor analytic procedures. However, L. C. Miller (1976) sounds a note of caution and cites data to substantiate his concern. Some 64 phobic children and their matched controls were rated by their parents on various commonly accepted behavior rating scales such as the Louisville Behavioral Check List and the ensuing data subjected to factor and multiple discriminant analysis. Without going into details, it will suffice here to draw attention to his conclusion, that instrument factors elicited by factor analysis in psychotherapy change studies may well be little more than statistical artifacts. A multiple discriminant analysis is suggested as a more appropriate technique for the study of both classification and change itself.

Considerable attention has been given to the development of various observational systems, especially for working with children. Thus, Ross and Zimiles (1976) have developed what they call the Differentiated Child Behavior Observational System (DCB) for the systematic recording of children's interactions in ongoing classroom activities. DCB is designed for live use in the classroom by trained observers who encode children's interactional behaviors on both timed and change-of-behavior bases. One distinctive feature of their system is the emphasis on the substantive aspects of the children's interactions, the content as well as the source and direction of each entry. In addition, unlike most other approaches, the DCB is applicable to the informal open classroom as well as to the more traditional setting. Current work is concerned with defining the coding procedures and expanding their coverage, cross-validating previous findings with a new set of equally diverse classrooms and estimating the magnitude of error attributable to variation among observers and classroom situations.

Observer ratings are subject to a particular kind of correlational bias stemming from the shared assumptions about traits and behavior possessed by the raters (Berman & Kenny, 1976). Bruner and Tagiuri (1954) labeled these assumed correlations "implicit theories of personality"; others refer to them as logical errors or halo effects. Raters appear to possess assumptions concerning the concurrence of rated items, and these assumptions can introduce systematic distortion when correlations are derived from the ratings. Thus, whenever a researcher wishes to use raters or observers to assess any form of association between behaviors or between traits, the possibility of correlational bias arises. It is difficult in such situations to determine whether the intercorrelations obtained from the ratings are due to the assumptions and biases of the rater or to the actual behavior of the persons being rated.

In similar fashion, correlational bias can occur in the judgments and ratings made by clinicians, and a variety of suggestions have been made for the minimization of this effect. Suggested strategies include the use of carefully defined behavioral terms on the rating scale, rating all persons on one trait at a time and the computation of correlations from the mean ratings of a number of observers. However, as Berman and Kenny point out, these simple techniques may well be ineffective and, in practice, the majority of researchers who employ observer ratings either ignore or dismiss the problem of correlational bias and continue to report correlations derived from uncorrected ratings. They do not even attempt to minimize this particular effect.

Much of the evidence of a bias in ratings is circumstantial rather than experimental and alternate explanations are not hard to come by. Thus, one might even question whether crorelational bias in ratings occurs at all. One obvious way to resolve this issue and highlight any bias that occurs in ratings is to manipulate experimentally the actual correlation between items that are being rated by observers and then to examine the correlational bias which may appear under these conditions. Although their data are confined to normal subjects in a laboratory situation, Berman and Kenny's findings clearly indicate that implicit assumptions concerning the co-occurrence of traits can have a systematic effect on immediate as well as delayed ratings. Moreover, the degree of this correlational bias was found to be constant not only across different levels of actual correlation but also across ratings made at different points in time.

This demonstration of correlational bias has major implications for the use of human observers and raters. The suggested solutions of Berman and Kenny include the elimination or minimization of human observers altogether. Much valuable information can be obtained by mechanical coding as long as the devices introduced are relatively unobtrusive. Another possibility, which still permits the individual experimenter to play an active role in the investigation, is to videotape actors performing the various behaviors performed in a rating scale. These videotapes could then be presented to observers in such a manner than there would be no correlation between the performances of one behavior and any of the other behaviors.

Among the more interesting scales for recording behavior with psychiatric patients is that of Tarlow and his associates. The Verbal Report Form (VRF), still under development, generates a reliable measure of conversation and verbal behavior for use in helping service persons test the progress of hospitalized psychiatric persons. In one recent study (Tarlow, Alevizos & Callahan, 1976) the CRF was able to discriminate between three contrasted groups of patients and normals by using the number of inappropriate responses checked by three groups of raters. Requiring a minimum of training and mechanical intervention, such devices offer considerable promise in the extention of objective report forms to the hospitalized psychiatric patient.

Tittler, Anchor and Weitz (1976) point to a further advantage of direct behavioral assessment over the self-report in that it lends itself to the measurement of states or transient quantities. Being anchored in immediate experience, behavioral techniques should be more sensitive to small short-term changes in the state of the individual. In the study reported by these authors, both behavioral and self-reported devices were employed to measure states of openness. The hypothesis generated was that behavioral methods would be more sensitive to actual changes in level of openness than self-report measures. Two self-report measures of openness and two behavioral measures of openness were given to 50 students prior to and immediately following one of four treatment procedures. Contrary to prediction, none of the measures indicated an increase in openness for those subjects who had undergone openness-promoting treatments. However, when the data were broken down more closely in terms of individual examiners, systematic differences were noted from examiner to examiner. Examiner differences seems to be the other side of the coin from correlational biases and are of probably equal relevance.

Tittler et al. suggest three possible types of examiner influence: One, the subject gradually perceives the examiner as being receptive to what is being measured; two, the examiner creates a presonal ceiling effect in his subjects by encouraging openness during the pre-test; three, the examiner can elicit resistance by pressing for openness. While applicable primarily to the measurement of openness, their conclusions would seem to be generally applicable.

Objective behavioral assessment techniques have been most extensively applied in the assessment of social skills (Eisler, 1977; Hersen & Bellack, 1976 b; see also our Commentaries to Sections II and VIII). Somewhat arbitrarily, Eisler divides his procedures for assessing social skills into objective and subjective categories. (But as he points out, objectively and subjectively defined social behaviors are really on a continuum. To the extent that the interpersonal behaviors can be precisely specified to outside observers in advance of the rating procedures, the measuring process is objective; to the extent that the judges decide for themselves whether the observed behaviors reflect various definitions of social skill, the process is subjective). Subjective measures appear to possess greater social validity than any simple objective measures of social skill. When using the more highly specified objective measure, it is necessary to demonstrate that the measured behaviors bear significant relationship to the skills which are being assessed, either by correlational analysis or by the ability to discriminate between groups of individuals who do or do not have the skill under investigation. In most situations, concludes Eisler, it is better to use a combination of the two.

Eisler delineates a variety of methods for evoking social interpersonal performance. Situations which most closely approximate the subject's real-life situation are more likely to elicit his actual interpersonal response. This goal may be obtained either by role-playing the social situation or by involving the individual's real-life interactional partner in the assessment situation. Both strategies possess certain methodological and practical advantages and disadvantages. Among the more novel strategies for coping with some of the limitations of conventional role-playing is that of Forgione (1976) who developed the use of life size mannequins in the behavioral assessment of child molesters. While neatly circumventing prohibitions against the use of children even for diagnostic purposes and offering some potential as a therapeutic device, the use of models introduces a complicating new dimension whose parameters are almost entirely unknown.

As yet, comparatively little is known about the effects of variations in role-playing methodology on the assessment of either assertive or social behaviors. To this end, Galassi and Galassi (1976) investigated the effects of role-playing variations on the assessment of assertive behavior in college students, comparing taped with live stimulus presentations and the number of subject responses required (single vs. multiple). While the results are of interest, it is the fact that such parameters are being systematically investigated which is of primary concern here. Future research in assertion training and social skill develpment might well direct greater attention to the effects of the methodology employed on the subject's performance. For example, Bellack, Hersen and Turner (in press) examined the validity of role-playing tests for social skills with psychiatric patients. Again, while their findings are of interest in their own right, it is the fact that attention is being given to such parameters that is of relevance here.

Although in-vivo observation is the ideal strategy for securing meaningful data about client functioning, in many circumstances it is either impractical or infeasible. It is for such situations that the laboratory analogue has been developed. For example, the Behavior Avoidance Test of Lang and Lazovik (1963) has become a standard procedure for assessing fear. In similar fashion, the use of contrived situations is becoming standard strategy for the assessment of social skills.

In their comprehensive review of the behavioral assessment and treatment of alcoholism, Nathan and Briddell (1977) delineate three distinct kinds of behavioral measures of drinking in laboratory settings. The first utilizes objective operant indices in the experimental laboratory for the study of the relative reinforcement values of alcohol, money and socialization. Most of the early studies were carried out primarily with male alcoholics and it is only recently that the techniques have been extended to the study of females. For example, Tracey, Karlin and Nathan (1976) made an experimental analysis of chronic alcoholism in four women, calling into question earlier findings with respect to men alone. Women alcoholics demonstrate a singular rather than biphasic pattern of alcohol consumption and remain "maintenance" drinkers throughout the period programmed for drinking. However, the study is limited to four subjects who may well differ in socioeconomic status, as well as drinking characteristics themselves, from the male alcoholics previously studied. Also, it is a far cry from laboratory studies of drinking to the drinking behavior of individuals in the more real-life situations.

The second behavioral strategy currently under development involves the use of "taste tests." These require subjects to taste a variety of alcoholic and nonalcoholic beverages and to rate the beverages along taste dimensions. However, the real purpose of the procedure is to measure actual alcohol consumption without the subject's being aware of what is being measured. Alcohol taste rating tasks have been used to explore the effects of distress, expectancy and modeling influence in the consumption of alcohol. The third development, historically speaking, pertains to the development of drinking at experimental bars established within laboratory settings—one more step towards an approximation of the natural environment.

As Nathan and Briddell note, the trend is towards greater and greater approximation of the natural environment as a substitute for working in the natural environment itself. At the present time, most of the long-term assessment of alcohol drinking behavior in the natural environment is non-behavioral in nature, relying on general questionnaires, such as the MMPI, or tests derived especially for measurement of so-called alcoholic personalities, such as the Alcadd and the Manson. These two latter measures are of debatable validity and susceptible to most of the difficulties associated with non-behavioral personality assessment that have been repeatedly noted throughout this Series.

Of the new behavioral assessment procedures developed for the measurement of the drinking pattern of alcoholics in the natural environment, one of the more important is that of Sobell and Sobell (1973a, 1973b, 1976) (See Franks & Wilson, 1976). Also noteworthy is the Drinking Profile of Marlatt (1976), a 19-page questionnaire completed during a standardized interview and designed to yield an intensive behavioral profile of drinking preferences, rates and patterns, as well as the motivational and reinforcement variables associated with drinking.

Clinical assessment with children has shown an increasingly ecological trend in recent years, a movement towards direct examination of the child and the social environment in which he behaves. Children seem to present a great variability of behavior across diverse settings: the home, the classroom nad the local sweetshop are very different worlds, probably operating under different systems and calling for different patterns of behavior. This presents a difficult problem for the professional faced with the assessment of children's behavioral and emotional problems. Assessment must be specific to the setting in which the problems have been observed to occur. If the problem is evident in the home and school, assessments must be made in both settings and it cannot be assumed that the findings will be similar.

To sample the problem child's behavioral interactions in a variety of real-world settings, Wahler, House and Stembaugh (1976) developed a manual which focuses on three facets of ecological assessment: 1) an interview format designed to set the stage for the observational sample procedure; 2) an observational procedure for use by those adults who are members of the child's natural community; and 3) a standardized recording system for use by the clinician or some other impartial observer. The systematic application of such techniques is likely to receive considerable attention within the coming years.

Among the alternative methods of assessment that have been developed, we focused last year upon the work of Moos, Barker and their associates. One such approach is to assess the environment of any particular setting through the shared perceptions of members of that setting along various environmental dimensions. This "perceived environment" approach has been extended by Moos and his colleagues to a variety of psychiatric, correctional and high-school settings. Several studies have focused on the correlates of perceived environment and the relationship of the perceived environment to selected outcome variables. Thus, Trickett and Moos (1974) found consistent relationships between perceived environment of the high-school classroom and student satisfaction with the environment. However, despite the increasing credibility of the notion of perceiving environment as a useful approach to environmental assessment, certain methodological issues remain.

For example, Kaye, Trickett, and Quinlan (1976) raise the question of whether the perception of persons in a setting corresponds with their behavior in that setting, or might members be responding to the environment in terms of what Alkar (cited by Kaye et al.) describes as a "shared myth." This issue is of particular importance in interpreting correlational studies based solely on self-report of participants in selected environments.

To this end, Kaye et al. employed a multitrait, multimethod matrix approach to the environmental assessment of the high school classroom. Their study investigated the relationship of a measure of perceived environment of the classroom to alternative methods of assessing an environment. Global ratings by reliable outside observers and a content analysis of discrete teacher-student interactions were also used. To the extent that systematic relationships exist among these different methods, it is their claim that the perceived environment is neither an artifact of measurement nor a "shared myth" of the perceivers.

The findings are more complicated than the authors perhaps expected. Certain predictions did not occur and some unanticipated findings emerged, suggesting that the various methods for assessing psychosocial environments have to be used with caution and sophistication. Nevertheless, their findings highlight the importance of using multiple methods to capture the qualities of psychosocial environment. It is the particular nature of the environment dimension to be measured that determines the most appropriate set of methods.

Among the more novel applications of behavioral assessment procedures in the natural environment, we might include the extension of these techniques to the assessment of sports spectator behavior. Traditional methods, based on well documented theories of collective behavior, suffer from a variety of limitations (Cheffers, Lowe & Harrold, 1976). Mechanical strategies for measuring and recording changes in crowd noise and behavior, such as noise fibrillators or telemetric heart reactors are possibilities which exist only in the remote future. The Individual Reaction Gestalt (IRG) of Cheffers et al. is a behaviorally based device for measuring and predicting sports spectator behavior. Based on techniques of interactional analysis and a methodology introduced by Flanders in 1960 for the study of teacher-pupil classroom interactions, its implementation depends on training groups of observers to code behavior. An alternative to the opinion questionnaires and other psychometric devices traditionally used in measuring such phenomena, it offers several major advantages: The researcher can draw an accurate picture of the total crowd behavior while still investigating in detail any particular individual; it is relatively easy to train observers; it requires little apparatus other than a flowchart recording form. Its particular value is that it can look at randomly selected individuals set against the totality of the surrounding crowd environment. While methodological problems with respect to validity and reliability still remain partially unresolved, this is a method of considerable promise.

Behavioral observational procedures are also useful in cross-cultural studies. For example, there is the assertiveness pull scale of Kagan and Carlson (1975), used to assess the development of assertiveness of young children from Anglo-American as contrasted with Mexican-American cultures. Such devices may also be used for longitudinal studies as well as cross-cultural comparisons (e.g. Avellar & Kagan, 1976). We single out these studies primarily to draw attention to the need for cultural differences to be taken into account in the study and practice of assertiveness and assertion training, an area distinguished primarily by the speed with which practice has leapt ahead of data.

ANALOGUE MEASURES

Nay (1977) provides a comprehensive survey of the use of analogue measures to circumvent the limitations of direct monitoring in the natural environment. There is always the possibility that the observer's presence will contaminate the environment, and environments such as home settings or certain out of doors conditions can place major restrictions on any sustained observational efforts. The analogue situation requires the client or subject to respond to stimuli that simulate those to be found in the natural environment. Although raising serious questions about validity and observer effect, analogue situations provide the investigator with a less costly and more practical alternative method of collecting information.

Nay organizes his review into five distinctive categories of analogue measurement: First, there is the pencil-and-paper analogue in which the client is required to make a written statement of what he *would* say or *would* do in response to a stimulus scene. Paper-and-pencil analogues can be given to many individuals at one setting, they require little or no training or apparatus and they can be carried out under virtually any circumstance. They are also readily amenable to quantification. Their major disadvantage is that they are far removed from the natural situation, and a respondent's written description of what he would do in a situation may be very different from what he actually would do.

Second, there are audiotape analogues, in which the stimulus items are presented in an exclusively auditory format. These can provide the respondent with a much more natural segment of behavior while retaining many of the advantages of administration and quantification offered by pencil-and-paper analogues. They are also easy to modify and can be used in virtually any setting. Videotape analogues, the third category, are similar to audiotape analogues, with the advantage of the visual dimension. Disadvantages include increased costliness to produce, cumbersomeness and the complexities which arise with any sophisticated form of instrumentation.

Next comes what Nay terms the enactment analogues, such as the Behavioral Avoidance Test in which the respondent is required to interact in the laboratory with relevant persons, stimuli or objects usually present in the natural setting. The outstanding advantage of the enactment approach is that the assessor is systematically able to record the client's behavior in response to the relevant stimuli, making it considerably less artificial than the approaches described thus far.

Role-playing analogues, Nay's fifth category, have already been discussed. Suffice to note their greater flexibility for the assessor in the presentation of criterion stimuli than any of the analogues so far reviewed. The major disadvantage is probably the potential lack of concordance between stimuli presented in the role-play situation and criterion stimuli found in the natural environment. Furthermore, any role-play approach is limited by the client's ability to act.

Nay highlights some of the besetting issues in analogue assessment: issues of validity and reliability, primarily. Although the correlation between clinic and laboratory measures is often significant, few investigators have systematically compared measurements in the clinical setting to criterion behaviors in the natural environment.

Two parallel progressions are noted by Nay in his roughly hierarchical categories: as the cost of administration increases, so the similarity of the analogue stimuli to those found in the natural environment is concomitantly enhanced. The cost-benefit ratios involved await investigation.

By way of concluding this discussion of assessment in the natural environment, we draw attention to Kent and Foster's (1977) point that, just as a photograph is often casually accepted as a mirror of the scene it depicts without the realization that the final picture is an intricate product of equipment, photographer and developing process as well as the scene itself, so many investigators erroneously view direct observation recording as the purest and most direct portrayal of behavior.

PHYSIOLOGICAL ASSESSMENT

Physiological assessment may take the form of indirect indices of change in behavior, (e.g., blood alcohol level or urine analysis) or direct measurement of psychophysiological response systems. Despite cogent criticisms by Wolff and Merrens (1976—see Franks & Wilson, 1976), many investigators consider physiological measures an essential component of the assessment process (e.g. Barlow, 1977; Borkovec, Weerts & Bernstein, 1977; Kalman & Feuerstein, 1977). As far as the assessment of social skills is concerned, there is some difference of opinion regarding the utility of physiological measures, particularly with respect to the assumption of a direct relationship between a particular emotional state and actual behavior (Eisler, 1976). This is very evident in studies which use heart-rate or pulse-measures to assess social anxiety. As Bandura (1969) long ago pointed out, emotions experienced phenomenologically are rarely accompanied by a corresponding diversity of physiological response pattern; different emotional states are cognitively identified and discriminated in terms of the external social situation rather than internal somatic cues. And correlations among physiological indicators themselves tend to be low.

There is no necessary relationship between general physiological arousal and self-report of specific emotional states. Physiological indicators would appear to be among the least reliable in terms of predicting complex social behavior. Furthermore, they are difficult to obtain, special apparatus and training are required, and the procedures involved are typically intrusive with regard to the natural quality of the social interactions under study. Their major value, according to Eisler, is in group analogue studies where individual differences in response to experimental conditions are relatively unimportant and the artificiality of their presence can be tolerated more readily.

Physiological measures have been employed in only one assertiveness training study, in which manually assessed pulse rate was used as a crude measure of autonomic arousal before and after role-playing (McFall & Marston, 1970). And Borkovec, Stone, O'Brien and Kaloupek (1974) successfully discriminated between socially anxious and nonanxious subjects on the basis of heart-rate arousal. Thus, heart-rate may be a valid measure with persons who are unassertive due to debilitating anticipatory social anxiety. However, in general, Rich and Schroeder are pessimistic with respect to the future of physiological measures in the identification of different response classes of assertiveness and suggest that physiological assessment would do well to focus on anticipatory arousal and its reduction through assertion training.

The future of physiological assessment depends in part upon increasingly sophisticated instrumentation. At least in principle, instruments could be developed which are vastly more sensitive, in all respects, than any human sense organ. Unfortunately, the application of instrumentation to the study of human behavior is relatively recent and the published reports are spread over a wide and diverse range of journals, few of which are read by behavior therapists. Furthermore, meaningful selection of the appropriate instrument, at best a difficult challenge to the technically unsophisticated mental health professional, is made virtually impossible in many instances due to the paucity of technical information made available. To take one particular example from Rugh and Schwitzgebel's (1976) excellent survey, out of 44 pieces of biofeedback advertising literature, 21 failed to provide adequate specifications.

OUTCOME EVALUATION

Finally, we turn to assessment of outcome. The last paper to be reprinted in this Section, by Minkin and his associates, suggests a need to supplement traditional behavior analysis measurement systems by some form of social validation. Behaviors, especially socially important behaviors, are even more complex than we had suspected, and outcome evaluation is probably one of the complicated facets of the overall assessment process.

The many technical and methodological advances in the field contribute to the increasing sophistication in the application of assessment procedures to outcome evaluation. For example, the problem-oriented medical record (POR) (Weed, 1969—see also Franks & Wilson, 1976) has been adapted for psychiatric problems (Grant & Maletsky, 1972; Smith, Hawley & Grant, 1974). But in its customary format, the Weed system is maximally useful for the identification of problem areas only in those situations where patient independence is limited and observation facilities are close by. Now, Wolff and Epstein (1977) have extended the range and effectiveness of the system to situations in which controls are fewer and essential records not readily accessible. Their modification permits immediate recording of essential information in the environment where the behavior occurs and the transfer of this information to a permanent record with minimal effort.

While this simple modification of a proven system lends itself well to the ongoing evaluation of change and outcome, considerable refinements are indicated if POR strategies are to achieve that precision which one has learned to expect from a carefully conducted behavioral analysis. In the words of Katz and Woolley (1975), "problem-oriented records should not be constructed as a panacea for solving complex psychiatric problems. They do not guarantee high standards of quality, but they do provide potential use for reorganizing existing patient records so that relevant clinical information can be utilized most effectively."

In Section X, we draw attention to the regrettable failure to submit many self treatment programs to any form of controlled evaluation. A similar argument applies to the many tape cassettes, videotapes and even films which are readily available for use either in conjunction with a therapist or on an over-the-counter basis. It is perhaps with this in mind that Kwiterovich and Horan (1977) took a hard look at a frequently used but rarely evaluated film entitled "Assertive Training for Women: A Stimulus Film," produced by Pearlman, Coburn, and Jakubowski-Spector (1973) for the American Personnel and Guidance Association.

Kwiterovich and Horan randomly assigned 48 women solicited through university-wide advertisements to one of four conditions in a Solomon type design which allows for an examination of experimental treatment, the effects of pretesting, and the interactions between these factors. The experimental treatment consisted of viewing the film and participating in the structured discussions as recommended in the leader's guide. Women in the placebo control condition observed and discussed a quite different film entitled "Focus on Behavior: The Social Animal" which dealt with group pressures in more general terms. Half of the women were pretested and all were posttested on the Rathus Assertiveness Scale and a modification of the Action Situation Inventory (Friedman, 1968). Follow-up data were gathered six weeks after treatment by an experimentally blind male confederate who requested that they "join an organization which would stop inflation by asking American women to give their jobs to unemployed American men." An experimentally blind judge listening in on an extension phone logged a series of response measures. Once again, the finding—no significant difference between experimental and control treatments on any of the behavioral ratings—is of less relevance in this section of the Annual Review than the fact of the evaluation process itself.

It seems extraordinary to us that behavioral programs be evaluated by other than behavioral means. For example, a well-designed and conducted behavioral program for training hyperactive children, utilizing various combinations of modeling, self-verbalization and self-reinforcement techniques, was recently evaluated exclusively by a battery of conventional non-behavioral tests (Douglas, Parry, Marton, & Garson, 1976). It would be interesting to speculate about how easy it would have been to devise a more appropriate form of evaluation and perhaps utilize the conventional battery, in addition, if the investigators had so desired.

Increasing attention is being given to the methodological and statistical issues involved in evaluation. Kaplan and Litrownik (1977) note the neglected or inappropriate use of multivariate techniques in the assessment of multiple outcome criteria in behavioral research. Walker and Hops (1976) stress the use of normative behavioral observation data as a standard in the evaluation of treatment effects produced in other settings. It is important to have an established standard or criterion level in order to judge whether treatment has achieved its goals. Without it, it becomes difficult to reach any definitive conclusions with respect to the effectiveness of the various treatment procedures. Peer normative data may be used as a standard for evaluating treatment effects administered either within the regular classroom or in special settings followed by reintegration into the regular classroom. Thus, such data can provide an operant measure of appropriate child behavior in any given classroom at any given point in time, together with measures of variability and trends in operant level over time as a function of changes in classroom stimulus conditions. Measures of stimulus conditions during follow-up periods also make interpretation of generalization and maintenance effects much more meaningful.

No matter how benignly intended, evaluation within an institutional setting is a delicate matter. There is always the possibility of an evaluation process being viewed as a threat by the staff concerned, and few positive changes are then likely to occur. As a contribution to the resolution of this dilemma, Herendeen, Demster and Wimer (in press) have developed a method for focusing on the performance of the unit as a whole rather than that of any individual staff member, considerable care always being taken to explain what is going on to the authorities and staff involved. Hopefully, this prevents the vicious cycle of pinpointing error, attributing blame and feeling threatened from originating in the first place. But even this strategy is not sufficient. "De-individualized" program evaluation, if ill timed or ill conceived, can still lead to unrealistic rejection when group or facility performance fails to match up to promise (Zusman, 1976).

Although rarely reported, the investigator can often learn as much from failure as from success. As in the well choosen title of Skopec and Cassidy's (1976) clinical contribution to LeBow's (1976) text book of behavior therpay for nurses, "sometimes our plans go awry." Reasons for failure are not always to be found exclusively within the vagaries of the experimental design *per se*. Skopec and Cassidy separately describe two behavioral programs that failed. Each touches upon obstacles to success that only a close look at the specific situation by an observer intimately familiar with the complexities of the total setting could detect, let alone anticipate. Contributing factors can lie as much in our individual styles, as in subtle quirks of the situation which are beyond our control, as in the niceties of the experimental design, the nature of the disorder or even the patient himself.

In a thoughtful paper which discusses the use of criterion referenced measurement principles in the evaluation of behavior modification studies, Rosenfiield and Houtz (1976) define evaluation as the process of obtaining information on which to base decisions. In behavior modification studies, these decisions typically involve the type of behavior to be selected for modification, the types of procedures involved, where the modification is to be applied, the consequence of the modification to the individual and to the environment and so forth. Rosenfield and Houtz's concern is with the building of a model for the evaluation of behavior modification studies based on the relationships between the types of decisions made in such studies and the principles of criterion referenced measurement and instruction.

Criterion referenced measurement (Gronlund, 1973) shares several characteristics with behavior modification procedures: Both stress specification of objectives in behavioral terms; in both, the tasks used in evaluation should have a direct relationship to the procedures; and both require a system of storing and reporting of performance based on clearly and objectively defined tasks. Rosenfield and Houtz note three additional characteristics of criterion referenced measurement which have received little attention from behavior modifiers: the specification of a domain of relevant behaviors to be assessed; the specification of the standards of performance; and the sampling of the performance under representative conditions. It is these latter characteristics, so Rosenfield and Houtz believe, which provide information crucial to the types of decisions made by teachers or clinicians in behavior modification programs. More to the point, they propose—but do not test—a model whereby these strategies can be integrated into the development and evaluation of behavior modification programs.

Finally, for those whose interests are primarily practical, we draw attention once again to a useful introductory manual by Gelfand and Hartmann (1975) entitled: "Child Behavior: Analysis and Therapy." Their concluding chapter, geared towards the beginning clinician, spells out in detail how to assess the effects of treatment programs.

SINGLE-CASE EXPERIMENTAL DESIGNS AND THE PRACTITIONER

Behavior therapy has not only generated significantly *more* systematic outcome research than any other therapeutic approach (Shapiro's [1976a] peculiar reasoning notwithstanding), it has also resulted in the development of different research strategies for addressing the critical question of whether specific methods are effective (cf. Kazdin & Wilson, in press). One of the most valuable research strategies has been single-case experimental design, a methodology deriving from the operant conditioning emphasis on the single subject and its eschewal of statistical analyses of data. As noted at the onset of this Section, Hersen and Barlow's (1976) thorough review of this methodological approach will prove extremely useful to applied researchers. However, single-case experimental designs are often uncritically advocated and accepted where important limitations exist, and it is this point that we take up now.

The Limitations of Single-Case Experimental Designs

In the paper reprinted in Section II of this volume, Bandura presents a critical analysis of the limitations of single subject designs. The purpose here is not to repeat all of Bandura's criticisms but to focus on the issues of the generality of findings from single-case designs and their applicability to clinical practice (see Wilson, 1977c). The answer to the generality question that Hersen and Barlow propose is the replication of single-case experiments. The direct replication strategy tests the efficacy of a single method administered by the same therapist in the same setting on a particular problem with more than one client. If the treatment is demonstrably effective with all clients, the results are easily interpretable. Problems in interpretation arise, however, when the results are not that clear-cut. Sidman (1960) states that failure to replicate results with all subjects does not detract from the successes achieved in some subjects. However, as Bandura notes, there is a danger in attributing the successes to the manipulation of the reinforcement contingencies and dismissing replicative failures as due to the inadequate use of otherwise effective reinforcers. In these instances, it is possible that the observed changes in behavior are due to the influence of unobserved or uncontrolled factors that happened to covary with the treatment manipulation in the successful cases.

Hersen and Barlow summarize the problem of mixed replicative results as follows: "If one success is followed by two or three failures, then neither the reliability of the procedure nor the generality of the finding across clients has been established, and it is probably time to find out why. If two or three successes are mixed in with one or two failures, then the reliability of the procedure will be established to some extent, but the investigator must decide when to begin investigating reasons for lack of client generality" (p. 335). In trying to find out the reasons for the mixed results, the investigator faces the same difficulty encountered in group methodology. Like technique-oriented group studies, direct replication strategies require homogeneous clients. Yet this happy state of affairs seldom occurs. If the treatment is effective with all clients despite this heterogeneity, interpretation of the data is easy. But if the results are mixed, the investigator does not know whether the method is of limited utility or whether any one of a number of causes of interclient variability was responsible for the inconsistent treatment outcome.

Interpretation of single-case experimental designs is uncomplicated when the target behaviors are stable during pretreatment baseline assessment and target behaviors during treatment do not overlap with baseline performance. However, such clear-cut clinical effects are not always obtained. Most treatments are not that powerful when applied separately because clinical disorders are maintained by several interacting variables and hence not every determinant is controlled. Excessive variability of client behavior across different phases of the study makes it difficult to determine significant behavior change.

Excessive variability in treatment outcome is not uncommon in clinical practice. In the tradition of operant research, most single-subject designs have been used under highly controlled conditions (e.g., the classroom or a hospital ward). As they are extended to less controlled conditions in clients' natural environments, the variability in the data can be expected to increase, and less than dramatic changes in behavior can be anticipated. To disregard outcomes of this nature might be to overlook reliable effects that could have theoretical and/or clinical significance. Partly in response to problems of this nature, recent attention has been focused on the use of statistical analysis of single-case designs.

Even if the data from direct replications can be unambiguously interpreted, the problem of generalizing the results from the individual case to a more general population of clients remains. The solution proposed by Hersen and Barlow is *systematic replication*. Systematic replication is defined as the attempt to replicate the findings from direct replication studies, varying the therapists who administer the procedures, the type of clients, the nature of the target behavior, the setting in which treatment occurs, or any combination thereof. But there are difficulties with this strategy. The question is: When is a systematic replication series finished? Or put differently, when can the investigator decide that the generality of a finding has been scientifically established?

Single-subject methodology provides no guideline for answering this crucial question. Hersen and Barlow suggest that a systematic replication series is never over, that knowledge gained in this fashion is cumulative, and that investigators and treatment methods vary in terms of the relative amount of confidence therapists can place in them. But this involves subjective judgment, and it is clear that there are disagreements among therapists about what constitutes "relatively effective" treatment in this sense.

According to Hersen and Barlow, one of the major advantages of single-case experimental designs is that this approach "tends to merge the role of scientist and practitioner" (p. 356). Superficially, a closeness of the single-subject design to clinical practice may be seen. Unlike group outcome research with its statistical analyses of mean performance across subjects, single-subject methodology addresses the individual, who is also the practicing therapist's concern. Because of the focus on the individual subject, clinical problems that tend to be relatively rare or idiosyncratic can still be rigorously investigated. However, as Wilson (1977c) argues, the thesis that single-case experimental designs are the means of merging the roles of scientist and practitioner fares poorly under more critical scrutiny.

In fact, the ethical, practical, and methodological difficulties inherent in establishing cause-effect relationships using single-case experimental designs are not significantly fewer than in between-group outcome research. Professional ethics dictate that the client be fully informed as to whether he is participating in a research project or receiving therapy. The therapist's activities must be identified as one or the other. If it is therapy that the client is receiving, many of the critical requirements of single-case experimental designs are difficult, if not impossible, to meet. In essence, all single-case experimental designs necessitate baseline observations, holding certain conditions constant at different times, and intervening selectively in a limited manner at any one point. This clearly conflicts with the priority in any service delivery setting, which is to treat the client's problems in as effective and efficient manner as possible. The use of any reversal design is clearly unethical in this context. Clinically relevant change, produced at the least possible cost (in terms of time, effort, money, and emotional stress), is the goal of *clinical practice* (see Azrin, 1977). Identifying the determinants of behavior change is of little relevance to the therapist or the client in this setting. The latter is a *scientific* concern that need have no immediate bearing on the behavior of the practitioner.

In response to the foregoing view, it is often stated that practitioners are accountable and that their methods should be evaluated to ensure that they are effective. Single-case experimental designs are said to provide one means of conducting evaluation of this sort in the applied setting. However, this assertion confuses the function of scientific evaluation of behavior change methods with what the practitioner who applies these methods can and should do with respect to data gathering and treatment evaluation.

The ethical obstacles to conducting single-case experimental designs have already been noted. The practical problems involved are virtually insuperable. Consider some of the characteristics of single-subject methodology. One is the observation of overt behavior. Behavior is assessed directly either in the situation of interest or in simulated circumstances where the behavior is sampled under laboratory conditions. Daily observations of this nature are usually reported. Obviously, these methodological demands exceed the capabilities and resources of the practitioner.

It is clear that experience bears out the conclusion that adequate single case experimental designs are not to be the activities in which therapists engage. The plea has been made that therapy techniques other than those of behavior therapy be submitted to analysis in single-case experimental designs. Bergin and Strupp (1970) called for much the same policy in their advocacy of new directions in psychotherapy research. Yet the available evidence shows quite clearly that non-behavioral methods have not been evaluated in this fashion. The reason is that they are used preponderantly by practitioners, not scientists. Similarly, practicing behavior therapists have shown little interest in using single-case experimental designs. These designs are used by a limited number of experimentally-minded clinical investigators with a primary commitment to research. They tend to work in experimental-clinical settings that facilitate—even encourage—this type of applied research. An excellent example is the prolific group at the University of Mississippi Medical School whose applied research using single-subject methodology comprises a good portion of the material in the Hersen and Barlow book (1976). This group of talented, research oriented investigators can hardly be viewed as full-time or regular practitioners. It is interesting to note that one of the major advantages Hersen and Barlow see in single-case experimental designs is the facility with which they yield publishable data. This concern reveals the difference between this group of clinical researchers and practitioners in general. What practitioner would view publication of data as a major reason for using a particular method? In proposing (a) rapid publication and (b) the merging of the roles of the scientist and the practitioner as two of the major reasons for adopting single-case experimental designs, Hersen and Barlow are trying to have their cake and eat it too.

In short, single-case experimental studies, conducted properly according to strict methodological and ethical requirements, will virtually always be done as research. The foregoing in no way detracts from the usefulness of single-case experimental designs in the scientific analysis and evaluation of treatment methods. It does clarify when, how, and for what purpose such research might be best employed. In this sense, it is on a par with between-group methodology; in both instances, basic laboratory experiments will help identify the mechanisms of behavior change and thereby facilitate the development of more effective methods. These methods will then be applied by practitioners in the uncontrolled clinical setting, unencumbered by the numerous methodological constraints that make possible the identification of behavior change processes but which exist only in the experimental or laboratory setting.

SECTION IV: ASSESSMENT AND EVALUATION

6

TOWARD A TASK ANALYSIS OF ASSERTIVE BEHAVIOR

Robert M. Schwartz

Indiana University

and

John M. Gottman

University of Illinois

The present study analyzed the components of assertive behavior. Assertiveness problems were conceptualized in terms of a task analysis of the topography of competent responding. One hundred and one subjects who spanned the range of assertiveness, measured by McFall's Conflict Resolution Inventory, responded to three sets of situations requiring refusal of an unreasonable request. Content knowledge of an assertive response, delivery of the response under two conditions, heart rate, self-perceived tension, and the incidence of positive and negative self-statements were assessed. Differences on these variables between low-, moderate-, and high-assertive groups were analyzed to determine the nature of the response deficit in nonassertive subjects. Low-assertive subjects differed from moderate- and high-assertive subjects

---

Reprinted with permission from *Journal of Consulting and Clinical Psychology*, 44, 6, 910-920, 1976.

The authors wish to thank Pam Kegg, Robert Setty, Jacob Pankowski, Jim Miser, and Alex Braitman for their help in running subjects and collecting data; Richard McFall for providing materials for the present investigation; and Richard McFall and Donald Meichenbaum for providing helpful criticism of the article.

on a role-playing assessment requiring them to deliver an assertive response, but they did not differ from moderate- and high-assertive subjects on their knowledge of a competent response or on hypothetical delivery situations. No significant differences in heart rate were observed between low-, moderate- and high-assertive subjects; however, higher self-perceived tension was found in low- compared to moderate- and high-assertive subjects. The present behavior task analysis study is recommended as a clinical assessment study preliminary to investigations comparing behavior change interventions.

Response acquisition approaches to assertion training are based on a skill-deficit model. According to this view nonassertive subjects are people with specific limited capabilities in a specific set of social situations. This approach is best characterized by McFall and Twentyman (1973), who wrote that

> The therapeutic objective is to provide patients with direct training in precisely those skills in their response repertoires. Very little attention is given to eliminating existing maladaptive behaviors; instead, it is assumed that as skillful, adaptive responses are acquired, rehearsed, and reinforced, the previous maladaptive responses will be displaced and will disappear. (p. 199)

A basic question has remained unresolved in response acquisition approaches, namely, what is the specific nature of the deficit in nonassertive subjects? Component analyses of assertion training programs (e.g., McFall & Twentyman, 1973) provide one approach to this question. Presumably, if modeling does not add significantly to the treatment effect, then the response deficit could not have involved a lack of exposure to skillful models.

Although the component analysis approach is useful in creating efficient interventions, there are several problems with its potential theoretical contribution toward specifying the nature of the response deficit. A treatment component, if effective, may be totally unrelated to the nature of the problem it treats (Buchwald & Young, 1969). For example, although aspirin ameliorates headaches, headaches are not a result of an aspirin deficiency. Furthermore, treatment components rarely can claim to deal with only one deficit at a time. For example, an effective coaching component may simultaneously result in response shaping, confidence building, and cognitive restructuring.

It may seem in the negative case (e.g., the failure of models to enhance the training effect as shown in McFall and Twentyman, 1973) that some insight is gained about what the deficit is not. However, in the negative case, the information gained is provocative at best. For example, why does modeling fail to enhance the treatment program? Is it because nonassertive subjects have seen many models of assertive behavior in their day-to-day experience and that the information provided by the models is redundant? How does the information conveyed by models differ from that provided by coaching? Is it more inductive than deductive? Is it more sketchy? Or is the modeling component poorly designed? What specifically is the response deficit that would make modeling ineffective and coaching effective? Therefore, even in the negative case, a component analysis does not specify the response deficit with precision.

An alternative strategy for specifying the response deficits in nonassertive subjects is suggested by the research of Gagné (1969) in the design of a remedial mathematics program. Suppose that some fourth-grade children in a city were incompetent in long division. Tests of addition, subtraction, multiplication, and the knowledge of remainders could be given to both children who could and could not do long-division problems. The intervention program would depend on the specific performance discrepancy obtained from this "task analysis" study. Such a study begins by specifying the likely components of a competent response and then testing the extent to which performance on the components discriminates between competent and incompetent populations.

The purpose of the present investigation was to determine what components are necessary in order to perform a competent assertive response. The assertive response was defined to include measurable responses from the cognitive, physiological, and overt response classes. Low-assertive, moderate-assertive, and high-assertive subjects were compared to determine which components of assertive behavior differentiated between groups within the three response classes mentioned above. For the purpose of this study, the definition of assertive behavior has been limited to refusal behavior, that is, refusing an unreasonable request.*

The components assessed within the cognitive system included positive and negative self-statements, that is, innerstatements or thoughts that would make it easier or harder to deliver a convincing refusal. When

* In a pilot study with 60 undergraduates, a general assertion scale (Galassi, DeLo, Galassi, & Bastein, 1974) was administered with McFall and Lillesand's (1971) CRI. The correlation between the two scales was .72, so it is likely that the inability to refuse an unreasonable request is strongly related to general assertion problems.

confronted with unreasonable requests, it is possible that assertive people make self-statements that are adaptive in terms of their ability to refuse. The unreasonable request may also elicit self-statements in nonassertive subjects that focus on the fear of being disliked or on having a moral responsibility to help everyone regardless of the situation. Meichenbaum found that test-anxious clients (Meichenbaum, 1972), speech-anxious clients (Meichenbaum, 1971), and phobic clients (Meichenbaum, 1971) produce negative self-statements that are maladaptive in terms of the desired performance. In the present study, the cognitive self-statements as they relate to the assertion situations were assessed by the Assertiveness Self-Statement Test (ASST) devised for this study.

Within the physiological system, the component measured by the present investigation was heart rate. In treating nonassertive subjects, McFall and Marston (1970) found that behavior rehearsal resulted in a reduction in heart rate measured after McFall's Behavior Rehearsal Assertion Test (BRAT); control groups demonstrated an increase in heart rate. Since a reduction in heart rate appears to be an outcome of McFall's treatment program, it has been used as the physiological measure in the present study. In addition, subjects were asked to rate their self-perception of tension on a 7-point scale after performing assertive responses.

To separate knowledge of the content of a competent response from its delivery three sets of problematic situations that require an assertive response were administered to the subjects. To assess the content knowledge of the response, the Assertiveness Knowledge Inventory (AKI) was devised. This inventory presents unreasonable requests in written form and requires a written refusal response to determine whether the subject knows what an assertive response entails. It was assumed that the written nature of the task would minimize other possible response components (e.g., physiological arousal or negative self-statements) that might occur as the task approached reality. To assess the ability to deliver the response orally under limited circumstances, the Hypothetical Behavioral Role-Playing Assertion Test (HYPO) was devised. These situations were presented on audiotape and an oral response was required, but the subjects were told to imagine that they were only modeling a good assertive response to show a friend how to do it. The task assessed the ability to construct an assertive response and deliver it orally under hypothetical and "safe" circumstances. Again, an attempt was made to make the situation unrealistic to reduce possible responses from other classes that may be elicited by the real situation. Finally, a shortened form of the Behavioral Role-Playing Assertion Test (the Reduced Behavior Re-

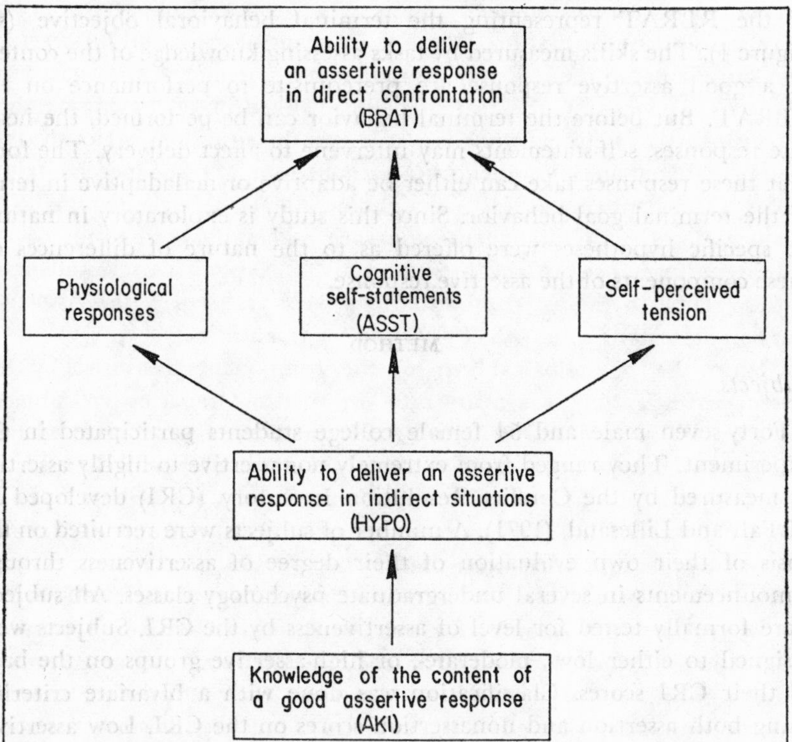

FIGURE 1. Hypothetical task analysis of the assertive response. (Boxes lower on the flowchart represent prerequisite behaviors of mediating process for competent performance.)

hearsal Assertion Test; RBRAT) was used to assess the content and delivery of the assertive response under circumstances that simulated reality as much as possible. Here subjects were told to imagine that they were being confronted with an unreasonable request and to respond orally as though they were actually talking to the person making the request. This task was designed to determine the subject's ability to construct and deliver an assertive response under circumstances that approximate real life.

These specific components of assertive behavior all appear to be relevant to successful performance. The relationship of these components can be conceptualized in a hierarchical task analysis, with performance of the RBRAT representing the terminal behavioral objective (see Figure 1). The skills measured by tasks assessing knowledge of the content of a good assertive response are prerequisite to performance on the RBRAT. But before the terminal behavior can be performed, the heart rate responses, self-statements may intervene to affect delivery. The form that these responses take can either be adaptive or maladaptive in terms of the terminal goal behavior. Since this study is exploratory in nature, no specific hypotheses were offered as to the nature of differences on these components of the assertive response.

METHOD

Subjects

Forty-seven male and 54 female college students participated in the experiment. They ranged from extremely nonassertive to highly assertive as measured by the Conflict Resolution Inventory (CRI) developed by McFall and Lillesand (1971). A number of subjects were recruited on the basis of their own evaluation of their degree of assertiveness through announcements in several undergraduate psychology classes. All subjects were formally tested for level of assertiveness by the CRI. Subjects were assigned to either low-, moderate-, or high-assertive groups on the basis of their CRI scores. Classification was done with a bivariate criterion using both assertion and nonassertion scores on the CRI. Low assertives had to earn an assertion score of 13 or less *and* a nonassertion score of 18 or more; moderate assertives had to earn an assertion score of between 10 and 20 *or* a nonassertion score of between 11 and 17; and high assertives had to earn an assertion score of 21 or more *and* a nonassertion score of 10 or less. There were 32 low assertives, 41 moderate assertives, and 28 high assertives, with approximately equal numbers of males and females in each group.

Procedure

Subjects were introduced to the experiment and told that the purpose was to find out more about how people react in situations requiring assertive behavior in order to develop a training program to help people who have a problem in this area.

While subjects filled out the CRI, their heart rate was recorded to obtain a base rate for later comparisons. They also indicated their level of tension on a 7-point scale to provide a base rate of self-perceived tension. After subjects were administered the CRI and randomly assigned to a counterbalancing order, they were presented with three sets of stimulus situations in which they were confronted with unreasonable requests. The three sets of situations were presented in counterbalanced order for all groups, and heart rate was again recorded before and during the first and last situations on the RBRAT. After responding to all the assertive situations, the ASST was administered to assess the positive and negative self-statements.

Dependent Measures

The subjects' written and tape-recorded responses on the AKI, HYPO, and RBRAT were rated independently by two "blind" judges using a 5-point scale from 1 (unqualified acceptance) to 5 (unqualified refusal; McFall & Twentyman, 1973). Rater intercorrelation on the AKI was .92, and a t test indicated that there was no difference between the two raters, $t(88) = .27$, $p = .79$. Rater intercorrelation on the HYPO was .56, and there was no difference between raters, $t(88) = .27$, $p = .79$. Rater intercorrelation on the BRAT was .90, and there was no difference between the two raters $t(88) = .39$, $p = .70$. Overall reliability (as measured by interrater correlation) on the three tasks was .79.

Heart Rate

Heart rate was measured using a spatially displaced finger plethysmograph that activated a photoelectric cell. It was placed on the ring finger of the nonwriting hand. A base rate was taken while the subject was filling out the CRI. Recordings were later made before and during the first and sixth RBRAT situations.

Self-perceived Tension

Subjects were asked to rate how nervous they felt on a scale from 1 to 7 (1 = not all nervous and 7 = extremely nervous). This measure was taken during the CRI as a base rate and immediately after the first and sixth RBRAT situations.

Cognitive Self-statements

Immediately after responding to all of the 18 assertive situations, the subject was given the ASST. This is a 34-item questionnaire with 17 positive self-statements that would make it easier to refuse the request and 17 negative self-statements that would make it harder to refuse. Examples of each are as follows:

Positive: I was thinking that it doesn't matter what the person thinks of me; I was thinking that I am perfectly free to say no; I was thinking that this request is an unreasonable one.

Negative: I was worried about what the other person would think about me if I refused: I was thinking that it is better to help others than to be self-centered; I was thinking that the other person might be hurt or insulted if I refused.

Subjects were asked to indicate on a scale from 1 to 5 how frequently these self-statements characterized their thoughts during the preceding assertive situations (1 = hardly ever and 5 = very often).

The ASST was consensually validated on an independent sample of 37 college students. Only those items that obtained a 90% agreement as to whether they were positive or negative in terms of facilitating or interfering with refusal behavior were used.

Subjects were also asked to respond to an item that asked them to indicate which of four sequences best characterized their thought process in terms of the order in which they made positive and negative self-statements. The sequences were as follows: Coping (— +), at first negative and later positive; unshaken doubt (— —), at first negative and later negative; unshaken confidence (+ +), at first positive and later still positive; giving up (+ —), at first positive and later negative. This was intended to assess whether subjects tended to sequence their positive and negative self-statements in different ways at different levels of assertiveness.

Problematic Situations

The situations were worded similar to the following: You have been standing in the ticket line at the movie theater for about 20 minutes. Just as you are getting close to the box office, three people who you know only slightly from your dorm come up to you and ask if you would let them cut in front of you.

All situations were taken from the CRI. Situations within each task were selected from the CRI to representatively sample refusal items with varying situational contexts, difficulty, and to whom the refusal was directed (to a close friend, friend, or acquaintance). The three tasks were sets of situations that differed in the following ways:

1. *For the AKI,* six situations were presented in written form, and the subjects were required to respond in writing with what they thought was a "model" refusal response. The AKI was designed to assess the subject's

content knowledge of a good assertive response. CRI items were 2, 14, 20, 24, 27, and 30.

2. *For the HYPO,* six situations were presented on tape. In responding to the situations orally, the subjects were told to imagine that a friend had given in to an unreasonable request because the friend did not know how to refuse. The subjects were asked to imagine that the friend wanted to know what to say at the time. The subject's response was tape recorded. CRI items were 4, 6, 10, 25, 31, and 35.

3. *For the RBRAT,* six situations were presented on tape in an attempt to create a simulation of a real situation. The subjects were told to imagine in as much detail as possible that they were being confronted by an unreasonable request. They were told to respond naturally as though they were actually talking to the person making the request. CRI items were 12, 16, 22, 29, 32, and 35.

Since all situations for the three inventories were taken from the CRI, it is important to ask whether the three inventories have similar psychometric properties. To answer this question an independent sample of 60 undergraduates took the CRI. Nonassertion scores were computed for the CRI. Also, the total number of items on which the subject said he or she would not refuse, and the total number of items on which the subject expressed discomfort were computed separately for the AKI, HYPO, and RBRAT. A principal components analysis found one large nonassertion factor that accounted for 54.30% of the variance. This factor had a high loading for CRI nonassertion (.85) and high loadings for AKI, HYPO, and RBRAT discomfort scores (.85, .65, and .79, respectively) but lower loadings for refusal scores on the AKI, HYPO, and RBRAT (.27, .50, and .50, respectively). Hence, discomfort scores were used to test whether assertion items of differential discomfort had been assigned to the three inventories. A repeated measures F test resulted in an F ratio of .70, $p > 50$, with refusal means of 2.30, 2.43, and 2.52, respectively, for the AKI, HYPO, and RBRAT. Therefore, it appears that the three inventories do, in fact, have similar psychometric properties.

RESULTS

Data were analyzed for each dependent variable using a 3×6 analysis of variance design with three groups (low, moderate, and high assertiveness) and six orders of administration of the AKI, HYPO, and RBRAT situations. There were no significant Groups × Order interactions. Results are presented separately for the order and groups main effects.

Order Effects

Significant order main effects were obtained for the knowledge of content (AKI) situations, $F(5, 83) = 2.90$, $p = .019$, and for the RBRAT situation, $F(5, 83) = 3.96$, $p = .003$. Subsequent tests using Tukey's honestly significant difference (HSD) test show that performance on the AKI was best for those subjects who received the AKI last; that is, after the HYPO and BRAT, Tukey's HSD = 3.98, obtained difference (83) = 4.38, $p < .05$. Performance on the RBRAT was best for those subjects who received the RBRAT last (i.e., after responding on both the AKI and the HYPO), Tukey's HSD = 4.93, obtained difference (83) = 6.44, $p < .05$.

Group Differences

The main effects for the assertiveness independent variable were as follows:

Knowledge of content (AKI). No significant differences were obtained between low-, moderate-, and high-assertive groups on the AKI, $F(2, 83) = 2.17$, $p = .19$.

Indirect delivery (HYPO). No significant differences between low-, moderate-, or high-assertive groups were obtained on the HYPO situation, $F(2, 83) = .44$, $p = .65$.

Direct delivery (RBRAT). Groups did differ significantly on the RBRAT, $F(2, 83) = 8.26$, $p = .008$. Using the Tukey HSD, all pairwise comparisons among the means on the RBRAT were made. Only the high- and low-assertive groups differed significantly, Tukey's HSD = 3.99, obtained difference = 5.38, $p < .01$.

Heart rate. Pulse was recorded first as a baseline and then before and during RBRAT Situations 1 and 6. No significant differences were obtained for base pulse, $F(2, 83) = 1.34$, $p = .27$, RBRAT 1 before pulse, $F(2, 83) = .28$, $p = .76$, RBRAT 1 during pulse, $F(2, 83) = .55$, $p = .58$, RBRAT 6 before pulse, $F(2, 83) = .42$, $p = .66$, or RBRAT 6 during pulse, $F(2, 83) = .65$, $p = .53$.

To investigate the trials effect, a one-way repeated measures analysis of variance was performed. All groups showed significant changes over trials—for low assertives, $F(4, 124) = 5.98$, $p < .001$; for moderate assertives, $F(4, 160) = 6.13$, $p < .001$; and for high assertives, $F(4, 108)$

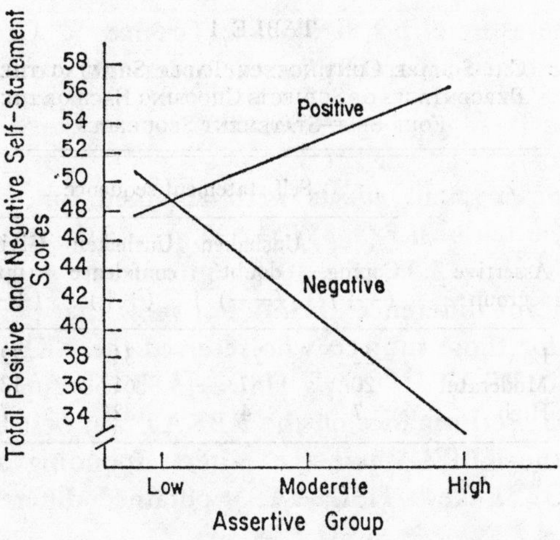

FIGURE 2. Positive and negative self-statement scores as measured by the ASST (85 = highest possible score).

= 5.18, p = .001. For each group, pairwise comparisons among trial means were performed to determine which changes over trials contributed to the significance. No groups differed from CRI base heart rate to before RBRAT 1, indicating that the pulse reading was reliable. Even though all groups increased their heart rate from before RBRAT 1 to during RBRAT 1, only the low-assertive group demonstrated a significant increase, HSD = 4.31, obtained difference (60) = 4.88, df = 60, $p < .01$. By RBRAT situation 6, no group increased their heart rate significantly from before to during the situation. For low assertive, HSD = 4.31, obtained difference (60) = 3.38, $p > .05$; for moderate assertive, HSD = 3.87, obtained difference (60) = 2.37, $p > .05$; for high assertive, HSD = 4.97, obtained difference (60) = .71, $p > .05$. Therefore, whatever differences in heart rate increases may have existed between low-, moderate-, and high-assertive subjects on Situation 1, these differences no longer existed by Situation 6.

Self-perceived tension. Low-assertive subjects consistently reported themselves to be more nervous than high assertives, with moderate assertives falling midway between. This was true for base tension, $F(2, 83) = 6.57$, p = .003, post-RBRAT 1 tension, $F(2, 83) = 5.38$, p = .007, and for post-RBRAT 6 tension, $F(2, 83) = 5.51$, p = .006. Using a one-way analysis of variance of average tension on RBRAT Situations 1 and

TABLE 1

CHI-SQUARE CONTINGENCY TABLE SHOWING THE PERCENTAGES OF SUBJECTS CHOOSING EACH OF THE FOUR SELF-STATEMENT SEQUENCES

	Self-statement sequence			
Assertive group	Coping (−+)	Unshaken doubt (−−)	Unshaken confidence (++)	Giving up (+−)
Low	22	22	34	22
Moderate	20	7	61	12
High	7	4	82	7

6 combined, groups again differed significantly, $F(2, 98) = 6.05$, $p < .01$. Using the Tukey HSD test, it was found that low- and moderate-assertive subjects differed in self-perceived tension, HSD = .91, obtained difference (60) = 1.06, $p < .05$; low- and high-assertive subjects also differed, HSD = 1.15, obtained difference (60) = 1.28, $p < .01$. The moderate- and high-assertive subjects, however, did not differ significantly on self-perceived tensions, HSD = .91, obtained difference (60) = .22, $p > .05$. Three repeated measures analyses of variance were performed to assess the trials effect. All three groups of subjects reported less tension on RBRAT Situation 6 than on RBRAT Situation 1: For low assertives, $F(1, 31) = 6.00$, $p = .019$; for moderate assertives, $F(1, 40) = 4.42$, $p = .039$; and for high assertives, $F(1, 27) = 5.29$, $p = .028$.

Cognitive self-statements (*ASST*). Significant differences were found between low-, moderate-, and high-assertive subjects on positive self-statements, $F(2, 83) = 6.53$, $p = .003$. Even stronger differences were found on negative self-statements, $F(2, 83) = 36.25$, $p = .00001$ (see Figure 2). High-assertive subjects had more positive and fewer negative self-statements than low-assertive subjects; moderate-assertive subjects fell midway between.* The Tukey HSD test indicated that only the low- and high-assertive groups differed significantly on positive self-statements, HSD = 6.41, obtained difference (60) = 7.99, $p < .01$. On negative self-statements, however, all groups differed significantly as

* The self-statements that distinguished low and high assertives the most tended to fall into the following categories: (a) concern about negative self-image and fear of being disliked and (b) other-directed versus self-directed—concern for the other person's position, feelings, and needs.

shown by the following pairwise comparisons among the groups—for low- and moderate-assertive groups, HSD = 5.63, obtained difference (60) = 8.08, $p < .01$; for moderate-and high-assertive groups, HSD = 5.63, obtained difference (60) = 7.81, $p < .01$; for low- and high-assertive groups, HSD = 5.63, obtained difference (60) = 15.89, $p < 0.1$.

To test for an interaction between groups and self-statements, a repeated measures analysis of variance was performed with two levels of self-statements (positive and negative). A significant interaction was obtained, $F(2, 98) = 29.82$, $p < .0001$.

To investigate differences between positive and negative self-statements within groups, a t test for matched samples was performed. The low-assertive group had more negative than positive self-statements, but this difference was not significant, $F(1, 31) = 1.77$, $p = .190$. On the other hand, the moderate group had significantly more positive than negative self-statements, $F(1, 40) = 24.65$, $p = .001$. The high-assertive group also had significantly more positive than negative self-statements, $F(1, 27) = 66.51$, $p < .0001$.

To investigate whether the assertive groups differed in the way they sequenced positive and negative self-statements, a chi-square contingency table test was performed and found to be significant, $\chi^2(6) = 16.01$, $p = .025$. A greater percentage of the high-assertive subjects checked the item characterized by "unshaken confidence" (++) than the low-assertive subjects, with the moderate subjects falling midway in between (see Table 1). Within the low-assertive group, there were individual differences in the sequence of positive and negative self-statements, with no preference shown for any of the sequences (excluding unshaken confidence). In fact, the alternative sequences were chosen by equal (22%) percentages of low-assertive subjects. Those in the moderate group not characterized by "unshaken confidence" did show a preference for the coping sequence (—+), with 20% choosing this sequence.

In addition to the assertive and nonassertive scores on the CRI, McFall and Lillesand (1971) calculated the difference between the assertive and nonassertive scores. Difference scores in the present investigation ranged from a low of —24 to a high of 34. In an attempt to gain greater descriptive and predictive precision, a polynomial regression was performed for positive and negative self-statements on assertiveness. The relationship between assertiveness and both positive and negative self-statements was best described by a linear function; for positive self-statements, $F(1, 97) = 63.1$, $p < .01$. Neither the quadratic nor the cubic terms were significant (see Figures 3 and 4).

DISCUSSION

Items selected from the CRI to form the AKI, HYPO, and RBRAT did not differ significantly on perceived discomfort. Discomfort scores loaded highly on the CRI nonassertion factor. The three tests thus have similar psychometric properties, and the absence of between-group differences on the AKI and HYPO and their presence on the RBRAT have important implications in describing the nature of the response deficit in nonassertive subjects.

Nonassertive subjects did not differ from highly assertive subjects in their ability to construct a written assertive response (AKI) or to verbally deliver the assertive response in hypothetical, and therefore safe, situations (HYPO). Although results on the HYPO must be interpreted with caution because of reduced interrater reliabilities, the finding of no group differences on both the HYPO and AKI indicates that perhaps low-assertive subjects do not suffer from a content knowledge deficiency or from an inability to deliver an assertive response, in the sense of merely knowing (formulating and articulating) the response. Nonassertive subjects do, however, lack the ability to perform these components of the task when confronted with a situation more similar to the real stimulus situation.

Since the population of the present investigation was similar to that of McFall and his associates, perhaps the effective components of coaching and rehearsal do not involve teaching the content of a good assertive response or the method of delivering it as narrowly defined above. Instead, the coaching and rehearsal component may focus on those dimensions of delivery skill that are involved in real-life situations. This raises the question of exactly which dimensions of delivery skill are necessary for competent assertive behavior in real life and what specifically was operating in the treatment program used by McFall and his colleagues. Order effects obtained on the RBRAT and AKI suggest that the assessment procedure was itself an intervention that enhanced the performance of all subjects on the RBRAT when the RBRAT followed the AKI and HYPO, and on the AKI when the AKI followed the RBRAT and HYPO. This suggests that mere practice in responding may be beneficial without coaching or rehearsal.

The present study suggests that physiological differences do not exist between low-, moderate-, and high-assertive groups. This may partially account for the results of an experiment comparing desensitization with assertion training. Bouffard (1973), in a 2 × 2 factorial design, studied

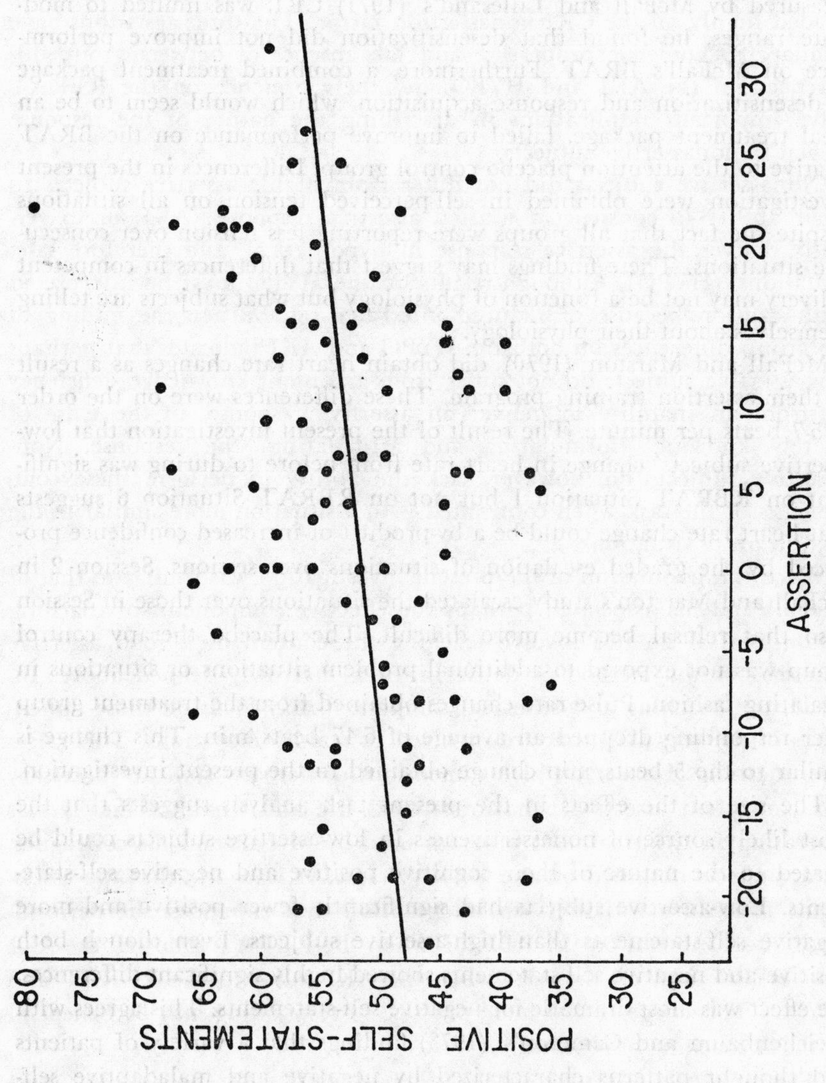

FIGURE 3. Polynomial regression of negative self-statements on CRI assertion difference score.

the relative effectiveness of group desensitization, group response acquisition training, and the combined procedures compared to an attention placebo control group. Although Bouffard's range of assertiveness, as measured by McFall and Lillesand's (1971) CRI, was limited to moderate ranges, he found that desensitization did not improve performance on McFall's BRAT. Furthermore, a combined treatment package of desensitization and response acquisition, which would seem to be an ideal treatment package, failed to improve performance on the BRAT relative to the attention placebo control group. Differences in the present investigation were obtained in self-perceived tension on all situations despite the fact that all groups were reporting less tension over consecutive situations. These findings may suggest that differences in competent delivery may not be a function of physiology but what subjects are telling themselves about their physiology.

McFall and Marston (1970) did obtain heart rate changes as a result of their assertion training program. These differences were on the order of 5-7 beats per minute. The result of the present investigation that low-assertive subjects' change in heart rate from before to during was significant on RBRAT Situation 1 but not on RBRAT Situation 6 suggests that heart rate change could be a by-product of increased confidence produced by the graded escalation of situations over sessions. Session 2 in McFall and Marston's study escalated the situations over those in Session 1 so that refusal became more difficult. The placebo therapy control group was not exposed to additional problem situations or situations in escalating fashion. Pulse rate changes obtained from the treatment group after responding dropped an average of 6.47 beats/min. This change is similar to the 5 beats/min change obtained in the present investigation.

The size of the effects in the present task analysis suggests that the most likely source of nonassertiveness in low-assertive subjects could be related to the nature of their cognitive positive and negative self-statements. Low-assertive subjects had significantly fewer positive and more negative self-statements than high-assertive subjects. Even though both positive and negative self-statements showed highly significant differences, the effect was most dramatic for negative self-statements. This agrees with Meichenbaum and Cameron's (1973) findings that a variety of patients had thought patterns characterized by negative and maladaptive self-statements. It is worth noting that not one low-assertive subject in the present investigation had cognitive self-statement scores that were similar to those to the high-assertive group. This demonstrates an extremely

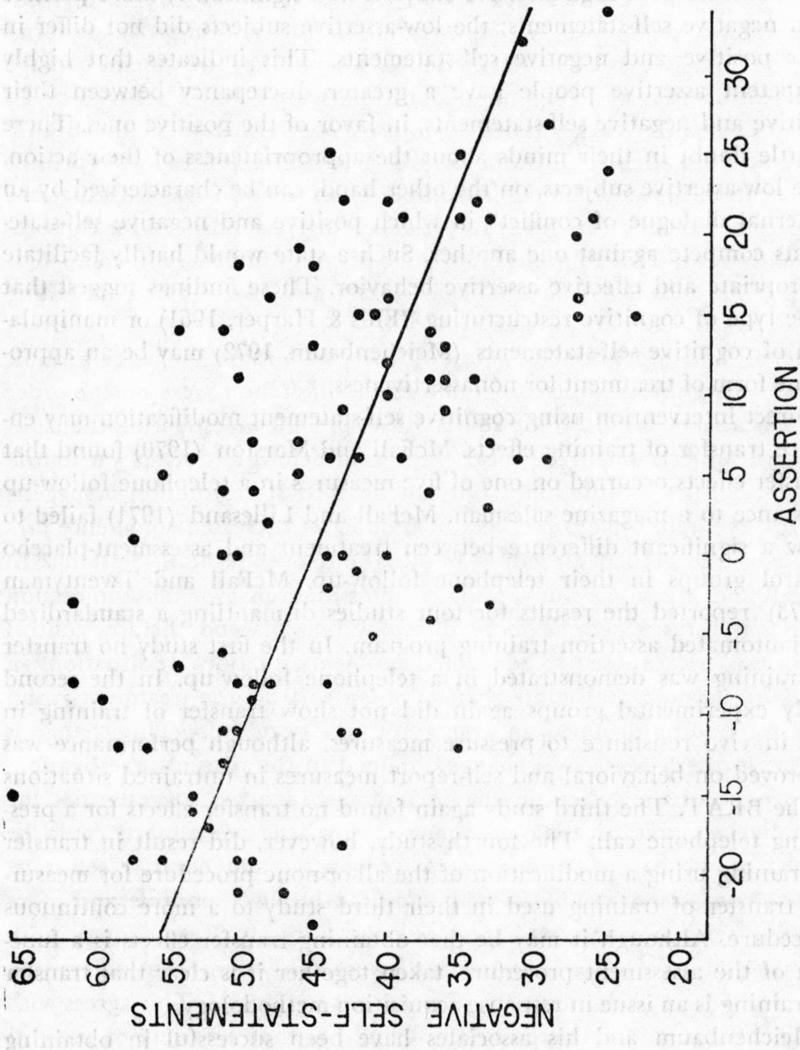

FIGURE 4. Polynomial regression of positive self-statements on CRI assertion difference score.

strong and consistent group difference that was not spuriously produced by averaging the data.

Comparing positive and negative self-statements within the groups, the moderate- and high-assertive subjects had significantly more positive than negative self-statements; the low-assertive subjects did not differ in their positive and negative self-statements. This indicates that highly competent assertive people have a greater discrepancy between their positive and negative self-statements, in favor of the positive ones. There is little doubt in their minds about the appropriateness of their action. The low-assertive subjects, on the other hand, can be characterized by an "internal dialogue of conflict" in which positive and negative self-statements compete against one another. Such a state would hardly facilitate appropriate and effective assertive behavior. These findings suggest that some type of cognitive restructuring (Ellis & Harper, 1961) or manipulation of cognitive self-statements (Meichenbaum, 1972) may be an appropriate form of treatment for nonassertiveness.

Direct intervention using cognitive self-statement modification may enhance transfer of training effects. McFall and Marston (1970) found that transfer effects occurred on one of five measures in a telephone follow-up resistance to a magazine salesman. McFall and Lillesand (1971) failed to show a significant difference between treatment and assessment-placebo control groups in their telephone follow-up. McFall and Twentyman (1973) reported the results for four studies dismantling a standardized semiautomated assertion training program. In the first study no transfer of training was demonstrated in a telephone follow-up. In the second study experimental groups again did not show transfer of training in two in vivo resistance to pressure measures, although performance was improved on behavioral and self-report measures in untrained situations of the BRAT. The third study again found no transfer effects for a pressuring telephone call. The fourth study, however, did result in transfer of training using a modification of the all-or-none procedure for measuring transfer of training used in their third study to a more continuous procedure. Although it may be that obtaining transfer effects is a function of the assessment procedure, taken together it is clear that transfer of training is an issue in response-acquisition methodology.

Meichenbaum and his associates have been successful in obtaining transfer effects using a coping self-statement intervention with hospitalized schizophrenics (Meichenbaum & Cameron, 1973), speech-anxious subjects (Meichenbaum, Gilmore, & Fedoravicius, 1971), and test anxiety (Meichenbaum, 1972). Glass, Gottman, and Shmurak (1976) collaborated in a study of the relative effectiveness of coaching and rehearsal versus cognitive self-statement modification in a dating skills program for girl-shy college males. They found that the greatest transfer effects to untrained laboratory role-playing situations, and ratings made by females the subjects called for a date, were obtained by the cognitive self-statement intervention. These findings are consistent with the current task analysis study and suggest that transfer of training effects may be enhanced with a cognitive self-statement assertion training intervention.

REFERENCES

BOUFFARD, D. L. *A Comparison of Response Acquisition and Desensitization Approaches to Assertion Training.* Unpublished doctoral dissertation, Indiana University, 1973.

BUCHWALD, A. M., & YOUNG, R. D. Some comments on the foundations of behavior therapy. In C. M. Franks (Ed.), *Behavior Therapy: Appraisal and Status.* New York: McGraw-Hill, 1969.

ELLIS, A., & HARPER, R. A. *A Guide to Rational Living.* Englewood Cliffs, N.J.: Prentice-Hall, 1961.

GAGNE, P. M. Curriculum research and the promotion of learning. In R. E. Stake (Ed.), *AERA Curriculum Monograph Series No. 1.* Chicago: Rand McNally, 1967.

GALASSI, J. P., DELO, J. S., GALASSI, M. D., & BASTEIN, S. The college self-expression scale: A measure of assertiveness. *Behavior Therapy,* 5:165-171, 1974.

GLASS, C. R., GOTTMAN, J. M., & SHMURAK, S. H. Response acquisition and cognitive self-statement modification approaches to dating skills. *Journal of Counseling Psychology,* 23:520-526, 1976.

MCFALL, R. M., & LILLESAND, D. B. Behavior rehearsal with modeling and coaching in assertion training. *Journal of Abnormal Psychology,* 77:313-323, 1971.

MCFALL, R. M., & MARSTON, A. R. An experimental investigation of behavior rehearsal in assertive training. *Journal of Abnormal Psychology,* 76:295-303, 1970.

MCFALL, R. M., & TWENTYMAN, C. T. Four experiments on the relative contribution of rehearsal, modeling, and coaching to assertion training. *Journal of Abnormal Psychology,* 81:199-218, 1973.

MEICHENBAUM, D. H., Examination of model characteristics in reducing avoidance behavior. *Journal of Personality and Social Psychology,* 17:298-307, 1971.

MEICHENBAUM, D. H. Cognitive modification of test-anxious college students. *Journal of Consulting and Clinical Psychology,* 39:370-380, 1972.

MEICHENBAUM, D. H., & CAMERON, R. Training schizophrenics to talk to themselves: A means of developing attentional controls. *Behavior Therapy,* 4:515-534, 1973.

MEICHENBAUM, D. H., GILMORE, J. B., & FEDORAVICIUS, A. Group insight versus group desensitization in treating speech anxiety. *Journal of Consulting and Clinical Psychology,* 36:410-421, 1971.

SECTION IV: ASSESSMENT AND EVALUATION

7

DEVELOPMENT AND FACTOR ANALYSIS OF A SOCIAL ANXIETY INVENTORY

Frank C. Richardson

University of Texas at Austin

and

Donald L. Tasto

Stanford Research Institute

A social anxiety inventory composed of 166 items drawn from hierarchies and lists of items used in the treatment of social anxiety by behavior therapists across the United States was constructed and factor analyzed. The method of factor analysis involved a rotation to an orthogonal structure producing seven conceptually clear factors accounting for 43% of the variance. The factors were named as follows: (1) fear of disapproval or criticism by others, (2) fear of social assertiveness and visibility, (3) fear of confrontation and anger-expression, (4) fear of heterosexual contact, (5) fear of intimacy and interpersonal warmth, (6) fear of conflict with or rejection by parents, and (7) fear of interpersonal loss. A revised 100-item scale built around a core of items correlating highly with these factors was briefly described, and possible uses for the scale in behavioral research, assessment, and therapy were discussed.

In recent years, a number of general Fear Survey Schedules and specific fear questionnaires have been developed and refined for the purposes of behavior therapy assessment and research. Tasto, Hickson, and Rubin (1973) have standardized and scaled the 122-item Fear Survey Schedule to provide normative data for use by both researchers and psychotherapists. Psychometric data have been reported for specific fear questionnaires dealing with fears of snakes, spiders, mutilation, and public speaking (Klorman, Weerts, Hastings, Melamed, & Lang, 1974), test anxiety (Suinn, 1969), and mathematics anxiety (Richardson & Suinn, 1973) intended to promote comparability of assessment of fears and changes in them due to treatment by different researchers. All of these self-report inventories are designed to tap the verbal-cognitive component of anxiety or fear reactions to specific stimulus events or situations. This paper describes the development and factor analysis of an inventory designed to assess this component of fear reactions to situations and events in the domain of social relationships.

Inadequate or distressful social relationships are widely regarded as either the substance or a primary cause of many forms of psychopathology. Lazarus (1971) has stressed that psychotherapy involves the "unlearning or relearning of basic interpersonal as well as situational sources of anxiety (p. 15). From a social learning perspective fear reactions to social or interpersonal situations may: (1) represent relatively automatic emotional reactions conditioned to social stimuli based upon prior (unpleasant or traumatic) experience; (2) be viewed as negative states of arousal that are actively self-generated by irrational thinking or panicky thoughts and images (Bandura, 1971; Meichenbaum, 1974); or (3) be considered negative emotional byproducts of ineffective behavior, covert and motor, that fails to successfully cope with the demands of the environment and secure rewards from it (Goldfried & D'Zurilla, 1969). Depending upon the individual case, the fear reaction itself, irrational thinking, ineffective interpersonal behavior, or some combination of these may form the target for treatment. The present inventory was designed to permit persons to report, across a wide variety of social situations, the experienced fear or anxiety that is often associated with disturbed social relationships.

Watson and Friend (1969) have developed scales to measure two different aspects of "social-evaluative anxiety," the Social Avoidance and Distress (SAD) scale and Fear of Negative Evaluation (FNE) scale. The SAD scale has proved useful as a measure of individual differences in general or trait social anxiety in several social-psychological (Byrne,

1971) and therapy outcome (Meichenbaum, Gilmore, & Fedoravicius, 1971) studies. For many persons, however, social anxiety reactions may be situation specific (Mischel, 1968, 1973), and Watson and Friend (1969) acknowledge that "The potential item universe from which items were selected for the FNE and SAD was intended to be all social situations, though only a few situations were unsystematically sampled by the items actually chosen." The present scale samples social or interpersonal situations more broadly and systematically. Such a scale eventually might both provide a valid measure of general social anxiety and permit identification of more specific social stimuli that elicit fear reactions in different individuals.

CONSTRUCTION OF THE INVENTORY

About two-thirds of the 166 items finally included in the present form of the inventory are brief, single phrase or sentence descriptions of social situations or events taken from hierarchies of items used in the treatment of social anxiety problems by behavior therapists across the United States. In the fall of 1970, we wrote each member or affiliate listed in the Membership Directory of the Association for Advancement of Behavior Therapy and published a note in *Behavior Therapy* requesting copies of such hierarchies or lists of items used in the treatment of social or interpersonal anxieties, construed very broadly, by any form of behavior therapy. Over 90 separate hierarchies used in systematic desensitization or assertive training or related treatment procedures, along with various other kinds of training and treatment materials, were contributed. About half concern assertiveness towards peers or parents, dealing with criticism, public speaking, heterosexual activities, or being in crowds or public places.

The remainder came from an additional pool of possible items generated from a variety of sources. These included other social anxiety scales and fear surveys, some of the literature on social anxiety, traditional personality theories, and the authors' clinical experience. Most of the items finally chosen refer to overt social happenings, such as social situations or the interpersonal acts of oneself or others. A few refer to feelings or thoughts in a social situation, such as "Feeling very angry towards your parents." The final 166 items were chosen to represent a wide variety of the kinds of social situations or interpersonal events that do not usually involve objective danger or harm, but commonly elicit a great deal of anxiety or fear.

Method

The inventory, entitled the *Social Reaction Inventory,* was administered to 155 male and 240 female undergraduates at two large state universities. Subjects wre asked to rate on a five-point Likert scale how much anxiety they currently felt in the situations described by the inventory's 166 items. A rating of "1" for an item indicated "Not at all," a rating of "2" indicated "A little," "3" indicated "A fair amount," "4" indicated "Much," and "5" indicated "Very much." Directions for completing the inventory included the following:

> Please indicate for each item how much *anxiety* or related feelings each situation causes you. It is important to distinguish between feelings of anxiety or fearfulness and other kinds of strong emotional reactions. For example, a number of the items refer to situations that may make you feel *angry,* but not anxious at all. Then you should indicate that you feel no anxiety. Of course, some situations may make you feel both angry and anxious—then you should respond just in terms of the anxious part of your feelings. Very often feelings that we would naturally describe with the words "disturbed," "unpleasant," or "upset" are closely related to anxiety and fearfulness. Usually, you should treat these feelings as part of anxiety and respond to each item in terms of how much *anxiety* or disturbance it causes you to feel.

Means, standard deviations, and various distribution statistics were calculated for subjects' responses to each item and for their total scores on the scale. Factor analysis was utilized to determine whether and which social stimuli cluster together in their capacity to evoke anxiety in this population. Subjects' scores on the items were first intercorrelated using the product-moment method. The resulting matrix of intercorrelations was factored using the method of principal axes. Twenty factors, accounting for 57% of the total variance, were rotated using the verimax method.

RESULTS

Subjects' mean scores on each of the items ranged from 1.43 to 4.07, while item standard deviations ranged from 0.79 to 1.55. The mean of the 166 mean item scores was 2.75.

For almost all items, the distribution of subjects' scores for that item was platykurtic, with statistically significant kurtosis coefficients in most cases. About three-fourths of the item score distributions were positively

TABLE 1

Items, Means, and Standard Deviations of the 10 Social Anxiety Inventory Items with the Highest Item Means

Item	Mean	*SD*	Item—factor correlations
Thoughts of losing a girl/boyfriend or spouse	4.07	1.28	.40 VII
Being told that something you said or did made someone very unhappy, upset, or sick	3.93	1.03	.27 I; .23 VI
The thought of forgetting or failing to perform some important responsibility	3.87	1.00	.30 III; .29 I
Your mother says something to the effect: "You don't really love me"	3.76	1.28	.68 VI
Watching an argument between members of your family	3.62	1.10	.41 VI
Your father says something to the effect: "You don't really love me"	3.55	1.36	.70 VI
Thoughts about possibly having offended someone or hurt their feelings	3.54	.98	.30 I
Saying goodbye to good friends or family whom you may not see for a long time	3.54	1.32	.30 VI
A friend accuses you of taking advantage of or "using" him/her	3.49	1.09	.37 I
Giving a speech before a group of relative strangers	3.47	1.21	.67 II

TABLE 2

Percentage and Cumulative Percentage of the Total Variance Represented by the First Seven Factors

Factor	Percentage	Cumulative percentage
I	27.566	27.566
II	4.692	32.258
III	2.745	35.003
IV	2.240	37.243
V	2.086	39.239
VI	1.793	41.122
VII	1.484	42.606

skewed, most significantly so. There was a strong tendency for the distributions of scores on items with very high item means to be negatively skewed. The distribution of subjects' total scores was platykurtic and positively skewed.

Several of the 10 highest mean items (Table 1) did not correlate highly with any of the major factors derived in the factor analysis, perhaps indicating that they do not reflect social anxiety. But it may be of interest to note what kinds of situations in the inventory evoke the most fear from college students.

Seven conceptually clear factors emerged from the factor analysis, accounting for 42.606% of the variance (Table 2).

For factors I, II, and III the eight or nine items, with their factor loadings, that correlate most highly with that factor are presented, followed (below the dotted line) by several additional items that seem to clarify the scope and meaning of the factor (Table 3). For the remaining four factors all the items, with their factor loadings, that correlate .35 or above with the factors are presented. Two additional items on factor V and two on factor VII correlated between .27 and .34 with those factors. The items are included because they appear to be conceptually related to the factors and suggest additional items for a revised scale.

Factor I appears to be defined by fears relating to *disapproval or criticism* by others. This factor accounts for the largest percentage of the variance and may represent the most common type of social anxiety. The items suggest a widely generalized fear of criticism or disapproval from others.

Factor II seems to reflect fears of *social assertiveness and visibility.* Its items refer to a variety of social situations involving assertiveness in the form of initiating an interaction, expressing one's beliefs or opinions, or standing up for one's rights, or else to being in situations of social visibility or responsibility that may, presumably, call for assertiveness.

Factor III is composed of items focusing on *confrontation and anger-expression.* These items refer to very specific situations involving feeling angry towards others or angrily confronting them. These functionally important behaviors are often thought of as part of social assertiveness, but none of the items listed in Table 3 loaded heavily on both factors II and III.

Factor IV clearly relates to fears of *heterosexual contact.* Two intriguing items refer to fears of being liked by a member of the opposite sex or doing something impulsively in a social context which may lead to such contact.

Factor V is composed of items that appear to deal with *intimacy and interpersonal warmth.* Only a few items in this version of the scale touched on this theme, but it may represent an important dimension of social anxiety.

Factor VI refers clearly to fears of *conflict with or rejection by parents.* Generally, the mean scores on these items, in this college population, were quite high.

TABLE 3

Social Anxiety Inventory Items and Factor Loadings Representing the First Seven Factors

Item	Factor loading
FACTOR I	
Someone calls something you have said or done "stupid"	.68
Someone acts as if they dislike you	.66
Being "put down" or ridiculed	.63
Someone acts as if you have hurt their feelings	.61
Someone says, "You could have done better"	.61
You say hello to someone you are acquainted with and they appear to ignore you	.61
You are friendly to someone and they give you the cold shoulder	.60
You buy a present for someone and they indicate that they don't like it	.59
....	
A person in authority (teacher, supervisor, parent) acts as if they disapprove of you	.56
In a discussion you raise a question and it is ignored by the group	.53
You remind someone to do something and they act mad at you	.50
Worrying about whether or not you are dressed properly for a social occasion	.49
Feelings of inferiority and inadequacy as compared with other people you are with	.46
Several people are talking about a social event to which you might have been invited, but were not	.42
Someone says that they like your brother or sister better than you for some reason	.41
FACTOR II	
Giving a speech before a group of relative strangers	.67
Being interviewed for a job	.67
Expressing a controversial opinion in a group or meeting	.65
Attending a fairly large party at which you are expected to take an active part in the conversation	.65
Being asked to be the leader in a group or meeting	.64
Talking with someone you would like to impress	.63
Speaking to someone in authority	.63
You approach a member of the opposite sex at a party and say something like: "If you're not busy, why don't you sit down and talk for a minute?"	.63
Being expected to explain your part of a job to a visitor whom the boss wants to impress	.61
....	
Feeling like you are the center of attention	.53
Starting up a conversation with a stranger on a train or plane	.52
Several friends ask you to make an important decision	.49
Telling a parent or supervisor that they are being interfering and will have to give you more freedom	.41
FACTOR III	
Telling a job associate that you are angry with him (her)	.59
You angrily tell off a waitress who has been impolite and incompetent	.54
You angrily confront a friend who has broken a promise and inconvenienced you	.49

TABLE 3 (*continued*)

Item	Factor loading
You angrily tell an interfering friend to "mind his/her own business"	.48
Someone you are out with is embarrassing you by his/her behavior. You feel compelled to say something about it	.45
You have to decide between two people for a job whose qualifications are equal	.44
Someone says, "You are getting too angry," or "Control yourself"	.43
You know that someone is lying to you, and you have to confront them	.41
....	
Telling someone they have hurt your feelings	.38
You tell a person they have hurt your feelings	.38
FACTOR IV	
Being caressed all over by a member of the opposite sex. You are both nude	.86
Caressing a member of the opposite sex all over. You are both nude	.82
Engaging in complete sexual intercourse with a member of the opposite sex	.76
Necking and making out heavily, fully clothed, with a member of the opposite sex to whom you are attracted	.75
A member of the opposite sex (not a spouse) you are getting to know indicates he or she would like to have sexual intercourse with you	.61
Dancing with and embracing someone of the opposite sex, fully clothed	.55
Someone acts as if he or she likes you a lot on short acquaintance	.42
Doing something social impulsively, on the spur of the moment	.32
FACTOR V	
A friend tells you he/she is very depressed and wants to talk over some problems with you	.68
Someone askes you for advice about an important personal problem of theirs	.63
Warmly complimenting a co-worker on a job	.47
Someone acts as if he or she likes you a lot on short acquaintance	.33
Asking for advice about a problem	.27
FACTOR VI	
Your father says something to the effect: "You don't really love me"	.70
Your mother says something to the effect: "You don't really love me"	.68
One of your parents implies that you are neglecting them and acts hurt	.67
Your mother or father acts cold towards you.	.65
Your father gets mad at you and criticizes you angrily	.64
Your mother or father acts cold towards you	.65
Feeling very angry towards your parents	.46
Watching an argument between members of your family	41
FACTOR VII	
At a party your date/spouse strikes up a warm and friendly conversation with a member of the opposite sex	.67
Your date/spouse keeps staring at some other person of the opposite sex who seems quite attractive	.63
Thoughts of losing a girl/boyfriend or spouse	.40
Your spouse or girl/boyfriend praises another person who is more successful in some way than you are	.39
You hold up your hand to say something in a class or meeting and are ignored by the teacher or leader	.34
Being concerned that someone will hurt your feelings	.27

Factor VII apparently reflects fears of *interpersonal loss.* Most of the items refer to the loss of a girl or boyfriend or spouse, and the first three items listed, which deal directly with this kind of loss, have exceptionally high item means.

DISCUSSION

Many of the items from the 166-item social anxiety inventory can be divided among seven distinct factors.* These are fears of disapproval or negative evaluation, social assertiveness and visibility, confrontation and anger-expression, heterosexual contact, intimacy and interpersonal warmth, conflict with or rejection by parents, and interpersonal loss. In general, the items making up these factors appear to form a promising core of items for the construction of an inventory to assess social fears and anxiety. Factors V and VII, dealing with fears of intimacy and interpersonal warmth and fears of interpersonal loss, are composed of only a few items. These factors need to be developed, but intuitively they seem to represent important features of social interaction which often do elicit anxiety that has serious consequences for behavioral functioning. The sets of items in Table 3 that load highly on and define the other five

---

* We have constructed a revised scale consisting of 100 items. These are the 65 items from Table 3, a few additional items from the original scale loading on factors I, II, and III, and a number of new items designed to tap the dimensions tentatively indicated by factors V and VII. This scale is being administered to a new sample of university students to cross-validate the factor structure obtained in this first study and obtain reliability data. The relationship between the factors obtained will be explored and a higher order factor analysis performed on the data. Some validity investigations, including correlation of the scale with other self-report scales, will be undertaken. The assumption that rating anxiety to these items predicts important consequences for behavioral functioning must also be investigated. Finally, the scale will be standardized, item analyzed, and scaled in an appropriate manner to provide normative data for use by researchers and psychotherapists. Of course, the present results and this new standardized scale may be limited in applicability to a college of young adult population.

A refined and standardized scale of this type would appear to have many uses. These include assessment at the beginning of therapy to identify problem areas, facilitate the choice of a therapeutic strategy, and assist in the building of hierarchies for desensitization or assertive training; measurement of some of the outcomes of treatment for social anxiety and social skill deficits; and applied research to determine the classes or dimensions of social interactions with respect to their potential for eliciting anxiety in different populations; and to investigate the relationship between social anxiety and other aspects of adjustment and behavioral functioning. A scale of this type, with distinct, conceptually pure factors, could prove especially useful in measuring the *generalization* of fear reduction from certain kinds of social stimuli dealt with specifically in treatment to *other* stimuli in the domain of social interaction.

factors may provide a satisfactory means of assessing the verbal-cognitive component of fear reactions to basic and functionally important dimensions of social relationships and situations.

REFERENCE NOTE

1. MEICHENBAUM, D. Clinical implications of modifying what clients say to themselves. Unpublished manuscript, University of Waterloo, 1974.

REFERENCES

BANDURA, A. *Principles of Behavior Modification.* New York: Holt, Rinehart & Winston, 1969.

BYRNE, D. *The Attraction Paradigm.* New York: Academic Press, 1971.

D'ZURILLA, T. J., & GOLDFRIED, M. R. Problem solving and behavior modification. In C. M. Franks & G. T. Wilson (Eds.), *Annual Review of Behavior Therapy Theory and Practice.* New York: Brunner/Mazel, 1973.

GOLDFRIED, M. R., & D'ZURILLA, T. J. A behavioral-analytic model for assessing competence. In C. D. Spielberger (Ed.), *Current Topics in Clinical and Community Psychology.* New York: Academic Press, 1969. Vol. I.

KLORMAN, R., WEERTS, T. C., HASTINGS, J. E., MELAMED, B. G., & LANG, P. D. Psychometric description of some specific fear questionnaires. *Behavior Therapy,* 5:401-409, 1974.

LAZARUS, A. A. *Behavior Therapy and Beyond.* New York: McGraw-Hill, 1971.

MEICHENBAUM, D., GILMORE, J. B., & FEDORAVICIUS, A. Group insight vs. group desensitization in treating speech anxiety. In C. M. Franks & G. T. Wilson (Eds.), *Annual Review of Behavior Therapy Theory and Practice.* New York: Brunner/Mazel, 1973.

MISCHEL, W. *Personality and Assessment.* New York: Wiley, 1968.

MISCHEL, W. Toward a cognitive social learning reconceptualization of personality. *Psychological Review,* 80:252-283, 1973.

RICHARDSON, F. C., & SUINN, R. M. The mathematics anxiety rating scale: Normative data. *Journal of Counseling Psychology,* 19:551-554, 1973.

SUINN, R. M., The STABS, a measure of test anxiety for behavior therapy: Normative data. *Behavior Research and Therapy,* 7:335-339, 1969.

SUINN, R. M., & RICHARDSON, F. C. Anxiety management training: A nonspecific behavior therapy program for anxiety control. *Behavior Therapy,* 2:498-510, 1971.

TASTO, D. L., HICKSON, R., & RUBIN, S. E. Scaled profile analysis of fear survey schedule factors. In C. M. Franks & G. T. Wilson (Eds.), *Annual Review of Behavior Therapy Theory and Practice.* New York: Brunner/Mazel, 1973.

WATSON, D., & FRIEND, R. Measurement of social-evaluative anxiety. *Journal of Consulting and Clinical Psychology,* 33:448-457, 1969.

WATSON, D., & THARP, R. *Self-directed Behavior.* Monterey, Calif.: Brooks/Cole, 1972.

It might also be used to assess the outcomes of such very general skill training approaches as problem solving training (Suinn & Richardson, 1971) in terms of their effects in certain specific areas of functioning.

SECTION IV: ASSESSMENT AND EVALUATION

8

THE SOCIAL VALIDATION AND TRAINING OF CONVERSATIONAL SKILLS

Neil Minkin, Curtis J. Braukmann, Bonnie L. Minkin, Gary D. Timbers, Barbara J. Timbers, Dean L. Fixsen, Elery L. Phillips, and Montrose M. Wolf

University of Kansas

Three reliably measured components of conversation—questioning, providing positive feedback, and proportion of time spent talking—were identified and validated as to their social importance. The social validity of the three conversational behaviors was established with five female university students and five female junior-high students. Each was videotaped in conversations with previously unknown

---

Reprinted with permission from the *Journal of Applied Behavior Analysis,* 9, 127-139, No. 2 (Summer, 1976). Copyright 1976 by the Society for the Experimental Analysis of Behavior, Inc.

Portions of these data were presented at the eighty-first Annual Convention of the American Psychological Association, Montreal, Canada, September 1973. This manuscript is based upon a thesis submitted by the senior author to the Department of Human Development, University of Kansas, in partial fulfillment of the requirements for the M.A. degree. This research was supported by grants MH13664 and MH20030 from the National Institute of Mental Health (Center for Studies in Crime and Delinquency) to the Bureau of Child Research and the Department of Human Development of the University of Kansas. The authors express their appreciation to Hector Ayala, Patrizia Braukmann, Richard Goldstein, Steven King, Kathryn Kirigin, John Lutzker, Dennis Maloney, Howard Rosenfeld, Larry Russell, Mitchell Taubman, John Werner, and a number of others who contributed to this study.

adults. The conversational ability of each girl was evaluated by a group of 13 adult judges who viewed each tape and rated each conversant "poor" to "excellent" on a seven-point rating scale. The average ratings of the girls correlated at r = 0.85 with the specified behavioral measures. These procedures were replicated with additional subjects and judges and yielded a correlation of r = 0.84. The high correlations between ratings and the objective measures suggested that the specified conversational behaviors were socially important aspects of conversational ability. Employing a multiple-baseline design across the behaviors of asking questions and providing positive feedback, an attempt was made to train four girls who used these behaviors minimally to engage in the behaviors in conversations with adults. Adult judges were again employed to rate randomly selected samples of the girls' skills in pre- and posttraining conversations. The average ratings of the girls before training were lower than both the university girls and the junior high-school girls. After training, the girls' conversational abilities were rated substantially higher than those of their junior high-school peers. These rating data validated the benefits of the training and the social importance of the behavioral components of questions and feedback in conversation. The authors suggest that it may be necessary for traditional behavior analysis measurement systems to be supplemented by social-validation procedures in order to establish the relationship between "objectively" measured behaviors and complex classes of behavior of interest to society.

DESCRIPTORS: social validation procedures, conversational behavior, social interaction behaviors, predelinquents

The effectiveness of applied behavior analysis depends on careful specification and measurement of the behavior of interest. Many behaviors dealt with by behavior analysts are easily specified and measured, e.g., working arithmetic problems correctly (Felixbrod and O'Leary, 1973) or climbing on a climbing apparatus (Harris, Wolf, and Baer, 1964). However, some behaviors are more complex and difficult, especially socially important behaviors that include numerous component parts. These behaviors are often described in vague generalities, which do not provide a basis for measurement. For example, empathy is considered to be an important characteristic of an effective counsellor (Truax and Carkhuff, 1967), yet what exactly constitutes empathy and thus, what behaviors should be taught to counsellor trainees, is debatable (Coleman, 1964; Haase and Tepper, 1972; Smith, 1973). To quantify empathy, researchers have attempted to specify the behavioral components and to validate their importance through the ratings of relevant judges *i.e.,* experienced counsellors.

Haase and Tepper (1972) asked experienced counsellors to rate the empathy level of a counsellor who was modelling various specified behavioral components of empathy on videotaped segments of simulated counselling situations. The results indicated that several nonverbal behaviors, including eye contact, bodily orientation toward the client, and the distance of the counsellor from the client correlated highly with the ratings. This outcome indicated that these components were "valid" aspects of empathy according to the judgment of experienced counsellors. The specification of behavioral components and validation of their importance by relevant judges is a procedure that might be used to define other complex social interaction skills.

Finding a high positive correlation between the specified behaviors and the ratings of skill levels by relevant judges does not rule out the possibility that some important behavioral components of the skill remain unspecified. In addition, frequency levels, duration levels, and critical interaction patterns of the behaviors may be important variables. Given these possibilities, training that increases levels of the specified and validated behaviors may not increase ratings of the skill level by relevant judges. Validation that training did increase judged skill level might be obtained by asking relevant judges to rate an individual's skill level both before and after training.

Thus, the specification and training of complex social behaviors that involve subjective dimensions seems to require four steps: (1) specification of the potentially relevant behavioral components, (2) social validation of the importance of each of the behavioral components, (3) training of the components, and (4) social validation that increases in the specified behavioral components resulted in increased level of judged skill. The purpose of the present research was to carry out these steps in a training program designed to improve the conversational skills of predelinquent girls.

I. SPECIFICATION AND SOCIAL VALIDATION OF CONVERSATIONAL BEHAVIORS

Two sets of conversational samples were obtained to permit the reliable specification and social validation of some important behavioral components of conversation. The first set was used to identify and to measure conversational behaviors, to provide normative information on the conversational behavior of junior-high and university females, and to determine the relationship between the conversants' behavior and ratings of conversational skill by relevant judges.

SAMPLE 1

Subjects

Five junior high-school students and five university students, all female, ranged in age from 12 to 20 years. The junior-high students were in the eighth and ninth grades and the university students were freshmen and sophomores. The junior-high girls volunteered in response to an announcement made in a study hall by the vice-principal of a local junior high school. The university girls responded to an announcement made in a sorority house by one of the sorority sisters.

Setting and Apparatus

The setting was a 3.6 by 4.2 m room that contained two chairs positioned at an angle of 45 degrees with respect to one another. A video camera and microphone, placed approximately 1.5 m in front of the two chairs, were connected to a Sony 2200 videotape recorder and monitor located in an adjoining room not visible from the chairs.

Procedure

Each of the 10 subjects was videotaped in two 4-min conversations, producing a total of 20 sample conversations. In each conversation, the subject and an adult previously unknown to the subject were alone in the room. The sequencing of conversations was arranged so that no subject would have two consecutive conversations. Each subject conversed with a different male or female adult during each conversation. On entering the room, the conversants were asked to be seated and given the following verbal instructions by one of the experimenters:

> "We would like you to speak with each other for a short period of time. You may talk about anything you wish. You will be told when to begin and when to stop."

The videotape unit was then turned on. The experimenter said, "You may begin now" and left the room. At the end of 4 min, the videotape unit was turned off, the experimenter re-entered the room, informed the conversants that time was up, and thanked them for participating. Each conversant then received $2.00 for having participated.

Definitional specification, recording, and reliability. After informally reviewing the 20 videotaped sample conversations, the experimenters noted that the university students had asked more questions and had given more positive feedback than the junior-high students. In some conversations, one person spoke a great deal or very little. Based on these informal observations, the conversational behaviors of questioning, positive feedback, and time talked were reliably specified using the following procedure.

Two or more naive observers simultaneously viewed the videotaped conversations. They were given a written definition of the behavior and written instructions on how to record the behavior. An interval procedure was used to record conversational questions and positive conversational questions and positive conversational feedback by dividing each of the 4-min conversations into 24, 10-sec intervals. An audiotape, which signalled the beginning and end of each interval, was synchronized with the videotape for each conversation. The observers were instructed to score an occurrence in each 10-sec interval in which the behavior being observed occurred at least once. The written definitions of a conversational question and positive conversational feedback were modified several times until naive observers could agree at least 85% of the time that the behavior did or did not occur. To control for observer bias (Arrington, 1943), new observers were employed each time the written behavioral definition was changed. The time-talked measure was recorded by counting the cumulative number of seconds spoken by each of the conversants. This definition proved to be immediately reliable.

A "conversational question" was defined to include: (a) any command by the subject, (b) any question by the subject, (c) any "question of clarification" by the subject, and (d) any statement by the subject that in effect functions as a question.

Examples: following a statement by the other conversant, such as "I go to K.U.," an example of (a) (above) would be "Tell me more about that," (b) (above) "How long have you gone there?," (c) (above) "K.U.?," or "Oh, really?," or "You do?," and (d) (above) "So you are in college," or "In other words you are a student."

"Positive conversational feedback" was defined as a brief utterance of no more than three words that indicated that the subject either (a) approves, (b) concurs, or (c) understands what the other conversant is saying or has just said.

For example, if the other conversant were to say: "I think blue is the best color," examples of (a) (above) would be "That's nice," "good," or "interesting," (b) (above) "I agree," "I know," "mm-hmm," and "right," (c) (above) "oh," or "hmm," or "blue" (a repetition of part of what was said unless intoned as a question). This utterance can be neither a "conversational question" nor a response to a "conversational question," and may or may not be directly followed by further utterances by the subject.

The reliability of the measurement system was assessed 128 times throughout the study. Four types of reliability computations were used: point by point, occurrence, nonoccurrence, and gross. Point-by-point agreement (Wolf and Sherman, Note 1) was calculated by dividing the total number of intervals of agreements by the total number of intervals of agreements and disagreements. Agreement as to occurrence (Bijou, Peterson, and Ault, 1968) was calculated by dividing the total number of intervals in which there was agreement that the behavior occurred by the total number of intervals in which there was agreement and disagreement that the behavior occurred. Agreement as to nonoccurrence was calculated by dividing the total number of intervals in which there was agreement that the behavior did not occur by the total number of intervals in which there was agreement and disagreement of the nonoccurrence of the behavior. The gross method (Wolf and Sherman, Note 1) of determining reliability was also used to compare the totals of the observers' observations. The gross per cent agreement was calculated only for the time-talked behavior by dividing the larger total into the smaller total.

Agreement on the recording of conversational questions was assessed on 48 occasions. Mean point-by-point agreement was 94% (range: 83% to 100%). Mean occurrence agreement was 90% (range: 75% to 100%), and mean nonoccurrence agreement was 91% (range: 66% to 100%).

Reliability on the recording of positive conversational feedback was assessed 50 times. Mean point-by-point agreement was 92% (range: 80% to 100%). Mean occurrence reliability was 89% (range: 66% to 100%), and mean nonoccurrence agreement was 90% (range: 66% to 100%). Interobserver reliability for time talked was assessed 30 times. The mean gross agreement was 98% (range: 88% to 100%).

RESULTS

During the 24 intervals of a 4-min conversation, the university subjects averaged 7.7 intervals in which they asked at least one conversational question, 7.4 intervals containing at least one instance of positive conversational feedback, and spoke an average of 128 sec. The junior-high subjects averaged 0.8 intervals containing a conversational question, 3.2 intervals of positive conversational feedback, and spoke an average of 100.4 sec.

Social Validation

Judges and setting. Adult residents of the subjects' local community observed the 20 sample conversations and rated the conversational ability of each subject. The purpose was to determine whether the specified behavioral components were viewed as socially important variables of conversation.

The 13 adults who volunteered to serve as judges were seven males and six females. They ranged in age from 19 to 51 years, mean age, 26. Nine judges were full or part-time university students at the graduate or undergraduate level. The four other judges included a gas-station attendant, two homemakers, and a Pinkerton guard. The judges observed and rated the conversational ability of the subjects in a university conference room where two Sony series 2200 videotape monitors were used to display the taped conversations.

Procedures. The 20 sample conversations were arranged in random order, with the provision that no subject would appear in two consecutive conversation sequences. Finally, all conversations were transcribed onto two videotapes, each containing 10 conversations in the randomly determined order.

Two groups of judges consisting of six or seven people viewed the tapes. The first group viewed and rated the randomized conversations in an order from one to 20. The second group viewed and rated the tapes in a counter-balanced order, first, conversations 11 through 20 were viewed, then conversations one through 10.

Before viewing the tapes, each judge was given a rating by making a mark along a seven-point bi-polar semantic differential scale (Osgood, Suci, and Tanenbaum, 1957) with the poles labelled "excellent" and "poor." The judges were also instructed to rate independently, and to try not to be influenced by the conversant's age or appearance. They were also told that they could go back and change any rating at any time. The judges received $4.00 each for their participation in the approximately 2.5-hour rating session.

A composite behavioral score was calculated for each conversant in each conversation in a manner that gave equal weight to a conversant's score on each of the three individual measures. While a score for conver-

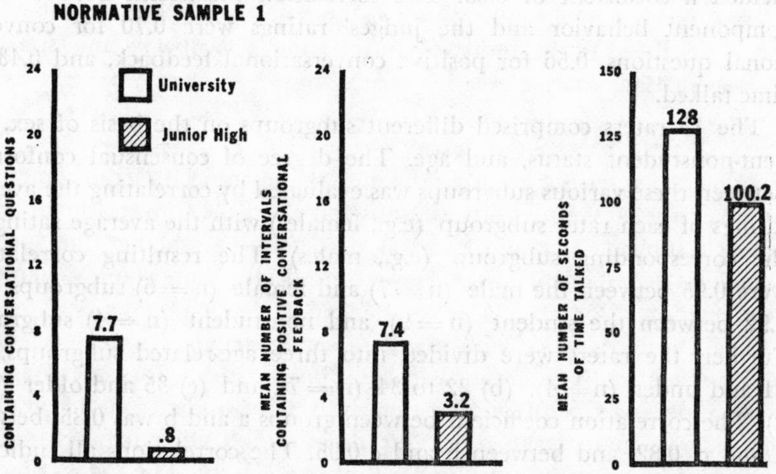

FIGURE 1. Normative Sample 1. The left graph shows the mean number of 10-sec intervals that contained at least one conversational question asked by university females (left bar) and junior-high females (right bar) during their respective 4-min conversations with adults. The center graph shows the mean number of 10-sec intervals during the 4-min conversations that contained at least one instance of positive conversational feedback by the university females (left bar) and junior-high females (right bar). The right graph shows the mean number of seconds talked by the university and junior-high females during their respective conversations.

sational questions and positive conversational feedback could range from 0 to 24 (24, 10-sec intervals in 4 min), the time-talked score could range from 0 to 240 (240 sec in 4 min). Thus, to assure equal weighting, it was necessary to transform the time-talked scores. By dividing the total number of seconds talked by 10, the potential range of scores was also made 0 to 24. The composite score was computed by adding the conversational question and positive conversational feedback scores to the transformed score for time talked. For example, if a conversant had seven intervals in which she asked questions and seven intervals in which she emitted positive conversational feedback and spoke 103 sec, her composite score would be 24.3 ($7 + 7 + 10.3$).

Results. The mean rating by the judges of the university subjects was 5.25, with a rating of one being "poor" and a rating of seven being "excellent". The mean rating of the junior-high subjects was 3.4. The correlation between the composite behavioral score and the judges' rating yielded a coefficient of 0.85. The correlation coefficients between each component behavior and the judges' ratings were 0.70 for conversational questions, 0.56 for positive conversational feedback, and 0.43 for time talked.

The 13 raters comprised different subgroups on the basis of sex, student-nonstudent status, and age. The degree of consensual conformity between these various subgroups was evaluated by correlating the average ratings of each rater subgroup (e.g., females) with the average ratings of the corresponding subgroup (e.g., males). The resulting correlations were 0.95 between the male ($n = 7$) and female ($n = 6$) subgroups, and 0.92 between the student ($n = 9$) and nonstudent ($n = 4$) subgroups. Further, the raters were divided into three age-related subgroups, (a) 21 and under ($n = 4$), (b) 22 to 34 ($n = 7$), and (c) 35 and older ($n = 2$). The correlation coefficient between groups a and b was 0.85, between a and c, 0.82, and between b and c 0.95. The correlations all indicated a high degree of consensus among the various rater subgroups.

To determine the extent of interjudge agreement or reliability, the Kendall coefficient of concordance (W) was employed (Siegel, 1956). In using this test, rankings of all 20 conversations were obtained from each judge by rank ordering the conversations from highest rated to lowest rated by that judge. The resultant score of $W = 0.61$ was significant at the < 0.001 level. This may be interpreted to mean that each of the judges applied essentially similar standards in evaluating the conversations.

To provide some estimate of intrajudge agreement (the agreement of a judge with himself), Pearson product moment correlations were computed between each judge's ratings of one of the conversations of each conversant and the remaining conversation of each conversant. The resulting correlations for each of the 13 judges were transformed into a single correlation coefficient using a Fisher Z transformation (Guilford, 1965). The resultant $r = 0.68$ suggests an overall consistency between the judge's ratings of individual conversants across their two conversations.

SUMMARY

The first part of this study indicated that some of the behavioral components of conversation could be specified and reliably measured. Data from the normative samples of conversation indicated that the university subjects used more of the specified components than the junior-high subjects. It also appeared that subjects who emitted more of the specified component behaviors were considered better conversationalists by adult members of the local community. Further, there appeared to be consensual agreement between the various raters and subgroups of raters as to relevant judgments of conversational ability. The 0.85 correlation coefficient between the composite behavioral score and the judges' ratings suggested a strong relationship between the specified behavioral components and how one was evaluated as a conversationalist. However, it was possible that the high correlation might have been a "chance" occurrence, due to the fact that the behavioral definitions were developed from the same tapes that were rated, and consequently the correlation might have been unique to that sample (Blumenfeld, 1972). Thus, a replication was necessary to verify the results.

SAMPLE 2

Subjects

Five junior-high and five university females ranged in age from 12 to 20 years. The junior-high students were in the eighth and ninth grades and the university students were freshmen and sophomores. As with the girls who participated in the first sample, the junior-high girls volunteered through an announcement made in a study hall and the university girls responded to an announcement made in a sorority house.

Setting, Apparatus, and Procedures

The setting, apparatus, and procedures were identical to those reported for Sample 1.

RESULTS

The results indicated that the university subjects averaged 7.8 intervals in which they asked at least one conversational question, 8.3 intervals containing at least one instance of positive conversational feedback, and spoke an average of 137.7 sec. The junior-high subjects averaged 1.1 intervals in which they asked conversational questions, 3.6 intervals containing at least one instance of positive conversational feedback, and spoke an average of 113.4 sec.

Social Validation

Judges. Fifteen local community residents, seven males and eight females, volunteered to serve as judges. They ranged in age from 19 to

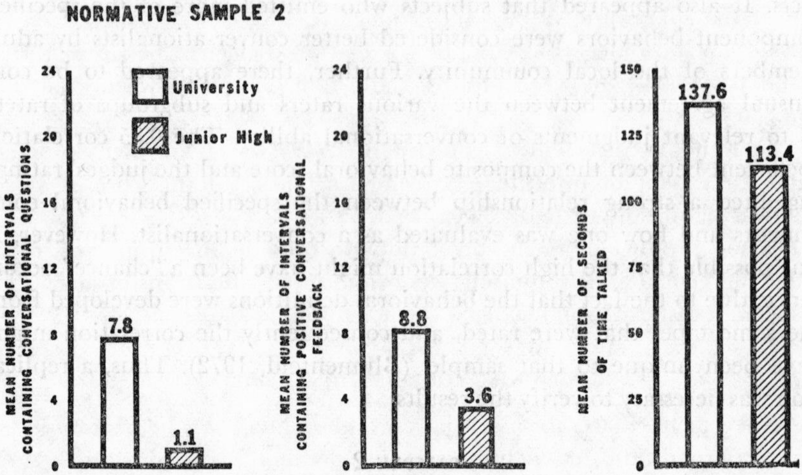

FIGURE 2. Normative Sample 2. The left graph shows the mean number of 10-sec intervals that contained at least one conversational question asked by university females (left bar) and junior-high females (right bar) during their respective 4-min conversations with adults. The center graph shows the mean number of 10-sec intervals during the 4-min conversations that contained at least one instance of positive conversational feedback by the university females (left bar) and junior-high females (right bar). The right graph shows the mean number of seconds talked by the university and junior-high females during their respective conversations.

58 years, average age, 27. This group of judges consisted of 10 graduate and undergraduate students, one student teacher, two homemakers, one bookkeeper, and one university housemother.

Setting, apparatus, and procedures. The setting, apparatus, and procedures were identical to those reported for Sample 1.

Results. The mean rating by the judges of the university subjects was 5.0, with one being "poor" and seven being "excellent." The mean rating for the junior-high subjects was 3.7. The correlation between the composite behavioral score and the judges' ratings was 0.84. The correlation coefficients between each component behavior and the judges' ratings was 0.63 for conversational questions, 0.64 for positive conversational feedback, and 0.65 for time talked.

Correlations to determine consensual conformity between the various subgroups yielded coefficients of 0.76 between the male $(n = 7)$ and the female $(n = 8)$ subgroups, 0.79 between the student $(n = 10)$ and nonstudent $(n = 5)$ subgroups. The raters were also divided into three age-related subgroups (a) 21 and under ($n = 8$), (b) 22 to 34 ($n = 4$), and (c) 35 and older ($n = 3$). The correlation coefficient between groups a and b was 0.94, between groups a and c, 0.75, and between groups b and c, 0.78.

The Kendall coefficient of concordance (W) was again used to determine the extent of interjudge agreement. The resultant score of $W = 0.46$ was significant at the < 0.001 level.

Pearson product moment correlations to provide an estimate of intrajudge agreement with himself were computed and transformed. The Fisher Z transformation yielded a coefficient of $r = 0.61$.

II. TRAINING CONVERSATIONAL SKILLS

Achievement Place for Girls is a residential group home for six to eight court-adjudicated delinquent and predelinquent girls. Interested residents of the community make up the Board of Directors, who are responsible for establishing the major goals of the program. The goals are carried out by professional teaching-parents who live in the home and have primary responsibility for the treatment and care of the girls (Phillips, Phillips, Fixsen, and Wolf, 1974). One major goal of Achievement Place for Girls is teaching social-interaction behaviors that the community views as being important for successful relationships.

Subjects, Setting and Apparatus

Four girls in the Achievement Place program volunteered to participate in this aspect of the research. The girls ranged in age from 12 to 14 years and were in the seventh through the ninth grades. The teaching-parents recommended asking these girls to participate on the basis that they were "generally deficient" in social communication skills with adults.

The setting and apparatus were identical to those in which Samples 1 and 2 were obtained.

Procedures

A multiple-baseline design (Baer *et al.*, 1968) across the behaviors of conversational questions and positive conversational feedback was used to analyze effectiveness of the training procedures. Each subject participated in three to six 4-min baseline conversations with previously unknown adults. The conversants received the same instructions as those participating in collection of the normative data. The baseline conversations involved two after-school sessions of approximately 1.5 hour and each girl was paid $1.00 before the session.

The procedure for training conversational questions consisted of three parts: instructions with rationale, demonstration, and practice with feedback. Instructions with rationale consisted of describing the behavior, giving oral and written examples of the behavior, explaining the importance of the behavior in conversation, and asking the girls why they felt the behavior was important. Demonstration consisted of two experimenters modelling the behavior in a sample two-person conversations. In practice with feedback, 4-min interactions with one of the experimenters were videotaped to allow feedback to each girl on the amount of the target behaviors she had engaged in. When the girls met the experimenter-established criterion (16 instances of conversational questions in each of two consecutive 4-min conversations with one of the experimenters) the girls were asked to participate in additional conversations with unknown adults, earning $0.10 for each conversational question they would ask.

When the girls had demonstrated proficiency in asking conversational questions, they were taught to give positive conversational feedback. The procedure for teaching positive conversational feedback was identical to that employed in the teaching of conversational questions: instructions with rationale, demonstration, and practice with feedback. On meeting the experimenter-established criterion of 16 instances of positive conversational feedback in two consecutive 4-min conversations with one of the experimenters, the girls were informed of the opportunity to engage in more conversations with unknown adults. They each continued to receive $0.10 for each instance of positive conversational feedback.

One girl, Kim, did not participate in the group training session. Kim was trained in part by viewing a videotape of the instructions and demonstrations provided in the group training session. The practice and feedback components of the training were identical to the group sessions. Again, a multiple-baseline design was used across Kim's behavior.

RESULTS

In baseline, Kim asked questions in an average of three of the 24 intervals and in each conversation gave positive conversational feedback in an average of two intervals. In the posttraining sessions, she asked questions in an average of 13 intervals and gave positive feedback in an average of 11 intervals.

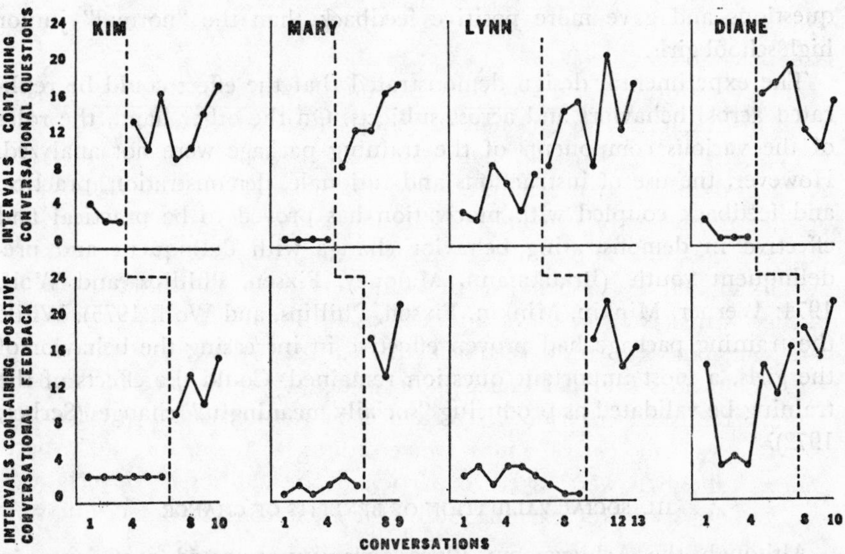

FIGURE 3. The number of 10-sec intervals that contained at least one conversational question (upper graphs) and the number of 10-sec intervals that contained at least one instance of positive conversational feedback during conversations with previously unknown adults for the four Achievement Place girls. The vertical dashed line represents where training was introduced.

Mary did not ask any questions in her baseline conversations and had an average of 0.8 intervals in which she gave positive feedback. In her posttraining sessions, she asked questions in an average of 15 intervals and averaged 17 intervals of positive feedback.

Lynn, in her baseline sessions, asked questions in an average of five of the 24 intervals and gave positive feedback in an average of 1.7 intervals. In her posttraining sessions, she averaged 18 intervals in which she asked questions and averaged 17 intervals in which she gave positive feedback.

Diane averaged 0.5 intervals containing questions and averaged 9.2 intervals containing positive feedback in baseline. In posttraining sessions, Diane asked questions in an average of 12 intervals and gave positive feedback in an average of 18 of the 24 intervals.

SUMMARY

Training effectively increased the use of conversational behaviors. After training, the Achievement Place girls consistently asked more questions and gave more positive feedback than the "normal" junior high-school girls.

The experimental design demonstrated that the effect could be replicated across behaviors and across subjects. On the other hand, the roles of the various components of the training package were not analyzed. However, the use of instructions and rationale, demonstration, practice, and feedback coupled with motivation has proved to be practical and effective in demonstrating behavior change with delinquent and predelinquent youth (Braukmann, Maloney, Fixsen, Phillips, and Wolf, 1974; Werner, Minkin, Minkin, Fixsen, Phillips, and Wolf, 1975). While the training package had proven effective in increasing the behavior of the girls, a most important question remained. Could the effects of the training be validated as producing "socially meaningful" change (Serber, 1972)?

III. SOCIAL VALIDATION OF BENEFITS OF CHANGE

Although the Achievement Place girls demonstrated proficiency in using the specified and validated behaviors, the qualitative effects of the training remained unknown. Thus, an attempt was made to determine if the girls were viewed as better conversationalists after training.

Subject, Setting, and Apparatus

The 15 adults who viewed and rated the second set of normative samples served as judges. The setting and apparatus were identical to those used in the rating procedures of the second set of normative samples.

Procedures

One baseline and one posttraining videotaped conversation for each Achievement Place girl were randomly selected for judging. The eight conversations were then randomly ordered, with the provision that no subject would appear in two consecutive conversational sequences.

Immediately after rating the 20 conversations constituting the second set of normative samples, the judges viewed and rated the baseline and posttraining conversations of the Achievement Place girls. The first group of judges viewed and rated each conversation in an order from one to eight. The second group viewed and rated the tapes in a counterbalanced order, i.e., first conversations five through eight, then conversations one through four. The judges were not informed that Achieve-

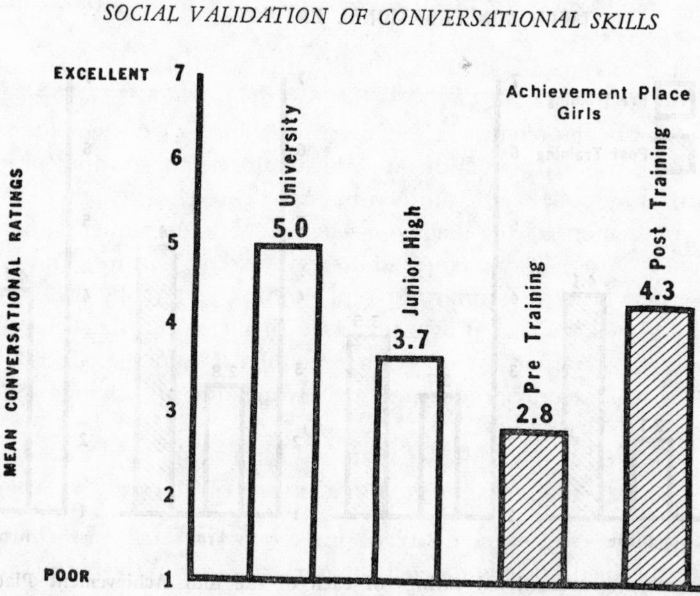

FIGURE 4. The four bars respectively represent the mean ratings of the conversational ability of the university females, junior-high females, Achievement Place females before training and the Achievement Place females after introduction of the training package, as judged by residents of their local community using a seven point bi-polar scale with the poles labelled *poor* and *excellent*.

ment Place girls were involved in the last eight conversations and no distinction was made between the 20 normative sample tapes and the last eight videotapes.

RESULTS

Figure 4 shows that the average rating of the Achievement Place girls before training was 2.8 and the average rating of their conversational ability after training rose to 4.3.

Figure 5 shows that the individual rating for each Achievement Place girl increased after training. Before training, Diane received an average rating of 2.1, which rose to 4.2 after training. Fourteen of the 15 judges rated Diane as a better conversationalist; one judge's rating remained the same. Before training, Mary received an average rating of 2.7 and after training it rose to to 3.5. Twelve judges rated Mary as a better conversa-

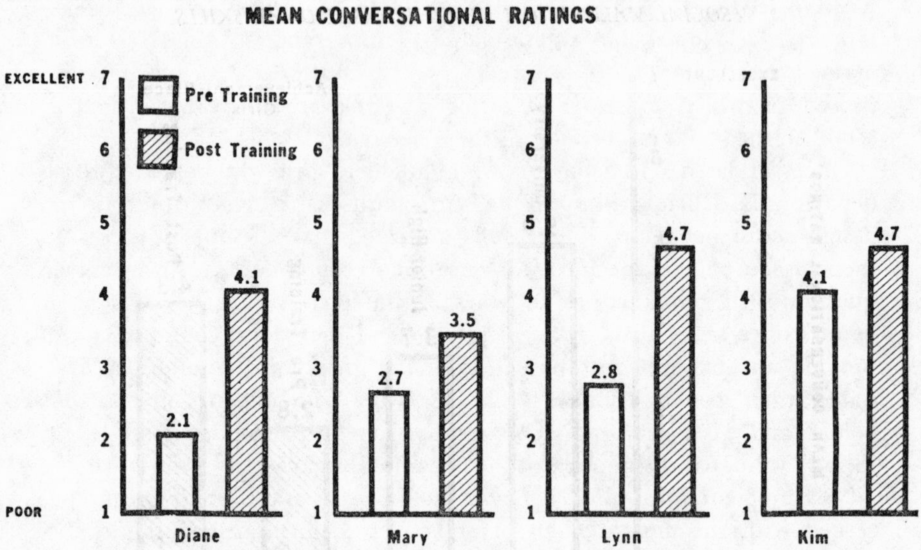

FIGURE 5. The mean conversational ratings of each of the four Achievement Place females before and after introduction of the training package as judged by residents of their local community using a seven-point bi-polar scale with the poles labelled *poor* and *excellent*.

tionalist, two rated her ability as the same, and one rated her ability to have decreased. Lynn averaged 2.8 before training and 4.7 after training. Eleven judges rated improvement and four judges' ratings remained the same. Kim's average rating before training was 4.1 and after training was 4.7. The rating change seen for Kim was less dramatic than for the other girls. Nevertheless, seven judges rated improvement, five judges' ratings remained the same, and three judges rated her ability to have decreased.

GENERAL DISCUSSION

The results suggest that some of the behavioral components of conversation can be reliably specified and socially validated as being important. The results also suggest that the specified components can be trained and the benefits of increases in the behavior of the trainees can also be socially validated.

Videotaped conversations of "normal" junior-high and university females provided normative information about their conversational behaviors. The older females generally asked more questions, gave more positive feedback, and spoke more. Reliable definitions of these behaviors were developed, but their relational importance to conversation remained unknown. Thus, to quantify conversation, a social-validation procedure, which consisted of ratings, by relevant judges, was used to establish the social importance of these behaviors.

Once validated, the behaviors were taught to girls who appeared to be behaviorally deficient in speaking with adults using a multiple-baseline design across behaviors. The results indicated that all subjects increased their usage of the specified conversational components. However, the question still remained as to whether the girls would be considered better conversationalists by adult members of their local community. To provide an answer, adult judges from the girls' local community evaluated their conversational skills by rating videotaped conversations before and after training. The results, showing increased skill levels, socially validated the benefits of the behavioral increases.

Measurement in applied behavior analysis has traditionally been concerned with the measurement of objectively defined behaviors, i.e., behaviors that could be reliably recorded as to their presence or absence by independent observers. As behavior analysis expands into more complex realms of behavior, the social validity of objectively measured behaviors will become a more significant issue. As we attempt to deal with more complex behaviors we may inadvertently choose to measure behavioral components that are not relevant to the complex behavior of interest to society. Thus, our traditional objective measurement procedures will have to be supplemented by methods to establish the relationship of the specified objective components to the complex class of behavior. Social validation is one such method.

For example, affection might be considered a complex social behavior. If the goal of a behavior analyst is to teach a parent to be more affectionate towards his child, it might be necessary to specify the important component behaviors of affection. Some of the components might include touching, smiling, and hugging. To validate the social importance of these behaviors, four steps might be used. First, gathering sample parent-child interactions. Second, developing and recording reliable definitions of specific interactant behaviors. Third, employing relevant judges, e.g., other parents, randomly selected if possible, to rate the sample interactions and evaluate each parent as to the amount of affection shown to the child within the interaction. The evaluation instrument might be a bi-polar rating scale with the poles labelled as to the amount of affection shown. Step four would involve correlating the ratings of the judges with a composite score of the objectively measured behaviors of the parents. The subsequent coefficient would indicate the level of relationship of the specified objectively measured components of affection to the common English "meaning" of affection as rated by the judges. In the present study, the use of a composite behavioral score produced a measure highly correlated with the ratings.* Some of the important behavioral components of creativity, conversation, and affection, as well as other complex classes of social behaviors, could probably be identified through the use of social-validation procedures.

Social-validation procedures can also be used to identify and describe subsequent benefits of a behavior change. Traditionally, behavior analysts have evaluated the effectiveness of their training procedures almost exclusively in terms of their ability to modify objectively defined behaviors. However, training procedures that increase objectively defined behaviors may not necessarily produce an increase in the perceived skill of the subject according to relevant judges. The teaching of socially validated behaviors does not necessarily produce socially valid changes. Again, evaluations by relevant judges could be a means of verifying the benefits of behavior change. Evaluations of a subject both before and after training would provide the behavior analyst with information as to the effectiveness of his intervention procedures.

Since the present research was conducted in a structured training setting, rather than in the natural environment, the degree to which equally beneficial changes in conversational skills can be produced in the natural setting is a question for future research. Future research should also examine a wider range of relevant judges, including peers and the youths themselves.

REFERENCE NOTE

1. Wolf, M. M., & Sherman, J. A. In D. Hursh, J. Wildgen, B. Minkin, N. Minkin, J. Sherman, and M. Wolf (Eds.), *The Principles and Procedures of Behavior Modification*. Lawrence, Kansas: Project MORE, 1973.

REFERENCES

Arrington, R. E. Time sampling in studies of social behavior: A critical review of techniques and results with research suggestions. *Psychological Bulletin*, 40:81-124, 1943.

Baer, D. M., Wolf, M. M., & Risley, T. R. Some current dimensions of applied behavior analysis. *Journal of Applied Behavior Analysis*, 1:91-97, 1968.

* Each of the components was given an equal weighting in the composite score in this study. There are more statistically sophisticated procedures for assigning relative weights that involve regression equations.

BIJOU, S. W., PETERSON, R. F., & AULT, M. H. A method to integrate descriptive and experimental field studies at the level of data and empirical concepts. *Journal of Applied Behavior Analysis,* 1:175-191, 1968.

BLUMENFELD, W. S. I am never startled by a fish. *American Psychological Association Monitor,* 3:14, 1972.

BRAUKMANN, C. J., MALONEY, D. M., FIXSEN, D. L., PHILLIPS, E. L., & WOLF, M. M. An analysis of a selection interview training package for predelinquents at Achievement Place. *Criminal Justice and Behavior,* 1:30-42, 1974.

COLEMAN, J. C. *Abnormal Psychology and Modern Life.* 3rd ed. New York: Scott Foresman & Co., 1964.

FELIXBROD, J. J., & O'LEARY, K. D. Effects of reinforcement of children's academic behavior as a function of self-determinant and externally imposed contingencies. *Journal of Applied Behavior Analysis,* 6:241-250, 1973.

GUILFORD, J. P. *Fundamental Statistics in Psychology and Education.* 4th ed. New York: McGraw-Hill, 1965.

HAASE, R. F., & TEPPER, D. T. Nonverbal components of empathetic communication. *Journal of Counseling Psychology,* 19:417-424, 1972.

HARRIS, F. R., WOLF, M. M., & BAER, D. M. Effects of adult social reinforcement on child behavior. *Young Children,* 20:8-17, 1964.

OSGOOD, C. E., SUCI, G. J., and TANNENBAUM, P. H. *The Measurement of Meaning.* Urbana: University of Illinois Press, 1957.

PHILLIPS, E. L., PHILLIPS, E. A., FIXSEN, D. L., & WOLF, M. M. *The Teaching-Family Handbook.* Lawrence: University of Kansas Press, 1974.

SIEGEL, S. *Nonparametric Statistics for the Behavioral Sciences.* New York: McGraw-Hill, 1956.

SERBER, M. Teaching the nonverbal components of assertive training. *Journal of Behavior Therapy and Experimental Psychiatry,* 3:179-183, 1972.

SMITH, H. C. *Sensitivity Training: The Scientific Understanding of Individuals.* New York: McGraw-Hill, 1973.

TRUAX, C. B., & CARKHUFF, R. R. *Toward Effective Counseling in Psychotherapy.* Chicago: Aldine, 1967.

WERNER, J. S., MINKIN, N., MINKIN, B. L., FIXSEN, D. L., PHILLIPS, E. L., & WOLF, M. M. Intervention Package: Analysis to prepare juvenile delinquents for encounters with police officers. *Criminal Justice and Behavior* 2:55-83, 1975.

Section V

BEHAVIOR THERAPY WITH CHILDREN AND ADOLESCENTS

Commentary

The literature on behavior therapy with children is both huge and diverse. Aside from the behavioral journals themselves, papers on the behavioral treatment of children are to be found in journals devoted to children's problems in general (e.g., *Journal of Abnormal Child Psychology*), to specific problems in children (e.g., *Journal of Autism and Childhood Schizophrenia*), and to journals that focus on education and the schools (e.g., *Journal of School Psychology*). Still other papers are scattered across different journals by virtue of the specific theoretical or practical issues they pertain to, such as the *Journal of Personality and Social Psychology*, the source of one of the papers reprinted in this Section. From our review of these various literature sources we have chosen to concentrate on four major areas of interest to behavior therapists concerned with children: training parents and teachers in behavioral skills and management; behavior modification in the classroom; specific disorders among children, such as self-injurious behavior and hyperactivity; and behavior therapy with the families of delinquents.

TRAINING PARENTS AND TEACHERS IN BEHAVIORAL MANAGEMENT SKILLS

Parents as Behavior Change Agents

The use of parents as behavioral mediators—in the Tharp and Wetzel (1969) sense—in behavior modification programs for children has been widespread, and much of the literature on this topic has been discussed in previous volumes in this Series (see the 1974, 1975, and 1976 volumes). The first paper in this Section—by Lavigueur—describes the experimental analysis of the use of siblings as an adjunct to the modification of children's behavior by parents in the home setting. Controlled evaluations of the effects of training groups of parents to implement behavioral procedures have been infrequent. Sadler, Seyden, Howe, and Kaminsky (1976) report the evaluation of parents groups that incorporate both behavioral and humanistic (Rogerian) methods. In all, their 13 groups consist of a total of 277 parents. Almost half of the parents were referred by community agencies for children's problems such as "mental retardation, emotional disturbance, learning disabilities, behavior disorder, and similar categories" (p. 158). The remainder complained of less severe problems with their children.

The parents expressed high approval of the eight session weekly program, increased their rates of positive reinforcement toward their children, increased compliance rates among their children, and were successful in improving specifically targeted responses as well as more general behavior in their children. While these results seem to suggest that parent training groups are remarkably effective, several caveats are in order before interpreting these data. In the first place, there was no control or comparison group (s) of parents. Secondly, all data are based upon parents' own ratings or estimates of their own behavior and that of their children. Sadler et al. report a reliability check between husband and wife ratings, but this still falls short of providing independent verification of the effects reported. A third problem is that "only those parents who completed both pre- and posttests were selected for analysis." This raises the possibility that those parents who were not included were less successful. Dropouts and subjects that do not complete all assessments are almost always those who have benefited less from treatment than those who complete the program. Lastly, the range of children's problems dealt with was so heterogeneous that, even if more objective measures had been obtained, it would still be difficult, if not impossible, to interpret them unequivocally. The evaluation of treatment programs—whatever their specific nature—requires that the target behavior be clearly specified and sufficiently homogeneous to be interpreted meaningfully (Kazdin & Wilson, in press). Other findings of Sadler et al. are that parents of younger children were less likely to dropout, that the attendance of both parents enhanced their continued participation in the program, and that charging a fee increased attendance.

On a different, and in many ways more informative, note for the practitioner, Cole and Morrow (1976) describe their *failures* in a program of training small groups of parents in behavioral management skills. Thirty-nine families participated in these 10 weekly group programs. The children whose problems were the target of change were predominantly "normal" youngsters whose ages ranged from 10 to 16 years. Specific target behaviors included the completion of chores and homework assignments, arriving at school on time, putting clothes and toys away, eliminating bedwetting, and decreasing quarrels and fights with siblings and peers. Cole and Morrow report that the program was effective in changing target behaviors in most families. However, they give an impressionistic account of two sorts of parents whose own behavior interfered with their ability to implement behavioral procedures successfully with their children.

The first pattern of parent behavior that impaired program effectiveness involved marital conflict. As a result of discord between the two parents, specific problem behaviors were unlikely to be agreed upon and specific procedures were not implemented. The second pattern involved what Cole and Morrow refer to as "insensitive authoritarian coerciveness." This latter pattern consisted of a) parents' inflexible insistence that their children abide by rigid codes of conduct, combined with the punitive enforcement of such behavior, and b) an insistence that the parents were always right and that the child submit to all adult dictates. Although impressionistic and lacking in systematic documentation, practitioners who have implemented behavioral programs in real-life settings will readily resonate to these difficulties. Moreover, they discuss some useful suggestions for coping with these parental obstructions. Anecdotal observations indicate that parents who insist on rigid standards and that the child submit to adult wishes are particularly sensitive to what others will think of *them*—the parents. Their behavior toward their children appears to be heavily influenced by their perceptions of what is likely to win approval or disapproval from others. Cole and Morrow suggest the use of peer-group influence through modeling and behavior rehearsal to teach alternative conceptions and behaviors.

There have been several reviews of parents as change agents for their children over the past few years, and now Reisinger, Ora, and Frangia (1976) add another. Their review spans three different conceptual approaches—behavioral, psychodynamic, and client-centered. There is not much new in Reisinger et al.'s coverage of behavior modification. They emphasize the importance of generalization of clinic-taught behaviors across different situations and behavior disorders, and conclude that the evidence in support of this generalization is limited. Parents have been shown to transfer skills learned in the clinic to other situations, but Reisinger et al. point out that most of these data are confounded by the investigators' presence during these observations. Whether parents actually do implement these skills across situations, the authors maintain, has yet to be established. The review of non-behavioral approaches is useful, and the acceptance of the hypothesis that parents *cause* their children's disturbances as a de facto truth is criticized. It is important to remember that success in employing parents to modify their children's disturbed behavior does not necessarily mean that these behaviors developed *because* of parental influence. Reisinger et al.'s conclusion might help serve as an antidote to thoroughly unprofessional pronouncements that hold parents directly responsible for their children's disorders: "In view of the absence of evidence which would indict parents of disturbed children, current views of the parental contribution for or against therapeutic gains seem to be based more on therapist training and treatment model expectation than on actual parental behavior" (p. 116).

Gloglower and Sloop (1976) compared two strategies in training groups of parents who had requested assistance in management of children's problems such as temper tantrums and noncompliance. The first strategy consisted of teaching parents the principles of behavior modification for four of the 10 weekly sessions, the remaining six sessions being devoted to changing specific target behaviors. The second strategy consisted of concentrating solely on changing specific target behaviors. The data show that parents who received general instruction in behavior modification principles in addition to supervision in changing specific target behaviors appeared to show greater progress on more measures than parents trained according to the second strategy. Aside from parents' own descriptions of their behavior, videotapes of posttreatment parent-child interactions provided objective measures of the effects of the two strategies. A five month follow-up lends further weight to the significance of this study. Finally, the results indicate that knowledge of behavior modification as evaluated by a test of operant principles is not tantamount to evidence of the ability of parents to implement the procedures in the home situation. This point is elaborated below.

Child abuse is a major problem that appears to have attracted little in the way of systematic behavioral research and therapy. Jensen (1976) outlines a conceptual model for the behavioral treatment of parents who physically abuse their children. The basic premise is that these parents lack the skills to manage ordinary child behavior and then resort to violence to "deal with perceived deviance." Teaching parents more appropriate parenting skills would reduce or eliminate child abuse. Of course, we must point out the obvious, namely, that many parents who lack adequate child management skills nonetheless do not become child abusers. Clearly, other factors must be involved.

Jensen describes a program for training social workers and nurses to set up behavioral programs with such parents, but presents no data. On the basis of anecdotal reports, Jensen "cryptically" concludes—the term is his, not ours—that behavior modification procedures for the correction of child abuse can be taught to social workers and nurses, that it is a useful intervention in "certain child abuse cases," that careful study rather than moral outrage is necessary to deal with child abuse, and that intervention for child abuse should be moved out of the Community Mental Health Center into the community in which the family lives. These recommendations are difficult to fault. Now if what is often said were only done. . . .

Teachers as Behavior Change Agents

In addition to parents, teachers have often been employed as behavior change agents in behavior modification programs in the classroom. As with parent training programs, teachers are frequently trained to carry out behavioral procedures through inservice workshops of one sort or another. The critical question, one that has not received enough systematic attention, is: Do teachers who attend these workshops behave any differently when they return to their classrooms? If the findings of Bowles and Nelson (1976) are typical, the use of workshops as a means of training teachers to implement behavioral principles and procedures requires rethinking.

In the first phase of the Bowles and Nelson study, teachers who participated in an inservice workshop on behavior modification were compared to a control group that received no didactic instruction in behavioral principles. Not surprisingly, the teachers who received instruction in behavior modification performed significantly better on a paper-and-pencil test of their knowledge of behavior modification than the control group. However, there was no difference between the two groups in terms of their actual behavior in the classroom. This failure to demonstrate significant effects of workshop training on teachers' behavior in the classroom setting occurred despite the fact that each workshop participant was required to complete a case study requirement. In other words, each workshop participant had to select a specific target behavior in his or her classroom for modification along the lines discussed and reviewed in the workshop. This case study requirement is a common assignment in workshops based on the responsive teaching model. Yet the skills presumably acquired in the course of conducting the case study did not generalize to the routine classroom situation. Science workshops on behavior modification are directed at altering behavior in the classroom rather than questionnaire responses. These findings are likely to give those who conduct such workshops routinely pause for thought.

In the second phase of their study, Bowles and Nelson provided teachers with bug-in-the-ear training in their own classrooms. Unlike the workshop format, this method resulted in significant change in the teachers' behavior in the classroom. In spelling out the implications of these data for the future conduct of workshops, Bowles and Nelson suggest several alternative procedures. One is to provide more direct in-class training, possibly using bug-in-the-ear feedback. Another is to provide videotaped feedback and graphs of observational data, or to encourage self-monitoring of teacher behavior. As a variation of the usual inservice training model, follow-up consultation might be offered the workshop participant. However, the suggestion that we focus on changes in the behavior of target children rather than teacher behavior is far more controversial and quite infeasible in many classroom situations.

A practical concern with how behavioral consulting with teachers is most effectively accomplished is the subject of Dorr's (1977) paper. Thus, he recommends situations in which principals are strong and decisive. Once they accept the program they are likely to ensure that it is carried out properly, whereas laissez-faire leaders do not provide sufficient supervisory control (see also Rollins, McCandless, Thompson, and Brassell, 1974—reprinted in Franks & Wilson, 1975, for further evidence on the important role played by principals in behavior modification programs in the classroom). Dorr recommends against the use of jargon or an insistence on the use of precise "scientific" language; references to basic animal studies are to be avoided. Emphasizing the virtues of "diplomacy" over "orthodoxy," Dorr notes that "Very few teachers will subject themselves to the training necessary to become a crack behavioral technician (i.e., mastering charting procedures, collecting masses of data, using ABA designs, etc.). Insistence on this kind of purity would leave the children of most teachers virtually untouched by positive behavioral procedures. Because our goal is to communicate effective approaches to as many teachers as possible, it is far wiser to use procedures that are palatable to teachers, even if they are not always elegant in the academic sense" (p. 101). We concur with this sensible recommendation. Evidence supporting Dorr's impressions about the hazards of using in-group jargon to describe behavioral procedures in the classroom has been presented by Woolfolk, Woolfolk, and Wilson (1977). Moreover, among others, Woolfolk et al. (1977) point out that, aside from needlessly offending most people's sensibilities, behavior modification terms such as "control," "shaping," and "programming" behavior all convey the notion that behavior is under unidirectional regulation by the environment, an *assumption* that has been widely contested and is by no means shared by all behavior therapists.

"Towards humanizing . . . classroom behavior management" is the theme of Zimmerman and Zimmerman's (1976) paper which similarly grapples with the problem of how best to approach teachers in the attempt to implement behavior modification programs in the classroom. To the extent that there are still behavior modifiers who inflexibly insist upon teachers' using "precise" behavioral jargon, the Zimmermans' self-disclosing account of the ills that befell them in this respect should serve as a salutary lesson. Their advocacy of the use of experiential procedures designed to heighten self-awareness will be of interest to the practitioner. Role-playing, reflection, and Gestalt-type group techniques are all endorsed with a view to more effectively recognizing teachers' problems and helping them to use behavioral methods. According to Zimmerman and Zimmerman, they have even renamed their course, "Humanistic Classroom Management," focusing on values and communication. From a strategic point of view, there is much to recommend their suggestions. What is important now is to conduct the appropriate research to evaluate how best to implement behavioral methods in the classroom, being bold enough to experiment with such non-behavioral methods as self-awareness training.

BEHAVIOR MODIFICATION IN THE CLASSROOM

In 1967, reacting to evidence that the initial gains of children who had participated in program Head Start had not been maintained in the public school, the U.S. Congress established Project Follow Through.

This project was designed to provide economically disadvantaged children with a more sustained program of remedial education that would hopefully result in lasting benefits. As a quasi-experimental, longitudinal program, the effects on educational achievement and other behaviors of 22 intervention programs based upon different educational and developmental theories were evaluated. Two of these 22 programs were behavioral in nature, deriving from the University of Kansas and the University of Oregon respectively. The importance of this evaluation of behavior modification in the classroom is obvious. Much of the research indicating the efficacy of behavioral procedures in changing classroom behavior has been demonstrative in nature, conducted under highly controlled conditions that do not obtain in the normal classroom. Furthermore, long-term follow-ups of the effects of these programs are almost totally lacking (cf. Keeley, Shemberg, & Carbonell, 1976).

Stallings (1975) has described an evaluation of seven of the programs used in Project Follow Through, including the two behavioral programs, one based on cognitive developmental theory, one on the English open classroom model, and three others drawn from the models of Piaget, Dewey, and the English Infant Schools. Among other reasons, these seven programs were chosen for evaluation because they were implemented in at least five different locations across the country. The two major questions addressed by Stallings were a) Were these different programs implemented successfully in accord with their respective assumptions across the different locations? and b) did these different programs significantly influence children's behavior?

The results show that the seven programs were implemented successfully. For example, regardless of where the behavioral programs were utilized, they were readily identified as similar to each other and different from other programs and non-program comparison classrooms. With respect to outcome, the two behavioral programs resulted in greater gains in first-grade reading than the other five programs and non-Follow Through classes. Similarly, the two behavioral programs produced more improvement in math scores than the other programs or non-program classes. Other dependent measures indicated that children in the behavioral programs tended to accept responsibility for their failures but not their successes. Stallings attributes lower absence rates and higher scores on a nonverbal problem-solving test of reasoning (the Raven's Coloured Progressive Matrices) "to more open and flexible instructional approaches in which children are provided a wide variety of activities and materials and where children engage independently in activities and select their own groups part of the time" (p. 106). The overall conclusion reached by Stallings is that the seven Follow Through models "are bringing different strengths to their pupils, and each is bringing advantages not usually found in traditional classrooms" (p. 106).

A commentary on Stallings' stdudy by Resnick and Leinhardt (1975) is useful in that it helps place it in perspective as well as emphasizing its importance. They point out that most outcome research on comparative instructional programs has failed to determine whether the programs were implemented appropriately and has rarely demonstrated differential efficacy between programs. Yet this apparent lack of differences between different programs runs counter to observation and common sense. The answer, they suggest, lies in the fact that the research evaluation strategies were inappropriate. Certain criteria must be met if research is to discriminate among potentially effective programs. First, actual classroom practices have to be documented and related to specific outcome goals. Second, multiple measures, including academic, social, and attitudinal effects need to be sampled in outcome studies. According to Resnick and Leinhardt, Stallings presents the first major published report that attempts to meet these criteria. (There is a striking parallel between many of the problems of traditional program evaluation research in education and the problems that have obscured potentially important differences among psychological treatments in the psychotherapy outcome literature [cf. Kazdin & Wilson, in press]. Moreover, Resnick and Leinhardt's recommendations about documenting the adequacy of testing of the treatment programs as well as multiple measures of specific functioning similarly are consistent with Kazdin and Wilson's suggestions for improved outcome research in psychotherapy and behavior therapy.)

Because the Stallings study represents such a significant outcome study of educational programs it deserves careful, critical scrutiny. There are methodological problems with the study. Thus, the conclusion about programs having been successfully and consistently implemented is heavily dependent on observations that were open to bias and some unreliability. Each observer made observations on the adequacy of program implementation in only one classroom at only one location. This results in a program × observer confound. Since each observer was local to the region where the program was instituted, he or she probably knew the nature and aims of the program and thus might have biased accounts of how well it was implemented. This problem was not due to a methodological oversight as much as it was dictated by the practical and economic difficulties of carrying out a complicated study.

Another problem with this study and Stallings' conclusions concerns the measurement of social behaviors such as independence, cooperation, and initiative. It is perhaps inaccurate, note Resnick and Leinhardt, to label these behaviors as *outcome* measures; rather, they reflect the extent to which the different programs were successful in creating a classroom environment consistent with their assumptions. Thus, the open classroom setting facilitated these behaviors, whereas in the structured classroom children were not given as much opportunity to engage in these behaviors. The data fail to indicate whether children in the open classroom would initiate these social behaviors in another, more neutral setting. Nor do they establish that the occurrence of these child-initiated activities facilitate learning—an important reservation. Furthermore, there is no way of assessing how children in the structured behavioral programs might have acted had they been exposed to a less structured environment. It is one thing to observe behavior that occurs in one situation, quite another to make inferences about what could occur under different environmental circumstances.

The use of group contingencies in behavior modification in the classroom was discussed in last year's volume (Franks & Wilson, 1966, pp. 451-453). Since then, Hayes (1976) has published a review of the literature on this topic. Consistent with previous evaluations, Hayes concludes that group and individual reinforcement systems appear to be equally effective, although she emphasizes methodological shortcomings in many of the studies on which this conclusion is based. Among others, we have voiced concern about the possible side effects of group contingency programs. Indeed, we quoted Martin's (1972) view that group reinforcement systems be used only in "severe situations where traditional methods fail and where the teacher makes special efforts to control the severity of the pressure [exerted by other children on the individual child]" (p. 57). Hayes is less reserved about the utility of group contingencies, and does not even address Martin's specific concerns. According to Hayes, both positive and negative side effects on the individual child's sociometric status have been shown, the critical variables in this process remaining to be identified. The unpredictability of this fact alone would seem to indicate greater caution in the use of group contingencies than Hayes conveys. On the positive side, cooperative interactions among children in a group reinforcement program have been noted, and Hayes suggests how these might be put to constructive use.

Finally, Hayes suggests that the potential long-term effects of group contingencies raise important moral and sociological issues. Group consequences that purportedly develop strong mutual peer control and subordinate individual achievement are starkly contrasted with programs for the individual. The implication is that it is the Soviet school system versus the American free enterprise ethic. While we agree that the long-term (as well as the short-term!) effects of group contingency programs be monitored closely, the distinction between "the group" versus "the individual" is overdrawn.

The roles of parents and teachers as behavior change agents have already been discussed. Scott and McLaughlin (1976) review the use of peers in classroom management. Attention from peers seems to be a potent reinforcer for children, one that can result in beneficial behavior change. Moreover, peers have been shown to function effectively as contingency managers in the regulation of other children's behavior. The practical possibilities of these findings are obvious, the prospect of certain children assisting the teacher in the implementation of behavioral programs being an appealing one. However, Scott and McLaughlin also note the ethical issues raised by the prospect of using peers as "contingency managers." There is, as yet, relatively little evidence about the effects of the child's functioning as a contingency manager on that child's own social and academic behavior. The data available are encouraging, indicating that children may benefit both socially and academically by acting as contingency managers. Furthermore, other children may even prefer peers as contingency managers. However, considerable caution and careful evaluation of possible side effects will be necessary to evaluate the broader implications of using peers as behavior change agents in the classroom or in other situations. Specifically, the evolving nature of the interpersonal relationships among children in these different roles will need to be assessed.

Last year we discussed the overjustification hypothesis and the criticism of token reinforcement programs that it has generated (Franks & Wilson, 1976, pp. 447-451). We suggested that the basic weakness in the arguments of critics such as Levine and Fasnacht (1974) is that it is predicated upon external reward of high frequency behaviors that are intrinsically reinforcing. Ideally, a token economy should not be used in such circumstances, but only when there appears to be no other alternative to increasing the frequency of low or even non-existent behaviors. Moreover, appropriately used, tangible rewards are faded out as rapidly as possible so that the target behaviors are maintained by naturally occurring contingencies (cf. O'Leary & O'Leary, 1976).

The second paper reprinted in this Section—by Greene, Sternberg, and Lepper—provides a more relevant test of the overjustification hypothesis under conditions more closely resembling a well-designed token reinforcement program. Their fundamental premise is that, to the extent that token programs are commonly used for *relatively* low rates of target behavior (as opposed to non-existence of the behaviors), the possibility exists that external reward undermines intrinsic interest. Greene et al.'s results fail to settle the issue, but they do indicate that multiple-trial external reinforcement procedures as are used in token programs may produce overjustification effects. However, the failure to uncover any apparent overjustification effect in their high interest group—the one that the theory must predict an effect for—creates difficulties for the theory. As the authors point out, even in this study the token reinforcement procedures employed differed from those that are normally found in practice. Given the fact that the critical variables that produce overjustification effect are still somewhat unclear, these procedural differences might be extremely important.

Greene et al. emphasize that not all external rewards are predicted to undermine subsequent intrinsic interest, as we may have suggested in last year's volume. Rather, it is said to be the information that rewards convey about the individual's motivation, competence, and likelihood of future reinforcement that is the critical determinant of the overjustification effect. Regardless of the specific fate of this currently controversial hypothesis, to the extent that it encourages rigorous research on how cognitive activities mediate external rewards it will have served a useful purpose.

SPECIFIC CHILDHOOD DISORDERS

Hyperactivity

The case for developing an effective psychological treatment as an adjunct or an alternative to pharmacotherapy with hyperactive children is compelling. Drug treatment does not help all hyperactive children, nor does it foster appropriate social and academic growth. At best, it makes it possible. Moreover, there are problems with drug-related side-effects (cf. Ayllon, Layman, & Kandel, 1975—reprinted in Franks & Wilson, 1976). O'Leary, Pelham, Rosenbaum, and Price (1976) showed that a behavioral treatment program with hyperactive children (average

age of eight years) attending normal or non-remedial classes was significantly more effective than a no treatment control group. The behavioral program used consisted of the following steps: 1) specification of each child's daily classroom goals; 2) praising the child for efforts to achieve those goals; 3) end-of-day evaluation of the child's behavior relevant to the specified goals; 4) sending the parents a daily report card on their child's daily progress; and 5) rewarding the child for improvement. Constant contact and good communication among therapist, parent, and teacher were a part of this program. Although no attempt was made to alter the child's behavior at home, O'Leary et al. note that behavioral programs could readily be adapted to this end. While these results are encouraging, it must be remembered that the control group was not a stringent one. However, on the basis of available data, the comparative efficacy of behavioral programs for hyperactive children is impressive (e.g., Ayllon et al., 1975).

Christensen (1975) investigated the combined effects of Ritalin and a token reinforcement procedure in the treatment of hyperactive, institutionalized retarded youths whose ages ranged from 9 to 16 years. Using a within-subject design, a baseline phase was followed sequentially by the behavioral program plus the drug, and the behavioral program plus a placebo under double-blind conditions. Following a reversal to baseline conditions, the same treatment conditions were repeated. The results show that the behavioral plus placebo condition produced significant decreases in disruptive behavior and increased work-related activities. Substituting the Ritalin for the placebo resulted in very limited additional therapeutic benefits. Although this study provides additional evidence for the usefulness of behavioral procedures in the treatment of hyperactivity, it does not represent an adequate test of drug treatment. In the first place, standardized doses of Ritalin were administered instead of individually titrating the drug dose. In the second place, the effects of Ritalin alone were never observed.

Self-Injurious and Psychotic Behavior

The third article reprinted in this Section is by Carr, Newsom, and Binkoff. As the authors point out, the several published successes in which contingent reinforcement programs reduced or eliminated self-injurious behavior must be balanced against the documented cases where reinforcement methods have been ineffective (see Romanczyk & Goren, 1975, for example). The results of Carr et al.'s careful experimental analysis of the possible antecedent stimuli governing self-destructive behavior take us one step closer to beginning to understand this disturbing phenomenon. The authors also appropriately caution therapists not to assume immediately that a contingent reinforcement program is the preferred method in all cases, but to conduct a searching behavioral analysis of the individual child's problems.

Aversion conditioning of one sort or another has been commonly used to treat self-injurious behavior (cf. Bachman, 1972—reprinted in Franks & Wilson, 1974). Duker (1976a) reports the treatment of a profoundly retarded, 16-year-old female who banged her head against the wall. Both punishment and an escape-avoidance conditioning method were effective in decreasing self-injurious behavior. However, only the escape-avoidance conditioning procedure resulted in generalized treatment effects. The results of the punishment contingency appeared short-lived when the contingency was withdrawn. Duker offers an explanation for the differential effectiveness of these two methods, while in a response to this paper, Gathercole (1976) points out the desirability of reinforcing behaviors that are incompatible with self-injury. In a further comment, Duker (1976b) states that this procedure, while sound in principle, is often not feasible in large, under-staffed wards.

Frankel and Simmons (1976) speculate about the processes responsible for the acquisition and maintenance of self-injurious behavior in retarded and schizophrenic children. They conclude that self-injurious behavior "is learned in low-functioning children as a coercive alternative for obtaining adult attention. Treatment literature, particularly studies in which time-out interventions were employed, offered some support for the acquisition of self-injurious behavior within both escape avoidance and shaping paradigms. In literature on primates as well as human epidemiology, the possibility of unconditional respondent origins for this behavior has been suggested. Finally, in studies where punishment was used, some evidence has been offered for conditional reinforcing and discriminative stimulus control of pain in the maintenance of this behavior" (p. 519).

The problem in Frankel and Simmons' conceptualization, evident in the preceding quotation, is that they are drawing conclusions about the *acquisition* of behavior on the basis of *treatment* outcome. A logical error is committed. Knowledge about how behavior might be modified is not tantamount to evidence about how it originally developed, a point repeatedly emphasized in the literature (e.g., Davison, 1969; Rimland, 1964). At best, Frankel and Simmons' review evaluates the relation of treatment variables to outcome. Even here, however, a thorough methodological appraisal of the treatment outcome literature would unquestionably reveal numerous inadequacies with respect to basic design, inadequate controls, lack of follow-up, and other problems.

Lichstein and Schreibman (1976) review the use of electric shock in the treatment of autistic children. All 12 studies reviewed indicated that electric shock was "highly effective" in reducing or eliminating undesirable behavior. Focusing particularly on the side effects of punishment procedures using shock, Lichstein and Schreibman conclude that most side effects are positive in nature, including response generalization, enhanced social behavior, and "positive emotional behavior." A limited number of negative side effects were reported. Recognizing the reservations that are held about aversion procedures, the authors point out that we cannot afford to ignore any treatment approach that may be of help to autistic children. Their point that decisions about the use of aversion procedures should be based on the rational evaluation of the specific child's problem and alternative treatments rather than the practitioner's own emotional biases is well taken.

Proposed similarities (theoretical and/or procedural) between behavior therapy and psychodynamic therapy are presented perennially, as this Series has frequently observed. However, it is rare that the argument is made with respect to such a severe disorder as childhood autism. Referring to Bettelheim's (1967) treatment approach as an exemplar of the psychodynamic approach, Helm (1976) tries to develop the procedural similarities between the two methods. His case is unconvincing. The tacit assumption that attention to the relationship between the therapist and child is inevitably psychodynamic in nature is quite misleading, as Wilson and Evans (1976) have shown. His conclusion, that both behavioral and psychodynamic aspects of intervention are important, and "that both play a role in virtually all therapeutic efforts" is clichéd and unsubstantiated by the available experimental literature. Unsuccessful as a whole, Helm's paper contains an interesting historical reference to a case report by Witmer of the treatment of a psychotic child over 50 years ago.

Childhood Asthma

Creer, Renne, and Christian (1976) provide an informative description of the contributions of behavioral methods to the treatment of childhood asthma at the Children's Asthma Research Institute and Hospital

(CARIH) in Denver, Colorado. The role of systematic desensitization in reducing panic attacks and fear of needles or oxygen tents, the use of reinforcement procedures in the management of malingerers, and strategies for generalization of improvement to the home environment are described. In terms of the latter, Creer et al. note that "the degree of success ultimately achieved in rehabilitating children is often tied directly to the degree of success in rehabilitating their families" (p. 231). Parent training, based on behavioral principles, is an important part of the program.

Teaching children with asthma to use the emergency respiratory equipment is another crucial aspect of the treatment program at CARIH. Renne and Creer (1976) have reported an innovative study in which they used reinforcement principles to train children to use the Intermittent Positive-Pressure Breathing (IPPB) apparatus. This device delivers broncodilator medication to the lungs under positive pressure. Specific components of the behavior—attention, diaphragmatic breathing, and proper handling of the equipment—were identified and explicitly shaped using a multiple-baseline design. These procedures were effective in teaching the children how to use the IPPB and resulted in significantly greater relief of asthma symptoms. This increased efficacy of the medication had substantial benefits. More intense forms of therapy, such as hospitalization or the administration of corticosteroids were required less frequently. That drugs, such as the corticosteroids, could be reduced is especially significant in view of their often adverse side effects. In a second study, nurses were rapidly trained to instruct children along similar behavioral lines, thereby increasing the efficiency and feasibility of the program.

Conduct Disorders

The fourth paper reprinted here is Kent and O'Leary's controlled outcome study of the behavioral treatment of conduct problem children. There are several important features of this paper to which attention should be drawn. First, it represents an excellent example of the problem-oriented, treatment package evaluation strategy in outcome research (see Kazdin & Wilson, in press). While the program was structured, treatment components were clearly specified and the methods flexible enough so that the therapist could tailor them to deal with the particular problems of individual children. Moreover, the component parts of the program had each been developed empirically in controlled laboratory research by O'Leary and his associates. Very often, treatment packages consist of so many different methods that it is impossible to determine what the behavior change agents are (see Franks & Wilson, 1976, pp. 388-389; Kazdin & Wilson, in press).

Second, the intervention program is *feasible* from the practitioner's point of view. Kent and O'Leary clearly point out and describe how most behavior modification programs in the classroom have relied upon resources that are simply not available to the average clinician. It is difficult to over-emphasize the relevance of research of this nature that takes well-established methods, proven effective in changing behavior in the laboratory, and determines how to maximize their effects in a realistic fashion in real-life settings. In an important extension of this line of research, Kent and O'Leary (1977) have shown that a team of Ph.D. and B.A.-level therapists working together are as effective as Ph.D. therapists alone in administering the intervention program. Indeed, teachers reported that they preferred working with the Ph.D./B.A.-level team. (The successful replication of the Kent and O'Leary study reprinted here by other therapists attests to the operational precision with which it was described—a further indication of a useful treatment package).

A third characteristic of the Kent and O'Leary study is that they included a no treatment control group. The fact that this group seemed to "catch" the experimental group in terms of improvement in behavior in the classroom at follow-up emphasizes the importance of appropriate control groups in an area of behavioral research in which such controls have typically been sorely lacking. Lastly, this is one of the relatively few studies that has included a long-term follow-up. Once again, behavior modification in the classroom has been a research area in which the focus has almost always been on short-term effects of a demonstration-type study (see Keeley, Shemberg & Carbonell, 1976).

BEHAVIOR THERAPY WITH THE FAMILIES OF DELINQUENTS

The final paper reproduced in this Section—by Alexander, Barton, Schiavo, and Parsons—presents data that are not exactly common fare among reports of behavior modification intervention programs, namely, therapist factors in treatment outcome. The apparent importance of therapist behaviors on treatment outcome should not necessarily be unexpected; nor are these effects inconsistent with a social learning model (cf. Wilson, 1977 d; Wilson & Evans, 1976, 1977). Other strands of evidence indicating the influence on outcome of the therapist's behavior have become apparent. For example, as discussed in Section II of the present volume, Mathews et al. (1976) found some support for the role of a therapist effect on the outcome of such structured methods as imaginal and *in vivo* flooding. Also, Stuart and Lott (1972—reprinted in Franks & Wilson, 1974) appealed to therapist factors in accounting for their outcome data. It is important to reiterate Alexander et al.'s point that relationship factors alone do little to change the behavior of the sort of delinquent they have described (see Parsons & Alexander, 1973—reprinted in Franks & Wilson, 1974). This is clearly indicated by the essential failure of a client-centered treatment program to effect improvement.

Stuart, Tripodi, Jayaratne, and Camburn (1976) compared behavioral contracting to a no treatment control group in the modification of the behavior of predelinquents. The youths were treated together with their families. As described by Stuart et al., the behavioral contracting procedure required the therapist to act as a mediator who: "1) creates an environment in which each person is free to express his or her desires, 2) offers a rationale for changing behavior so that each participant can make concessions without losing face, and 3) then provides a structure for carrying these negotiated changes into the natural environment of community living" (p. 245). Attempts to alter the youths' behavior at school consisted of cooperation with teachers in devising contingency contracts that specified mutual responsibilities. In particular, a report card method was employed in which teachers would rate each youth's behavior during the day and parents would administer consequences at home. Although the no treatment control group received no formal therapy, families in this condition were not discouraged from seeking help elsewhere. Apparently, about one-fifth of these families sought other forms of assistance.

The results are disappointing. On neither of the two objective methods of outcome—academic performance and attendance at school—was the behavioral contracting group superior to the control group. Indeed, both groups showed lower rates of school attendance after therapy than at pretreatment. Subjective ratings by the youths' families and their teachers did indicate that the behavioral group produced greater improvement, but in view of the lack of change on the objective measures and the methodological limitations of the subjective ratings, these data must be interpreted with great caution. Stuart et al. suggest that one reason for the lack of success of their behavioral contracting program was that teachers did not comply fully with the program. In other words, teachers often failed to indicate that a youth had misbehaved during school periods so as to avoid a confrontation with that youth who knew that he would be faced with negative consequences at home for a bad report.

Finally, Stumphauzer (1976) presents a brief overview of the history of behavior therapy with delinquent youths and reviews different behavioral procedures for intervening in the community setting to prevent or modify delinquent behavior.

SECTION V: BEHAVIOR THERAPY WITH CHILDREN AND ADOLESCENTS

9

THE USE OF SIBLINGS AS AN ADJUNCT TO THE BEHAVIORAL TREATMENT OF CHILDREN IN THE HOME WITH PARENTS AS THERAPISTS

Henry Lavigueur
Concordia University

The use of a sibling as a therapeutic aid to home parental management of a disruptive child was investigated in two families, using a multiple baseline technique. Having both siblings and parents act as therapists is advantageous in modifying a child's disruptive behaviors when inappropriate behaviors have a history of sibling reinforcement. However, in one of the families the undesirable behaviors of the target child were inappropriately attended to more frequently by his parents than by his sibling. The appropriate behaviors of the treated child appeared to be manipulable by parental treatment alone in both families. The sibling behavior modifier exhibited improvement in the specific behaviors which he treated in the target child. A more generalized reduction in the sibling's inappropriate behav-

---

Reprinted with permission from *Behavior Therapy*, 7, 602-613, 1976.

This article is based on a part of a doctoral dissertation submitted to the Department of Psychology at the University of Illnois in 1973. Sincere appreciation is expressed to committee members Sidney Bijou, Frank Costin, Donald Shannon, and Ralph Swarr for their valuable contributions to this study. Special thanks are extended to Warren Steinman, who, as thesis supervisor, provided help and encouragement in bringing the research to completion.

> ior occurred in the family in which the sibling was a more consistent behavior modifier. In the family wherein the sibling was inconsistent in his performance as a therapist, a correction in the preferential parental attention to the target child (which had resulted from treatment) recovered his performance. Sibling relations improved concomitantly with the sibling's treating the target child in a more positive manner.

The attention of a problem child's peer group may influence his behavior more than similar stimulation provided by adults (Browning & Stover, 1971; Buehler, Patterson & Furniss, 1966; Patterson, Littman & Bricker, 1967; Patterson, Note 1). Furthermore, the effectiveness of using peers as behavior modifiers in institutional settings has been well demonstrated (Browning & Stover, 1971; Solomon & Wahler, 1973; Wahler, 1967; Weisen, Hartley, Richardson & Roske, 1967). To date, there has been no controlled home investigation employing children as change agents for their siblings.

The "helper therapy principle" (Reisman, 1965) predicts advantageous consequences to anyone taking on a therapeutic role in the form of better adjustment and broadened perspective. Several studies specifically indicate the beneficial influence on the interpersonal and task-oriented behavior of school children used as change agents for peers (Freeman, 1971; Hawkinshire, 1963). But why would the peer acting as a helper show increased adjustment? Pearl (Note 2) proposes that he develops "a stake in the system" and therefore feels it more necessary to follow the system's code. The stake in the system may be an increased return in attention to the peer who is placed in a therapeutic role of giving approval. Charlesworth and Hartup (1967) and Weiss (1966) indicate that the amount of social reinforcement given by an individual seems to be positively related to the amount that individual receives from others. Thus, it might be predicted that using peers as change agents of disruptive behaviors of another child should contribute to the reciprocity and maintenance of a treatment program.

The present study examines the use of siblings as therapeutic aids to home parental management (via positive reinforcement, extinction, and time-out procedures) of a child who is considered disruptive. We ask two questions: Is a treatment program which includes siblings as behavior modifiers more effective than parental treatment alone in modifying the behavior of a child designated as a conduct problem? What are the benefits to the sibling acting as a modifier?

METHOD

Subjects. In each of two families, a target child was designated as a particular problem by his parents. Another child, who acted as a therapeutic aid, was less of a conduct problem, although exhibiting some undersirable behaviors of his or her own.

Family A was a working-class, black family with two daughters. The parents complained that the 12-year-old target child was withdrawn and hostile, sarcastic and evasive, participating little in household duties and activities. They described her 10-year-old sibling as being more extraverted, verbal, and a great help around the house. Family B was a white, upper-middle-income family with three sons, ages 10, 9, and 3. The father was a professional, the mother a housewife. The 9-year-old target child was described by his parents as rude, tense, and a demanding child. The 10-year-old sibling who served as a therapeutic aid was described as an easy-going child whose behaviors did not constitute a particular problem.

PROCEDURE

An observation rating scale was employed within the home by two experimentally naive undergraduate students. One was present during all intervention sessions, the second during about half the sessions to ascertain reliabilities. Observations were made only when all family members were present. Precautions were taken to minimize the reactivity of family members to having observers in the home (cf. Johnson & Bolstad, 1973, 7-67; Lytton, 1973). Several prebaseline visits allowed the families to habituate to the observers' presence. To decrease their anxiety and embarrassment, parents were given a thorough explanation of the use of observation and informed that the observers were student research participants as opposed to experts in child rearing.

The behavioral categories presented in Table 1 were used to record the appropriate and inappropriate behaviors of the target child and sibling and the attention paid to these behaviors by the home therapists (the attention of both parents as well as the attention given by the sibling to the target child). Observers sampled three types of child-home therapist (s) interaction: target child-parent (both mother and father, each recorded separately) interaction, sibling-parent interaction, and target child-sibling interaction.

During 45 min of continuous recording, each type of interaction was observed consecutively for only 3 min before sampling 3 min of each of the other two types. Five such sequences during each session provided

15 min of each of the three interactions. Rates of behavior for the target child during each session are based on 30 min of observation whereas rates for the sibling are based on 15 minutes. A single occurrence of any behavior merited recording during a 20-sec observation interval, no matter what the duration of that occurrence.

Therapeutic treatment of the target child was carried out by the parents and sibling under the direction of the experimenter. The study was divided into five phases:

Baseline: Ten sessions of parents, target child, and sibling interacting in their usual fashion at home.

Parental treatment 1. During the next five observation sessions parents were instructed and cued by the experimenter to reinforce one of the target child's appropriate behaviors, positive verbalizations, and to ignore or time-out one of his inappropriate behaviors, negative verbalizations. Only in Family B were negative verbalizations sufficiently intense and disruptive to necessitate time-out.

During observation sessions, a "go-ahead" hand motion indicated to parents that they were to give the target child attention and praise. A "stop" hand motion signaled parents to withdraw their attention by avoiding body, eye, and verbal contact. The experimenter's pointing to the child's bedroom cued parents to use time-out, that is, to take the target child to his room. As parents learned to respond appropriately to the target child's behavior on their own, the cueing system was used less frequently.

At the end of each session parents were given specific suggestions (e.g., "Do not look at Johnny when he is muttering under his breath as this will tend to increase this behavior") or constructive praise (e.g., "I like the way you told Johnny to go to his room—you weren't overly emotional nor did you give him long explanations concerning what he did wrong").

Parental and sibling treatment I. During the next five sessions, parents continued to differentially reinforce (or time-out) the target child's verbalizations. However, the sibling was also instructed by his parents to attend to positive verbalizations and ignore negative verbalizations of the target child. With the experimenter present, the sibling was told that his brother (or sister) was currently having conduct problems which might get him in trouble and that the sibling could help him overcome these problems. The parents role-played positive and negative verbalizations and how the sibling should respond to these behaviors. It was emphasized that, in the future, the sibling might have similar problems and that the target child might then help him. Parents were encouraged

TABLE 1

The Observation Rating Scale

Child row (target child or sibling):
Inappropriate behaviors

(a) Negative verbalizations—rude verbalizations (e.g., "Shut up," "None of your business," "Who asked you "); evasiveness in answers to parents' questioning; screaming (vocalizations louder than conversational level excluding sounds appropriate to toys such as planes, guns, etc.)

(b) Noncompliance—not following orders; not responding (neither verbally nor by gestures) when spoken to. (This category was only employed in Family B.)

(c) Aggression—pushing someone else's property over or destroying it; hitting; kicking; shoving; pinching; slapping; attempting to strike; biting; pulling hair; *but not*: (1) striking oneself; (2) throwing ball, airplanes, or pillows (even at people) as these are play objects.

(d) Negative affect—crying; dragging feet and lowered head when these are not customary postures; making faces whether or not at others (typical of this would be frowning, sticking out tongue, pushing out lips in combination with squinting).

Appropriate behaviors

(a) Positive verbalizations—all speech directed to another person which is not negative.

(b) Spontaneous verbalizations—that non-negative speech which is not made in response to another person's previous question, order, or statement and therefore initiates a new conversation.

(c) Helping—following orders or carrying out household duties, whether by request or spontaneously. (This category was only employed in Family B.)

(d) Offering help—a verbal proposal of help (e.g., "May I get it for you?," "I'll do the dishes this time."); spontaneous initiation of a helping response. (This category was only employed in Family A.)

(e) Positive affect—smiling, laughing, singing, humming, dancing.

(f) Playing—engaging in a pleasurable activity which involves cooperative interaction with another child (e.g., playing ball, cards, building toy airplanes together but excluding television-watching and other such autonomous activities).

Therapist row (s) (mother, father, or sibling):

(a) Negative attention—physical restraint or negative physical contact (hitting, striking, pinching) initiated by the therapist towards the child; critical verbal comments or high intensity verbalizations (yelling, screaming, scolding, or raising voice) directed towards the child; keeping child from doing activity, sending to room, use of time-out.

(b) Positive attention—praising the child; smiling at the child; initiating a play activity with the child; non-negative physical contact with the child.

(c) Neutral attention—all verbal attention (including orders and commands) to the child which is neither negative nor positive.

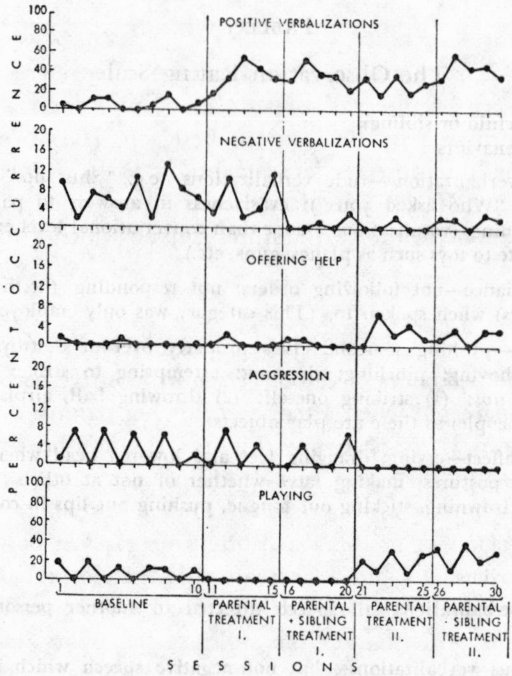

FIG. 1. Percentage of occurrence over time of the target child's behaviors in Family A.

to praise the sibling for carrying out his work, letting him know specifically how he was being helpful.

Parental treatment II. During the five sessions of this phase, the previous parental and sibling handling of verbalizations continued. However, the parents were now instructed and cued to reinforce a second appropriate behavior (offering help in Family A, helping in Family B) and to ignore (or time-out) a second inappropriate behavior (aggression in Family A, noncompliance in Family B). Again, Family A parents did not use time-out as the aggressive behavior of the target child, shoving and back-slapping of the sibling, was not sufficiently intense to disrupt family interaction.

Parental and sibling treatment II. All previous parental and sibling contingencies were still employed during this final five session phase. The sibling was now instructed and reinforced for attending to the second appropriate behavior and ignoring the second inappropriate behavior of the target child.

RESULTS AND DISCUSSION

Reliability was calculated by dividing intervals of agreement between the two observers by intervals of agreement plus intervals of disagreement and multiplying by 100 (Bijou, Peterson, Harris, Allen, & Johnson, 1969). The interobserver agreement on each of the 13 categories ranged from 83 to 95%. Calculations were performed on data pooled from the 25 sessions in the two families during which a second observer was present.

Family A

The desirable behaviors of the target child, positive verbalizations and offering help, increased when attended to by her parents during Parental Treatments I and II, respectively (Figure 1). One undesirable behavior of the target child, negative verbalizations, decreased only under the therapeutic manipulation of her sibling during Parental and Sibling I.

The sibling behavior modifier exhibited increases in positive verbalizations and offering help and a decrease in negative verbalizations when she began to treat these behaviors (Figure 2). No parallel change was noted in parents' attention to the sibling's behaviors during these periods.* Improvements in the sibling's behavior appear to be the outcome of her acting as a behavior modifier, rather than an outcome of parental handling of her behavior.

When the sibling modified negative verbalizations in the target child during Parental and Sibling I, not only her own negative verbalizations but also her own aggression and negative affect * decreased. Again, it should be noted that there was no change in parental attention to these behaviors. The target child's negative verbalizations decreased concomitantly with the sibling's treatment of this behavior but her aggression and negative affect only decreased concomitantly with parental treatment of the former behavior. This suggests that acting as a behavior modifier may be a more powerful treatment strategy for reducing generalized negative behavior than being the recipient of behavior modification efforts of significant others.

During the final two treatment periods, during which no specific

* Tables indicating the percentage of the target child's and sibling's behaviors attended to (positively, neutrally and negatively) by other family members may be obtained in full from the author upon request.

* Negative affect is not included in Figs. 1 and 2 since this behavior correlated with aggression in both the target child ($r = .621$, $p < .005$) and the sibling ($r = .546$, $p < .005$) over the 30 sessions of the study (Pearson Product Moment).

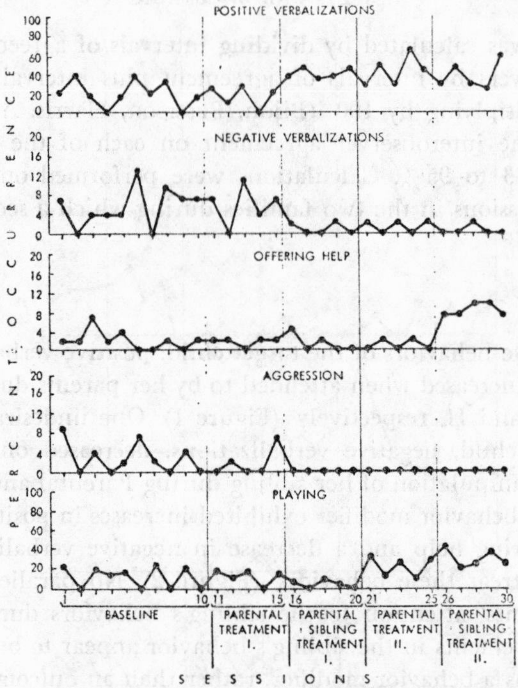

FIG. 2. Percentage of occurrence over time of the sibling's behaviors in Family A.

manipulation took place for the purpose of increasing their playing together, the two girls began playing more. Specific behavior improvements in both children generalized to play behavior which was not treated.

Family B

Unlike the Family A sibling, who consistently modified her interactions with the target child according to the treatment plan, the Family B sibling exhibited some reversal to baseline interaction during Parental Treatment II (Figure 4). For example, during this period, he responded with negative attention to 5% of the target child's positive verbalizations (as compared to baseline and Parental and Sibling Treatment I rates of 5 and 0%, respectively). Nevertheless, most of the improvement in the sibling's behavior can be traced to his acting as a behavior modifier. The sibling exhibited increases in positive speech and helping

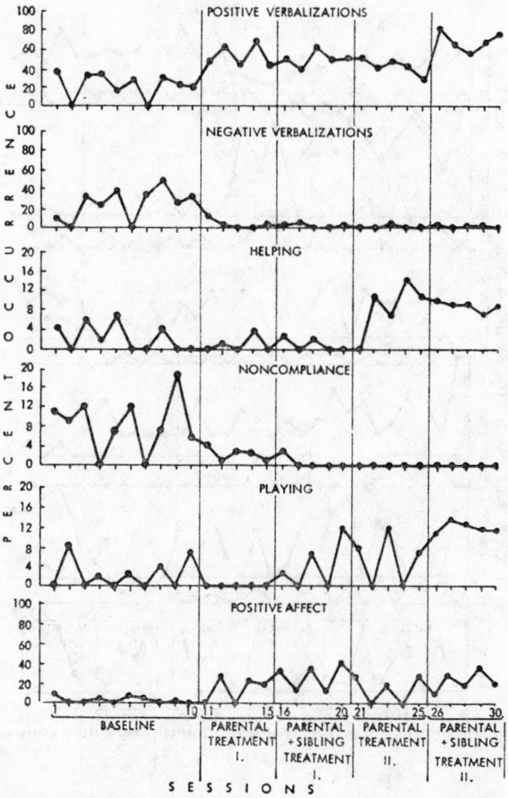

FIG. 3. Percentage of occurrence over time of the target child's behaviors in Family B.

and decreases in negative verbalizations and noncompliance when he began to treat these behaviors.

The target child's positive verbalizations and positive affect increased during Parental Treatment I and his helping behavior increased during Parental Treatment II, demonstrating that parental attention influenced the frequency of these desirable behaviors. However the target child showed most positive affect during Parental and Sibling Treatments I and II, those periods when the sibling reinforced him differentially for appropriate behavior (Figure 3).

In Family A, the sibling's acting as a behavior modifier led to an immediate decrease in all of the sibling's negative behaviors whereas the application of behavior modification techniques to the target child only decreased that negative behavior of the target child which was specifically

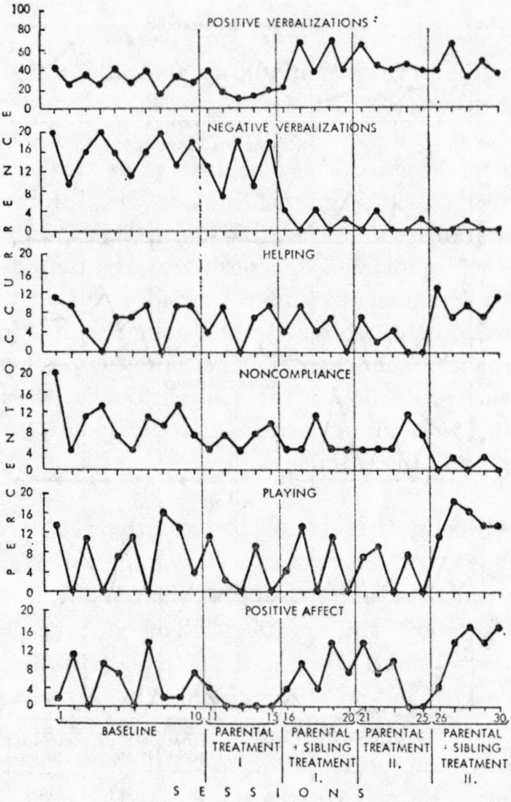

FIG. 4. Percentage of occurrence over time of the sibling's behaviors in Family B.

treated. However in Family B the target child decreased all his aversive behaviors* (including noncompliance which continued receiving inappropriate parental attention) simultaneously with parental treatment of negative verbalizations, whereas the sibling did not show less noncompliance, until the period when he acted as a behavior modifier for this behavior. One hypothesis is that the Family B sibling did not enact the role of behavior modifier as the Family A sibling had. In fact, as noted above, there was greater inconsistency in the sibling performance as a behavior modifier over time.

* Negative affect and aggression in both the target child ($r = .594$, $p < .01$; $r = .672$, $p < .005$, respectively) and in the sibling ($r = .644$, $p < .005$; $r = .781$, $p < .005$, respectively) were correlated with their respective rates of negative verbalizations over the 30 sessions of the study (Pearson Product Moment).

One contributing factor to this inconsistency may have been the marked preferential treatment of the target child which was noted in Family B once parental treatment began. For example, while during baseline the mother in Family B attended equally to the positive verbalizations of both children, during the first three treatment periods she attended positively to 9% and neutrally to 56% of the target child's positive verbalizations while attending positively to only 1% and neutrally to only 18% of the sibling's positive verbalizations. When, upon the experimenter's request, parents equalized attention to the two children during Parental and Sibling II, the sibling regained his performance as an effective behavior modifier. Furthermore his positive affect, which had decreased to zero during the last two sessions of Parental Treatment II, concomitantly with his reverting from therapeutic interaction with the target child, exhibited its highest frequency. Both children's play also increased.

It is also noteworthy that during baseline the Family A sibling reinforced a much greater percentage of the target child's inappropriate behaviors than did the Family B sibling. The Family A sibling had attended neutrally to 60% and negatively to 50% of the negative verbalizations of the target child whereas the Family B sibling had attended neutrally to only 17% and negatively to only 28% of the negative verbalizations of his brother. Meanwhile the Family B parents paid somewhat more attention to inappropriate behavior of the target child than did the Family A parents. This may be why the Family A target child's negative verbalizations did not decrease until treated by the sibling, whereas parental treatment alone was sufficient to eliminate all inappropriate behaviors of the Family B target child.

It is essential to take into account the family "dynamics" prior to home intervention. One cannot assume that any given technique will be equally effective when applied without knowledge of the agent's value as a social reinforcer. Nevertheless, employing the sibling as a behavior modifier led to improvement in the behavior of the helper as well as the interaction of the children in both families.

The rate of spontaneous verbalizations (those verbalizations not preceded by others' comments) of the target child and the sibling in Family A, as well as the target child and the sibling in Family B correlate highly and significantly with their respective rates of positive verbalizations over all 30 sessions. Thus, increases in verbalizations were not merely a result of increased parental elicitation of speech after treatment began.

CONCLUSIONS

Having both siblings and parents act as home therapists is advantageous in modifying a child's disruptive behaviors when inappropriate behaviors have a history of sibling reinforcement. Undesirable behaviors may be inappropriately attended to more frequently by parents than by siblings in some families. Much of the literature suggests that the disruptive behaviors of a problem child are strongly reinforced by his peer group (Browning & Stover, 1971; Buehler et al., 1966; O'Leary & O'Leary, 1972; Patterson et al., 1967; Patterson, Note 1). However, these studies deal with institutionalized children and their peers who have been officially labeled as deviant or disturbed. The present study deals with siblings within the home environment wherein the behaviors of concern are probably different both in type and magnitude as well as the differing function of adults (who are parents as opposed to mental health workers) in supporting these behaviors.

The appropriate or prosocial behaviors of the treated child were manipulable by parental management alone in both families.

The benefits accruing to the sibling have been consistently observed. Both increases in the specific appropriate behaviors he was instructed to attend to in the target child and decreases in the specific inappropriate behaviors he ignored were demonstrated. However a more generalized reduction in the inappropriate behaviors of the helper (as predicted by Reisman, 1965) occurred only in the family in which the sibling had been a greater dispenser of reinforcers in the first place and where he was proved to be a more consistent behavior modifier over time. Bolstad and Johnson (1972) indicated that children involved in self-observation and reinforcement decreased their disruptive classroom behavior to a greater extent than children who experienced externally managed reinforcement. A child's acting as a behavior modifier, which necessitates his monitoring his own behavior, may result in a more generalized decrease in his or her disruptive conduct than would the application of contingencies to specific behaviors.

In the family wherein the sibling was inconsistent in his performance as a therapist, a correction in the preferential parental treatment of the target child (which had resulted from treatment) recovered his performance. The highest rates of appropriate behaviors and lowest rates of inappropriate behaviors were then observed. Furthermore the children played together more. Perhaps when they were no longer competing for parental attention, i.e., not jealous of each other, more amiable interaction was possible. Parents, worrying about the development of a particular child and putting much effort into helping him, may ignore other children in the family of whose adjustment they are more assured. Employing siblings as therapists, thereby getting them to cooperate in treatment, would seem to be one way around this problem. However, this study suggests that parents may have to be specifically instructed to avoid such pitfalls.

REFERENCE NOTES

1. PATTERSON, G. *State Institutions as Teaching Machines for Delinquent Behavior.* Unpublished mimeo paper, Child Study Center, University of Oregon, 1963.
2. PEARL, A. *Youth in Lower Class Settings.* Paper presented at the Fifth Symposium on Social Psychology, Norman, Oklahoma, 1964.

REFERENCES

BIJOU, S. W., PETERSON, R. F., HARRIS, F. R., ALLEN, K. E., & JOHNSTON, M. S. Methodology for experimental studies of young children in natural settings. *The Psychological Record,* 19:117-210, 1969.

BOLSTAD, O. D., & JOHNSON, S. M. Self-regulation in the modification of disruptive classroom behavior. *Journal of Applied Behavior Analysis,* 5:443-454, 1972.

BROWNING, R. M., & STOVER, D. O. *Behavior Modification in Child Treatment.* Chicago: Aldine-Atherton, 1971.

BUEHLER, R. E., PATTERSON, G. R., & FURNISS, J. M. The reinforcement of behavior in institutional settings. *Behavior Research and Therapy,* 4:157-167, 1966.

CHARLESWORTH, R., & HARTUP, W. Positive social reinforcement in the nursery school peer group. *Child Development,* 38:993-1002, 1967.

FREEMAN, D. S. Effects of utilizing children with problem behaviors as modifiers of their peers. *Dissertation Abstracts International,* 32: (1-B), 557-558, 1971 (July).

HAWKINSHIRE, F. Training procedures for offenders working in community treatment programs. In B. Guerney (Ed.), *Psychotherapeutic Agents: New Roles for Nonprofessionals, Parents, and Teachers.* New York: Holt, Rinehart & Winston, 1969.

JOHNSON, S. M., & BOLSTAD, O. D. Methodological issues in naturalistic observation: Some problems and solutions for field research. In L. A. Hamerlynnck, L. C. Handy, and E. J. Mash (Eds.), *Behavior Change: Methodology, Concepts, and Practice.* Champaign, Ill.: Research Press, 1973.

LYTTON, H. Three approaches to the study of parent-child interaction. *Journal of Child Psychology and Psychiatry,* 14:1-17, 1973.

PATTERSON, G. R., LITTMAN, R. A., & BRICKER, W. Assertive behavior in children: A step toward a theory of aggression. *Society for Research in Child Development Monographs,* 32:No.5, 1967.

REISMAN, F. The "helper" therapy principle. *Social Work,* 10:27-32, 1965.

SOLOMON, R. W., & WAHLER, R. G. Peer reinforcement control of classroom problem behavior. *Journal of Applied Behavior Analysis,* 6:49-56, 1973.

WAHLER, R. G. Child-child interactions in free-field settings: Some experimental analyses. *Journal of Experimental Child Psychology,* 5:278-293, 1967.

WEISEN, A. E., HARTLEY, G., RICHARDSON, C., & ROSKE, A. The retarded child as a reinforcing agent. *Journal of Experimental Child Psychology,* 5:109-113, 1967.

WEISS, R. Some determinants of emitted reinforcing behavior: Listener reinforcement and birth order. *Journal of Personality and Social Psychology,* 3:489-492, 1966.

SECTION V: BEHAVIOR THERAPY WITH CHILDREN AND ADOLESCENTS

10

OVERJUSTIFICATION IN A TOKEN ECONOMY

David Greene,

Carnegie-Mellon University

Betty Sternberg

School of Education, Stanford University

and

Mark R. Lepper

Stanford University

A token economy was designed to discover whether demonstrably effective reinforcement procedures would also produce an overjustification effect, indicated by a significant

---

Reprinted with permission from the *Journal of Personality and Social Psychology*, 1976, Vol. 34, No. 6, 1219-1234.

This report is based on the first author's doctoral dissertation at Stanford. The second author generated the experimental materials and supervised the day-to-day operation of the experiment. The third author was chairman of the dissertation committee and participated actively in all phases of the study. Support came from National Institute of Mental Health Grants MH 24134 to Mark R. Lepper and MH 12283 to the Social Psychology Training Program at Stanford.

Grateful acknowledgement is made to Daryl J. Bem and J. Merrill Carlsmith for their contributions as members of the dissertation committee; to Stephen M. Johnson, Susan Roth, Richard Schulz, and Robert S. Siegler for their comments on an earlier draft; to John Delgado, principal, and M. Sue Bailey and Ann Jefferson, teachers at the McKinley School, for their gracious cooperation and assistance; and to Sandra Dubriel and Katie Godfrey for their help with data collection.

decrement in posttreatment engagement with previously reinforced activities, in the absence of perceived tangible or social rewards. Three different experimental token economy groups were compared with a single control group. Following baseline observations, a treatment phase was initiated, during which differential reinforcement was made contingent upon time spent with designated "target" activities. During this phase, subjects in all three experimental groups spent significantly more time with these activities than did the nondifferentially reinforced control subjects. Subsequently, after differential reinforcement was withdrawn, subjects in two of the three experimental groups spent significantly less time with their target activities than control subjects did, demonstrating that multiple-trial contingent reinforcement procedures are capable of producing overjustification effects. The relationship between these findings and the problem of achieving generalization of treatment effects from token economies is discussed.

Principles from attribution theory (Kelley, 1973) and self-perception theory (Bem, 1972), taken together, suggest that a person's intrinsic interest in an activity may be decreased by inducing him to engage in that activity as an explicit means to some extrinsic goal—a proposition that has been called the "overjustification" hypothesis (Lepper, Greene, & Nisbett, 1973). If the justification provided to induce a person to engage in an activity were perceived to be unnecessarily high or otherwise psychologically "oversufficient," the person might come to infer that his actions were motivated by the contingencies of the situation, rather than by an intrinsic interest in the activity itself. Thus, a person induced to undertake an inherently desirable activity as a means to some ulterior end would not longer regard the activity as an end in itself.

To test this hypothesis, Lepper et al. (1973) introduced an attractive drawing activity into children's nursery school classrooms during "free play" periods and unobtrusively recorded measures of the children's interest in the activity. Youngsters showing initial interest were randomly assigned to one of three conditions. In the expected-award condition, children were asked to engage in the activity in order to obtain an extrinsic reward, a "Good Player" certificate; in the unexpected-award condition, they engaged in the same activity and received the same reward, but had no knowledge of the reward until after they had finished the activity; and in the no-award condition, children neither expected nor received a reward, but otherwise duplicated the experience of subjects in the other conditions. These experimental treatments were administered in a room apart from the classrooms. Two weeks later, the drawing materials were again placed in the children's classrooms, and unobtrusive measures of post-experimental interest were recorded. As predicted, subjects who had agreed to engage in the activity in order to obtain the award subsequently spent significantly less time playing with the materials than did subjects in either of the other two conditions. Relative to their uniform baseline levels of interest, subjects in the expected-award condition showed a significant decrease from baseline to postexperimental observations, while subjects in the other two conditions showed no significant change.

This finding has been subject to considerable further scrutiny. On the one hand, its generality has been confirmed across a substantial number of procedural variations and subject populations. Deci and others (cf. Deci, 1971, 1975), for example, have obtained comparable results by paying college subjects to solve puzzles. Similarly, Lepper and Greene (1975) found that the presence of adult surveillance as well as the expectation of reward could decrease children's subsequent interest in playing with a target activity. On the other hand, it is clear that anticipated rewards will not undermine intrinsic motivation if they are not salient to the subject (Ross, 1975). Thus, in its current formulation (Lepper & Greene, 1976), the overjustification hypothesis applies to (a) activities of at least some initial interest to a subject, (b) conditions which make salient to a subject the instrumentality of engaging in a particular activity as a means to some extrinsic end, and (c) measures of subsequent engagement in situations where subjects do not expect extrinsic rewards.*

Overjustification Studies and Token Economies

One important question raised but not answered in the present overjustification literature is its relevance to the systematic use of tangible reinforcement procedures in applied settings (Kazdin & Bootzin, 1972; O'Leary & Drabman, 1971). At first glance, the finding that salient expected rewards may undermine intrinsic interest seems like a direct attack on the token economy establishment (cf. Levine & Fasnacht, 1974). However, a typical token reinforcement program and a typical overjustification study differ from each other in a number of potentially important ways. A consideration of these differences will help to elucidate the rationale for the present study.

* An extensive discussion of some relevant conceptual and definitional issues in the overjustification literature is available elsewhere (Lepper & Greene, 1976).

The most obvious difference is between subjects selected for low rates of appropriate behavior versus subjects selected for high rates of appropriate behavior. Since the overjustification hypothesis presumes at least some intrinsic interest in a target activity, its domain would seem to exclude token economies whose subjects will not engage in appropriate behavior without extrinsic reinforcement (e.g., Ayllon & Azrin, 1965). To the extent that subjects in token economy programs are commonly selected for relatively (vs. absolutely) low rates of appropriate behavior, however, the applicability of the overjustification hypothesis remains an empirical issue.

A second major difference between token economies and overjustification studies is of potentially greater theoretical interest: the use of multiple-trial reinforcement procedures and the demonstration of a reinforcement effect via such procedures. These essential features of token economy programs have been notably absent from overjustification experiments. Indeed, two recent studies have sought to demonstrate that an overjustification effect would not occur when multiple-trial reinforcement procedures were employed. In one of these studies, Feingold and Mahoney (1975) found that five children increased (rather than decreased) their performance of a play activity after having been reinforced for playing with it. In the other study, Reiss and Sushinsky (1975, Experiment 2) found that "preferences" among songs established by discrimination training procedures transferred to a recognizably similar posttest situation. Both studies appear to demonstrate that overjustification effects should not be expected when token economy procedures are employed. However, as Lepper and Greene (1976) have noted, these studies differ from previous demonstrations of overjustification effects in several other ways, making interpretation of their findings equivocal.

One such difference concerns the use of intrasubject (vs. between-groups) designs in these studies. Although control groups are typically not necessary to the explicit objectives of token economies (Kazdin, 1973; Sidman, 1960), they are absolutely essential to studies designed to distinguish among the various multiple effects of particular experimental procedures. In the Lepper et al. (1973) study, for example, the effect of the expected-award manipulation is distinguishable from other effects of the experimental procedures (e.g., social feedback, increased task engagement, familiarity with the activity) because the design included one group of subjects who received the same reward unexpectedly and another group of subjects who received no reward at all. Unfortunately, neither the Feingold and Mahoney (1975) nor the Reiss and Sushinsky (1975, Experiment 2) study included subjects who did not receive contingent or differential reinforcement. Therefore, the data from these studies cannot answer the question of whether their reward procedures per se would have increased, decreased, or had no effect on subjects' subsequent interest, relative to appropriate control conditions in which subjects engaged in the target activity without expecting contingent reward.

Furthermore, these studies were testing a "straw-man" version of the hypothesis. The overjustification hypothesis does not predict that all rewards, or even all expected rewards, will undermine subsequent intrinsic interest (Greene, 1975; Lepper & Greene, 1976; Lepper et al., 1973; Ross, 1975); nor does it delineate procedures. On the contrary, the overjustification hypothesis presupposes that the effects of rewards on subsequent behavior are mediated by the information they convey concerning (a) a person's perceived motivation for engaging in the activity, (b) the person's competence at the activity, and/or (c) the subsequent probability of further extrinsic reinforcement for engagement in the activity—all of which will necessarily depend on the context and manner in which the rewards are presented (cf. Bem, 1972; Feingold & Mahoney, 1975; Lepper & Greene, 1976). As one example, rewards contingent upon superior task performance, which provide an individual with significant information about his competence or ability at an activity, should be less likely to produce a decrement—or more likely to produce an increment—in subsequent intrinsic interest than rewards contingent upon task engagement per se (Deci, 1975; Lepper & Greene, 1976; Ross, 1976). Thus, an appropriate test of the overjustification hypothesis requires a comparison across experimental conditions in which other relevant factors have been held constant.

In addition, to provide data relevant to any hypothesis concerning intrinsic motivation, it is of central theoretical importance to distinguish between two classes of experimental settings: those in which extrinsic rewards are potentially available for the target activity versus those in which extrinsic rewards are not perceived to be available (Lepper & Greene, 1976; Lepper et al., 1973). There are, of course, many reasons why a person might engage in a target activity; however, the focus of the overjustification hypothesis is on intrinsic as opposed to extrinsic reasons. This distinction has been operationalized by defining intrinsically motivated behavior as that which occurs in the perceived absence of extrinsic rewards (Deci, 1971; Lepper et al., 1973; Ross, 1975). In the face of sufficiently powerful extrinsic rewards, individuals will often engage in activities in which they have no intrinsic interest. Therefore, assessments of subsequent intrinsic interest must be obtained in situations where subjects do not expect either tangible or social rewards to be contingent upon engagement in the activity.

Furthermore, to preclude such expectations, some provision must be made to minimize the confounding influence of potential artifacts, such as demand characteristics, subjects' reactivity to experimental procedures, and experimenters' expectancies (Johnson & Bolstad, 1973; Levine & Fasnacht, 1976). In social psychological experiments, failure to keep personnel "blind" to subjects' differential treatments may be sufficient grounds for outright rejection of a manuscript submitted for publication. In token economies, by contrast, personnel often have a justifiable "vested interest" in maintaining appropriate behaviors after tangible reinforcement has been withdrawn (O'Leary & Drabman, 1971). In perhaps the typical case, a teacher is trained in systematic observation techniques and contingent social approval behaviors as part of the token economy (Kazdin, 1973). In such a situation, it seems unreasonable to assume that the effects of this training will disappear when an attempt is made to reinstate pre-treatment baseline conditions, or that this situation provides an appropriate test of intrinsic interest (Lepper & Greene, 1976).

In short, a proper test of the relevance of the overjustification hypothesis to token economies requires a between-groups design and an experimental setting in which time spent with a target activity can reasonably be attributed to intrinsic motivation.

The Present Study

This kind of setting was created in two elementary classrooms by providing a time of day during which the entire class would partake of a set of four activities with a common focus. Within the set, individual children were free to choose which activities they would engage in. As long as no differential contingencies were imposed among the activities, we presumed that an individual's relative intrinsic interest in a particular activity was reflected in the time he or she spent playing with it. The dependent measure, then, was the amount of time spent playing with particular activities within the prescribed set. Given this situation, it was possible to introduce and later withdraw a system of reinforcement contingencies, and to observe its effects on children's immediate and subsequent interest in the various activities.

After baseline observations to determine initial relative preferences, children were randomly assigned to one of four groups, three experimental and one control. For subjects in each of the three experimental groups, two of the four available activities were designated on an individual basis as "targets." In the high-interest group, the target activities were the two which each child had played with most often during the baseline phase. In the low-interest group, they were the two which each child had played with least often during baseline. In the choice group, they were the two chosen by each child individually after the baseline phase. During the treatment phase of the study, then, each experimental subject was differentially rewarded for spending time with his or her two target activities. For subjects in the control group, all four activities were designated as targets. During the treatment phase, these children were contingently rewarded for time spent with any of the four available activities. Thus, all four groups of children received contingent reinforcement during the treatment phase of the study. The difference between experimental and control subjects was that experimental subjects were *differentially* rewarded for playing with their target activities, whereas control subjects were *nondifferentially* rewarded for playing with any of the four available activities.

Two features of this design are critical. First, since target activities were different for different subjects within the same experimental group, it was possible to keep all personnel in the study from knowing any child's experimental condition. Second, the nondifferentially rewarded group provided a basis of comparison for each of the three experimental groups, controlling for effects of time and repeated measurement such as practice effects, satiation, and regression to the mean. Post-treatment data from each of the three experimental groups could therefore be compared with data from a group of subjects whose experiences had been otherwise identical.

We expected to demonstrate a reinforcement effect during the treatment phase in all three experimental groups. This effect would be indicated by a significant increase in time spent with their target activities by each group of experimental subjects, relative to the time spent with appropriately matched or yoked activities by the subjects in the control group. We could then discover whether the same procedures that had produced a reinforcement effect would also produce an over-justification effect after the contingencies had been withdrawn. This effect would be indicated by a significant decrease in time spent with target activities by experimental subjects, relative to the time spent with appropriately matched or yoked activities by control group subjects.

METHOD

Experimental Setting and Subject Population

The study was conducted in an elementary school with an ongoing individualized mathematics program. During "math time," each child worked on one of 100 levels into which the elementary mathematics curriculum had been divided. A distinctive feature of the program was its explicit reliance on an elaborate system of extrinsic rewards, including a biweekly "Awards Assembly," when certificates and trophies were presented to all who had earned them since the last assembly. This system of extrinsic rewards provided a simple, natural way to deliver contingent extrinsic reinforcement during the treatment phase of the study.

Two classrooms served as the immediate experimental setting. Subjects were 44 fourth and fifth graders, selected after the baseline phase according to a procedure described below. The school population was predominantly of lower socioeconomic levels, with 40% of the families receiving welfare. Of the 44 subjects, 19 had Spanish surnames, 17 were Anglos, 7 were Black, and one was Asian. The mean total arithmetic grade equivalents on the California Test of Basic Skills for fourth graders and fifth graders, respectively, were 3.72 and 4.11 in the October preceding the study, and 4.51 and 5.54 in the May following the study.

Experimental Materials

The design required the constant availability of four different activities, comparable in initial interest. This requirement was met within the context of a "math lab." The four activities shared a common structure and format, each consisting of a set of manipulative materials, a sequence of "task cards" (instructing students how to use the materials) selected after extensive pretesting, and a folder containing "activity sheets." The specific materials were (a) geoboards (peg boards with rubber bands, to explore plane geometry); (b) Dienes blocks (cubes, bars, and larger cubes in different numerical bases); (c) attribute materials (items varying in color, shape, and size, to promote logical thinking and set theory ideas); and (d) tangrams (puzzle pieces in geometrical shapes, to be matched to various templates). Each child was provided with his own folder for each activity. Each folder was covered with a "log" sheet with columns headed "date," "time started," and "time finished." Each activity sheet had a place where the date on which it was completed was to be recorded. There were sufficient materials, task cards, and activity sheets to allow any child to choose to engage in any activity at virtually any time.

Procedure

Five school days before the first day of the baseline phase, the experimenter (the second author) introduced "some new math games" to each of two classrooms, in her capacity as administrator of the school's ongoing math program. For a regular, ½-hour period each day, she explained, four activities would be available for children to play with on their own, to help her "find out which games to use in our math program." One activity was introduced in some detail on each of 4 consecutive school days. After this training period, a 5th day was devoted to administering a simple questionnaire which asked about children's previous exposure to and anticipated liking of the four different activities.

Baseline. During the next 13 school days, children played with the four activities with no differential reinforcement contingencies, except with the constraint that each child was to try each of the activities at least once. At the end of this baseline phase, the amount of time children had spent with each activity was calculated. Children were then blocked into groups of four on the basis of the extent to which they had concentrated their time on their two most preferred activities and, within blocks, randomly assigned to conditions. A total of 51 children had been present in the two classes during the baseline period. Four children were dropped from the study, at the teachers' request, because of various learning problems; an additional three children, showing the most extreme concentrations of time on their two preferred activities, were eliminated to produce a balanced sample of 44 subjects. The sample included 11 subjects in each condition, 5 fourth graders and 6 fifth graders, or 5 boys and 6 girls.

Treatment. On the first day of the treatment phase, the experimenter handed out a sheet of paper to each child and asked the class to read it silently. She then went over this sheet, point by point, with the class, as follows:

> [The experimenter] is very proud of the way you have all been helping her. Now, she is going to help you!
>
> 1. If you work with certain games for 3 hours, [the experimenter] will give you credit on your math award sheet for having completed 1 math level. [The award sheet was the basis on which children were

given certificates and trophies at their Awards Assemblies.] (If you work 6 hours, you will get credit for 2 levels. If you work for 9 hours, you will get credit for 3 levels.) But, you'll only get credit if you write down correctly the time you start and stop, just as you have been doing. [Children had been recording data on their log sheets.]

2. [The observer] will be in this room every day during math lab to check on how well you keep track of the time you play with the games. If she finds that you do not record the time you played with the game correctly, you will not get any credit for playing with that game.

3. [An assistant] will keep track of how long you play with the games on a chart. [The experimenter held up before the class a 28 × 22 inch (.71 × .56 m) bright orange posterboard chart with the title, "New Levels Completed for Math Awards Assembly." Each child's name was entered down one side, and headings across the top indicated how many hours and levels were completed.] When you come to class on Wednesday and Friday, you will see how long you have played and how much longer you have to play to get credit for a level.

4. As soon as you reach the 3-hour point on the chart, your teacher will give you a paper to bring to your math teacher. This paper will tell your math teacher to enter Math Lab on your award sheet in your math profile.

5. Next [the experimenter] is going to give you a sheet with your name on it and the list of games for which she will give you credit toward your math award(s).

At this point, the experimenter handed out a sheet in the format of a personalized letter to each child in the class. After the date and greeting, it said

> You may play with any game you want to. Starting today, you will get 1 math level's credit for every 3 hours you play with: [the subject's target activities]. To help you remember, these folders have a big green X in the corner. [Target folders had been marked prior to class except as explained below.]

Subjects in the high-interest group were given the two activities with which they had spent the most time during baseline as their target activities. Low-interest group subjects were given the two activities with which they had spent the least time during baseline. For control subjects, all four activities were listed; thus, for these subjects, there remained no differential contingencies among the four activities. Subjects who had been assigned to the choice group were given a sheet with two blank lines. When all the sheets had been handed out, subjects in the choice group were asked to step outside the classroom with [the first author]. Meanwhile, the rest of the class proceeded to go to the math lab area as usual, where they found that the upper right corner of the log sheet on the cover of the folders for their target activities had been marked with a large green X.

Subjects in the choice group were told that they were being allowed to choose for themselves which two activities they would like to be the ones for which they could earn credit for levels. They were told to make the decision individually, and that different children might have different reasons for choosing their activities; in fact, each child might have a different reason for choosing each of his two activities. Many reasons were suggested, to emphasize the range of alternatives. Then these subjects were led back into their classroom and told to take the sheet with two blank lines to their seats, to think about their choices by themselves, and then to write their choices on the sheet and bring it to [the first author] at the back of the classroom. As each child did so, the now-designated target folders were marked with a large green X and all four folders were given to the child to bring over to the math lab area. From this moment on, children in all four experimental groups were treated alike.

The treatment phase continued for 12 more days. For the first 3 of these days, the classroom teachers went over the experimental instructions at the beginning of the math lab period. The chart providing feedback to the children was updated every Tuesday and Thursday evening, so that upon first arriving in class Wednesday and Friday mornings, children would typically take note of their progress.

Withdrawal. On the first day of the withdrawal phase, the experimenter said that others in the school were resenting the "unfair advantage" that this and the other class were enjoying, and that she was inclined to agree that it would be unfair to continue such an advantage any longer. Therefore, she was taking down the chart as a sign that working with math lab activities would no longer earn credit for math levels. In addition, the upper right corner of the log sheet on the cover of all the folders had been clipped off, removing the discriminative cue to what had been target activities. On the other hand, she continued, there was no reason to remove the math lab materials from the classrooms; in fact, the teachers had been really happy with the math lab period. Children could continue to help her by working as before, or by making up their own activity sheets, which she would use in other classrooms.

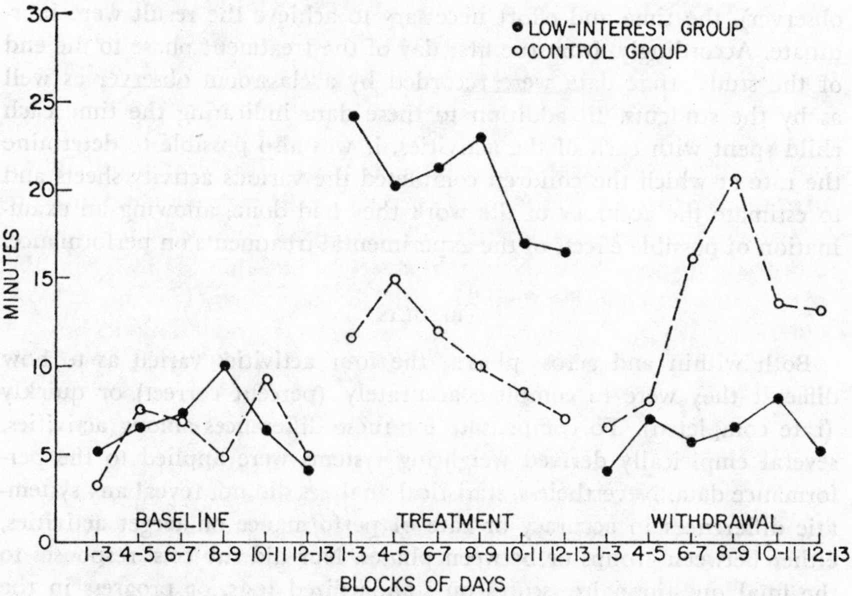

FIGURE 1. Mean time per day spent with target activities by low-interest group subjects and comparable data for control group subjects.

After the 13th day of the withdrawal phase, all the folders were removed from the classrooms. The next day, the experimenter administered a questionnaire, telling children that their preferences would determine which activities stayed in their rooms, with the other activities destined for other classrooms. Before children left school on the day of this last questionnaire, the folders for the two activities which each class had "voted for" were returned to the math lab areas.

Data Collection

The dependent variable of primary interest was the time spent by each subject with each of the activities. During the baseline phase, children were instructed to record the date and time whenever they took one of their folders from or back to the math lab area, on the log sheet on the cover of the folder. Their recording behavior was monitored carefully and social approval was delivered contingently when appropriate recording behavior was observed. Although this procedure produced acceptably reliable data (83% to 91% agreement with data recorded by a classroom observer), the time and effort necessary to achieve the result were inordinate. Accordingly, from the first day of the treatment phase to the end of the study, time data were recorded by a classroom observer as well as by the students. In addition to these data indicating the time each child spent with each of the activities, it was also possible to determine the rate at which the children completed the various activity sheets and to estimate the accuracy of the work they had done, allowing an examination of possible effects of the experimental treatments on performance.

RESULTS

Both within and across phases, the four activities varied as to how difficult they were to complete accurately (percent correct) or quickly (rate completed). To compensate for these differences among activities, several empirically derived weighting systems were applied to the performance data. Nevertheless, statistical analyses did not reveal any systematic differences in accuracy or rate of performance on target activities, either between groups or between phases. Nor did subjects' responses to the final questionnaire, scores on standardized tests, or progress in the school's regular math program show evidence of differences between groups. Although differences between groups on any of these global measures would have been of some interest, it is not surprising that none were found, since the differential contingencies in this study were designed to affect the amount of time spent with particular activities, rather than what was done with them. Significantly, there were no reliable differences between groups or between phases in the mean time spent per day on all four activities combined; instead, the effects of our experimental manipulations were apparent only on the measure of greatest interest, the amount of time children spent with their target activities.

Within-Group Comparisons

A primary concern of the study was the demonstration of a reinforcement effect for each of the three experimental groups during the treatment phase. The relevant data are presented in Figures 1-3. These figures show the mean time per day spent with target activities during the three phases of the study by subjects in each of the three experimental groups, as well as comparable data for control group subjects. For each of the three experimental groups it can be observed that: (a) the mean time per day spent with target activities during the baseline phase, though variable from day to day, was essentially stable across days; (b) time on target during the treatment phase was greater than it had been during the baseline phase; and (c) removal of the contingency resulted in a decrease in time on target from treatment to withdrawal. Both these shifts occurred for all but 2 of the 33 experimental subjects. In addition, *t* tests for correlated means established that all these within-group differences between phases were statistically significant at or beyond the $p <$ .01 level.* Thus, the differential contingencies produced a clear reinforcement effect in each of the three experimental groups.**

It should be noted that the data for control group subjects in Figures 1-3 represent three different sets of data from the same subjects. Each set of data was generated by following the rule that had determined which activities would be target activities for one of the experimental groups. For example, the control group data in Figure 1 show the mean time per day that these subjects spent with the two activities with which they spent the least time during the baseline phase, the "low-interest" activities of the control subjects. Similarly, data for control subjects in Figure 2 show the time they spent with their initially "high-interest" activities. The data for control subjects in Figure 3 show the time they spent with two activities yoked to the choices of target activities made by choice group subjects, in terms of the ranks of the chosen activities within each choice group subjects' baseline preferences. Since subjects were blocked before assignment to conditions, each experimental subject was matched to the control subject in the same block.

It should be clear that the data in Figures 1 and 2 for control group subjects are not independent, since for each subject the activities plotted in one figure are necessarily the two of the set of four not plotted in the

* All significance levels are based on two-tailed tests.

* The pattern of data for the low-interest group (Figure 1) is precisely that typically found in operant studies in applied settings. In fact, 1 of the 11 children in this group failed to respond to the treatment manipulation, a state of affairs quite familiar to researchers in this field (Kazdin & Bootzin, 1972; O'Leary, Becker, Evans & Saudargas, 1969). For the other 10 children in the group, the mean time per day with target activities during treatment was 22.4 minutes with a standard deviation of 8.2 minutes. For the "deviant" child, the mean time per day with target activities was only 1.2 minutes. Consequently, this subject's data were excluded from the low-interest group for purposes of subsequent between-groups comparisons. In addition, 3 subjects left school before the end of the study. Since all of them were in the control group, every effort was made to use all of the data whenever possible. Thus, for high-interest and choice group comparisons with control subjects during withdrawal, analyses are based on 9 subjects per cell, including 1 who left school after 5 of the 13 days of that phase; during the first two phases of the study, these comparisons are based on all 11 subjects in each group; and low-interest group comparisons which control subjects are based on 1 fewer subject per cell in each phase.

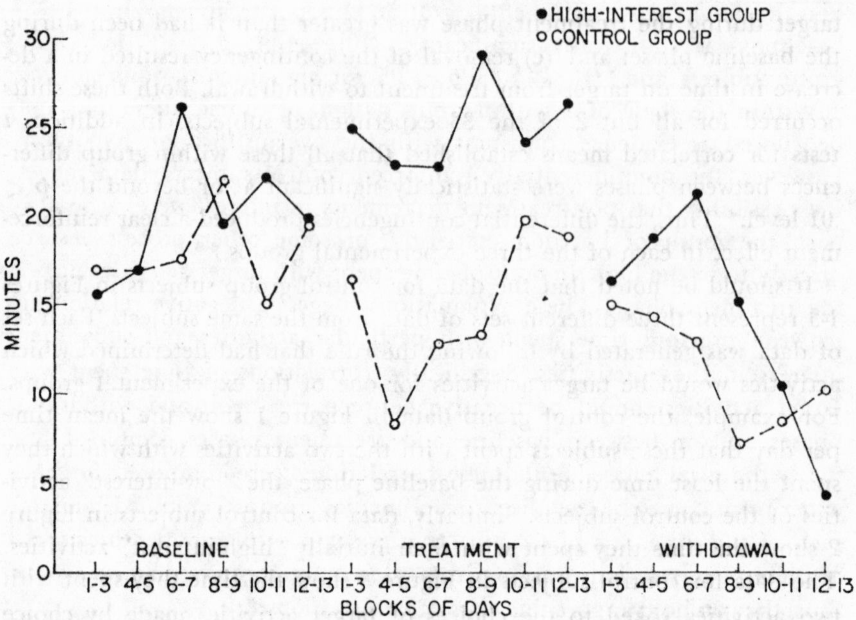

FIGURE 2. Mean time per day spent with target activities by high-interest group subjects and comparable data for control group subjects.

other figure. What is represented twice in these two figures, then, is basically a single effect: Differences in the likelihood of playing with different activities during baseline tended to diminish by the end of the study for subjects *not* exposed to differential contingencies during the treatment phase. Interestingly, there is no evidence of a shift in preferences for the activities yoked to the choices of choice group subjects (Figure 3). This difference between activities selected for initial extremity versus activities selected on a different basis is provocative, suggesting some kind of regression effect within the control group, although none of these within-group differences between phases (including baseline vs. withdrawal) attained statistical significance.

On the other hand, subjects in each of the three experimental groups spent less time with their target activities during the withdrawal phase than they had during the baseline phase. For the low-interest group this difference was not statistically significant, although inspection of Figure 1 suggests that interpretation of this lack of significance should make allowance for the restricted range between the initial baseline and zero.

For the other two experimental groups, this posttreatment drop below baseline was statistically significant, $t(10) = 4.14$, $p < .01$, for choice group subjects, and $t(10) = 2.38$, $p < .05$, for high-interest group subjects.

Within the logic of a within-group design, of course, these data may be viewed as evidence consistent with the overjustification hypothesis. However, the nondifferentially reinforced control subjects' data suggest the possibility that posttreatment decrements in interest were, at least in part, the result of boredom, satiation, or some other process ensuing directly from the high amount of time spent with target activities during the treatment phase. These explanations suggest a negative relationship between previous time spent with particular activities and subsequent interest in those activities. Specifically, correlations of time spent with target activities should be negative between treatment and withdrawal phases and/or between baseline and treatment phases combined and the withdrawal phase. Both these correlations were computed for each experimental group, the three experimental groups combined, and for each of the three sets of target activities for control group subjects. All of these 14 correlations were positive or no more negative than $r = -.05$; thus, they do not support this class of explanations.*

Between-Groups Comparisons

It should be emphasized, however, that within-group comparisons and between-groups comparisons are asking different questions. In the present study, our primary concern was whether any of the experimental treatments that produced a reinforcement effect would also produce an overjustification effect, as indicated by a significant decrease in time spent by experimental group subjects with their target activities, after the withdrawal of differential contingencies, relative to the time spent by control group subjects with appropriately matched or yoked activities. Since each experimental subject was matched with a control subject by the blocking procedure described earlier, *t* tests for correlated means were used to compare each experimental group with the control group during each

* In principle, of course, these correlations are not inconsistent with the possibility that all children proportionately lost interest in their initially preferred activities over time (Johnson, Note 1); this sort of explanation, however, does not account for the relative effects of the three experimental treatments. Moreover, studies designed explicitly to control for satiation have consistently found overjustification effects which could not be attributed to effects of increased task engagement (e.g., Calder & Staw, 1975; Lepper & Greene, 1975; Ross, 1975; Ross, Karniol, & Rothstein, 1976).

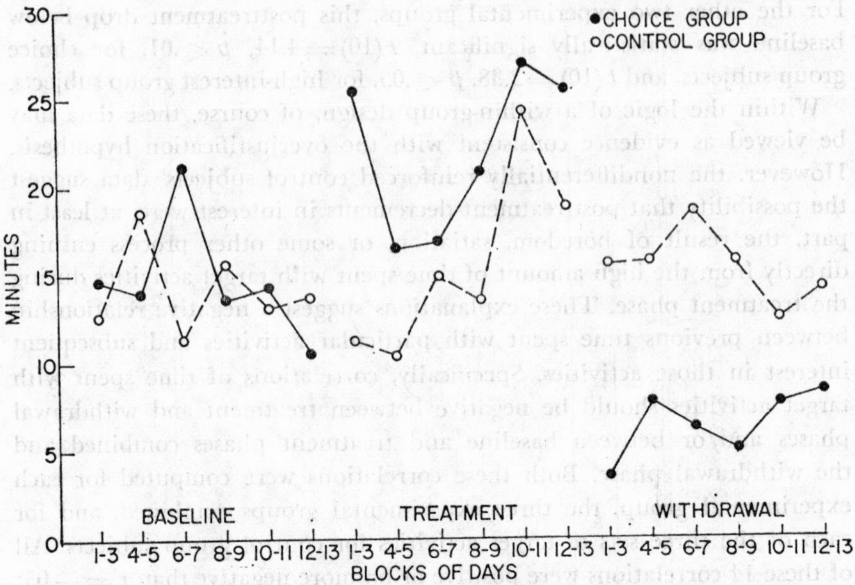

FIGURE 3. Mean time per day spent with target activities by choice group subjects and comparable data for control group subjects.

phase. These comparisons, as well as the cell means on which they are based, are presented in Table 1.*

During the baseline phase, of course, experimental and control subjects did not differ in the time they spent with the activities which would subsequently be designated as targets for experimental subjects. During the treatment phase, experimental group subjects spent significantly more time with their target activities than did the subjects in the control group ($p < .05$ or less in each case). During the withdrawal phase, subjects in two of the three experimental groups spent significantly less time with their target activities than did control group subjects matched or yoked to them. Although high-interest group subjects' time on target was significantly below their baseline level, $t(10) = 2.38$, $p < .05$, they did not differ from control subjects ($t < 1$). Subjects in the low-interest group and in the choice group, however, spent significantly less time with their target activities than did control subjects matched or yoked to them,

* Each of the nine comparisons in Table 1 was also made separately for boys and girls and for fourth- and fifth-graders. In each of the four sub-groups of subjects, the pattern of means is strikingly similar to that of Table 1 (see Greene, 1974).

TABLE 1

MEAN MINUTES PER DAY SPENT WITH TARGET ACTIVITIES BY EXPERIMENTAL SUBJECTS DURING EACH PHASE AND COMPARISONS WITH CONTROL GROUP SUBJECTS

Target Activities	Phase		
	Baseline	Treatment	Withdrawal
High-probability during baseline			
Experimental (HI)	19.3	25.6	14.7
Control (C)	17.8	15.0	13.0
Chosen after baseline			
Experimental (CH)	14.5	21.9	6.8
Control (C)[a]	13.8	14.8	16.1
Low-probability during baseline			
Experimental (LO)	6.7	22.4	3.5
Control (C)	6.1	10.6	11.7
t tests			
HI vs. C ($n = 11$)[b]	1.57	2.83*	<1
CH vs. C ($n = 11$)[b]	<1	2.46*	3.55**
LO vs. C ($n = 10$)[b]	1.15	3.54**	2.54*

[a] Target activities were yoked to ranks of preferences of activities chosen by experimental subjects.
[b] Comparisons during the withdrawal phase are based on two fewer subjects per cell.
* $p < .05$.
** $p < .01$

$t(7) = 2.54$, $p < .05$, and $t(8) = 3.55$, $p < .01$, respectively.* Thus, the same procedures which produced a reinforcement effect during the treatment phase also produced a posttreatment decrement in time spent with target activities (an overjustification effect) for subjects in two of the three experimental groups.

DISCUSSION

The present findings indicate that, under some conditions, multiple-trial contingent reinforcement procedures are capable of producing posttreatment decrements in engagement with previously reinforced activities. These results, obtained over the course of a 13-day period following the removal of demonstrably effective token programs, are clear evidence that overjustification effects are not limited to single-trial, "noncontingent" reward procedures, as Reiss and Sushinsky (1975) have contended. Instead, together with data from other studies of the subsequent effects of multiple-trial reinforcement procedures (Brownell, Colletti, Ersner-Hershfield, Hershfield, & Wilson, in press; Colvin, 1973; Johnson, Bolstad, & Lobitz, 1976; Meichenbaum, Bowers, & Ross, 1968), the present results demonstrate that the use of powerful systematic reward procedures to promote increased engagement in target activities may also produce concomitant decreases in task engagement, in situations where neither tangible nor social extrinsic rewards are perceived to be available.

These data are sufficient to indicate that the simple distinction between single-trial versus multiple-trial reinforcement procedures does not provide an adequate account of the conditions under which overjustification effects will be obtained. Unfortunately, however, the differences in results across the three experimental conditions do not allow an unambiguous conclusion concerning the effects of differences in subjects' levels of initial interest in the present situation. On the basis of previous laboratory data on overjustification (e.g., Calder & Staw, 1975), one would expect overjustification effects to be more likely among subjects rewarded for engagement in activities of relatively higher (vs. relatively lower) initial interest. Instead, during the withdrawal phase, high-interest subjects showed no less interest than control subjects, while low-interest subjects showed significantly less subsequent interest than control subjects. In part, this

* These differences between group means were paralleled by differences in the number of individual subjects in each group whose time with target activities decreased from baseline to withdrawal. This decrease occurred for 8 of 11 high-interest subjects versus 6 of 9 control subjects' "high-interest" activities, 7 of 10 low-interest subjects versus 3 of 8 control subjects' "low-interest" activities, and 9 of 11 choice group subjects versus 3 of 9 control subjects' activities yoked to their choices.

reversal stems from the unanticipated general drift exhibited by control subjects over the course of the experiment, in which initial preferences tended to diminish over time. Therefore, interpretation of these particular differences is more problematic than would have been the case had control subjects' preferences remained constant throughout the study. On the one hand, this difference between the high- or low-interest groups may reflect a genuine effect of the interest manipulation; on the other hand, it may equally well reflect the relative insensitivity of the present design for assessing changes which parallel the temporal trends in the control condition.

In particular, the results of a recent doctoral dissertation (Colvin, 1973) indicate that some caution is appropriate in interpreting the present failure of the high-interest condition to produce a decrement in subsequent interest relative to control subjects, since Colvin's study provides a conceptual replication of the high-interest and control conditions in the present study and obtains clear evidence of significant overjustification effects on both within-group and between-groups comparisons. Colvin's subjects were elementary school children who had been selected for their demonstrated interest in art. They were asked to participate in the study on a voluntary basis and then randomly assigned to one of two experimental conditions. Token reinforcement systems were introduced after baseline observations had determined the children's relative preferences between two sets of different art materials. In one group, children were contingently reinforced for time spent with their preferred materials; in the other group, children were noncontingently reinforced after each session. During this treatment phase, contingent token rewards proved highly effective in altering subjects' choices. Then, after 4 weeks, the token systems were abruptly terminated for both groups. Although the two groups did not differ in the percentage of time they spent with their preferred materials during the baseline phase, the group which had been contingently reinforced while the token systems were in operation spent significantly less time with these materials during an explicit "extinction" phase than did the group which had been noncontingently reinforced. In the latter group, moreover, initial activity preferences were maintained throughout the experiment. These findings provide evidence that token reinforcement procedures can produce decreases in posttreatment engagement with previously reinforced activities among subjects selected for an initial high interest in the activities.

At the same time, it should be noted that Colvin's study and the present one differed in several respects. For example, his procedure included two sets of art activities while ours included four sets of math activities, and his reinforcers were art and play materials while ours were rewards associated with the school's ongoing math program. In addition, Colvin's subjects were volunteers from a University School while ours were a "captive audience" from a public school population of relatively lower socioeconomic levels. It remains for further investigation to determine the significance, if any, of these differences in populations or procedures between the two studies.

Interestingly, compared to the data from the high-interest and low-interest conditions, subjects in the choice condition of the present study showed dramatic decreases in subsequent interest, which were apparent in both within-group and between-groups comparisons. Indeed, during the 13-day withdrawal phase, choice subjects' posttreatment engagement in the previously rewarded activities showed no overlap with baseline data from this same group or posttreatment engagement levels displayed by control subjects. In this light, it is important to note that the experimental procedure which distinguished this condition involved more than the provision of an opportunity for subjects to select the target activities for which rewards were to be provided. Specifically, in this condition subjects were asked individually to think about the activities and the reward program, and were asked to make a public statement of their desire to receive rewards contingent upon engagement in particular activities. Such a procedure, which elicits an overt commitment from the subject and explicitly directs the subject's attention to the consequences of his behavior (cf. Collins & Hoyt, 1972; Kiesler, Nisbett, & Zanna, 1969; Zanna, Lepper, & Abelson, 1973), is reminiscent of procedures employed in previous laboratory demonstrations of overjustification (e.g., Lepper et al., 1973), in which subjects are asked to make an explicit acknowledgment of the instrumentality of their engagement in a particular activity prior to undertaking the activity.*

* Note that the salience of instrumentality can and should be distinguished from the salience of particular rewards or contingencies. The distinction is analogous to Kruglanski's (1975) distinction between explanations of voluntary actions versus explanations of events or occurrences. In the former case, naive attribution is purposive or teleological, partitioning reasons into ends and means; specifically, distinguishing between endogenously (intrinsically) and exogenously (extrinsically) motivated actions. In the latter case, naive attribution is causal, distinguishing between personal and environmental explanations (cf. Heider, 1958; Jones & Davis, 1965). The overjustification hypothesis, of course, addresses the means-end distinction rather than the person-environment distinction (cf. Lepper, Greene, & Nisbett, 1973, p. 130). Therefore, the theoretically crucial issue is what makes instrumentality salient, rather than what makes particular stimuli salient (cf. Kruglanski, 1975, pp. 402-405).

Certainly, the possibility that variations in the manner in which token reward programs are presented may affect subsequent interest following the withdrawal of a relatively long-term reward program deserves further empirical investigation (cf. Feingold & Mahoney, 1975). It would seem particularly important to note that there may be two operationally distinguishable components or stages to a subject's response to reward manipulations. Most research has focused on parameters of reward (or tasks, or subjects), in the hope that a set of boundary conditions might be established for specific effects. A perhaps more basic question is, when do people engage at all in the kind of cognitive "work" postulated by attribution and self-perception theories? If variations in the manner in which token reward programs are presented in fact determine whether subjects ever think about their reasons for engaging in activities, a closer look at such variables may resolve apparent discrepancies in the literature.

Overjustification Effects and Contrast Effects

In language more common to the applied reinforcement literature, the present study and related investigations (e.g., Colvin, 1973; Johnson et al., 1976) provide direct evidence of "contrast" effects from token economy procedures. A contrast effect is said to occur whenever components of a multiple schedule of reinforcement interact, such that a change in behavior frequencies, produced by a change in one component of the multiple schedule, is accompanied by a change in behavior frequencies in the opposite direction under the other, unchanged component (Dunham, 1968; Freeman, 1971; Reynolds, 1961). Operationally, then, any response suppression relative to baseline, following multiple-trial reinforcement procedures, is appropriately labeled an instance of "behavior contrast," as an empirical description of the directionality of the posttreatment effect. When, as in the present study, a between-groups design is used, the effect is typically described as "incentive contrast" (Black, 1968; Cox, 1975; Dunham, 1968). It should be emphasized that contrast effects are defined empirically, in terms of reinforcement procedures and behavior frequencies, rather than theoretically, in terms of particular hypothetical constructs or processes. Thus, there is no particular reason to suppose that all contrast effects with human subjects should necessarily be amenable to the same theoretical explanation (cf. Johnson et al., 1976).

Overjustification effects, on the other hand, are defined in terms of a specific set of theoretical constructs, rather than any particular observable manifestation of them. Overjustification effects have been demonstrated, for example, as a consequence of the imposition of a variety of extrinsic constraints, including "enforced rehearsal" (Rosenhan, 1969), surveillance (Lepper & Greene, 1975), externally imposed deadlines (Amabile, DeJong, & Lepper, 1976), and salient, expected rewards (e.g., Deci, 1971; Lepper et al., 1973; Ross, 1975), as well as multiple-trial contingent reinforcement procedures (Colvin, 1973; the present study). Similarly, the predicted consequences of these manipulations have been assessed by diverse dependent measures, including qualitative indices of task performance (e.g., Garbarino, 1975; Kruglanski, Friedman, & Zeevi, 1971; Lepper et al., 1973) and questionnaire instruments (e.g., Calder & Staw, 1975; Kruglanski, Alon, & Lewis, 1972), as well as behavioral measures of subsequent intrinsic interest (e.g., Deci, 1971; Lepper et al., 1973; Ross, 1975). It would appear, therefore, that overjustification effects and contrast effects should be characterized as constituting two conceptually distinct domains which partially overlap. Within the overjustification domain, behavioral effects which eventuate from multiple-trial contingent reinforcement procedures may be accurately described as instances of behavioral or incentive contrast. Conversely, within the contrast domain, the overjustification hypothesis affords one plausible theoretical account for at least some of the effects with human subjects (cf. Johnson et al., 1976).

Further study of the possible role of cognitive mediation in contrast effects would seem to be warranted by the current literature on attempts to achieve generalization from token economy programs. A recent scholarly review of this literature (Kazdin, 1975) offered the following appraisal:

> Amid the enthusiasm over the progress already made in token economy research and the exciting trends, there remains a major void. There have been relatively few advances in developing a behavioral technology which can be used effectively to maintain behavior and to ensure transfer of training to settings where contingencies are not rigidly programmed. (p. 263)

In this context, the clear implication of an attributional perspective is to favor strategies for achieving generalization of treatment effects that focus on subjects' cognitions about their reasons for engaging in target behaviors, rather than strategies that focus on programming the post-treatment environment (Greene, 1974; Kopel & Arkowitz, 1975; cf. Kazdin, 1975; Kazdin & Bootzin, 1972). From this perspective, generalization to nonprogrammed settings is more likely to occur when training procedures induce subjects to make endogenous rather than exogenous attributions (Kruglanski, 1975) about their reasons for engaging in target behaviors. Exemplary of such procedures are: (a) the use of minimal and naturally available rather than overly powerful and arbitrary reinforcers (e.g., O'Leary, Drabman, & Kass, 1973), (b) the use of various "fading" techniques in which extrinsic rewards are gradually phased out (e.g., Drabman, Spitalnik, & O'Leary, 1973), and (c) the use of self-control and self-reinforcement techniques to replace or supplant externally imposed reinforcement programs (e.g., Brownell et al., in press; Drabman et al., 1973).

In the present study, of course, theoretical objectives dictated some departures from informed token economy practice (cf. Kazdin, 1975; O'Leary, in press), which should be acknowledged in any attempt to evaluate the applied significance of the present findings. For example, to provide a situation in which either increases or decreases in relative interest would be apparent, the present study employed "normal" subjects and a limited set of four mathematics activities of comparable initial interest. Similarly, to assess the effects of the reward system per se—with other potentially confounding factors (e.g., feedback about one's competence) held constant—the present reinforcement contingencies were based on time spent with target activities rather than a performance-based criterion. Nor was any attempt made to withdraw the reward system gradually or otherwise induce subjects to attribute their behavior during the treatment phase to intrinsic factors.

Thus, the procedures employed in the present study do not constitute an optimal strategy for achieving generalization of treatment gains to unprogrammed settings. Had the program been designed to promote subjects' feelings of competence via performance-contingent reinforcement, or to enhance subjects' feelings of personal responsibility for their behavior via extended "fading" procedures, for example, the results might well have been different. Considerable caution should therefore be exercised in extrapolating from the present study, and the present results should not be taken as evidence that sensitively designed token reinforcement systems will always, or even typically, produce decrements in subsequent intrinsic interest.

At the same time, however, the present study also differed from most existing token programs in its aim to distinguish between intrinsically and extrinsically motivated behavior. Consequently, there was no attempt made to maintain treatment gains by substituting either contingent social approval or other naturally available reinforcers for the withdrawn token system; on the contrary, every effort was made in the present study to eliminate such extrinsic incentives during the posttreatment phase. Indeed, to accomplish this objective, classroom personnel were kept "blind" to subjects' treatment conditions throughout the study, and were explicitly instructed not to provide any differential social reinforcement contingent on a child's choice of activities. From a theoretical point of view, these were the departures from typical token economy practice that merit the greatest attention. Given the applied objectives of token reinforcement programs, their implementation has rarely provided the theoretically appropriate conditions for testing the overjustification hypothesis (Greene, 1974; Lepper & Greene, 1974). But if the same reinforcement procedures may have quite different effects on intrinsic as opposed to extrinsic motivation, research presumed to evaluate token reinforcement programs should include measures capable of assessing intrinsic as well as extrinsic motivation.

Conclusions

A proper test of the relevance of the overjustification hypothesis to applied token reinforcement programs requires a between-groups design and an experimental setting in which time spent with an activity can reasonably be attributed to intrinsic (vs. extrinsic) motivation. The present study included these features in an applied reinforcement program extending over 9 weeks in two public elementary school classrooms. In two of the three experimental conditions, demonstrably effective multiple-trial reinforcement procedures produced posttreatment decrements in intrinsic interest in previously reinforced activities, relative to nondifferentially reinforced control subjects. These findings demonstrate that typical token economy procedures are capable of producing overjustification effects under some conditions. Precise specification of these conditions awaits further research.

REFERENCE NOTE

1. Johnson, S. M. Personal communication, November 25, 1974.

REFERENCES

Amabile, T. M., DeJong, W., & Lepper, M. R. Effects of externally imposed deadlines on subsequent intrinsic motivation. *Journal of Personality and Social Psychology,* 34:92-98, 1976.

Ayllon, T., & Azrin, N. H. The measurement and reinforcement of behavior of psychotics. *Journal of the Experimental Analysis of Behavior,* 8:357-383, 1965.

Bem, D. J. Self-perception theory. In L. Berkowitz (Ed.), *Advances in Experimental Social Psychology* (Vol. 6). New York: Academic Press, 1972.

BLACK, R. W. Shifts in magnitude of reward and contrast effects in instrumental and selective learning: A reinterpretation. *Psychological Review,* 75:114-126, 1968.

BROMWELL, K., COLLETTI, G., ERSNER-HERSHFIELD, R., HERSHFIELD, S. M., & WILSON, G. T. Self-control in school children: Stringency and leniency in self-determined and externally-imposed performance standards. *Behavior Therapy,* in press.

CALDER, B. J., & STAW, B. M. Self-perception of intrinsic and extrinsic motivation. *Journal of Personality and Social Psychology,* 31:599-605, 1975.

COLLINS, B. E., & HOYT, M. F. Personal responsibility-for-consequences: An integration and extension of the "forced compliance" literature. *Journal of Experimental Social Psychology,* 8:558-593, 1972.

COLVIN, R. H. *Imposed Extrinsic Reward in an Elementary School Setting: Effects on Free-operant Rates and Choices.* Unpublished doctoral dissertation, Southern Illinois University, 1973.

COX, W. M. A review of recent incentive contrast studies involving discrete-trial procedures. *The Psychological Record,* 75:373-393, 1975.

DECI, E. L. Effects of externally mediated rewards on intrinsic motivation. *Journal of Personality and Social Psychology,* 18:105-115, 1971.

DECI, E. L. *Intrinsic Motivation.* New York: Plenum, 1975.

DRABMAN, R. S., SPITALNIK, R., & O'LEARY, K. D. Teaching self-control to disruptive children. *Journal of Abnormal Psychology,* 82:10-16, 1973.

DUNHAM, P. J. Contrasted conditions of reinforcement: A selective critique. *Psychological Bulletin,* 69:295-315, 1968.

FEINGOLD, B. D., & MAHONEY, M. J. Reinforcement effects on intrinsic interest: Undermining the overjustification hypothesis. *Behavior Therapy,* 6:367-377, 1975.

FREEMAN, B. J. Behavioral contrast: Reinforcement frequency or response suppression? *Psychological Bulletin,* 75:347-356, 1971.

GARBARINO, J. The impact of anticipated reward upon cross-age tutoring. *Journal of Personality and Social Psychology,* 32:421-428, 1975.

GREENE, D. Immediate and subsequent effects of differential reward systems on intrinsic motivation in public school classrooms (Doctoral dissertation, Stanford University, 1974). *Dissertation Abstracts International,* 35:4626B, 1974. (University Microfilms No. 75-6854).

GREENE, D. Comment upon Feingold and Mahoney's "Reinforcement effects on intrinsic interest: Undermining the overjustification hypothesis." *Behavior Therapy,* 6:712-714, 1975.

HEIDER, F. *The Psychology of Interpersonal Relations.* New York: Wiley, 1958.

JOHNSON, S. M., & BOLSTAD, O. D. Methodological issues in naturalistic observation: Some problems and solutions for field research. In L. A. Hamerlynck, L. C. Handy, & E. J. Mash (Eds.), *Behavior Change: Methodology, Concepts, and Practice.* Champaign, Ill.: Research Press, 1973.

JOHNSON, S. M., BOLSTAD, O. D., & LOBITZ, G. K. Generalization and contrast phenomena in behavior modification with children. In E. J. Mash, L. A. Hamerlynck, & L. C. Handy (Eds.), *Behavior Modification and Families.* New York: Brunner/Mazel, 1976.

JONES, E. E., & DAVIS, K. E. From acts to dispositions. In L. Berkowitz (Eds.), *Advances in Experimental Social Psychology* (Vol. 2). New York: Academic Press, 1965.

KAZDIN, A. E. Methodological and assessment considerations in evaluating reinforcement programs in applied settings. *Journal of Applied Behavior Analysis,* 6:517-531, 1973.

KAZDIN, A. E. Recent advances in token economy research. In M. Hersen, R. M. Eisler, & P. M. Miller (Eds.), *Progress in Behavior Modification* (Vol. 1). New York: Academic Press, 1975.

KAZDIN, A. E. Recent advances in token economy research. In M. Hersen, R. M. Eisler, & P. M. Miller (Eds.), *Progress in Behavior Modification* (Vol. 1). New York: Academic Press, 1975.

KAZDIN, A. E., & BOOTZIN, R. R. The token economy: An evaluative review. *Journal of Applied Behavior Analysis,* 5:343-372, 1972.

KELLEY, H. H. The processes of causal attribution. *American Psychologist,* 28:107-128, 1973.

KIESLER, C. A., NISBETT, R. E., & ZANNA, M. P. On inferring one's beliefs from one's behavior. *Journal of Personality and Social Psychology,* 11:321-327, 1969.

KOPEL, S. A., & ARKOWITZ, H. The role of attribution and self-perception in behavior change: Implications for behavior therapy. *Genetic Psychology Monographs,* 92:175-212, 1975.

KRUGLANSKI, A. W. The endogenous-exogenous partition in attribution theory. *Psychological Review,* 82:387-406, 1975.

KRUGLANSKI, A. W., ALON, S., & LEWIS, T. Retrospective misattribution and task enjoyment. *Journal of Experimental Social Psychology,* 8:493-501, 1972.

KRUGLANSKI, A. W., FRIEDMAN, I., & ZEEVI, G. The effects of extrinsic incentives on some qualitative aspects of task performance. *Journal of Personality,* 39:606-617, 1971.

LEPPER, M. R., & GREENE, D. Turning play into work: Effects of adult surveillance and extrinsic rewards on children's intrinsic motivation. *Journal of Personality and Social Psychology,* 31:479-486, 1975.

LEPPER, M. R., & GREENE, D. On understanding "overjustification": A reply to Reiss and Sushinsky. *Journal of Personality and Social Psychology,* 33:25-35, 1976.

LEPPER, M. R., GREENE, D., & NISBETT, R. E. Undermining children's intrinsic interest with extrinsic rewards: A test of the overjustification hypothesis. *Journal of Personality and Social Psychology,* 28:129-137, 1973.

LEVINE, F. M., & FASNACHT, G. Token rewards may lead to token learning. *American Psychologist,* 29:816-820, 1974.

LEVINE, F. M., & FASNACHT, G. Reply. *American Psychologist,* 31:90-92, 1976.

MEICHENBAUM, D. H., BOWERS, K. S., & ROSS, R. R. Modification of classroom behavior of institutionalized female adolescent offenders. *Behavior Research and Therapy,* 6:343-353, 1968.

O'LEARY, K. D. Token reinforcement programs in the classroom. In T. Brigham & C. Catania (Eds.), *The Analysis of Behavior: Social and Educational Processes.* New York: Irvington-Naiburg/Wiley, in press.

O'LEARY, K. D., BECKER, W. C., EVANS, M. B., & SAUDARGAS, R. A. A token reinforcement program in a public school: A replication and systematic analysis. *Journal of Applied Behavior Analysis,* 2:3-13, 1969.

O'LEARY, K. D., & DRABMAN, R. Token reinforcement programs in the classroom: A review. *Psychological Bulletin,* 75:379-398, 1971.

O'LEARY, K. D., DRABMAN, R. S., & KASS, R. E. Maintenance of appropriate behavior in a token program. *Journal of Abnormal Child Psychology,* 1:127-138, 1973.

REISS, S., & SUSHINSKY, L. W. Overjustification, competing responses, and the acquisition of intrinsic interest. *Journal of Personality and Social Psychology,* 31:1116-1125, 1975.

REYNOLDS, G. S. Behavioral contrast. *Journal of the Experimental Analysis of Behavior,* 4:57-71, 1961.

ROSENHAN, D. Some origins of concern for others. In P. A. Mussen, J. Langer, & M. Covington (Eds.), *Trends and Issues in Developmental Psychology.* New York: Holt, Rinehart & Winston, 1969.

ROSS, M. Salience of reward and intrinsic motivation. *Journal of Personality and Social Psychology,* 32:245-254, 1975.

ROSS, M. The self-perception of intrinsic motivation. In J. H. Harvey, W. J. Ickes, & R. F. Kidd (Eds.), *New Directions in Attribution Research*. Hillsdale, N.J.: Erlbaum, 1976.

ROSS, M., KARNIOL, R., & ROTHSTEIN, M. Reward contingency and intrinsic motivation in children: A test of the delay of gratification hypothesis. *Journal of Personality and Social Psychology*, 33:442-447, 1976.

SIDMAN, M. *Tactics of Scientific Research*. New York: Basic Books, 1960.

ZANNA, M. P., LEPPER, M. R., & ABELSON, R. P. Attentional mechanisms in children's devaluation of a forbidden activity in a forced-compliance situation. *Journal of Personality and Social Psychology*, 28:355-359, 1973.

SECTION V: BEHAVIOR THERAPY WITH CHILDREN AND ADOLESCENTS

11

STIMULUS CONTROL OF SELF-DESTRUCTIVE BEHAVIOR IN A PSYCHOTIC CHILD

Edward G. Carr,

University of California, Los Angeles

Crighton D. Newsom

Camarillo State Hospital

and

Jody A. Binkoff

University of California, Santa Barbara

This study attempted to isolate some of the stimulus variables that controlled the self-destructive behavior of a psychotic child. In Experiment 1, the child was exposed to several demand and nondemand situations. In Experiment 2, the situation containing demands was modified so that

---

Reprinted with permission from *Journal of Abnormal Child Psychology,* 4, 2, 1976.

This investigation was supported in part by USPHS Research Grant 11440 from the National Institute of Mental Health. The research was conducted while the first author held a postdoctoral fellowship from the Medical Research Council of Canada. The authors thank Jon and Lynn Killion and Dennis Russo for their help in data collection and Ivar Lovaas, Laura Schreibman, and Robert Koegel for their many helpful criticisms. The encouragement and support of Tim's parents during the course of this study are sincerely appreciated.

demands now occurred in the context of a positive, ongoing interaction between the child and the adult therapist. The rates of self-destructive behavior underwent several orderly changes: (1) Rates were high in demand situations and low in nondemand and modified-demand situations; (2) rates decreased sharply when a stimulus correlated with the termination of demands was introduced; and (3) rates of self-destruction typically showed gradual increases within each of those sessions which contained only demands. These results were interpreted as suggesting that (1) self-destruction, under certain circumstances, may be conceptualized as an escape response which is negatively reinforced by the termination of a demand situation and (2) certain modifications of the social environment may provide discriminative stimuli for behaviors other than self-destruction, thereby decreasing this behavior.

A number of children diagnosed as psychotic, retarded, or brain-damaged exhibit self-destructive behavior, that is, behavior which results in physical injury to the child's own body. The most prevalent forms of self-destruction are head-banging, face-slapping, and biting of the hands, arms, or shoulders. Because such behavior poses a physical threat to the child's well-being, as well as preventing him from participating in normal social and academic activities, the problem has been the focus of a great deal of research. The majority of such research has been concerned with altering the *consequences* of self-destructive behavior. Thus, investigators have reduced the frequency of self-destructive behaviors by utilizing extinction (Lovaas & Simmons, 1969); timeout (Wolf, Risley, & Mees, 1964; Hamilton, Stephens, & Allen, 1967); positive reinforcement of behaviors incompatible with self-destruction (Lovaas, Freitag, Gold, & Kassorla, 1965; Peterson & Peterson, 1968); and punishment (Tate & Baroff, 1966; Lovaas & Simmons, 1969; Corte, Wolf, & Locke, 1971).

The literature cited above makes it clear that by manipulating the consequences of self-destruction, it is possible to achieve considerable control over this behavior. Nevertheless, one occasionally encounters children who, for various reasons, respond poorly to some or all of the above interventions (Bachman, 1972). The present study dealt with just such a child. The treatment failures cited underline our imperfect understanding of self-destructive behavior and provide an incentive to seek new interventions. In the present case, the casual observation that the child's self-destructive behavior appeared to worsen considerably whenever he was placed in a demand situation led us to consider the possibility of an intervention based on appropriate manipulations of antecedent stimuli (such as demands) rather than consequences. By concentrating the experimental analysis on antecedent stimulus variables, it might be possible not only to develop effective procedures for decreasing self-destruction but also to discover new functional relationships relating to the motivation of self-destructive behavior. Accordingly, we designed two experiments to study the effects of stimulus variables on self-destructive behavior. In Experiment 1 we attempted to isolate those stimulus situations which seemed to be particularly conducive to high rates of self-destructive behavior. In Experiment 2 we sought to modify the stimulus properties of those situations so as to reduce the frequency of this behavior.

Experiment 1

METHOD

Subject

Tim was 8 years old and had a diagnosis of schizophrenia, childhood type, with associated mental retardation. His Stanford-Binet IQ was 66 (mildly retarded range). He had limited expressive and receptive speech and understood only simple commands and requests. He had some social behavior; for example, he would occasionally talk to adults or show signs of affection such as kissing. He could imitate rather extensively and had adequate self-care skills. Visual hallucinations may have been present, since he was occasionally observed to stare into space while talking and gesticulating vigorously. He often engaged in self-stimulatory behavior (primarily body rocking). His self-destruction began when he was 2 years old. Typically, he would hit his head and face with his closed fist or the palm of his hand at various times throughout the day. The intensity of his self-destructive behavior was seldom great but he would often bruise or cut his face through the cumulative effect of many hours of hitting. Before we saw Tim, he had received several unsuccessful forms of treatment for his hitting, including drugs (Mellaril, Ritalin, and Thorazine), restraints (hands tied behind the back), contingent electric shock, extinction, timeout, and reinforcement of incompatible behaviors. We were alerted to Tim's problem by his teachers, who complained that his self-destructive behavior worsened considerably whenever he was put in a classroom situation.

Apparatus and Recording Technique

All sessions were conducted in one of two 2.4- by 3.7-m experimental rooms, one with a red carpet and one with a brown carpet. Henceforth, these rooms will be referred to as the red room and the brown room, respectively. At one end of each room was a one-way mirror. On the ceiling behind the child and out of his sight was a small, 6-w, green light bulb which was used to signal the start and finish of each session to the adult (experimenter). During sessions, the door to the room was locked. In all sessions, the adult and the child sat facing each other near the one-way mirror, except during the Free Time condition (see below), in which Tim was not required to sit in his chair.

In the observation rooms adjacent to each experimental room, recordings were made on button panels wired to an Esterline Angus multiple pen recorder in a soundproof box. Six observers (four of whom were naive to the purposes of the study) were randomly assigned to record at various times throughout the study.

Two behaviors were recorded: self-hitting and compliance. Self-hitting was defined as any blow delivered to the face or head with the closed fist or the palm of the hand. Compliance was defined as a correct response to a command within 5 sec; the list of commands is given below. Hitting and compliance were not mutually exclusive behaviors: It was possible for Tim to hit himself while in the act of complying and, in fact, he sometimes did.

A minimum of one reliability check was taken during each condition of an experiment. In Experiment 1 there was a total of 15 reliability checks, and in Experiment 2, there were 10. Each reliability observer was naive to the purpose of the experiment in progress. The response definitions were communicated verbally to each of the observers a few minutes before the start of a session. The reliability index was the percentage of agreement between the two observers, calculated by dividing the smaller total frequency by the larger total frequency. In Experiment 1, the mean interobserver reliability for hitting frequency was 91% (range: 75% to 100%) and for compliance to mands, 100%. In Experiment 2, reliability on hitting was 99% (range: 95% to 100%) and for mand compliance, 100%.

Procedure

In Experiment 1, we assessed the effects of three different stimulus conditions on the rate of Tim's hitting. These conditions were the following.

TABLE 1

Stimuli Used in Experiments 1 and 2

List of tact stimuli	
The walls are white.	The birds are singing.
My pants are soft.	The lights are on.
There are flowers in the garden.	The grass is green.
It's sunny today.	I have two eyes.
List of mand stimuli	
Do this (hold arms out).	Do this (touch knees).
Point to the window.	Point to the door.
Touch your leg.	Touch your shoe.
Do this (clap hands).	Do this (arms up in the air).

Free Time. This condition was intended to approximate those periods of the day on the ward when Tim was not engaged in any structured activity. He was free to roam about the room, to sit, or to lie down. If he talked to the adult, the adult would answer him politely and briefly, avoiding a conversation. (This restriction also held for the Tacts and Mands conditions described below.) Such interactions were rare. At all other times, the adult would avoid eye contact or talking. No demands were placed on Tim.

Tacts. This condition served as a control for the effects of verbalizations per se on self-destructive behavior. The adult presented a series of simple declarative sentences, none of which required a response from Tim (e.g., "The grass is green"). A list of these tacts (Skinner, 1957) appears in Table 1. Each session consisted of 20 tact presentations whose order changed daily. The adult presented the tacts at the rate of once every 30 sec on the average, irrespective of Tim's ongoing behavior. The adult would call the chlid's name, look him in the eye, smile, and deliver the tact. The adult would then look away and avoid eye contact or talking.

Mands. This condition was intended to approximate a structured classroom therapy situation. Tim was presented with a series of 20 commands (e.g., "Point to the door"), which appear in Table 1. These mands (Skinner, 1957) were very similar to mands we had observed Tim to carry out correctly and easily on the ward. The method and order of presenting the mands was the same as that described for the tacts with the following modifications. If Tim responded correctly to a mand, the adult would pat him on the leg and praise him. (In other, nonexperimental situations, we found this combination of social reinforcers to be effective for Tim.) If he responded incorrectly or failed to respond within 5 sec, the adult would look away from him. When the adult was not presenting mands to Tim, he would avoid eye contact or talking with Tim.

The sessions in each of the above three conditions were conducted in the following manner. Tim was brought to either the red or the brown room first (the order varying from day to day) and a 10-min component would be run. At the end of the first component, the adult would announce, "Okay, let's go," and unlock the door to the room. The adult and child would then walk down a hall to the other room and the next component would begin 35 min later. Each set of two components constituted a session. Sessions were carried out 5 days per week, one to two sessions per day, the minimum time between sessions being 4 hours.

The experimental design used to assess the effects of mands on self-destructive behavior was a multiple schedule design (Leitenberg, 1973) with reversals in each component. The red and brown rooms constituted the two stimulus components of the multiple schedule. In each component, the Free Time condition served as the baseline. The mands condition was introduced into and removed from one of the components at a time while the baseline condition was in effect in the other. The Mands condition was replicated across components (i.e., in both the red and the brown room). The Tacts condition, as noted above, served as a control for the effects of verbalizations per se on self-hitting, and was conducted in the brown room. (This point is discussed further below.) Finally, during sessions 6 and 20—27, an adult who was naive to the purpose of the study carried out the various conditions. (For all other sessions, the adult in the room with Tim was knowledgeable about the purpose of the experiment.)

Marker Stimulus Sessions. During the course of Experiment 1, it became clear that the verbal stimulus used by the adult to end the sessions had a profound effect on rate of self-hitting. Therefore, after the three conditions described above had been completed, a fourth condition was conducted (in the red room) to assess the effect of this stimulus on self-hitting. The first 10 min of each session were identical to the Mands condition described above. However, at the 10-min point in each session, the adult presented a marker stimulus (so named because it was used to "mark" the 10-min point.) For two of the sessions the marker stimulus was "Okay, let's go," the stimulus which normally ended all sessions. For the remaining two sessions the marker stimulus was "The sky is blue," a stimulus which had never been used before to end a session.

Once the marker stimulus was presented, no more mands were given but hits were recorded for an additional minute, during which the adult would remain seated. Thus, these sessions lasted for 11 min, at the end of which the adult would unlock the door to the room and leave with Tim. The order of the marker stimulus sessions was: "Okay, let's go" (first and fourth sessions), and "The sky is blue" (second and third sessions).

RESULTS AND DISCUSSION

Figure 1 shows the number of hits per min, over sessions, in the brown and red rooms (top and bottom panels, respectively) for the various experimental conditions. Hitting occurred at a high rate during the Mands conditions and at a near-zero rate during the Free Time and Tacts conditions. The effects of the Mands and Free Time conditions on rate of hitting were the same irrespective of the room used (brown or red) or the adult who was present (informed or naive).

Figure 1 (top panel) shows that during the first Free Time condition in the brown room, hitting occurred at a mean rate of .5 hits per min and remained at that level (.4 hits per min) during the Tacts condition (sessions 5—7). However, with the introduction of Mands, hitting abruptly increased and continued to rise over sessions 8—10 (mean rate, 60.5 hits per min). When the Free Time condition was reinstated in session 11, hitting immediately fell to a near-zero level and remained low over the remaining sessions in that condition (mean rate, .9 hits per min). Reinstatement of Mands by the naive adult in sessions 22—24 resulted in another sharp increase in hitting rate (mean rate, 84.1 hits per min), which fell again during the final Free Time condition (mean rate, .5 hits per min). A similar pattern of responding was seen in the red room (Figure 1, bottom panel), where the mean hitting rates during the first Free Time, Mands, and second Free Time conditions were 1.3, 47.1, and 1.2 hits per min, respectively. Thus, the abrupt reversals in hitting rate which occurred across sessions with the change from Free Time to Mands and vice versa were characteristics of Tim's behavior in both the brown and the red room.

Perhaps even more striking than the changes which occurred *across* sessions were the changes which occurred *within* sessions. Consider, for example, session 22. In the brown room, a Mands condition was in effect first and Tim hit himself 711 times. A few minutes later, the second component of session 22 was run in the red room where Free Time was in effect, and Tim hit himself 3 times. These sharp reversals in hitting

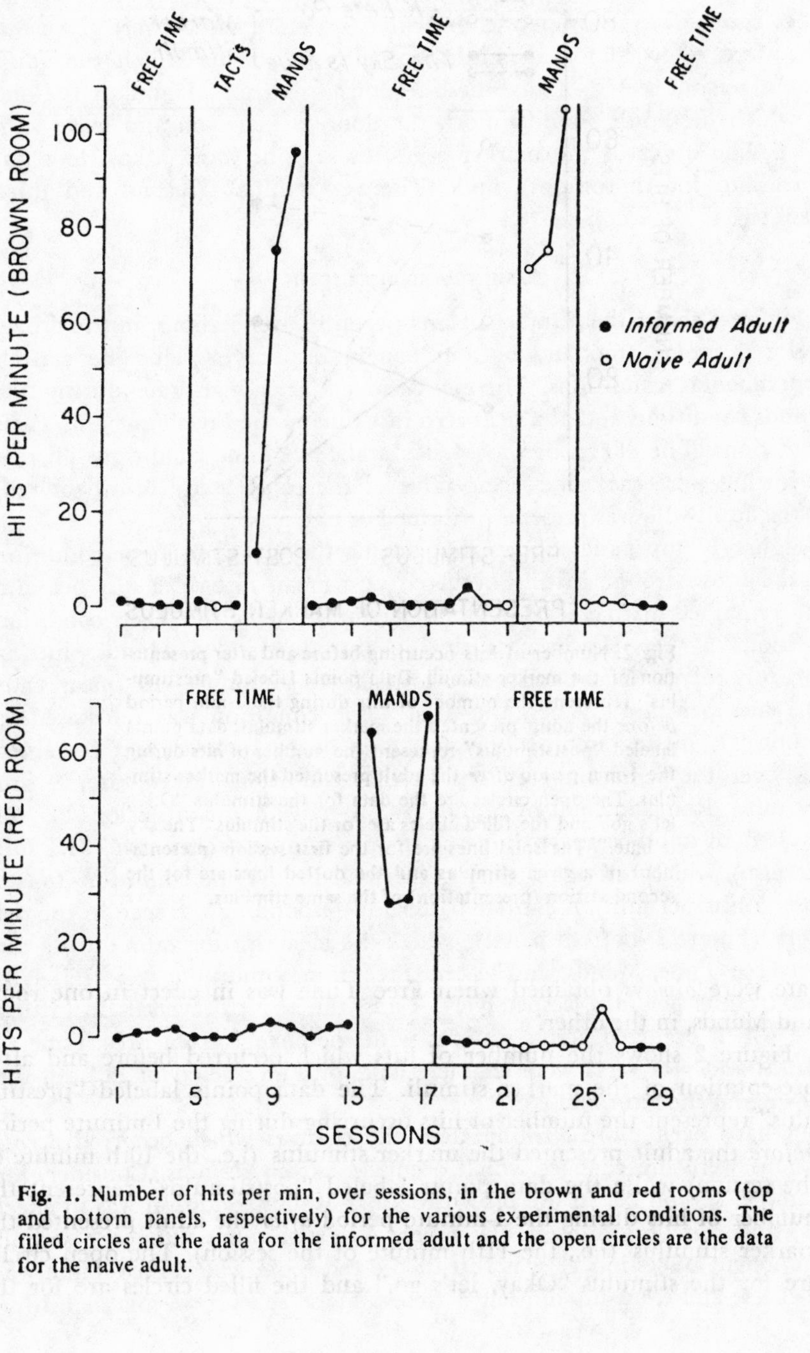

Fig. 1. Number of hits per min, over sessions, in the brown and red rooms (top and bottom panels, respectively) for the various experimental conditions. The filled circles are the data for the informed adult and the open circles are the data for the naive adult.

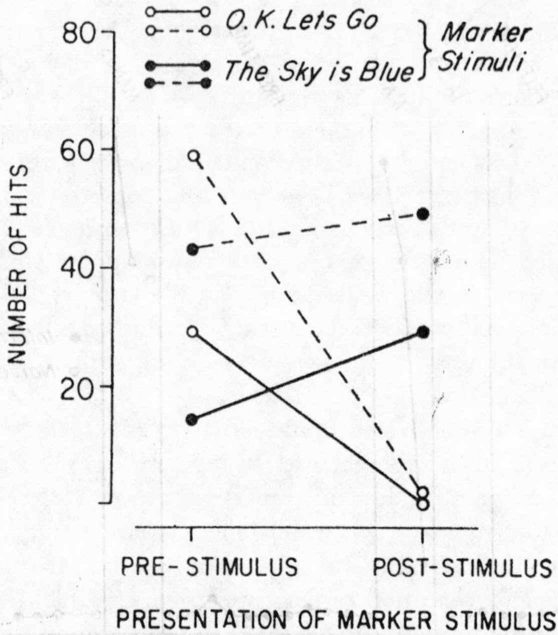

Fig. 2. Number of hits occurring before and after presentation of the marker stimuli. Data points labeled "prestimulus" represent the number of hits during the 1-min period *before* the adult presented the marker stimulus; data points labeled "poststimulus" represent the number of hits during the 1-min period *after* the adult presented the marker stimulus. The open circles are the data for the stimulus "O.K., let's go" and the filled circles are for the stimulus "The sky is blue." The solid lines are for the first session (presentation) of a given stimulus and the dotted lines are for the second session (presentation) of the same stimulus.

rate were *always* obtained when Free Time was in effect in one room and Mands, in the other.

Figure 2 shows the number of hits which occurred before and after presentation of the marker stimuli. The data points labeled "prestimulus" represent the number of hits occurring during the 1-minute period *before* the adult presented the marker stimulus (i.e., the 10th minute of the session) while the data points labeled "poststimulus" represent the number of hits during the 1-minute period *after* the adult presented the marker stimulus (i.e., the 11th minute of the session). The open circles are for the stimulus "Okay, let's go," and the filled circles are for the stimulus. "The sky is blue." Finally, the solid lines on the graph are for the first session with a given stimulus and the dotted lines are for the second session with the same stimulus.

The figure shows that when the marker stimulus which normally ended the session ("Okay, let's go") was presented, the number of hits abruptly decreased to a near-zero level. The hitting decreased from 29 and 59 hits in the prestimulus period to 1 and 2 hits, respectively, in the post-stimulus period. However, when a marker stimulus which had not previously been used to end a session ("The sky is blue") was presented, the number of hits increased somewhat. The hitting increased from 14 and 43 hits in the prestimulus period to 29 and 49 hits, respectively, in the poststimulus period.

Experiment 1 demonstrated that a situation in which demands occur can be discriminative for high rates of self-destructive behavior. It was possible, of course, that any differences in the rate of self-destructive behavior in the Mands versus Free Time conditions might have been due simply to the fact that the adult presented verbal stimuli to Tim during the Mands condition but not during Free Time. Thus it might be that *any* verbal stimuli (whether they were mands or not) would have increased hitting. To control for this possibility, we had an adult present tacts to Tim. The fact that Tim's hitting was negligible in the Tact condition is evidence that not *all* verbal stimuli are discriminative for self-destruction.

Another important point is that the naive adult was able to replicate the results of the informed adult. This fact demonstrates that the data which were generated were not a function of some idiosyncracy in the informed adult's manner of conducting the sessions.

EXPERIMENT 2

In Experiment 1, we isolated a stimulus situation, namely the presentation of demands, which was discriminative for high rates of self-destructive behavior. In Experiment 2, we sought to modify the demand situation so as to bring the hitting under control.

METHOD

The subject, apparatus, and reliability measurement were the same as in Experiment 1.

Procedure

In Experiment 2, we assessed the effect of two different methods of mand presentation on the rate of Tim's hitting. These methods were as follows.

Mands. This condition was identical to the Mands condition of Experiment 1 (see above).

Mands Plus Positive Context. This condition was the same as the Mands condition with one important exception. When the adult was not presenting a mand to Tim, the adult, instead of remaining silent, would relate a simple story to him which concerned some familiar object or event (such as going swimming). The adult was instructed to deliver the story in an animated, cheerful manner, and to be as entertaining as possible. Each story was elaborated upon long enough to fill the entire intermand interval. There were 10 such stories. The order of story presentation and the specific wording of each story varied from session to session but the themes of the stories did not. Each story was presented twice in a session. When a mand was due to be presented, the adult simply stopping telling the story and delivered the mand. In a sense, the mands were "slipped into" a positive context.

All sessions were conducted in the red room. Each session was of 10-min duration, at the end of which the adult would announce, "Okay, let's go." Sessions were run 5 days per week, no more than twice a day, with the minimum time between sessions being 4 hours.

We employed a reversal design to study the effects of Mands versus Mands Plus Positive Context (with an informed adult conducting the sessions). The Mands condition served as the baseline for six sessions, and was followed by the Mands Plus Positive Context condition for four sessions, and finally, the Mands condition was reinstated for two sessions. The pattern of alternating between Mands and Mands Plus Positive Context was repeated with a naive adult conducting the sessions.

RESULTS AND DISCUSSION

Figure 3 shows the number of hits per min, over sessions, for the experimental conditions. Hitting occurred at a high rate during Mands and generally at a low rate during Mands Plus Positive Context. The mean hitting rates for the first, second, and third Mands conditions were 50.3, 55.0, and 84.1 hits per min, respectively, while the mean rates for the corresponding Mands Plus Positive Context conditions were 4.0, 11.7, and 2.0 hits per min, respectively. The change from Mands to

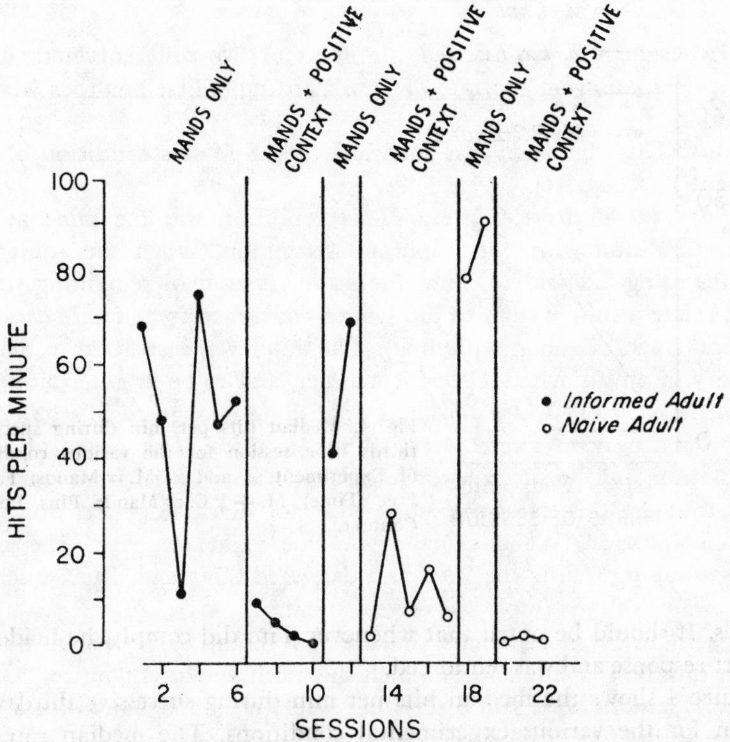

Fig. 3. Number of hits per min, over sessions, for the Mands versus Mands Plus Positive Context conditions. The filled circles are the data for the informed adult and the open circles, the data for the naive adult.

Mands Plus Positive Context was *always* marked by an abrupt decrease in hitting rate while the change from Mands Plus Positive Context to Mands was *always* marked by an abrupt increase. These relationships were the same whether the adult who was present was informed or naive.

The Pearson product—moment correlation coefficient computed for the relationship between frequency of hitting and frequency of compliance was —.82. There was thus a strong tendency for high hitting rates to be associated with low compliance rates and vice versa. Mean compliance was 96% during Mands Plus Positive Context and 45% during

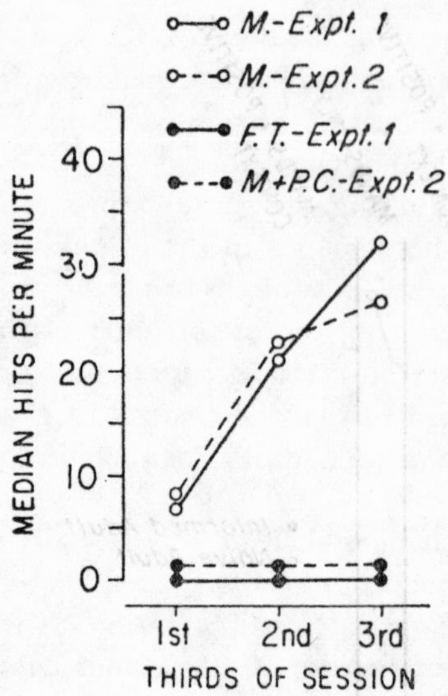

Fig. 4. Median hits per min during successive thirds of a session for the various conditions of Experiments 1 and 2. M. = Mands; F.T. = Free Time; M. + P.C. = Mands Plus Positive Context.

Mands. It should be noted that whenever Tim did comply, he made the correct response and was reinforced.

Figure 4 shows the median hits per min during successive thirds of a session for the various experimental conditions. The median rates reported for the Mands and Free Time conditions of Experiment 1 were a combination of all the data collected for each of these conditions and were not separated according to which room the session was conducted in. This averaging was justifiable since Tim's performance under a given condition was essentially the same in the two rooms.

During the Mands conditions, the median rate of hitting increased steadily from a low level during the first third of a session to a high level by the final third of a session. In Experiment 1, the median rates in the first, second, and final thirds of a session were 6.6, 21.3, and 32.1 hits per min, respectively, and in Experiment 2, the rates were 7.5, 22.6, and 26.5 hits per min, respectively. This pattern of gradually increasing hitting through the course of a session occurred for 70% of the Mands sessions in both Experiments 1 and 2. In contrast, the rate of hitting in the Free Time and Mands Plus Positive Context conditions remained essentially the same across thirds of a session. The median rates in the first, second, and final thirds of a session in the Free Time condition were .1, .2, and .2 hits per min, respectively, and the corresponding rates in the Mands Plus Positive Context condition were 1.3, 1.1, and 1.4 hits per min, respectively. Only 28% of the sessions in the Free Time condition and 17% of the sessions in the Mands Plus Positive Context condition showed the pattern of gradually increasing hitting which characterized the majority of the sessions in the Mands conditions.

In Experiment 2, we showed that by altering the stimulus properties of a demand situation (i.e., presenting the demands in the context of a cheerful, positive, ongoing interaction), it was possible to bring the problem behavior under control without sacrificing the opportunity of presenting demands to the child, as is essential in teaching situations. Additionally, our naive adult control demonstrated that the changes in Tim's behavior were not an artifact of the informed adult's manner of conducting the sessions.

We can speculate on how stimulus changes such as those occurring during the Mands Plus Positive Context condition of Experiment 2 might work to control self-destructive behavior in a demand situation. It will be recalled that commands were a salient feature of the Mands conditions and that these stimuli were discriminative for high rates of hitting. Once Tim started such hitting, he generally continued throughout the session. It is plausible that high rates of self-destructive responding are discriminative stimuli for additional self-destructive responses and that such responses become chained to one another in a manner analogous to that reported for lower organisms in the reinforcement schedule literature (Ferster & Skinner, 1957; Reynolds, 1968). If this hypothesis is true, it may be that the major role of the stories in the Mands Plus Positive Context condition was that of providing stimuli for behaviors *other* than self-destruction (thus breaking up the response chain). The laughing, smiling, and talking which Tim exhibited during the Mands Plus Positive Context sessions may be examples of just such behaviors. Our results may also be related to those typically obtained in counterconditioning studies (Jones, 1924; Wolpe, 1958), in which certain stimuli, known to control behaviors incompatible with an undesirable target behavior, are deliberately introduced into the therapeutic setting.

GENERAL DISCUSSION

It should be noted that Tim differed from many self-destructive children described in the literature in that he was only mildly retarded and had language as well as some social skills. His pattern of self-destruction might therefore be more characteristic of higher functioning children. Given this possible limitation, the data presented above on the stimulus control of self-destructive behavior may nevertheless have implications for theories of the motivation of self-destructive behavior. Specifically, several aspects of the data suggest that Tim's self-destructive behavior in the Mands conditions may best be conceptualized as *escape responding.* The strongest evidence for this interpretation are the data of Figures 2 and 4. First, Tim's rate of hitting dropped dramatically following presentation of the stimulus "Okay, let's go" (Figure 2). This stimulus was always used to terminate sessions and was thus highly discriminative for the termination of demands. A stimulus which is consistently paired with the absence of an aversive event is technically referred to as a "safety signal." Typically, operant escape responding is reduced in the presence of a safety signal (Azrin, Hake, Holz, & Hutchinson, 1965; Hineline & Rachlin, 1969). The fact that Tim abruptly stopped hitting himself whenever the adult said, "Okay, let's go," suggests that the stimulus functioned as a safety signal for him, indicating that the demands had ended and no further escape responses (self-hits) were necessary. Further, it is important to note that the stimulus "The sky is blue" (which was never before used to terminate sessions and therefore could not have become a safety signal) did not reduce the rate of hitting.

Secondly, if one regards as a negative reinforcer the termination of a session which contained demands, then it is possible to think of each session (in the Mands conditions) as a fixed-interval 10-min schedule of escape. That is, after a fixed interval of 10 min the session ended, and any hitting which occurred at that time was negatively reinforced by the termination of the demands. In the animal literature, fixed-interval schedules of escape have been shown to generate a rate of responding which gradually increases throughout the fixed interval (Azrin et al., 1965; Hineline & Rachlin, 1969). Examination of Figure 4 shows that during the Mands conditions of Experiments 1 and 2, Tim's rate of hitting gradually increased throughout the session, a fact which is again consistent with an escape hypothesis. It is noteworthy that in the Free Time condition (which did not contain demands and therefore would not be expected to generate escape responding) Tim's rate of hitting remained unchanged throughout the session. Finally, we may consider the self-destructive behavior in the Mands Plus Positive Context condition. If we make the plausible assumption that the cheerful, amusing stories which the adult told to Tim in this condition prevented that condition from becoming aversive as the Mands conditions were assumed to be, then again we would expect no motivation for escape responding. The unchanging rate of hitting for this condition, shown in Figure 4, may reflect the lack of aversiveness of the Mands Plus Positive Context condition.

Third, if the demand situations are aversive, as an escape interpretation requires, one might expect considerable negative emotional behavior in these situations. In fact, we noticed that Tim appeared very "anxious" and whined a great deal during the Mands conditions. On the other hand, in the Free Time, Tacts, and Mands Plus Positive Context conditions, which we have suggested were not aversive, he smiled and laughed and, in general, seemed quite happy. These observations are hampered, of course, by the fact that they are only anecdotal and must therefore be interpreted with caution. However, these observations do suggest one direction for further research. It is possible that through continued association with a positive context, the mands might eventually lose their aversive properties and the positive context could be faded out. If this effect could be produced, it might no longer be necessary to establish routinely a positive context each time the child was placed in a demand situation.

The most prevalent conceptualization of self-destructive behavior states that this behavior is maintained by positive social reinforcement such as adult attention (Lovaas et al., 1965; Lovaas & Simmons, 1969). We suggest that in some cases it may be that self-destruction serves an escape function and is maintained by the negative reinforcement which is produced by the termination of a demand situation. The possibility of multiple determination of self-destructive behavior has an important treatment implication. If self-destruction which is in fact being maintained by negative reinforcement is incorrectly assumed to be maintained by positive reinforcement, the therapist may treat the problem with extinction or timeout, techniques which involve removing all attention from the child. Unfortunately, these procedures also involve the termination of all demands, and thus the therapist would inadvertently be negatively reinforcing self-destructive behavior, making it worse. Thus, the teacher who dismisses a child from the classroom because the child is hitting himself may, in a sense, be giving the child just what he wants. This analysis should make clear the importance of always performing a functional analysis of such behaviors and not merely assuming that all behaviors which share a similar topography also share a similar set of controlling variables.

REFERENCES

Azrin, N. H., Hake, D. F., Holz, W. C., & Hutchinson, R. R. Motivational aspects of escape from punishment. *Journal of the Experimental Analysis of Behavior*, 8:31-44, 1965.

BACHMAN, J. A. Self-injurious behavior: A behavioral analysis. *Journal of Abnormal Psychology,* 20:211-224, 1972.

CORTE, H. E., WOLF, M. M., & LOCKE, B. J. A comparison of procedures for eliminating self-injurious behavior of retarded adolescents. *Journal of Applied Behavior Analysis,* 4:201-213, 1971.

FERSTER, C. B., & SKINNER, B. F. *Schedules of Reinforcement.* New York: Appleton-Century-Crofts, 1957.

HAMILTON, J., STEPHENS, L., & ALLEN, P. Controlling aggressive and destructive behavior in severely retarded institutionalized residents. *American Journal of Mental Deficiency,* 71:852-856, 1967.

HINELINE, P. N., & RACHLIN, H. Notes on fixed-ratio and fixed-interval escape responding in the pigeon. *Journal of the Experimental Analysis of Behavior,* 12:397-401, 1969.

JONES, M. C. The elimination of children's fears. *Journal of Experimental Psychology,* 7:382-390, 1924.

LEITENBERG, H. The use of single-case methodology in psychotherapy research. *Journal of Abnormal Psychology,* 82:87-101, 1973.

LOVAAS, O. I., FREITAG, G., GOLD, V. J., & KASSORLA, I. C. Experimental studies in childhood schizophrenia. I. Analysis of self-destructive behavior. *Journal of Experimental Child Psychology,* 2:67-84, 1965.

LOVAAS, O. I., & SIMMONS, J. Q. Manipulation of self-destruction in three retarded children. *Journal of Applied Behavior Analysis,* 2:143-157, 1969.

PETERSON, R. F., & PETERSON, L. R. The use of positive reinforcement in the control of self-destructive behavior in a retarded boy. *Journal of Experimental Child Psychology,* 6:351-360, 1968.

REYNOLDS, G. S. *A Primer of Operant Conditioning.* Glenview, Ill.: Scott, Foresman, 1968.

SKINNER, B. F. *Verbal Behavior.* New York: Appleton-Century-Crofts, 1957.

TATE, B. G., & BAROFF, G. S. Aversive control of self-injurious behavior in a psychotic boy. *Behavior Research and Therapy,* 5:281-287, 1966.

WOLF, M. M., RISLEY, T. R., & MEES, H. Application of operant conditioning procedures to the behavior problems of an autistic child. *Behavior Research and Therapy,* 1:305-312, 1964.

WOLPE, J. *Psychotherapy by Reciprocal Inhibition.* Stanford, Calif.: Stanford University Press, 1958.

12

A CONTROLLED EVALUATION OF BEHAVIOR MODIFICATION WITH CONDUCT PROBLEM CHILDREN

Ronald N. Kent and K. Daniel O'Leary

State University of New York at Stony Brook

A behavioral intervention program for conduct problem children with both behavioral and academic difficulties in elementary school was evaluated. Subjects were randomly assigned to treatment ($n = 16$) and a "no-contact" control group ($n = 16$). A standardized 20-hour treatment program involving the child, his parents, and his teacher was provided by Ph.D. clinical psychologists. Both observational recordings and teacher ratings of social and academic behavior demonstrated that significantly greater behavioral improvement had occurred for treated than for control children. However, at a 9-month follow-up, the control group had improved sufficiently that these differences in social be-

---

Reprinted with permission from *Journal of Consulting and Clinical Psychology*, 44, 4, 586-596, 1976.

This project was supported by Grant MH-21813 from the National Institute of Mental Health. The authors are indebted to Sandra Armel and Joan Fisher for their assistance with the research; Kenneth Kaufman, Susan O'Leary, Lisa Serbin, and Mary Starke who served as therapists and consultants for the project; Sharon Foster and Joyce Sprafkin for their editorial assistance; William Morrison for statistical consultation; and Ruth Shepard who served as the administrative associate. Particular thanks go to Raymond Barber, Middle County School District, as well as to the school psychologists and teachers who participated in this project, for their continued support and encouragement.

havior were no longer significant. Although no differences existed between treated and untreated children in achievement test performance or grades at termination, follow-up revealed that the treated subjects had significantly better achievement scores and grades 9 months after termination. Ratings of therapists by teachers and parents were uniformly positive, and there were no dropouts during the 3-4-month course of treatment.

Recent reviews have unequivocally documented the efficacy of behavior modification procedures with a variety of child problems in the home (Patterson, 1969; Wahler, 1976) and classroom (O'Leary & O'Leary, 1976). The effects of such interventions are substantial and replicable, providing strong support for the efficacy of a behavioral approach to child treatment. However, the context of most behavioral treatment investigations may have contributed substantially to the positive outcomes reported. In general, the effects of specific behavioral intervention procedures have been assessed on a research basis. The special advantages likely to accrue in such a context are particularly clear in the classroom literature. Teachers involved in classroom projects have received college course credit or stipends in return for their participation (Becker, Madsen, Arnold, & Thomas, 1967; Kaufman & O'Leary, 1972; Walker & Buckley, 1972). Further, the teacher's execution of experimental procedures has frequently been monitored on a regular basis by research personnel. Such monitoring provides an opportunity for immediate feedback when the experimental procedures are not adequately implemented through misunderstanding or lack of motivation. Advantages such as these, unavailable to the clinician, may have contributed to an overestimation of the value of child behavior modification in outpatient settings.

During the last 5 years, a few scattered investigations of behavioral treatment for children have been conducted under circumstances similar to those of the clinician in private practice or at a community clinic. These studies are characterized by treatment of actual clinical referrals, reasonable limits on therapist time and resources, and the use of multiple treatment procedures, rather than a single technique.

In 1969, Tharp and Wetzel provided initial evidence of the effectiveness of outpatient behavior modification with 77 predelinquent children. Eight specially trained paraprofessionals labeled *behavior analysts* provided consultation to "mediators," including parents and teachers, in establishing contingencies for a wide range of problem behaviors at home and in school. Behavioral data collected by behavior analysts in conjunction with the mediators revealed that 89% of the problem behaviors were reduced in frequency by 50% or more during the course of therapy. Similarly, ratings by the mediators more than 9 months after the termination of contact with the behavior analyst reflected improvement in 76% of the problem behaviors. However, school grades revealed no effect of the treatment program at 6-, 12-, and 18-month follow-up evaluations.

O'Leary, Turkewitz, and Taffel (1973) reported similar rates of improvement in an outpatient training clinic using behavior modification for a variety of child problems. Seventy cases treated by clinical psychology interns for a median of 15 weeks were evaluated at termination by their therapist and at follow-up by their parents. Therapist ratings indicated improvement in 81% of the problems treated. Similarly, parent ratings collected an average of 6 months later reported improvement in 77% of the problems treated.

Fo and O'Donnell (1974) reported a controlled treatment evaluation using indigenous nonprofessionals as change agents. These adults served as "buddies" for youths, 11-17 years old, who were referred for behavioral and academic difficulties. The study employed three treatment conditions: noncontingent relationship, contingent social approval, and contingent social and material reward. A fourth condition provided a no-treatment control group. Data were collected on five subjects in the noncontingent relationship group and on seven subjects in each of the other groups. The results of this study clearly demonstrated the effectiveness of the two contingency conditions in reducing school truancy during two consecutive 9-week intervention periods. In contrast, truancy rates of children in the relationship and control conditions changed little from baseline during the corresponding period of time. Social behavior problems, such as fighting and not doing chores, were only treated in six children who received social and material reinforcement. Clear reductions in these behaviors are thus difficult to evaluate in the absence of objective ratings and a control group. The "buddy system" produced no effect on school grades.

Patterson (1974) evaluated a behavioral treatment program for children who displayed problems in the home. With his graduate students and associates, Patterson treated and evaluated treatment efficacy on 27 children for home and school difficulties. Intervention included training in behavioral procedures for all parents and consultation with school personnel for 14 of the children who additionally had significant problems in school. Total treatment time per case averaged 31.5 hours in the home and 28.6 hours in the classroom. In addition, Patterson provided an average of 1.9 hours of consultation during the 12-month follow-up period. The effects of treatment were evaluated in both the home and the school by independent observational recordings. In the home the rate of deviant behaviors was reduced 43% to a level Patterson defined as "within the normal range" (one half of the standard deviation of normals from the mean for normals). This reduction was maintained at a 12-month follow-up. In the classroom the rate of appropriate behavior increased 29% from baseline to termination of treatment and was maintained at that level at a 4- to 6-month follow-up.

These four investigations are unusual in the behavioral literature since they provide evaluations of treatment procedures that are clearly relevant to the outpatient child and family clinician. Unfortunately, each of these studies suffered from several major research liabilities that preclude clear and unequivocal interpretation of the findings. Perhaps the most serious limitation was the absence of a matched control group or subjects randomly assigned to conditions in all the studies except that of Fo and O'Donnell (1974). That study, however, lacked a follow-up evaluation. There is currently no empirical basis for assuming that behavioral problems of children in school or at home remain unchanged either quantitatively or qualitatively over time. It is possible that children are referred for treatment during particularly difficult periods and that some of the problems would be solved without professional aid.

With the exception of Patterson (1974), a second critical limitation was the absence of reliable and objective measures of change obtained from persons other than the therapist or client. Evaluations of treatment success by Tharp and Wetzel (1969) and O'Leary, Turkewitz, and Taffel (1973) were based entirely on reports by the participants in therapy. Fo and O'Donnell (1974) provided seemingly objective measures on school attendance but not for changes in more complex social behaviors. Perceptions of improvement by parents and teachers are certainly valuable measures of the substantive impact of treatment. In fact, objective documentation of change in the absence of positive reports from parents and teachers might well be viewed as an indication of overly specific measurement procedures that detect results of little practical significance. However, evaluations of therapy must demonstrate that more than perceptions of therapy participants have been altered.

The absence of evidence indicating maintenance of behavioral improvement after termination of therapist contact is also striking. Patterson (1974) is one of the few investigators who collected systematic follow-up data. He obtained observational recordings during follow-up periods of 12 months in the home and 6 months in the classroom. Conclusions based on these follow-up data in the home vary considerably depending on the method of data analysis (Kent, 1976; Reid & Patterson, 1976). Patterson found that only 14 of the 27 treated children manifested sufficient school difficulties to warrant school-based treatment. Follow-up data in the classroom were obtained for 10 of these children at 1-3 months *or* 4-6 months following treatment. There was a significant increase for these 14 children from baseline to follow-up, but in the absence of a control group one does not know whether these changes would have been greater than changes in a matched nontreated control group.

All of the studies described involved treatment of children for problems at school. However, only Tharp and Wetzel (1969) provided a measure of academic improvement, and they did not obtain significant grade improvement. Although grades are subject to bias, the absence of either grade or standardized achievement test changes in behavior therapy outcome studies argues strongly for the need for greater emphasis on changing academic behavior if long-term academic and social effects are to be obtained.

The purpose of the present investigation was to provide a comprehensive evaluation of child behavior modification for school problems under typical outpatient clinical circumstances. Specifically, the design features of the present study included (a) objective measures of change from independent evaluators as well as ratings by clients, (b) multiple measures of academic as well as behavioral change, (c) random assignment of referred children to treatment and a no-contact control condition, (d) a 9-month follow-up evaluation, (e) a highly structured therapy program that specified each of the intervention procedures and when they were to be implemented in a 55-page manual, and (f) a homogeneous population of children in Grades 2-4 referred for the combination of conduct problems and academic difficulties. The present study provides data on 32 children and teachers in their respective classrooms in six schools and on treatment by four therapists. With the exception of intermittent data collections, the present investigation simulated outpatient behavioral treatment of children with conduct problems and academic difficulties. Children referred by their school and parents were treated by Ph.D. psychologists. Consultation with teachers at the schools and with parents and children in the clinic was limited to a total of 20 hours of direct contact per case. All children were treated in the context of normal classrooms with 30-32 children. None of the participants (parent, teacher, or child) received any incentive for their role in therapy. Objective research measures that provided intermittent indications of improvement or lack thereof were unavailable to therapists until after termination of treatment. After the termination of therapy and three or four follow-up visits to our facility to discuss continuation of the tutoring with a certified teacher, there were no subsequent contacts between the therapist and the schools, parents, or children except a therapist report that was sent to the school.

METHOD

Referral Procedures

The program was described to teachers as an intervention for second-, third-, and fourth-grade children with conduct problems (Peterson, 1961; Quay, 1972) in the classroom. They were told that the program was particularly designed to deal with aggressiveness, inattention, impulsiveness, lack of motivation, and reading or math problems. The nature of the data collection throughout the project was described, noting that the purpose of behavioral and academic measures was to evaluate the effects of a combination of therapeutic procedures whose individual merit had been successfully documented. However, children with an IQ of less than 80, physical handicaps, or current placement in a special class were not eligible for treatment. Teachers were asked to refer one or more children manifesting *both* behavioral and academic difficulties, although it was stated that only one child in any classroom could receive treatment. Further, it was noted that after completion of the referral process three of the schools in the district would randomly be assigned treatment while children selected from the remaining three schools in the same district would provide a control group.

Subjects

One hundred and four children were referred from 53 classrooms. Teachers referred from 1 to 4 children, and approximately 75% of all teachers chose to refer at least one child. When a child was referred, his teacher was asked to complete the School Behavior Checklist, and a trained observer obtained standardized recordings of his behavior in the classroom. In addition, reading and math sections of the California Achievement Test (CAT) were administered to small groups of referred children by a certified teacher employed by the investigators. On the basis of these measures, children were ranked, within each classroom and within each school, on severity of problems. In making such judgments, observational data weighed most heavily; ratings on the aggression factor of the School Behavior Checklist, second; and CAT reading scores, third. On the basis of random assignment of participating schools to treatment and control conditions, the 16 most severe cases in each condition were selected for participation.

Treatment Program

A highly structured yet flexible treatment program was developed in consultation with the therapists and described in detail in a 55-page therapy manual.* The structure of the therapy manual provided a basis for replication of treatment procedures by other investigators as well as by applied personnel, including bachelor's degree therapists during the second year of this project.

The treatment involved four successive phases: assessment, school intervention, home intervention, and withdrawal of treatment procedures. The total therapist contact time for each case was limited to 20 hours, with approximately 3-4 hours allotted for assessment, 8 hours for school intervention, 7 hours for home intervention, and 2 hours for treatment withdrawal.

Assessment

Children were randomly assigned to therapists except when conflicts of parents' and therapists' respective schedules occurred. Initially, therapists were given written descriptions of the child by the teacher, standardized scores from the School Behavior Checklist, and a detailed questionnaire concerning the child's problems completed by the parents. The first contact was with parents and focused on current and historical difficulties as well as other related family problems (e.g., divorce, alcoholism). Subsequently, the therapist met with the child to establish rapport and to allay concerns about therapy. Additionally, the verbal section of the Wechsler Intelligence Scale for Children was administered to the child. Assessment of the child's difficulties at school usually involved two therapist visits to discuss current problems and their possible determinants and to observe the class. Although observation was probably quite reactive, altering the behavior of the child, and his teacher, as well as that of other children in the class, valuable information about class

* This manual is available for $2 payable to State University of New York at Stony Brook.

structure, interaction of the child with his peers, and the teacher's child management repertoire were usually obtained.

Finally, to provide more objective indices to the therapist, teacher, and parent about the child's progress, a daily report was developed by the therapist in conjunction with the teacher. Four or five salient problem behaviors, of which at least two were academic in most cases (e.g., completing an assignment, doing a certain number of problems in a particular lesson, or bringing in homework), were selected for daily evaluation by the teacher. In some instances, behaviors initially chosen were changed after repeated evaluations by the teacher revealed that other problems were more salient.

School Intervention

Three basic factors were emphasized in treatment of school difficulties: (a) systematic use of praise and other forms of positive teacher attention (e.g., a pat on the back or wink) to shape the child's academic and social behavior; (b) reduction of threats and reprimands audible to the whole class and substitution of occasional reprimands audible only to the child; and (c) parental praise, encouragement, and special privileges, such as extra television, desserts, or reading to the child, when the child evidenced improvement on the daily report completed by the teacher. In three cases in which these procedures were judged ineffective, an hourly report with back-up rewards and privileges in class was also used.

Home Intervention

Although social and academic improvement in school was the primary focus of therapy, consultation regarding behavior management was provided to parents as a basis for assisting their children with homework and tutorial materials. Parents were instructed to praise appropriate behavior, ignore inappropriate behavior whenever possible, and to restrict privileges, contact with peers, and television viewing for brief periods of time when punishment was necessary. In addition, the therapist discussed the undesirable effects of angry scoldings and corporal punishment as well as the advantages of the infrequent use of punishment. The applicability of these procedures to receipt of the daily report and to tutorial sessions represented the primary focus of several therapy sessions. Prior to initiating tutorial sessions, therapists modeled appropriate teaching skills, viewed the parents' attempts to work with the child, and provided extensive feedback. When it was judged that a parent was able to work with the child in a positive and supportive manner, daily tutorial sessions of 20-30 minutes each evening were initiated. Eleven parents worked with their child in reading, and 4 parents worked with their child in math. (One set of parents was judged too punitive to tutor despite extended counseling to effectively work with their child.)

In all 16 cases the mother assumed the major responsibility for the home intervention program, and very often she came for appointments unaccompanied by the child's father. At each appointment with a parent, the child met with the therapist for 20-30 minutes of the hour. On the average, therapists spent about 4 hours, or 20% of their total direct contact time, alone with the child. Frequent contact with the child allowed continual monitoring of the child's feelings about the treatment program as well as discussion to increase the child's motivation and involvement in treatment. In the context of this structured treatment program, a variety of family problems including marital conflicts, pending divorces, parental depression, and alcoholism required the therapists to provide supportive therapy for parents. Nonetheless, the primary focus of each office visit involved discussion of the child, emphasizing school-related problems. This priority was clearly indicated to all parents at the outset of therapy.

Treatment Withdrawal

The final stage of therapy involved the withdrawal of explicit reward procedures, such as class consequences, and the phasing of daily reports to twice weekly or weekly reports. Parents were asked to continue daily tutorial sessions, and both parents and teachers were encouraged to maintain contingent praise for appropriate behavior.

In most cases, treatment began in January 1973 and ended in May 1973. Following the termination of therapist contact, a certified teacher met with 14 of the 16 children and their mothers on three to four occasions during the summer of 1973. During these meetings the teacher monitored the child's progress, provided supplementary materials, and encouraged both parents and children to continue their daily tutorial sessions for the duration of the summer. At a minimum, these brief summer contacts were designed to lessen or prevent "backsliding" in academic skill so frequently reported during a summer vacation.

Outcome Measures

The selection of dependent measures was intended to reflect improvement in academic skills as well as in social behavior in the classroom. A variety of measures based on teacher reports as well as more objective and reliable measures of behavioral and academic functioning were employed. If only teacher reports were to reflect improvement as a function of treatment, it would seem that a biasing of rating rather than actual change in the child might have occurred. Conversely, if only objective measures reflected the effects of treatment, these instruments could be viewed as focusing on circumscribed aspects of classroom behavior. Only convergence of teacher evaluations and objective assessment would allow unequivocal descriptions of treatment effects.

Two observational codes of disruptive classroom behavior were used in the present study. The code used during selection of children has been used and described in a variety of previous investigations (Drabman, Spitalnik, & O'Leary, 1973; O'Leary, Drabman, & Kass, 1973; O'Leary, Kaufman, Kass, & Drabman, 1970).* A second code specifically designed for use in open or semistructured classrooms prevalent in Middle Country School District was employed in assessing the level of disruptive behavior at termination of therapy and follow-up. The nine categories of behavior comprising this later code were interference with others, extended vocalization, noncompliance, physical aggression, verbal aggression, self-stimulation (e.g., rocking, masturbation), day-dreaming, solicitation of teacher attention, and time off task (not attending). In addition, a composite measure of disruptive behavior was computed by summing the frequencies of the nine categories of behavior. Codes 1 and 2 were applied in obtaining comparisons of the target child with other same-sex, nonreferred "comparison children" selected at random from the class. Measures of comparison children provided an index of the "normal" level of disruptive activity in a particular classroom during a particular activity. During the selection period, using Code 1, observers made three 20-minute observations for each target child. Using Code 2, observers made two 20-minute observations at the end of treatment and six 20-minute observations for each target child at follow-up. In addition, 10 randomly selected comparison children were observed for 2 minutes each during every observation session. All observers were kept uninformed as to whether the children they were observing were receiving treatment.

The School Behavior Checklist (Miller, 1972) was employed to provide standardized teacher description of the target child's behavior at school. Three factorially derived dimensions of this checklist evaluated were as follows: (a) Aggressiveness, (b) Low Need Achievement (assessing motivation), and (c) Academic Disability (assessing academic skills). Ratings

* Occurrence reliability for Code 1, used in subject selection, was consistently above .75.

on the School Behavior Checklist were obtained at the time of referral, at midtreatment in April, at the end of treatment, and at follow-up.

In addition, teacher ratings of global academic and of behavioral change were obtained to provide an overall indication of the teacher's perceptions of these two general areas of classroom activity. Similarly, teacher ratings of up to five *specific* target behaviors selected by the teacher as particularly relevant to the referred child were obtained. Teachers rated global and specific behavior change on a 9-point scale ranging from "1 = dramatically worsened," to "5 = no change," to "9 = dramatically improved." Global and specific behavior ratings were obtained at midtherapy (about mid-April), posttherapy (the third week in June), and at follow-up (approximately 9 months later).

As an objective measure of academic skill, the reading and math sections of the CAT were administered to small groups of children in the schools by a certified teacher. Alternate forms of the CAT were administered at referral, following treatment, and at a 6-month follow-up in November and December. As a measure of academic performance, as evaluated by the teacher, grades for all children were obtained in the seven basic elementary school subjects at the end of the year prior to treatment, at the end of treatment, and at the end of the follow-up year. At termination of the treatment program, questionnaires concerning the procedures and their perceived effectiveness were distributed to parents, teachers, and therapists.

RESULTS

Observational Recordings

During each observation session, recordings were obtained of the disruptive behavior of a random sample of comparison children as well as that of the target child. Measures of the behavior of other children in the classroom provided a norm of that classroom. In analysis of observational recordings, the average behavior rate of comparison children in each classroom was subtracted from the rate of the target child. This measure provided an index of the extent to which the target child was more disruptive than his peers.

Independent a priori tests (Kirk, 1969) were used to test the differences between treated and control target children at termination and at follow-up. At termination, four of nine individual behavioral categories revealed significant differences between treated and control children. Children who had received treatment were less likely than controls to

TABLE 1

Composite Observation (Target—Comparison)

Group	Posttherapy	Follow-up
Treated	14.95	18.95
Control	47.27	14.47

interfere with their classmates, $t\,(24) = 2.36$, $p < .025$, solicit the teacher's attention, $t\,(24) = 3.52$, $p < .001$, fail to attend to the assigned task, $t\,(24) = 2.72$, $p < .010$, and daydream, $t\,(24) = 2.84$, $p < .005$.*

The composite measure of disruptive behavior representing the total of all nine categories of disruptive behavior also revealed a significant difference between treated and control children, $t\,(24 = 3.04$, $p < .005$. The average difference between treated children and their own class controls was 14.93 instances of disruptive behavior per 100 15-sec observation intervals. This compares favorably with a difference between the non-treated children and their own class controls of 47.27. These indices reflected a 68% difference in rates of disruptive behavior between treated and control children at termination of therapy (see Table 1).

On the other hand, follow-up comparisons of treated and control children 9 months later provided a stark contrast with the immediate effects of therapy. None of the nine individual categories or the composite revealed significant differences. The control children were significantly different from randomly selected peers during treatment, whereas the treated children were not. However, neither treated nor control children were significantly different from randomly selected peers during follow-up.

The reliability of the observational recordings of target and control children by each observer was assessed for the entirety of one observation session of 40 minutes out of an average of every three sessions. Reliability was calculated on the basis of simultaneous recordings of children in their respective classrooms by two observers. An occurrence reliability measure was computed by dividing the number of agreements on the occurrence of each category of behavior during each observation interval by the total number of agreements and disagreements.

For the nine observational categories, average reliability coefficients

* Variations in degrees of freedom in the article are due to failure of teachers to complete certain ratings, absence of academic targets for some children (teacher ratings), incomplete grades, or movement from the school district.

were interference with others, .78; extended vocalization, .92; noncompliance, .79; verbal aggression, .83; solicitation of teacher, .87; daydreaming, 1.00; physical aggression, .44; self-stimulation, .56; time off task, .78; and the composite of the nine categories, .81. The two categories with the lowest reliabilities, physical aggression and self-stimulation, were particularly low in frequency, revealing no significant treatment effects and contributing little to the overall composite measure.

School Behavior Checklist

A priori tests were employed to evaluate differential improvement for treated and control subjects. The School Behavior Checklist scales used here were Aggression, Low Need Achievement, and Academic Disability. For the analyses, all raw scores were converted to standardized scores based on the normative data of Miller (1972).

For Aggression, there were significant differential improvement rates from pretherapy to midtherapy for the treated and control groups, $t(52) = 3.29$, $p < .005$ (see Footnote 3). Similarly, there was differential improvement from pretherapy to posttherapy, $t(52) = 3.16$, $p < .005$. During the follow-up year with new teachers, there were no significant differences between the treated and control subjects (see Table 2). On Low Need Achievement, there were significant differential improvement rates from pretherapy to posttherapy for the treated and control groups, t (52 =22.17, $p < .025$. There were no differences attributable to treatment at midtherapy or at follow-up. Finally, there were no significant differences between treated and control subjects on Academic Disability at any point in the program.

Teacher Ratings

A priori tests were employed to evaluate ratings of specific behavioral and academic target behaviors and of global behavioral and academic functioning. These ratings were obtained at midtherapy, posttherapy, and follow-up. The midtherapy ratings revealed significant differences between the treated and control groups on all four ratings as follows: specific behavior, $t(26) = 3.67$, $p < .001$; specific academic, $t(20) = 5.65$, $p < .001$; global behavior, $t(23) = 2.30$, $p < .025$; and global academic, $t(22) = 3.00$, $p < .005$. At posttherapy, ratings of specific behavior, t $(26) = 4.00$, $p < .001$, and specific academic, $t(20) = 2.08$, $p < .05$, revealed significant differences between treated and control groups. At follow-up there were no significant differences between the groups (see Table 3 and Footnote 3).

TABLE 2

School Behavior Checklist

Scale	Pretherapy	Midtherapy	Posttherapy	Follow-up
Aggression				
Treated	3.00	1.71	1.76	1.91
Control	2.60	2.96	2.94	1.68
Low Need Achievement				
Treated	1.75	.96	1.06	1.21
Control	1.36	1.40	1.19	.87

TABLE 3

Problem Behavior Ratings

Item	Midtherapy	Posttherapy	Follow-up
Specific behavior			
Treated	6.91	7.05	5.93
Control	5.88	5.94	5.62
Specific academic			
Treated	6.85	5.74	6.45
Control	5.10	6.10	6.78
Global behavior			
Treated	7.08	7.00	5.87
Control	6.23	6.46	5.73
Global academic			
Treated	6.83	6.42	6.73
Control	5.83	6.00	6.20

TABLE 4

California Achievement Test

	Reading Comprehension	
Time	Treated	Control
Pretherapy	1.99	2.20
Posttherapy	2.26	2.64
Follow-up	3.21	2.78

California Achievement Test

A priori tests were employed to evaluate the Vocabulary, Reading Comprehension, Computation, and Math Concepts and Problem sections of the CAT. Comparison of change from pretreatment to termination revealed no significant differences between treated and control children. At follow-up 6 months later (approximately 12 months after the pretest), scores of treated children had improved 1.22 years from the pretest in reading comprehension. This gain was significantly greater than the 5.6-month improvement manifested by control children, $t(58) = 2.54$, $p < .01$ (see Table 4 and Footnote 3). The other sections of the CAT revealed no significant differences at follow-up.

Grades

A priori tests were employed to evaluate improvement from grades assigned at the end of the year preceding treatment with grades at posttreatment and at the end of the follow-up year. Grades were obtained for seven subjects required for all second-, third-, and fourth-grade children: reading, writing, spelling, math, social studies, English, and science. Five levels of grades were assigned : excellent, good, satisfactory, poor, and failing. For the purposes of analysis, these five grades were assigned numerical equivalents from 5 to 1, respectively. No significant effect of treatment was evident in grades assigned at termination. At follow-up, however, significantly greater improvement from pretreatment levels in grades of treated children was obtained in reading, social science, and math. Improvement in reading grades averaged .75, from 2.25 to 3.00 for treated children versus a decrement from 2.91 to 2.73 for control children, $t(42) = 2.26$, $p < .025$ (see Footnote 3). Similarly, improvement in math grades averaged .25 for treated children (from 2.33 to 2.58) compared to no change for control children, $t(40) = 2.93$, $p < 2.005$. Finally, improvement in social studies grades averaged .34 for treated children as compared with a deterioration of .50 for control children, $t(40) = 2.10$, $p < .025$. (See Table 5).

Teacher Evaluation of Therapist and Therapy Procedures

Teachers were asked, after termination of treatment, to evaluate their therapist and his approach on a number of 7-point scales. On the average, teachers indicated that the procedures were quite helpful ($M = 5.0$; 1 = not helpful, 7 = very helpful) and that they would be likely to continue to employ these procedures with other children in the future ($M = 6.1$;

TABLE 5

Grades

Subject	Pretherapy	Posttherapy	Follow-up
Reading			
Treated	2.25	2.67	3.00
Control	2.91	3.00	2.73
Math			
Treated	2.33	2.25	2.58
Control	3.00	2.40	2.30
Social studies			
Treated	2.58	3.00	2.92
Control	2.90	3.30	2.40

1 = will definitely not employ procedures, 7 = will definitely employ procedures). In addition, the teachers indicated that they would recommend participation in the treatment program to other teachers ($M = 5.8$; 1 = definitely would not recommend participation, 7 = definitely would recommend participation). Finally, teachers described their therapists as likable ($M = 6.5$; 1 = unlikable, 7 = likable), committed ($M = 6.4$; 1 = uncommitted, 7 = committed), competent ($M = 6.5$; 1 = incompetent, 7 = competent), and concerned with their problems ($M = 6.3$; 1 = unconcerned, 7 = concerned).

Parent Evaluation of Therapist and Therapy Procedures

Parents were similarly asked to evaluate their therapist and his approach on 7-point scales. On the average parents felt strongly that their child's school behavior had improved ($M = 6.1$; 1 = dramatically worsened, 7 = dramatically improved) as had his school work ($M = 6.3$; 1 = dramatically worsened, 7 = dramatically improved). They indicated that, as parents, they were quite likely to continue to use the treatment procedures in the future ($M = 5.9$; 1 = not likely to use, 7 = extremely likely). On an interpersonal level parents reported that the child strongly liked the therapist ($M = 6.1$; 1 = strongly disliked; 7 = strongly liked). The parents themselves described the therapist as likable ($M = 6.9$; 1 = extremely unlikable, 7 = extremely likable), committed ($M = 6.7$; 1 = extremely uncommitted, 7 = extremely committed), competent ($M = 7.0$; 1 = extremely incompetent, 7 = extremely competent), and concerned with their problems ($M = 6.2$; 1 = not at all concerned, 7 = extremely concerned).

Dropouts from Treatment

There were no instances in which children, parents, or teachers failed to complete the treatment program extending over a period of 3-4 months. Further, 14 of the 16 treated children elected to participate in the optional weekly tutorial program offered during the summer following termination of treatment. The 2 children who did not participate were not in the Stony Brook area during the summer.

Unfortunately, some dependent measures were unavailable during the follow-up period. Two children, one treatment and one control subject, moved out of the state during the follow-up period. None of the follow-up measures were collected for these children. Two other children, both in the control group, moved sufficiently far out of the school district that although the CAT could be administered repeated observation was not feasible. The teachers of one treatment child and two control children refused to participate in the follow-up observational procedures. These were teachers who had not been involved in the treatment program but who had received children who participated the previous year. Their refusal prevented collection of observational and teacher checklist data on these three children. Finally, grades for five treatment and five control children were unavailable due to such factors as incomparable grading systems or incomplete transfer of records from previous schools.

DISCUSSION

The present study provides clear evidence of the effectiveness of behavior modification procedures under ordinary outpatient circumstances. Measures of academic achievement, grades, direct observation in the classroom, and teacher ratings all indicated significantly greater improvement in treated than untreated children. As such, the measures provide some converging evidence of the positive effects obtained.

Divergences among the measures, however, also merit consideration. Although there were significant differences in observed rates of disruptive behavior in the classroom for treated versus untreated children immediately following treatment, these differences were absent at follow-up. Conversely, although there were no significant differences between treated and control children in academic achievement at termination of therapy, as reflected by grades and scores on the reading and math sections of the CAT, there were significant differences favoring the treated children at follow-up.

The absence of academic differences at termination of therapy may have reflected that parent tutoring had only been provided for 10-12 weeks, on the average, prior to posttreatment evaluation. Continuation of parent tutoring during the summer, with occasional support and direction from a teacher, may largely account for academic improvement evident at follow-up. On the other hand, lack of differences between treated and untreated children in level of disruptive behavior in the classroom at follow-up may have been a result of the unavailability of therapists subsequent to formal treatment for occasional consultation with the new teacher when difficulties arose. Patterson (1974) routinely provides therapist intervention when required during the follow-up period. In contrast, the resources of the current project only permitted a written therapy report for the new teacher during the follow-up year. In many cases additional therapist contact with families and intervention for child problems in the home may have facilitated continued improvement at school. There is some evidence suggesting that a child's behavior in the home is related to behavior at school (Patterson, 1974; Wahler, 1969). A variety of anecdotes from the current study describing disruptiveness that was clearly related to parent-child arguments at home and fighting with siblings suggest that, at least on occasion, difficulties at school were caused by ongoing problems at home, such as parent-child arguments and fighting with siblings. Furthermore, a recent study by Johnson and Lobitz (1974) documented the significant relationship between observed rates of disruptiveness at home and marital conflict. It seems in retrospect that, in many cases, additional consultation with the family would have enhanced treatment effects.

The previous discussion does not imply that 20 hours of consultation per case is not beneficial. It does suggest, however, that with certain cases many more hours may be needed. The 20 hours of consultation in the present study was divided almost equally between the parent and teacher, and the majority of parent consultations involved discussion of the child's progress in school. It seems apparent that even in a clinical research study varied lengths of treatment are necessary. Based on this study, however, it appears that certain clients were very well served by 20 hours of consultation, whereas others may need at least double that number to produce lasting improvement in the schools.

Ratings of personal attributes of the four therapists by teachers and parents indicated that they were almost uniformly well received. It was particularly heartening to find such positive evaluations of therapists on personal attributes, such as warmth, understanding, and empathy, considered important in almost any therapeutic endeavor.

The strong behavioral improvement of the control group, as documented by observational recordings and teacher ratings on the School Behavior Checklist, was a completely unanticipated finding. If a control group had not been included in the current project, the effects of treatment would have been evaluated by measuring improvement from pretreatment scores. A reliance on such measures would have led to the conclusion that treatment produced clear behavior improvement that was maintained with very slight deterioration 9 months after the termination of therapy. Such a conclusion bears a striking resemblance to the report of Patterson (1974), which is based on within-subject change in the absence of a control group matched for rates of disruptive behavior. It is clear that behavioral rates of disruptive children must not be assumed to be constant over long periods of time. Particularly in view of the increasing emphasis on maintenance of behavior change after withdrawal of treatment programs (O'Leary & O'Leary, 1976), untreated control groups seem to be an essential aspect of a sound experimental design.

As noted earlier, the research literature indicates that behavior modification with children produces some of the most substantial and consistent changes of any behavioral intervention procedure and, thus, any psychological treatment. The present study indicates that these procedures can indeed be effective even in ordinary outpatient treatment circumstances but perhaps not as dramatically as has been suggested by previous research.

REFERENCES

Becker, W. C., Madsen, C. H., Arnold, C. R., & Thomas, D. R. The contingent use of teacher attention and praise in reducing classroom behavior problems. *Journal of Special Education*, 1:287-307, 1967.

Drabman, R. S., Spitalnik, R., & O'Leary, K. D. Teaching self-control to disruptive children. *Journal of Abnormal Psychology*, 82:10-16, 1973.

Fo, S. O., & O'Donnell, C. R. The buddy system: Relationship and contingency conditions in a community intervention program for youth with professionals as behavior change agents. *Journal of Consulting and Clinical Psychology*, 42:163-169, 1974.

Johnson, S. M., & Lobitz, G. K. The personal and marital status of parents as related to observed child deviance and parenting behavior. *Journal of Abnormal Child Psychology*, 2:193-207, 1974.

Kaufman, K. F., & O'Leary, K. D. Reward, cost, and self-evaluation procedures for disruptive adolescents in a psychiatric hospital school. *Journal of Applied Behavior Analysis*, 5:329-333, 1972.

Kent, R. N. A methodological critique of "Interventions for boys with conduct problems." *Journal of Consulting and Clinical Psychology*, 44:297-299, 1976.

Kirk, R. E. *Experimental Design: Procedures for the Behavioral Sciences.* Belmont, Calif.: Wadsworth, 1969.

MILLER, L. C. School Behavior Checklist: An inventory of deviant behavior for elementary school children. *Journal of Consulting and Clinical Psychology,* 38:134-144, 1972.

O'LEARY, K. D., DRABMAN, R. S., & KASS, R. E. Maintenance of appropriate behavior in a token program. *Journal of Abnormal Child Psychology,* 1:127-138, 1973.

O'LEARY, K. D., KAUFMAN, K. F., KASS, R. E., & DRABMAN, R. S. The effects of loud and soft reprimands on the behavior of disruptive students. *Exceptional Children,* 37: 145-155, 1970.

O'LEARY, K. D., TURKEWITZ, H., & TAFFEL, S. J. Parent and therapist evaluation of behavior therapy in a child psychological clinic. *Journal of Consulting and Clinical Psychology,* 41:279-283, 1973

O'LEARY, S. G., & O'LEARY, K. D. Behavior modification in the school. In H. Leitenberg (Ed.), *Handbook of Behavior Modification and Therapy.* Englewood Cliffs, N.J.: Prentice-Hall, 1976.

PATTERSON, G. R. A community mental health program for children. In L. A. Hamerlynck, P. O. Davidson, & L. E. Acker (Eds.), *Behavior Modification and Ideal Mental Health Services.* Alberta, Canada: University of Calgary, 1969.

PATTERSON, G. R. Intervention for boys with conduct problems: Multiple settings, treatments, and criteria. *Journal of Consulting and Clinical Psychology,* 42:471-481, 1974.

PETERSON, D. R. Behavior problems of middle childhood. *Journal of Consulting Psychology,* 25:205-209, 1961.

QUAY, H. C. Patterns of aggression, withdrawal, and immaturity. In H. C. Quay & J. S. Werry (Eds.), *Psychopathological Disorders of Childhood.* New York: Wiley, 1972.

REID, J. B., & PATTERSON, G. R. Follow-up analyses of a behavioral treatment program for boys with conduct problems: A reply to Kent. *Journal of Consulting and Clinical Psychology,* 44:299-302, 1976.

THARP, R. G., & WETZEL, R. J. *Behavior Modification in the Natural Environment.* New York: Academic Press, 1969.

WAHLER, R. G. Setting generality: Some specific and general effects of child behavior. *Journal of Applied Behavior Analysis,* 2:239-246, 1969.

WAHLER, R. G. Deviant child behavior within the family. In H. Leitenberg (Ed.), *Handbook of Behavior Modification and Therapy.* Englewood Cliffs, N.J.: Prentice-Hall, 1976.

WALKER, H. M., & BUCKLEY, N. K. Programming generalization and maintenance of treatment effects across time and settings. *Journal of Applied Behavior Analysis,* 5:209-224, 1972.

SECTION V: BEHAVIOR THERAPY WITH CHILDREN AND ADOLESCENTS

13

SYSTEMS-BEHAVIORAL INTERVENTION WITH FAMILIES OF DELINQUENTS: THERAPIST CHARACTERISTICS, FAMILY BEHAVIOR, AND OUTCOME

James F. Alexander, Cole Barton,
University of Utah

R. Steven Schiavo
Wellesley College

and

Bruce V. Parsons
Institute of Therapeutic Psychology, Santa Ana, California

A clinical setting was used to evaluate therapist characteristics, therapist process, and family process in a short-term systems-behavioral model of family intervention. Families

Reprinted with permission from *Journal of Consulting and Clinical Psychology*, 44, 4, 656-664, 1976. Copyright 1976 by the American Psychological Association.
Portions of this study were presented at the National Convention of the Association for the Advancement of Behavior Therapy, Chicago, November 1974. This research was supported by a Biomedical Sciences Support Grant, U.S. Public Health Service Grant RR07092.

> were designated by one of four degrees of therapy outcome. These designations were supported by nonreactive recidivism data and independently derived process data in which improved families showed greater supportive communications. A priori assessments of therapists' structuring and relationship skills were strong descriptors of outcome variance. The data suggest that therapist relationship skills, heretofore overlooked in the behavior modification literature, may be crucial determinants of therapy success.

Theorists, researchers, and clinicians investigating the variables that differentially contribute to therapy outcome have generally dealt with three areas: client variables, intervention models and techniques, and the service delivery system (i.e., therapists). Traditional 1:1 psychotherapies have received the greatest attention, requiring large volumes to simply summarize and synthesize the extensive literature (see Bergin & Garfield, 1971; Meltzoff & Kornreich, 1970; Sager & Kaplan, 1972; Strupp et al., 1974). The newer family therapy approaches, particularly those with a systems-behavioral perspective in natural environments, have a less well-developed data base, though literature has been developed for unique client populations (e.g., Alexander, 1974; O'Leary, O'Leary, & Becker, 1967; Patterson, McNeal, Hawkins, & Phelps, 1967; Patterson, Ray, & Shaw, 1968; Spark & Brody, 1970; Stuart, 1969; Wynne, 1970; Ray, Note 1). Different therapy models and technologies have also been compared (Alexander & Parsons, 1973; Bergin & Strupp, 1970; Gurman, 1974; Parsons & Alexander, 1973), though again the data are sparse.

Notably absent in family therapy literature, however, are concept and research papers covering therapist variables and other aspects of the service delivery system. Partly because of its emphasis on scientific underpinnings, the systems-behavioral family approaches have generally used a journal article format for dissemination, with treatment procedures described as independent variables in a method section. As a result, the technology of behavior change (time-out, shaping, modeling, contracting, etc.) are reasonably well understood, and their effectiveness has been demonstrated in a variety of contexts (e.g., Parsons & Alexander, 1973; Patterson et al., 1968; Stuart, 1971).

On the other hand, relatively little attention has been paid to the *process* through which consultants (or trainers, or therapists) motivate parents, nurses, teachers, and institutions to apply these principles (Hartmann, 1975). In the field of delinquency, for example, Stuart (1971) has clearly defined elements of "good behavioral contracts"; Parsons and Alexander (1973) have explained the use of token systems, verbal conditioning, and bibliotherapy; Alexander (1974) detailed principles of good communications; and Thorne, Tharp, and Wetzel (1967) have clarified the concepts of shaping and contingency. What Stuart failed to do, however, was to detail how therapists get families to negotiate ("great efforts were expended . . .") ; Parsons and Alexander did not describe how to get families to use tokens and books; and Thorne et al. simply stated that "These parents were persuaded . . . (p. 23)." In other words, we know little about which factors determine whether technology will be adopted.

Thus, although family therapy conferences and informal discussions often cover such topics as "resistant parents," inefficient therapists, and high dropout rates, rarely are such topics the focus of formal research programs. The present study was designed as an initial attempt at studying the process of systems-behavioral interventions with delinquent families, based on the contention that although the principles of behavior change are reasonably well established, the processes through which clients accept these principles are not. Stated differently, the project represents a change in focus from intertherapy comparisons of outcome (see Alexander & Parsons, 1973; Parsons & Alexander, 1973) to an intratherapy identification and evaluation of variables that differentially contribute to changes in therapy process and outcome.

Meltzoff and Kornreich (1970) have pointed out that many studies of psychotherapy show limited relevance due to several constraints. First, carefully controlled studies are typically performed in an analogue format, making it difficult at best to generalize findings to true clinical situations. Second, independent and dependent variables are typically derived from relatively specific theoretical constructs, and it is often difficult to apply these idiosyncratic measures to other therapeutic situations due either to their questionable validity or their esoteric nature. Finally, and perhaps most critically, it is not often demonstrated that investigations of psychotherapy have any relation to "real-world" outcomes. In an effort to meet these objections, this study was performed with actual therapists and clients in a treatment setting. The measures of therapist characteristics were selected on the basis of their face validity and previous empirical research, and therapy process measures were also derived from prior published research. Additionally, several measures of therapy outcome were used to provide indices of successful versus nonsuccessful treatment.

Therefore, an intervention program was examined that had already been demonstrated to significantly modify family interaction and reduce recidivism over no-treatment controls and two alternative treatments (Alexander & Parsons, 1973). A new sample of therapists was then trained and assigned cases as in the original study, with the goal of focusing on therapist behavior, while holding the formal aspects of the treatment program constant (all therapists were similarly trained), and intervening in a homogeneous client population. This strategy was designed to determine the degree of outcome variance accounted for by certain therapist characteristics.

METHOD

Subjects

Twenty-one families were seen during the project period, representing referrals from District 2 of the Utah Juvenile Court, the Utah Youth Services Bureau, Salt Lake Community Mental Health, and calls directly to the Psychological Clinic (University of Utah, Department of Psychology). The range of referral problems (primarily "soft delinquency," i.e., runaway, ungovernable, truancy, and curfew), sex distribution (10 males, 11 females), age (13-16 years), and socioeconomic status were comparable to those represented in the original therapy outcome studies (Alexander & Parsons, 1973; Parsons & Alexander, 1973). These families were seen by 21 therapists (14 males and 7 females). Comparable to the original studies, therapist experience ranged from second-year students with almost no prior therapy experience ($n = 6$) to PhDs with extensive experience ($n = 2$). The remainder of the therapists were third- and fourth-year graduate students with 1-2 years of therapy experience. (Few, however, had prior experience with the intervention approach used in the present project.)

As referrals were received, families were randomly assigned to therapists based on common schedules of time availability. All sessions were audiotape recorded with the family's consent, and sessions were directly observed through one-way mirrors (with the exception of two families who refused).

Intervention: Training and Process

Prior to the treatment phase of the project, therapists were given a 10-week training course using reading materials, lectures, group discussions, observation of training videotapes, and role playing. During the project, therapists also received direct live supervision and weekly group meetings to discuss specific techniques, intervention strategies, etc.

As described in Alexander and Parsons (1973), the intervention model involved the referred delinquent and his/her parents seen together. Therapists were trained to modify family communication patterns and interaction sequences by modeling, prompting, and reinforçing clear communication of substance as well as feelings, with clear presentation of demands and alternative solutions.

Therapist training emphasized verbal activity, directiveness, and clarity to interrupt repetitive maladaptive sequences; to change the family's focus from one of past attributes ("he's always . . .") to that of present and future behaviors; and to adopt a style of positively reinforcing acceptance behaviors rather than punishing (via blaming, restricting, etc.) unacceptable ones (Alexander, 1974; Parsons & Alexander, 1973).

The goal of these manipulations was for the family to develop techniques of reciprocal contingency contracting, initially with the active assistance of the therapist, later spontaneously without therapist intervention. In this process the focus was not on "delinquent" target behaviors per se but on the family system *functions* served by the delinquency, such as maintaining adolescent-parent distance and independence and maintaining parental role relationships (Alexander, 1974; Malouf & Alexander, 1974).

Dependent Measures

The objective criterion of remaining versus dropping out of therapy was used to distinguish between poor and good outcomes. Further distinctions were made within each of these groupings as follows:

Outcome 1. In the first session both the therapist and the family made no movement toward changes in communication patterns, reduction of complaints, or contract negotiation. Families terminated against therapist judgment, failing to attend the second session (n = 4 families).

Outcome 2. The family attended several sessions but terminated against advice. During sessions the family attempted changes in communication and contracting but could not successfully change interaction style. Complaints continued at termination (n = 5 families).

Outcome 3. The family continued in treatment until end of project forced termination by the therapist. Positive changes in communication, contracting, and complaints were demonstrated, though families still lacked the ability to spontaneously solve problems without assistance (n = 5 families). Of these, two requested continued treatment and were seen by their therapist under the auspices of another agency. Five indicated they desired neither referral nor further treatment.)

Outcome 4. Termination was jointly agreed to by therapist and family, based on complaint cessation, spontaneous problem-solving ability, and effective communication (n = 7 families).

Therapist characteristics. At the conclusion of the 10-week training phase, the training supervisor rated trainees on eight 5-point scales.* These ratings were based on direct behavioral observations of the trainees during training sessions (role playing, group interaction, and interviews). It should be emphasized that these ratings were made prior to direct treatment, thus were completely independent of family outcomes. As such they constituted an a priori assessment of process characteristics, a form of "prediction" of how therapists would behave in therapy. (a) Affect-behavior integration was the degree to which trainees characteristically related family expression of affect to behavioral sequences and vice versa. (b) Humor was the degree to which trainees characteristically used humor to relieve tension and relabel sequences. (c) Warmth was reflected by the frequency of use of smiling, active listening, forward lean, and social chitchat before and after sessions. (d) Directiveness was the frequency of verbal and nonverbal commands, instructions, physical rearrangement of chairs, and interrupting family interaction sequences. (e) Self-confidence was measured by eye contact and forward lean when giving directions, voice level, references to program, and/or personal effectiveness. (f) Self-disclosure was the degree to which trainees characteristically referred to their own reactions, past history, and current life. (g) Blaming was the frequency of using and reinforcing negative labels, attribution of malevolent intent, and complaining, and (h) Clarity was the degree to which trainees characteristically used short, specific, and clear communications, and behaviorally specific comments (as opposed to complex conceptualizations).

Independent ratings by the project intern and supervisor demonstrated an overall effective percentage of agreement of 75%. Agreement increased to 92% when the dimensions were collapsed into low rates of the behavior (Categories a and b), moderate rates (c), and high rates (d and e).

Interaction behavior. Three 15-minute samples of audiotape-recorded therapy interactions were selected for each family, representing the first portion of the initial interview, and the first portion of the next to last

* The complete rating manuals can be obtained from the first author.

session. (These data, of course, were unavailable for the four familes that terminated after one session.) Using the manual developed by Alexander (1973; see Footnote 1), these tapes were content coded for rates of family defensive and supportive communications, which had been previously demonstrated to distinguish delinquent from normal ("adaptive") family interaction (Alexander, 1973).

Defensive communication consists of verbal and extraverbal behaviors that are threatening or punishing to others and reciprocally invite and produce defensive behaviors in return. Characteristic of such communications are behaviors that are evaluative, controlling, and involve the use of strategies that are indifferent, superior, dominating, and meant to impress others. Supportive communications (defined as genuine information seeking and information giving, spontaneous problem solving, empathic understanding, and equality) tend to produce lowered anxiety, clearer communications, and more productive interactions in and among others (Alexander, 1973; Gibb, 1961). During the rating of therapy sessions, family members were assigned scores ranging from 1 to 4 for both defensiveness and supportiveness. These scores reflected raters' judgments of the rate of each type of behavior in the sessions as either never occurring (1), occurring infrequently (2), occurring often (3) or constituting almost all the behavior expressed by that person (4).

Raters participated in 10 2-hour training sessions and were trained to a criterion of 90% effective agreement. During the actual rating process, 12 independent reliability probes (different raters listening to the same tapes at different times) generated an effective percentage of agreement of 91.2%. In the present analysis, intrafamily communications on each of the two dimensions were summed and divided by the number of family members. The means were then reflected as a ratio (family supportiveness/defensiveness).

RESULTS

Outcome Measures

Although the initial outcome measures involved only a slight degree of therapist judgment, the possibility of bias was of some concern. Thus, two independent nonreactive measures of outcome were developed: subsequent recidivism of the referred delinquent in the family and supportiveness/defensiveness family process measures. The convergence of these measures with the primary outcome measures was evaluated.

Recidivism. Juvenile court and community mental health records

TABLE 1

Rereferral Rates for Families in Each Outcome Condition

Condition	n	Rereferral n	Rereferral %
1	5	3	60
2	4	2	50
3	5	0	0
4	7	0	0

were searched for indices of subsequent referral 12-15 months following intervention. Table 1 contains the number of families in each primary outcome designation and the number and percentage of families with subsequent court or mental health center contacts. As seen in the table, the poor outcome conditions (1 and 2) showed high recidivism rates of 60% and 50%, respectively. Alternatively, good outcome conditions (3 and 4) showed no recidivism at all. The overall rate (23.8%) of recidivism for this sample of families closely corresponds with a recidivism rate of 26% found in an earlier therapy outcome study with the same therapeutic model (Alexander & Parsons, 1973). The data support the outcome designations in the present study and additionally suggest that present replication reflects impact comparable to prior treatment programs.

Family process measures. It was expected that independently defined good versus poor outcome families would reflect differential rates of supportive and defensive process measures, as reflected by supportiveness/defensiveness ratios.

Table 2 displays family supportiveness/defensiveness ratios for each outcome group (1, 2, 3, 4) during the first part of the initial session (Phase A), the last part of the initial session (Phase B), and the next-to-last session (Phase L). Since Outcome Group 1 families attended only a first session, 3 × 3 analysis of variance for unequal N with therapy sessions as a repeated measure was performed for Outcome Groups 2, 3, and 4 (Kirk, 1968) across all three phases (see Table 3).

As seen in Table 3, there were main effects associated with outcome

TABLE 2

GROUP MEANS BY SESSION FOR FAMILY AND THERAPIST SUPPORTIVENESS/DEFENSIVENESS MEASURES

Outcome group	Therapy session		
	A	B	L
1	70.2	68.2	
2	66.8	64.8	58
3	74.6	62.2	87.8
4	78.4	67	151.7

groups, $F(2, 18) = 5.25$, $p < .05$, and sessions, $F(2, 36) = 7.79$, $p < .01$, as well as an Outcome Groups × Sessions interaction, $F(4, 36 = 5.12$, $p < .01$. Since the interaction was statistically significant, tests were performed for simple main effects (Kirk, 1968).

Results of these tests showed that supportiveness/defensiveness ratios were not significantly different at Phase A, $F(2, 54) = 1.21$, *ns*, or Phase B, $F(2, 54) = 1$, *ns*, in the first session. These data suggest that the intervention, and not initial differences, were responsible for the significant differences found in family process by the next-to-last session, $F(2,54) = 14.28$, $p < .01$. Further, as independently derived and evaluated measures of adaptive family interaction (Alexander, 1973), they provide additional support for the outcome designations.

Therapist Characteristics

Relationship and structuring dimensions. The pretherapy supervisor ratings of therapist's skills were investigated as therapist-derived determinants of therapy outcome. Affect-behavior integration, warmth, humor, blaming, self-disclosure, directiveness, self-confidence, and clarity ratings were correlated with outcome, and the data were examined from the intercorrelation matrix presented in Table 4.

Blaming, self-disclosure, and clarity scores were removed from consideration due to low correlations with outcome (*rs* = .35, .44, and .29, respectively), and due to high correlations with other rated dimensions (for blaming and humor, $r = .69$; for self-disclosure and warmth, $r = .86$;

TABLE 3

FAMILY SUPPORTIVENESS/DEFENSIVENESS RATIO ANALYSIS OF VARIANCE SUMMARIES

Source	SS	*df*	MS	*F*
Between	1.085.39	15		
Outcome Groups (A)	97.75	2	48.88	3.81*
Subjects within groups	166.98	13	12.84	
Within	600.37	32		
Sessions (B)	117.67	2	58.84	5.63**
A x B	154.58	4	38.65	3.70*
Sessions x Subjects within groups	271.88	26	10.46	

* $p < .05$
** $p < .01$

for clarity and self-confidence, $r = .64$). Since these dimensions correlated poorly with outcome and highly with other dimensions, it was felt that these scores would add little predictive value beyond that contained in the remaining scores.

Further inspection revealed that there were two apparent blocks of scores that were highly intercorrelated. Affect-behavior integration, warmth, and humor intercorrelations ranged from .63 to .81 (all *ps* < .05), with an average correlation of .70. Directiveness and self-confidence intercorrelated .76 ($p < .05$). Most intercorrelations between separate dimensions within these two blocks were nonsignificant (*rs* ranged from —.09 to .49), with the exception of a significant correlation between self-confidence and affect-behavior integration ($r = .54$, $p < .05$). Collapsing the remaining scores within each of these two blocks (affect-behavior integration + warmth + humor: directiveness + self-confidence) into two global mean scores for each therapist, and then correlating them, generated correlation of .35 (*ns*). Therefore, these data demonstrated apparent groupings of intercorrelated scores that were statistically independent. For purposes of further analysis, individual scores within blocks were collapsed into mean scores for each of two dimensions. Arbitrarily, and yet supported by some face validity, these were labeled relationship and structuring dimensions.

Kerlinger and Pedhazur (1973) argued that continuous data such as these are optimally evaluated by multiple regression procedures. Since these data represented a narrow range of scores (1-5), it was felt the tests would be conservative. For subsequent analyses, the relationship and structuring global mean scores were entered as independent variables

TABLE 4

Correlation Matrix of Therapist Characteristics and Outcome

	Relationship dimension					Structuring dimension		
	1	2	3	4	5	6	7	8
Outcome	.60*	.35[a]	.57*	.65*	.44[a]	.62*	.58*	.29[a]
1. Affect-behavior integration		.39	.72	.67	.54	.19	.54	.36
2. Blaming			.63	.69	.43	.11	.06	−.03
3. Warmth				.81	.86	−.01	.17	−.07
4. Humor					.63	.41	.49	.21
5. Self-disclosure						−.06	−.02	−.09
6. Directiveness							.76	.56
7. Self-confidence								.64
8. Clarity								

[a] Removed from consideration due to low correlation with outcome.
* $p < .05$.

TABLE 5

MULTIPLE REGRESSION MEANS COMPARISONS BETWEEN THERAPISTS FOR RELATIONSHIP AND STRUCTURING SKILLS

Source	*df*	*SS*	*MS*	*F*
Relationship skills				
Total regression	3	10.1913	3.3971	5.01*
Regression due to poor (1 & 2) vs. good (3 & 4)	1	8.0277	8.0277	11.84**
Regression due to 3 vs. 4	1	2.0606	2.0606	3.04***
Regression due to 1 vs. 2	1	.1031	.1031	<1
Residual	17	11.5292	.6781	
Total	20	21.7205		
Structuring skills				
Total regression	3	10,042.4470	3,347.4823	3.81*
Regression due to poor (1 & 2) vs. good (3 & 4)	1	6,598.3950	6,598.3950	7.92*
Regression due to 3 vs. 4	1	192.3075	192.3075	<1
Regression due to 1 vs. 2	1	3,251.7450	3,251.7450	3.70***
Residual	17	14,932.5520	878.3854	
Total	20	24,975.00		

* $p < .05$.
** $p < .01$.
*** $.05 < p < .10$.

against the dependent variable, outcome (1, 2, 3, 4), in multiple regression analyses.

Relationship and structuring dimensions as predictors of outcome. The first analysis was performed to determine the predictive value of relationship and structuring scores on outcome. Jointly, relationship and structuring scores accunted for 59.65% of the variance in outcome, $F(2, 18) = 26.61$, $p < .01$. The partialing of the intercorrelated effects of the structuring dimension from the relationship dimension yielded a significant effect, $F(1, 18) = 6.69$, $p < .05$, indicating that prediction was significantly enhanced by inclusion of both variables. Singly, relationship skills alone accounted for 44.6%, $F(2, 18) = 7.26$, $p < .05$, of the variance in outcome, whereas structuring skills alone accounted for 35.8%, $F(2, 18) = 5.03$, $p < .05$. Structuring skills, however, with the intercorrelated effects of relationship skills partialed out, accounted for 15% of the outcome variance.

Orthogonal vector coding for unequal N was used for therapist group means comparisons of the relationship and structuring dimensions (Kerlinger & Pedhazur, 1973). The results are summarized in Table 5. There were significant differences between poor outcome (1s and 2s) and good outcome (3s and 4s) therapists, $F(1, 17) = 11.84$, $p < .01$, on the relationship dimension. There was no significant difference within poor outcome (1s vs. 2s) therapists ($F < 1$, *ns*), whereas the difference within good outcome (3s vs. 4s) therapists approached significance, $F(1, 17) = 3.04$, $.05 < p < .10$.

The same analysis was performed for the structuring dimension. There were significant differences between poor outcome (1s and 2s) and good outcome (3s and 4s) therapists, $F(1, 17) = 7.92$, $p < .05$. There was no difference between 3s and 4s ($F < 1$, *ns*), whereas the difference between 1s and 2s approached significance, $F(1, 17) = 3.70$, $.05 < p < .10$.

DISCUSSION

In discussing the effects of behavioral approaches to changing behavior, Marston (Note 2) indicated that behaviorists are continually confronted with evidence of behavior change that has occurred with little, if any, involvement of reinforcement as described by learning theory technologies. He suggested that it is becoming increasingly important to define and examine these additional, and to date nonspecific, aspects of therapeutic situation that facilitate behavior change. In a study of an intervention program similar to the one used in the present investigation, Stuart and Lott (1974) empirically demonstrated the importance of examining the behaviors of therapists within the therapy process. Specifically, in studying the effects of behavioral contracts with delinquents, they found that contract features tended to depend more on individual therapists than on characteristics of the client. In addition, since contract features were unrelated to treatment outcome, Stuart and Lott (1974) concluded that

> other factors, either in the treatment (such as facilitation of communication) or in the techniques of service delivery (such as the process of negotiating behavioral contracts) are the real determinants of treatment outcome. (p. 487)

The results of this study suggest useful methodological and substantive directions in attempting to isolate and demonstrate these determinants. In evaluating families in therapy, the process measures of supportiveness and defensiveness toward the end of therapy seemed to appropriately describe the effectiveness of intervention. These data converged with objective (dropout) data and therapist evaluations of family outcome, as well as the nonreactive outcome measure of recidivism.

The findings regarding the predictive variance found in therapist characteristics were unanticipated and perplexing in light of our previously published research on this intervention model. It was expected that the therapist skills of greatest consequence to outcome would be those emphasized in training manuals (Alexander, 1974; Malouf & Alexander, 1974) and formal descriptions of the model (Alexander & Parsons, 1973; Parsons & Alexander, 1973). These skills have been depicted as more technical or structured dimensions of a modification technology.

Instead, it was the global quality of relationship skills that made the most significant contribution to outcome variance. One explanation of this finding may be that there is a potential statistical artifact arising from selection of therapists and their training. Because of the importance placed on therapist structuring skills in this intervention model, it was possible that by the end of the pre-therapy training phase therapists had already been "trained to criterion," resulting in a relatively homogeneous sample with respect to these skills.

However, the data offer an alternative interpretation. First, the data indicate that there are differences between good and poor outcome therapists in structuring skills, arguing that therapists are not homogeneous on this dimension. What is perhaps more interesting, though only suggestive due to significance levels, is that the poor outcome therapists appear to differ from less poor therapists on this dimension, whereas better outcome therapists are homogeneous. These data suggest that perhaps structuring skills are a necessary condition to insure that families will return for therapy, though not sufficient to insure successful therapy.

Relationship skills also differentiate good from poor outcome therapists. However (though only suggestive due to significance levels), poor outcome therapists appear homogeneous, whereas the best outcome therapists appear different from good ones. An interpretation is that therapist relationship skills may determine the qualitative distinction between good versus best outcomes.

However, relationship skills alone are apparently ineffective in modifying delinquent families. Prior research has clearly demonstrated that a client-centered intervention program, as compared to the intervention program evaluated here, failed to modify familiy interaction patterns (Parsons & Alexander, 1973) or reduce recidivism below the rate of no-treatment controls (Alexander & Parsons, 1973). Thus, a focus on relationship skills alone, at least with an adolescent (delinquent) family population, failed to demonstrate any impact on outcome. Instead, it appears that the effects of relationship skills on the part of the therapist are most likely enhanced, if not elicited, by a well-structured therapeutic agenda and operational framework. Conversely, without the superimposed structure represented in the present systems-behavioral model, therapists (especially relatively inexperienced ones) would be operating in a climate in which relationship-building behaviors have little impact on behavior change.

Finally, it is essential to note that the therapist skills described in this study represent dimensions derived from an assessment of in vivo process characteristics during training, not some global personality attribute or profile derived from standard personality inventories that have been found to have poor predictive value compared to in vivo supervisors' ratings (Bergin & Jasper, 1969). A great deal of subsequent research, evaluating specific sequential effects of selected therapist's behaviors, is necessary to determine the crucial dimensions and how they operate. Expanding the matching to sample philosophy to include therapist training programs would require identifying those therapist behaviors associated with successful treatment outcome and shaping therapists to perform those behaviors while reducing the rate of behaviors found to negatively correlate with successful treatment. Further, it should be noted that family characteristics undoubtedly influence outcome, no matter which skills the therapist exhibits. In the present study, the identified therapist characteristics accounted for only 60% of outcome variance, and it is probable that with a more heterogeneous family population "error variance" would be even greater.

In summary, the methodological constraints in the present design do not allow for direct causal interpretations of the impact of therapist behaviors on changes in family interaction and outcome. However, the results are sufficiently compelling to suggest the necessity of expanding the intervention model examined here, and all those with related philosophies and techniques, to include a formal focus on therapist behaviors. Although the intervention techniques stressed by the model have proven effective (Alexander & Parsons, 1973; Parsons & Alexander, 1973), the current study indicates that therapist characteristics, to date almost ignored in the literature, also have major effects on the results of these techniques.

REFERENCE NOTES

1. Ray, R. S. *The Training of Mothers of Atypical Children in the Use of Behavior Modification Techniques*. Unpublished master's thesis, University of Oregon, 1965.

2. Marston, A. R. *Parables for Behavior Therapists*. Paper presented at the Second Annual Southern California Behavior Modification Conference, Los Angeles, October 1970.

REFERENCES

Alexander, J. F. Defensive and supportive communications in normal and deviant families. *Journal of Consulting and Clinical Psychology*, 40:223-231, 1973.

Alexander, J. F. Behavior modification and delinquent youth. In J. C. Cull & R. E. Hardy (Eds.), *Behavior Modification in Rehabilitation Settings*. Springfield, Ill.: Charles C Thomas, 1974.

Alexander, J. F., & Parsons, B. V. Short-term behavioral intervention with delinquent families: Impact on family process and recidivism. *Journal of Abnormal Psychology*, 81:219-225, 1973.

Bergin, A. E., & Garfield, S. L. (Eds.). *Handbook of Psychotherapy and Behavior Change: An Empirical Analysis*. New York: Wiley, 1971.

Bergin, A. E., & Jasper, L. G. Correlates of empathy in psychotherapy: A replication. *Journal of Abnormal Psychology*, 74:477-481, 1969.

Bergin, A. E., & Strupp, H. H. New directions in psychotherapy research. *Journal of Abnormal Psychology*, 76:13-26, 1970.

Gibb, J. R. Defensive communications. *Journal of Communications*, 3:141-148, 1961.

Gurman, A. S. The effects and effectiveness of marital therapy: A review of outcome research. In H. H. Strupp et al. (Eds.), *Psychotherapy and Behavior Change: 1973*. Chicago: Aldine, 1974.

Hartmann, D. P. Recent trends in child behavior modification. In W. T. McReynolds (Ed.), *Behavior Therapy in Review*. New York: Aronson, 1975.

Kerlinger, F. N., & Pedhazur, E. J. *Multiple Regression in Behavioral Research*. New York: Holt, Rinehart & Winston, 1973.

KIRK, R. E. *Experimental Design: Procedures for the Behavioral Sciences.* Belmont, Calif.: Brooks/Cole, 1968.

MALOUF, R. E., & ALEXANDER, J. F. Family crisis intervention: A model and technique of training. In R. E. Hardy & J. C. Cull (Eds.), *Therapeutic Needs of the Family.* Springfield, Ill.: Charles C Thomas, 1974.

MELTZOFF, J., & KORNREICH, M. *Research in Psychotherapy.* New York: Atherton Press, 1970.

O'LEARY, K. D., O'LEARY, S., & BECKER, W. C. Modification of a deviant sibling interaction in the home. *Behavior Research and Therapy,* 5:113-120, 1967,

PARSONS, B. V., & ALEXANDER, J. F. Short-term family intervention: A therapy outcome study. *Journal of Consulting and Clinical Psychology,* 41:195-201, 1973.

PATTERSON, G. R., MCNEAL, S., HAWKINS, N., & PHELPS, R. Reprogramming the social environment. *Journal of Child Psychology and Psychiatry,* 8:181-195, 1967.

PATTERSON, G. R., RAY, R. G., & SHAW, D. A. Direct intervention in families of deviant children. *Oregon Research Institute Research Bulletin,* 8:No. 9, 1968.

SAGER, C. J., & KAPLAN, H. S. (Eds.). *Progress in Group and Family Therapy.* New York: Brunner/Mazel, 1972.

SPARK, G. M., & BRODY, E. M. The aged are family members. *Family Process,* 9:195-210, 1970.

STRUPP, H. H., et al. (Eds.), *Psychotherapy and Behavior Change: 1973.* Chicago: Aldine, 1974.

STUART, R. B. Operant-interpersonal treatment for marital discord. *Journal of Consulting and Clinical Psychology,* 33:675-682, 1969.

STUART, R. B. Behavioral contracting within the families of delinquents. *Journal of Behavior Therapy and Experimental Psychiatry,* 2:1-11, 1971.

STUART, R. B., & LOTT, L. A., JR. Behavioral contracting with delinquents: A cautionary note. In C. M. Franks & G. T. Wilson (Eds.), *Annual Review of Behavior Therapy and Practice: 1974.* New York: Brunner/Mazel, 1974.

THORNE, G. L., THARPE, R. G., & WETZEL, R. J. Behavior modification techniques: New tools for probation officers. *Federal Probation,* June 1967, 21-27.

WYNNE, L. C. Communication disorders and the quest for relatedness in families of schizophrenics. *American Journal of Psychoanalysis,* 30:100-114, 1970.

Kirk, R. E. *Experimental Design: Procedures for the Behavioral Sciences.* Belmont, Calif.: Brooks/Cole, 1968.

Mason, R. E., & Alexander, J. F. Family crisis intervention: A model and technique of training. In R. E. Hardy & J. G. Cull (Eds.), *Therapeutic Needs of the Family.* Springfield, Ill.: Charles C Thomas, 1974.

Meltzoff, J., & Kornreich, M. *Research in Psychotherapy.* New York: Atherton Press, 1970.

O'Leary, K. D., O'Leary, S., & Becker, W. C. Modification of a deviant sibling interaction pattern in the home. *Behaviour Research and Therapy,* 5:113-120, 1967.

Parsons, B. V., & Alexander, J. F. Short-term family intervention: A therapy outcome study. *Journal of Consulting and Clinical Psychology,* 41:195-201, 1973.

Patterson, G. R., McNeal, S., Hawkins, N., & Phelps, R. Reprogramming the social environment. *Journal of Child Psychology and Psychiatry,* 8:181-195, 1967.

Patterson, G. R., Ray, R. S., & Shaw, D. A. Direct intervention in families of deviant children. *Oregon Research Institute Research Bulletin,* 8(No. 9), 1968.

Sager, C. J., & Kaplan, H. S. (Eds.) *Progress in Group and Family Therapy.* New York: Brunner/Mazel, 1972.

Spark, G. M., & Brody, E. M. The aged are family members. *Family Process,* 9:195-210, 1970.

Strupp, H. H., et al. (eds.) *Psychotherapy and Behavior Change 1973.* Chicago: Aldine, 1974.

Stuart, R. B. Operant-interpersonal treatment for marital discord. *Journal of Consulting and Clinical Psychology,* 33:675-682, 1969.

Stuart, R. B. Behavioral contracting within the families of delinquents. *Journal of Behavior Therapy and Experimental Psychiatry,* 2:1-11, 1971.

Stuart, R. B., & Lott, L. A. Behavioral contracting with delinquents: A cautionary note. In C. M. Franks & G. T. Wilson (Eds.), *Annual Review of Behavior Therapy Theory and Practice 1973.* New York: Brunner/Mazel, 1974.

Thorne, G. L., Tharp, R. G., & Wetzel, R. J. Behavior modification techniques: New tools for probation officers. *Federal Probation,* 31:21-27, 1967.

Wynne, L. C. Communication disorders and the quest for relatedness in families of schizophrenics. *American Journal of Psychoanalysis,* 30:100-114, 1970.

Section VI

ADDICTIVE BEHAVIORS: ALCOHOLISM, OBESITY, CIGARETTE SMOKING AND DRUG ADDICTION

Commentary

ALCOHOLISM

Outcome Studies

In our 1974 volume we had occasion to reprint Hunt and Azrin's (1973) successful implementation of a community-reinforcement treatment program for alcoholics (see Franks & Wilson, 1974). Among other commendable features, the unusually high improvement rates described by Hunt and Azrin and the inclusion of an independently conducted follow-up at six months after treatment stamp this as one of the most convincing sources of support for the efficacy of a behavioral treatment approach for alcoholism. The first paper reprinted in this Section, by Azrin, represents an extension of the community-reinforcement approach to alcoholism. Azrin describes several improvements in the treatment package used, including the introduction of techniques to ensure the self-administration of Antabuse, and the systematic use of the Buddy system—a social support strategy that Alcoholics Anonymous (AA) has always had as a cornerstone of its treatment program. The results of Azrin's program are encouraging, with behavior therapy shown to be significantly more effective than the control treatment even at a two year follow-up. The magnitude as well as the breadth of improvement across different domains of client functioning are striking.

Last year also saw the publication of Sobell and Sobell's (1976) two year follow-up data from their heavily publicized study. The one year follow-up of the original study was reprinted in our 1975 volume, together with a discussion of the adequacy of the design of the study and the evaluation procedures used (cf. Franks & Wilson, 1975). The results two years after termination of treatment are still very impressive. As at previous follow-up evaluations, the controlled drinking-experimental (CD-E) group was significantly different from the controlled drinking-control (CD-C) group. For the entire second year of follow-up, the CD-E subjects functioned well for an average of 89.61% of all days as compared to a mean of 45.10% of all days for the CD-C subjects. The difference between the no drinking-experimental (ND-E) and no drinking-control (ND-C) subjects approached but did not reach significance at either the eighteen month or two year follow-ups. Over the entire second year of follow-up ND-E subjects functioned well for a mean of 64.60% of all days, while ND-C subjects functioned well for a mean of 45.13% of all days.

Differences between experimental and control group subjects were found not only for drinking behaviors but for other adjunctive measures of functioning as well. An evaluation of adjustment to interpersonal relationships and problem situations revealed the same pattern of results as for drinking. Subjects in the CD-E group were classified as significantly more improved than CD-C group members at each follow-up over the two year period. Subjects in the ND-E groups were rated as significantly more improved than ND-C subjects during the first year, but not during the second year of follow-up. With regard to vocational status only the CD-E subjects differed from their controls during the second year of follow-up.

The Azrin study reprinted here and Sobell and Sobell's (1976) study represent the best comparative outcome evidence that behavior therapy is an effective treatment method for alcoholism. The results obtained must rank among the most favorable—and in the case of the Sobell and Sobell findings on controlled drinking, the most controversial—ever reported. Furthermore, as relatively sophisticated controlled outcome studies they provide good examples of the requirements and difficulties of conducting rigorous research on complex behavior disorders such as alcoholism. For all these reasons these two impressive studies demand searching evaluative scrutiny (see Kazdin & Wilson, in press; Nathan & Briddell, 1977).

In both studies the comparison treatment condition consisted of routine therapy offered by a State Hospital. The adequacy of this alternative treatment can be questioned. For example, it can be argued that almost any novel treatment program introduced into such conventional therapy settings would capitalize on the placebo factors of renewed interest, optimism, and enthusiasm the treatment staff might display. In other words, the two treatments being compared might not have been valued equally highly by the therapists who administered them and/or the clients that participated in the different programs. Clients in the control treatment condition in the Azrin study received didactic information on the negative effects of alcohol and were encouraged to join Alcoholics Anonymous, the workings of which were explained. Beyond this it is not clear what real therapeutic elements there were in the control treatment. On face value it would be difficult to argue that such a program could have equated for the many placebo influences generated by the community-reinforcement program. One reviewer has suggested an iatrogenic effect of relegating some clients to routine treatment while assigning others to a novel program (Emrick, 1974). Specifically, Emrick (1974) observes that 40% of the clients in Sobell and Sobell's (1976) control groups expressed resentment at having been deprived of the experimental treatment at the two year follow-up. Another 20% reported that they had initially experienced feelings of resentment but then felt better. The possibility exists that the difference between the behavior therapy and control groups was in some part a function of the negative reaction of control group clients as well as the improvement shown by the behavior therapy group clients.

Both studies used very broad therapy programs comprising diverse treatment techniques. The difficulty in determining the effective agents of therapeutic change has been discussed by Nathan and Briddell in connection with the Sobell and Sobell study. The therapy package included techniques that have little or no independent empirical support, such as electrical aversion conditioning. Yet the treatment package produced marked changes in alcohol consumption during the course of follow-up but not during treatment. Specifically, clients drank to excess during non-shock "probe" test periods but showed controlled drinking and even abstinence following the completion of the program. Interpretation of treatment effects is further complicated by the fact that follow-up involved a lengthy and intensive ongoing relationship between one of the investigators and the clients. It is probable that this follow-up procedure was reactive and might well have contributed in important but unspecified ways to successful outcome at follow-up.

Subjects were not randomly assigned to groups in the Sobell and Sobell study, confounding the type of treatment goal with subject selection factors. Clients were selectively assigned to the controlled drinking conditions because they had requested it, had significant social support in their natural environment, and/or had successfully practiced controlled drinking in the past. Comparisons between controlled drinking and abstinent conditions are thus confounded. Since behavior therapy was significantly superior to routine treatment during the second year of follow-up only within the controlled drinking condition, an interaction between subject selection factors and the long-term efficacy of behavior therapy is indicated.

Lastly, both the Azrin and Sobell and Sobell studies exemplify the sort of multiple measurement of treatment outcome—including personal, social, vocational, and physical criteria in addition to the amount and pattern of alcohol consumption—that is necessary in evaluating therapy for alcoholics (see Section VIII, Franks & Wilson, 1975). In the Sobell and Sobell study, however, follow-up measures were obtained by one of the main investigators, making it impossible to rule out the effect of unintentional bias.

Predictably, the issue of controlled drinking has continued to generate professional controversy. In contrast to the excellent results reported by Sobell and Sobell, Ewing and Rouse (1976) report the failure of an attempt to develop controlled drinking in a group of alcoholics. To summarize, of 35 referrals, 10 patients attended the program only once before dropping out, while another 11 terminated in less than six sessions on the grounds that the program involved too much effort "and that it would be easier to stop drinking altogether." The remaining 14 patients attended at least six sessions, nine of them completing 12-24 sessions. The weekly treatment sessions were closely modeled on the Lovibond and Caddy (1970) discriminated aversion conditioning procedure. Aside from this discriminated aversion conditioning treatment, other therapeutic measures included asking the patients to keep a daily diary of any drinking, instructing them how to modify their drinking behavior by mixing and sipping drinks rather than gulping straight alcohol, encouraging the participation of spouses or girlfriends, and occasionally having the therapists model moderate social drinking during a session.

All patients learned to discriminate blood alcohol levels (BALs) and developed controlled drinking patterns during the therapy program. However, at follow-ups ranging from 27 to 55 months after treatment, *none* had maintained the controlled drinking pattern. According to Ewing and Rouse, "not all patients required hospitalization for their drinking and not all patients necessarily showed such lengthy, or as many episodes of, loss of control as they might have experienced before the treatment program. However, for the alcoholic, even one bout of loss of control can be damaging in many ways and, we believe, represents a poor outcome of therapy" (p. 131). All except one of the patients eventually decided to become abstinent, nine of them successfully so at the time of follow-up (either through AA or Antabuse). Ewing and Rouse arrive at the following conclusion: "Based on our experiences with these patients and a long-term follow-up, we hace concluded that, in our hands at least, further attempts to inculcate controlled drinking by such methods are unjustified. Some of the optimistic claims that have been made by other workers may have been premature. It should be noted that no similar treatment program has yet reported a follow-up greater than 24 months' duration" (p. 134).

There are several major problems with this inadequate study. At best, all Ewing and Rouse can conclude is that *discriminated aversion conditioning* does not effectively result in the maintenance of controlled drinking. They ignore the crucially important fact that other methods are available and have been used to develop controlled drinking (cf. Sobell & Sobell, 1976). The Lovibond and Caddy (1970) study has been severely criticized, and it is highly improbable that aversion conditioning is useful for developing either controlled drinking or abstinence (Wilson, in press b). Aversion conditioning almost certainly was *not* the agent of change in the Sobell and Sobell study. Rather, it seems likely that the teaching of social skills, assertive responses, and problem-solving competencies through behavior rehearsal was a major factor. There is a wide agreement that these behavioral methods should be part of an effective behavioral program (e.g., Nathan & Briddell, 1977; O'Leary & Wilson, 1975). Yet Ewing and Rouse seem to have omitted any serious attention to these vital areas. The most that was done—and details are lacking—was to encourage spouse or partner participation in a less than systematic fashion. The primary focus of the Ewing and Rouse program was on discriminated aversion. Accordingly, a plausible alternative reinterpretation of their data is that they simply reflect the results of an inadequate therapy program that does not adequately reflect current behavior therapy, whether the goal be abstinence or controlled drinking.

A second consideration is that treatment outcome has to be appraised in terms of the initial induction of change, its generalization to other situations, and its maintenance over time. Since no explicit maintenance strategy was employed, it is not surprising that the initial treatment produced improvement did not persist. A third factor is the inadequacy of the way in which maintenance data are described. Ewing and Rouse acknowledge that "loss of control" (a vague descriptor) drinking occurred less frequently than before treatment. However, they dismiss this apparent improvement by asserting their belief that "even one bout of loss of control represents a poor outcome." This reasoning is steeped in now largely discredited assumptions of "loss of control" (cf. Hamburg, 1975; Lloyd & Salzberg, 1975; Pomerleau, Pertschuk, & Stinnet, 1976), and represents a retreat into global, qualitative judgments of outcome as opposed to more quantitative indices of specific drinking patterns (cf. Sobell & Sobell, 1976). Finally, there was no control group. It is quite possible that a control group that received abstinence training might have responded in much the same way. The fact that nine of the subjects eventually succeeded in becoming abstinent does not permit the conclusion that a goal of abstinence would have resulted in superior results compared to controlled drinking.

In sum, this is a largely anecdotal report with inadequate outcome measures that tests a method that is *a priori* limited or inappropriate. As a result it fails to contribute to the determination of the efficacy of controlled drinking. Worse, the precipitous and unwarranted conclusions that are drawn from such inadequate data seem likely to muddle the troubled waters still further.

Caddy and Lovibond (1976) conducted a more detailed investigation of the discriminated aversion conditioning method. They compared three therapy conditions in the treatment of 60 alcoholics: 1) discriminated aversion plus self-regulation, education, and psychotherapy; 2) self-regulation, education, and psychotherapy without the discriminated aversion conditioning; and 3) discriminated aversion conditioning alone. In the discriminated aversion conditioning, subjects received a painful electric shock to the larynx on 80% of the occasions they exceeded a BAL of 0.05% during treatment sessions. Self-regulation included training in specific self-control techniques such as stimulus control and instructions to the effect that alcohol abuse could be brought under client control. The nature of the psychotherapy condition is far from clear, and this is one of the problems in interpreting the results of this study. However, it appears to have included general support, some discussion of marital problems, and relaxation training (hardly the usual psychotherapy technique!). There were 10 two hour therapy sessions in all, although the combined group received more overall therapist contact.

The combined treatment group showed greater improvement at posttreatment and at a six months follow-up than either the self-regulation or discriminated aversion conditioning groups alone. Eighty percent of the combined group were estimated to be complete successes or moderately improved at follow-up. The discriminated aversion conditioning treatment fared most poorly. At six month follow-up, 70% of this group showed no improvement. This treatment condition approximates most closely the behavioral treatment method employed by Ewing and Rouse, indicating still further the lack of relevance of that study to the resolution of the question of the feasibility of training controlled drinking. A substantial dropout rate complicates interpretation of Caddy and Lovibond's findings. Five subjects in the combined group, four in the self-regulation group, and seven in the aversion conditioning group failed to complete the full course of therapy, giving an overall attrition rate of approximately 26%.

Two treatment studies emphasized training the alcoholic to cope more effectively with stressful situations. Pomerleau, Pertschuk, Adkins, and Brady (1976) compared a multifaceted group behavior therapy program with traditional group psychotherapy in the treatment of middle-income problem drinkers. A one year follow-up showed no significant difference between the two groups in terms of number of patients who abstained. However, behavior therapy resulted in significantly reduced alcohol consumption and significantly less attrition during treatment compared to traditional group psychotherapy. Foy, Miller, Eisler, and O'Toole (1976) demonstrated that teaching alcoholics social skills resulted in more effective interpersonal behavior (e.g., refusing drinks) in alcohol-related situations after the patients were discharged from the hospital. The potential significance of this finding is highlighted by Marlatt's (1973) finding that social pressure from former drinking associates was a major factor associated with relapse.

O'Leary, O'Leary, and Donovan (1976) have reviewed studies on social skills acquisition and the development of interpersonal competence in alcoholics. They conclude that prealcoholic teenagers are less socially skilled than their light drinking and nondrinking counterparts. According to O'Leary et al., male prealcoholics appear to lack adequate models for socially appropriate masculine behavior and adopt a simplistic, hypermasculine stance early in life. This stance in turn becomes increasingly maladaptive and is further reinforced as more sophisticated social responses are required of the prealcoholic. Additionally, since they tend to choose heavy drinkers as friends, prealcoholics are less likely to have socially appropriate peer models available to them during the late adolescent and early adult years.

Aversion therapy for alcoholism is still a focus of activity. Wiens,

Montague, Manaugh, and English (1976) report the results of emetine-based chemical aversion conditioning with 261 alcoholics at a one year follow-up. (The details of this study are discussed in an earlier volume in this Series—see Franks and Wilson, 1975.) Consistent with Lemere and Voegtlin's (1950) findings, 63% had remained abstinent. Wiens et al.'s data were drawn from the records of the Raleigh Hills treatment facility in Portland, Oregon, for the year of 1970. A comparable analysis of the data for the year 1971 indicated an abstinent rate of 59% at the one year follow-up (Wiens, 1976). This figure is based on 98% of the patients, a remarkably high penetration rate for a follow-up study in an area where massive attrition is usually the case (see Franks & Wilson, 1975).

The Raleigh Hills Hospitals' results, obtained with patients who are relatively advantaged, are encouraging. However, reservations must be had about the nature of the assessment of treatment outcome in these studies. In the Wiens et al. study, for example, 164 of the 261 patients were evaluated as abstinent or not on the basis of their hospital charts. Forty-one were contacted by mail, and 35 by telephone. The reliability and validity of these measures are unknown. The value outcome data could be improved by independent assessment of more detailed measures of alcohol consumption during follow-up. Nonetheless, the detailed reporting of clinical outcome data from treatment settings is a relatively rare occurrence, and this commendable practice is to be encouraged.

Glover and McCue (1977) compared electrical aversion conditioning with a control group that received routine hospital treatment. There was no difference between treatments for patients between the ages of 20 and 40 years. For patients over the age of 40 years electrical aversion conditioning appeared to be superior. Among other problems, patients were not assigned randomly to groups and some patients received additional treatment in the form of relaxation training. As a result it is difficult to interpret these findings in any meaningful way.

Wilson and Tracey (1976) compared electrical aversion conditioning with aversive imagery in the treatment of chronic alcoholics. The use of single-subject methodology and objective assessment of the subjects' alcohol consumption in a semi-naturalistic laboratory setting allowed a fine-grained analysis of individual response patterns. The two methods did not differ from each other, and both were relatively ineffective in decreasing drinking. However, when a relatively mild shock (the same stimulus that had been ineffective in the respondent conditioning paradigm) was made contingent on each drink the subjects took, alcohol consumption was effectively suppressed. The latter finding replicates Wilson, Leaf, and Nathan's (1975) results on the efficacy of punishment in the regulation of drinking by alcoholics. The failure to demonstrate the efficacy of aversive imagery suggests that a technique like covert sensitization may be less useful than some investigators have previously surmised.

Wilson and Tracey (1976) showed that, when the punishment contingency was in effect, even after subjects had been "primed" with alcohol, no drinking was observed. These data provide still further evidence that the traditional disease theory of alcoholism is untenable. The major assumption of this theory is that loss of control, or involuntary drinking, is governed by a physiological addictive process which is triggered by the ingestion of alcohol. The present data support a view of loss of control drinking as learned behavior, differing only in rate and quantity of alcohol consumed from normal social drinking. Finally, Peters (1976) provides a delightfully engaging account of aversion conditioning from a nineteenth century case report—an extract from one of Chekhov's stories!

An overall appraisal of the application of behavior therapy to alcoholism is presented by Litman (1976). Aside from some incisive analyses of the shortcomings of most behavioral studies to date, Litman offers some constructive suggestions about future directions. In particular she emphasizes how operant conditioning formulations have ignored the role of cognitive factors in alcohol abuse (see also Wilson, 1977).

Assessment of Alcohol Problems

The study of the ad lib drinking habits of alcoholics in the laboratory setting has proved very useful in the assessment of determinants of excessive drinking. Reviewing the advantages of behavioral assessment methods that involve alcohol consumption in the laboratory, Nathan and Briddell (1977) state that they are "reliable, analogous to drinking behavior outside the laboratory, and salient to the problem of alcohol abuse. . . ." However, Lawson, Wilson, Briddell, and Ives (1976) point out that no validation study has been conducted to assess the relationship between drinking in a controlled setting and drinking in the natural environment.

In an initial investigation of this relationship, Lawson et al. allowed two male alcoholics *ad lib* access to their preferred alcoholic beverages during a seven day period on a controlled laboratory setting. During a subsequent 11 day period, alcohol was available in the laboratory only on alternate days, and 16 hour home visits were scheduled on the intervening days. Neither subject drank in the laboratory setting. One of the subjects became intoxicated the first time he returned home. A detailed behavioral assessment with this subject had indicated that his relationship with his wife was a major source of conflict and a likely determinant of drinking. Of considerable interest in view of the loss of control notion of alcoholism, this subject displayed no interest in drinking upon his return to the laboratory—with its free access to alcohol—despite the fact that on two occasions he was still intoxicated. Clearly, drinking is regulated by situation-specific psychosocial variables. Alcohol in the bloodstream of the alcoholic does not inevitably lead to alcohol abuse—it depends on the controlling cognitive and environmental influences. Adequate assessment of drinking patterns requires that the stimuli that normally govern drinking are present in the laboratory or real life situation.

Most treatment programs for alcoholics rely upon self-report of drinking behavior as the outcome measure. In some instances, it appears that self-report correlated well with behavioral measures of drinking (Sobell & Sobell, 1975). Recently, Sobell, Sobell, and Vanderspek (1976) compared self-report, clinical judgment, and physiological measures of blood alcohol concentration. They concluded that neither self-reports nor the clinical judgment of trained observers are adequate as a basis for treatment decisions when the person in question has a positive blood alcohol concentration. "While conjoint use of both self-report and judgment measures increases the probability of identifying instances when a subject has recently been drinking, a substantial incidence of false negative evaluations still occurs. This finding is not surprising when one considers that acquired tolerance to alcohol is likely to occur for clients of an alcohol treatment program who engage in extended drinking. Therefore, it is suggested that alcohol treatment programs, especially outpatient programs, should include breath analysis among their routine assessment procedures and also as part of any treatment outcome investigation" (Sobell et al., 1976).

Finally, Miller (1976) has reviewed different assessment methods for differentiating alcoholics, including special alcoholism scales, personality measures, psychophysiological indicators, and direct behavioral observations. Thus far, no completely satisfactory method for identifying alcoholism has emerged.

Conceptual Issues

As we have noted in previous volumes, the disease model of alcoholism has come under increasing attack. Pattison (1976b) presents an excellent review of the assumptions underlying the traditional disease model of alcoholism, and summarizes some of the recent experimental and clinical evidence that discredits these notions. Further evidence at odds with the disease conception of alcoholism that assumes that alcoholism is single entity marked by a progressive, irreversible disease process is presented by Clark and Cahalan (1976). A longitudinal study of white males shows greater variability in problem drinking than a unilinear model of alcoholism can encompass. Many individuals move in and out of severe drinking problems. Moreover, young males rather than older men display the highest rates of problem drinking. Clark and Cahalan suggest that the conceptual focus be shifted from viewing alcoholism as a disease entity to an emphasis on particular drinking problems. This position is consistent with the social learning analysis of alcoholism (e.g., Bandura, 1969), and has profound implications for research and treatment. Clark and Cahalan put it this way: "If an alcoholism-as-disease model is emphasized, public policy tends to be oriented around the individual as the locus of the disease; and alcoholism research and treatment accordingly take on a clinical and pathological emphasis. If, instead, the 'problems' approach is emphasized, there are fewer conceptual barriers to viewing the drinking problems as associated with disjunctions in the interactions between the individual and his environment—with considerable different implications for research and remedial measures" (p. 258).

Pattison (1976a) criticizes traditional treatment programs based on the premise that there is "*one* population of alcoholics, to be treated by *one* best method, resulting in *one* therapeutic outcome." Instead, Pattison presents a multivariate model emphasizing that there are several alcoholic populations, that may be treated by diverse methods, that may result in different outcomes. The different outcome goals stress the need for multiple measures of drinking and non-drinking behavior. More specifically, goals relating to drinking patterns are broken down into five possible outcomes: abstinence, social drinking, attenuated drinking, controlled drinking, and normal drinking. The specificity and operational clarity of this conceptual approach to alcoholism treatment goals should aid in moving research away from the "either/or" classification of "dry" or "drunk" that have served to obscure potential treatment difference in previous investigations.

Gilbert (1976) describes a view of drug and alcohol abuse as excessive behavior rather than disease process. Thus, he proposes that "pharmacology may not have very much to do with drug abuse," evidence for which has been emphasized recently by social learning theorists (cf. Marlatt, 1977; Wilson, 1977). The situational specificity of alcohol and drug abuse is a mainstay of this argument, and Gilbert cites data showing that skid-row alcoholics removed to a farm community where abstinence is enforced simply stop drinking without withdrawal symptoms. Moreover, they appear to be able to resume moderate drinking. As Gilbert observes, this suggests that "the former alcoholism was maintained largely by features of the skid-row environment rather than by physical dependence on alcohol."

Gilbert argues that viewing alcoholism as excessive behavior leads one to look for the causes of excessive behavior rather than the causes of alcohol abuse per se. It follows from this position that treatment should be directed at the causes of excessive behavior; merely reducing one excessive behavior (e.g., alcohol abuse) might result in its replacement by another excessive behavior. There is little evidence to support this notion. Members of AA are supposed to drink vast quantities of coffee, but the evidence is anecdotal and alternative interpretations other than excessive behavior are easily come by. There is better evidence that an increase in eating is associated with a decrease in cigarette smoking, but here again alternative explanations cannot be ruled out. At first blush, Gilbert's analysis sounds uncommonly like the old psychodynamic battle cry of "symptom substitution." The claim of symptom substitution has been shown to be a conceptual red herring, without empirical backing. However, ample evidence exists indicating that when one behavior changes, others may change as well. Behavior does not consist solely of discrete response patterns, nor does it take place in a social vacuum. The modification of behaviors other than the target response is therefore not unexpected and can be more parsimoniously accounted for than by postulating symptom substitution.

Gilbert suggests that the causes of excessive behavior could be related to specific schedules of reinforcement. In short, he suggests that excessive behavior could be seen as adjunctive behavior that is schedule-induced (Falk, 1972). Schedule-induced excessive behavior occurs when reinforcers are provided a deprived animal in small quantities and according to a specific time schedule; the excessive behavior is not related to the reinforcer (which need not be contingent upon behavior) and has been demonstrated in pigeons, rats, and people. Schedule-induced behavior is an extremely robust, generalizable phenomenon, the implications of which have not been explored with human problems. An examination of the conditions under which excessive alcohol consumption occurs, with schedule-induced adjunctive behavior in mind, might prove to be a useful research strategy.

OBESITY

Behavioral research and therapy with obese clients continue to be an extremely active area. Over the past year at least three books (Mahoney & Mahoney, 1976a; Stunkard, 1976b; Williams, Martin & Foreyt, 1976) and two major review articles (Leon, 1976; Stunkard & Mahoney, 1976) have been published. A thoughtful position paper by Stunkard (1976a) on the future prospects for broad-scale social-behavioral interventions is of particular importance. Commercial enterprises such as Weight Watchers, medical facilities, industry, trade unions, the government, the media, and the educational process are all evaluated as means for the more effective modification of obesity. Stunkard's explicit statement on the inevitability and desirability of efforts to control obesity passing from medical to non-medical agencies is particularly encouraging to those who are behaviorally committed.

Outcome Studies

The second paper in this Section—by Öst and Götestam—represents a rare comparative outcome study of the behavioral treatment of obesity with a long-term follow-up. The results are discouraging, for they indicate that the widely demonstrated superiority of behavioral treatment at posttreatment and over short-term follow-ups disappears by a one year follow-up. This is precisely the pattern of results that Hall and Hall (1974) discerned in their review of the behavioral treatment literature.

There are many informative aspects of this well-designed study by Öst and Götestam. First, it compares behavior therapy with an active alternative treatment approach—pharmacotherapy using fenfluramine. As Öst and Götestam point out, the alternative treatment in previous comparative studies has been some sort of verbal psychotherapy that is more accurately described as an attention-placebo treatment (e.g., Wollersheim, 1970). A second commendable feature of the Öst and Götestam report is their description of treatment-produced side effects. Among others, Stunkard (1976b) has reported the occurrence of emotional states such as depression in clients who have lost weight. As in the treatment of alcohol-related problems, outcome measures of programs for the modification of obesity should include multiple measures of weight loss *and* emotional, social, and physical well-being. Consistent with most of the behavioral studies, there were few side effects of the behavioral treatment in the Öst and Götestam study. Even the greater number of side effects experienced by subjects who received the fenfluramine seems very minor and inconsistent with the fears of those who suggest that serious emotional consequences are attached to successful weight loss. Another encouraging finding of the Öst and Götestam study is the positive and significant correlation between degree of habit change and percent of initial body weight lost. This suggests that there is a treatment-specific effect of the behavioral procedures employed.

Discouraging data are also reported by Hanson, Borden, Hall and Hall (1976). They compared a behavioral self-control program to two programmed text conditions differing only in the degree of therapist contact, an attention-placebo, and a no treatment control group. The three behavioral treatment groups were collectively superior to the control groups at post-treatment and at a 10-week follow-up, but not at a one year follow-up. There was a noticeable subject attrition rate during treatment (21.8%). Moreover, an additional 11% of subjects dropped out during follow-up. Since program dropouts are usually failures these results have particularly negative implications for long-term efficacy.

On a more positive note, Mahoney and Mahoney (1976b) report the results of the behavioral treatment of 13 obese subjects. Improvement at posttreatment was even more pronounced at a six month follow-up, after which weight loss stabilized at one and two year follow-ups. Aside from the lack of any controls, the fact that only seven and five subjects respectively—of the initial 13—were contacted at the two follow-ups vitiates the significance of the findings. Furthermore, it should be noted that Hanson et al. conducted their follow-up over the telephone and the Mahoneys obtained some of their data by mail. The validity of self-report of weight maintenance is not established.

Brightwell and Clancy (1976) report the results of the behavioral treatment of eight cases of obesity after one year. Two of the subjects dropped out of therapy, and the remainder showed sizeable weight losses. The percent of excess weight lost ranged from 18.3% to 41.3%, results that are comparable to Stuart's (1967) findings that have remained the most impressive in the literature to date. A two year follow-up of these six subjects indicated that two had continued to lose weight whereas the other four had regained weight but were still lighter than their initial pretreatment weight (Brightwell, 1977). Most investigators will place little store in results based on six subjects without any controls. However, they are reported here because they are on a par with Stuart's (1967) massively influential and still widely cited study. That, too, is an anecdotal report. The attrition rate in that series was 20%, similar to the 25% in the Brightwell and Clancy report. Subjects in the Stuart program were treated throughout a one year period, as in the Brightwell and Clancy program. The latter, however, involved far less therapist contact.

Musante (1976) describes an intensive outpatient treatment program with 229 unselected patients, all of whom had failed at other attempts at weight reduction and appeared to have entered the program as a last resort. The program is based on a 700 calorie diet served in a dining room where the patients eat their three meals a day. The diet is nutritionally sound, and Musante reports that patients express satisfaction and seldom feel hungry. The daily meals are the focal point of a behavioral treatment program modeled on that of Stuart (1967). This *in vivo* training program is the first large-scale attempt to modify directly eating behavior rather than instructing patients in what to do and then relying upon their self-reports about whether they complied with program prescriptions. In another technique innovation patients are presented with sample menus of 21 predesigned weekly meals. As Musante notes, "simply providing patients with a list of food groups or food exchange lists (Stuart, 1971) from which to construct diet meals may be too difficult a task. The prepared menu may insure a greater chance of success, in that it specifies the desired behavior in small steps, provides a specific concrete goal, and serves as immediate feedback to the patient on his performance in terms of food selection and preparation" (p. 200).

Over one half (53.7%) of the patients lost 20 or more pounds; 23.6% lost more than 40 pounds, and seven patients gained weight. Median length of treatment was just over 10 weeks, with an average weight loss per week of 2.3 pounds for women. Unfortunately, no follow-up data are presented. However, Musante's use of *in vivo,* direct retraining of more appropriate eating habits is an excellent idea that needs further exploration. In addition, really effective weight reduction programs will almost certainly have to follow this program's lead in tailoring treatment length to actual weight loss. Standardized programs that are of fixed duration, often without any maintenance strategies built in, may be providing an inadequate test of the power of behavioral treatment procedures. Yet these are the sort of programs that predominate throughout the behavioral treatment literature.

Rozensky and Bellack (1976) found that overweight subjects responded differently to treatment programs emphasizing self-control or a therapist-controlled financial contingency respectively. Subjects identified as high self-reinforcers on a pretreatment behavioral task did well in the self-control program but not the therapist-directed program, whereas the low self-reinforcing subjects appeared to do equally well. Balch and Balch

(1976) describe the use of health service personnel as therapists in behavioral weight reduction programs. Their findings indicate that these personnel might be as effective as more specialized professionals.

Preventing Treatment Dropouts. Treatment dropouts have almost invariably been a problem in weight reduction programs. Hagen, Foreyt, and Durham (1976) provide additional evidence that contingency contracting in the form of a financial deposit is an effective means of reducing attrition. Nash (1976) conducted an analysis of dropouts from a commercial weight reduction program and found that the person most likely to drop out of treatment was the one who had been involved in treatment previously. Neither juvenile onset nor excessive overweight was associated with treatment attrition rates.

Component Analyses. McReynolds and Paulsen (1976) compared a comprehensive behavioral self-control treatment to one emphasizing stimulus control procedures. There was no difference at posttreatment. The stimulus control program was significantly superior at three and six month follow-ups, but not at nine, 12, and 18 month follow-ups. Although all groups tended to regain weight increasingly after the three month follow-up, impressive rates of maintenance of treatment-produced weight loss of approximately 75% and 80% respectively were obtained at the one year follow-up. The superiority of a component part of the usual behavioral self-control treatment package over the complete program raises important theoretical and practical issues concerning the nature and effective ingredients of what have developed into standardized treatment programs. In another example, Green (1976) showed that self-monitoring of daily caloric intake resulted in as much weight loss over a short-term treatment period as that obtained with the now traditional multifaceted behavioral treatment program patterned after Stuart and Davis' program (1972).

Treatment Adherence

McReynolds and Paulsen's findings bring to the fore another issue that has not received any attention in the behavioral literature. As behavior therapy has matured, broad-spectrum or multifaceted treatments have been increasingly employed in the treatment of complex behavior disorders (e.g., Arzin, 1977; O'Leary & Wilson, 1975). The extreme of this emphasis on broad-scale interventions is Lazarus' (1976) multimodal approach. In short, he states that durable treatment effects are an increasing function of the extent to which the different modalities of the BASIC ID are treated with diverse treatment techniques. But is "more" always better, as Lazarus and many others suggest? Aside from the McReynolds and Paulsen data, other instances of combined treatments proving no more effective, and even less so, than single methods are reported in the literature. In the treatment of anxiety-related problems, for example, Meichenbaum, Gilmore, and Fedoravicius (1971) found that combining systematic desensitization with self-instructional training was slightly less effective than either of the two treatments applied singly. On the other hand, Sherman, Mulac, & McCann (1974) reported a synergistic effect of relaxation training and rehearsal feedback. The combined treatments were significantly more effective than either one used singly. While the empirical evidence is insufficient to permit a definitive answer, there are grounds for arguing that "more" is not inevitably better—it could even be counter-productive.

One problem might be that multimodal treatment packages involve conflicts among fundamental behavior change mechanisms. Another way to look at the use of multifaceted treatments is in terms of *adherence*. A striking characteristic of behavior therapy is that clients are always asked to *do* something, whether it be relaxing in a chair, monitoring daily caloric intake, or making assertive responses in public. The success of these behavioral methods is directly dependent on the degree to which they are implemented by the client (cf. Wilson & Evans, 1976). The systematic analysis of the variables that determine adherence—in both medical and psychological treatment programs—is just beginning (see Blackwell, 1976, for an excellent review of the area), but certain factors are apparent. With respect to adherence to medication regimens, for example, there is clear evidence that adherence drops when multiple medications are prescribed (Blackwell, 1976). The reasons are not clear, but possible mechanisms can be suggested. If clients are presented with a smorgasbord of different techniques—as is usually the case in the behavioral treatment of obesity—they might easily infer that adherence to at least one or two is sufficient. Their choice might not always be the desirable one, especially since they are likely to forego time-consuming and effortful but effective methods (e.g., self-monitoring of daily caloric intake).

The therapist might inadvertently contribute to this client behavior. There is evidence that the therapist's attitudes towards treatment procedures influence client adherence to those procedures. Thus, clients prescribed anti-psychotic drugs by a physician who did not believe fully in drug treatment showed lower adherence rates than patients treated by a physician who subscribed to their efficacy (Blackwell, 1976). It may be that, in instructing a client to engage in a number of different homework assignments, the therapist conveys the attitude that he or she does not expect 100% adherence to all tasks. However, if the therapist is intervening with a single technique, he or she is likely to be more decisive in conveying to the client the necessity of adhering to the assignment. For one thing, the therapist is obviously committed to that technique at that time and is likely to communicate enthusiasm and a belief in its efficacy. These "nonspecifics" are an important part of all successful treatments, including behavior therapy (Wilson, 1977d). Required to carry out a single task (or at least limited assignments), clients know that they are more easily accountable to the therapist the following session when homework assignments are reviewed. This whole discussion can be summarized by emphasizing that treatment outcome will depend on how well clients follow therapists' instructions, and that this might be critically influenced by *what* they are asked to do and *how* they are asked to do it. The latter could be affected by limited versus multimodal treatment approaches.

Of course, timing is an important parameter that cuts across the treatment process referred to above. Multiple interventions could be conducted in such a way as to encourage maximum adherence provided that the client is never overloaded—in both the psychological and practical sense—and the different instructions are appropriately integrated, at least from the client's perspective. This requires considerable therapist skill, and we suspect that many a behavioral program has proved ineffective for want of more judicious timing. Until we have a better understanding of the mechanisms of behavior change, advocacy of multifaceted treatment programs must be balanced by an awareness that "more" is not always better.

CIGARETTE SMOKING

It was once said that the identification of cigarette smoking as a cancer-causing substance did more to change the behavior of psychological researchers than the habits of cigarette smokers. Research activity on behavioral methods to help people to stop smoking has continued to improve. In a major review of the field, Bernstein and McAlister (1976) conclude that progress has been made. Specifically, they state that two treatment packages—a combination of specific and "nonspecific" treatment effects—are clearly superior to previous intervention strategies. These are a) rapid smoking within a positive social treatment context (e.g. Lichtenstein, Harris, Birchler, Wahl & Schmahl, 1973; Schmahl, Lichtenstein & Harris, 1972) and b) multicomponent interventions which more specifically program the teaching/reinforcement of nonsmoking behaviors along with smoking suppression tactics (e.g. Flaxman, 1976). The Lichtenstein et al. and Schmahl et al. studies were reprinted and discussed in earlier volumes in this Series (Franks & Wilson, 1973, 1974). Sensory deprivation procedures (e.g., Suedfeld & Ikard, 1974) which were discussed in last year's volume (Franks & Wilson, 1976), are also identified as particularly promising by Bernstein and McAlister.

One of the major problems remaining is a familiar one: the failure to develop effective strategies for the maintenance of treatment-produced reductions in smoking. As Bernstein and McAlister note, the "primary emphasis has been upon attempts to develop smoking behavior change techniques whose initial effects (perhaps supplemented by "booster" treatments) are strong enough to last forever. The appearance of multicomponent interventions indicates, however, that this somewhat illogical situation is beginning to change; researchers are at last recognizing that, if they are to reach the goal of long-term maintenance of nonsmoking behavior, the point at which a person stops smoking must mark the beginning of a new intervention phase, not the onset of follow-up" (p. 99).

Bernstein and McAlister make an interesting observation. They note that a recent Gallup poll showed that only 34% of people who wish to stop smoking are interested in attending a smoking clinic. The majority appear to favor a self-help program. Even if self-administered programs prove to be less effective than more formal therapist-directed procedures, there is still a place for them on the grounds of greater acceptability—and hence more probable influence—among certain segments of the population. The broader issues relating to self-administered treatments are discussed by Glasgow and Rosen (1977), Kazdin and Wilson (1977) and in Sections I and X of the present volume.

Outcome Studies

As with all the addictive behaviors, electrical aversion conditioning has been one of the methods investigated by behavior therapists. Russell, Armstrong, and Patel (1976) conducted a well-controlled study in which they randomly assigned 70 dependent, heavy smokers to one of the following five treatment groups: 1) electrical aversion conditioning, involving 10 20-trial sessions of shocks paired with the act of smoking; 2) simulated aversion conditioning with non-contiguous shocks; 3) non-shock smoking sessions to control for satiation effects; 4) simple support and attention from the therapist; and 5) no treatment.

Prior to these treatments, as part of the assessment procedure, self-monitoring and self-control instructions to subjects produced reductions in the rate of smoking by 12% and 26% respectively. All four treatments were significantly superior to no treatment. In fact, 61% of treated subjects stopped smoking compared to only 14% of those not treated. However, there was no difference among the four treatment methods. This finding is particularly damaging to electrical aversion conditioning. Russell et al. were careful to base their conditioning procedure on that of Marks and Gelder (1967) which had been successful in the treatment of sexual deviance. Both classical conditioning and operant conditioning components were incorporated into the procedure that apparently had the stamp of approval of such authorities on learning theory as Eysenck and Rachman. Russell et al. observe that the only way in which they might have failed to have provided aversion conditioning an optimal chance for success was in not administering more powerful shocks. However, the authors report that the shocks used were "as strong as is ethically justified or indeed practically possible in the clinical situation." Wilson and Tracey (1976) offered the same conclusion in describing the ineffectiveness of electrical aversion conditioning with alcoholics. Moreover, the claim that stronger shocks might have made the difference is contradicted by the lack of any clinical effect at the levels used.

Another finding of interest is that a simple 15 minute session with a therapist was as effective as a much longer session involving more intensive therapist contact. The indications were that it was the type of person rather than the treatment that influenced smoking behavior. Subjects who were depressed or disturbed in other ways tended to fare poorly, whereas those who expressed confidence about the outcome of treatment did well.

Berecz (1976) paired client-administered electric shock with cognitive representation of either the events that triggered the act of smoking or the actual smoking behavior itself. The results showed that treatment was totally ineffective with the four women it was used with, and apparently successful only with the three male clients who imagined the triggering cognitions. In view of these uninspiring results and the complete absence of controls—rendering the report uninterpretable in any event—Berecz's discussion of the potential value of this cognitive conditioning technique for cigarette smoking and other addictive problems is premature.

Lando (1976) compared a self-pacing technique, an aversion procedure approximating the rapid-smoking method (but see our comments on the possibly crucial differences between Lando's procedure and rapid-smoking in Franks & Wilson, 1976), and a non-aversion control method in the treatment of 40 chronic smokers. The aversion procedure was significantly more effective than the other methods in reducing smoking at posttreatment. However, a six month follow-up indicated that there were no differences among the three methods. Subjects who stopped smoking completely at posttreatment showed the most improvement at follow-up. Lando discusses possible reasons why he failed to obtain the maintenance of treatment-produced improvement reported by Lichtenstein et al. (1973—see Franks and Wilson, 1976).

One of the two treatment strategies identified by Bernstein and McAlister as particularly promising was a multifaceted treatment approach used by Flaxman (1976). Flaxman used a self-control package consisting of diverse techniques. These included developing a new hobby, playing with worry beads as a distractor, relaxation training, thought stopping, programming competing responses, self-reinforcement, the repetition of reasons for ceasing to smoke, and public statements of commitment to stop. Of subjects receiving this complicated package, those who used a target-date (two weeks after starting treatment) procedure for stopping did significantly better than those who stopped immediately or those who tried to taper off. At a six month follow-up 50% of subjects who used the target-date quitting procedure were abstinent. A group that practiced rapid-smoking in addition to all the above-mentioned methods showed an abstinence rate of 62%. Although these outcome figures are encouraging, the sort of omnibus treatment program used by Flaxman makes it virtually impossible to determine effective agents of change.

A self-control treatment program was also used successfully by McGrath and Hall (1976). They compared a self-management treatment package to self-monitoring and social reinforcement treatment and no treatment over the course of an eight week treatment program and three month follow-up. Both the self-management and self-monitoring (strangely viewed as an "attention-placebo" treatment by the authors) were significantly more effective in reducing cigarette smoking at posttreatment than no treatment. At follow-up, the self-management treatment was more effective than self-monitoring and social reinforcement. As McGrath and Hall point out, in terms of abstinence their treatments were relatively ineffective. However, markedly reduced consumption might prove to be a realistic goal (see Frederiksen, Peterson, & Murphy, 1976, below).

Two particularly encouraging aspects of this study should be noted. The first is the impressive maintenance of reduced smoking over the three month follow-up, the time when most relapse usually occurs. The second is the high correlation between subjects' report of implementation of self-control methods and treatment outcome. Together with Flaxman's results, this study provides some of the most convincing evidence to date for the efficacy of behavioral self-control procedures in the modification of cigarette smoking.

Kreitler, Shahar, and Kreitler (1976) compared the effects of systematic desensitization and satiation treatment on different types of cigarette smokers. The results showed no difference between the treatment methods or between "positive affect" and "negative affect" smokers. However, differences in subjects' cognitive orientation towards stopping smoking were strongly related to outcome irrespective of the type of treatment or smoker. Cognitive orientation scores were derived from a questionnaire that assessed subjects' beliefs about the problems involved in stopping smoking. As Kreitler et al. conclude, these findings provide evidence for the role of cognitive factors in the behavioral treatment of addictive behaviors. They might also have practical implications in terms of helping to identify those clients who might best benefit from treatment and in preparing others for a more effective response to therapy.

Frederiksen, Peterson and Murphy (1976) report an attempt to develop *controlled smoking,* namely smoking at or below a target level set by the individual smoker. The procedures of programmed delay and contingency contracting were compared in the treatment of 16 smokers in a multiple baseline design across subjects. Contingency contracting resulted in less attrition and better development and maintenance of controlled smoking over the six months follow-up period. Five of the eight subjects in the contingency contracting group smoked at 50% of their initial rate, with four of them smoking the relatively safe number of less than 10 cigarettes per day. Single-subject data from the multiple baseline design suggest that contingency contracting had a treatment-specific effect on smoking during treatment. However, subjects reported using the treatment procedures only occasionally during follow-up. Accordingly, it is difficult to attribute the successful maintenance that was obtained to the specific behavioral treatment.

Raw (1976) compared the effects of three interventions with smokers attending a chest clinic. The three interventions were a) advice from a chest physician to stop smoking; b) participation in an additional interview with a psychologist; and c) the wearing of a white laboratory coat by the psychologist during the interview. The chest physician's advice to quit smoking had a significant effect in decreasing smoking over a three month follow-up. The interview with the psychologist added nothing to this effect. However, wearing a white coat during the interview resulted in less subsequent smoking. Raw emphasizes the way in which the demand characteristics of the medical setting could be more effectively used to reduce smoking rates given the important part general practitioners might play in any preventative health system. Of additional clinical interest is the finding that a questionnaire designed to measure motivation to stop smoking proved to be a useful predictor of reduction of smoking. Given the dearth of effective predictor variables in behavior therapy, this might prove to be an important finding.

All the studies described thus far utilized between-group designs. Frederiksen (1976) advocates the use of single-case experimental designs. Although he presents an unduly favorable picture of the relevance of single-subject methodology, there is no doubt that the judicious use of these designs can provide an important link between uncontrolled clinical case reports, on the one hand, and well controlled between-group designs of the sort recommended by Bernstein and McAlister, on the other.

The relative merits of single-case experimental designs are discussed more fully in Section IV of this volume.

DRUG ABUSE

In last year's volume we reprinted Callner's (1975) review of behavioral treatment approaches to drug addiction. Almost every paper reviewed by Callner is methodologically inadequate, 74% of the papers being uncontrolled, individual case reports. A recent review of essentially the same domain of literature by Götestam, Melin, and Öst (1976) provides a similarly sobering appraisal. Götestam et al. conclude that of the 38 studies they evaluated, only five used *any* type of experimental control. However, one was a single group design, the other four single-subject designs that were very rudimentary. Not a single controlled group outcome study employing a control group was found, a telling comment on the lack of rigorous behavioral research in this area.

The catalogue of methodological shortcomings uncovered by Götestam et al. includes inadequate assessment and the absence of appropriate follow-up evaluations. The importance of multiple measures of specific drug-taking behavior and other facets of the patient's life has been emphasized in the preceding commentary (e.g., Pattison, 1976a). Yet only 37% of the studies reviewed by Götestam et al. included more than one type of measure in the assessment of treatment outcome. Only five studies reported the reliability of the outcome measure. Many studies described follow-up evaluations, but the assessment methods used to obtain follow-up information leave a great deal to be desired.

Reeder and Kunce (1976) compared two methods in the treatment of heroin addicts. In a "videomodel" treatment condition subjects viewed a series of videotapes designed to show a model displaying coping behavior in situations related to remaining drug-free. The skills that were modeled included asking for help, interviewing for a job, and solving problems related to staying drug-free. In the second treatment subjects viewed a videotaped lecture about coping behavior. All subjects met in small sub-groups and discussed the videotapes they had observed with an ex-addict psychological assistant. The results of this pilot study indicate that subjects who had viewed the "videomodel" tapes exhibited significantly better vocational outcomes at 90 and 180 days follow-ups. Unfortunately, the authors do not describe other aspects of the subjects' functioning, including their drug-related behavior. Yet the use of a coping model, a form of social influence that has been demonstrated to be very effective in changing other behaviors, appears to be a most appropriate treatment method for the rehabilitation of the drug addict.

In contrast to the dismal methodological scene pictured by Callner and Götestam et al., Epstein, Parker, and Jenkins (1976) describe a well-controlled study of a heroin addict. Using a multiple baseline design, the effects of covert sensitization were shown to decrease drug urges. It was also associated with maintenance of abstinence from heroin and increased assertiveness on the part of the client. Contingency contracting was employed to encourage the client to work and to pay back financial debts. A commendable six month follow-up indicated that the client was still abstinent, experienced no drug urges, and was financially independent.

The role of contingency management in a methadone maintenance treatment program is described by Melin, Andersson, and Götestam (1976). After they had been detoxified and placed on methadone, opiate addicts' hospital environment was restructured such that privileges were contingent upon the successful completing of specific target behaviors. The target behaviors included getting up in the morning, participation in the morning conference, making the bed, occupational therapy, gymnastics, exercise walks, and other such activities. Privileges included passes to leave the ward, receiving visitors. The institution of the contingency program increased the target behaviors which were observed to decrease during the accidental suspension of the program for three weeks. In classic reversal design style the target behaviors increased once the contingencies were re-introduced.

Several questions can be raised about this study. It does demonstrate that at least some behaviors of drug addicts maintained on methadone are amenable to modification through reinforcement contingencies. This is not unexpected, since countless demonstration-type studies have shown that the introduction of explicit reinforcement contingencies in a closed institutional setting will result in behavior change. Further demonstration projects of this kind are simply unnecessary—they are redundant. The crucial treatment issues are now known to be more complicated. A major question is the generalization and maintenance of change. This issue is not addressed by Melin et al. For example, the very success of the reversal of reinforcement contingencies shows that the behavior change was unlikely to endure once the specific, artificial contingencies were withdrawn. Again, the behavioral literature is full of such demonstrations—explicit attempts to develop transfer to the natural contingencies are relatively few. Finally, one must question the relevance of the target behaviors chosen for modification. They are relatively trivial, the sort of behavior that was typically modified in operant demonstration programs in the 1960s. The need now is for the development of behavioral repertoires that facilitate a return to the natural environment and coping skills that enable the former addict to remain drug-free and gainfully employed once released from the hospital. Tsoi-Hoshmand (1976) has proposed a behavioral competence training model for rehabilitation programs that bears on this recommendation, but there is little empirical support yet for this theoretically appealing model. And in a related development, Callner and Ross (1976) have identified a lack of assertiveness skills on the part of heroin and amphetamine users.

Contingency contracting now ranks as perhaps the most widely used behavioral treatment method with drug addicts. Frederiksen, Jenkins, and Carr (1976) applied contingency contracting to improve the relationship of a 17-year-old poly-drug abuser with his family. Behavioral assessment had indicated that drug-taking behavior was related to conflicts between the client and his family. Although drug use itself was never made the direct target of contingency contracts, it decreased markedly as the client and his mother and father began interacting more constructively. This case serves as a reminder that drug abuse may be maintained by a variety of different variables, and that a thorough behavioral assessment is essential if successful treatment is to result.

A major research advance in the assessment and modification of alcohol abuse was ushered in by the intensive study of the actual drinking behavior of alcoholics in the laboratory setting (e.g., Mendelson & Mello, 1966; Nathan & O'Brien, 1971). Meyer, McNamee, Mirin, and Altman (1976) describe the application of a similar operant analysis to the behavior of opiate addicts. The effects of narcotic antagonists (naloxone and naltrexone) on the self-administration of heroin by addicts were studied on a research ward where subjects—hard core addicts—had to earn points for heroin. In addition to behavioral analyses of the effects of the opiate antagonists, biochemical, psychophysiological, and social psychological aspects of the subjects' functioning are concurrently evaluated. The authors provide a frank and informative discussion of the difficulties involved in developing such a research program, and detail procedures that are to be recommended in winning widespread public and professional support for such research. Although the estimated cost for each subject per year is $20,000, the *quality* and *quantity* of research data to be derived from such an undertaking seem well worth it.

SECTION VI: ADDICTIVE BEHAVIORS: ALCOHOLISM, OBESITY, CIGARETTE SMOKING AND DRUG ADDICTION

14

IMPROVEMENTS IN THE COMMUNITY-REINFORCEMENT APPROACH TO ALCOHOLISM

N. H. Azrin
Anna State Hospital, Illinois

Summary — This study evaluated a modified Community-Reinforcement program for treating alcoholics. The previously tested Community-Reinforcement program included special job, family, social and recreational procedures and was shown to reduce alcoholism. To increase the effectiveness of the program further, the present study incorporated a buddy system, a daily report procedure, group counseling, and a special social motivation program to ensure the self-administration of Disulfiram (Antabuse). The alcoholics who received the improved Community-Reinforcement program drank less, worked more, spent more time at home and less time institutionalized than did their matched controls who received the standard hospital treatment including Antabuse in the usual manner. These results were stable over a 2-year period. The program appeared even more effective and less time-consuming than

---

Reprinted with permission from *Behaviour Research and Therapy*, 1976, Vol. 14, 339-348.

This research was supported by the State of Illinois Department of Mental Health and Grant No. 00457 from the National Institute of Mental Health. Grateful acknowledgement is expressed to J. Mallams and E. Kiphart who served as counselors, and to W. Anderson, E. Sauerbrunn, F. Chastain, J. Pullen, W. Simmons, C. Bingham, A. Orechwa, J. Westberg, and R. C. Steck all of whom contributed in a direct way to the successful completion of the study.

the previous program. The present results replicate the effectiveness of the Community-Reinforcement program for reducing alcoholism and indicate the usefulness of the additions to the program.

INTRODUCTION

A new method for treating alcoholics has been developed recently (Hunt and Azrin, 1973). This Community-Reinforcement procedure was based on a social learning theory model and consisted of the rearrangement of significant personal and community based reinforcers. Using a matched-control design, the study found that the percentage of (1) time spent drinking was 6 times greater for the control group, (2) time spent unemployed was 12 times greater for the control group, (3) time away from one's home was twice as high for the control group and (4) time spent institutionalized was 15 times greater for the control group, all as compared to the Community-Reinforcement group. This substantial effectiveness of the Community-Reinforcement program continued over a 6-month follow-up.

The Community-Reinforcement program contained four separate components each of which provided satisfactions that would interfere with drinking. (1) The counselor placed alcoholics in jobs which had characteristics that interfered with drinking such as being full-time, steady, satisfying and well-paying. (2) Marriage and family counseling procedures were used which increased the alcoholic's satisfactions in his marriage or family such that he would be involved more continuously and pleasurably in family activities. (3) A self-governing social club for abstinent alcoholics was organized for providing the clients with enjoyable social events especially during the evening hours and on weekends. (4) The alcoholic was primed into engaging in pleasurable hobbies and recreational activities that would provide an alternative to drinking.

Still some problems existed. One major problem was that few of the clients remained totally abstinent, but rather, experienced temporary lapses in which they started to drink. Some of these slips seemed to result from some temporary crisis such as a loss of a job or from some short-term impulse. One method of overcoming these short-term, impulsive slips is the drug Disulfiram (Antabuse) which reacts with alcohol to create an adverse physical reaction. The use of Antabuse as part of the treatment program would, therefore, eliminate impulsive drinking since the former alcoholic would be required to wait about a week after discontinuing the Antabuse before he could begin drinking again.

Antabuse has been available as a treatment for alcoholism and has undergone extensive clinical usage (Fox, 1967; Lundwall and Bakeland, 1971). However, a major problem with the use of Antabuse is the frequent reluctance of alcoholics to accept this medication. Billet (1964) noted the large number of dropouts that occur in Antabuse programs. The present program added special procedures for motivating and training the clients to use the Antabuse.

Another problem that can exist in the previous program occurs because the lapse into drinking may not be caused by some short-term crisis or impulse but rather may be a signal that further adjustments are necessary in the program. A solution to this problem might be to have the former alcoholic report regularly to the counselor who has learned to identify signals that problems have occurred. The program was revised to include procedures which taught the client how to identify and handle such crisis danger signals and also to provide regular reports to the counselor about his adjustment in anticipation of such crises.

Another problem in the previous program was that some of the clients continued to make occasional demands on the counselor for assistance in their new non-alcoholic life style, such as advice on repairing an automobile which was necessary for their employment. This type of problem was often better handled by a non-professional counselor who was more conveniently located to the client. The present program arranged for a "buddy" in the client's neighborhood to provide this advice.

Another general problem in the previous procedure was the duration of time needed for counseling. The new procedure reduced this problem by utilizing group counseling in which several alcoholics were counseled at the same time.

A question that was not answered in the previous study was whether the results with the new procedure were unique to the single counselor who provided the counseling. The present program used three different counselors to determine whether the benefits of the new program could be obtained by several different counselors.

In summary, the present study extended the previous Community-Reinforcement program for alcoholism by (1) the use of Disulfiram to inhibit impulsive drinking, (2) special motivational procedures for the continued usage of the Disulfiram, (3) the use of an early warning notification system to alert the counselor that problems were developing, (4) the use of a neighborhood friend-advisor to continue social support of the client after professional counseling had been terminated, (5) group counseling procedures to reduce the amount of counseling time per client and (6) the use of different counselors to determine the ability of different counselors to use the new procedure. As in the previous study, the experimental design employed random assignment of one member of each matched pair of clients into a control group.

METHOD

Subjects and Design

Twenty men who had been admitted for alcoholism treatment at a State Hospital were offered the chance to participate in this study. The criteria for selection were (1) an extensive record of alcoholism, (2) physiological symptoms of withdrawal from alcohol upon admittance, (3) availability, (4) capability of being matched with another currently hospitalized alcoholic, (5) between 20 and 60 years old, (6) residing within an hour's drive from the hospital. They were told that some would be randomly selected to receive a special community-based program which involved Antabuse and social and family counseling. The progress of all would be followed. The persons who were not selected would receive the regular hospital program. All twenty men agreed to participate. (One dropped out one week afterwards. He and his matched control were not used in the data analysis).

The clients were matched on the basis of a life-adjustment score that summed the score on each of five scales (5 points each) in each of the five areas of job satisfaction, job stability, family stability, social life and drinking history. A match required no more than two points difference in the total score; the ratings were done by four different counselors. Also, unanimous subjective agreement of the four counselors was a requirement that a match was warranted. A coin flip in the presence of three persons determined which member received the Community-Reinforcement counseling. The clients were assigned to the counselors on the basis of geographic location.

The clients in the control condition received the same housing, and other hospital services from other counselors but did not receive the Community-Reinforcement procedures. The control clients received instruction regarding alcoholism and its dangers, individual and group counseling, advice to take Antabuse, and encouragement to join an Alcoholics Anonymous group.

Reliability

During the counseling program, the three counselors from the Community-Reinforcement program maintained contact with both members of each pair and, for the purposes of increasing the validity of client self-report, at least one other person associated with each alcoholic, usually the wife and employer. The contact intervals varied between 4 times per week to once every 4 weeks with the median being once every two weeks. The regular information which was obtained by the counselor consisted of a day-by-day self-report on a 4-point rating scale for the areas of Antabuse administration, drinking, social life, family life and employment. If any doubt existed about the validity of the client's self-report, the counselors questioned the client until assurance was obtained. To obtain a measure of reliability, an independent follow-up survey was completed by a research assistant hired expressly for this task. The assistant was unaware of the nature of treatment, or of the nature of the research, but was instructed that follow-up information of former hospitalized patients was to be gathered. The reliability of all reports was greater than 95%.

Job Counseling

All of the clients were given intensive job counseling, using the same procedure as in the previous Community-Reinforcement Program. This job-finding counseling is described in a separate report in more detail (Azrin, Flores, and Kaplan, 1975). Some of the distinctive features of this type of job counseling were that it emphasized personal contacts, was done in a group setting, involved exchange of job leads among job-seekers, and was monitored closely in all feasible respects by the counselor. Relevant to the objective of counseling alcoholics, the type of jobs sought were those that were full-time, permanent, satisfying, well-paying and performed in a highly visible social contact.

Marital Counseling

Marital counseling was given to all of the married alcoholics, including those who were separated or contemplating divorce. The procedure used was the same as had been used in the previous Community-Reinforcement study and is described in more detail in a separate report on that procedure (Azrin, Naster and Jones, 1973). Some of the major features of this special marital counseling were that all areas of the marriage were counseled, both husband and wife were present, satisfactions were maximized for both partners, and the granting of satisfactions to a partner was done in the context of reciprocal satisfactions being received from that partner. Most relevant to the alcohol treatment, the wife of the alcoholic always included as one of her requests that her partner be totally abstinent from alcohol and that he request her to help him in doing so, including assisting him in taking his Disulfiram each day. As in the previous program "synthetic families" were arranged with a friend or employer for the unmarried clients and behavioral counseling provided for the client and its members.

Resocialization

The resocialization procedures were for the purpose of arranging for the client to have a happy and satisfactory social life with persons who would encourage him to remain sober. The problem which was presented by this objective was that most clients did not enjoy interactions with many social groups such as church and civic organizations where sobriety might be encouraged. More appropriate and enjoyable social companions were persons who had previous drinking problems but were presently maintaining their sobriety. One semi-formal association which met this criteria already existed: Alcoholics Anonymous. Thus, the clients were encouraged to attend AA regularly and special efforts were made to insure that the clients sampled AA at least once or twice. However, AA seemed to have certain limitations in the area of resocialization because meetings usually were held during the week, excluded non-alcoholics and did not especially facilitate general social and recreational interactions. Consequently, a special self-governing social club for alcoholics (Hunt & Azrin, 1973) was formed which met on the weekend and included activities such as card playing, dancing, picnics, pot-luck dinners and other recreations for both alcoholics and non-alcoholic guests.

Recreational Activities

The alcoholic clients were encouraged and assisted in developing hobbies and recreations of their choice which would insure their continued motivation to remain sober. (See Hunt and Azrin, 1973.)

Problem-prevention Rehearsal

To teach the client how to handle situations which, in the past, had led to drinking, he was given instructions and rehearsal during the counseling. First, he was asked to review all of those situations which, in the past, had created an urge to drink, such as an argument with his wife, children, employer or friends, or loss of his job or seemingly unjust accusations by police. He then acted out the scenes that typified these interactions and was given instruction and behavioral rehearsal in handling them more adaptively. Behavioral rehearsal was also used after a stressful problem occurred as instruction for prevention of similar problems in the future.

Early Warning System

A recurring problem in treatment had been that the client began drinking after some very stressful occurrences of which the counselor had been unaware. To keep the counselor or the peer advisor informed on a regular basis, the clients mailed a Happiness Scale to him each day. This scale was a normal part of the marital counseling procedure (Azrin, Naster and Jones, 1973) and involved the rating by both the client and his spouse of their happiness in each of 10 areas of their life. Both the client and his spouse exchanged their scales, and initialed each other's scale before sending them to the counselor. A modified scale was used for the non-married client.

The Antabuse Procedure

The distinguishing feature of the present Antabuse program was the special social arrangements for ensuring that the clients would find Antabuse therapy acceptable and convenient for use over a period of several months. These procedures were developed as a result of a common question: "If Antabuse is so good why doesn't everybody use it?" It appeared that Antabuse was not used as often as it could be because the clients (1) viewed it as a "crutch" which implied that the client suffered from a lack of character or will power; (2) viewed it as a coercive weapon which was used against them to force sobriety on them; (3) had not established the use of Antabuse as a regular "habit."

The first two problems were solved by teaching the client to view Antabuse usage in a positive manner. A central procedure in teaching this new viewpoint was that the client asked someone, usually the spouse, to help him remain sober by monitoring his Antabuse every day. Thus, instead of a "watchdog" with a coercive weapon the monitor was viewed as a "helper" or caring friend. Another new viewpoint that was taught was that Antabuse functioned as a chemical time-delay device which gave the client time to think over a decision rather than act impulsively. Also, since the wife's involvement was a crucial part of the procedure, and their mutual dependency is usually a new notion to them, she was instructed to rehearse all of the reasons that she should be involved with giving him the Antabuse, such as his sobriety meaning more happiness, work and money for her.

Several procedures were used to ensure that Antabuse would become a firmly established habit: (1) the time for taking Antabuse was linked to an already well-established habit or event such as mealtime, brushing one's teeth, or arriving home from work; (2) The spouse was involved in the administration of Antabuse each day so that she could remind him if he forgot, and if he should stop taking Antabuse she could notify the counselor so that pre-crisis therapy could occur; (3) Since the Antabuse routine was usually broken during interruptions such as vacations, weekends, sickness, running out of Antabuse supply, deaths in the family, and others, special counseling and rehearsal were given prior to, or during these events as to how to continue the "Antabuse habit" in spite of these potential interruptions; (4) To assure that the client received social support, he was to take the Antabuse only in the presence of his wife, peer advisor, or counselor. Every counseling session was initiated by having the client take the Antabuse pill which he did by mixing the pill into a preferred beverage such as coffee; (5) To assure ease of obtaining and using Antabuse, the counselor either referred the client to a physician who was knowledgeable and sympathetic regarding the use of Antabuse, or the counselor directly contacted the client's family physician and explained the role of the Antabuse in the counseling program.

Group Counseling

The clients were counseled in a group, rather than individually. The group usually included two to four clients, as well as their peer-advisors and spouses, depending on the type of counseling scheduled and the compatibility of the client's schedules. The counselor continuously encouraged the clients to provide answers to each other's questions, to comment on each other's progress, to provide individualized examples supportive of the counselor's statements, and to promote social activities among the clients outside of the counseling sessions. After the intensive counseling period, these group sessions were continued at intervals of about every 2 months, often as a part of a picnic or other recreational events.

Buddy Procedure

Arrangements were made for each client to have a peer-advisor who would meet with him regularly and provide advice and encouragement. The goal was to select a peer-advisor with the following characteristics: He should be a former alcoholic, have been sober for at least a year, reside near the client, or have been a former client in this program, be similar in age and social-economic status to the client, desire to help the client and be respected by the client, and agree to meet regularly with the client and to report regularly to the counselor. Regular meetings were arranged between the advisor and the alcoholic. In these meetings, the new client and the advisor discussed ways of solving problems that were pressing and relevant to staying sober, such as those of dating or having a place to go with dates, income tax, obtaining an automobile license and making new friends.

The Contracts

Written contracts were used to formalize the agreements between the clients and the counselors for all of the major procedures. These contracts were signed statements describing the assignment each person agreed to complete, the target date, the reasons for following the procedures and what remediation procedures the client would take if he deviated from his agreement. Contracts were made for taking Antabuse, attendance in the group sessions, marriage counseling, the daily reports required in the early warning procedure and for meeting with the peer-advisor.

RESULTS

Figure 1 shows that the mean percent of time spent drinking, unemployed, away from home, and institutionalized during the first 6 months for the control group and for the Community-Reinforcement group. The percent of time spent drinking was 2% for the Community-Reinforcement group and 55% for the control group. The percentage of time unemployed was 20% for the Community-Reinforcement group and 56% for the control group. The percentage of time spent away from the family or synthetic family was 7% for the Community-Reinforcement group and 67% for the control group. The percentage of time spent institutionalized was 0% for the Community-Reinforcement group and 45% for the control group. The *t*-test of differences for paired comparisons (Edwards, 1969) yielded significant differences ($p < 0.005$) for all measures. The dependent measures were calculated by dividing the number of days the patient was drinking, unemployed, out of home and institutionalized by the total number of days since discharge. For the drinking measure, time spent in an institution was not included. If a person had a job but did not work some days because of temporary weather conditions, illness, being on vacation or weekends or holidays, he was still considered to be employed full time on those days.

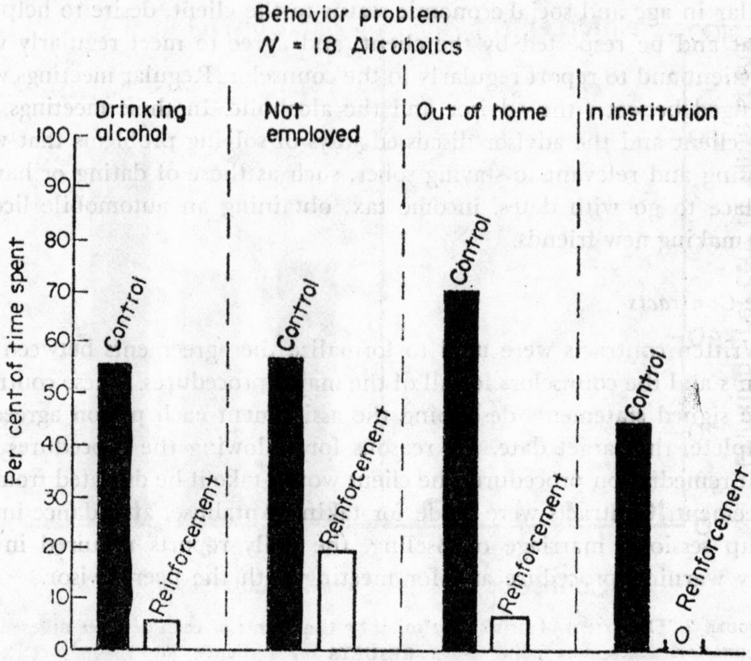

FIGURE 1. Comparison of the Community-Reinforcement clients and the Control clients on each of 4 measures. The "Drinking Alcohol" measure designates the percentage of days on which the client was drinking alcohol. The "Not Employed" measure designates the percentage of days which the client did not work. "Out of Home" designates the percentage of days the client was absent from his family or home. "In Institution" designated the time spent in a mental hospital or prison. The dark vertical bars are for the control group whereas the unshaded bars are for the clients who received the Community Reinforcement counseling. The period of time for the data was the first 6 months after discharge of the client from the hospital.

Figure 2 shows the results for the three different counselors during the first 6 months. For each of the 3 counselors, the clients in the control group drank at least 50% of the time whereas his clients in the Community-Reinforcement group drank less than 5% of the time.

Figure 3 shows the results of the 2-year follow-up of the clients. The clients continued to abstain from drinking at least 90% of the time of each 6-month period during the 2-year follow-up.

Figure 4 shows that the median counseling time was lower, and the percentage of time spent drinking was lower for the improved Commu-

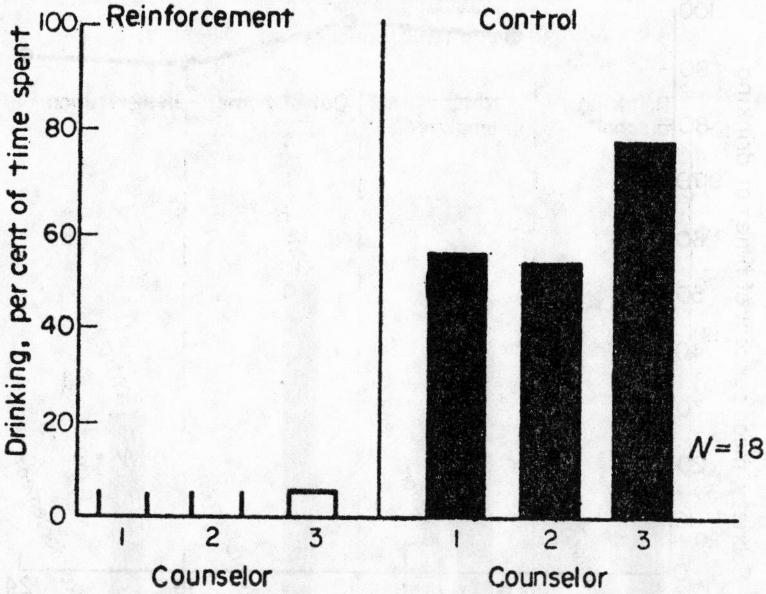

FIGURE 2. The extent of drinking alcohol by the clients of each of three different counselors. Each data point (vertical bar) is for 3 clients. The shaded vertical bars are for the control clients who were matched to the clients treated by the Community-Reinforcement method. The "O" designation means that no drinking occurred.

nity-Reinforcement procedures than for the previous procedures reported in Hunt and Azrin (1973). The median counseling time was 50 hours for the previous procedures and 30 hours for the improved procedures. The mean percentage of time spent drinking by clients in the reinforcement groups was 14% for the previous procedures and less than 2% for the improved procedures.

All 7 of the married clients remained married even though all had suggested the possibility of separation or divorce in the initial counseling sessions and one client couple was actually separated for a brief period. A "synthetic" family relationship with parents or relatives was arranged for the other two single clients.

The employment procedures rapidly secured jobs for all clients within 2 weeks of the instigation of the job-finding counseling. One client changed jobs twice during the 6-month period, using the employment procedures both times. After using the procedures a total of three times

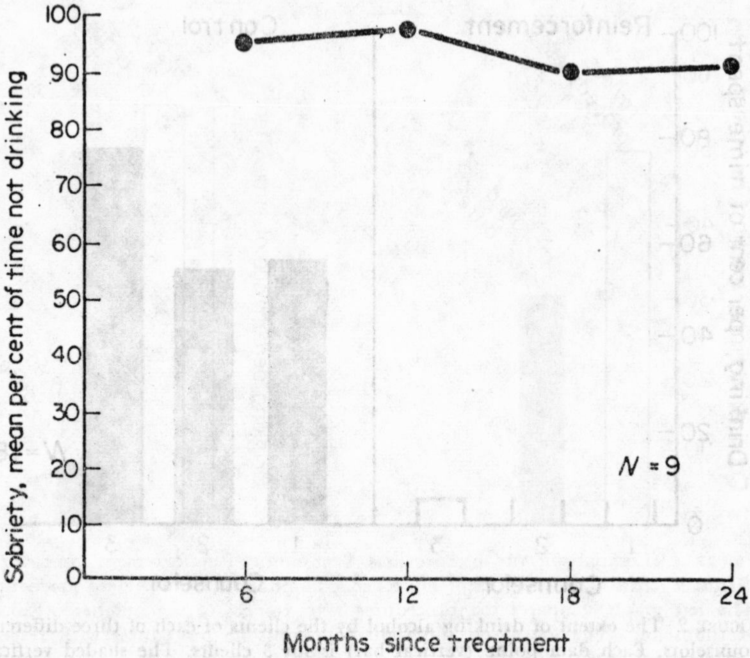

FIGURE 3. Long-term follow-up over 24 months. Each data point is for the 6-month period, beginning with discharge from the hospital.

in 6 months, he was quite enthusiastic about their effectiveness. This 52-year-old client worked more during the months following treatment than during any comparable previous period for the 10 years prior to counseling.

All of the clients in the reinforcement group established, or reestablished, regular significant social relations with social groups which supported their sobriety. All of the nine attended at least two AA meetings, at least one of the meetings at the previously established social club for alcoholics, and over half attended these on a regular basis.

A more personalized description of the results may be obtained from the following illustrative case history of one of the clients whose history and treatment outcome was fairly typical.

ILLUSTRATIVE CASE HISTORY

Carl was legally married, but had been separated from his wife for six months. He had been hospitalized for alcoholism twice in the past,

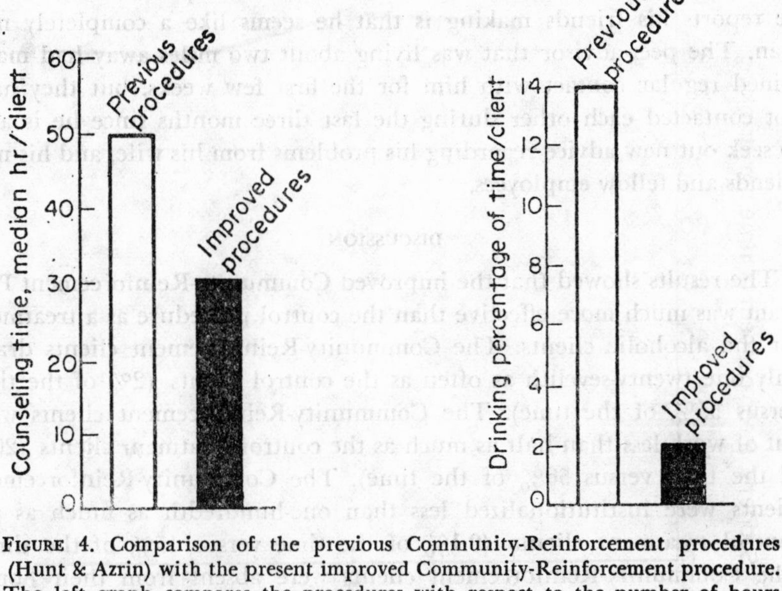

FIGURE 4. Comparison of the previous Community-Reinforcement procedures (Hunt & Azrin) with the present improved Community-Reinforcement procedure. The left graph compares the procedures with respect to the number of hours of counseling. The graph on the right compares the procedures with respect to the extent of drinking that resulted.

in addition to his current hospitalization. He had no close friends except for intimate "drinking buddies." He had not worked on a full-time basis during the last seven months. Carl was selected for the Community-Reinforcement Counseling. He took his Antabuse regularly, beginning with his stay in the institution. He obtained a job as a maintenance man in an apartment building that paid him $80.00 a week, which was more than he had ever earned previously. He enrolled in the special social club for alcoholics. Carl was persuaded to attempt to reinstate his marriage and received marital counseling with his wife who was also reluctant, but agreed to give it "one more chance." He was discharged from the institution immediately after obtaining the job, three weeks after his counseling had started. After his discharge, he continued taking the Antabuse with his wife's assistance for which he regularly thanked her. Carl drank only on one day during the year. He has worked full-time since his discharge except for one week when he changed to an even better job as a garage mechanic. He attended the social club about twice a month and also local Alcoholics Anonymous groups about once a month. He has reestablished old friendships and created new ones. The most frequent comment that he reports his friends making is that he seems like a completely new man. The peer-advisor that was living about two miles away had maintained regular contact with him for the first few weeks, but they have not contacted each other during the last three months since he is able to seek out new advice regarding his problems from his wife, and his new friends and fellow employees.

DISCUSSION

The results showed that the improved Community-Reinforcement Program was much more effective than the control procedure as a treatment for the alcoholic clients. The Community-Reinforcement clients drank only one twenty-seventh as often as the control clients (2% of the time versus 55% of the time). The Community-Reinforcement clients were out of work less than half as much as the control treatment clients (20% of the time versus 56% of the time). The Community-Reinforcement clients were institutionalized less than one-hundredth as much as the control treatment clients (0.1% of the time versus 45% of the time). The Community-Reinforcement clients were absent from their homes or synthetic homes only one-ninth as often as the control treatment clients (7% versus 67%). The post-treatment data of the control treatment clients demonstrates what a difficult population they were and what a poor prognosis they had. Even after the very intensive counseling provided in the control procedure, those clients were drinking 55% of the time, were unemployed 55% of the time, were away from their homes 60% of the time, and were confined to an institution 45% of the time. These results confirm the previous findings that the Community-Reinforcement Program is an effective method of treating alcoholic clients (Hunt & Azrin, 1973).

The improvements made in the Community-Reinforcement Program resulted in greater effectiveness and greater efficiency. Whereas the previous program resulted in the clients drinking 14% of the time after treatment, the improved program resulted in drinking only 2% of the time. Whereas the previous procedure required 50 hours for the average client, the improved Community-Reinforcement Procedure required only 30 hours.

The treatment procedure was used equally effectively by each of three different counselors, thereby demonstrating the efficacy of the procedures in spite of the inevitable individual differences in style between counselors.

The benefits to the clients were not transient. The 2-year follow-up showed that the initial benefits were maintained.

Several methodological difficulties have existed in interpreting the results of previous studies such as high drop-out rates, reliance on self-report of the client, the non-availability of a comparable control group, absence of follow-up data, etc. These methodological deficits have been so extensive (Miller, Pokorny, Valles, & Cleveland, 1970) that reviews of past evidence have concluded that no treatment for alcoholism has been shown to be effective (Hill and Blane, 1967; Wallgren and Barry, 1970). Very recently reinforcement-based treatments have emerged that have been effective and that do satisfy some of the methodological considerations (see review by Miller and Barlow, 1973). The present study also attempted to solve these very difficult methodological problems. A matched-control group with random assignment was used to ensure a comparable control group of clients for comparison. A separate observer was used who had no prior knowledge of which treatment the client had received; he obtained the data regarding drinking, working, etc. in addition to the corroborative data by family members, friends, employers, etc. The whereabouts of each client were pursued sufficiently to obtain the data regarding their adjustment for at least 24 months for all clients thereby providing the follow-up data. The procedure included methods of monitoring the clients and thereby prevented early drop-outs after treatment initiation.

The general approach of this improved method, as well as the initial method, is to rearrange the alcoholic's social environment such that other more reinforcing activities compete with drinking behavior. The client then is motivated to reject alcohol as a reinforcer because of the resulting loss of so many other reinforcers. In achieving this objective, the present method relied heavily on reinforcement and behavioral counseling procedures used for other problems such as identifying and maximizing reinforcers, reinforcer sampling and response priming (Ayllon & Azrin, 1968), reinforcement for competing reactions (Azrin and Nunn, 1973), structuring the learning setting, role-playing, negative consequences for the undesired response of drinking (Azrin and Holz, 1966), behavioral family counseling (Azrin, Naster and Jones, 1973), behavior rehearsal peer support (Azrin and Nunn, 1973) and reinforcement contracting (Sulzer, 1965). The primary objective was to use a counseling "package" which would be effective rather than a single type of procedure. Each of the component procedures was conceptually based on a reinforcement approach and standardized in its usage.

A recent development in the reinforcement therapies has been to teach alcoholics to control their drinking rather than to attempt total abstinence (Sobell and Sobell, 1973; Hedberg and Campbell, 1974). The present program is compatible with either objective except for the antabuse Procedure which must be omitted if the treatment goal is to achieve controlled drinking since even small amounts of alcohol will produce a reaction after taking Antabuse. The results of the previous Community-Reinforcement program which did not use Antabuse (Hunt & Azrin, 1973), suggests that the controlled drinking can be achieved by this approach even if the Antabuse is omitted.

REFERENCES

AYLLON, T., & AZRIN, N. H. *The Token Economy: A Motivational System for Therapy and Rehabilitation.* New York: Appleton-Century-Crofts, 1968.

AZRIN, N. H., FLORES, T., & KAPLAN, S. J. Job-finding club: A group-assisted program for obtaining employment. *Behav. Res. and Therapy,* 13:17-27, 1975.

AZRIN, N. H., & HOLZ, W. C. Punishment. In W. K. Honig (Ed.), *Operant Behavior: Areas of Research and Application.* New York: Appleton-Century-Crofts, 1966.

AZRIN, N. H., NASTER, B. J., & JONES, R. Reciprocity counseling: A rapid learning-based procedure for marital counseling. *Behav. Res. and Therapy,* 11:365-382, 1973.

AZRIN, N. H., & NUNN, R. G. Habit reversal: A method of eliminating nervous habits and tics. *Behav. Res. and Therapy,* 11:619-628, 1973.

BILLET, S. L. The use of antabuse: An approach that minimizes fear. *Med. Ann. D.C.,* 33:612-614, 1964.

EDWARDS, A. L. *Statistical Analysis.* New York: Holt, Rinehart and Winston, Inc., 1969.

FOX, R. *Alcoholism.* New York: Springer Publishing Co., 1967.

HEDBERG, A. G. & CAMPBELL, L. III. A comparison of four behavioral treatments of alcoholism. *J. Behav. Ther. and Exp. Psychiat.,* 5:251-256, 1974.

HILL, M. J. & BLANE, H. T. Evaluation of psychotherapy with alcoholics: A critical review. *Q. J. Stud. Alcohol,* 28:76-104, 1967.

HUNT, G. M. & AZRIN, N. H. A community-reinforcement approach to alcoholism. *Behav. Res. and Therapy,* 11:91-104, 1973.

LUNDWALL, L. & BAKELAND, F. Disulfiram treatment of alcoholism: A review. *J. Nerv. Ment. Dis.,* 153:381-394, 1971.

MILLER, B. A., POKORNY, A. D., VALLES, J., & CLEVELAND, S. E. Biased sampling in alcoholism treatment research. *Q. J. Stud. Alcohol,* 31:97-107, 1970.

MILLER, P. M. & BARLOW, D. H. Behavioral approaches to the treatment of alcoholism. *J. Nerv. Ment. Dis.,* 157:10-20, 1973.

SOBELL, M. B. & SOBELL, L. C. Individualized behavior therapy for alcoholics. *Behav. Therapy,* 4:49-72, 1973.

SULZER, E. S. Behavior modification in adult psychiatric patients. In L. Ullmann & L. Krasner (Eds.), *Case Studies in Behavior Modification.* New York: Holt, Rinehart and Winston, Inc., 1965.

WALLGREN, H. & BARRY, H. *Actions of Alcohol,* Vol. II. Amsterdam: Elsevier Publishing Co., 1970.

SECTION VI: ADDICTIVE BEHAVIORS: ALCOHOLISM, OBESITY, CIGARETTE SMOKING AND DRUG ADDICTION

15

BEHAVIORAL AND PHAMACOLOGICAL TREATMENTS FOR OBESITY: AN EXPERIMENTAL COMPARISON

Lars-Göran Öst and K. Gunnar Götestam

University of Uppsala, Sweden

Abstract — The effectiveness of behavior therapy in the treatment of obesity was compared to a pharmacological treatment (fenfluramine) and a waiting-list control condition. Subjects at least 15% overweight were obtained through a newspaper advertisement and randomly assigned to three groups with 15 in each. The subjects were weighed before, after and at a 12-months follow-up occasion. The results showed that all subjects reduced their initial weight significantly but they also regained most of their weight loss during the year after treatment. The between group comparisons indicated that the behavioral treatment was more effective than the pharmacological in reducing the subjects' overweight.

The problem of overweight and weight-reduction has attracted an increased interest from behavior therapists during the 1970's. When looking through the reference list of the latest review of the area (Bellack, 1975) one finds that between 1967-1969 one experimental study was pub-

Reprinted with permission from *Addictive Behaviors,* Vol. I, 331-338.

This research was supported in part by grant No. 97/72 P from the Swedish Council for Social Science research and Alfred E. Benzon A/S. We thank Charlotte Borella, Eva Sandström, Lotta Wadelius and Peter Lantz who served as therapist in this study.

lished each year. During 1970-1974 the number of published studies were 2, 5, 6, 5, and 9 respectively. Up to 1975 the total number of published experimental studies on behavioral treatment of obesity is 30. The increased rate of publications has also led to one literature review each year between 1972 and 1975 (Abramson, 1973; Bellack, 1975; Hall & Hall, 1974; Stunkard, 1972).

Different authors (e.g. Hall & Hall, 1974) have pointed out several methodological shortcomings in the studies of this field, which calls for cautiousness in drawing of conclusions. However, the general conclusion that can be drawn from these reviews is that the behavioral methods have been shown to reduce overweight effectively but the long-term results are still unclear. Furthermore only four studies (Harmatz & Lapuc, 1968; Levitz & Stunkard, 1974; Penick, Filion, Fox & Stunkard, 1971; Wollersheim, 1970) have made a direct experimental comparison between a behavioral and some other treatment for obesity, which permit only tentative conclusions concerning the relative efficiency of these methods. The conclusion that can be drawn from comparative studies is that the behavioral treatment applied in one study with psychiatric patients was more effective than group therapy (Harmatz & Lapuc, 1968), in another study with college students it was more effective than non-specific group therapy (Wollersheim, 1970), and in a third study with self-help subjects more effective than nutrition training of the usual self-help program (Levitz & Stunkard, 1974). The mean weight losses for the behavioral group in these studies with treatment periods of 6, 12 and 12 weeks were however not too impressive and hardly clinically significant (Jeffrey, 1974): 3.7 kg, 4.7 kg and 1.9 kg respectively.

There is to date no controlled experimental study comparing a behavioral treatment with a pharmacological method. Fenfluramine is chemically an amphetamine derivate but it lacks stimulant properties and thus the risk of developing physical and/or psychological dependence is considered less than for the other amphetamines used in the treatment of obesity (Chlouverakis, 1975). The drug has been found to be an effective weight reducing agent in some controlled studies (Lawson, Roscoe, Strong & Gibson, 1970; Munro, Seatin, & Duncan, 1966; Persson, Andersson & Deckert, 1973.)

The purpose of the present study was to compare the short and long-term effects of a behavioral treatment to those of an appetite suppressant drug (Fenfluramine) when these treatments were applied in a way that they realistically would be used in a clinical-therapeutic situation.

METHOD

Subjects and Design

Subjects for this study were obtained through advertising in the local newspaper. A total of 167 persons answered the advertisement. These persons were mailed a questionnaire about their present weight and height, work, home situation, eating habits and earlier attempts to reduce weight. A total of 112 persons answered the questionnaire and 76 of them fulfilled the criterion of at least 15% overweight. This group of persons was invited to a meeting (70 attended) where they were informed about the study (in general terms). Furthermore their weight and height were measured and they were given three forms: (1) a daily weight chart, (2) 14 baseline eating monitoring forms, and (3) 7 daily exercise forms. The participants were to monitor their weight for 14 days and their food intake and amount of exercise for 7 days. These forms were collected during a pretreatment assessment meeting where the persons (now 64) were weighed and presented with a 45-minute lecture on food and nutrition. From this pool of 64 persons who remained after baseline monitoring, 45 subjects were randomly assigned to three groups (with $n = 15$ in each): (1) Behavioral treatment, (2) Fenfluramine, and (3) Waiting-list control. This somewhat complicated procedure of not only having subjects in the first group collecting baseline data, was considered necessary in order to conceal from the subjects in group 3 that they were control subjects.

Subjects (38 females and 7 males) ranged in age from 17 to 63 with a mean of 40.9 yr. Three were students, while 32 were working and 10 were housewives. A classification of the subjects' socio-economic levels with respect to profession yielded no difference between the groups. Their percentage overweight at the start of treatment ranged from 15 to 62 with a mean of 35.2%.

Therapists

Three undergraduate students who had a thorough knowledge of Stuart & Davis (1972) method served as therapists for the behavioral group. Each of them treated 5 subjects who were randomly assigned to them. A physician experienced in the use of Fenfluramine treatment of obesity was the therapist for the second group.

Treatments

The subjects in group 1 received 20 sessions of 30 minutes (twice a week during the first four weeks and once a week during the last 12 weeks) while the subjects in group 2 received 8 sessions during the 16-week treatment period.

Group 1: Behavioral treatment. With a few modifications the treatment method applied for these subjects was that presented by Stuart & Davis (1972). Their treatment model consists of three parts: (a) situational control of overeating, (b) a diet management program, and (c) an exercise management program. The *situational control* of overeating included different steps that the subject was to learn in order to eliminate cues that initiate overeating (e.g. arranging to eat in only one room and at the same place in that room, avoiding the purchase of problematic foods, and making problematic eating as difficult as possible). Other steps were included to suppress cues that might lead to excessive food intake (e.g. minimizing the contact with excessive food, and controlling states of deprivation). Furthermore there were some steps to increase the probability of appropriate eating behaviors (e.g. providing acceptable alternative food choices, and making acceptable food more attractive). Finally, certain steps were applied to provide negative consequences for undesirable eating responses and positive consequences for appropriate responses (e.g. the provision of material and social reinforcement for following the program). The teaching of these steps took the first four sessions of the treatment program. The *diet management* program (sessions 5-7) consists of choosing an individual caloric level and a corresponding food plan based on the principle of food exchanges. The present study used four different food plans (1000, 1200, 1500, and 1800 kcal. respectively) while Stuart & Davis had seven (from 1200 to 2300 kcal.). After finding the estimated caloric requirement for the subject (depending on age and sex) in a table (Food and Nutrition Board, National Research Council, 1968) 500 kcal. are subtracted and the food plan nearest to this value is chosen. The subject also has to record (on a vinyl folder) everything she eats during the day and graph the total amount of calories together with her daily weight. In the *exercise management* program (session 8) the expenditure in the subject's daily living is increased and then regular physical exercises are introduced, e.g. cycling or swimming. The latter exercises are recorded by the subject on a daily exercise plan which is kept in the same vinyl folder as the food plan. Stuart & Davis recommended a relatively slow weight reduction. The diet management program should aim at a 1-lb reduction and the exercises at a ½-lb week, or a total of 0.7 kg/week.

Group 2: Fenfluramine. The subjects in this group recieved fenfluramine tablets (Ponderal) with a maximum dose of 60 mg twice daily. The dosage was gradually increased in the beginning and decreased at the end of treatment. To avoid overdosing, subjects received the exact number of tablets they were to take between two sessions at the end of each session. In addition to this pharmacological treatment the therapist also gave the subjects general advice about nutrition and exercises. The therapist of group 2 had no knowledge about the behavioral method.

Group 3: Waiting-list control. These subjects performed baseline recordings and attended a lecture on nutrition (the same as all other potential subjects) and were assessed at the same time as the other subjects. They were told that they could not receive treatment at the moment (due to the large number of applicants) and were placed on a waiting list for treatment at later time.

Assessments

Subjects were assessed before and after treatment, and at follow-up 12 months after the end of the 16-week treatment period. *Before* treatment the subjects' weight, height, daily food intake and exercise habits were obtained. *After* treatment the weight was measured. Furthermore questionnaires were answered by the subjects. Group 1-subjects recorded their food intake and exercise habits during one week. Group 2-subjects answered a form concerning side effects from the drug treatment. Finally, group 3-subjects were asked if they had tried to reduce their weight during the time period in question, if so what method they had used, and if the lecture on nutrition and exercises they attended in the beginning of the study had influenced them in any way. At *follow up* (after 1 yr) all subjects were weighed and group 1-subjects were asked if they had continued to follow the treatment program, and if not the causes for discontinuing.

From the assessment described above the following outcome measures were derived: (1) Weight in kg, (2) Percentage overweight (by reference to a table of average weights for different heights; Natvig, 1956), and (3) Weight-reduction index (Jefferey, 1974) defined as (weight lost/overweight in kg) $\times$ (initial weight/target weight) $\times$ 100.

Statistical Methods

The random assignment of subjects to the three groups resulted in significant differences in initial weight and percentage overweight between groups 1 and 3, and 2 and 3. To adjust for this the data were analyzed with analysis of covariance (with subsequent *t*-tests).

RESULTS

Attrition

Four subjects dropped out of the first (behavioral) group; three because of unexpected changes in their personal lives that had nothing to do with their participating in the study. They left the program 1, 3 and 6 weeks after the start. One subject was dropped because she attended only half of the sessions (and very irregularly). In the second group (fenfluramine) there were also four drop-outs, after 2, 4, 4 and 12 weeks respectively. One terminated because of a long-term gastroenteritis, one because of hypothyreosis, one was admitted to a psychiatric clinic because of depression, and one terminated because of side effects (tiredness) from the drug. In the third group (waiting-list control) four subjects dropped out; one became pregnant during the study and three did not show up for the post-treatment assessment. An analysis of these 12 dropouts (26.7%) did not yield any significant differences as to initial percentage of overweight. There were no further drop-outs between the end of treatment and the 1-yr follow-up.

Outcome Measures: Actual Figures

Table 1 presents an overview of the most important individual data. A general result of the analyses of covariance was significant F-values *both* between and within groups when the before vs. after differences were tested. When it comes to the before vs. Follow-up differences only the within-group F-values were significant.

Weight in kg. The mean weights for the three groups are shown in Table 2.

The means were significantly reduced in all three groups after treatment (group 1: $t = 6.90$; $p < 0.001$, group 2: $t = 4.12$; $p < 0.01$, group 3: $t = 2.89$; $p < 0.02$). The mean number of kilograms lost during the treatment were for group 1: 9.35 kg (S.D. 4.47), for group 2: 5.72 kg (S.D. 4.53) and for group 3: 3.51 kg (S.D. 4.04). The difference between the behavioral group and the control group was significant ($t = 3.91$, $p = 0.001$) while the difference between the behavioral and the fenfluramine groups did not reach significance ($t = 1.83$). The fenfluramine treated subjects did not however lose more weight than the waiting-list control subjects ($t = 1.08$).

At the one-year follow-up assessment both treatment groups had, compared to after treatment, increased their mean weight (group 1: $t = 3.57$; $p < 0.01$), group 2: $t = 5.45$; $p < 0.001$) while the small increase for the

TABLE 1

Initial Weight, Percent Overweight, Weight Loss and Weight-Reduction Index for Each Subject in the Three Groups. (Group 1 = Behavioral, 2 = Fenfluramine, 3 = Waiting-list)

Subject	Sex	Height (cm)	Initial weight	Percent overweight	Weight loss (Kg) after	Weight loss (Kg) follow-up	Weight-reduction index after	Weight-reduction index follow-up
G 1:1	F	160	86.0	45.5	—16.1	—19.6	86.1	106.4
2	M	171	91.0	34.8	—12.0	—1.6	68.9	9.2
3	F	167	86.2	35.1	—4.5	—7.7	27.0	46.4
4	M	176	104.0	46.5	—2.5	+3.5	11.7	0
5	F	173	102.5	51.5	—14.3	—6.3	61.9	26.5
6	F	154	80.6	46.5	—7.0	—3.1	39.7	18.0
7	F	166	76.8	21.7	—14.8	—8.7	131.8	77.5
8	F	159	74.0	26.7	—8.5	—1.5	68.6	12.7
9	F	164	76.9	24.4	—7.8	—0.9	64.5	7.4
10	M	179	106.1	44.9	—5.6	+1.4	24.7	0
11	F	161	72.4	21.3	—9.8	—6.3	93.1	60.0
Mean		166.4	87.0	36.2	—9.4	—4.6	61.6	33.1
SD		7.7	12.4	11.2	4.5	6.2	34.9	35.2
G 2:1	F	165	81.4	30.6	—2.8	+0.2	19.7	0
2	F	177	87.2	23.7	—0.2	+9.3	1.2	0
3	F	164	88.0	42.4	—1.3	—0.2	7.1	1.1
4	F	167	94.0	47.3	—1.6	+1.7	7.4	0
5	F	162	94.0	55.6	—6.4	—1.3	29.6	6.2
6	F	158	93.7	62.4	—4.2	—1.5	19.4	6.5
7	F	165	86.2	38.1	—8.7	—0.6	51.1	4.1
8	F	175	97.6	41.2	—9.1	—3.1	45.1	20.1
9	F	160	80.9	36.9	—9.2	—2.8	57.6	17.6
10	F	156	85.6	51.8	—15.3	—7.3	79.0	38.0
11	F	153	63.3	16.4	—4.1	—3.5	53.3	45.6
Mean		163.8	86.6	40.6	—5.7	—0.8	35.1	12.7
SD		7.4	9.4	13.7	4.5	4.1	24.5	16.0
G 3:1	F	164	87.4	41.4	—1.9	+0.4	9.9	0
2	F	162	69.5	15.1	—1.7	+2.0	21.9	0
3	F	167	76.9	20.5	—1.9	+0.9	18.1	0
4	F	162	74.4	23.2	—3.8	—8.1	33.3	71.2
5	F	149	66.1	26.1	+0.2	—2.6	0	22.9
6	F	162	75.2	24.5	+0.4	+1.3	0	0
7	F	166	82.8	31.2	—6.4	—12.5	42.0	83.1
8	F	151	73.0	37.7	—1.0	—0.4	6.9	2.8
9	M	189	123.2	53.6	—13.9	+3.4	49.3	0
10	M	184	95.1	24.0	—4.9	—10.6	33.5	71.4
11	F	162	72.4	19.9	—3.8	—0.4	38.4	4.0
Mean		165.3	81.5	28.8	—3.5	—2.4	23.0	23.2
SD		12.0	16.1	11.3	4.0	5.3	17.4	34.2

control group was insignificant. A further comparison between the initial and the follow-up means showed that the behavioral group was the only group with a significantly lower mean weight ($t = 2.43$; $p < 0.05$) at follow-up. The between-group comparisons after treatment yielded the following t-values: group 1 vs. 2: $t = 1.98$, group 1 vs. 3: $t = 2.89$; $p < 0.01$, and group 2 vs. 3: $t = 0.94$. At follow-up there were no significant differences between the groups.

Percentage overweight. The results for this measure (Table 2) were essentially the same as for weight with a significant decrease after treatment, a significant increase for groups 1 and 2 during the year after treatment, leaving only the behavioral group with a lower mean percentage of overweight at follow-up compared to before treatment. The between group comparisons for this measure also produced one significant difference. The percentage overweight of the behavioral group was significantly lower than the control group's ($t = 2.95$; $p < 0.01$). Again there were no significant follow-up differences.

Weight-reduction index. The result of the study in terms of this index which takes into account weight, height, amount overweight, target weight and weight lost is shown in Figure 1.

At post-treatment the difference between the behavioral (61.6) and fenfluramine (35.1) groups were significant ($t = 2.15$; $p < 0.05$) as well as between the behavioral and control (23.0) subjects ($t = 3.29$; $p < 0.01$). The index of the fenfluramine group was however not significantly different from that of the control group. At follow-up none of the differences was significant.

Supplementary Results

Eating and exercise habits. As the change of eating and exercise habits are explicit goals of the behavioral treatment applied for group 1 it is interesting to relate changes in this respect to the obtained weight losses. A rater, who was unaware of the patients' weight losses, compared the before and after recordings of food intake and exercise for each subject and ranged the subjects according to the degree of habit change. The variables influencing this ranking were, e.g. type of food eaten, composition of meals, distribution of food intake over the day, and the type and amount of exercise performed. A Spearman rank correlation between degree of habit change and percent of initial body weight lost yielded a significant coefficient of 0.59 ($p < 0.05$).

The mean weight loss (for group 1) at follow-up was 4.6 kg, an in-

Table 2. Weight in kg and per cent overweight for the three groups before, after and at follow-up. (Group 1 = behavioral, 2 = fenfluramine, 3 = waiting-list)

Group		Before (kg)	Before (%)	After (kg)	After (%)	Follow-up (kg)	Follow-up (%)
1	M	87.0	36.2	77.6	21.5	82.4	28.6
	SD	12.4	11.2	14.1	13.9	15.5	15.1
2	M	86.6	40.6	80.8	31.1	85.7	38.9
	SD	9.4	13.7	10.3	13.5	10.0	13.2
3	M	81.5	28.8	77.9	23.8	79.0	25.1
	SD	16.1	11.3	12.7	9.4	17.3	15.0

crease from posttreatment of 4.8 kg on the average. At the follow-up interview it was found that two subjects (S1 and S3) had continued to use the principles they were taught in the behavioral program. They had continued to lose weight: 3.5 and 3.2 kg respectively. Two other subjects (S7 and S11) had continued with the program for about 6 months and at follow-up they had increased their weight by 6.1 and 3.5 kg respectively. The seven other subjects had stopped using the principles shortly after the end of treatment and at follow-up they had a mean increase of +7.0 kg (range 3.9-10.4 kg). The difference in mean weight increase between those who continued ($n = 4$) with the program (mean = +0.72 kg) and those ($n = 7$) who discontinued (mean = +7.02 kg) was significant ($t = 3.12$; $p < 0.02$).

Side effects. Another factor of interest in evaluating the treatment methods is if they produce any negative side effects. Both the treatment groups were asked about this at the end of treatment. In the behavioral group two subjects had experienced no side effects whatsoever. Nine subjects had only once or twice during the treatment period experienced the following effects: hunger (7), nervousness (3), irritation (3), tiredness (2) and feebleness (2). The figures in brackets denote the number of times each effect was mentioned. The fenfluramine-treated subjects experienced negative effects of somewhat higher frequency and duration. The side effects reported were: tiredness (5), dryness in mouth (4), swollen fingers (3), diuretic effects (2) and dizziness (2).

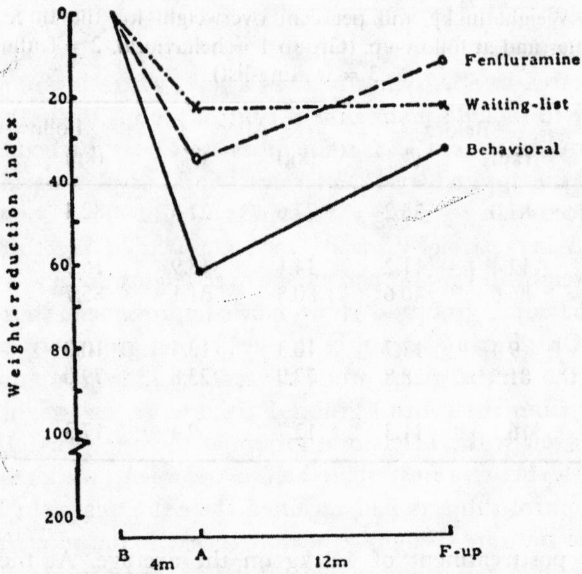

Fig. 1. Weight-reduction index for the three groups after treatment and at follow-up.

Control group. Since the control subjects who did not receive treatment also reduced their weight significantly it is interesting to take a closer look at them. Seven of the control group subjects had tried to reduce their weight at some time during the study (six by reducing calorie intake and increasing exercise, and one by weighing himself before and after every meal). Furthermore four subjects said that the baseline recording of food intake and exercises (which all potential subjects performed prior to randomization) had influenced their eating habits. Three subjects thought that the lecture on nutrition had influenced them in a positive way.

DISCUSSION

The amount of therapeutic contact differed between the treatment groups. The reason for this was the attempt to apply both treatment methods as they realistically would be used in a clinical setting, as this is the first study comparing a behavioral and a pharmacological treatment of obesity. The drug is supposed to be the active therapeutic agent in group 2 so it was not considered necessary to have more than 8 sessions for this group compared to 20 for group 1. On the other hand the control group probably was not a non-treatment group but rather a "minimal treatment" group. Jeffrey (1974) has stated that behavior therapy research in obesity has reached a level where it no longer would be necessary to include no-treatment control groups but rather compare the behavioral treatment with some other treatment method.

Which of the applied treatments (behavioral or pharmacological) was the most effective in reducing the subjects' weight? This question cannot be answered in a straightforward way. On two of the three outcome measures (weight in kg, and percentage overweight) there was a tendency for the behavioral group to show more improvement, but not significantly so. On the same measures the behavioral group was significantly better than the control group while the fenfluramine group did not differ significantly from the control group. Furthermore, on weight in kg and percent overweight the behavioral group, at the one year follow-up had a significantly better result than before treatment while the fenfluramine and control subjects had regained their pre-treatment levels. The last outcome measure, weight-reduction index, is the most fair since it takes into account not only weight and height, but also amount of overweight, goal and weight lost. On this index (which Jeffrey, 1974, recommended for comparisons across studies) the behavioral group was significantly better than the fenfluramine and control groups. Once again the fenfluramine subjects' result did not differ from the control subjects'. Taken together these results indicate that the behavioral method was more effective than the pharmacological in reducing the subjects' overweight.

At the one year follow-up all groups had increased their mean weight but the behavioral group still had a lower mean than before treatment, which was not the case for the other groups. The most plausible explanation for this weight gain in the behavioral group is that only some subjects had learned new eating and exercise habits to such a degree that they continued to use them on their own after the treatment period. It is also probable that the contingencies for following the program were weakened considerably when the treatment period ended. The self-control of the subjects may to a large extent have depended on external control, i.e. the contact with the therapist once a week. The subjects had probably not succeeded in transfering this controlling function to their natural environment. When applying these principles clinically it is very important to make a thorough behavior analysis of each individual client, especially concerning the contingencies in his/her natural environment which would support continued adherence to the program. Since the drug treatment for the second group did not aim for a change in eating habits, but less food intake due to the appetite-suppressing effects of the drug, it is understandable that these subjects regained weight when the drug was withdrawn.

Jeffrey (1974) described the need for long-term follow-up and stated that "Much of the recent enthusiasm for behavior modification approaches has been based on dramatic demonstrations of weight loss over short periods of time" (p. 624). The 30 experimental studies up to 1975 have a mean follow-up time of 18 weeks (range 0-2 yr). Hall & Hall (1974) in their review found that in studies with a short follow-up period (12 weeks or less) the differences between treatment and control groups remained significant while this was not the case in studies with longer follow-up periods. The results of the present study are in agreement with this conclusion.

The literature contains only two studies with a follow-up period of 1 yr or more. Hall (1973) reported a 2-yr follow-up on 10 subjects and concluded that "The results do not indicate a long-lasting effect from the behavioral treatment of obesity" (p. 648). Mahoney (1974) on the other side found that in the most successful of his treatment groups, 70% of the subjects maintained or improved their weight losses during the 1-yr follow-up period.

If the purpose is to compare behavioral methods with other types of treatments, e.g. psychotherapy or pharmacotherapy, future research in this area should attempt to optimize these treatments. The three comparative studies described earlier (Harmatz & Lapuc, 1968; Penick, Filion, Fox & Stunkard, 1971; Wollersheim, 1970) can hardly be said to have given the psychotherapeutic method a fair chance. Rather it seems as if these groups were used as nonspecific or attention-placebo conditions. If the purpose is to investigate a behavioral method it would be most desirable to design and evaluate techniques for mantaining the weight losses obtained after treatment. Another very urgent question that behavior therapists in this area should attend to is how effective behavioral treatments are for severely (75-100%) overweight persons. The research on college students has served its purpose and now we should turn our research efforts to clinically relevant populations.

REFERENCES

ABRAMSON, E. E. A review of behavioral approaches to weight control. *Behaviour Research and Therapy*, 11:547-556, 1973.

BELLACK, A. S., Behavior therapy for weight reduction. *Addictive Behaviors*, 1:73-82, 1975.

CHLOUVERAKIS, C. Dietary and medical treatments of obesity: An evaluative review. *Addictive Behaviors,* 1:3-21, 1975.

Food and Nutrition Board, National Academy of Sciences—National Research Council Recommended Daily Dietary Allowances, 1968.

HALL, S. M. & HALL, R. G. Outcome and methodological considerations in the behavioral treatment of obesity. *Behavior Therapy,* 5:352-364, 1974.

HARMATZ, M. G., & LAPUC, P. Behavior modification of overeating in a psychiatric population. *Journal of Consulting and Clinical Psychology,* 32:583, 1968.

JEFFREY, D. B. Some methodological issues in research on obesity. *Psychological Reports,* 35:623-626, 1974.

LAWSON, A. A. H., ROSCOE, P., STRONG, J. A., & GIBSON, A. Comparison of fenfluramine and metformine in treatment of obesity. *Lancet,* 2:437-441, 1970.

LEVITZ, L. S., & STUNKARD, A. J. A therapeutic coalition for obesity: Behavior modification and patient self-help. *American Journal of Psychiatry,* 131:423-427, 1974.

MAHONEY, M. Self-reward and self-monitoring techniques for weight control. *Behavior Therapy,* 5:48-57, 1974.

MUNRO, J. F., SEATON, D. A., & DUNCAN, L. J. P. Treatment of refractory obesity with fenfluramine. *British Medical Journal,* ii:624-625, 1966.

NATVIG, H. *Nye Hoyde Vekttabeller for Norske Kvinnor og Men.* Oslo, 1956.

PENICK, S. B., FILION, R., FOX, S., & STUNKARD, A. J. Behavior modification in the treatment of obesity. *Psychosomatic Medicine,* 33:49-55, 1971.

PERSSON, I., ANDERSSON, V., & DECKERT, T. Treatment of obesity with fenfluramine. *European Journal of Clinical Pharmacology,* 6:93-97, 1973.

STUART, R. B., & DAVIS, B. *Slim Chance in a Fat World.* Champaign, Ill.: Research Press, 1972.

STUNKARD, A. J. New therapies for the eating disorders. *Archives of General Psychiatry,* 26:391-398, 1972

WOLLERSHEIM, J. P. Effectiveness of group therapy based upon learning principles in the treatment of overweight women. *Journal of Abnormal Psychology,* 76:462-474, 1970.

Section VII

SEXUAL DISORDERS, MARITAL DISHARMONY, AND DEPRESSION

Commentary

SEXUAL DYSFUNCTION AND DEVIANCE

The Treatment of Sexual Dysfunction: Conceptual Issues

The publication of Masters and Johnson's (1970) best-selling book on human sexual inadequacy ushered in the era of the "sex therapies." Although there are frequently differences from one program to the next, the term "sex therapy" has come to denote an explicitly directive approach to the treatment of specific sexual behaviors ("symptoms"). The emphasis is on the here and now of the presenting problem(s) and therapy is typically very short-term. The enthusiastic reception of "sex therapy" by diverse medical and mental health professionals and nonprofessional groups (and, apparently, the public at large) has been dramatic, and treatment programs for the treatment of sexual dysfunction—some would say the enhancement of sexual repertoires—are widespread.

Two years ago (cf. Franks & Wilson, 1975), we cautioned that the rise of the "new sex therapy" raised important conceptual and clinical questions about the adequacy of treatment. Our current reservations appear as pertinent to the contemporary scene as they were then: The effective treatment of sexual dysfunction involves considerably more than instruction in the art of body massage and the expert use of vibrators. Inadequate interpersonal relationships and lack of personal communication are more often than not the reasons for sexual distress. Accordingly, "sex therapy" requires trained therapists who are skilled and experienced in the treatment of complex emotional disorders. "Sex therapy" is not to be divorced from a more comprehensive therapeutic framework. As

Bruni (1974) has aptly remarked: "Sex treatment as a subspecialty with separate practitioners and settings increases fragmentation of psychological and sexual functioning which is neither necessary nor advantageous to clients" (p. 277). In particular, we questioned the logic and clinical wisdom of the eclectic incorporation of the essentially behavioral treatment techniques of Masters and Johnson (1970) and others within a psychodynamic framework (e.g., Kaplan, 1974).

The importance of retaining sex therapy within the empirically supported conceptual framework of social learning theory goes beyond theoretical niceties or research applications. Of more immediate concern is that the failure to adopt a theoretically integrated and consistent approach could result in sex therapy being less effective than it might otherwise be. The reason is that behavior therapy is far more than a collection of useful therapeutic techniques. More importantly, it represents a particular way of conceptualizing clients' problems, it is characterized by a flexible problem-solving orientation that is based upon an educational as opposed to the quasi-disease model of behavior disorders, and is steeped in the method and substance of scientific psychology. Grafting behavioral techniques which, in any event, are constantly being modified, refined, and improved onto a psychodynamic treatment model is to lose distinguishing features of the behavioral approach, as we know it.

Brady (1976a) has reported a telling instance of the importance of placing the treatment of sexual dysfunction within a comprehensive behavioral assessment and modification program. A 27-year-old client was treated for frequent secondary impotence. The now almost standard therapy of graduated in vivo desensitization failed completely. The client went against the therapist's explicit instructions and drank before a session of sensate focus (alcohol consumption significantly decreases penile tumescence, Wilson, in press a); his wife similarly ignored instructions by engaging almost immediately in direct genital stimulation and urging her husband to attempt intercourse. Mutual recriminations inevitably followed these interactions. As soon as this self-defeating pattern of behavior became apparent, the therapist delved more deeply into the nature of the couple's marital relationship, commendably conducting analyses of actual behavioral interactions in the therapist's office. This assessment showed that the client was plagued by self-doubt and a lack of assertiveness; his wife, while she expressed warmth and support on occasion, was predominantly critical and aggressive in manner. A multifaceted behavioral treatment program of training in assertiveness and communication competencies, and contingency contracting aimed at securing adherence to the therapist's prescriptions produced significant improvement in the marital relationship over the following five months. However, the impotence persisted, and anxiety was still attached to sexual performance. At this point the original in vivo desensitization program was reintroduced with the result that the impotence was eliminated within a few weeks. A six month follow-up indicated successful maintenance of the couple's newfound sexual adequacy. This case replicates almost exactly the case of premature ejaculation discussed by Wilson and Evans (1977) in which Masters and Johnson's (1970) squeeze technique proved unsuccessful until the couple's interpersonal problems were resolved.

These and other clinical illustrations indicate that effective treatment of specific sexual disorders is, at least in some instances, dependent on improvement in other aspects of the clients' functioning so that competitive tendencies and lack of interpersonal communication do not preclude the successful implementation of specific sexual techniques. Thus, O'Leary and Wilson (1975), for example, have suggested that one explanation for what Masters and Johnson (1970) term their "clinical disaster area"—impotence—could be the failure to focus directly on frequently nonsexual sources of sexual dysfunction by using a broader range of behavioral methods including behavioral rehearsal, assertion training, and imaginal procedures such as systematic desensitization, covert modeling, and orgasmic re-conditioning.

In his discussion of this case, Brady (1976a) anticipates the obvious question of why a comprehensive behavioral assessment was not conducted at the outset. Had this been the case, treatment would have initially focused on the marital relationship rather than consisting of direct intervention with respect to impotence. Brady suggests that it is more efficient to try the least time-consuming strategy first, resorting to a more multifaceted and complex treatment program only if the problem does not yield readily. Moreover, he suggests that the use of a highly focused behavioral procedure also provides a powerful diagnostic and motivational test. As in this case, it may quickly expose resistances to treatment so that other, related features of the total clinical problem can be identified, assessed, and appropriately treated. While there will be those who reject this approach, it has considerable appeal for the busy practitioner intent on providing cost-effective treatment. If the therapist can detect clients the majority of whom respond to the direct treatment of sexual dysfunction, Brady's suggestion would appear to hold considerable merit. The ramifications of this issue are discussed more fully below.

The Results of Behavioral Treatment of Sexual Dysfunction

It is noteworthy that behavioral methods for treating sexual dysfunction have gained such ready acceptance, even among psychodynamically oriented therapists (e.g., Kaplan, 1974), despite the fact that there is little in the way of well-controlled outcome research attesting to their efficacy (cf. Kazdin & Wilson, in press). Masters and Johnson's (1970) clinical success rate of 81% at posttreatment and 75% at a five year follow-up is unprecedented. Additionally, as these authors note, these findings are strengthened by the not inconsequential fact that over 50% of their clients had tried previous psychotherapy without success, and the conservative manner in which they evaluated outcome (cf. O'Leary & Wilson, 1975). However, unequivocal demonstration of the efficacy of methods awaits controlled outcome research.

In comparative outcome studies, Obler (1973) showed that behavior therapy consisting of systematic desensitization and other behavioral methods was significantly more effective than either traditional group psychotherapy or no treatment in the treatment of a heterogeneous of sexual problems. Kockott, Dittmar, and Nusselt (1975) found systematic desensitization marginally superior to conventional medical treatment of impotence. Clients who did not respond to these therapies were then treated with a modified Masters and Johnson program that resulted in significantly greater improvement than systematic desensitization had. Marks (1976a) cites unpublished findings of Crowe (1976) showing that behavioral treatment is superior to both interpretive and supportive psychotherapy in producing improvements in couples' sexual adjustments. For the rest, the evidence for the efficacy of behavioral methods rests primarily on uncontrolled clinical reports (Kazdin & Wilson, in press; Marks, 1976). Particularly disappointing has been the tendency of major programs modeled on the Masters and Johnson (1970) format to forego the reporting of detailed outcome data (e.g., Hartman & Fithian, 1972; Kaplan, 1974). We have had occasion in earlier volumes of this Series (cf. Franks & Wilson, 1974, 1975) to criticize programs that fail to provide an account of their success rates, which, aside from their relevance to potential consumers of this service, would also serve a useful scientific purpose. Global, summary statements to the effect that the results obtained are comparable to those of Master and Johnson or of any other program are not good enough.

It is in this connection that the first paper that is reprinted in this Section, by Mathews, Bancroft, Whitehead, Hackmann, Julier, Bancroft, Gath, and Shaw, is of particular significance. It represents a controlled study of the behavioral treatment of sexual inadequacy under relatively routine service delivery circumstances. Moreover, it constitutes the first systematic attempt to conduct a component analysis of the effective agents of change in the Masters and Johnson-type program, and to evaluate the necessity for a dual-sex therapy team to conduct treatment. In contrast to the other clinical impressions of Kaplan (1974), Lazarus (1974), and others, Mathews et al. found that a modified Masters and Johnson-type program appears to be more effective when administered by a dual-sex therapy team. In view of the considerations of both efficacy and efficiency that attach to the resolution of this vital question of whether a dual-sex therapy is superior to the single therapist, hopefully the paucity of research on this issue will soon be remedied.

Two other findings in this study bear mentioning. The first is that the superiority of the directed practice, in vivo treatment over imaginal systematic desensitization lends further empirical support to the consistent findings that performance-based methods are more effective than those based upon verbal or imaginal operations (cf. Bandura, 1977a). The second concerns the marked variability in outcome of patients in the treatment with directed practice with minimum therapist contact treatment group. Mathews et al. suggest that there are those patients who will respond to straightforward behavioral techniques whereas others, distinguished mainly by interpersonal and communication difficulties, will not respond to this treatment. Indeed, it appears that the latter's problems might even be aggravated. This line of reasoning is consonant with Brady's (1976a) views discussed above.

The relatively poor showing of the treatment group that received minimum therapist contact and mailed instructions is significant on another count. "Do-it-yourself" treatment manuals, based on behaviorally oriented techniques, have recently begun to be marketed. A timely note of caution has been sounded by Rosen (1976c) concerning self-help manuals that have not been adequately evaluated. For example, Rosen points out that Barbach (1975) advises women with inhibitions about masturbating to prolong self-stimulation and exaggerate reactions, advice presumably based on a flooding strategy to reduce anxiety. However, there is no evidence to indicate whether self-administered flooding is effective. Evidence does exist that, under certain circumstances, anxiety is exacerbated rather than diminished by flooding (e.g., McCutcheon & Adams, 1975;

Stone & Borkovec, 1975). Sensitization of this sort could plausibly result from inappropriate self-stimulation of the sort that Barbach proposes (see Commentary, Section X).

Finally, if fault is to be found with Mathews et al.'s study, the adequacy of the outcome measures can be questioned. Relatively global ratings—whether by therapist, client, or even blind assessor—provide limited and often insufficiently discriminating information (cf. Franks & Wilson, Section IX, 1976; Kazdin & Wilson, in press). The unavailability of the data from the self-report diaries is unfortunate.

The behavioral treatment of orgasmic dysfunction was compared to a waiting list control group by Munjack, Cristol, Goldstein, Phillips, Goldberg, Whipple, Staples, and Kanno (1976). Twelve middle- to upper-class women with primary orgasmic dysfunction and 10 with secondary orgasmic dysfunction, whose average age was 29 years, and who were currently living with their husbands, were assigned to either an immediate treatment or a delayed treatment group. The treatment program consisted of heterogeneous techniques that were tailored to the individual case. Techniques included systematic desensitization, assertion training, modeling, cognitive restructuring, direct education using plastic models, in vivo homework assignments, and masturbation training using vaginal dilators and vibrators. Most patients were seen individually, without their husbands, about 75% of the time. All treatment was administered by two male therapists and one female therapist working alone. Outcome measures consisted of a number of personality questionnaires, an assessment interview with two blind assessors, and a "Sexual Adjustment Form" that sampled patients' reactions to specific aspects of sexual behavior as well as frequencies of sexual behaviors.

Treatment was significantly more effective than no treatment on several measures: a) the percentage of patients experiencing orgasm during at least 50% of sexual relations; b) the percentage of women reporting satisfactory sexual relations at least 50% of the time; c) patients' ratings of positive reactions to various sexual behaviors; and d) assessors' global clinical ratings of the women's sexual adjustment, as well as their feeling about sex. Only about one-third of the women were orgasmic in at least 50% of their sexual encounters at the end of the 20 sessions of treatment.

Somewhat predictably in terms of previous findings (McGovern, Stewart, & LoPiccolo, 1975, reprinted in Franks & Wilson, 1976), women with primary orgasmic dysfunction responded differently from those with secondary orgasmic dysfunction. At posttreatment, 22% of the primary and 40% of the secondary orgasmic dysfunctional patients were orgasmic in at least 50% of their sexual relations, whereas none were orgasmic before treatment. At follow-up, however, none of the primary orgasmic dysfunctional patients was orgasmic more than 50% of the time, whereas the percentage of secondary orgasmic dysfunctional patients had increased to 60%. In terms of global ratings at follow-up the secondary dysfunctional women were judged to be significantly more improved than those with primary dysfunction.

Munjak et al. report that the therapists considered the husbands' presence to be highly beneficial to treatment outcome, and thought that greater participation by the husbands in more treatment sessions might have resulted in less "resistance" on their part of some of the husbands. Many of the women with primary orgasmic dysfunction appeared to have significant non-sexual problems. As a result, Munjak et al. suggest that 20 therapy sessions were too few to treat the marital discord before tackling the sexual dysfunction. They recommend that "couples must either be highly selected for marital harmony (if treatment for a sexual dysfunction is be attempted directly and immediately) or first be treated for their interpersonal problems. Since marital and sexual problems are most often inextricable the combined problem should probably be treated by the same therapist or therapy team" (p. 502). It should be noted that the strategy that Munjak et al. advocate differs from Brady's (1976a) priorities in sex therapy. Finally, while these results provide some support for the general notion that behavioral treatment is superior to no treatment, the use of an omnibus, multifaceted program does not allow any determination of the effective agents of behavior change.

Fabbri (1976) has described a combined treatment approach featuring hypnosis and behavior therapy. The behavioral methods include systematic desensitization, in vivo graded assignments, and assertion training. Hypnosis was used to facilitate relaxation training and to heighten visual imagery. This program was applied mainly to single clients by one therapist. Of 78 cases of varied sexual dysfunctions, including impotence, premature ejaculation, and orgasmic dysfunction, 72% were estimated to have been successes as defined by "the state of being regularly functional." Unfortunately, Fabbri does not elaborate on what "regularly functional" means in operational terms. Changing the criterion of success to include cases that were functional (orgasmic?) "most of the time" rather than "always," a success rate of 91% was obtained. Uncontrolled clinical reports of this nature would be immeasurably improved by careful specification of what methods were applied to what problems in what sort of client. More detailed description of outcome measures must be reported if different clinical trials are to be related meaningfully to the broader context of the treatment of sexual dysfunction.

Obler's (1973) comparative outcome study demonstrated that a behavioral treatment package was significantly more effective than traditional psychotherapy. However, since Obler used visual presentations of anxiety-eliciting situations and assertion training in addition to systematic desensitization, it cannot be determined what the effective agents of change were. Moreover, since a variety of heterogeneous disorders were treated, it is unclear from Obler's findings whether specific methods are appropriate for particular problems. Wincze and Caird (1976) compared two of the specific components of Obler's therapy package—systematic desensitization and video desensitization—with a waiting list control group in the treatment of women with "'essential' sexual dysfunction with little or no evidence of 'situational' dysfunction" (p. 336). Approximately 75% of the women were non-orgasmic, although their primary presenting problem was excessive anxiety associated with most aspects of sexual behavior. The video desensitization consisted of visual presentation of precisely the same scenes that were described verbally during the desensitization hierarchy. Thus, the women were exposed to a standardized hierarchy that had been chosen from 30 pre-determined sexual scenes. Therapy lasted from four to 12 weeks. Following posttreatment assessment, the control group was assigned to either imaginal or video desensitization for a 4-12 week treatment course and then reassessed. Assessment consisted of interviews in which both partners evaluated their sexual behavior and which were rated on a five point scale ranging from "very much improvement" to "much worse." In addition, a number of anxiety questionnaires were completed by the women at home and mailed in to the therapist. Follow-up interviews were conducted 1-3 months after termination of therapy.

Video desensitization was superior to imaginal desensitization in terms of reduction in heterosexual anxiety at posttreatment, while both behavioral treatments resulted in significantly greater improvement on some measures than the control group. No improvement was evident in the control group during the waiting period; subsequent treatment, however, produced changes comparable to those shown by the initial desensitization treatment groups. Only 25% of the women who were non-orgasmic before treatment were orgasmic following therapy. The relative weakness of the outcome measures—global ratings based on interviews plus questionnaire responses—together with the absence of any attention-placebo control group makes unequivocal interpretation of these data difficult if not impossible. Moreover, as the authors themselves point out, regardless of the anxiety-reducing value of desensitization, it appears to be an unsatisfactory form of therapy if orgasmic functioning is the goal of therapy.

Yulis (1976) reported the treatment of 37 middle- or upper-class clients who were premature ejaculators. The average duration of their sexual problems was just over eight years. Treatment was closely modeled after the Masters and Johnson program, the client being treated together with his female partner by a dual-sex therapy team. The clients' assertive behavior was assessed in role-playing sessions, and assertion training was administered at the therapists' discretion. Thirty-three of the men (89%) reported a "very satisfactory sexual relationship" at a six month follow-up, self-reports that were confirmed by their partners. Very satisfactory sexual adjustment was defined as between 80-100% "ejaculation-controlled sexual encounters" (p. 356).

An informative feature of Yulis' report is the data on generalization of improved ejaculatory control to sexual intercourse with partners other than those who participated in the therapy sessions. Of 23 clients who described sexual contact with at least one non-treatment partner, nine experienced persistent difficulties in ejaculatory control in attempting intercourse with the non-treatment partner. All nine clients (five of whom were married) reported episodes of premature ejaculation with their treatment partners following unsuccessful encounters with non-treatment partners. Yulis suggests that the success of the 13 men who experienced no ejaculatory problems with non-treatment partners is attributable to the fact that 11 of these 13 men received assertion training. Of the 10 subjects who did not receive assertion training, seven experienced ejaculatory problems with non-treatment partners. Of course, these are post hoc analyses of the data, and are only suggestive at best. However, these findings once again emphasize the fact that treatment-induced improvement does not necessarily generalize to other situations. Specific steps must be taken to facilitate such generalization. Overall, the 89% success rate is encouraging and provides further clinical support for the unparalleled efficacy of the Masters and Johnson-type treatment for premature ejaculation, a disorder that was once considered to be extremely resistant to modification (cf. Hastings, 1967).

Group Behavioral Treatment of Sexual Dysfunction

Yulis (1976) suggests that his high success rate is due in part to the fact that his clients were relatively young. Schneidman and McGuire (1976) treated two groups of women suffering from primary orgasmic dysfunction, one above and the other below the age of 35 years. All women had stable partners and were college-educated. Treatment consisted of a modified Masters and Johnson-type program with the addition of a self-directed masturbation program and filmed instructions. Each group consisted of 10 couples and met for 10 weeks. At posttreatment, 70% of the women younger than 35 years were orgasmic with vibrator or partner stimulation, but none was orgasmic during intercourse. A six month follow-up indicated that the number of women who were orgasmic with masturbation had increased to 80%. Of the older women, 40% were orgasmic with masturbatory stimulation at the end of therapy. This figure had increased to 60% at the six month follow-up. Only one of the older women was orgasmic during intercourse.

Group behavior therapy of this nature appears to be more effective with younger women. The success rate with this group is comparable to Masters and Johnson's success rate of 83% for all clients with primary orgasmic dysfunction. However, the failure of the women's newfound orgasmic capacity to generalize to the coital situation is striking. Interestingly, Schneidman and McGuire report that the absence of orgasm during intercourse was *not* a major concern for the women. Barbach (1974) has reported that the generalization of orgasmic capacity to intercourse took place approximately eight months after the termination of treatment. Since couples reported that their sexual relationship was continuing to improve even after therapy, it is possible that a similar process might have occurred among the women treated by Schneidman and McGuire. Even if this were not to happen, however, the apparently satisfactory outcome of this study underlines the oft-stated point that there is more to sexual activity and enjoyment than orgasm during intercourse. The overall success of this therapy program in helping women to become orgasmic can be contrasted with the relative ineffectiveness of imaginal and vicarious desensitization (cf. Wincze & Caird, 1976).

Of clinical significance is Schneidman and McGuire's finding that some of their clients' male partners became increasingly anxious as the women became more sexually expressive. In four couples, the men, who had previously initiated sexual activity, became resistant and refused to cooperate in the treatment assignments. Indeed, in the group of women below the age of 35 years a special group meeting was held for their male partners in order to reduce anxieties and clarify treatment goals. The authors speculate that this was not the case in the older group since changes occurred more slowly. Suffice it to say that therapists need to be alert to the effects on the client's relationship with her partner as she becomes more sexually expressive. Other therapists have noted that some husbands have become impotent after their wives' sexual responsiveness was increased. This phenomenon exemplifies the fact that psychological functioning represents a continuous reciprocal interaction between people's behavior and its controlling environmental consequences, and reinforces Masters and Johnson's (1970) insistence that "there is no such thing as an uninvolved partner in any marriage in which there is some form of sexual inadequacy." Behavior change does not occur in a vacuum but within the context of an ongoing network of complicated social relationships. More often than not, the development of behavioral competence engenders positive, reinforcing social feedback; it may also, however, draw attention to behavioral deficits in a marital partner for whom the original problem was of functional value, and who will often require treatment in his own right.

In contrast to group therapy with clients with homogeneous sexual problems, as in the Schneidman and McGuire (1976) study (see also Kaplan, Kohl, Pomeroy, Offit, & Hogan, 1974, who treated premature ejaculators), Leiblum, Rosen, and Pierce (1976) have described the successful use of the group treatment format with couples with mixed sexual dysfunctions. The problems of this group included premature ejaculation, orgasmic dysfunction and secondary impotence. Following a 10 session modified Masters and Johnson program, five of the couples reported greatly improved functioning in terms of their sexual interaction and marital relationship. The one couple that failed to respond was marked by severe marital conflict from the outset. As in the Brady (1976a), Mathews et al. (1976), and Munjak et al. (1976) reports discussed above, marital discord appears to complicate the effective treatment of sexual difficulties.

Finally, the promising nature of these uncontrolled clinical reports suggests that group therapy with its obvious cost-effectiveness benefits be more systematically evaluated in controlled outcome studies.

Measurement and Modification of Penile Tumescence

The penile plethysmograph is clearly the most discriminating objective measurement of sexual responsiveness (cf. Barlow, 1977). However, there is evidence that penile tumescence in response to erotic material can be modified voluntarily under instructional control (e.g., Laws & Rubin, 1969). To the extent that penile tumescence is used to make judgments about sex offenders, this question of voluntary control or "faking" becomes an important issue. Quinsey and Bergersen (1976) investigated instructional control of penile tumescence in five normal males who received four tests of sexual preference in which their penile responses to slides that varied in age and gender were assessed. Two of the subjects were able to modify their penile responses significantly in the direction of the instructions, i.e., they increased their arousal to slides of young children while decreasing responsiveness to adult females. Quinsey and Bergersen observe that if normal subjects can voluntarily influence tumescence, there is no reason to believe that sex offenders cannot modify their responses in desired directions. While investigators involved in the assessment of deviant sexual behavior should be alert to this possibility, the data thus far indicate that child molesters, at any rate, do not "fake" their penile responses. For example, Quinsey, Steinman, Bergersen, and Holmes (1975) found that child molesters responded in the same manner as non-sex offender subjects in rating the sexual attractiveness of people, but were differentiated from normals in terms of their penile response to children.

The value of measures of penile tumescence in the assessment of sexual responsiveness among sex offenders has been clearly demonstrated by Abel, Barlow, Blanchard, and Guild (1977). Penile responses of rapists and non-rapists were monitored during audio descriptions of rape and non-aggressive sexual scenes. Only the rapists showed erections to rape descriptions. Moreover, this assessment procedure also discriminated those rapists that had the highest frequency of rape, those who had injured their victims, and those who had assaulted children.

The lack of correlation or desynchrony among verbal, physiological, and behavioral measures of fear has been well-documented (e.g., Borkovec, 1977; Lang, 1969; Rachman & Hodgson, 1974). Accordingly, it should not be too surprising to find that different measures of sexual responsiveness do not necessarily correlate with each other. Bancroft (1971), for example, obtained correlations between subjective estimates of sexual arousal and penile response to erotic pictures that ranged from 0 to 0.99.

Schaefer, Tregerthan, and Colgan (1976) had eight male subjects estimate their levels of erection while lying on their backs or sides. Penile tumescence was simultaneously monitored while subjects read either erotic or non-erotic material. Discrepancy between penile tumescence and subjective estimates of erection occurred at all levels of tumescence, with actual erection being consistently underestimated. Greater discrepancy was observed when subjects were reading non-erotic material. On the basis of this latter finding Schaefer et al. arrived at the following conclusion: "... it seems that subjects attend more strongly to psychological than to physiological cues when making... estimates. For example, estimates of 10 to 20% of total erection were not uncommon at 90% measured erection when non-erotic material was being read. If males *think* that they have an erection, they probably do; but they may also have one without realizing it" (p. 5). With respect to the measurement of sexual responsiveness in women using the vaginal photoplethysmograph, Wilson and Lawson (1976, 1977) showed that physiological measures did not correlate with subjective estimates, the latter being heavily influenced by psychological cues.

Different measures can be derived from the penile plethysmograph, including peak magnitude, latency to maximum arousal, and duration of various levels of tumescence. Quinsey and Harris (1976) found that peak magnitude, a relatively easy measure to take, was as useful as the more complicated area measure that incorporates all the parameters of the response—latency, recruitment, magnitude, and duration.

Penile tumescence in normal males can be significantly modified through instrumental conditioning procedures (cf. Rosen, 1973). There has been little research on the extension of biofeedback methods to cases of sexual dysfunction, however. Recently, Csillag (1976) reported the modification of erectile responses in six clients with primary and secondary impotence. All six clients showed significant improvement in erectile performance during the 16 biofeedback treatment sessions. Of potential clinical significance is the finding that the ability to achieve an erection apparently generalized from the laboratory setting to the clients' natural environment. Three clients were able to engage satisfactorily in sexual intercourse following treatment. One of the major difficulties with biofeedback procedures in general is the extent of generalization decrement that has been obtained across different target responses (Shapiro & Surwit, 1976). If the apparent generalizability of the instrumental conditioning of penile erection is replicated under better controlled circumstances, the results would carry theoretical as well as clinical significance.

Homosexual Behavior

Once the target of numerous attempts at modification using aversion conditioning and other behavioral methods, homosexuality tends to be conceptualized somewhat differently today. Specifically, the position has been taken that behavior therapists should not undertake to attempt heterosexual reorientation of homosexuals on the grounds that this implicitly endorses heterosexually biased views of homosexuals as "sick" people (cf. Davison, 1977). Less extreme statements have argued that heterosexual behavior is not necessarily the appropriate treatment goal for homosexuals, and that it is appropriate only for those clients who, with fully informed consent and cognizant of the different alternatives available to them, nevertheless wish to develop heterosexual skills and sexual responsiveness. Moreover it is recognized that improved homosexual adjustment is a legitimate goal of therapy (e.g., Bancroft, 1974; Wilson & Davison, 1974—reprinted in Franks & Wilson, 1975). Within this context, several treatment approaches for the alteration of sexual preferences in homosexuals have appeared during the past year.

Looking back over several years of research on the modification of homosexual orientation and behavior, McConaghy (1976) poses the question of whether homosexual orientation is irreversible. Summarizing the results of four major studies, McConaghy concludes that aversion therapies significantly reduced homosexual feelings and behavior, but failed to alter sexual orientation as defined by clients' penile tumescence responses to pictures of nude women. Although most subjects showed a statistically significant reduction in penile volume response to pictures of nude men, the reduction was relatively small. In all four studies over half the subjects continued to show penile responses indicative of a homosexual orientation after therapy.

McConaghy's interpretation of these data is curious. He suggests that "patients do not produce these changes consciously but that their motivation to show improvement with treatment may cause them to do so unconsciously" (p. 562). This unparsimonious "explanation" is, of course, no explanation at all. It would seem imprudent to rule out "conscious" motivation on the part of the subjects. We know that subjects can voluntarily inhibit erection (Laws & Rubin, 1969), and it is not difficult to understand why most subjects would wish to show decreased interest in nude male pictures. Aside from the general set to adhere to the demand characteristics of the therapeutic situation, many of the subjects McConaghy treated were in legal difficulties, and except for the fourth study, some had court sentences for sexual offenses pending. These subjects would seem particularly good candidates for "faking" reduced sexual interest in males.

McConaghy puzzles over the reason for the discrepancy between penile responses that failed to indicate much reduction in homosexual arousal and the greater reduction in homosexual feeling and behavior that was reported by subjects after treatment. But major questions about the adequacy of the measure of homosexual feeling and behavior can be raised. One problem is that these measures were derived from follow-up interviews. To quote McConaghy, "From their report at each interview of the amount of sexual interest they felt towards men and women and the amount and nature of their sexual fantasy and behaviour, an estimate was made of change in the patients' heterosexual and homosexual desire" (p. 557). It may be that subjects were reporting what they thought (or wished) the investigators to hear; the reason for the greater change on these subjective measures than on the more objective penile responses could well be that as global subjective measures, they are far more susceptible to "nonspecific" influences such as demand characteristics and suggestion (cf. Kazdin & Wilson, in press). McConaghy, however, dismisses an explanation of this sort, and advances a completely speculative interpretation account of aversion conditioning in largely discredited Pavlovian terms.

In contrast to McConaghy's findings, Freeman and Meyer (1975) have reported unusually successful results in the alteration of sexual preferences of male homosexuals. Nine homosexual clients who were either referred professionally or responded to a newspaper advertisement about the program were treated with a combination of electrical aversion conditioning and heterosexual conditioning over the course of 20 therapy sessions. In the latter, heterosexual slides (the conditioned stimulus) were paired systematically with attractive slides of attractive nude men (the unconditioned stimulus). Unlike previous studies on heterosexual conditioning of this nature, Freeman and Meyer claim to have produced sufficient conditioning to the point where a full erection was elicited by the heterosexual pictures (CS) alone by the end of therapy. This apparently successful classical conditioning of sexual arousal is significant in its own right. The fact that all nine clients reportedly maintained an exclusive heterosexual adjustment at a one year follow-up (18 months in seven of the cases) is of clinical significance. Perhaps the most remarkable aspect of this almost uniquely successful outcome is that four of the clients were "primary homosexuals" (Feldman & MacCulloch, 1971), i. .e, they had never experienced any heterosexual contact. Feldman and MacCulloch failed totally to modify the behavior of primary homosexuals, irrespective of the treatment used. Freeman and Meyer's results are quite unrepresentative of the behavior therapy literature on the treatment of homosexual behavior (cf. Bancroft, 1974), and it is plausible to assume that idiosyncratic client variables may have accounted for the results.

Ever since Davison's (1968) imaginative development of what was once, in more sexist times, described as "Playboy therapy" but is now referred to as *orgasmic reconditioning,* the procedure of pairing symbolic representation of desired sexual behavior with masturbation-induced orgasm has been one of the more popular behavioral techniques in the attempt to develop heterosexual responsiveness in homosexuals. Yet there is little in the way of empirical support for this technique. As Conrad and Wincze (1976) point out, the only evidence in its favor is flawed by one or more of the following problems: confounded treatment designs, lack of objective measurement, and exclusive reliance on self-report of behavior change.

Conrad and Wincze describe the treatment of four male homosexuals using orgasmic reconditioning with both psychophysiological and behavioral measures of outcome (the latter consisting of self-monitoring of daily sexual thoughts and behaviors). Although all four clients reported that their sexual adjustment had improved, their physiological and behavioral measures were unchanged. These findings are particularly troubling given that previous use has been dependent solely upon subjective reports of outcome. These results hardly demonstrate that the method is *not* a useful treatment method, but they do place the onus on behavioral investigators to demonstrate the efficacy of this widely favored technique in well-controlled studies.

Exemplifying many a multifaceted program for the treatment of homosexual behavior, Phillips, Fischer, Groves, and Singh (1976) emphasize a variety of procedures for developing heterosexual responsiveness rather than focusing on eliminating homosexual arousal. Featured among these techniques is orgasmic reconditioning, systematic desensitization, and assertion training.

Sexual Deviance and Problems of Gender Identity

Aversive behavior rehearsal is a technique for the treatment of exhibitionism in which the client is asked to expose himself in the treatment setting to people who know him. Providing valuable discussion of practical clinical procedures and concerns, Wickramasekera (1976) describes two variations of this procedure in the second paper in this Section. The one is an *in vivo* method, the other a vicarious procedure in which the client observes a videotape of another exhibitionist being treated with aversive behavior rehearsal. Wickramasekera reports that of 20 exhibitionists treated in this manner with only one to four sessions, all had ceased exposure completely in follow-ups ranging up to seven years. The brevity and apparent efficacy of this method are striking. Although there are those who object to such a method in principle on the grounds that it is "dehumanizing," little could be further from the truth provided appropriate informed consent procedures are scrupulously observed.

Consider, for example, the case of a client treated by one of the authors who had been a persistent exhibitionist for over 15 years, had failed to show any improvement after more than 10 years of psychodynamic psychotherapy, and had served six years in prison on account of his exhibitionism. Apprehended for exposing himself to juveniles, the client was due to receive a life sentence, at least in part because he was judged as incorrigible (diagnosed as such by at least one psychiatrist). In a case such as this, it would seem unethical and unprofessional conduct not to offer him the *choice* of treatment with a technique that is supported by at least some clinical evidence, albeit uncontrolled in nature. This is particularly true if what some interpret as more benign and less intrusive methods have already failed. Critics may sometimes lose sight of the consequences of *not* intervening in an effective manner.

Using a multiple baseline design, Brownell and Barlow (1976) demonstrated the treatment-specific effects of covert sensitization applied to an exhibitionist who also molested his step-daughter. Deviant sexual behavior was reduced only after it was the target of covert sensitization. The specificity of effect was further apparent from the fact that deviant sexual behavior was eliminated without affecting his sexual interaction with his wife and non-sexual contact with his step-daughter, both of which remained highly desirable. A problem with this study, however, is that the dependent measure consisted of self-report data. Although the authors suggest that self-report of sexual arousal is highly correlated with psychophysiological measures, the above (e.g., Conrad & Wincze, 1976; Schaefer et al., 1976) studies discussed demonstrate that this is not necessarily so.

In previous volumes in this Series (Franks & Wilson, 1975) we have discussed the problem of childhood cross-gender identification problems and the ethical and clinical issues they present. In further experimental investigations of this problem, Rekers, Yates, Willis, Rosen, and Taubman

(1976) demonstrated the successful change of childhood gender identity using pre-post assessment procedures. The mother of a five-year-old effeminate boy, identified as a high risk for adult transsexualism, was trained to reinforce "masculine" play behavior and to extinguish "feminine" play behavior in the clinic setting. Specifically, two cross-gender mannerisms were identified on the basis of videotape observation. These were 1) a flexed elbow, defined as standing with arms raised with a limp wrist; and 2) feminine running, defined as running with elbows flexed but arms turned away from the body with hands raised approximately to shoulder level. Specific fading procedures were employed to facilitate generalization of the more masculine behavior to situations in which the boy's mother was not physically present. The diagnosis at a 25 month follow-up was that the child was effeminate but not a gender identity problem.

The reliable differentiation between gender-identity problems and normal behavior of children is of crucial importance in therapy of this sort. Rekers and Yates (1976) have shown that the systematic observation of free sex-typed play of children between the ages of three and eight years can discriminate between normal and gender-identity of "feminoid" boys. The behavior of the feminoid boys was not significantly different from that of girls at that age. An important element of this procedure appears to be the play of the child when he is alone. Rekers (1975) found that only when the child was alone was sex-type play reliably correlated with the diagnosis of cross-gender identification.

MARITAL DISHARMONY

Until the 1970s the behavioral literature on the assessment and treatment of marital conflict was limited to one or two uncontrolled clinical reports. Within the last several years, however, there has been an upsurge in interest in behavioral marital therapy, and some significant research programs have been initiated. In our commentary in last year's volume on Greer and D'Zurilla's (1975—reprinted in Franks & Wilson, 1976) review of the area, we concluded that marital behavior therapy was characterized by numerous inadequacies, including anecdotal case reports, limited assessment of therapeutic effects, and poorly designed outcome studies, the absence of generalization and follow-up data (see also Commentary, Section X). Since then, at least four different reviews of behavioral approaches to marital discord and conflict have appeared (Glisson, 1976; Gurman & Kniskern, 1977; Jacobson & Martin, 1976; Patterson, Weiss, & Hops, 1976).

That the state of the art of behavioral marital therapy has not changed appreciably from our prior appraisal is evident from all four reviews. Patterson et al. (1976), for example, state that the area is, in the Kuhnian sense, a *pre*scientific one, with research designed to investigate marital interaction limited in both quality and quantity. Jacobson and Martin (1976) provide a comprehensive review and searching evaluation of the problems and progress in the field, particularly with respect to outcome data. Stuart (1969) reported follow-up data on behavioral marital therapy that indicated continuing improvement, but the lack of a control group and exclusive reliance on possibly unreliable self-report data render his findings suggestive at best. Jacobson and Martin observe that the research program of Patterson, Weiss and their associates at the Oregon Research Institute represents the most thorough investigation of behavioral assessment and treatment of marital conflict to date. This group has developed an important objective measure of marital interaction in the laboratory—the Marital Interaction Coding System (MICS). In this coding system interactions between partners are assessed on two dimensions: a rewardingness dimension or the degree to which the spouses emit rewarding rather than punishing actions toward each other; and a problem-solving dimension in which the efficiency of marital communication in solving mutual problems is evaluated. Both verbal and nonverbal responses are videotaped and reliably coded under a number of operationally defined categories. Specific changes have been demonstrated on the MICS following a broad behavioral intervention program. However, both Gurman and Kniskern (in press) and Jacobson and Martin point out that some of the changes obtained could be construed as negative or what Strupp and Hadley (1977) would refer to as deterioration effects. Although this group has collected follow-up data (Patterson, Hops, & Weiss, 1975), the lack of control groups and the fact that the follow-up data are based entirely on global self-reports obtained by telephone or mail suggest considerable caution in interpreting the results (cf. Patterson et al., 1976).

Azrin, Naster, and Jones (1973—reprinted in Franks & Wilson, 1975) asserted that their study was the first to validate experimentally a behavioral treatment approach to marital conflict. However, this study has been severely criticized (e.g., Cochrane & Sobol, 1976; Jacobson & Martin, 1976). In this study, couples received three weeks of a placebo treatment ("catharsis counseling") prior to a four week behavioral program. Jacobson and Martin point out that the credibility of the placebo treatment was not assessed, that the sole dependent measure was a global self-report estimate of marital happiness, and that behavioral treatment was confounded with order effects. In effect, the Azrin et al. study was a series of replicated AB designs that do not allow the determination of cause-effect relationships.

Jacobson's study (cited in Jacobson & Martin, 1976) comparing a behavioral treatment program similar to that used by the Oregon group with minimal treatment and waiting list control groups is more convincing. A particularly informative feature of this outcome study was the incorporation of a series of replicated single-subject experiments within the context of the overall between-groups design. In addition to general dependent measures that formed the basis for group comparisons, each couple monitored two specific target behaviors that were modified according to a multiple baseline design. The behavioral treatment resulted in significantly greater improvement in marital interaction as assessed by the MICS and self-report data. Neither generalization nor follow-up information is reported. The fact that Jacobson and Martin were led to conclude that this unpublished study, at least at the time their review was written, was the "only clinical study to date in evaluation of behavior change procedures for married couples which has employed a control group" (p. 549), is a significant commentary on the field in its own right.

Jacobson and Martin distinguish between the studies referred to above and what they designate as "analogue studies." The latter are said to be "analogue" research for two main reasons: a) subjects are couples recruited from the general population who are not necessarily distressed; and b) intervention methods have been directed towards one isolated target behavior rather than attempting to increase the overall level of satisfaction in the relationship. Laboratory studies of this sort have demonstrated that behavioral procedures such as positive reinforcement and simple charting and recording of interactions between spouses can effectively alter target interpersonal behavior. Reviewing all the research on the evaluation of behavioral marital therapy, Jacobson and Martin reach the following conclusion: "although not conclusive, [these studies] strongly suggest the efficacy of a treatment approach combining contingency contracting with direct training of communication skills in the clinical setting.... Furthermore, there is suggestive evidence that either of the two main components of this approach can be of some benefit when used alone . . ." (pp. 552-553). Similarly, Gurman and Kniskern (in press) conclude that there is suggestive evidence that behavioral treatment of marital conflict is effective. Interestingly, Gurman and Kniskern also conclude that this evidence in favor of behavioral interventions is no more compelling than that which supports non-behavioral couples' therapy. Indeed, they suggest that the latter is more persuasive, in part because of the emphasis in behavioral studies on so-called "analogue" research. A discussion of the relative merits of "analogue" research is beyond the scope of the present commentary—but see Bandura (1977a) and Kazdin and Wilson (in press).

The third paper reprinted in this Section—by Liberman, Levine, Wheeler, Sanders, and Wallace—is a rare exception to Jacobson and Martin's finding of the absence of outcome studies with a control group. In this instance, behavioral treatment was compared with an alternative treatment in a comparative outcome study. Despite the small size of the subject samples, the Liberman et al. study represents an impressive demonstration of the efficacy of behavioral treatment methods. The inclusion of follow-up data is one of its commendable features. Another is the assessment of outcome using multiple objective and self-report measures. The results, showing a significant difference on direct observational data but not on the self-report data, assume special importance in view of the exclusive reliance on self-report data in previous behavioral studies describing follow-up data (e.g., Azrin et al., 1973; Patterson et al., 1975; Stuart, 1969). Other noteworthy features of the study are Liberman et al.'s analysis of the behavioral treatment program as a cost-effective, feasible approach in typical community clinic settings and their discussion of possible therapist bias. The fact that only the direct behavioral and not self-report measures of outcome differentiated between the two groups indicates that the difference is not attributable to demand characteristics or any other "nonspecific" effect associated with the therapists. Rather, it provides discriminant validity for the efficacy of the specific behavioral procedures.

With multiple measures one would not be surprised to learn that specific methods may have different effects on different measures. Thus, Gurman and Kniskern, in their analysis of the Liberman et al. study, assert that "deterioration effects" were noted for the behavioral treatment program on two dependent measures (number of "pleases" and "marital activities"), and on one ("marital activities") for the interactional treatment. With respect to the marital activities, both treatment groups reported decreases in overall frequency from the month prior to treatment to the last month of treatment. However, this figure has to be interpreted in the context of both groups expressing less desire for change in the frequency of marital activities at the end of treatment. It appears arbitrary to categorize the decrease in frequency as a deterioration effect, and other interpretations are at least as plausible.

Finally, the Jacobson and Martin and Patterson et al. reviews of the behavioral marital therapy literature are primarily focused on specific treatment models and techniques and their empirical and clinical evaluation. Glisson (1976) makes the argument that additional theory testing and development have been relatively ignored to the detriment of the field. His position is considered more fully in the Commentary to Section X of the present volume.

DEPRESSION

The last paper to be reprinted in this Section is Eastman's critical evaluation of behavioral formulations of depression. Depression is one of the most common of the behavior disorders, but it remains poorly understood. Somewhat surprisingly, behavioral investigations of depressive reactions have been relatively sparse in number and, for the most part, very rudimentary in nature. Eastman's analysis of behavioral formulations leaves no doubt as to their numerous inadequacies. In general, they are imprecisely stated such that they are untestable. Thus, while views such as Lazarus' (1968) have been undeniably heuristic in prompting further investigation, their scientific value is limited. Eastman's own synthesis is, of course, quite speculative, and it remains to be seen whether his attempt to state testable propositions serves as a useful basis for research.

Several other problems with what—with the exception of Seligman's learned helplessness model—are inchoate behavioral formulations are noted by Eastman. These include sloppy conceptualizations of anxiety and its role in the development and maintenance of depression, the absence of controlled research, and the reliance on anecdotal case studies in much of the behavioral dialogue on depression thus far. The only systematic research on depression has been restricted mainly to animal studies and Seligman's studies with less than severely depressed college students. Interestingly, Eastman fails to refer to Beck's (1967, 1976) theory and research on depression. Although Beck himself describes his theory and consequent therapy as "cognitive," his concepts and methods are increasingly being included under the broad rubric of "cognitive behavior modification" (cf. Mahoney & Arnkoff, in press; Wilson, in press d). The ultimate goal of cognitive therapy is the development of rational, adaptive thought patterns. Cognitive therapy progresses through the following phases:

a. clients become aware of their thoughts;
b. they learn to identify inaccurate or distorted thoughts;
c. these inaccurate thoughts are replaced by accurate, more objective cognitions;
d. therapist feedback and reinforcement are a necessary part of this process.

The specific procedures used to accomplish these therapeutic objectives are both behavioral and cognitive in nature. The former include the prescription of an explicit activity schedule, graded tasks aimed at providing success experiences, and various homework assignments. The latter include techniques such as "distancing" and "decentering." Distancing is the process of regarding thoughts objectively. Decentering is the ability to separate oneself from the occurrence and impact of external events.

Beck's cognitive theory of depression has much to recommend it. Unlike most of the behavioral formulations reviewed by Eastman, Beck's theory is clearly stated and scientifically testable. Most importantly, Beck and his colleagues have conducted a well-controlled comparative outcome study of cognitive (behavior) therapy versus imipramine, the pharmacological treatment that is widely considered to be the treatment of choice with depressives (Rush, Beck, Kovacs, & Hollon, 1977). Cognitive (behavior) therapy resulted in significantly greater improvement at a long-term follow-up. Moreover, Rush et al.'s study showed that imipramine treatment was associated with a significantly greater dropout rate during therapy. The details of this impressive study will be consideerd in greater detail in next year's volume in this series.

Eastman emphasizes a particularly important point that is overlooked in many behavioristic formulations, namely that the *"meaning that the frequency and type of behavior have for the individual is crucial"* (emphasis added). An exclusive preoccupation with overt behavior is simply insufficient for accounting for the phenomena of depression. Eastman indicates that frequency of behavior alone is not necessarily related directly to levels of depression, and it is a commonplace clinical observation that certain individuals report moderate to severe depression even though to the objective onlooker they appear quite competent and successful. Specifically, the individual's perception of his or her functioning may be more fundamental than actual overt behavior. Yet until Beck's and Seligman's contributions, little if any attempt was made to pay serious attention to cognitive factors. As Seligman, Klein, and Miller (1976) conclude in their review of depression, the cognitive theorists such as Beck "have shown a refreshing disinclination to engage in etiological speculation and have contributed a great deal to descriptions of thinking in depression, an area that has been neglected by both psychoanalysts and behaviorists for too long. Their work must play an integral role in any comprehensive theory of depression" (p. 174).

Seligman et al. provide an evaluation of several different treatment approaches to depression. A telling comment on psychotherapy is that no controlled studies comparing its efficacy with alternative treatment methods (e.g., cognitive or drug therapy) or even with no treatment have been reported. The inclusion of a no treatment control group seems especially important in view of Seligman et al.'s observation that psychotherapy is usually a long-term treatment whereas most forms of depressive reactions are often short-term disorders. However, Seligman et al.'s appraisal of behavioral treatments is equally sobering: ". . . all of the studies to date have been case studies . . . the lack of sufficient numbers of subjects, the lack of control groups, the use of therapists and patients as raters of improvement, and the lack of adequate follow-up preclude the evaluation of the effectiveness of these procedures" (p. 184).

Seligman's learned helplessness model of depression is well-known, and is discussed in Eastman's review. In short, the essence of Seligman's position is that the symptoms, etiology, cure, and prevention of learned helplessness parallel those of depression. This schema is presented in Table 1.

Eastman has pointed out that predictions from the learned helplessness model have been tested on animals and with college students. It is currently fashionable to denigrate or even dismiss entirely the results of laboratory investigations using subjects recruited for the purpose of the study. Such research is often referred to as "analogue research." Suffice it to say that many of the objections raised in connection with laboratory studies are equally pertinent to clinical studies, and that, in several instances, laboratory studies confer unique advantages over tests in the applied clinical arena (see Kazdin & Wilson, in press). Moreover, a standardized laboratory paradigm for testing the effect of a particular intervention—such as Klein and Seligman's (1975) use of success experiences to reverse the impact of learned helplessness—seems to be an invaluable first step in identifying important mechanisms of behavior change. Instead of being preoccupied with whether these subjects are "real patients," as whether their depression is the "real" clinical depression, investigators could, as Seligman et al. suggest, profitably employ the labora-

TABLE 1

Learned Helplessness	Depression
Symptoms	
1. Passivity.	1. Passivity.
2. Difficulty learning that responses produce relief.	2. Negative cognitive set.
3. Dissipates in time.	3. Time course.
4. Lack of aggression.	4. Introjected hostility.
5. Weight loss, anorexia, social and sexual deficits.	5. Weight loss, anorexia, social and sexual deficits.
6. Norepinephrine depletion and cholinergic activity.	6. Norepinephrine depletion.
7. Ulcers and stress.	7. Ulcers(?),[a] cholinergic activity and stress (?).
	8. Feelings of helplessness.
Cause	
Learning that responding and reinforcement are independent.	Belief that responding is useless.
Cure	
1. Directive therapy: forced exposure to responding producing reinforcement.	1. Recovery of belief that responding produces reinforcement.
2. Electroconvulsive shock.	2. Electroconvulsive shock.
3. Time.	3. Time.
4. Anticholinergics and norepinephrine stimulants (?).	4. Norepinephrine stimulants and anticholinergics (?).
Prevention	
Inoculation with mastery over reinforcement.	(?)[a]

a "?" means "unknown." Reprinted from Seligman, Klein & Miller (1976).

tory paradigm to compare the relative effects of different change strategies on the phenomena of learned helplessness.

Any viable explanation of depression will have to account for the fact that some individuals become depressed following apparent successful attainment of desired goals, such as a promotion, or newfound wealth. The learned helplessness model can accommodate this phenomenon by postulating that these successful people become depressed because they perceive that they are being rewarded independently of their behavior—the reinforcement is noncontingent or uncontrollable. In a partial test of this prediction, Benson and Kennelly (1976) compared the performance of subjects exposed to uncontrollable aversive stimuli and uncontrollable positive outcomes. Whereas uncontrollable aversive stimuli produced learned helplessness as predicted by Seligman, uncontrollable reinforcements did not.

Regardless of the ultimate fate of the learned helplessness model—only continued experimental research will determine this—it has served a valuable heuristic function in generating new ideas and encouraging research efforts. Aside from its relevance to clinical behavior therapy and depressive reactions, the learned helplessness model has an important bearing on long-standing theoretical issues in the field of learning. Learned helplessness is a cognitive theory of learning and challenges existing stimulus-response (S-R) models. Levis (1976) is quick to emphasize that the learned helplessness model has fulfilled these functions, and, restricting himself to the animal conditioning studies, offers an alternative S-R interpretation. However, the importance of cognitive factors in the assessment and modification of human depression seems impossible to deny, as we have mentioned above, and the role of cognitive concepts in explanations of behavior change has received persuasive empirical support (e.g., Bandura, 1977a, 1977b). The cognitive nature of the learned helplessness model is in line with this more recent conceptual emphasis in behavior therapy.

Finally, Coyne (1976b) has proposed an interactional description of depression. According to this conceptualization, the depressed person's social environment is a critical factor in maintaining depressed behavior. This view is close to that of Lewinsohn and his colleagues (Lewinsohn, 1974) who hold that the depressed individual's lack of social skills is a key factor in the development of depression. Coyne suggests that the apparent behavioral deficits of depressed persons are due to the fact that other people in the depressed person's social environment are unwilling to interact with them and that depressed persons do not have the necessary skills to overcome this. Coyne (1976a) had normal subjects engage in a telephone conversation with either a depressed patient, a nondepressed patient, or a normal patient. Subjects who had spoken to the depressed patient were subsequently more depressed, anxious, and rejecting themselves. In terms of social learning theory, with its emphasis on reciprocal determinism, behavior, including depressive reactions, is a function not only of its environmental consequences but also of the person's social skills and the manner in which external events are centrally mediated. An interactional view is fundamental, but more complex than Coyne suggests (see Bandura, 1977b).

SECTION VII: SEXUAL DISORDERS, MARITAL DISHARMONY, AND DEPRESSION

16

THE BEHAVIORAL TREATMENT OF SEXUAL INADEQUACY: A COMPARATIVE STUDY

Andrew Mathews, John Bancroft, Antonia Whitehead, Ann Hackmann, David Julier, Judy Bancroft, Dennis Gath and Phyllis Shaw

University Department of Psychiatry, The Warneford Hospital, Oxford, England

Summary — Thirty-six couples complaining of sexual difficulties were treated with one of three methods: (1) systematic desensitization plus counselling, (2) directed practice—based on that of Masters and Johnson—plus counselling, (3) directed practice with minimal contact. Both members of each couple were seen together, but half in each treatment group were treated by a single therapist and half by a therapist pair. Differences in outcome among the groups were not highly significant, but consistent trends were found which suggested that the combination of directed practice and counselling was associated with most change, particularly when two therapists were involved.

Since the publication of "Human Sexual Inadequacy" (Masters & Johnson, 1970) there has been a marked increase in optimism and en-

Reprinted with permission from *Behaviour Research and Therapy*, 1976, Vol. 14, 427-436.

thusiasm for the treatment of sexual dysfunction in couples. Masters & Johnson base their report on the treatment of nearly 800 patients, 300 of whom had been followed up for five years, and they claim success rates considerable in excess of previous reports, the lowest being that of 60-70 percent for impotence. However, in the absence of any objectively defined criteria of success, or controlled comparison with alternative treatments, it is difficult to be certain to what extent their high success rates may be an artefact of the assessment procedure or self-selection of patients, and to what extent they reflect a significant advance in treatment techniques (Laughren & Kass, 1975). The present study was planned as a controlled evaluation of a modified version, more suitable for ordinary national health service clinics, and at the same time as a preliminary investigation of the part played by the different components of this treatment. We distinguished between two main components, one of which can be called "directed practice" and the other "counselling." The first, directed practice, is described by Masters & Johnson in some detail and includes general guidelines for giving and receiving pleasure, as well as techniques tailored to specific problems. The "counselling" component is less clearly described, although it is said to be of importance in changing attitudes that block the directed practice. The relative importance of these two components is of both theoretical and clinical interest.

The three methods used in the present study were chosen to contrast these two components used separately and in combination. One treatment included both components, within our N.H.S. clinic modification, using once-weekly visits. Another contained the directed practice component, but counselling was minimized by using a "correspondence course" approach with instructions sent by post. As it was not considered practical to use counselling alone, the remaining treatment combined counselling with systematic desensitization. This last treatment thus allows a comparison of directed practice with an alternative behavioral approach, both in combination with counselling. In summary, the three treatments consisted of (1) systematic desensitization with counselling, (2) directed practice with counselling and (3) directed practice with minimal counselling.

In all treatments both partners of a dysfunctional couple were involved, as the directed practice techniques could not be applied to a single patient. It remained possible to investigate the need for a dual-sex therapist team, which is emphasized by Masters & Johnson. Since the use of two therapists doubles the cost in professional time, it seemed worthwhile to test whether two therapists achieved better results than one in any of the treatments investigated.

METHOD

Design of the Study

Patients presenting for treatment of sexual difficulties, with partners willing to participate in treatment, were allocated at random to one of three treatment procedures and to either one or two therapists, within a balanced factorial design. The members of each couple were first interviewed and their difficulties rated by one of two psychiatrists who remained blind throughout to treatment and to therapist. The screening psychiatrist decided which member of the couple appeared to be the main complainant (i.e. had the greater degree of sexual dysfunction) and the sex of the main complainant was balanced across treatments and therapists. Where couples were assigned to one therapist, the therapist was of the same sex as the main complainant.

The first meeting with the therapists was scheduled for about four weeks after screening and assessment to allow time for a baseline period of self-assessment using diaries of sexual behavior. Treatment began similarly in all treatments, with a detailed sexual history taken from each partner separately, followed by a round table discussion involving both partners together. Physical examinations were arranged to take place between the first and second visits; in the case of female patients this took place at a nearby family planning clinic so that any contraceptive problems could also be dealt with at this point.

The different treatments then began, either with once-weekly visits to the Department, or with a weekly exchange of letters, and continued for a further ten weeks. At the end of this time a further four weeks elapsed before each couple was seen again by the independent psychiatric assessor, and a final interview with assessor and then therapist (s) was scheduled after a further three months, making a total follow-up period of four months.

Patients

Thirty-six couples were included, 18 of whom were classified as primarily male problems, and 18 as female. Of the male complainants, 13 had experienced some erectile failure and 12 had some degree of premature ejaculation, with 8 patients reporting both. Ejaculatory incompetence occurred in only one patient. With the female complainants, failure to experience orgasm was common (13 patients), in contrast to vaginismus, with only one case in the sample. The most typical complaint was that of generally low interest in, and arousal by sexual relations, occurring to some degree in 17 out of the 18 female complainants. The husbands of the female complainants reported fewer sexual difficulties themselves; only 3 had experienced erectile failure in appropriate circumstances, although 8 had some premature ejaculation. Wives of male complainants, on the other hand, were more severely affected: all 18 had some orgasmic difficulty, and 13 had some lack of sexual interest or arousal. Couples with the man as the main complainant were older (see Table 1) and had co-habited correspondingly longer, although the mean duration of the problem (5.2 years, range 1-22) was not different. About two thirds of all the patients had experienced a more satisfactory relationship previously; in half of the total this was with the present partner.

Twenty-three of the 36 couples were referred from G.P.'s, and the rest from Family Planning Clinics and the Marriage Guidance Council, as well as psychiatrists and physicians in the region. A few individuals (9 out of the total of 72) were being currently treated for some other psychological disturbance, usually with minor tranquilizers, and in all, 17 had been so treated at any time. Women were more likely to have been treated than were men (see Table 1).

Screening of Patients and Preparation for Treatment

On referral, all couples were interviewed by one of the two independent psychiatrists, who took both a general and sexual history from both partners separately, and ensured that selection criteria were met. In addition to making ratings of the present relationship and giving some pencil and paper tests, the independent assessor asked both partners to keep a diary of sexual contact over the next three-week period; couples were also given a written description of the time course and general principles of treatment, but this did not mention specific procedures.

Patients Not Completing Treatment

Of the patients who were seen during the period of study but were not included among the 36 couples treated, 9 attended but were considered unsuitable or refused treatment and 7 entered treatment but did not complete it. In the case of the 9 couples who attended but did not enter treatment, the most common reason was that the problem did not seem

Table 1. Means of pre-treatment variables showing significant pre-treatment differences between male and female complainant couples

	Male complainant couples		Female complainant couples	
Partner	Male	Female	Male	Female
Age (yr)	38.3	35.7	32.2	28.0
Length of co-habitation (yr)	13.3		6.4	
Frequency of other disturbance	3	4	1	9

to be primarily a sexual one, but rather general marital disharmony or some other psychological disturbance. Of the 7 couples who started but did not complete treatment, 2 separated during the study, 4 reported difficulties in meeting requirements for home practice, and one patient was thought too depressed to continue.

Therapists

There were six therapists, three male and three female, all being either clinical psychologists or psychiatrists. They were divided into dual-sex teams and each team treated at least one couple before the main study to familiarize them with working together in carrying out treatment procedures. Before and during the study, all therapists met regularly on a weekly basis to discuss problems arising from treatment, and to help in keeping procedures constant across therapists.

Treatments

Manuals were prepared giving an outline of desensitization and practice instructions, together with aims and limits of counselling discussion, while leaving therapists some freedom to alter the emphasis to suit individual needs. All treatments began with one session of history taking, which concentrated on sexual development, history of the problem, and current sexual attitudes and behavior. In the second session a week later, the "round table discussion," the therapist(s) attempted to summarize and integrate the account given by both partners, and to resolve any discrepancies. Once an agreed account was achieved, the therapist(s) continued by giving a brief descriptive explanation of possible causes of the problem, emphasizing the attitudes and behavior brought by both partners to the relationship, rather than the responsibility of either partner alone. Couples were reassured that given the right conditions the sexual dysfunction was reversible, and the specific procedures to be employed were described and discussed.

Treatment 1—Systematic Desensitization Plus Counselling

In the second session or "round table discussion" the principles of systematic desensitization and hierarchy formation were explained and the couple were asked to prepare hierarchies before the next session. The early sessions thereafter were mainly concerned with training in relaxation and desensitization, and whenever possible, this was carried out with both partners using a joint hierarchy of sexual situations. Desensitization could be carried out separately with non-overlapping items, or if one partner was making slower progress, the other was sometimes involved in a "helping" role (e.g. by presenting imaginal items). The couple were asked to practice relaxation at home and to repeat the imaginal desensitization that had taken place during treatment sessions. They were encouraged to set aside time for regular physical contact, but to limit their sexual behavior to those items that had been successfully "desensitized." In the last few sessions the imaginal desensitization was mainly carried out by the patients at home, the sessions with the therapist being principally used for general sexual counselling and discussion of problems that had arisen at home during desensitization practice. Any attitudes or beliefs that emerged as relevant or obstructive to progress were discussed, and attempts made to modify them using the counselling approach. Emphasis was always laid on the importance of free communication of sexual feelings between partners.

Treatment 2—Directed Practice Plus Counselling

At the second session (round table discussion) a complete ban was placed on intercourse and genital stimulation and instructions* (termed "sensate focus" by Masters & Johnson) were given for pleasuring by caressing other body parts. These instructions were first discussed, and were then given in a standard written form so that the couple could take them away. This first stage required each partner to alternate in actively caressing or passively receiving caresses, while avoiding specifically sexual areas. The second stage, usually given on week two, included instructions to guide the partner's hand during pleasuring, and from week three onwards, contingent on satisfactory reports of progress, therapists went on to add further stages related to the specific problem. In the case of premature ejaculation for example, the woman was instructed to stimulate the man's genitals gently, to stop immediately on his signal that ejaculation was close, and then "squeeze" the penis by opposing finger and thumb on either side of the coronal ridge. In the case of erectile impotence or lack of genital sexual response in the woman, instructions for "non-threatening" genital caressing with lotions were given, each partner guiding the other's hand to produce the most pleasurable sensations.

The couple were usually advised to adopt the "female superior" posi-

* Available from the first author on request.

tion in later stages and gradually progress to penile insertion and intercourse when appropriate.

Counselling took the same form as in Treatment 1 and as far as possible the time available for discussion was similar, with generally more time devoted to it in the later sessions.

Treatment 3—Directed Practice with Minimum Contact

The first two treatment sessions took the same form as that described previously, but at the end of the second interview couples were told that only occasional visits to the clinic would be necessary and week-by-week instructions would be sent by post. Thereafter the only contact with the couples was one mid-treatment visit (i.e. the seventh week of treatment) and one end-of-treatment visit, each lasting about forty minutes. Between these, instructions for directed practice were sent every week, together with a letter, signed by the therapist(s), containing brief comments, specific suggestions, and a set of questions about practice sessions, to be completed and returned at the end of the week. During the mid- and end-of-treatment visits, discussions concerned practical problems arising from practice; therapists avoided all discussions of attitudes or more general sexual feelings.

Measures

Ratings of general and sexual relationship were completed by the independent psychiatrist before and after treatment, and at follow-up, using a five-point scale from completely satisfactory (1) to completely unsatisfactory (5), similar to those previously described by Gelder and Marks (1966). Partners were then asked to rate themselves and their spouses on a semantic differential (to be reported elsewhere) and to fill in a questionnaire concerning intercourse and love-making frequency over the previous three months. This included questions about any difficulties encountered in erection, ejaculation, discomfort during penetration, lubrication and orgasm.

Therapists completed similar ratings to those made by the independent assessor from their own notes made at the beginning and end of treatment, four weeks later (pre) or earlier (post) than the assessor, so that only at follow-up were these ratings directly comparable. Reliability data for assessor and therapist are given in Table 2. Most reliability figures are acceptable, with the notable exception of assessor-therapist disagreement on amount of change in the general relationship rating. Therapists also made five-point ratings of a number of specific areas of sexual function, but only some of these scales subsequently showed a satisfactory range of scores. The scales analyzed were, for the male partner, enjoyment of sexual activity, erection (impotence) and premature ejaculation; for the female partner, enjoyment of sexual activity, interest in and arousal during sexual activity and orgasmic capability.

Self-report diaries were completed separately for the three weeks before assessment, to indicate the frequency and satisfaction derived by each partner from three behavioral categories of sexual contact: non-intimate but affectionate, intimate caressing, and sexual intercourse. In the event it proved difficult to obtain complete records on this measure from all patients, and the results were not analyzed. Instead, each partner was asked to complete a five-point rating scale of the present state of both general and sexual relationship and the extent of improvement from worse (—1) to very much improved (3), at post-treatment and follow-up.

RESULTS

Analysis

Outcome measures were analyzed using an analysis of covariance suitable for a factorial design, unless the distribution of scores made this unsuitable, when a non-parametric median test was applied to change scores from each treatment group. Otherwise, separate analyses were conducted at post-treatment and follow-up, using the pre-treatment score as a co-variate, so that the influence of pre-treatment status on outcome was removed statistically. The factorial design allowed the examination of possible effects due to treatment, to therapist number (single same sex, or dual-sex team), to the sex of the main complainant, and to the interaction between these three factors.

Ratings of General and Sexual Relationship

No significant differences between treatments were found, either at post-treatment or at follow-up, on covariance analysis of independent assessors' or therapists' ratings, or patients' own self ratings of general and sexual relationship. The assessors' ratings of sexual relationship are shown in graph form in Figure 1, and it can be seen that the mean change in Treatment 2 (directed practice with counselling) is approximately twice that in Treatment 1 (desensitization with counselling). The lack of significance of this difference suggests great variation of response within the treatments, and this is illustrated in Table 3. Both treatments

Table 2. Means (and standard deviations) of independent assessors' and therapists' ratings for general and sexual relationship and inter-rater reliability, at each occasion of measurement

General relationship Ratings (1–5)	Pre-treatment	Post-treatment	Follow-up	Change Pre–F.U.
Independent Assessor	1.58 (0.68)	1.79 (0.88)	1.97 (1.08)	0.39 (0.94)
Therapist (Same sex)	2.15 (1.12)	1.67 (0.93)	1.88 (1.12)	0.28 (0.78)
Reliability Ass. × Th.	0.42	0.58	0.63	0.15
Reliability Th. × Th.	0.85	0.95	0.91	0.91
Sexual relationship Ratings (1–5)	**Pre-treatment**	**Post-treatment**	**Follow-up**	**Change Pre–F.U.**
Independent Assessor	4.10 (0.67)	2.99 (1.43)	3.13 (1.61)	0.97 (1.38)
Therapist (same sex)	3.94 (0.92)	2.99 (1.44)	3.01 (1.59)	0.93 (1.39)
Reliability Ass. × Th.	0.65	0.86	0.95	0.82
Reliability Th. × Th.	0.79	0.95	0.99	0.92

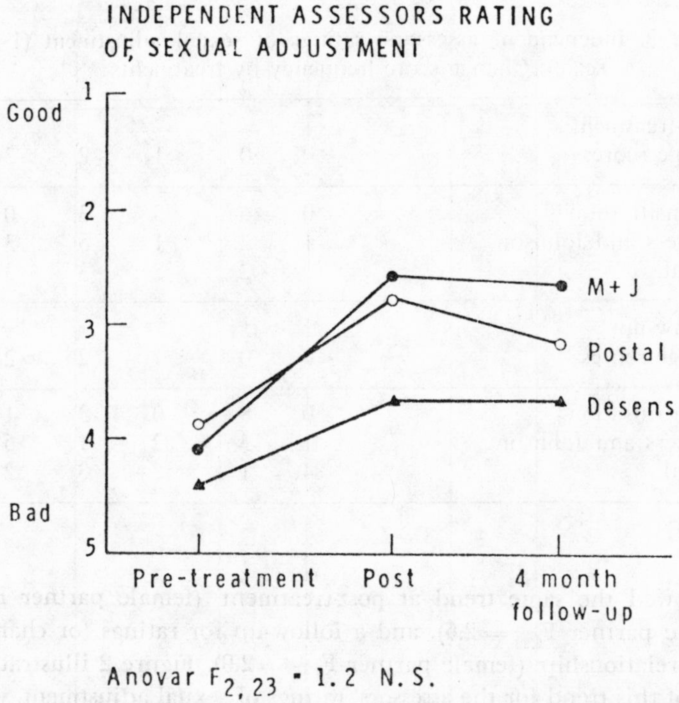

FIGURE 1. Mean sexual adjustment ratings made by the independent assessor at pre-treatment, post-treatment, and follow-up, for each treatment group.

using directed practice as described by Masters & Johnson seem to be associated with wider variation in response than the desensitization based treatment. In particular it is noticeable that the postal form of directed practice seems to be associated with a greater number of couples getting worse or relapsing on follow-up.

Examination of the possible differences due to therapist effect, the sex of the main complainant, or interactions between these factors and treatment group, also failed to show clearly significant results. However, some consistent trends emerged, which taken individually could not be considered significant, but which in combination appear more convincing.

Interactions between treatment group and number of therapists at between the 5% and 10% levels were found for the independent assessors' ratings of sexual relationship at post-treatment ($F_{2,23} = 2.5$) and at follow-up ($F_{2,23} = 3.1$). The patient's rating of change in sexual relation-

Table 3. Independent assessors' ratings of sexual adjustment (1–5 scale): Change score frequency by treatments

Post-treatment change scores	<0	0	⩽1	⩽2	>2
Desensitisation	0	6	3	3	0
Masters and Johnson	1	2	1	5	3
Postal	2	2	2	3	3
Follow-up change scores	<0	0	⩽1	⩽2	>2
Desensitisation	0	8	0	3	1
Masters and Johnson	1	3	2	1	5
Postal	4	1	2	3	2

ship showed the same trend at post-treatment (female partner $F_{2,23} = 2.9$; male partner $F_{2,23} = 2.6$), and a follow-up for ratings for change in general relationship (female partner $F_{2,23} = 2.9$). Figure 2 illustrates the nature of this trend for the assessors' ratings of sexual adjustment, which, taken with the other results, is consistent with the conclusion that the outcome of directed practice with counselling (Treatment 2) is enhanced by the use of a dual-sex therapy team, unlike either of the other treatments.

There was also a tendency for couples from which the woman had been judged the main complainant, to rate their own sexual relationship at follow-up to be worse than couples in whom the man had been considered the main complainant (male partner, $F_{1,23} = 2.8$; female partner, $F_{1,23} = 3.8$). This was in agreement with therapist ratings of follow-up sexual adjustment which also favored male complainant couples ($F_{1,23} = 3.0$).

Therapist Ratings of Sexual Function

Unlike pre-treatment measures of general and sexual relationship, ratings of specific sexual functions, as might be expected, did show pre-treatment differences associated with the sex of the main complainant. Among the men, those who had been designated as main complainants tended to be rated as enjoying sexual contact less ($F_{1,24} = 4.8$, $p < 0.05$)

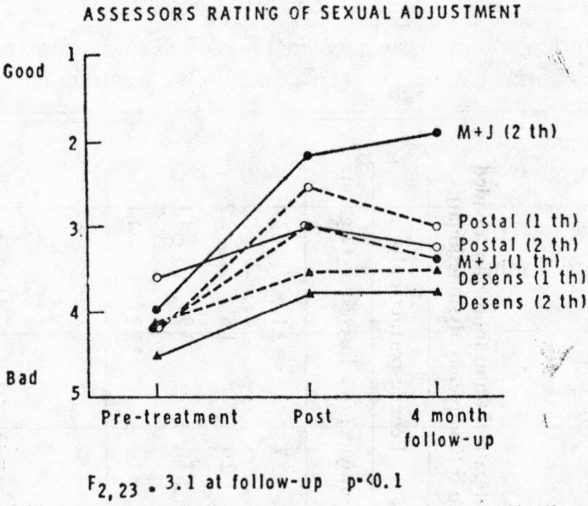

FIGURE 2. Mean sexual adjustment ratings made by the independent assessor, divided by treatment group and number of therapists.

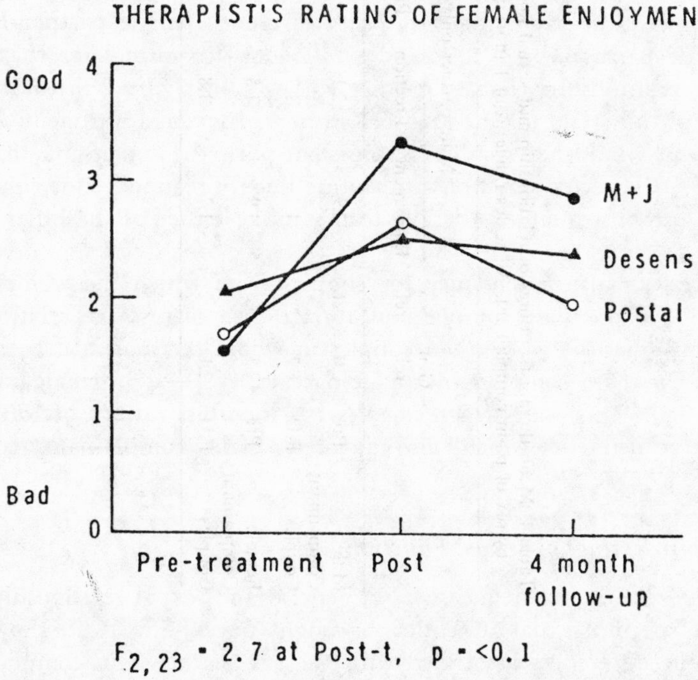

FIGURE 3. Mean sexual enjoyment ratings made by therapists at pre-treatment, post-treatment and follow-up, for each treatment group.

Table 4. Mean therapists' ratings of relationship and sexual function at pre-treatment and follow-up, divided by sex of main complainant. All scales range from 1 (normal function) to 5 (completely dysfunctional)

		Gen. rel.	Sex rel.	Male partner only			Female partner only		
				Enjoyment	Erection	Premature	Enjoyment	Interest	Orgasm
Male Complainant Couples	Pre	2.0	4.1	2.9	2.1	2.7	2.7	2.1	3.4
	F.U.	1.7	2.8	1.7	1.7	1.5	2.0	1.8	2.9
Female Complainant Couples	Pre	2.3	3.8	1.9	1.5	1.6	3.8	3.9	4.1
	F.U.	2.1	3.2	1.7	1.8	1.3	3.2	3.2	4.1

Table 5. Frequencies of couples in each treatment group reporting increases in S.I. frequency at follow-up

	Increase	Same/ Decrease
Desensitisation	3	9
Masters and Johnson	8	4
Postal	3	9

$\chi^2 = 5.8$, $p < 0.1$.

and as having more problems with premature ejaculation ($F_{1,24} = 8.0$, $p < 0.01$). Of the women those judged to be the main complainant were also rated as enjoying sexual contact less ($F_{1,24} = 5.0$; $p < 0.05$) and to have less sexual interest ($F_{1,24} = 19.8$; $p < 0.001$).

After treatment, ratings of male sexual function showed no remaining differences associated with original status as main complainant owing to relative gains in these patients. However, among women, those orginally designated as main complainants were still relatively worse off (see Table 4). This suggests that female patients with severe sexual dysfunction profited less from treatment than male patients, although the nature of the data makes this conclusion difficult to justify statistically. On the orgasm scale, for example, of 18 female complainants, only 2 were rated to have improved orgasmic response at follow-up. Only one measure showed any evidence of statistical trends associated with type of treatment: therapist ratings of female enjoyment of sexual contact. Directed practice with counselling was associated with most post-treatment change on this measure, and desensitization with least change ($F_{2,23} = 2.7$, $p < 0.1$) as can be seen in Figure 3.

Frequency of Sexual Contact

Estimates made by the two partners of love-making frequency agreed reasonably well (for S.I., $r = 0.87$). Because of the large number of zero scores, main effects were examined using a median test by comparing numbers of couples reporting increased frequency of intercourse with those reporting no change or decreases. This revealed a trend in favor of directed practice with counselling, compared with the other two treatments, but again only at a 10% level (Table 5).

Prediction of Outcome

Examination of pre-treatment descriptions and ratings made by assessors failed to show significant associations between outcome and age, type or duration of problem, existence of a previous more satisfactory relationship, duration of cohabitation or number of children. However, there was a tendency for less change to occur in sexual function when initial general relationship was poor ($r = 0.42$, $p < 0.01$) and a non-significant trend in the same direction when one member of the couple had been treated for other psychological disturbance.

DISCUSSION

Whilst changes in individual outcome measures are limited and do not show highly significant differences between treatments, the consistency of trends is striking, and suggests that Treatment 2 (i.e. directed practice plus counselling) is generally superior to Treatments 1 and 3. This would imply that both components of Treatment 2, directed practice and counselling, are of importance in determining overall outcome. An important reason for the lack of clearer differences among treatments is the considerable variability in outcome, especially with Treatment 3. This is of some interest as it suggests that while there are couples who respond favorably to simple behavioral directions, there may be others, perhaps those in whom interpersonal or communication difficulties are more important, whose problems are aggravated by this approach when used alone. If so, it would be of some importance to recognize the characteristics that distinguish these two outcome groups.

Treatment 1, systematic desensitization plus counselling, showed mainly small changes and there seems little justification for using imaginal desensitization, except possibly in those cases where there is a strong phobic element. It may be argued that the Masters & Johnson approach has a great deal in common with desensitization as used clinically (Laughren and Kass, 1975). Obviously there are some similarities; the behavioral limits set by the hierarchy would have a similar anxiety reducing effect to the ban on intercourse and genital contact. The graded approach used by Masters & Johnson has a hierarchical quality to it. In clinical practice desensitization in imagination is usually combined with graded practice *in vivo*: in our treatment behavioral instructions were deliberately limited to general encouragement to try out "desensitized" behavior. It is possible, therefore, that a greater emphasis on graded practice in Treatment 1 may have produced results more comparable with Treatment 2. However, there are also important differences between directed practice as described by Masters & Johnson, and the type of directed practice normally associated with desensitization. In the Masters & Johnson approach, behavioral steps are guided by the occurrence of mutual pleasure, rather than the avoidance of anxiety. The emphasis laid on communication between the partners during practice, and on giving and receiving pleasure, may be more appropriate to maintaining a mutually satisfying relationship than behavior solely dictated by desensitization hierarchies. However, further research would be necessary to establish which, if any, of the various techniques in Masters & Johnson's directed practice have effects different from that of *in vivo* desensitization.

The nature of the change occurring in couples whose treatment was rated relatively successful, was often surprisingly unclear. This seems particularly true of "female complainant" couples, where changes in orgasmic function were disappointingly few, even when there was general agreement that the sexual relationship had improved. One possibility is that some parts of treatment, particularly the mutual exchange and communication aspects of directed practice, succeeded in increasing sexual enjoyment, despite failure to attain orgasm. Several trends in our data point to a more generalized disturbance in female complainants, with a greater degree of residual dysfunction at the end of treatment. There is also evidence that, irrespective of the sex of the main complainant, the outcome of treatment was poorer when the sexual dysfunction was associated with a more widespread disturbance in the relationship.

The comparison between one and two therapists, while inconclusive, suggests that the fuller Masters & Johnson approach benefits from the use of two therapists. It remains debatable whether the superiority, if real, is sufficient to justify the general adoption of dual therapist teams for this treatment. It may be possible with further research to identify the circumstances in which two therapists are especially useful. This would not only be clinically desirable, but might also help in clarifying the nature of the underlying therapeutic process.

ACKNOWLEDGEMENTS

This research was supported by grants from the Medical Research Council. U.K. (to A. Mathews, D. Julier and P. Shaw) and from the Mental Health Trust and Research Fund (to A. Whitehead). We wish to thank Dr. Margaret Whitty for help in carrying out physical examinations.

REFERENCES

GELDER, M. G. & MARKS, I. M. Severe agoraphobia: A controlled trial of behavior therapy. *Br. J. Psychiat.*, 112:309-319, 1966.

LAUGHREN, T. P. & KASS, D. J. Desensitization of sexual dysfunction: The present status. In Gurman & Rice (Eds.), *Couples in Conflict*. New York: Aronson, 1975.

MASTERS, W. H. & JOHNSON, V. E. *Human Sexual Inadequacy*. London: Churchill, 1970.

SECTION VII: SEXUAL DISORDERS, MARITAL DISHARMONY, AND DEPRESSION

17

AVERSIVE BEHAVIOR REHEARSAL FOR SEXUAL EXHIBITIONISM

Ian Wickramasekera
University of Illinois

The aversive behavior rehearsal (ABR) technique is a specific procedure for the management of chronic sexual exhibitionism. The *in vivo* ABR (I-V-ABR) makes an appointment for the patient to come into the clinic and expose himself at a specific time and place to people who know of him. The vicarious aversive behavior rehearsal (V-ABR) technique arranges for a chronic exhibitionist to observe via video tape the I-V-ABR treatment of a fellow exhibitionist. Twenty chronic exhibitionists have been treated with one to four sessions with the above methods, and none has relapsed to date in follow-ups ranging up to 7 years.

Aversive Behavior Rehearsal (ABR) (Wickramasekera, 1972) is a technique for the management of chronic (repeated offenders as defined by police records) sexual exhibitionism in a specific subset of exhibitionists. The technique or a variant has been independently replicated (Serber, 1970; Reitz & Keil, 1971; Stevenson & Jones, 1972).

METHOD

In Vivo ABR (I-V-ABR) Procedure

It is indicated for patients who are introverted, anxious, moralistic, and probably contra-indicated for the extroverted, sociopathic type of

---

Reprinted with permission from *Behavior Therapy,* 7, 167-176, 1976.

patient whose trait anxiety level is low. It elicits the patient's symptom (exhibitionism) under conditions which overlap substantially with the naturally occurring event, but with certain critical alterations. (1) The "exposure" is deliberately planned by therapists and patient several weeks in advance. (2) The "exposure" is enacted under conditions of reduced anonymity. (3) During enactment, the behavior is subjected by the patient and therapist to cognitive-verbal exploration of associated affect, bodily sensations, and fantasy. The goal is to elicit and "demytholigize" any autistic fantasies that may cognitively mediate the exhibitionism in the natural habitat. Conditions are arranged to increase the probability that the patient will take a pedestrian, critical, and analytic view of what he is doing during the act of "exposure." It has been hypothesized (Wickramasekera, 1972) that sexual exhibitionism occurs under internal conditions of increased fantasy involvement (Sarbin & Coe, 1972) and reduces critical judgment (Hilgard, 1965). These patietns show reduced critical judgment when they use public places, compulsively return to the same place with their car license plates clearly visible, and in numerous other ways temporarily ignore situational dangers. A cognitive shift from fantasy involvement to a critical pedestrian view may alter the future probability of exhibitionism under the internal (moods of self-pity, boredom, anger, failure) and external (warm weather, parks, girls in short skirts) conditions which set the stage for exposure. In some respects, the above intervention is equivalent to reducing the probability of "hypnotic" behavior under specific internal and external conditions which may operate as discriminative stimuli, for hypnotic behavior as it has been conceptualized by some writers (Sarbin & Coe, 1972; Wickramasekera, 1976).

Vicarious ABR (V-ABR) Procedure

A promising variant of the ABR procedure, Vicarious Aversive Behavior Rehearsal (V-ABR), is based on instructing and situationally arranging for an exhibitionistic patient to observe a videotape of a real exhibitionist being processed *in vivo* through the ABR procedure. The V-ABR procedure is probably indicated for the same type of patients who benefit from the *in vivo* ABR procedure, but who cannot be processed through the entire I-V-ABR for one or more of the following reasons: (1) deficient in the motivation necessary to go through the *in vivo* ABR; (2) medical contra-indications which require that the patient be exempt from the severe stress of the ABR procedure (e.g., positive history of cardiovascular or CNS complications; e.g., angina pectoris,

TABLE 1

Flow Chart of ABR Procedure

I. Initial Diagnostic Interview
  A. Collect following facts and formulate relationships
    1. First event (age, circumstances), frequency (in remote and recent past and present), locations, time of day or night, duration of episode, ages and sex of observers (special features).
    2. Masturbation, ejaculation, associated rituals, and fantasies; triggering events (e.g., conflict, failure, weather, female clothing, daydreams, and fantasies).
  B. Present treatment plan and alternatives with prognosis. Present intervention as research, not routine treatment. State side effects, patient reads article on ABR. State restriction on intercourse for 3 weeks following Procedures I and II.

II. Psychological and Psychophysiological Tests
  A. MMPI, Eysenck Personality Inventory, Taylor Manifest Anxiety Scale, Spiegel Eye Roll Test of Hypnotizability, SHSS Form A, Hypnosis Attitude Scale, Protestant Ethic Scale.
  B. Respiration, GSR, EMG, Heart Rate. Baseline and response to standardized stimuli.

III. Medical Tests and Physical Examination (any contra-indications?)

IV. Discuss Treatment Plan with Significant Others and Lawyer. Read and Sign Consent for Treatment and Videotape Forms.

V. Procedure I (40 min. of self-disclosure, intensive self-exploration, and confrontation of which approximately 20 min. is actual physical exposure).

VI. Procedure II (40 min. of intensive self-disclosure, self-exploration, and confrontation of which approximately 20 min. is actual physical exposure).

VII. Follow-up (3 weeks later) with Observation of Video Tape of Procedure I while monitored psychophysiologically (heart rate, EMG, GSR, respiration). Retake MMPI.

VIII. Follow-ups at following Intervals: Three weeks after treatment (view neutral and aversive video tape). Thereafter, 2, 6, 9, and 12 months, and once each year.

cardiac decompensation, hypertension, epilepsy, etc.); (3) patient with weak reality contact, marginal adjustment, or who is prepsychotic or acutely disturbed. The V-ABR is offered only to those patients who have carefully considered and refused the *in vivo* ABR procedure or to those who are judged likely to be hurt by the *in vivo* ABR.

Components I-IV have diagnostic utility but also appear to potentiate certain active ingredients in the behavior influence process. These ingredients include self-disclosure, self-exploration, commitment, structuring of positive expectations, and giving the patient responsibility for making the technique work (demand characteristics), etc., which have been empirically demonstrated to be effective variables in both the psychotherapy and the social psychological research literature (Strupp & Bergin, 1972; Goldstein, Heller & Sechrest, 1966).

Component I, section A, elicits and shapes the patient's self-exploratory and self-monitoring behaviors from very specific topics (e.g., first events of exposure, age) to a very general form of self-monitoring and exploration (identification of triggering events). At this more general level, the patient is attempting to relate the onset of his symptom to internal events (e.g., conflict, failure, self-pity, boredom) and environmental events (e.g., the warm weather, specific location, length of women's skirts, types of female clothing). The identification of these internal and external antecedents or triggering events is important in terms of helping the patient develop an "early warning" system for his post-therapy prophylactic use. Component I, section B, essentially involves selling the patient on the ABR technique, but doing so in a cautious and ethical manner. Previously observed side effects are described (repeated nightmares, temporary anxiety or depression, secondary impotence) and the requirement of abstinence from sexual intercourse for 3 weeks after treatment is presented.

Components II and III are mainly intended to enable an eventual more precise and objective specification of the type of patient for whom this procedure is indicated or contra-indicated. It has been hypothesized (Wickramasekera, 1972) that trait anxiety, hypnotizability, the degree of socialization, and autonomio lability are implicated in the probability of certain sexual deviations. In addition, the combination of extensive psychological, psychophysiological, and medical tests may create the therapeutic expectation in the patient that grave and healing events are about to occur. The psychophysiological tests currently involve: (a) a 15-20 min adaptation period, (b) a 10-min baseline period, (c) the discharge of a cap pistol from 3 ft. behind the subject at about the level of his head, (d) instructions to solve simple mental arithmetic problems and to read aloud the titles of the books in the bookcase across the room from him, (e) instructions to the subject to visualize with his eyes closed a pleasant and relaxing scene (e.g., soaking in the bathtub, sipping a martini while relaxing by a fire, etc.), and (f) instructions to visualize with eyes closed the last time he was arrested for indecent exposure.

Component IV is the culmination of a series of progressively more tightly interlocking tacit behavioral commitments to change. It requires the patient to make a full disclosure of his deviation, its frequency and chronicity to significant others (parents, wife, etc.), and his lawyer. It also challenges him to persuade them of the wisdom of undergoing the ABR procedure and, in the process of so doing, he appears to strengthen his own commitment. This component closes with the patient signing a release to videotape his naked body for the "advancement of science" and releasing me of all responsibility for possible negative consequences. Components I-IV may take as many as four to eight 50-min sessions.

Components V and VI involve approximately two, 40-min sessions of full self-disclosure, self-exploration, and self-confrontation in the presence of five mental health professionals (social workers, senior medical students, psychiatric nurses, psychology interns) in a large room with a one-way mirror and videotaping of the entire proceedings. It is sometimes hinted at this point that there may be other authorized observers (e.g., referring probation officer, arresting law officer, etc.) on the other side of the mirror. I open the session in a kind, but grave manner and become progressively more obnoxious and confronting as the session progresses. I begin by putting a series of rapid questions to the patient (Please state your name, age, address, marital status, occupation, children (names and ages), wife, religion, specific deviant sexual acts, associated rituals and locations, objects of exposure, etc.).

The patient is instructed to cue specific acts of exposure and masturbation. The use of numbers appears more effective in securing compliance under stress than verbal requests. The patient is told, "When I say *one,* you will unzip your pants and lower your underpants; when I say *two,* you will get a firm grip on your penis (use patient's own word); when I say *three,* you will start to masturbate ("jack-off")."

During and between exposures the patient is pointedly questioned by all the team members individually and requested to attend to different parts of his body or their legs, breasts, crotches, hips, etc. For example, he might be asked to respond to all or some of the following questions and instructions: What is your mood when you expose yourself? What triggers the mood? What do you see now as you look at yourself in the mirror? Describe what you think we see as we look at you right now. What do you think we are feeling, thinking, etc. as we look at you now? How do your hands feel? How does your head, legs, penis, stomach, etc., feel? Give your penis a voice; let it talk to us. Tell us about the man you are in your public life. Tell us about your private life. What are your masturbatory fantasies?

During components V and VI, the patient is asked to disrobe and robe several times while encouraged to explore the relationship between current feelings, moods prior to exposure, during exposure and their relationship to antecedents, consequences and immediate situational factors. He is frequently relieved to be asked to "zip up," or pull up his pants, but this relief is short-lived because, soon afterwards, he is asked to disrobe again. At the close of the session, the patient is frequently in tears, trembling, weak, and nauseous. I dismiss the team and change abruptly into a warm, kind, supportive figure who wipes his eyes and fetches him a drink of water. I express, sincerely and freely, my admiration for the courage and strength he demonstrated during the previous "hell"; and I leave him in doubt for a few days as to whether another procedure will be required.

The primary contraindications for another procedure are massive sympathetic arousal during the first procedure, "insightful" verbalization with active patient participation, and any (rare) evidence of bizarre behavior during or after the procedure. The primary indication for a second procedure is marginal arousal and "unauthorized" psychological escape behavior while physically present (dissociation). If a second procedure is scheduled, we begin by asking specific details about cognitive, affective, and motor reactions during and after the first procedure, particularly, immediate and delayed reactions. The session continues with some variation on previous material, any new material, or loose ends from the previous session. To disrupt any persisting dissociation, team members approach the patient physically and ask him to describe physical details about other team members, their clothing or body, etc.

RESULTS

In *in vivo* ABR procedure has been offered to 25 patients. Five have refused at the onset or not completed the I-V-ABR or V-ABR. Sixteen have been treated with the *in vivo* ABR, and four with vicarious ABR. The number of treatment sessions with the *in vivo* ABR have varied from one to four. In the last 2 yr we have never used more than one treatment session. Prior to treatment, the 16 patients had been symptomatic for 4 to 25 yr with rates of exposure varying from 1 to 20 per month. The follow-up ranged from 3 months to 7 yr. Patients in the vicarious ABR group had been symptomatic for 7 to 13 yr. No patient treated with the ABR procedure has reported exposing himself, nor have we detected any relapse. All patients report having between one to four brief and easily terminated thoughts of exposure at least once in 3 months. Eight reported mild to severe anxiety when thoughts of exposure fantasies reduced dramatically, with quality and duration "feeling" vastly different from the pretreatment fantasies. The follow-ups for the vicarious ABR are too brief for inclusion here.

The follow-ups are based on four kinds of data: (1) Verbal report during the periodic individual interviews. Many patients report that, prior to their follow-up treatment, their anxiety level increases and the previous ABR procedure is reactivated in memory. These regular follow-up sessions strengthen the ABR procedure and should be regarded as part of it. (2) Private interviews with significant others (wife, employers, parents, etc.) or telephone calls are used at the time of the patient's follow-up interview to check on the patient's verbal report. (3) Search of police records of indecent exposure in the three surrounding counties are used to verify the patient's verbal report. (4) The patient is shown the results of a video-physio evaluation procedure which is done 3 weeks after the ABR treatment. Immediately after the video-physio evaluation procedure (explained in detail later), the patient is shown the chart records of his psychophysiological reactions to the ABR technique. This increases the credibility of the treatment effects. Routine psychophysiological testing (heart rate, GSR, respiration) during the periodic follow-up interview is presented to the patient "to detect how much of the previous conditioning persists." Some patients perceive this new procedure as a "lie detector test" and this may contribute further to the inhibition of the deviant behavior. During this procedure, the patient is instructed following a baseline determination to expose himself in fantasy and casually asked, while still connected to the instrument, the number of times he exposed himself since the last follow-up.

The *in vivo* ABR appears to have side effects observed between *in vivo* ABR procedures I and II or immediately after treatment. These include moderate to mild anxiety, tension, and depression of 1 to 4 weeks duration, and these disappear after 5 weeks. Repeated nightmares in which the ABR procedure or a variant of it is rehearsed in sleep, have been reported by three patients. Secondary impotence of brief duration has been reported by three patients. Temporary loss of interest in sex has been reported by approximately 10 *in vivo* ABR patients. All symptoms appear to have cleared up 2 months after treatment.

To reduce secondary impotence we prohibit sexual intercourse for 3 weeks after *in vivo* ABR procedure I. The mechanism of erection is primarily parasympathetic and, hence, a temporary state of massive sympathetic arousal (post-treatment anxiety and tension) is probably antagonistic to effective sexual functioning. Residual anxiety usually

TABLE 2

Flow Chart of Video-Physiograph Assessment Procedure

1. Adaptation and baseline (20 min.)	3. Aversive TV tape (8 min.)
2. Control TV tape (8 min.)	4. Return to baseline (8 min.)

subsides by the third week after treatment. About one-half the patients will disassociate during procedures I and II to avoid the impact of the aversive reality that has been carefully arranged for them. They will not attend or become "numb" to the full impact of the aversive reality. This "unauthorized form of escape behavior" (Azarin & Holz, 1966) has been terminated by insisting forcefully that the patient describe the present physical reality (color of female's eyes, hair, shape of their breasts, legs, clothes, etc.), his own physical reactions, his current autistic fantasies, and his speculations about the thoughts and feelings behind the females' faces. I can usually estimate the intensity of the aversion generated by how severe is the exhaustion or tension headache *I* feel after the procedure.

To determine the psychophysiological consequences of being processed through the ABR procedure and being reminded of it (memory stimulated by observation of the video tape record of their treatment), the following instructional and situational arrangements are made: The patient, told to return to the therapist's office for "a test" approximately 3 weeks after the last in vivo ABR procedure, is connected to a physiograph (screened from the patient) while he sits quietly on a comfortable recliner. In front of the subject, approximately 8 ft. away, are two videotape monitors. The monitor above is programmed to show a portion of the videotape (aversive tape) of the patient's treatment. The monitor below is programmed to show a "neutral" or control tape (a portion of the initial diagnostic interview by the present therapist of the patient). After connection to the physiograph, the patient is given 20 min to adapt and "relax." The control tape is then activated remotely for 8 min. The aversive tape is activated remotely and allowed to run for 8 min. The subject, previously instructed to observe both tapes carefully, is not informed about the contents of the videotapes or the order in which they will be shown. After 8 min of exposure, the aversive tape is switched off and the subject is instructed to relax for 10 min prior to disconnection from the physiograph which has been monitoring and re-

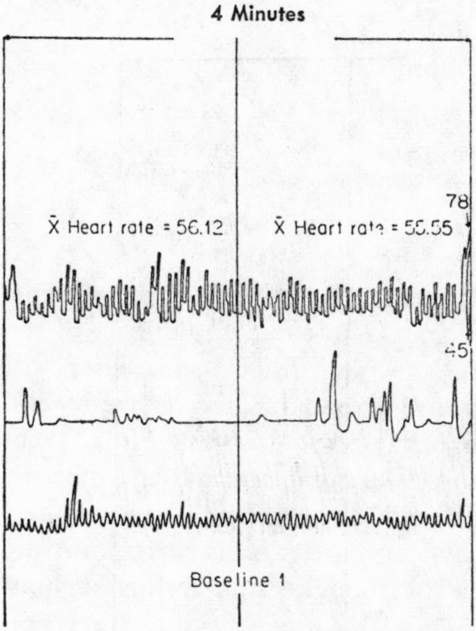

FIGURE 1A

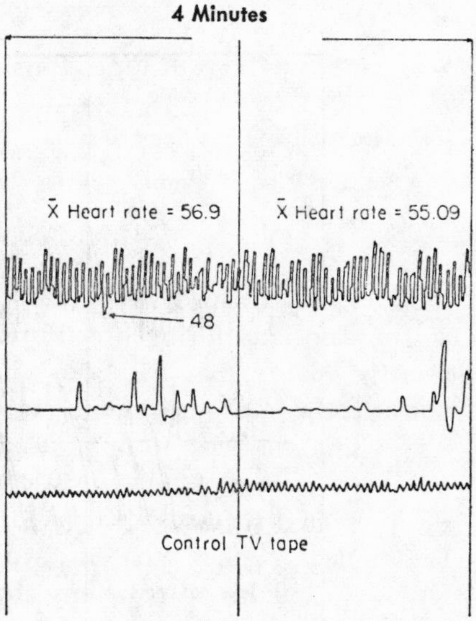

FIGURE 1B

cording his heart rate (BPM), respiration, and GSR during the adaptation, observation, and relaxation periods.

The purpose of the control tape is to determine the psychophysiological consequences of simply orienting to and observing a videotape of one's self while connected to a physiograph. Inspection of the physiograph record during the exposure to control and aversive tape sequences indicates clear and significant differences in heart rate, Galvanic Skin Response (GSR), and respiration.

The figures show psychophysiological changes occurring in a white male adult during two baseline periods and while observing an aversive (a videotape of himself behaviorally rehearsing sexual exposure and masturbation in the presence of three females and two males) tape. The upper trace is of heart rate (BPM), the middle trace of GSR, and the bottom trace is of respiration. Paper speed is 6 in./min. This patient's record was selected because he demonstrates physiological changes in all three response systems (heart rate, GSR, respiration). Not all subjects tested to date demonstrate clear changes in all three response systems. As implied by Lacey (1959), individual patients appear to show response profiles.

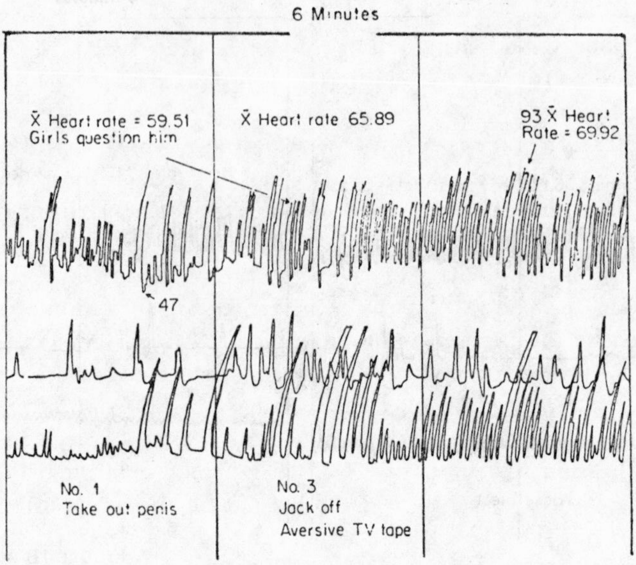

FIGURE 1C

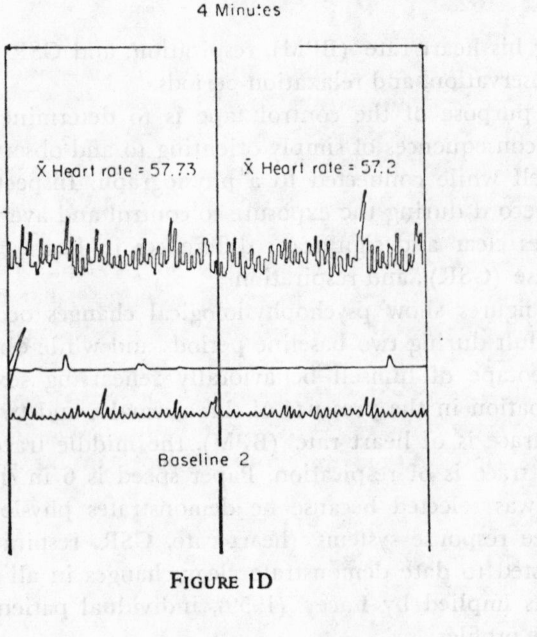

FIGURE 1D

DISCUSSION

Instructionally and situationally, the ABR procedure arranges for the elicitation of strong aversive internal consequences (typically patients report or manifest one or more of the following before, during, or immediately after the procedure: trembling, nausea, lightheadedness, palpitations, weakness, cramps, butterflies in stomach, headaches, tightness in chest, etc.) in the patient. "Voluntary" participation (Wickramasekera, 1971) ensures that the patient actively generates the aversive consequences in himself. The aversion is installed inside the subject and outside his control, so the aversive contingency cannot be easily dismantled by the patient, as for example, with a portable and remotely controlled shock generator. It has been speculated (Wickramasekera, 1972) that the procedure may involve interoceptive conditioning. The suggestion that, if aversion is attached to internal cues, the gradient of generalization will be flatter (Miller, personal communication, 1973) may explain the apparently reliable transfer of the suppression of exhibitionism from the clinical situation to the patient's natural habitat.

If the ABR technique is continued over several sessions, the patient will desensitize to the technique. Hence, treatment should cease with a brief "resensitization" (Wickramasekera, 1970).

Many exhibitionists are quiet, nonassertive, moralistic individuals who take few risks in their "public" lives, but become daring figures during their "private" exhibitionistic episodes and fantasies. Their public image may be one of respectability, caution, reliability, and industry, whereas in their private feelings they are desperately bored, resentful, self-pitying individuals whose fantasies are defiant and dangerously exciting.

During procedures I and II, the patient frequently develops "insight" into this inconsistency between his public and private lives and is strongly encouraged to act in more adaptive risk taking and assertive ways in his public life (e.g., asking for a raise or promotion, speaking back to his wife, boss or a peer, changing jobs, trying a love affair). It appears likely that the inhibition of aggressive, sexual-novelty, and excitement needs increases episodically the probability of maladaptive expression (indecent exposure) of such deprivations.

REFERENCE NOTE

1. MILLER, N. E. Personal communication, 1973.

REFERENCES

AZRIN, N. H., & HOLZ, W. C. Punishment. In W. K. Honig (Ed.), *Operant Behavior, Areas of Research and Application*. New York: Appleton-Century-Crofts, 1966.

GOLDSTEIN, A. P., HELLER, K., & SECHREST, L. B. *Psychotherapy and the Psychology of Behavior Change*. New York: Wiley, 1966.

HILGARD, E. R. *Hypnotic Susceptibility*. New York: Harcourt, Brace & World, 1965.

LACEY, J. E. Psychophysiological approaches to the evaluation of psychotherapeutic process and outcome. In E. A. Rubenstein & M. B. Parloff (Eds.), *Research in Psychotherapy*. Washington, D.C.: APA, 1959.

MASTERS, W. H., & MASTERS, V. E. *Human Sexual Inadequacy*. Boston: Little Brown, 1970.

MILLER, N. E., & MURRAY, E. J. Displacement and conflict: Learnable drive as a basis for the steeper gradient of avoidance than of conflict. *Journal of Experimental Psychology*, 43:227-231, 1952.

MILLER, N. E. Liberalization of basic S-R concepts: Extension to conflict behavior, motivation and social learning. In S. Koch (Ed.), *Psychology: A Study of a Science* (Study 1, 2). New York: McGraw-Hill, 1959.

MILLER, N. E. Some implications of modern behavior therapy for personality change and psychotherapy. In D. Byrne & P. Worchel (Eds.), *Personality Change*. New York: Wiley, 1964.

MOWRER, O. H. *The New Group Therapy*. Princeton, N.J.: Van Nostrand, 1964.

ORNE, M. T. Hypnosis, motivation and the ecological validity of the psychological experiment. In W. J. Arnold & M. M. Page (Eds.), *Nebraska Symposium on Motivation*. Lincoln: University of Nebraska Press, 1970, pp. 187-265.

REITZ, W. E., & KEIL, W. E. Behavioral treatment of an exhibitionist. *Journal of Behavior Therapy and Experimental Psychiatry*, 2:67-69, 1971.

SERBER, M. Shame aversion therapy. *Journal of Behavior Therapy and Experimental Psychiatry*, 1:213-215, 1970.

STEVENSON, J., & JONES, I. H. Behavior therapy techniques for exhibitionism. *Archives of General Psychiatry*, 27:239-241, 1972.

STRUPP, H. H., & BERGIN, A. E. Some empirical and conceptual bases for coordinated research in psychotherapy. In H. H. Strupp & A. E. Bergin (Eds.), *Changing Frontiers in the Science of Psychotherapy*. Chicago: Aldine-Atherton, 1972.

TRAUX, C. B., & CARKHUFF, R. *Toward Effective Counseling and Psychotherapy*. Chicago: Aldine, 1967.

WICKRAMASEKERA, I. The application of learning theory to the treatment of a case of sexual exhibitionism. *Psychotherapy: Theory, Research and Practice*, 5:108-112, 1968.

WICKRAMASEKERA, I. Desensitization, resensitization and desensitization again. *Journal of Behavior Therapy and Experimental Psychiatry*, 1:257-262, 1970.

WICKRAMASEKERA, I. The effect of "hypnosis" and task motivational instruction in attempting to influence the voluntary self-deprivation of money. *Journal of Personality and Social Psychology*, 19:311-314, 1971.

WICKRAMASEKERA, I. A technique for controlling a certain type of sexual exhibitionism. *Psychotherapy: Theory, Research and Practice*, 9:207-210, 1972.

WICKRAMASEKERA, I. (Ed.). *Biofeedback, Behavior Therapy and Typnosis: Potentiating the Verbal Control of Complex Human Behavior*. Chicago: Nelson Hall, 1976.

SECTION VII: SEXUAL DISORDERS, MARITAL DISHARMONY, AND DEPRESSION

18

MARITAL THERAPY IN GROUPS

A Comparative Evaluation of Behavioral and Interactional Formats

Robert Paul Liberman, Jan Levine, Eugenie Wheeler,

Nancy Sanders and Charles J. Wallace

Camarillo-Neuropsychiatric Institute (UCLA) Research Center,
Oxnard Community Mental Health Center
Oxnard, California

ABSTRACT

A comparative evaluation was conducted in a community mental health center between two types of brief, marital therapy in groups. The experimental group of four couples was exposed to behavioral methods based on social learning principles. The primary interventions were (1) training the spouses in discriminating and monitoring the occurrence of pleasing events and behaviors; (2) behavioral rehearsal of communication skills using prompting, modelling, feedback, and "homework" assignments; and (3) contingency contracting. The comparison group of five couples was led in an interactional format with the leaders encouraging ventilation of feelings, problem-solving through discussion, and mutual support and feedback. Both groups were led by the same three clinicians.

Reprinted with permission from *Acta Psychiatrica Scandinavica,* Supplement 266, 1976.

Outcome was measured on multiple levels before, during and immediately after treatment. Follow-up assessments were conducted at one, two, and six months after treatment. Response measures included the self report by clients on marital satisfaction; on consumer satisfaction with the treatment experience; on their observations of pleasing behaviors given and received as recorded on wrist counters; and direct observation of client via "live" time-sampling and coding of videotapes of problem-solving discussions before and after treatment. Results showed few differences between groups on the self-report measures; however, there were significant improvements by both groups on these measures after treatment which were maintained into the follow-up evaluation. The direct observational data indicated that the members in the behavioral group displayed significantly more positive and mutually supportive verbal and nonverbal behaviors in their interaction as a result of treatment.

INTRODUCTION

Marital separation and divorce and their sequelae in the life events of the involved family members comprise the greatest stress on the psychological and physical functioning of individuals. Research on the stress produced by alterations in life style associated with separation and divorce, such as work and financial changes, sexual, problems, change in residence and social activities, and revision of personal habits indicates that psychiatric and physical illnesses frequently occur in individuals experiencing these events (Holmes & Masuda, 1973; Holmes & Rahe, 1967). Even when not followed by separation or divorce, marital discord and conflict are widely prevalent in our mobile culture with its changing values and the diminishing strength and cohesiveness of nuclear and extended families. There were 715,000 divorces in the United States in 1972 and it has been estimated that forty million married couples need counseling (Kuhn, 1973).

Although marital therapy has been practiced for over thirty years, empirical evaluations of the process and outcome of clinical interventions with married couples have been scanty and poorly designed (Olsen, 1970; Gurman, 1973). The professional specialty of marriage counseling has proceeded with a great amount of vigor but without much rigor. Less than one-third of reported outcome studies on marital therapy have used control groups and only two have compared differing types of therapy (Crowe, 1973; Hickman, 1970). Relatively few studies have employed behavioral observations, independent raters, or multidimensional assessments. The most frequently used outcome criteria have been patients' self-reports and global ratings of change, of dubious reliability and validity when relied upon alone.

The behavioral approach to marital conflict has generated new treatment techniques aimed at increasing the level of reciprocity or mutually reinforcing exchanges between husband and wife (Weiss, Hops, and Patterson, 1973; Stuart, 1969; Knox, 1971; Azrin, Naster & Jones, 1973; Liberman, 1970). Because of the recency of the application of social learning principles to marital dyads, clinical research in this area has not yet advanced beyond the stage of single case reports, laboratory analog studies, and non-factorial, single-group studies. Despite its embryonic stage, behavior therapy with married couples has already shown clinical promise with an accumulated improvement rate in five studies of 95 percent for 36 couples.

The present research was undertaken to subject the initially favorable results of behavior therapy with married couples to a more rigorous experimental test by evaluating the outcome of brief, marital group therapy using contrasting formats in two groups. One group was led in an interactional format while the other group engaged in behavioral rehearsal of communication skills and contingency contracting. The hypothesis was that the couples in the group receiving more directive, behavioral interventions would display greater improvement and change. Furthermore, the research was conducted in a typical community mental health center where marital problems constituted a significant proportion of outpatient referrals and where a mandate existed to provide services that would minimize or prevent family disorders. The behavioral treatment for married couples was designed so that the clinical team at the mental health center could continue to use and evaluate the methods if the treatment proved effective.

METHODS

Subjects

Subjects were recruited for the groups by requesting referrals of married couples interested in improving their marriages from the clinical staff of the Oxnard Mental Health Center, from local clergymen, and from physicians in private practice. A total of 14 couples were screened, all meeting the criteria set for admission into the groups. The criteria were:

1. living together
2. contemplating separation or divorce but willing to postpone definite plans for action for the duration of treatment
3. not psychotic
4. not addicted to drugs or alcohol.

Four couples dropped out after the pre-testing but before the first group session for the following stated reasons:

1. one husband decided he did not want to discuss his marriage in a group
2. one wife felt that her husband needed to change on his own and that she did not need any help herself
3. one couple felt that their schedules were too hectic to permit their weekly participation
4. one couple tired of the baseline data collection procedures and lost interest in participating.

The fourth couple withdrew two days prior to the first session of the Behavioral Group to which they had been assigned. Because of the time element, it was not possible to replace them and this group began with four couples whereas the Interactional Group began with five couples. One couple in each group had temporarily separated in the past.

Couples were assigned consecutively as they were referred with the Behavioral Group starting six weeks in advance of the Interactional Group. While the couples within each group were heterogeneous with regard to social class and age, the averages for each background variable were similar for the two groups. Occupations of the group members varied from policeman to attorney to machinist. The average income for couples in both groups was approximately $1,000 per month. Members from both groups averaged 13 years of education and 14 years of marriage. The modal number of children in the families was two.

Based upon responses to the initial administration of the Marital Pre-Counseling Inventory (Stuart, 1973), the participants in the groups claimed unhappiness on a broad range of marital dimensions. Major dissatisfactions were claimed for social, affectionate, and sexual interactions with each other; management of children, free time, and finances; sharing of household responsibilities; and social interaction with friends and relatives.

Therapists

All sessions of both groups were led by the same three therapists—a male psychiatrist, a female psychiatric social worker, and a female mental health nurse. Each had 4 years of experience in conducting therapy groups for married couples using both behavioral and non-directive, interactional, insight-oriented methods. The three therapists met for 30 minutes prior to and after each group meeting to plan strategy and tactics, review progress, and to divide responsibilities equally for leadership and interventions.

There was no fee for the married couples beyond an attendance-contingent, refundable $15.00 deposit. One dollar was refunded for attendance at each of the first eight treatment sessions with the remainder refunded at the ninth session if perfect attendance had been maintained. During the screening and orientation process, each couple met the group leaders who attempted to cordially and enthusiastically generate favorable therapeutic expectations for the group experience.

Response Measures

A multidimensional battery of dependent measures was used in the assessment of outcome in the married couples groups. Self-report as well as direct observational data were collected before, during, and after the nine therapy sessions. Most of the measures were derived from the marital assessment battery developed and validated by Weiss, Hops, & Patterson (1973). An outline of the response measures with their associated levels of behavior is provided in Table 1.

Targeting and Recording "Pleases." Referring to a universal list of behaviors which one spouse can do to please the other, instructions were given to couples during the initial orientation session regarding their counting daily the number of "Pleases" each gives and receives. The list, which each spouse kept, made clear that a "Please" was any action, behavior, or verbal expression by one spouse directed to the other which is viewed by the recipient as making his/her life, day, or moment easier or more pleasant. Behaviors and behavioral consequences that qualified as "Pleases" could be divided into instrumental activities (e.g., doing chores, making a meal) and affectional behaviors (e.g., a compliment, a kiss or hug).

"Pleases" received and given were event recorded by each spouse on two wrist counters respectively. At the end of each day, the totals on the wrist counters were transferred to a data sheet and the wrist counters were re-set to zero. The couples were told that it was appropriate to thank their partners when they received a "Please" or to mention it when they gave a "Please," but they were asked not to compare counters

TABLE 1

Response Measures Used to Assess Outcome of Married Couples Groups

Response Measure	Levels of Behavior	When Recorded	How Recorded
Marital Adjustment Test	Interpersonal	Self-report	Pre, Post, 1 mo., 6 mo. follow ups
Areas of Change	Interpersonal	Self-report	Pre, Post, 2 mo., 6 mo. follow ups
Marital Pre-Counseling Inventory	Interpersonal & Family System	Self-report	Pre, Post
Marital Activities Inventory	Intrapersonal & Interpersonal	Self-report	Pre, Post
Hours Together	Interpersonal	Self-report	Daily
Shared Recreational Activities		Self-report	Daily
Counting "Pleases" Received & Given	Quasi-Interactional	Self-report & Spouse-report	Daily
Looking, Smiling, Touching	Interactional	Observer	Each session
Marital Interaction Coding System	Interactional	"Blind" Observer	Pre, Post
Therapy Evaluation Questionnaire	Consumer Satisfaction	Self-report	Post

on their daily totals. It was explained to couples from both groups that one purpose of the therapy group was to teach people to concentrate on the good, helpful, and pleasant interactions in their marriage, rather than dwell on the bad or unpleasant events. The baseline recording of "Pleases" began immediately after the initial orientation meeting and continued until the final group meeting. It should be noted that the dual recording of "Pleases" received and given provides an opportunity to compute inter-spouse agreement on their awareness and detection of pleasing interchanges.

Hours Together and Shared Recreational Activities. Each couple was asked to keep a record of the total number of waking hours spent together each day. At the end of each day, they were instructed to discuss how many hours had been spent together, reach a consensus to the nearest half-hour, and record that on their data sheet. Each person was also asked to record the number of different recreational activities shared with his/her spouse each day. This was accomplished by having each person review a list of 50 recreational activities and to check off those that applied. The partners were to tabulate this data independently and were told not to compare results. These records were kept from the initial orientation interview to the last group meeting.

Four nights a week the mental health center's secretary telephoned each couple and asked each person to report the data on "Pleases," hours, together, and shared recreational activities which had been collected since the previous phone call. Each week the couples were expected to bring their data sheets to the group meeting. If a person did not have any data to report when the secretary called, nothing was said; however, if data were not returned at a group meeting, the individual was reminded of the importance of recording these events. It should be evident that the tracking of "Pleases," hours together, and shared recreational activities comprise potential interventions for change as well as dependent measures of outcome.

Marital Activities Inventory. This inventory is designed to measure how frequently a person engages in 85 different recreational, self-enhancing, affectional, or utilitarian activities alone or together with spouse or others (Weiss, Hops, & Patterson, 1973). Examples include playing golf or tennis, talking about friends or relatives, and gardening. The respondent indicates how many times, during the past month, he/she engages in each activity alone, with spouse, and with others. Secondarily, the respondent notes whether he/she would like to share each activity with his/her spouse more frequently, less frequently, or the same as in the past month. This questionnaire was administered to group members before and after the nine therapy sessions.

Marital Pre-Counseling Inventory. This inventory (Stuart, 1973) is a comprehensive questionnaire designed to collect information on various aspects of a person's marriage. The questions deal with issues such as sexual satisfaction, areas of congruence and mutual understanding, child management, and communication effectiveness. The questionnaire was administered before and after the nine therapy sessions.

Areas of Change Questionnaire. This questionnaire (Weiss, Hops, & Patterson, 1973) is used to determine from each person:

1. How much self would like spouse to change
2. How much self thinks spouse would like self to change

3. How well the two partners understand each other as measured by the congruence between self's rating of 1 and spouse's rating of 2 above.

These three measures are obtained by having each person indicate whether he/she would like his/her spouse to perform each of 34 behaviors more frequently, less frequently, or continue at the current rate. A second section asks each person to estimate, using the same scale, how his/her spouse responded on the same questions asked in the first section. By comparing self's estimates of spouse's responses with the *actual* responses made by spouse, an "understanding" or congruence score can be obtained for each person. This test was administered to the subjects before the therapy group began, immediately after it terminated, at a 2-month follow-up, and again at a 6-month follow-up.

The Marital Adjustment Test. This widely used marital evaluation instrument (Locke & Wallace, 1959) is designed to measure a person's general marriage happiness and satisfaction. The abbreviated version of the test was used in this study. The items deal with such questions as how frequently a person agrees with his spouse on issues of finances, friends, and sex; how many interests the person shares with his/her spouse; how frequently a person confides in his/her spouse; and how frequently a person wishes he/she had not married his/her spouse. A total "happiness" or marital adjustment score can be derived with the maximum number of points possible being 158. Scores of 100 or above almost always indicate a non-distressed marriage. This test was administered to all subjects before the group began, immediately after it ended, and at 1-month, 2-month, and 6-month follow-ups.

Non-Verbal Behavioral Observations. During each group session, observations were made to determine how frequently each person (1) looked at his/her spouse, (2) looked and smiled at his/her spouse, and (3) touched his/her spouse. This was accomplished by observing each person during 25, five-second intervals at each group meeting. The observations were done by a research assistant who sat unobtrusively in a corner of the room where the group was meeting. The couples had all met the observer during the pre-tsting session and had been told to anticipate her presence. They were told, however, not to engage her in any group discussion.

Each group meeting included five observation periods. The observation periods began after the meeting had been in progress for 10 minutes, 30 minutes, 50 minutes, 70 minutes, and 90 minutes. At the beginning of each observation period, the first person on the observer's attendance sheet was observed for five seconds. During the following 10 seconds, the assistant recorded whether or not each of the above nonverbal behaviors occurred during the 5 second interval. The next person on the attendance sheet would then be observed for 5 seconds, and the behaviors that occurred were recorded during the 10 seconds that followed. This continued until each person had been observed five times during each period. The observations procedure was then discontinued until it was time for the next observation period to begin.

During five of the group sessions, a second research assistant attended in order to measure reliability of the observational data. This was accomplished by having the lead observer tap her stopwatch with a pencil at the beginning of an observation interval. She would then tap it twice at the end of five seconds, and the two observers would record independently their behavioral observations. The percent of effective agreement between raters was computed.

Marital Interaction Coding System (MICS). The MICS (Weiss, Hops, & Patterson, 1973) is a system which has been developed to objectively record verbal and non-verbal behaviors that occur as marriage partners attempt to resolve a marital problem in a discussion format. Every behavior which is emitted and that can be classified into one of the system's 28 behavioral categories is recorded sequentially in 30-second blocks. Examples of the different categories are disagreement, approval, acceptance of responsibility, criticism, compromise, and humour.

Two videotapes were made of each couple that participated in the research study—one before the group began and another during the week after it was over. During the first taping sessions, standardized instructions were read to each couple in which the couple were told to discuss their feelings and opinions on a pre-selected topic for ten minutes and try to reach some agreement. The assigned topics varied, depending on what area the couple had indicated as being a major source of conflict in the previously scored Areas of Change questionnaire.

During the second taping session, standardized instructions were again read to each couple, but the assignment of a discussion topic was done somewhat differently. Each couple was given a list of topics which are common sources of conflict in marriage. They were told to choose one about which they disagreed but not one which had been discussed during any meeting of the workshop. The couple was then videotaped while discussing their topic for ten minutes.

The videotapes of all 18 conversations were then edited so that the conversations appeared in random order. Two naive, "blind" and trained raters from the Oregon Research Institute coded the tapes using the MICS. Interaction was coded for both husband and wife on separate lines in units of 30 seconds. Scores were reported as frequency of each behavioral category and then were normalized for total output of verbal and non-verbal behaviors. Reliability of coding was expressed as average percentage agreement for a 30 second line. Inter-rater reliability was obtained for five of the eighteen videotapes.

Consumer Satisfaction. A final measure of outcome was a 14 item questionnaire which tapped the group members' satisfaction with the treatment and their attitudes toward improvements that had been accomplished. Examples of questions were, "Do you feel that the group was worth the time you invested in it?"; "Would you recommend the group to a friend?"; and "After completing the group, how do you rate your new abilities to cope with marital conflict?" The three items described above were scored for comparative purposes between the two groups, with 14 points being the maximum positive score obtainable.

Treatment Procedures

Both groups met for 8 weekly, 2 hour sessions and then for a follow-up session one month later. The main differences between the two groups were the use of behavioral rehearsal for direct training of communication skills, and contingency contracting in the Behavioral Group and their absence from the Interactional Group. The interventions used with the two groups are listed in Table 2.

Behavioral Group. The members of the behavioral group received training in three areas:

1. specifying and acknowledging how each spouse could "please" the other in reciprocal ways
2. engaging in behavioral rehearsals to learn more constructive verbal and non-verbal communication
3. negotiating an agreement on a contingency contract.

Practice was prompted in each of these tasks during the sessions and "homework" assignments were given to extend the practice into the home. Each week chapters from a programmed text on *Improving Communication in Marriage* (Human Development Institute, 1967) was assigned to the spouses in the Behavioral Group. These chapters were to be read at home out loud in a dyadic, alternating, and responsive manner. The material provided instructions, examples and practice in ways to express

TABLE 2

Outline of Treatment Interventions for Behavioral and Interactional Groups

Interventions	Groups Behavioral	Interactional
Orientation to group with instructions to promote therapeutic expectations	Yes	Yes
Contingency deposit for attendance	Yes	Yes
Phone calls from clinic secretary	Yes	Yes
Discriminating and counting "Pleases" with graphic feedback	Yes	Yes
Tenderness film	Yes	Yes
Catharsis, ventilation, sharing of feelings	Limited	Yes
Verbal insight on marital relationship	Limited	Yes
Communication skills training using behavioral rehearsal, modeling, prompting, and feedback	Yes	No
Contingency Contracting	Yes	No

positive and negative feelings directly, constructively, and honestly. The final negotiation and agreement phase of the contingency contracting was supervised by the leaders in sub-groups of individual couples while the remainder of the behavioral procedures were carried out in the group-as-a-whole. A session-by-session description of the format and interventions used for the Behavioral Group follows. A more complete *Leader's Guide* to behavioral marital therapy in groups is available from the senior author (Liberman, 1975).

SESSION 1

1. Introductions and orientation to group, confidentiality, and importance of completing records and assignments were covered.

2. Problems and goals were targeted by prompting each member to translate general and vague dissatisfactions and desires to operational, behaviorally specific ones.

3. Graphs of "Pleases" that were counted and reported during the pre-group baseline period were reviewed. The rationale for exchanging "Pleases" and becoming more aware of the good aspects of their relationship was presented. The importance of reciprocity (vs. coercion) in marriage was highlighted by six slides of comic strip cartoons illustrating humorous but conflicted marital situations. The members were urged to report their giving and getting "Pleases" accurately rather than to make themselves look good or to please the leaders.

4. Training in communication skills was begun with behavioral rehearsals of (a) how to spontaneously initiate "Pleases" and (b) how to verbally and non-verbally acknowledge "Pleases" when they are given. The partners were shown, in scenes modeled by the therapists, how to catch your spouse doing something nice and the pitfalls of taking "Pleases" for granted. For example, each spouse was required to complete a response to their partner, "I like it when you do. . . ." Many of the rehearsals focused on the critical times of the day when initiating and acknowledging "Pleases" have disproportionately high impact on subsequent interactions; for example, upon awakening in the morning (e.g., "Can I bring you a cup of coffee in bed?"), and when greeting after work in the evening (e.g., "I've been looking forward to seeing you all day.") .

5. Homework Assignments:

(a) Each spouse was instructed to continue the counting of "Pleases" received and given using wrist counters as described above. Members were also instructed to try to *double* their baseline average number of giving "Pleases" on one randomly assigned day during the next week. In addition, they were told to acknowledge all "Pleases" received on that day by giving their spouse "warm fuzzies," which were small, soft, colorful cotton balls. These assigned days, different for each partner in a pair, were termed "Love Days" (Weiss, Hops, & Patterson, 1973).

(b) Each couple was instructed to engage in a 10 minute daily "Executive Session" during which they were to practice giving and acknowledging "Pleases." An "Executive Session" was defined as a period of conversing together without distractions at a designated time and place.

SESSION 2

1. Homework assignments were reviewed. Graphs of "Pleases" were publicly displayed and comparisons of the past week's data were made with the previous baseline data. Any effects of "Love Days" were focused on as were the discrepancies between "Pleases" given by each and perceived as having been received by the other. Each member was encouraged to give specific examples of "Pleases" given and received during the week. Each couple reviewed their experiences in having "Executive Sessions."

2. An educational film, "Tenderness" (Serber & Laws, 1974), was shown and discussed. This 20 minute film graphically depicts, with an annotative narration, a couple exchanging caresses, embraces, kisses, and verbal feedback on what was physically satisfying. Discriminations are highlighted between correct vs. incorrect ways of exchanging verbal and nonverbal tenderness.

3. Behavioral rehearsal followed the content of the film in focusing on ways to improve communication between spouses regarding the exchange of physical affection. Mutual hand massage was used as a way of demonstrating and practicing how to ask for and acknowledge pleasing physical affection. After modelling by leaders, each patrner took 3-5 minute turns

at massaging their spouse's hands with instructions to directly and affirmatively request how they want to be massaged and to give audible, verbal, positive feedback to their spouse on what feels good. Subsequently each spouse practiced, with modelling and feedback by the leaders, how to ask for sex in positive ways, and how to "turn on" his/her partner verbally and through non-sexual, physical contact.

4. Homework Assignments:

(a) Counting "Pleases" and "Love Days" were continued as in session one.

(b) Executive Session: Each couple was instructed to spend 10 minutes each day practicing massage with verbal feedback. Each partner was instructed to initiate sex at least once during the next week.

SESSION 3

1. Homework assignments were reviewed as in Session 2.

2. Behavioral rehearsals focused on two types of interactions which were aimed at priming and reinforcing reciprocity:

(a) Asking for a "pleasing behavior" from your spouse (e.g., "It would make me feel good if you would do. . . .").

(b) Giving "Pleases" and positive feedback to spouse when he/she does something that pleases you (e.g., "When you do (say) . . . , it makes me feel great!").

3. The *Marital Contracting Exercise* leads couples in a stepwise fashion from the identification of personal needs and desires in the marriage to the negotiation of sets of behavioral responsibilities and their consequential privileges in a mutually agreed upon contingency contract. In developing the contract openly in the group, spouses establish specific behavioral commitments for self and other, empathize, bargain, and compromise with each other. The structured, stepwise elements in this exercise are described in detail in another publication (Weathers and Liberman, 1975). The exercise leads to a "parallel, explicit exchange, *quid pro quo*" model of a contract in which each spouse can separately initiate changes in desired behaviors and receive contingent rewards irrespective of the compliance or noncompliance of the other spouse (Weiss, Birchler, & Vincent, 1974). The exercise was carried out over a period of three group sessions. In this session the exercise was begun by each spouse choosing a behavior or action by self that pleases the other. This is followed by each spouse choosing a behavior or action of other that will please self. After exchanging the latter, each spouse has two potential behavioral responsibilities that represent actions or expressions that would please their partner.

4. Homework Assignments:

(a) Counting "Pleases" and "Love Days" were assigned as above.

(b) "Executive Sessions": For 10 minutes or more each day couples were instructed to practice giving "Pleases" and acknowledging them.

SESSION 4

1. Reviews were made for homework on "Pleases" and "Executive Sessions" by going around the group and having each couple describe their experiences.

2. Behavioral rehearsals focused on expressing negative feelings directly and spontaneously. Examples of this element of interpersonal communication include:

(a) Accusativeness and indirect expressions of anger or resentment vs. directly "owning up" to feelings (e.g., "You're a bitch," [indirect, accusative] vs. "When you do . . . it makes me mad and boil up inside," [direct, "owning up"]).

(b)Distinctions among passive-aggressive withdrawal, appropriate assertiveness, and aggressiveness.

(c) Sulking and withdrawal vs. direct and spontaneous expression of feelings.

3. The second phase of the *Marital Contracting Exercise* builds empathy by requiring both parties to state how they would feel if their partner actually would carry out the behaviors chosen as responsibilities in the first phase. Each spouse is prompted by the group leaders to indicate how much the behavioral responsibility of their partner would be valued, how hard it would be to carry out, and how much it would be appreciated. Next, each spouse sets the costs of carrying out his/her two designated responsibilities by ordering them according to degree of difficulty.

4. Homework Assignments:

(a) Counting "Pleases" and "Love Days" were assigned as above.

(b) "Executive Sessions": Couples were instructed to practice expressing negative feelings directly to each other for at least ten minutes each day.

SESSION 5

1. "Pleases" and "Executive Sessions" were reviewed as above.

2. Behavior rehearsals focused on learning how to empathize with your spouse. Each person was shown how to reflect back what his/her spouse said to the latter's satisfaction before going on with his/her side of the conversation. This empathy exercise had the effect of slowing down acrimonious interactions, thereby inhibiting the branching off into irrelevant and pent-up recriminations.

3. The *Marital Contracting Exercise* proceeds by each spouse choosing a behavioral privilege or reward that would please self and one that would please his/her partner. These privileges can include engaging in pleasant activities alone or with spouse as well as purchasing or consuming certain goods. After exchanging privileges chosen for and accepted by their partners, each spouse has two potential rewards to match with correspondingly weighted responsibilities. The final stage of the exercise

involves bargaining and compromising between marital dyads with the schedule of the exchange process (i.e., how much privilege is contingent upon how much of performed responsibilities) being made explicit. Bonuses for consistent fulfillment of responsibilities and penalties for infractions and failure to fulfill responsibilities can be added.

4. Homework Assignments:

(a) Counting "Pleases" and "Love Days" were continued as above.

(b) Each spouse was instructed to monitor his/her completed contract on data check lists provided. In addition, the clinic secretary asked each spuose to report the progress of his/her compliance with the terms of the contract during each between-session phone call.

(c) "Executive Sessions" were to focus on the empathy exercise for at least ten minutes each day.

SESSION 6

1. "Pleases," "Executive Sessions," and contracts were reviewed by going around the group.

2. Behavioral rehearsals dealt with reactions to unexpected hostility, bad moods, displaced anger, and persistent negative behavior from one's spouse. Through modelling, rehearsal, prompting, and feedback, each spouse was shown a variety of tactics helpful in defusing potentially destructive and coercive situations. These tactics included:

(a) giving repeated, persistent "Pleases" and "melting" negative feelings through these positive responses

(b) ignoring the negative behavior and diversion into positive activities or reinforcers.

(c) a brief time-out or "cooling off" period taken by the target of the negative feelings. This maneuver helps to develop equitable distance between spouses by asking for and structuring time apart. In taking a time-out from a potentially angry interchange, the person must indicate the following:

(1) that he/she cannot tolerate the continued negative feelings by "owning up" directly to his/her feelings and expressing them, without accusation, to the partner

(2) that he/she is taking a brief time-out to help cool the situation

(3) where he/she is going (e.g., around the block or into another room)

(4) how long he/she will be gone

(5) that upon returning, he/she will be pleased to discuss the conflict, argument, or unpleasantness and try to resolve it by using an "Executive Session."

3. Contracts were renegotiated and amended as needed.

4. Homework Assignments:

(a) Counting "Pleases" and "Love Days" were continued as above.

(b) Monitoring of the contract was continued.

(c) "Executive Sessions" were to be scheduled to practice dealing with negative feelings.

SESSIONS 7 AND 8

1. "Pleases," "Love Days," "Executive Sessions," and contracts were reviewed in the group.

2. Behavioral rehearsals reviewed special areas of need for each couple.

3. Contracts were renegotiated and amended as needed.

4. Homework Assignments:
   (a) Counting "Pleases" and "Love Days" were continued as above.
   (b) Monitoring of the contract was continued.
   (c) "Executive Sessions" were encouraged to focus on the special areas of marital communication that still posed problems for each couple.

SESSION 9

(1 month later)

This session was a review and follow-up with the leaders using themselves as "consultants" to the couples who wished or required additional training in communication or contracting skills.

Interaction-Insight Group. The aims of the therapists for the Interactional Group were.

1. To establish cohesiveness through encouraging group members to ventilate feelings and share similar problems.

2. To use empathy, warmth and concern with each other and with the group members as models for spouses.

3. To assist the couples to describe their problems and dissatisfactions more specifically and clearly without mutual recriminations and blaming.

4. To suggest ways that the couples could improve their relationships by changing their responses to each other at home. Advice was given on how to move from coercive to reciprocal exchanges.

5. To provide insight and awareness into their interpersonal behavior and self-defeating ways by giving feedback. Interpretations were made from an interpersonal, reality based framework, not from a psychodynamic one.

The leaders prompted the group members to respond to each other and to offer suggestions for helping one another. Emphasis was placed on ventilating feelings directly and spontaneously, giving positive and negative feedback to each other, and asking directly for what they wanted from each other. Intermember interaction and mutual support was encouraged, prompted, and "reinforced."

Each group session was begun by reviewing the individual graphs reflecting their exchange of "Pleases" during the previous week. Since the graphs were extended weekly in an ongoing fashion, it was possible to place each week's "Pleases" in the perspective of the past weeks' exchanges. There were frequent explanations of the importance of reciprocity in marriage and the necessity to give "Pleases" in order to receive them. In the second session, there was a showing of the "Tenderness" film with an introduction to the importance of specificity and directness in asking for and acknowledging physical affection and sex; however, there was no massage exercise as in the Behavioral Group.

The leaders were careful to avoid any behavioral rehearsal or roleplaying and contingency contracting in the Interactional Group. While problems were pinpointed and suggestions for change specifically made, the Interactional Group received no exposure to behavioral rehearsal or contracting, and there were no "homework" assignments given between sessions, except for the weekly counting and reporting of "Pleases."

RESULTS

Attendance was 100 percent for the Behavioral Group members while four of the ten members of the Interactional Group missed seven of the meetings, an attendance rate of 92 percent. From the point of view of faithfulness in reporting daily data, the Behavioral Group members were more regular and reliable in their reports to the clinic secretary and on their report sheets. For the self-report of "Pleases" given and received, "Shared Recreational Activities," and "Hours spent together," the members of the Behavioral Group provided data more often than their counterparts in the Interactional Group on 30 of 32 comparisons during treatment and baseline periods ($p < 0.001$, sign test).

In the Behavioral Group, the leaders discovered that they had inadvertently programmed too many interventions and activities into the session formats. As a result, some sessions went 15 minutes overtime and were gripped by a sense of hurriedness. For example, the weekly review of "Pleases," using graphic feedback and group interaction, took up 20-30 minutes of each session for both groups. The pace was more relaxed

TABLE 3

Examples of the Contingency Contracts Developed by the Couples in the Behavioral Group

Couple	Contingencies: Responsibilities	Contingencies: Privileges
1 Wife	To greet husband affectionately every day when he comes home from work To plan budget Sundays at 1 p.m. for ½ hr.	Husband will express his feelings and thoughts to me daily at lunch or after work Husband will give me a massage for 20 min
1 Husband	To express approval for something that wife does well once/week To call wife on phone every night from work between 9.30 - 10.00 p.m.	Wife will initiate plans for all leisure time on Saturday Wife will be more pleasant in the morning and will fix a breakfast for every 2 phone calls
2 Wife	To comply or refuse in a friendly way to a request each day To initiate sex once/week	Husband will do same Husband will tolerate my friends and be positive when discussing them
2 Husband	To converse with wife on 5 of 7 days for 5 min. each time on a topic of her choice To go to church with wife once/month	Wife will listen to my views on future work and residence plans once/week for 20 min. Wife will give me a massage every other day for at least 5 min. for 30 days following church attendance
3 Wife	To tolerate and forgive husband's mistakes To allow husband 2 hr/wk to play with son alone	Husband will do same Husband will take me to lunch or dancing once/week
3 Husband	To complete weekly chores without reminders To give wife advance notice when working late To get car serviced once/week	Wife will go for pleasure ride in car with me for 30 min once/week Wife will respond in a friendly way when given notice about late working Wife will help to plan household repairs and chores
4 Wife	To clean one room of house to husband's satisfaction each week To massage husband 3 times/week	Husband will express approval of work once/day Husband will reciprocate the same
4 Husband	To ask about wife's feelings 1-2 times/day To spend 3 hr/week doing something together with whole family	Wife will tolerate or say something nice about two of my friends Wife will initiate sex 3 times/week

in the Interactional Group with the leaders finding more time to encourage the group members to react to each other as experiences and issues were shared. Without a fixed curriculum of pre-planned interventions, the leaders felt more spontaneous during their sessions with the Interactional Group. However, it is of interest that the Behavioral Group developed an esprit and cohesiveness which led to two spontaneous "reunions" at two and twelve months after termination.

The leaders found the members of the Behavioral Group responsive to instructions and prompts during the weekly exercises in communication skills and during the contingency contracting exercise. In Table 3 are listed the clauses or contingencies of the contracts agreed to by the four couples in the Behavioral Group. Compliance to the terms of the contracts varied from couple to couple, with an average fulfillment rate of 72 percent. Two couples (1 and 4) followed through flawlessly while the other two couples met their contract terms sporadically.

Shortly after the Interactional Group ended, one couple separated. This came about principally because the wife, who had come to every meeting including the final three in the absence of her husband, gained assertive skills through encouragement from the leaders and the group members and decided to set limits on her husband's actions in carrying on an extra-marital affair. Their separation lasted six months during which time the wife developed friendships of her own and started college. They reconciled seven months after the group's termination. One couple from Behavioral Group had a brief one month separation nine months after treatment ended, ostensibly in the wake of the wife's returning to graduate school, thereby outdistancing her husband careerwise. After 4 sessions of additional counseling they reconciled.

"Pleases" Counted as Given and Received. In Table 4 are listed 20 examples of "Pleases" received by husbands and wives. Couples varied in the extent to which they reported graphic examples of "Pleases" that they had given and received each week. With few exceptions, the marital partners did not follow through with their "Love Day" assignments in either group. From their anecdotal statements it appeared that the requirement to keep track of daily "Pleases" on wrist counters was experienced as a burdensome and easily forgotten task. Once the initial novelty wore off, the group members kept their wrist counter tallies in a *pro forma* manner which kept the letter but not the spirit of the task.

There was enormous variation from spouse to spouse in the number of "Pleases" which were reported as both given and received. In Table 5

TABLE 4

Examples of "Pleases" Received from Spouse and Recorded by Members of Both Marital Therapy Groups

"Pleases" received from wives and recorded by husbands	"Pleases" received from husbands and recorded by wives
1. Asked if I needed anything from the store.	1. Called to say he loved me.
2. Came out to greet me when I came home.	2. Called to tell me when he would be home and asked how I was.
3. Fixed an especially nice dinner.	3. Gave me a nice, long hug.
4. Went to a ball game with me.	4. Listened attentively to my complaints.
5. Suggested going on a picnic.	5. Gave me a super back-scratch.
6. Helped me stay on my diet.	6. Played with our son.
7. Listened to my work problems.	7. Got out my sewing machine and ironing board.
8. Said that I was sexy and that she was proud of me.	8. Patted my knee.
9. Called me at work and asked how I felt.	9. Cuddled in bed with me in the morning.
10. Was very affectionate in the evening.	10. Cooked his own dinner.
11. Talked and held hands in bed feeling close.	11. Washed the dishes.
12. Let me take a walk alone while she managed the children.	12. Let me have coffee while he took care of our son.
13. Gave me a nice back rub.	13. Called to tell me he would be working overtime.
14. Helped me find a tool I had misplaced.	14. Shopped with me for birthday presents and invited me out to dinner.
15. Brought me coffee in bed.	15. Repaired water sprinkler.
16. Held dinner until 9 p.m. for me.	16. Told me what a great day he had with the family.
17. Agreed to diet with me.	17. Brought home small gifts for everyone as a surprise.
18. Talked openly about her feelings.	18. Fixed cheese omelets for breakfast —my favorite!
19. Let me sleep late.	19. Made reservations for a show.
20. Supported me in controversy with our son.	20. Helped our son with algebra without getting angry.

TABLE 5

Number of "Pleases" Given and Received as Reported by Spouses Attending Behavioral and Interactional Groups. Variations in Number of Reporting Days Occurred Because Baseline Periods Varied from Couple to Couple and Some Spouses Failed to Report Data on Occasional Days.

			Treatment period	
	Baseline Mean (Range)	Weeks 1+2 Mean (Range)	Weeks 3+4 Mean (Range)	Weeks 5+6+7 Mean (Range)
Reporting Days				
Behavioral	14.1 (6-24)	13.4 (12-14)	13.4 (12-14)	15 (7-21)
Interactional	10.4 (7-13)	13.7 (13-14)	13.1 (9-14)	13.9 (7-21)
Pleases Given/Spouse/Day				
Behavioral	5.9 (0-14)	4.4 (0-16)	4.4 (0-16)	3.8 (0-16)
Interactional	4.1 (0-19)	4.1 (0-19)	4.2 (0.16)	4.9 (0-12)
Pleases Received/Spouse/Day				
Behavioral	9.1 (0-51)	6.3 (0-33)	5.9 (0-18)	5.0 (0-15)
Interactional	5.7 (0-13)	4.9 (0-19)	5.0 (0-15)	5.9 (1-14)

is listed the mean number of "Pleases" for members of the two groups during baseline and three intervals of treatment.

With the large amount of inter-individual variance, there were no statistically significant differences within groups over time or between the groups on raw numbers of "Pleases." It is of note that for members of both groups, the number of "Pleases" reported as *received from spouse* regularly exceeded the number reported as *given to spouse,* by a factor of 1.2 to 1.5.

To evaluate the degree to which recorded "Pleases" might operationally reflect reciprocity between spouses, correlation coefficients were calculated among the various combinations of "Pleases" given and received. The sources and types of data used for these Pearson product-moment correlations are presented in Table 6.

During the baseline recordings, 33 and 50 percent of all possible correlation coefficients were statistically significant at beyond the 0.05 level for the Behavioral and Interactional Groups respectively. During the treatment period 80 percent of the possible correlation coefficients for the

TABLE 6

Mean Pearson product-moment correlation coefficients for wrist counter recordings of "Pleases" given and received. These correlations approximate operational measures of reciprocity between spouses in the Behavioral (N = 8) and Interactional (N = 10) Groups. The correlations were calculated for each individual by using the available daily reports of "Pleases" given and received. The correlations were then averaged across the members in each group for the baseline and treatment periods. In determining statistical significance the degrees of freedom were based on the number of couples.

Sources of Recorded "Pleases"	Baseline Period Behavioral	Baseline Period Interactional	Treatment Period Behavioral	Treatment Period Interactional
Within each spouse				
Self: No. "Pleases" given to spouse / Self: No. "Pleases" received from spouse	.55	.64	.61	.61
Across Spouses				
Self: No. "Pleases" given to spouse / Other: No. "Pleases" received from spouse	.15	.41	.42	.39
Self: No. "Pleases" given to spouse / Other: No. "Pleases" given to spouse	.04	.55	.23	.37
Self: No. "Pleases" received from spouse / Other: No. "Pleases" received from spouse	.12	.39	.36	.26

couples in the Behavioral Group were statistically significant at beyond the 0.05 level. During the treatment period, 73 percent of the possible correlation coefficients were statistically significant for the Interactional Group. Most of the correlations were of low magnitude, indicating rather poor reliability or agreement between the spouses on their detection and recording of pleasing events. The comparison which led to the highest correlations in both groups, thereby serving as the relatively best indicator of reciprocity, was the number of "Pleases" recorded as received by each spouse vs. the number of "Pleases" recorded as given by the same spouse.

There are no statistically significant differences in the correlations between groups or within groups from baseline to treatment periods. For each mean correlation, there was an increase in "reciprocity" for the Behavioral Group and a decrease for the Interactional Group from baseline to treatment periods.

Hours Together, Shared Recreational Activities, and Marital Activities Inventory. While there was a large amount of inter-individual and intra-individual variation on the reported number of waking hours spent together with spouse, little difference was noted between the group means, or within each group over time from baseline through treatment. Couples from both groups averaged 6.4 hours spent together each day. Most of the intra-individual variation in hours together stemmed from working days vs. weekends and holidays. The average number of daily shared recreational activities was 3.5 with a range from 0 to 15 depending upon the couple. Even within each couple there was poor agreement in their separate reports. The group means, however, were fairly similar and did not show any systematic changes from baseline through treatment. The mean scores for the Marital Activities Inventory were similar for the two groups. While the members from both groups reported *decreases* in the total number of Marital Activities from the month prior to the group to the last month of the group, at the same time members from both groups indicated *less desire for change* in the frequency of marital activities at the time of termination.

Marital Pre-Counseling Inventory. For each of the sub-scales of this Inventory, a split-plot, factorial ANOVA was performed with one "between subjects" variable (type of therapy), and one "within subjects" variable (pre- vs. post-therapy periods) (see footnote p. 494). There were no statistically significant differences found for any of the comparisons.

Areas of Change Questionnaire. The two halves of this questionnaire require the respondent to indicate how much he/she wants changes in his/her spouse and also how much change he/she thinks his/her spouse wants in him/her. Thus, each person states his/her own desire to have changes made by spouse and also projects an estimate for his/her spouse's desires for changes in self. The data from each person's own desire for change in his/her spouse showed no statistically significant differences either between treatment groups or within groups over time from pre- to post-testing. However, the estimates or projections made about his/her spouse's desires for change did show a statistically significant difference among the scores obtained at the four measurement points irrespective of the treatment group involved ($F = 6.36$, $p < 0.01$, ANOVA). Tukey's HSD test indicated that the pre-test scores were significantly higher than all of the post-test scores ($p < 0.01$) but that there were no differences among the post-test scores done at time of termination, two months, and six months after termination. This signifies that, for both groups, there was felt to be less desire for change from one's spouse after termination of treatment.

By comparing the desires for changes expressed by a husband with his wife's estimate of his desires for changes, an "understanding" or congruence score could be ascertained. This score reflects the degree of understanding or empathy by each spouse and is a measure of the state of their relationship. For example, if a husband stated that he wanted his wife to give *much more attention* to his sexual needs and she, in turn, indicated that it would please her husband if she paid *much more attention* to his sexual needs, the wife would be given an optimal score for understanding or congruence on that item. The same calculation could be made for a husband's understanding score. These "understanding" scores were analyzed by means of a split-plot, factorial ANOVA with one between subjects variable (type of treatment) and one within subjects variable (testing times). Results indicated significant differences among the testing times ($F = 10.79$, $p < 0.01$) and a significant interaction between the types of treatment and the testing times ($F = 3.36$, $p < 0.05$). Degrees of freedom were based on the number of spouses. Further analysis of the interaction using a test of simple main effects indicated that the Behavioral Group partners developed significantly closer understanding or congruence from pre- to post-therapy. No such improvement in understanding occurred in the Interactional Group.

Marital Adjustment Test. The means for the Locke-Wallace MAT administered before and after therapy and at one, two, and six month follow-ups are presented in Table 7. Seven of eight in the Behavioral Group and eight of ten in the Interactional Group showed increases in their marital satisfaction from before to after therapy. The pre-therapy scores are similar to those reported by others who have used this test to evaluate their treatment of distressed couples (Kuhn, 1973; Weiss, Hops, & Patterson, 1973). A split-plot, factorial ANOVA was performed with comparisons for type of therapy and for change over time at the various measurement periods. The F ratio for the time variable indicated that

TABLE 7

Mean Scores of the Locke-Wallace Marital Adjustment Test for the Behavioral (N = 8) and the Interactional (N = 10) Groups

	Pre-therapy	Termination	Follow-ups 1 Month	2 Month	6 Month
Behavioral Group	74.5	92.3	91.0	96.5	93.4
Interactional Group	64.6	84.0	88.0	93.7	91.5

TABLE 8

Group Means per Session and Individual Ranges in Time-Sampled Observations of Nonverbal Behavior Expressed by One Spouse to Another During Treatment Sessions

	Behavioral Group Means	Ranges	Interactional Group Means	Ranges
Touches	3.80	(0.13-9.88)	2.00	(0.0 -5.0)
Looks	2.90[a]	(1.38-4.50)	1.02	(0.29-2.00)
Looks and Smiles	0.88[a]	(0.38-1.38)	0.34	(0.0 -1.00)

[a] Behavioral Group's mean significantly greater than Interactional Group's mean $p < 0.001$ (t test).

there were significant differences in the scores of both groups across the five time periods ($F = 9.74$, $p < 0.01$). Tukey's HSD test revealed that the pre-therapy scores were significantly lower than all of the post-therapy scores ($p < 0.01$) and that there were no significant differences among the post-therapy scores. The improvement in marital satisfaction obtained by members from both groups tended to stabilize and be maintained from the time of termination to the six month follow-up point. The MAT scores obtained from the three couples from the Behavioral Group who attended the one year, spontaneous reunion indicated that their improvement in reported satisfaction was sustained at the same level as at the six month follow-up.

Observations of Nonverbal Behavior. The group means and interindividual ranges for "Touches," "Looks," and "Looks and Smiles" (Eisler, Hersen, & Agras, 1973) are presented in Table 8. The average percent effective agreement between raters for all three of the nonverbal behaviors was 67.3 with a range of 54.5 to 78.6 percent from the initial observational period to the final one. If the initial session, during which the second rater was being trained, is excluded, the inter-rater agreement rises to 72.5 percent. For each of these nonverbal behaviors, a split-plot, factorial ANOVA was performed with one "between subjects" variable (type of therapy), and one "within subjects" variable (mean for sessions 1 plus 2 vs. mean for sessions 7 plus 8). For "Touches" there was no significant difference between groups using the overall mean. However, the Behavioral Group's mean for sessions 1 and 2 was significantly higher than that of the Interactional Group ($F = 7.77$, $p < 0.01$). These differences were not apparent during sessions 7 and 8. Neither group showed statistically significant changes from sessions 1 and 2 to sessions 7 and 8.

The data on "Looks" given by one spouse to another indicated that there was a statistically significant difference between the groups. Using the overall mean, the members of the Behavioral Group looked at each other more often than their counterparts in the Interactional Group ($t = 4.95$, $p < 0.001$). The analysis of data from sessions 1 and 2 as well as from sessions 7 and 8 revealed that the marital partners in the Behavioral Group gave more "Looks" to each other during the initial two sessions and the final two sessions of the treatment than those in the Interactional Group ($F = 11.44$, $p < 0.01$). "Looks and Smiles" exchanged between partners also differentiated the two groups. Results indicated significant differences for both types of treatment ($F = 15.99$, $p < 0.01$) and measurement times ($F = 12.46$, $p < 0.01$) and for the interaction of the two variables ($F = 6.75$, $p < 0.01$). Analysis of the interaction using a test of simple main effects indicated that the spouses in the Behavioral Group looked and smiled at each other significantly more during the first two sessions but not the last two sessions. The overall number of "Looks and Smiles" for the Behavioral Group was significantly higher than that for the Interactional Group ($t = 3.65$, $p < 0.001$). It should be noted that the communication skills training which comprised an important part of the Behavioral Group's interventions focused directly on these nonverbal behaviors; thus, on occasion, the time-sampled observations were of "Looks," "Touches," and "Smiles," that were being prompted by the group leaders. Since, during any single observation period, often none and not more than one couple were engaged in role-playing, the nonverbal data reveal more about the outcome rather than the process of training in communication skills.

Marital Interaction Coding System (MICS). From the 18 pre-and post-therapy videotapes, 5 were chosen by a table of random numbers for inter-rater reliability. Percent effective agreement averaged 78 and ranged from 73 to 85 percent. As in the study reported by Weiss, Hops, & Patterson (1973), six collective categories were formulated by grouping discrete codes. In Table 9 are presented the collective categories with their constituent codes and the group means for the pre-therapy and post-therapy assessments of the video-tapes. Given the normative data compiled by Weiss and his colleagues on the MICS (Weiss, Hops, and Patterson, 1973), Levels I, IV, and V would be expected to increase and levels II, III, and VI would be expected to decrease as a function of treatment.

Split-plot factorial ANOVA's were performed to test for differences between groups and for differences over time within groups. Level I, "Problem Solving," showed a significant interaction between the time periods and the treatment. Tests of simple main effects revealed that the only statistically significant comparison was that the members of the Interactional Group had a higher percentage of "Problem Solving" acts than the members of the Behavioral Group prior to the start of therapy ($F = 4.57$, $p < 0.05$). However, there were no differences after therapy. Neither group changed significantly from pre- to post-therapy although the increase in "Problem Solving" by the Behavioral Group members approached statistical significance ($F = 3.02$, $p < 0.10$). There were no statistifically significant interactions or comparisons for Level II, "Problem Description," behaviors.

Level III or "Negative Verbal Behaviors" showed a significant interaction between measurement times and the treatments ($F = 9.41$, $p < 0.01$) A test of simple main effects indicated that the Behavioral Group members decreased their "Negative Verbal Behaviors" to a statistically significant degree from pre- to post-therapy ($F = 9.51$, $p < 0.01$). The Interactional Group showed no correspondingly significant change. There were no statistically significant differences between the groups at either pre- or post-therapy. No significant interactions appeared for behaviors in Level IV, "Positive Verbal."

Levels V and VI, "Positive and Negative Non-Verbals" respectively, showed results favoring the Behavioral Group. For Level V there was a significant interaction between the variables of time and treatment ($F = 12.57$, $p < 0.01$). A test of simple main effects indicated that the Behavioral Group members increased their output of "Positive Non-Verbals" from pre- to post-therapy ($F = 11.47$, $p < 0.01$) and that the Behavioral Group was higher than the Interactional Group after therapy ($F = 7.37$, $p < 0.01$). There were no differences between the groups before therapy and the Interactional Group did not significantly change from pre- to post-therapy. For Level VI there was a significant interaction between the variables of time and treatment ($F = 7.73$, $p < 0.01$). A test of simple

TABLE 9

Comparison of Pre- and Post-therapy mean (normalized) MICS level Scores for Behavioral and Interactional Groups. The means are expressed as a fraction of the subtotals for verbal and nonverbal interaction coded by the MICS. The levels are mutually exclusive but only 21 of the 28 categories of the MICS are included in the Levels. Therefore, verbal and nonverbal subtotals add up to less than 1.00 each.

	Behavioral Group		Interactional Group	
	Pre	Post	Pre	Post
Level I: Problem-solving (Accept responsibility, Compromise, Problem solving)	0.14	0.23	0.27[a]	0.21
Level II: Problem Description (Negative Solution, Problem description, Solution past)	0.24	0.30	0.29	0.32
Level III: Negative Verbal (Complaint, Criticism, Deny Responsibility, Excuse, Put Down)	0.23	0.08[b]	0.13	0.19
Level IV: Positive Verbal (Agree. Approval, Humor)	0.04	0.06	0.07	0.04
Level V: Positive Nonverbal (Assent, Laugh, Positive physical contact, Smile)	0.27	0.51[b,c]	0.36	0.25
Level VI: Negative Nonverbal (no response, Not tracking, Turn off)	0.35	0.12[b,d]	0.29	0.38

[a] Interactional Group pre-therapy score significantly higher than Behavioral Group pre-therapy score ($p < 0.05$).
[b] Behavioral Group's pre- and post-therapy scores significantly different ($p < 0.01$).
[c] Behavioral Group's post-therapy score significantly different from Interactional Group's post-therapy score ($p < 0.01$).
[d] Behavioral Group's post-therapy score significantly different from Interactional Group's post-therapy score ($p < 0.05$).

main effects indicated that the Behavioral Group members decreased their output of "Negative Non-Verbals" from pre- to post-therapy ($F = 8.45$, $p < 0.01$) and that the Behavioral Group was lower than the Interactional Group after therapy ($F = 5.72$, $p < 0.05$). There were no differences between the groups prior to therapy and the Interactional Group showed no significant change from pre- to post-therapy.

Consumer Satisfaction. On the three questions from the Therapy Evaluation Questionnaire designed to assess satisfaction with the group, there was almost complete agreement by members of both groups that their experiences were beneficial and helpful. All but one of the members in both groups "felt that the group was worth the time invested" and "would recommend their group to a friend." Seven of eight in the Behavioral Group and eight of ten in the Interactional Group indicated that they had improved "somewhat" or "much" in their abilities to cope with marital conflict. Of the methods in the Behavioral Group, the role-playing of communication skills was viewed as most helpful. All but one member in each group felt that their communication skills had improved as a result of the group therapy.

DISCUSSION

This clinical experiment adds to the sparse number of empirical evaluations of marital therapy. It represents the first comparative study of two different approaches to marital group therapy using multidimensional or multilevel measures of outcome and reflects the "state of the art" in research on marriage counseling. The external validity of the findings is increased by virtue of the experiment being carried out in a typical community mental health center with a psychiatric nurse and social worker serving as co-therapists for the two groups. The interventions and assessment battery were tested in the crucible of a common clinical setting rather than in an academic laboratory. Thus, the study serves as an example to others that meaningful research can be tied to clinical practice with only a small expenditure for special resources. A part-time research assistant performed "live" observations during the sessions and helped in the pre- and post-testing of the couples. The videotapes were made on half-inch Sony equipment which is available to most community mental health centers and counseling clinics. The tapes were rated by an already trained coder from another part of the country who was "blind" to the purposes of the study and to the order and group assignment of the couples of the tapes. The cost of rating the pre- and post-therapy videotapes was only $120 including the reliability assay. Thus, the methods of treatment and evaluation as well as the results are generalizable and applicable to most settings where marital therapy is conducted. Rather than collecting dust in journals, research on marital therapy should be integrated with clinical practice, thereby avoiding the schism which has plagued psychotherapy research for the past thirty years.

Turning to the outcome data, it can be summarized by stating that both groups showed significant improvement in their self-reported marital satisfaction from pre- to post-therapy, but only the members of the Behavioral Group demonstrated improvements in their directly observed interactions. This would be an expected finding if one views subjectively expressed marital satisfaction as a variable more responsive to desires to please the therapists, acquiescent response sets, suggestions and advice, and attention-placebo interventions. Another self-reported index of satisfaction with treatment, the consumer satisfaction questionnaire, also reflected nearly unanimous, positive feelings by members of both groups regarding their therapy. On the other hand, the interactional level of behavior, as measured by the observations of nonverbal behavior during the sessions and the MICS before and after therapy, reflects goals that were specifically targeted for direct intervention in the Behavioral Group and for indirect intervention in the Interactional Group. Advice, in-group spontaneous interactions, interpretations, and encouragement to change marital communication failed to produce the detectable improvements which were formed in members of the group which received direct training via behavioral rehearsal. In Table 10 the major differences in outcome between the two groups are summarized.

It might be speculated that the differences between the groups would have been larger and detectable in other levels of measurement in favor of the Behavioral Group had the training in discriminating and acknowledging "Pleases" been limited to that group only. This was not done originally because the authors wished to use the recorded "Pleases" as a dependent measure as well as an intervention. However, the daily event-recorded "Pleases" proved to be an unreliable measure as well as insensitive to the treatments. While the correlation coefficients reflecting inter-spouse agreement on the frequency of recorded "Pleases" were statistically significant, their magnitudes were a relatively low 0.40 during treatment. Despite the therapists' focusing on the reports of "Pleases" and emphasizing in both groups the importance of pinpointing and counting "Pleases" for 20-30 minutes each session, the number reported actually declined in the Behavioral Group and remained fairly steady in the Interactional Group over the nine weeks of treatment. The failure of the "Pleases" records to increase with treatment is at odds with the data reported by Weiss, Hops, & Patterson (1973). Using a similar measure, "Pleasures," these workers found an increase from baseline to post-intervention in ten couples. The disparity in results may be a function of the differences in the way that the data were recorded by the spouses. In the current study, the "Pleases" were counted every day for the duration of treatment, while in the Weiss et al. study, counting was apparently done for only one week prior to and after treatment. The increase found by Weiss and his colleagues may have been a more valid reflection of at-home changes or may have partially come from a desire to please the therapists. The decreasing or fairly constant counts in the current study may reflect adaptation, bore-

TABLE 10

Major Differences in the Results Obtained Between the Behavioral and Interactional Groups

Outcome Measure	Summary of Comparative Results
Attendance	Behavioral Group = 100% vs. Interactional Group = 92%.
Reporting data from homework assignments	Behavioral Group members more regularly provided data on "Pleases," "Hours Together," and "Shared Recreational Activities."
Areas of Change Questionnaire	Behavioral Group members, after treatment, showed significantly greater understanding or congruence in their estimation of how their spouse actually wanted them to change.
Nonverbal Interaction coded during treatment sessions	Behavioral Group members "looked" and "looked & smiled" at their spouse significantly more often than members of the Interactional Group.
Marital Interaction Coding System (MICS)	Behavioral Group members showed significant decreases in "Negative Verbal" and "Negative Nonverbal" and increases in "Positive Nonverbal" categories at post-therapy assessments as compared to pre-therapy. Behavioral Group members showed significantly more "Positive Nonverbal" and less "Negative Nonverbal" behaviors than those in the Interactional Group at the post-therapy assessment.

dom, unreliability, and the aversiveness of continuing to count discrete events for such a long period of time.

Having the spouses separately count "Pleases" given and received enabled the authors to carry out a correlational analysis of the concept of reciprocity in marriage; that is, the hypothesis that each marital partner *receives* positive reinforcement from his/her spouse in proportion to the amount of positive reinforcement *given* to his/her spouse. While the number of "Pleases" recorded as received from spouse reliably exceeded the number recorded as given to spouse, the correlation coefficients between these data exceeded 0.60 during treatment. Given the relatively low level of agreement between spouses on the frequency of occurrence of "Pleases," the reciprocity hypothesis can only be given a small degree of support from the data of this study. More directly observed measures of marital interaction will be necessary to confirm or disconfirm the reciprocity hypothesis. The members in the Behavioral Group showed a tendency toward increases in reciprocity from baseline to termination which was not found in the Interactional Group.

A recent behavioral analysis of the determinants of marital satisfaction suggests that decreasing displeasurable behaviors may be a better means of improving marital adjustment (Wills, Weiss, and Patterson, 1974). The authors found that "Displeases" accounted for 65 percent of the explainable variance in rated satisfaction and that the immediate tendency to reciprocate displeasurable acts was stronger than that for pleasurable behaviors.

The measures of marital "togetherness" failed to show any change with treatment. This is in agreement with the data obtained by Weiss and his colleagues and may reflect a common intervention strategy in marriage counseling wherein the therapist advises the couple to seek outlets and satisfactions in recreational and social activities outside of the marital dyad or family unit. In fact, the leaders of the two groups in this study spent two hours during three separate sessions outlining a four point program for recreational and social participation—solitary participation, participation in the marital dyad, participation with the family, and participation with friends. This explanation for the lack of change in the absolute amount of mutual time and activities is supported by the finding that couples from both groups expressed less desire for altering these mutual experiences at the time of termination.

The roughly equivalent improvement in marital satisfaction on the Locke-Wallace test among members of both groups coincides with the findings reported by other marriage counselors. In the study by Weiss et al. (1973) the mean increase in scores on the Locke-Wallace test was almost 40 points while in the current study the increases were 20-30 points. In an evaluation of eight hours of marriage counseling for 39 clients, Kuhn (1973) found a mean increase of 14 points in the Locke-Wallace Marital Adjustment Test. It is reassuring to note that the rise in marital satisfaction detected immediately after therapy was completed was sustained throughout the six month follow-up period in both groups. The Areas of Change Questionnaire also revealed improvements in marital satisfaction as perceived in each other's spouse. The failure to find statistically significant improvements in the Marital Pre-Counseling Inventory is puzzling. However, positive changes, especially in those individuals who reported the largest increase in satisfaction on the Locke-Wallace test, were found but were not large enough in magnitude to be statistically significant.

At the interactional level, training in communication skills given directly through behavioral rehearsal in the Behavioral Group led to more frequent mutual interest as shown by non-verbal, orienting responses. These differences between the groups were detected from the first session onward since the training in communication skills for the Behavioral Group began in the first session. The data from the MICS is the "hardest" result showing the superiority of the outcome for the Behavioral Group. In each collective category, the Behavioral Group's means change in a desirable direction whereas the means from the Interactional Group showed deleterious changes in five of the six categories or levels. While differences between the group means in Level I (Problem Solving) did not reach statistical significance, seven of eight members of the Behavioral Group exhibited increases in this category while only three of ten in the Interactional Group did likewise. The orders of magnitude for the mean changes in the Behavioral Group's MICS categories were roughly similar to those found by Weiss et al. (1973) in the only other published report of MICS data.

The findings from this multidimensional outcome study call into question the inferences of improvement made by marriage counselors and therapists who in the past have utilized only self-reported measures of change by the clients. In the current study 80 percent of the Interactional Group and 88 percent of the Behavioral Group reported improvement in subjectively felt satisfaction with their marriages. Almost all members from both groups gave positive testimonials to the helpfulness of their therapy experiences which compares favorably with the 70 and 76 percent consumer satisfaction reported by Targow & Zweber (1969) and Burton & Kaplan (1968) respectively. However, only in the Behavioral Group was significant improvement measured in the problem-solving interactions observed by an independent rater who "blindly" coded pre- and post-therapy videotapes of spouses' conversations. In other words, only in the Behavioral Group were the members' cognitive changes correlated with changes in overt, marital interaction. In a review of the literature through 1972, Gurman (1973) found that behavioral marital therapy was associated with an improvement rate of 93 percent, greater than the approximately 70 percent improvement rates reported by nonbehavioral counselors and therapists. The apparent superiority of the behavioral approaches was qualified by the fact that only 19 cases, a small number, were involved. The present study, together with recently published and unpublished reports of behavioral marital therapy by Weiss et al. (1973), Azrin et al. (1973), and Crowe (1976), more than treble, the number of cases while substantiating the same high rate of effectiveness of the behavioral approach.

One criticism of the present study might be that the therapists who led both groups were biased in favor of the behavioral methods. While the senior author, who served as a co-therapist, has a strong behavioral orientation, the other two therapists had many years of training and experience in non-directive and interpretative modes of therapy. They were specifically trained to use behavioral methods for the current study. It might be argued that the differences favoring the Behavioral Group could be explained by greater enthusiasm for the behavioral methods by the leaders which was communicated to and benefited the couples in the Behavioral Group. Strands of evidence against this Hawthorne or placebo effect as an explanation for the differences come from the facts that both groups evinced similar improvements in self-reported marital satisfaction and the same, extremely high consumer satisfaction with the different methods. Additional evidence against a systematic bias by the therapists in favor of the Behavioral Group comes from the data on "Pleases." Both groups received the same instructions and feedback on their exchange of "Pleases" and both groups showed similar results. Differences, hence, appear to have been the result of the specific use of direct training methods in communication skills and contingency contracting.

It should be pointed out that there are few feasible ways out of the dilemma of controlling for attributes of the therapist in psychotherapy outcome research. If one uses different therapists, each with his/her own particular bias and expertise, the criticism could be raised that the "real" differences in the personalities and non-specific qualities of the therapists were not properly matched or controlled. Certainly the problem of expectation bias confounding the results of comparisons in psychotherapy research, including behavior therapy, requires more work at developing approximations to better controlled designs (Kent, O'Leary, Diament, & Dietz, 1974). One design that helps to control for therapist bias is to use therapists who are experienced and committed to their separate and distinctly different methods and then train them to employ each other's methods. If a non-behavioral clinician obtains better results using behavior therapy, then the superiority of the behavioral methods is more convincingly demonstrated. Unfortunately, it is difficult to find the setting and therapists that would be flexible enough to support this type of cross-over treatment.

Perhaps of greater importance to the advancement of research in marital therapy is the need for more naturalistic and direct measures of marital interaction. While self-reported satisfaction on questionnaires remains a critical criterion for outcome, of greater validity would be direct observations of the marital dyad. Some possible directions for developments in outcome measures are the scoring of role playing of critical problem situations that might be standardized; the unobtrusive observation of couples conversing in a waiting room; and the use of random activation of home-based audio and/or videorecorders.

Since a major purpose of the research was to evaluate the effectiveness of the behavioral procedures in marital group therapy, it would be useful to trace the further evolution of the treatment and evaluation package since the completion of the study. Ten additional groups have been run using somewhat altered procedures. Because the event recording of "Pleases" was so time-consuming for the clients and leaders, and was viewed by the clients as the least helpful aspect of the program, it has been replaced by the simpler recording of a single "Please" each day on a sheet of paper titled, "Catch Your Spouse Doing Something Nice and Let Him/Her Know About It," (Turner, 1972). The spouses are encouraged to exchange these sheets at the end of each day to acquaint their partner with the event they discriminated as a "Please." This change in format has increased the regularity of recording and speeded up the review of "Pleases" at each therapy session.

More time has been devoted to training in communication skills since the clients have indicated that this is the most important module in the program and because it is now felt that repeated practice and overlearning may facilitate the durability and generality of improvement. The contracting procedure is used selectively for clients who have progressed in their communication skills to the point of being able to negotiate, compromise, assert their desires and feelings, and deal with unexpected unpleasantness. Experiences have accumulated which suggest that contingency contracting is worth just about the paper it's printed on without the family members having adequate interpersonal communication skills. In the ongoing screening of clients, the Areas of Change Questionnaire and the Marital Pre-Counseling Inventory are used for the initial assessment. The effectiveness of treatment is gauged by the post-therapy administration of the Marital Adjustment Test, and completion of goals given weekly to the clients.

ACKNOWLEDGEMENTS

This work was supported in part by Grant No. MH-26207 from the NIMH Mental Health Services Research and Development Branch. The authors acknowledge the support and helpfulness of Drs. Rafael Canton and Sarah Miller (past and present Directors of Mental Health Services in Ventura County); Dr. Stephen Coray (Director, Ventura County Health Services Agency); Dr. Louis Jolyon West (Professor & Chairman, Department of Psychiatry, UCLA School of Medicine); and Drs. Howard Davis, Marie MacNabola, Frank Ochberg, and Mr. James Cumiskey of the NIMH.

The opinions stated in this article are those of the authors alone and do not represent the official policy of the Ventura County Health Services Agency or the Regents of the University of California.

FOOTNOTE

The results from the various dependent measures were analyzed using an unweighted means, split-plot factorial analysis of variance (ANOVA). This statistical technique allowed determination of answers to the following questions:

1. Were there significant differences between therapy groups on the pre-test results?
2. Were there significant differences between the therapy groups on the post-test results?
3. Were there significant differences between the pre- and post-test results for the Behavioral Group?
4. Were there significant differences between the pre- and post-test results for the Interactional Group?

Source tables for the variance and their respective degrees of freedom are available from the senior author.

REFERENCES

AZRIN, N. H., NASTER, B. J., & JONES, R. Reciprocity counseling: A rapid learning-based procedure for marital counseling. *Behavior Research and Therapy*, 11:365-382, 1973.

BURTON, G., & KAPLAN, H. M. Group counseling in conflicted marriages where alcoholism is present: Clients' evaluation of effectiveness. *Journal of Marriage and the Family*, 30:74-79, 1968.

CROWE, M. J. Conjoint marital therapy: Advice or interpretation? *Journal of Psychosomatic Research*, 17:309-315, 1973.

CROWE, M. J. A comparison of three forms of marital therapy: Behavioral Contracting vs. confrontational-interpretative vs. supportive approaches. Paper presented to the annual meeting of the British Assn. of Behavioral Psychotherapy, Exeter, England, 1976.

EISLER, R. M., HERSEN, M., & AGRAS, W. S. Effects of video tape and instructional feedback on nonverbal marital interaction: An analog study. *Behavior Therapy*, 4:551-558, 1973.

GURMAN, A. S. The effects and effectiveness of marital therapy: A review of outcome research. *Family Process*, 12:145-170, 1973.

HICKMAN, M. E. Facilitation techniques in counseling married couples toward more effective communication. *Dissertation Abstracts*, 31:2107, 1970.

HOLMES, T. H., & MASUDA, M. Life changes and illness susceptibility. In J. P. Scott (Ed.), *Separation and Depression*. Washington, D.C.: American Assn. for the Advancement of Science, Publication No. 94, 1973, pp. 161-186.

HOLMES, T. H., & RAHE, R. H. The social readjustment scale. *Journal of Psychosomatic Research*, 11:213-218, 1967.

Improving Communication in Marriage. Atlanta, Ga.: Human Development Institute, 1967.

KENT, R. N., O'LEARY, K. D., DIAMENT, C., & DIETZ, A. Expectation biases in observational evaluation of therapeutic change. *Journal of Consulting and Clinical Psychology*, 42:774-780, 1974.

KNOX, D. H. *Marriage Happiness*. Champaign, Ill., Research Press, 1971.

KUHN, J. R. *Marriage Counseling: Fact or Fallacy?* Hollywood, Calif.: Newcastle Publishing Co., 1973.

LIBERMAN, R. P. A behavioral approach to family and couple therapy. *American Journal of Orthopsychiatry,* 40:106-118, 1970.

LIBERMAN, R. P. Behavioral marital therapy: Group leader's guide. Unpublished manuscript. Available from BAM Project, 840 West 5th Street, Oxnard, Ca. 93030. 1975.

LOCKE, H. J., & WALLACE, K. M. Short marital-adjustment and prediction tests: Their reliability and validity. *Marriage and Family Living,* 21:251-255, 1959.

OLSON, D. H. Marital and family therapy: Integrative review and critique. *Journal of Marriage and the Family,* 32:501-538, 1970.

SERBER, M., & LAWS, R. Tenderness. A film produced by Behavioral Alternatives, San Luis Obispo, Ca. Available from Diane Serber-Corenman, Atascadero State Hospital, Atascadero, Ca.

STUART, R. B. *Marital Pre-Counseling Inventory*. Champaign, Ill.: Research Press, 1973.

STUART, R. B. Operant-interpersonal treatment for marital discord. *Journal of Consulting and Clinical Psychology,* 33:675-682, 1969.

19

BEHAVIORAL FORMULATIONS OF DEPRESSION

Clive Eastman

University of Birmingham, Birmingham, England

Six current behavioral formulations of depression are reviewed and criticized on the grounds of the narrowness of their conception, their frequently ambiguous initial expression in the literature, and the limited range of reinforcement parameters with which they deal. A decision model is presented that attempts to integrate these formulations into a coherent whole, whilst revealing the temporal and logical relations between them.

This paper has two aims: first, to review six current behavioral formulations of depression and, second, to propose an integration of these theoretical positions into a single explanatory model. Traditional psychiatric definitions, diagnostic classifications, and formulations of depression are not considered, whilst animal models are introduced only where essential.

UNDERLYING ASSUMPTIONS

Before turning to the behavioral formulations themselves, it is well to be aware of the assumptions, at least the more important assumptions,

---

Reprinted with permission from *Psychological Review*, 1976, Vol. 83, No. 4, 277-291.

I wish to express my thanks to Anne Broadhurst for her many helpful comments during the preparation of this paper.

that underlie them. Behavioral formulations being founded in learning theory, their basic assumption is that depression is a consequence of the reinforcement contingencies of which the individual's behavior is a function. More particularly, the depressed person is considered to be on what amounts to an extinction trial (Lazarus, 1968). The prime datum is the frequency of behavior, rather than its topography (Ferster, 1973). Thus, the functional analysis of an individual's depression involves a close examination of the physical and social stimulus fields in which he operates (Kanfer & Saslow, 1965). As Lazarus (1968) has succinctly put it: "One cannot ascribe to learning, response patterns which have no logical antecedents" (p. 83). Characteristically (one might say by definition), affective and cognitive factors do not directly enter into these theoretical formulations, not because they are insignificant data, but because they are less accessible, less manipulable than environmental stimuli. "There is a priority . . . for the general variables which determine the overall availability of behavior" (Ferster, 1966, p. 351).

This raises several fundamental problems. It is accepted by clinicians that the major, indeed the defining, characteristics of depression include behavioral and affective components. The behavioral formulations focus exclusively on behavior, regarding the low rate of response-contingent positive reinforcement as a cause of the feeling of depression. But the direction of causation is not certain. On a priori grounds it is equally possible that a reduction in the frequency of positively reinforcible behavior follows the feeling of depression. In the majority of cases, the frequency of behavior and the affective components of depression do seem to shadow one another closely, but there are exceptions. Ferster (1965) pointed out: "Whether a man who moves and acts slowly is 'depressed' or merely moving slowly is not easily or reliably determined by observing his behavior alone" (p. 9). Thus the elderly may exhibit a relatively low frequency of behavior when compared with the middle-aged or the young, but they are not necessarily depressed. Lewinsohn and MacPhillamy (1974) showed that a lower frequency of potentially pleasant activities, in the elderly, was not associated with lower enjoyability ratings. In contrast, depressed individuals exhibited both reduced frequency and reduced enjoyability ratings.

If the frequency of behavior were directly related to the level of depression, we should expect the patient who has undergone spinal surgery (and has to remain quite immobile for weeks on end) to become depressed. Conversely, we should expect the extremely busy individual to be the last person to become depressed: Neither case holds. The meaning that the frequency and type of behavior has for the individual is crucial. This point has been labored because few of the papers cited in this review make even passing reference to cognitive factors in depression. However, under certain circumstances depression could be regarded as an adaptive response, by virtue of the "secondary gains" that accrue: the social reinforcement from a concerned family or neighbors and the reduced demands made upon those who occupy a "sick" role. We shall see that several theorists do regard secondary gains as important factors in the maintenance of depression.

No attempt has been or will be made in this paper to define "depression," since nobody has yet proposed a generally accepted "complete" definition. It may be that the crucial defining characteristic of clinical depression is a relative or absolute decrease in norepinephrine available at brain receptor sites. Costello (1972a) refers to depression resulting from both behavioral and "endogenous biochemical and neurophysiological changes" (p. 241) and mentions norepinephrine. Seligman (Note 1) tentatively defines depression in terms of behavioral, affective, cognitive, and biochemical (norepinephrine) factors.

In the following discussion of the behavioral formulations of depression, "depression" is to be understood as a syndrome that includes (at least) a reduced frequency of goal-seeking behavior plus an associated negative affective state. It will become clear that the unequivocal, unambiguous statement of a formulation in the literature is rare. More often, a formulation is stated in such general terms that it is untestable and is restated in ways so different that the reader is left wondering whether not one but several separate formulations are being proposed. This is reflected in the disparate interpretations that different writers may give when referring to the same formulation.

SIX BEHAVIORAL FORMULATIONS OF DEPRESSION

Inadequate Reinforcement

The formulation of depression that has received the most attention in the literature is centered round the notion that depression is a function of inadequate reinforcement. This imprecise rubric designates a category in which there are at least two major variants: (a) reduction of reinforcement and (b) reduced frequency of social reinforcement.

Reduction of Reinforcement

Lazarus (1968) sees depression as "a function of inadequate or insufficient reinforcers" (p. 84). This could mean a reduced frequency of reinforcement, a poor quality of reinforcement, or an insufficient total amount of reinforcement, in unit time. It is equally possible that all of these aspects could apply at the same time, so the intended meaning of this formulation remains an open question. It is clear from the rest of his paper that Lazarus has in mind reinforcers in general, referring to money, position, love, health, etc. Burgess (1969) regards depression as a function of "reduced reinforcement" (p. 193). However, though she includes all types of reinforcement in her formulation, it is not apparent whether she is particularly concerned with frequency, total quantity, or both.

Reduced Frequency of Social Reinforcement

The majority of theorists have conceived of depression as a function of a reduced frequency of social reinforcement (Hersen, Eisler, Alford, & Agras, 1973; Lewinsohn & Graf, 1973; Lewinsohn, Weinstein, & Alper, 1970; Lewinsohn, Weinstein & Shaw, 1969; Liberman & Raskin, 1971; McLean, Ogston, & Grauer, 1973; Shipley & Fazio, 1973). As a consequence, therapy consists of social skills training and involves the patient's family in the therapeutic process since the family is a major source of social reinforcement.

The maintenance of established depression is mentioned in six of the above nine papers (Burgess, 1969; Lazarus, 1968; Lewinsohn & Graf, 1973; Lewinsohn et al., 1969, 1970; Liberman & Raskin, 1971). It is said to result from secondary social gains—for example, the attention and assistance that occupants of the "sick" role often receive from their family and friends. As Burgess (1969) points out, by the time the patient seeks clinical aid, he may not be suffering from reinforcement deficiencies, since "he obtains frequent reinforcements as a consequence to the emission of depressive behaviors" (p. 193). In terms of the low frequency of "performing behaviors" (to use Burgess's phrase), the client would seem to be on something akin to a schedule that reinforces low rates of behavior. Consequently, the thrust of Burgess's therapy is to instigate the nonreinforcement of depressive behaviors and, conversely, to establish performing behaviors, stressing task completion and contingent reinforcement.

Lewinsohn et al. (1969) propose a more complex maintenance sequence. They agree that social environments initially provide reinforcement but suggest that eventually people "avoid . . . [the depressive] as much as possible, thus decreasing his rate of receiving positive reinforcement and further accentuating his depression" (p. 232). Could it be that

Burgess has been treating depression in the earlier "secondary gains" maintenance stages?

Hersen et al. (1973) imply that maintenance is due to the decrease in reinforcement: "The decrease of positive reinforcement in the genesis and maintenance of depression has previously been documented" (p. 396). They then cite Lazarus (1968), Lewinsohn et al. (1969), and Liberman & Raskin (1971). But as we have seen, only Lewinsohn et al. take this position, and then only as part of a two-stage maintenance process.

It must be made clear that the two-part categorization mentioned above conceals the true complexity of the positions taken in most of the cited papers. To illustrate, I shall discuss Lazarus's (1968) paper in some detail.

Lazarus presents what I take to be three different formulations of depression in his relatively short paper. The first is that "depression is often a consequence of 'anxiety that is unusually intense or prolonged'" (p. 84). Though this does not sound like a behavioral formulation, it probably is one, since anxiety is itself "viewed as a response to noxious or threatening stimuli" (p. 84). Particular importance is attached to separating anxiety from depression during diagnosis and "to stress[ing] that they usually have different antecedents" (p. 84). The particular difficulty here is that not all theorists regard anxiety as a mediating factor between noxious stimuli and depression. Indeed, later, Lazarus lists (without dissent) three of the factors suggested by Ferster (1965) as giving rise to depression. One of these factors is "punishment and aversive control" (p. 85). Presumably, in order to maintain his position in respect to anxiety, Lazarus would have to argue that Ferster has unwittingly identified an antecedent of anxiety and that the latter mediates depression.

The second formulation is that "depression may be regarded as a function of inadequate or insufficient reinforcers. . . . A depressed person is virtually on an extinction trial. Some significant reinforcer has been withdrawn. There is a loss and deprivation" (pp. 84-85). The problem is to decide just what these statements amount to; is it one formulation or several? In the context of "extinction trials," "withdrawal" would appear to signify an absence of reinforcers. Likewise, "loss and deprivation" probably indicates an absence. But how do "inadequate or insufficient" fit in? Later, when discussing specific methods of treatment, Lazarus elaborates on "the generic conception of depression as a consequence of inadequate or insufficient reinforcement" (p. 86). He then goes on to talk about the "withdrawal . . . loss . . . expected loss or any anticipation of a nonreinforcing state of affairs" (p. 86). It would follow that unless the withdrawn reinforcer is replaced by a substitute, the overall frequency and total quantity of reinforcement in unit time would be reduced. In fact, Lazarus does not specifically mention the frequency of reinforcement.

Lazarus's third formulation is introduced in the context of therapy. "Depressed patients . . . need to learn a way of recognizing and utilizing certain reinforcers at their disposal" (p. 85). Again, this might not look like a separate formulation, but here Lazarus seems to be introducing the notion of distorted perception or cognition. Maybe he has in mind Ferster's (1966) suggestion that depression can result from the removal of an environmental stimulus, the removal of a discriminative stimulus for goal-seeking behavior. It could equally well mean that there is a filtering out or rejection of such stimuli signaling the availability of reinforcers. When describing his own use of behavioral deprivation and retraining, Lazarus says, "The schema of depression elaborated in the previous sections is that a chronic and/or acute non-reinforcing state of affairs can result in a condition where the person becomes relatively refractory to most stimuli and enters a state of 'depression' " (p. 88). Maybe the third formulation, if it is a formulation, is a foretaste of this latter vein in which "most stimuli" lose their reinforcing potential: a general loss of reinforcer effectiveness. But even in this last statement, it is not clear whether the fact that "the person becomes relatively refractory to most stimuli" is a necessary precondition for depression. Lazarus may be suggesting that the loss of reinforcer effectiveness and depression occur simultaneously, not sequentially.

Lazarus's (1968) paper was chosen from among several eligible examples by other theorists on the grounds of complexity; it appears to offer several formulations. Regretfully, it seems to me that Lazarus's formulations, and those of some of the other authors mentioned, are untestable in their current expressions, though their heuristic value can hardly be questioned. The very complexity of the problems involved makes it doubly difficult to offer precise formulations without, coincidentally, being dogged by the spectre of oversimplification. It is probably too much to expect that one formulation will be universally applicable to depression, but it is a pity when communication difficulties obscure what might be substantial contributions to our understanding of an important phenomenon.

Reinforcement parameters. All nine papers cited so far are open to the criticism that they display a curious narrowness of outlook regarding reinforcement parameters. There has been a concentration on either the withdrawal of reinforcers (they cease to be available) or on the reduced frequency of reinforcement. In the laboratory, where there is just one major source of exogenous reinforcement, the withdrawal of the reinforcer leaves the animal without any reinforcers. Human beings have many sources and types of reinforcers potentially available so that, other things being equal, the total removal of one reinforcer *may* reduce the overall frequency of reinforcement. Conversely, the frequency of reinforcement can be reduced without totally removing any one reinforcer. Whilst it is legitimate to concentrate on either withdrawal or frequency, it is essential to bear in mind that they can be related. Though the removal of a single significant reinforcer may be a highly visible triggering event, the long-term reduction of reinforcement frequency may be much more difficult to detect; the latter may involve no cataclysmic withdrawal of any one reinforcer.

Given that reinforcement is delivered, frequency is but one of four governing parameters. In a meticulous behavioral analysis of depression, Moss and Boren (1972) list four interrelated parameters of reinforcement: frequency, duration, magnitude and the amount of behavior required to obtain the reinforcer (the response cost). They give clinical examples corresponding to each of the parameters. The whole set is subsumed under the generic title of "Insufficient positive reinforcement" (p. 582). My contention is that in all of the previous nine papers, at least three of the four parameters have been ignored or, in the case of Lazarus (1968), possibly collapsed into the rubric of "inadequate or insufficient reinforcement" (p. 86). Moss and Boren also note that the withdrawal of a positive reinforcer involves two interrelated parameters: time or duration (permanent, prolonged, or brief withdrawal) and contingency (whether or not the withdrawal is contingent upon behavior). In practice, it may be very difficult or even impossible to decide which one (or combination) of these parameters is implicated for a particular patient. But awareness that several parameters do exist, and awareness of their identities, should facilitate the search for the factors of which depression is a function, as well as having implications for therapy.

Loss of Reinforcible Behavior

In characteristically erudite papers, Ferster (1966, 1973) emphasizes a loss of reinforcible behavior as the common denominator of depressed people. "Loss of behavior" is here used as a shorthand for "reduction in the frequency of reinforcible behavior." As possible experimental analogues of depression, he mentions (1966) three laboratory conditions that reduce the frequency of behavior: (a) an environment that can only be altered by emitting a very large amount of behavior, (b) aversive stimuli, especially conditioned aversive stimuli, and (c) a sudden large environmental change (a behavior-controlling stimulus is lost).

Ferster (1973) undertook a functional analysis of depression, producing a comprehensive appraisal of two broad classes of circumstances that can give rise to a loss of reinforcible behavior in man: (a) aversively motivated behaviors becoming prepotent and displacing reinforcible behaviors—for example, escape and avoidance and (b) "direct" reduction of the frequency of reinforcible behavior by means of "basic processes" such as the erratic presentation of reinforcers, inappropriately timed reinforcement, large and sudden environmental changes, and generalized and suppressed anger leading to a loss of social reinforcement. In this same paper, the point is made that "we cannot expect that there will be one cause of depression or a single underlying psychological process, because behavior is a product of so many psychological processes" (p. 861). Ferster's is essentially a two-level analysis of depression, in which the "loss of reinforcible behavior" is a unifying higher level concept whose antecedents are to be found at the lower level.

Loss of Reinforcer Effectiveness

Costello (1972a) proposed that the depressed person's general loss of interest in the environment is a function of a general loss of reinforcer effectiveness. Two antecedents are suggested: (a) endogenous biochemical and neurophysiological changes and/or (b) the disruption of a behavioral chain, such disruption resulting from, for instance, the loss of one reinforcer in that chain. He further suggested that the "reinforcer effectiveness of all the components of the chain of behavior is contingent upon the completion of the chain at either an overt or a covert level" (p. 241). (For example, the withdrawal of a reinforcer, or the removal of a discriminative stimulus for behavior, disrupts an ongoing chain of behavior, giving rise to a general loss of reinforcer effectiveness.) Costello regards a loss of reinforcer effectiveness as the fundamental mechanism underlying depression.

Lazarus (1972) criticized this formulation on the grounds that "it is usually difficult to determine whether . . . [it] is an effect or a cause of depression" (p. 249). He further suggested that it has preventive implications, in that one should avoid "single, pivotal reinforcements . . . [and provide] 'alternative routes' in the event that any chain of behavior is broken or blocked" (p. 250). Costello (1972b) replied that it is not that the person's behavior is under the control of one stimulus, but that stimuli, responses, and reinforcers are mutually interdependent and that "if there is a general loss of reinforcer effectiveness, there are no other available reinforcers" (p. 251). It follows that there is no remedy! He notes, however, that for most people this "is usually a temporary matter" (p. 252) and suggests that the stronger the mutual interdependence of a depressed person's behavior, the longer it will take for reinforcers to become effective again. Presumably they become effective again as a result of some sort of restructuring of the interdependencies.

Lewinsohn and MacPhillamy (1974), in their study of the relationship between age and engagement in pleasant activities, found that "a decrease in subjective enjoyability is uniquely associated with being depressed" (p. 293). They pointed out that this result is consistent with Costello's formulation.

Moss and Boren (1972) described three conditions that can lead to insufficient positive reinforcement, the third being the "interruption of a chain of behavior leading to positive reinforcement" (p. 585). They defined a chain of behavior as a complex 'sequence of behaviors, often topographically unrelated, developed and maintained by positive reinforcement" (p. 585). They gave an example of a patient who became severely depressed when the possibility of attaining a superordinate, long-term goal was removed. This represented the breaking of a chain of behavior before its successful completion. Since the Moss and Boren situation was one in which behavior was under the control of one superordinate stimulus, the likelihood of depression being precipitated could presumably have been avoided by adopting a Lazarus type of "preventive" measure. Hence, one would avoid single superordinate goals, having several (preferably unrelated) equally important targets, possibly with chains of behavior cross-linked (so that if one target disappeared, the chain directly subserving that defunct target could be transferred to a different goal).

Costello's position is difficult to conceptualize clearly. For Costello (1972a), a general loss of reinforcer effectiveness can result from "the loss of one of the reinforcers in the chain" (p. 241). He stresses the "interdependence between stimuli, responses, and reinforcers" (p. 244). He suggests that for some people, the general loss of reinforcer effectiveness may occur more readily and more often: "Perhaps for them the mutual interdependence of their behavior is particularly strong and needs to be weakened" (p. 252), though he admits that he cannot say how.

One way to conceive of this situation is as a network rather than as a chain. In fact, Costello mentions that chains of behavior are usually called "patterns of behavior" in sociological literature. Consider a tightly stretched net, made of some elastic filament. The knots in this net represent behaviors, stimuli, and reinforcers, while the filaments between them represent the interdependencies. If a single knot is excised, a large hole appears; the net effectively collapses. This represents the disruption of the relationships between behaviors, stimuli, and reinforcers that Costello calls a "loss of reinforcer effectiveness." If the net is only loosely stretched in the first place and if there are inbuilt holes (some behaviors, etc., are not interrelated with others), then the removal of one knot will have only a small effect on the total.

The problem with Costello's (1972a) formulation is that it is not explicit, it operates at an unspecified level of organization and, as he admits, "There is no experimental evidence to support or embarrass this hypothesized interdependence between stimuli, responses and reinforcers which is suggested by observation of depressed people" (p. 244). The prognostic implications of Costello's formulation are bleak: For the depressed person, nothing is reinforcing, nor can a substitute be found. An obvious embarrassment for the hypothesis is that depressed individuals do recover.

Costello regards the disruption of chains, or patterns, of behavior as the root cause of the loss of reinforcer effectiveness; but Ferster (1973) posited that a reduced frequency of some activities could lessen the effectiveness of reinforcers such as eating, sports, and sex. Thus, if there was a decline in the frequency of social behavior, a by-product could be a reduced frequency of sports, eating, and sex, given that these activities involve a "complex collateral social repertoire" (p. 858). Thus Ferster, like Costello, points out that behaviors are related in complex ways, but Ferster's is a less embracing concept. He neither talks in terms of a general loss of reinforcer effectiveness nor about the disruption of behavioral chains. He suggests that some behavioral patterns will be common to a number of other behavioral patterns. For example, walking is common to shopping, sports, sightseeing, visiting friends, and so forth. Losing the ability to walk would render these dependent activities much less probable. But what if the common behavior is all-pervasive? What if we are talking about social behavior in general? Then, surely, one might expect a widespread decline in general activities, since social behavior is the bulwark upon which so much other behavior depends. Thus, a general loss of reinforcer effectiveness should result.

The question remains: Are Costello and Ferster talking about the same process? In view of the uncertainties about Costello's formulation, an assured answer cannot be given to such a question. Assuming that these processes actually exist, it seems likely that they operate at different levels of organization. Ferster's formulation involves the loss of a common element from processes that may in all other respects be quite different. Costello is concerned with the disruption of purposeful, goal-directed chains of behavior in which stimuli, responses, and reinforcers are so intimately interconnected that the loss of one destroys the whole. Presumably this sort of catastrophe would only occur in the Ferster model if the common element was a highly pervasive one such as social behavior.

Aversive Control

The frequency of behavior can be reduced by aversive stimuli, particularly the conditioned aversive stimuli that precede the aversive event (Ferster, 1966). Moss and Boren (1972) identified two typical ways in which aversive control is associated with depressive behavior: (a) directly, where the aversive event is a reduction of positive reinforcement and (b) indirectly, where punishment, avoidance, or escape may suppress behaviors that would have been followed by positive reinforcement. They, too, stress that clinical cases of depression (as against animal analogues) "more often involve secondary . . . aversive stimuli often associated with a reduction of positive reinforcement rather than with the application of a primary aversive stimulus" (p. 586).

Since the straightforward reduction of positive reinforcement has been dealt with earlier in this paper, it is omitted from further discussion here.

Lazarus (1968) would seem to be in disagreement at this point. He insists that anxiety and depression usually have different antecedents, anxiety being a response to aversive stimuli and depression being a function of inadequate or insufficient positive reinforcement. However, he notes that depression can result from "anxiety that is unusually intense or prolonged" (p. 84). The problem is that if reduction of positive reinforcement is regarded as aversive, then anxiety and depression share the same antecedents. Likewise, inadequate or insufficient reinforcement (which Lazarus identifies as the antecedent of depression) can result from the operation of aversive stimuli (which are identified by Lazarus as the antecedents of anxiety). Until Lazarus defines the crucial differences between anxiety and depression, further speculation would seem to be unprofitable.

Moss and Boren (1972) highlighted one problem with the aversive control of behavior: "maintaining a continuing threat of presentation of the aversive stimulus in a situation denying escape" (p. 586). The work of Seligman and his co-workers appears to provide a solution to this difficulty.

Learned Helplessness

"Learned helplessness"—a belief in one's own helplessness—was first introduced into the literature by Seligman, as an animal analogue of reactive depression. Overmier and Seligman (1967) subjected dogs to a series of inescapable electric shocks, prior to escape-avoidance training in a shuttle box. Two thirds of these previously shocked dogs did not learn to escape by shuttling, whereas 90% of the control (not previously shocked) dogs did learn. The inability of these inescapably shocked animals to learn shuttling behavior has been designated "learned helplessness." It was also shown that dogs could be "immunized" against learned helplessness by first exposing them to escapable electric shocks, allowing them to develop and establish reliable shuttling behavior. When such dogs were later exposed to inescapable shocks and then placed in a shuttlebox, they learned to shuttle—they were not helpless.

Seligman (1972, 1973, 1975) has suggested that learned helplessness and reactive depression have in common a belief in one's own helplessness, and he proposes learned helplessness as a model of depression. Wolpe (1972) discussed three sets of circumstances in which depression is seen: (a) as a consequence of severe and prolonged anxiety, (b) as an exaggeration and prolongation of the normal reaction to loss, and (c) as a consequence of failure to control interpersonal situations (such failure being due to the effects of neurotic anxiety). He feels that Seligman's experiments "provide a basis for understanding human reactive depressions and for suggesting new methods of treating them" (p. 367). In a criticism of Ferster's (1973) paper, Lazarus (1974) insisted, "The main point about depressed persons is not only the absence of immediate positive reinforcement but a singular lack of hope of receiving future rewards" (pp. 360-361). This, too, sounds like learned helplessness. Melges and Bowlby (1969) also subscribe to this model in their statement that "the depressed person believes that his plans of action are no longer effective in reaching his continuing long-range goals" (p. 690). In his 1972 paper, Seligman added the caveat that "since most of the evidence for depression is largely anecdotal and selected, experimental tests in man on the helplessness theory of depression are needed" (p. 411).

In an experiment with undergraduate subjects, Miller and Seligman (1973) measured the change in expectancies for success following reinforcement in chance and skilled tasks (success and failure being covertly manipulated by the experimenter). The results showed that (a) depressed subjects (those with Beck Depression Inventory scores of at least nine) were less affected by success experiences than nondepressed subjects; (b) depressed and nondepressed subjects were affected equally by failure experiences; and (c) depressed and nondeprssed subjects were both affected more by success than by failure. The first result agrees with clinical observations that depressives selectively forget or devalue success. The second and third results are contrary to clinical observations that depressives exaggerate failures. The authors suggested that the clinically discordant findings might result from the nature of the tasks used and from some special characteristics of college students.

These results provide some measure of support for the learned helplessness model of depression, support of a plausible but indirect type. The measured dependent variable was "expectancy of success," which correlated with the depth of depression as measured by the Beck Depression Inventory. But though the total expectancy change on the skilled task was in the expected direction (negatively correlated with depression), it was not statistically significant and accounted for only 9% of the variance. This may have been a function of the mild level of depression represented by the subjects, in that the depressed group's mean Beck Depression Inventory score was 16.5, whereas the mean score for "moderate" depression is 25.4. The fact remains that no attempt has been made to replicate these results using a depressed patient group.

It is unfortunate that no attempt was made in this experiment to measure any increases in depression that might have occurred as a result of experiencing failure and, presumably, learned helplessness. If such increases had been found, some extra weight would have been added to Seligman's hypothesis. It could be that the differences found are a function of the depth of psychopathology in general, in that the subjects were chosen on the basis of their high or low depression scores. Miller and Seligman recognized this problem and noted that it was being researched.

Hiroto and Seligman (1975) investigated the generality of learned helplessness in man and found that pretreatments with insoluble discrimination problems, or an inescapable aversive tone, produced both failure to escape and failure to solve anagrams. Thus, generalization across behavioral and cognitive modalities was successfully demonstrated.

Seligman (1975) claims that helplessness and depression can result not only from noncontingent aversive stimulation but also from noncontingent positive reinforcement. He points to the difficulty that the "loss of reinforcers" theory has in accounting for depression following goal attainment, and believes that this phenomenon can be accommodated by the helplessness theory. He argues that depressed, successful people believe that they are currently rewarded not for what they are doing, but for who they are or what they have previously achieved.

To date, the animal studies of learned helplessness all seem to have used primary aversive stimuli—for example, electric shocks or very loud noises. However, the major visible precipitating events that give rise to human depression are not usually primary aversive stimuli but, typically, a sudden reduction of reinforcement or the operation of conditioned aversive stimuli. Since the reduction of positive reinforcement is considered to be an aversive event (Ferster, 1966; Moss & Boren, 1972), learned helplessness could possibly be induced by suitable manipulation of positive reinforcement. If the nine theorists mentioned in the first section of this review are correct, one would expect depression to result. Here, surely, "learned helplessness" appears to be just a synonym for "depression." In fact, Seligman (1973) says, "I suggest that . . . what depression is—is the belief in one's own helplessness" (p. 44). The difficulty is that if, as it appears, Seligman is here *defining* depression as learned helplessness, then there is no formulation to test. Any manipulation that results in depression would, by definition, result in learned helplessness.

Seligman (1975) argues that perception of the self as a controlling individual is a fundamental factor in self-esteem and that a perceived loss of control results in a feeling of helplessness. It is by means of this notion that the depression of the newly promoted corporation chairman is explained: Most of his responsibility is delegated and everything is done for him, with the result that he perceives himself as less in control over the immediate situation. It is also used to explain the depression that some "beautiful" women experience (they are showered with reinforcers because of their looks and not as a result of their own endeavors).

My own inclination is to add an important proviso: that perceived loss of control does not necessarily produce helplessness unless the loss is absolute. By "absolute" I mean that no alternative or compensating behaviors are available. Thus, Smith is only likely to feel helpless if, having lost control of his car, he can neither gain control nor jump clear. In terms of Mandler's interruption theory (Mandler & Watson, 1966), when an integrated response sequence is interrupted, a common response is to substitute an alternative segment that can be completed. Mandler argues that this avoids or reduces the arousal resulting from the original interruption.

Is the ad libitum fed laboratory animal the animal analogue of the "beautiful woman" syndrome? If so, such animals should be depressed, except that they never did have control over the availability of food. Genuine loss of control could be established by feeding animals exclusively on an operant schedule from the earliest possible age, continuing this schedule well into maturity, and then making food noncontingently available at all times. The first phase would effectively produce animals that had "always" had control over their food supplies, whilst the second phase would constitute a complete loss of control. Seligman would, presumably, predict that helpless animals would be produced by such manipulations.

In fact, the experiment suggested above is very similar to one reported by Mandler & Watson (1966). Hungry animals were rewarded with a large food pellet when they made correct brightness discriminations in a Y-maze. They were subsequently placed on an extinction schedule and run in the maze; half the group were food deprived, the remainder were satiated. The result was that the satiated animals "exhibited extremely excited behavior during extinction which increased with successive trials" (p. 267). Mandler explained the results in terms of his interruption theory, a concept that will be mentioned again in the context of the model presented toward the end of this paper.

GENERAL CRITICISMS OF THE BEHAVIORAL FORMULATIONS AND RESEARCH

There are several general criticisms that arise from the six behavioral formulations of depression and from the associated research. The majority of the research has been concerned with developing treatments based upon behavioral formulations. Thus, Lewinsohn and his co-workers have developed assessment procedures based on the premise that depression results from a reduced rate of social reinforcement. Whilst research into effective treatments is essential, fundamental research is needed (a) to isolate the critical factors in existing formulations and (b) to suggest new formulations. This could include treatment studies, but, again, identification of the essential treatment parameters would shed light on the sources of the depression per se. My concern is not that there are too many treatment studies, but that there are too few published fundamental studies. A further problem with treatment-based studies is that they are frequently case studies involving very few subjects, using incompletely defined treatments, sometimes using different treatments for each subject, and with no controls or replications. This is not the stuff with which a systematic body of knowledge is built.

Fundamental research into depression seems to have been confined to animal studies and the learned helplessness formulation. As mentioned earlier, Seligman's human studies have involved college students, a fact that Seligman suggested may account for his equivocal results. Animal analogues, whilst useful and suggestive, are limited. Ferster (1966) has highlighted the problem in terms of whether the notion of "psychosis" can be applied usefully to animals; he doubts whether it can. More fundamentally, to what extent do animals (especially infraprimates) share human affective states? It is evident that this is an important question, even considering behavioral formulations, because, as discussed above, the overall frequency of overt behavior is not necessarily indicative of the inner, affective state of the organism; but the affective component of human depression is surely one of its crucial defining characteristics.

With respect to the behavioral formulations themselves, most of the major criticisms have arisen during the course of this review. Some of the problems that emerged concerned the role of anxiety, the direction of causation, the use of students as subjects, the predominance (until recently) of anecdotal case studies, the rarity of controlled experiments, and the fact that the maintenance of depression is often ignored.

A major criticism that applies to many of the papers discussed is that the formulations are so imprecisely expressed that they are untestable and, consequently, of uncertain scientific value except, maybe, heuristically. Likewise, an imprecise restatement of an initially unclear formulation can leave the reader wondering whether two quite different formulations are intended rather than just one. A further difficulty arises with respect to the theorist who has published on the same topic area over a number of years and whose thinking on that topic has undergone various developments; Lazarus is a case in point. At the time of this writing, one cannot be sure whether Lazarus regards his earlier formulations as currently valid, or whether his most recent contribution supersedes all previous ones.

Synthesis

At this point, one might ask whether these different behavioral formulations of depression can be understood as operating via a common mechanism and, if so, whether a synthesis can be achieved. Costello (1972a) tentatively suggested that a general loss of reinforcer effectiveness is the "fundamental mechanism" (p. 242) through which depression is produced, whilst Seligman's "learned helplessness" also appears to be a contender for this same fundamental status.

An alternative tack would be to integrate the various formulations into a structured whole, but it appears that this has not been attempted. The object would be to represent the state of knowledge and theorizing, to make explicit some of the possible relationships between the formulations, and possibly, to reveal inconsistencies and gaps in our present knowledge. As with any conceptual model, it would only be one of many possible arrangements, and would make no claim to represent any ultimate "truth."

INTEGRATION OF THE BEHAVIORAL FORMULATIONS INTO A SINGLE CONCEPTUAL MODEL

The remainder of this paper is devoted to an attempted integration of the behavioral formulations of depression into a single conceptual model. The model is intended to operate only at the level of individual reinforcers or, possibly, groups of reinforcers, and not at the level of behavioral "chains" or "patterns." For this reason it does not, for example, attempt to account for the undoubted lack of interest that the depressed individual has in reinforcers in general, since a more speculative and higher level of analysis would be required for that task. The goal is to outline a logical model that permits rational decisions to be made in the light of previous experience. Obviously, this is not to suggest that human decision making is uniformly logical or always at a conscious level. The model is simply a device for drawing various formulations into closer proximity, one with the other, whilst suggesting logical relations between them that may not have been considered before. The full model includes two decision paths: one concerned with goal-seeking behavior (the positive reinforcement half) the other with avoidance and escape behavior from either primary or conditioned aversive stimuli. The simpler positive reinforcement half is introduced first, followed by the full model.

The Positive Reinforcement Half of the Model

Figure 1 represents the positive reinforcement half of the model. The passage of time should be understood to run down the page. Thus, the earliest temporal event occurring in successful goal-seeking behavior is to look for a discriminative stimulus (S^d), whilst the last event is to obtain positive reinforcement (S+ve). It is not suggested that the 10 serial events, which constitute the central spine, represent a definitive analysis of the stages involved in uninterrupted, successful goal-seeking behavior. The present concatenation was simply devised to subsume as many behavioral formulations as possible.

Excepting "functional depression," all of these formulations lead to the suppression of goal-seeking behavior (bottom left of Figure 2). They all operate over a substrate of extinction. This simply reflects the fact that the prime purpose of these formulations is to account for the observed reduction in the frequency of goal-seeking behavior displayed by depressed individuals. Since this is an attempted synthesis of current behavioral models, behavior must be seen either to achieve its goal (S+ve) or to fall short. Falling short, as a result of whatever cause, is here labeled "suppression of goal seeking behavior" and is assumed to be associated with depression.

It is interesting that even at this level of analysis, which excludes behavioral chains and patterns in the Costello sense, a "loss of reinforcer effectiveness" is still conceivable. Notice, though, that this is a loss of individual reinforcer effectiveness: not a general loss. The learned helplessness that is represented in this half of the model arises from a belief that efforts to obtain positive reinforcement will be unsuccessful: It does not have its origins in traumatic exposure to primary aversive stimuli.

There is one negative outcome from the central spine of the model that leads to goal attainment. ("Negative outcome" means a negative answer to a question that represents a central column event.) When positive reinforcement is noncontingently available, when behavior is unnecessary, functional depression is feasible. Doubtless, most wild rats engage in far more food-obtaining behavior than their ad libitum fed laboratory cousins. In this restricted sense, the latter are displaying the behavioral symptoms of functional depression.

The four feedback loops, to the left of the central spine, permit decisions to be made in the light of previous experience; they are learning loops. For example, the answer to the questions representing the third event ("Is S+ve likely to be available?") will be some function of previous experience with actual availability versus signaled availability. Of course, it is possible for an S^d to be present in the absence of the associated S+ve. Putting money into an empty coffee machine is an example of this situation. The effectiveness of a reinforcer is a function of the response cost that is, in its turn, a function of the amount of behavior needed to obtain that reinforcer. If the quality, quantity, frequency, or intensity of the behavior required is excessive (in the light of the frequency, quality, or quantity, etc. of the reinforcer), the reinforcer will lose its effectiveness.

The two remaining feedback loops provide the information needed to assess the likely effectiveness of the available behavior. When such behavior is judged unlikely to succeed in its aims, learned helplessness can result. This notion is entirely consistent with interruption theory, and has been expressed by Mandler (1975):

> Whenever a search of appropriate action systems indicates that, because of past experience or the generalized evaluation of personal competence, no actions are available that will achieve desirable ends, then helplessness and hopelessness will result. These means and ends need not be associated with the avoidance of aversive events, they may just as well relate to the unattainability of desirable states. (pp. 211-212)

"Helplessness," in the above quotation, refers to situational anxiety, whilst "hopelessness" means transituational helplessness.

The few remaining features in this half of the model are explained in the context of the full model.

The Full Model

Figures 1 and 2 comprise the full model. The two halves are assumed to operate largely in parallel over the total time course. There is no reason why this should be the case in practice, but the essential point is that with the exception of "functional depression," given an aversive discriminative stimulus ($S_{av}{}^{d}$), the positive part of the model stops until the aversive half inputs to the event labeled "goal seeking behavior." The aversive stimuli affect behavior, not the presence of an S^{d} or S+ve. Therefore, in this model the (aversive) withdrawal of S+ve is kept conceptually distinct from primary or conditioned aversive stimuli.

It is apparent that the first three events in the "aversive" half are mirror images of the first three in the "positive" half. These three negative outcomes in the aversive half lead not to the suppression of behavior but permit goal-seeking behavior to proceed; indeed, they may invigorate such behavior.

The effectiveness of the S_{av} is represented in terms of its effect on the goal-seeking behavior. This is one of the interconnections between the two halves of the model. If, as a result of the S_{av}, the goal-seeking behavior actually available is less than that required to obtain the S+ve, the S_{av} is effective. Clearly, the effectiveness of the S_{av} will at least depend on the strength and frequency, etc., of the goal seeking efforts which, in their turn, will depend on the effectiveness of the S+ve. This illustrates some of the complex interactions involved in the total "system" represented in the model. The present scheme also allows for the possibility of improved goal-seeking behavior contingent on the perceived absence of an S_{av}^{d}, or the presence of an ineffective S_{av}, or the probable unavailability of a signaled and effective S_{av}. The remainder of the aversive half is concerned mainly with avoidance behavior, escape behavior, and learned helplessness.

Successful avoidance and successful escape maneuvers are both shown as "opening the gate" (indicated by a positive sign) for positive goal seeking. Of course, though they open the gate, they may have such a depleting effect on the organism that the remaining behavior available for goal seeking is inadequate. It would follow that the S_{av} was effective, after all. Learning in the avoidance and escape columns is achieved, as elsewhere, by feedback loops.

It should be pointed out that if the organism receives the full force of the S_{av}, the effect is to close the gate on goal-seeking efforts (indicated by a negative sign). There is no question of invigoration since, by definition, the full S_{av} is effective in suppressing goal-oriented behavior.

Finally, the model shows two consequences of the belief than escape from the S_{av} would be unsuccessful. If the organism actively acquiesces as a result of this belief, the S_{av} is avoided, but goal seeking behavior is suppressed. The threat is successful. Seligman has drawn attention to an alternative consequence of the same belief: learned helplessness. In this case, the organism passively acquiesces but fails to escape from the threatening situation. This results in the full force of the S_{av} being felt. In terms of the current model, the helpless animal is locked into a circular system whose distinguishing events run in the following temporal sequence: (a) Is escape likely to be successful? (b) No, (c) $\triangle S_{av}$ (the organism receives a small increment of the total S_{av}), (d) Is escape attempted? (e) No, (f) S_{av}, (g) Is escape likely to be successful? and so on. Given a sufficient number of trials with inescapable aversive stimuli, this loop will become very strongly established. The Seligman cure, forcing the traumatized animal to escape, is shown as a short-circuiting of the helplessness loop. Likewise, spontaneous recovery can be represented by a successful escape attempt in the midst of the loop, maybe as a result of random behavior. An escape would be both adaptive and, presumably, highly rewarding; thus, learning should be relatively rapid. "Immunization" can be conceptualized as a process that establishes a strong and change-resistant "normal" escape sequence or "plan."

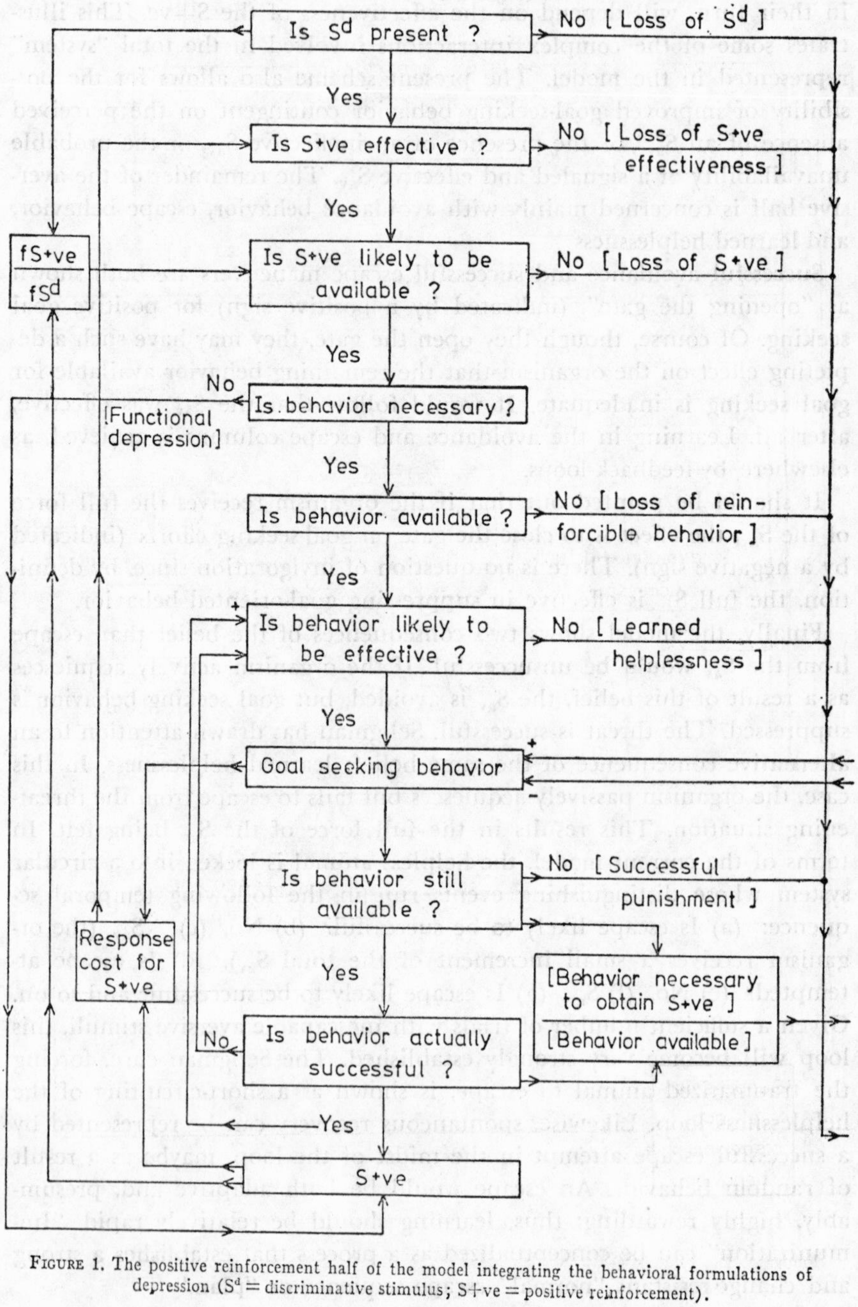

FIGURE 1. The positive reinforcement half of the model integrating the behavioral formulations of depression (S^d = discriminative stimulus; S+ve = positive reinforcement).

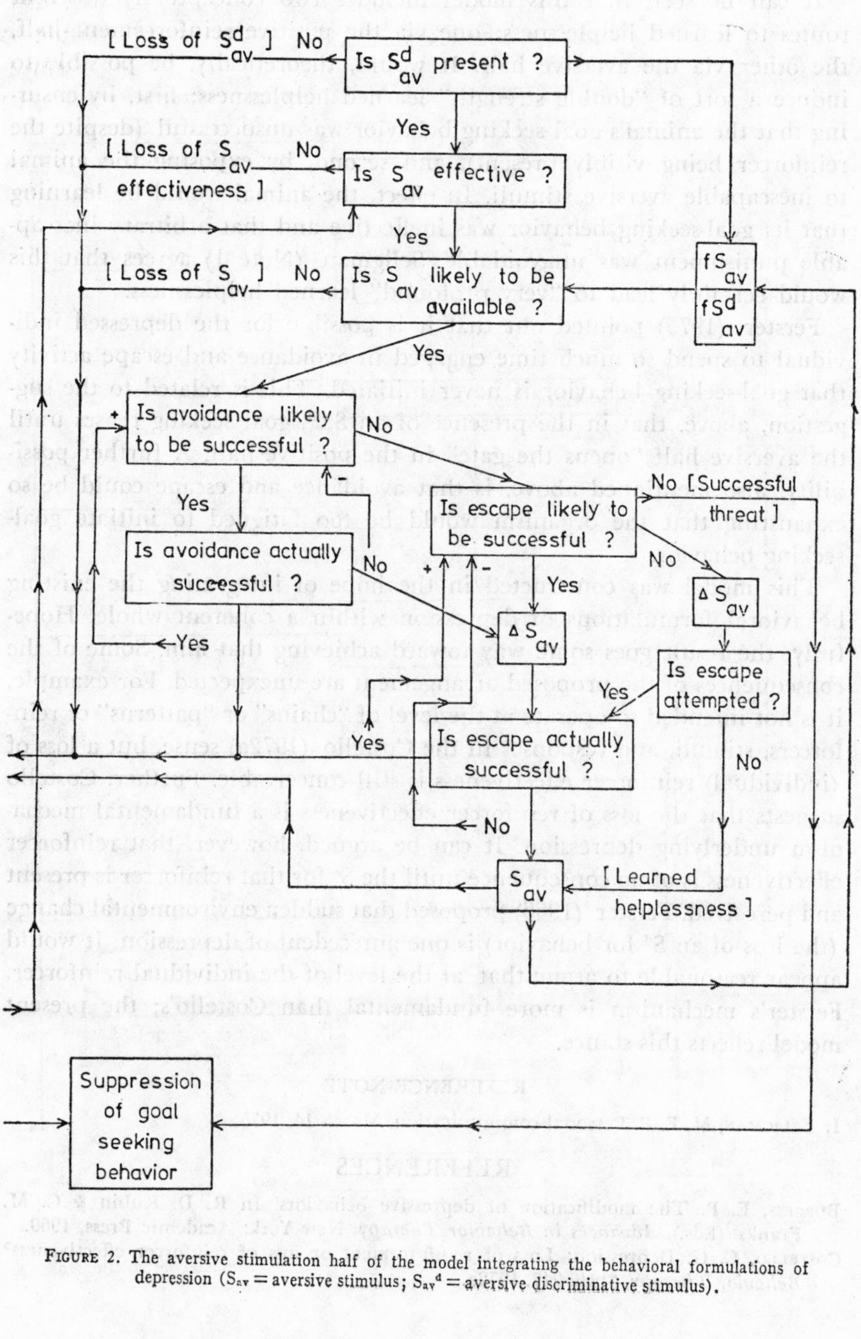

FIGURE 2. The aversive stimulation half of the model integrating the behavioral formulations of depression (S_{av} = aversive stimulus; S_{av}^{d} = aversive discriminative stimulus).

It can be seen that this model includes two conceptually different routes to learned helplessness: one via the positive reinforcement half, the other via the aversive half. It would, theoretically, be possible to induce a sort of "double strength" learned helplessness: first, by ensuring that the animal's goal seeking behavior was unsuccessful (despite the reinforcer being visibly present), and second, by exposing the animal to inescapable aversive stimuli. In effect, the animal would be learning that its goal-seeking behavior was ineffective and that arbitrary inescapable punishment was unavoidable. Seligman (Note 1) agrees that this would certainly lead to "very profound" learned helplessness.

Ferster (1973) pointed out that it is possible for the depressed individual to spend so much time engaged in avoidance and escape activity that goal-seeking behavior is never initiated. This is related to the suggestion, above, that in the presence of an S_{av}^{d}, goal seeking ceases until the aversive half "opens the gate" in the positive half. A further possibility, also mentioned above, is that avoidance and escape could be so exhausting that the organism would be too fatigued to initiate goal-seeking behavior.

This model was constructed in the hope of integrating the existing behavioral formulations of depression within a coherent whole. Hopefully, the result goes some way toward achieving that aim. Some of the consequences of the proposed arrangement are unexpected. For example, it is not intended to operate at the level of "chains" or "patterns" of reinforcers, stimuli, and responses in the Costello (1972a) sense, but a loss of (individual) reinforcer effectiveness is still conceivable. Further, Costello suggests that the loss of reinforcer effectiveness is a fundamental mechanism underlying depression. It can be argued, however, that reinforcer effectiveness is of no consequence until the S^d for that reinforcer is present and perceived. Ferster (1966) proposed that sudden environmental change (the loss of an S^d for behavior) is one antecedent of depression. It would appear reasonable to argue that, at the level of the individual reinforcer, Ferster's mechanism is more fundamental than Costello's; the present model reflects this stance.

REFERENCE NOTE

1. SELIGMAN, M. E. P. Personal communication, March 14, 1975.

REFERENCES

BURGESS, E. P. The modification of depressive behaviors. In R. D. Rubin & C. M. Franks (Eds.), *Advances in Behavior Therapy*. New York: Academic Press, 1969.

COSTELLO, C. G. Depression: Loss of reinforcement or loss of reinforcer effectiveness? *Behavior Therapy*, 3:240-247, 1972a.

COSTELLO, C. G. Reply to Lazarus. *Behavior Therapy,* 3:251-253, 1972b.

FERSTER, C. B. Classification of behavioral pathology. In L. Grasner & L. P. Ullmann (Eds.), *Research in Behavior Therapy.* New York: Holt, Rinehart & Winston, 1965.

FERSTER, C. B. Animal behavior and mental illness. *Psychological Record,* 16:345-356, 1966.

FERSTER, C. B. A functional analysis of depression. *American Psychologist,* 28:857-870, 1973.

HERSEN, M., EISLER, R. M., ALFORD, G. S., & AGRAS, W. S. Effects of token economy on neurotic depression: An experimental analysis. *Behavior Therapy,* 4:392-397, 1973.

HIROTO, D. S., & SELIGMAN, M. E. P. Generality of learned helplessness in man. *Journal of Personality and Social Psychology,* 31:311-327, 1975.

KANFER, F. H., & SASLOW, G. Behavioral analysis: An alternative to diagnostic classification. *Archives of General Psychiatry,* 12:529-538, 1965.

LAZARUS, A. A. Learning theory and the treatment of depression. *Behaviour Research and Therapy,* 6:83-89, 1968.

LAZARUS, A. A. Some reactions to Costello's paper on depression. *Behavior Therapy,* 3:248-250, 1972.

LAZARUS, A. A. On "A functional analysis of depression." *American Psychologist,* 29: 360-361, 1974.

LEWINSOHN, P. M., & GRAF, M. Pleasant activities and depression. *Journal of Consulting and Clinical Psychology,* 41:261-268, 1973.

LEWINSOHN, P. M., & MACPHILLAMY, D. J. The relationship between age and engagement in pleasant activities. *Journal of Gerontology,* 29:290-294, 1974.

LEWINSOHN, P. M., WEINSTEIN, M. S., & ALPER, T. A behavioral approach to the group treatment of depressed persons: A methodological contribution. *Journal of Clinical Psychology,* 26:525-532, 1970.

LEWINSOHN, P. M., WEINSTEIN, M. S., & SHAW, D. A. Depression: A clinical-research approach. In R. D. Rubin & C. M. Franks (Eds.), *Advances in Behavior Therapy.* New York: Academic Press, 1969.

LIBERMAN, R. P., & RASKIN, D. E. Depression: A behavioral formulation. *Archives of General Psychiatry,* 24:515-523, 1971.

MANDLER, G. *Mind and Emotion.* New York: Wiley, 1975.

MANDLER, G. & WATSON, D. L. Anxiety and the interruption of behavior. In C. D. Spielberger (Ed.), *Anxiety and Behavior.* New York: Academic Press, 1966.

MCLEAN, P. D., OGSTON, K., & GRAUER, L. A behavioral approach to the treatment of depression. *Journal of Behaviour Therapy and Experimental Psychiatry,* 4:323-330, 1973.

MELGES, F. T. & BOWLBY, J. Types of hopelessness in psychopathological process. *Archives of General Psychiatry,* 20:690-699, 1969.

MILLER, W. R. & SELIGMAN, M. E. P. Depression and the perception of reinforcement. *Journal of Abnormal Psychology,* 82:62-73, 1973.

MOSS, G. R. & BOREN, J. H. Depression as a model for behavioral analysis. *Comprehensive Psychiatry,* 13:581-590, 1972.

OVERMIER, J. B. & SELIGMAN, M. E. P. Effects of inescapable shock upon subsequent escape and avoidance responding. *Journal of Comparative and Physiological Psychology,* 63:28-33, 1967.

SELIGMAN, M. E. P. Learned helplessness. *Annual Review of Medicine,* 23:407-412, 1972.

SELIGMAN, M. E. P. Fall into helplessness. *Psychology Today,* 7:43-48, 1973.

SELIGMAN, M. E. P. *Helplessness.* San Francisco: Freeman, 1975.

SHIPLEY, C. R. & FAZIO, A. F. Pilot study of a treatment for psychological depression. *Journal of Abnormal Psychology,* 82:372-376, 1973.

WOLPE, J. Neurotic depression: Experimental analog, clinical syndrome, and treatment. *American Journal of Psychotherapy,* 25:362-368, 1972.

Section VIII

BEHAVIOR MODIFICATION IN INSTITUTIONAL SETTINGS

Commentary

BEHAVIOR MODIFICATION IN CORRECTIONAL INSTITUTIONS

The use of behavior modification in the prisons has been at the center of controversies over the ethical and legal implications of behavioral methods. The first paper reprinted in this Section—by Milan and McKee—provides a sound discussion of the ethical issues involved whenever *any* treatment or rehabilitation program is introduced into a correctional institution. As we have emphasized in previous volumes, there is little that is unique to behavioral methods when it comes to ensuring the personal and civil rights of individual prisoners or patients. A high standard of professionally competent, ethically proper conduct should characterize all forms of interventions in institutional settings. Thus, Milan and McKee detail carefully thought out policies regarding informed consent, the freedom of the individual offender to withdraw from the program without adverse or punitive effects, and the role of professional and peer reviews in maintaining high quality programs that do not abuse the prisoner's legitimate rights.

For the rest, Milan and McKee demonstrate that, with the exception that the correctional officers could not implement the full range of explicitly aversive procedures at their disposal, a benign token reinforcement program is a more effective motivator than more traditional methods. The results of their study show that the token program was the effective agent in producing behavior change. As is now so predictable about token economies, the prisoners' behavior dropped off markedly as soon as the contingencies were withdrawn. Milan and McKee comment that this should surprise no one, and that a more comprehensive rehabilitative effort will need to be made to foster those behaviors in the prison that will be useful (intrinsically motivating?) upon the prisoner's return to the real world. At the risk of being churlish, we would add that the demonstration that a token reinforcement program was more effective than praise alone and/or noncontingent reinforcement, as indicated by a reversal design, comes as no surprise either. There are now countless demonstrations—usually with reversal designs—of the power of reinforcement contingencies within a tightly controlled environment to alter specific target behaviors. This has been established across numerous populations with diverse problems; provided the conditions were properly arranged it was bound to have the effects demonstrated by Milan and McKee. In short, we know this much. What we do not seem to know that much about is the "comprehensive rehabilitative effort" that Milan and McKee refer to—the means of developing durable behavioral competencies that will generalize to the natural environment. As we have said before, it is now time to move on from demonstration-type projects of the effects of reinforcement contingencies on specific target behaviors using simple reversal designs and to focus on the real problems facing those who are involved in integrating former prisoners and mental hospital patients back into the community to stay and to function at some reasonable level. The latter point should be emphasized. Substituting the back-alley for the backward in an effort to get people out of institutions does not solve the problem.

The important conceptual and practical role of behavioral mediators in behavior modification programs is emphasized in Section V of this volume where we discuss the contributions of parents, teachers, and childhood peers to behavior change. Smith, Milan, Wood, and McKee (1976) report a study in which the correctional officer was employed as a behavioral mediator. According to Smith et al., the behavioral mediator in a correctional setting is one who (1) grasps "the basic principles of the social learning approach to the understanding and remediation of human problems; (2) recognizes the role of objectivity, consistency, and reliability in the day-to-day operation of a behavior modification program; and (3) demonstrates the ability to integrate the theoretical orientation and requisite skills by conducting, under the supervision of a qualified professional, an actual behavior change project" (pp. 346-347). In their study, officers received both formal didactic and practical on-the-job training in a variety of behavioral procedures, including "identifying, defining, observing, recording, and graphing behavior; positive reinforcement and punishment; time-out; escape; avoidance; extinction and stimulus control; schedules of reinforcement; and shaping, chaining, and fading" (p. 348). Behavioral observation data indicate that officers who had received this training displayed significantly greater interaction with inmates than officers who had not been trained. Furthermore, trained officers used positive reinforcement significantly more than untrained officers in their interactions with inmates. The officers stated that the training had helped them in their duties, while inmates showed a tendency —albeit statistically not significant—to rate trained officers more favorably than untrained officers (see also Commentary, Section I).

Although the changes observed in the officers' behavior cannot be unequivocally attributed to the behavioral program because of the absence of specific controls, Smith et al. have demonstrated the potential value of employing correctional officers as behavior change agents. Finally, it is noteworthy that Smith et al.'s training program was successful in changing the officers' behavior in the target setting, namely their interactions with inmates. As discussed in our Commentary to Section V, workshops for teachers are often ineffective in altering teachers' actual behaviors toward their children. The fact that Smith et al. deliberately supplemented didactic sessions with practicum training in the applied setting was undoubtedly a major factor in their success.

Kandel, Ayllon, and Roberts (1976) demonstrate that a token reinforcement program with two inmates who had been jailed for violent crimes resulted in significant increases in academic performance. Despite a long history of academic failure and a lack of motivation to remedy these deficiencies, both inmates made substantial progress in mathematics and English. The most extraordinary result reported by Kandel et al. was that one of the inmates passed 9th through 12th grade algebra in only 14 days! The small *n,* lack of controls and no follow-up render this demonstration suggestive rather than conclusive, but the data do encourage further application of incentive systems to build performance skills in prisoners that will be functional in their adjusting to society upon their release from prison.

The introduction of an improved token reinforcement program into temporary detention centers for youths was evaluated by Gambrill (1976) in the course of an inservice training program in behavioral principles for the staff. The behavioral procedures significantly reduced the administration of disciplinary actions on the part of the staff and seemed to meet with the approval of the detained youths. However, as Gambrill points out, the lack of necessary controls makes it impossible to rule out the influence of numerous other factors in accounting for the results.

Ross and Price (1976) have reviewed some of the conceptual issues in the application of behavioral methods in correctional settings. They draw attention to the possible occurrence of overjustification effects in such programs (see Section V for a discussion of the overjustification hypothesis). Specifically, they suggest that prisoners are especially likely to view their behavior as under direct control of external contingencies. As a result, they argue that the prisoner will not attribute any behavior change to himself (or intrinsic motivation) and that behavior change observed in the institutional setting will not persist. Milan and McKee's results showing the deterioration in performance as soon as the token economy was withdrawn are consistent with Ross and Price's analysis. This concern about how prisoners understand and perceive the influence process is not only an ethical imperative, it may also be an important element in the generalization and maintenance of program-produced behavior change (cf. Greene, Sternberg, Lepper, reprinted in Section V).

BEHAVIOR MODIFICATION IN PSYCHIATRIC HOSPITALS

As part of the enthusiasm for community mental health centers and their rapid expansion in the U.S. after the Community Mental Health Act of 1963, partial hospitalization was advanced as an alternative to inpatient care. Luber and Hersen (1976) discuss the therapeutic potential of partial hospitalization from a behavioral perspective and outline the procedural elements of their own program which is organized explicitly along behavioral lines. The second paper reproduced in this Section is by Austin, Liberman, King, and DeRisi, and they describe a comparative evaluation of two types of partial hospitalization programs.

Although considerable resources have been invested in the creation of mental health clinics throughout the country, Austin et al. point out that their study is one of the first to evaluate the comparative effectiveness of such a service delivery system. Their study is distinguished by the inclusion of a two year follow-up, a rare feature of any treatment outcome study, and the results are very encouraging for behavior therapy. An interesting methodological point is highlighted by Austin et al.'s paper. They discovered that the non-behavioral eclectic treatment condition in fact included a behavioral component—one of the therapists had independently sought and received training in behavior modification and was busily applying it with her patients! As Kazdin and Wilson (in press) point out, *it is essential that the treatments as implemented in any comparative outcome study are consistent with their original specifications.*

Interpretation of many outcome studies is clouded if not impossible because of overlapping treatment procedures (see also Azrin, 1977).

Social Skills Training

Hersen and Bellack (1976b) summarize the empirical status and clinical implications of social skills training with chronic psychiatric patients.* They point out that a sizeable body of research has consistently shown that psychiatric patients' post-hospital adjustment will be heavily influenced by their level of social skills. Reviewing the outcome data from available clinical studies, Hersen and Bellack (1976b) conclude that "inpatient psychiatric populations appear to respond positively to such training, including some psychotic patients whose more florid symptomatology had previously been controlled with psychotropic medication. Not only are improvements seen in target behaviors specifically dealt with but there are indications that overall improvements in general psychopathology (e.g., anxiety, somatic preoccupations, self-concept) may accompany such changes. There are other indications that when training in hospital is such that it approximates (via behavior rehearsal) real-life situations, then there is a greater likelihood that in-hospital changes will transfer to the patient's natural environment following discharge" (p. 571).

Using a multiple baseline design, Hersen and Bellack (1976a) demonstrated that social skills training resulted in significant improvement in interpersonal functioning in two male chronic schizophrenics. These therapeutic gains were maintained at a two month follow-up, but the generalization of treatment effects was not assessed. If social skills training is to result in significantly improved functioning by chronic patients in the natural environment after discharge from the hospital, the generalization of therapeutic effects to novel situations in the real world has to be demonstrated. Bellack, Hersen, and Turner (1976) assessed the generalization of the effects of social skills training on three chronic schizophrenics in a partial hospitalization setting. Unlike the majority of studies on social skills training, particularly laboratory-based studies, these three patients received a considerable amount of skills training—25, 26, and 31 sessions respectively. Generalization from trained to untrained and to novel situations was demonstrated. Furthermore, maintenance of

* Social skills training with less severely disturbed, predominantly normal or neurotic populations is discussed in Section II. Two competent reviews of the use of objective behavioral assessment of social skills, by Eisler (1977) and Hersen and Bellack (1976a) respectively, are discussed in our Commentary to Section IV.

treatment-produced improvement was observed in two of the patients at a two month follow-up. As Bellack et al. themselves comment, the generalization that was observed in this study was in the context of contrived role-playing situations in the laboratory. The effects of social skills training on similar interpersonal responses in the natural environment need to be determined. The authors also point out that the content and goals of their social skills program were predetermined rather than geared to any normative or objective pattern of functioning. The advantages of the latter are discussed more fully by Goldsmith and McFall (1975—reprinted in Franks & Wilson, 1976).

Several other papers over the past year have addressed the generalization of therapeutic changes in patients in psychiatric hospitals. Using social skills training, Frederiksen, Jenkins, Foy, and Eisler (1976) successfully modified abusive verbal outbursts in two inpatients. Therapeutic improvement on the target behaviors generalized to novel role-playing situations within the laboratory context and also to interpersonal situations on the hospital ward. The latter finding is encouraging, particularly as hospital staff rated these changes as substantial—ratings Frederiksen et al. refer to as evidence for "social validity."

Liberman, McCann, and Wallace (1976) review the issues involved in the generalization of behavioral treatment with psychotics, and suggest several specific procedures that may facilitate generalization. These may be summarized as follows:

a) Target behaviors should be selected that are *functional* for the individual upon re-entry into the natural environment;

b) Social reinforcers such as praise and approval should be paired systematically with tangible rewards so as to establish more natural sources of support for newly developed behavior;*

c) Tangible reinforcers should be faded out gradually;

d) Actual characteristics of the natural environment should be incorporated into the treatment setting prior to discharge. Liberman et al. cite as examples of such a strategy having patients cook their own meals, use the telephone and public transfortation, and other *functional* activities. (This sort of behavior is frequently absent from limited behavioral programs that are designed to shape-up simple behaviors that have little functional value in the real world);

---

* Caulfield and Martin (1976) establish the word "good" as a reinforcer for chronic schizophrenics by pairing it with the termination of censure.

e) Patients should be gradually reintroduced into the natural environment;

f) Patients' relatives and/or caretakers should be taught to continue the reinforcement procedures begun in the hospital;

g) Patients should be taught self-regulatory skills such as self-reinforcement;

h) Reinforcement in the hospital setting should be intermittent and delayed;

i) New behaviors should be "over-learned" so as to make them resistant to extinction;

j) Patients should be involved in their treatment program, planning therapy goals and evaluating progress. According to Liberman et al., "This helps to shift the perceived locus of control from external to internal, and makes it more likely that the patient will attribute clinical progress to his or her own efforts" (p. 495).

Modeling is a fundamental component of social skills training as described by Bellack et al. (1976), Frederiksen et al. (1976) and Hersen and Bellack (1976a). Jaffe and Carlson (1976) compared symbolic modeling via videotape with direct instructional control and an attention-placebo control condition in the initiation of appropriate social behavior. Both modeling and instructions were equally effective in producing greater change than the control group. Jaffe and Carlson conclude that "elaborate modeling treatments may not be justified" in some treatment programs in view of the success of the more economical instructional approach. However, this conclusion does not follow easily from their study. Subjects were called upon to perform relatively simple tasks. It is quite possible that these behaviors were in the subjects' repertoires and that under direct instigation—either through modeling or instructions—they engaged in more of this behavior than a group that did not receive direct instigation. There is a convincing body of evidence that modeling is far more effective than simple instructions in the acquisition of new responses and skills (Rachman, 1976a; Rosenthal, 1976). In conceptualizing observational learning as an influence process, it is imperative to distinguish between the acquisition and the performance of behavior if faulty conclusions are to be avoided. The effects of modeling on the behavior of institutionalized retarded children were demonstrated by Marburg, Houston, and Holmes (1976). Consistent with previous research on the determinants of modeling effects, children who observed multiple models showed significantly greater behavior change and generalization of change than children who observed a single model.

Token Economies

Token economies seem to be viewed as less exciting, less effective, and more complicated than was once the case. The days when it was thought that token reinforcement procedures represented a major clinical breakthrough in the rehabilitation of the chronic, unmotivated back-ward patient now seem rather distant. Criticisms of the token economy abound, some well-grounded and others unfounded. Significantly, responsible researchers within the field of behavior therapy have added their misgivings about the therapeutic potential of token economies to Davison's (1969) original critique of the literature. In what follows we consider three different forms of criticism of token economies in institutional settings that have appeared this past year.

Hersen (1976) concludes that, to implement a token economy in most institutional settings, "an artificial state of deprivation must be achieved." Rewards such as ward passes, sleeping and room arrangements, and social privileges that were once administered noncontingently are removed and made contingent upon the performance of specific target behaviors. The reason for this, Hersen suggests, is that most institutions do not have the resources to provide additional rewards to those that are already part and parcel of the routine functioning of the institution. This issue of absolute versus contingent rights is discussed more fully by Wexler (1973—reprinted in Franks & Wilson, 1974).

As a second major shortcoming of token economies, Hersen notes that the efforts of token programs rarely generalize to other settings. In fact, it is almost redundant these days to emphasize this difficulty with token economies. Part of the problem is that specific generalization strategies have never been included in narrowly conceived programs that have repetitiously demonstrated the modification of mostly simplistic behaviors across many types of patients. While these studies are easier to complete, they have become largely irrelevant to the purpose of rehabilitating the chronic patient. As noted elsewhere in this volume—not to mention time and again throughout this Series—attention must be concentrated on producing significant generalization and maintenance of meaningful, functional target behaviors. Liberman et al.'s (1976) recommendations in this respect might well be followed.

Hersen's third criticism of token economies echoes part of Levine and Fasnacht's (1974) conclusion—token economies may result in token learning. Or as Hersen puts it, do patients in these programs learn new behaviors or do they learn how to earn tokens? We considered Levine and Fasnacht's argument in last year's volume (Franks & Wilson, 1976). Ideally, of course, in earning tokens patients are supposed to learn functional skills. Clearly this does not always happen.

An observation that will come as a surprise to many is Hersen's contention that the implementation of a token economy program results in a loss of control by the staff over the patients. Hersen's rationale is that, in the token program, decisions that affect patients "follow programmatic lines rather than being made more subjectively." Indeed, he suggests that this is the reason that many administrators in hospitals are unwilling to support token economy programs in their institutions. A majority of people undoubtedly view token economy programs as a means of increasing control over patients, and hold that the advantages it offers staff and administrators in managing patient behavior—as distinct from effectively treating patients—is the reason token economy programs have been so widely adopted in institutions (e.g., Page, Caron, & Yates, 1975). The apparent discrepancy between these two views may be resolved when it is realized that Hersen is referring to the ideal implementation of token programs that have as their explicit aim the betterment of the patients and their return to some sort of real adjustment in the community—not more efficient methods for the staff to keep order on the wards.

The question about what patients learn in a token economy has also been raised by Gagnon and Davison (1976). They make the case that patients learn to apply to mental life a "metric prevalent in commerce." This might produce order of a kind in the hospital setting—what we might label simple patient *management* rather than *treatment*—but fares poorly in equipping patients for re-entry into the real world outside the hospital. Gagnon and Davison put it thus: "The success of token economies in mental hospitals rests on the fact that patients are not suffering from economic irrationality, and that they will learn to adapt pre-existing economic modes of behavior to deal with token environments. However, the other promise of the asylum is that, after the experience of order within it, the mad will be released into the outside world, having regained that which had been lost. In this sense, the token economy teaches the wrong things—the first is that the world is just and the second that good behavior is generally rewarded. What everyone knows is that sometimes the world is just and sometimes it isn't, and that sometimes good behavior is rewarded and sometimes it is not" (p. 534).

The third criticism of token economies in a state mental hospital is exemplified by Bilken's (1976) account of being a participant observer for five months in a token economy program in a locked state ward for "so-called chronic schizophrenic women." Biklen claims to have reviewed the literature and consulted widely with behavioral psychologists about token economies, as a result of which he concludes that the program he observed is *typical* of behavior modification. His specific conclusions are as follows: First, that the criteria for rating patients were highly subjective and open to bias. Second, that patients were deprived of certain rights in order to create contingent rewards. This, he argues, puts the experimenters in a position of intensified control over the patients. Third, he condemns the sole use of overt behavior as a dependent measure as deplorable (he objects particularly to the nature of the target behaviors). Fourth, patients were not involved in the design and implementation of the program, they reacted with anger, and they specifically rejected the token economy program.

It is unfortunate that Biklen's interesting approach to commenting upon a token economy program is marred by an obvious bias against behavior modification. Let us consider his various conclusions. First, there is nothing novel about describing the faults—methodological or otherwise—about a single study in any approach. The real question is to what extent a specific problem in a particular study is representative of the field as a whole? Regrettably, Biklen simply alleges that he reviewed the literature on token economy programs without evidencing the fruits of a scholarly review. For example, there are many token reinforcement programs where behavioral observations have been objective and where sources of obvious bias have been precluded (cf. Kazdin, 1977). Biklen leaves the misleading impression that no such study exists. Second, Biklen is correct in noting the deprivation of patients in order to create contingencies, but here again balance demands some reference to previous discussions of this problem by behavior therapists and the existence of more acceptable alternatives. Third, no one will disagree with Biklen that target behavior such as children's games are demeaning and silly. Among others, we ourselves have criticized this tendency in far too many token economy programs to focus on trivial behaviors. But to suggest that such foolish activities as those described by Biklen are representative of the majority of behavior modification programs is misguided. Biklen's final point is a cogent one. We, too, have witnessed many a token economy program that was set-up without any attempt to encourage patients' participation in the design, implementation, or goals of the program. What Biklen does not mention, however, is that this is not only ethically questionable, it is also bad behavior modification. An important tenet of behavior therapy is that the patient participate actively in treatment to the fullest extent possible. This includes patients in psychiatric institutions (cf. Bandura, 1969). Obviously, the program Biklen describes was deficient in many respects, including the apparent failure to listen to patients' complaints and to solicit their suggestions about how the program could be improved.

As a closing note, we might add that Biklen's description of the various activities the patients engaged in, the lack of meaningful contact they had with staff, and the overall unresponsiveness of the institution to their personal views is far more typical of the squalid emptiness and iatrogenic atmosphere of the typical non-behavioral state hospital back-ward. Those who have worked in or even visited the typical locked ward will know that the depressing phenomenon of well-intentioned volunteers leading adult patients in "'Farmer in the Dell,' 'London Bridge is Falling Down,' and the 'Bunny Hop,' as well as a paper airplane flying contest" (Biklen, 1976, p. 56) was well-entrenched before Ayllon and Azrin tried to devise effective ways of interrupting the appalling consequences of the institutionalization syndrome.

In his comments on token economy programs, Hersen (1976) suggests social skills training allied to self-control methods as an alternative behavioral approach to token reinforcement programs. Claeson and Malm (1976) compared a social skills training program ("training in activities of daily living [ADL]") with and without a concurrent token economy program. The patients were 50 male chronic schizophrenics who had been hospitalized from four months to 40 years. Assignment to groups was made on a random basis. The ADL program consisted of modeling, behavior rehearsal, and educational techniques. Most patients in both treatment groups improved to the point where, according to Claeson and Malm, they possessed "the minimum amount of social skills necessary for living in the community outside the hospital." Somewhat surprisingly in terms of previous findings, the ADL plus token economy group showed significantly better performance at a one-year follow-up. In contrast to Gagnon and Davison's (1976) thesis, Claeson and Malm suggest that the token economy "taught the patients how to respond better to the reinforcement systems of the community."

In a commentary on the Claeson and Malm study, Hall (1976) points out that the absence of an immediate positive effect of the token economy program makes it difficult to attribute the differences between the two groups at the one year follow-up to the token economy per se. Hall also draws attention to what he terms "the relatively luxurious nature of the reinforcers available to the token patients"—day trips from Sweden to

Denmark, beef steaks, sleep until late on Saturday or Sunday with coffee in bed, and other choice items! These reinforcers and the behaviors they were contingent upon are a far cry from the mindless children's games observed by Biklen.

BEHAVIOR MODIFICATION IN NURSING-HOME AND OTHER RESIDENTIAL SETTINGS

There is little reason to suppose that the behavior of the elderly in nursing-homes is not susceptible to the influence of reinforcement contingencies. Using an ABAB design, Baltes and Zerbe (1976) demonstrated the expected, namely that eating behavior in two nursing-home residents could be significantly affected by reinforcement contingencies. As we have said before, we know this much. The implementation of Baltes and Zerbe's recommendations about training the staff of these residential homes in behavioral principles, and teaching the residents themselves the principles of behavioral self-control is the sort of research that is needed now in preference to demonstration-type studies of well-established findings. In contrast to the very specific target behavior that was the focus of the Baltes and Zerbe study, Langer and Rodin (1976) addressed themselves to the effects of choice and decision-making in the aged. Elderly residents of a nursing home showed significant improvement when encouraged by the staff to make decisions and assume responsibility—albeit limited—for their actions. Langer and Rodin point in the direction that behavioral programs with the aged might well move: "The practical implications of this experimental demonstration are straightforward. Mechanisms can and should be established for changing situational factors that reduce real or perceived responsibility in the elderly. Furthermore, this study adds to the body of literature . . . suggesting that senility and diminished alertness are not an almost inevitable result of aging. In fact, it suggests that some of the negative consequences of aging may be retarded, reversed, or possibly prevented by returning to the aged the right to make decisions and a feeling of competence" (p. 197).

No behavioral program can be implemented successfully in an institutional setting unless the staff is well-trained and motivated to cooperate in the specific behavioral procedures involved. One of the problems is that inservice training workshops by themselves are not enough to ensure the necessary staff performance (see our discussion of this issue in Sections I, V, IV). Specific contingencies have been placed on staff performance in behavioral programs, using rewards such as money bonuses. Although these methods have been successful in altering staff behavior, the practical difficulties and economic costs involved in such procedures make it unlikely that they will be widely used or approved of. Iwata, Bailey, Brown, Foshee, and Alpern (1976) have reviewed the difficulties inherent in the different methods that have been used to maintain high level staff behavior and have reported the results of a cost-effective method based upon reinforcers available in the institution.

In brief, staff at a residential facility for the retarded became eligible for a weekly lottery if they had satisfied their performance criteria. In the lottery they could win the opportunity to rearrange their days off for the following week, which usually meant that they could have another weekend off. This method proved to be more effective than administering specific staff assignments. It is economical and it can be implemented on a large scale.

Sanson-Fisher, Seymour, and Baer (1976) evaluated the effects of training the staff of a residential facility for delinquent girls to reinforce presocial changes in the residents' verbal behavior. Limited improvements were effected. However, these changes in the girls' behavior were not maintained after training ended, nor did they generalize to situations in which the staff were not present. Sanson-Fisher et al. conclude that staff training of this nature should be supplemented by training delinquent youths in self-control strategies as well as involving their peer group in the behavioral program. Once again, this study, like so many others discussed in this volume, highlights what is perhaps the most important and challenging task in contemporary behavior therapy, namely the development of effective strategies for the generalization and maintenance of treatment-produced change.

SECTION VIII: BEHAVIOR MODIFICATION IN INSTITUTIONAL SETTINGS

20

THE CELLBLOCK TOKEN ECONOMY: TOKEN REINFORCEMENT PROCEDURES IN A MAXIMUM SECURITY CORRECTIONAL INSTITUTION FOR ADULT MALE FELONS

Michael A. Milan and John M. McKee

Rehabilitation Research Foundation, Montgomery, Alabama

Two experiments were conducted (1) to explore the application of token reinforcement procedures in a maximum security correctional institution for adult male felons and (2) to determine to what extent the reinforcement procedures disrupted the day-to-day lives of inmate participants. In Experiment I, an expanded reversal design revealed that the combination of praise and token reinforcement was more effective than the combinations of praise and noncon-

---

Reprinted with permission from the *Journal of Applied Behavior Analysis,* 9, 253-275, No. 3 (Fall 1976). Copyright 1976 by the Society for the Experimental Analysis of Behavior, Inc.

This research was supported by the U.S. Department of Labor, Manpower Administration, under Contract 21-01-73-38. Organizations undertaking such projects are encouraged to express their own judgement freely. Therefore, points of view or opinions stated in this report do not necessarily represent the official position or policy of the Department of Labor or other federal agencies mentioned herein. Portions of these data were presented at the meetings of the Southeastern Psychological Association in 1971 and 1972. The authors express their appreciation to Larry F. Wood, Robert L. Williams, Jerry J. Rogers, and Lee F. Hampton for their valuable assistance in this research, and to Charles Petko for his aid in the preparation of this report.

tingent token award or direct commands on four common institutional activities. The latter two combinations were not found to be any more effective than praise alone. Experiment II, which also employed a reversal design, indicated that the high levels of performance observed during the token reinforcement phases of Experiment I could be attained without subjecting participants to undue hardship in the form of increased deprivation of either social intercourse or the opportunity to engage in recreational and entertainment activities. Client safeguards are discussed in detail.

DESCRIPTORS: token economy, contingent *versus* noncontingent, daily activities, prison inmates, adults

A beginning has been made in the use of the principles and technology of applied behavior analysis with adult and juvenile offenders in institutional settings. The CASE (Contingencies Applicable to Special Education) projects conducted at the National Training School for Boys in Washington, D.C., aimed to increase the academic skill of youths and to prepare as many as possible either to return to school or pass the high school equivalency examination (Cohen and Filipczak, 1971; Cohen, Filipczak, and Bis, 1967). To meet these objectives, the CASE team established a 24-hr learning environment based on the principles of applied behavior analysis. Academic skills and IQs increased, as measured by standardized tests, and positive attitudinal changes were also observed. Moreover, once released the youths stayed out of trouble and out of institutions for longer periods of time than the national average. The eventual recidivism figure was not, however, different from that of comparable releasees (Filipczak and Cohen, Note 1).

Similarly, a ward was opened at Walter Reed Army Hospital, Washington, D.C., to treat soldiers diagnosed as having character or behavior disorders (Boren and Colman, 1970; Colman and Boren, 1969). The treatment program was based on the assumption that these men had failed in the military, and previously in civilian life, because of deficits in their behavioral repertoire. The program's objective was to teach soldiers the education and recreation skills, personal habit patterns, such as planning and performing consistently, and interpersonal skills that would make their presence and performance important to other members of their military unit.

In follow-up, the performance of 46 men released from the Walter Reed project was compared to that of 48 comparable soldiers who received either routine disciplinary action or general psychiatric treatment. Of the soldiers in the Walter Reed group, seven had completed their tour and 25 were functioning in a unit (69.5% "success"), while 14 had either been administratively discharged from duty, were AWOL, or were in a stockade (30.5% 'failure"). Of the comparison group, one had completed his tour and 12 were on active duty (28.3% "success"), while 33 were administratively discharged or in a stockade (71.7% "failure") (Colman and Baker, 1969).

The early work of the Experimental Manpower Laboratory for Corrections (EMLC), operated by the Rehabilitation Research Foundation and located at Draper Correctional Center in Elmore, Alabama, developed and implemented efficient and effective methods of encouraging adult offenders to excel in remedial academic instruction and vocational skill training (Clements and McKee, 1968). Contingency management procedures generated increases in both the quantity and quality of academic work performed in the classroom. Overall progress in the program was substantial: offenders enrolled in the projects averaged gains of 1.4 grades per 208 hr of programmed instruction. High school equivalencies were earned by 95% of those who qualified for and took the GED, and nine former students entered college after leaving prison (McKee and Clements, 1971).

Studies such as these are only the beginning of a behavioral analysis of the problems confronting the criminal justice system. The scope of problems to which this approach has been applied is circumscribed, and the evaluative research that has been conducted, although promising, is certainly not conclusive. The work done suggests, however, that this approach has the potential of being as productive when applied to the behavior of clients of the criminal justice system as it has been in the mental health, health-related, and educational professions. It is particularly unfortunate, therefore, that the Task Force on Corrections of the National Advisory Commission on Criminal Justice Standards and Goals (1973) suggests otherwise:

> Most techniques of behavior modification have been generated either in the mental hospital or for educational use. Although their application to the correctional situation is not necessarily inappropriate, sufficient attention has not been given to the nature, scheduling, and limits of the reinforcement repertory available in the correctional apparatus. Thus, the use of tokens for behavior reinforcement in a reformatory may not be a suitable application of an approach that works in mental hospitals, where the problems of manipulation for secondary gains are not so prominent (p. 516).

Comments such as these reflect the reluctance of members of the criminal justice community to acknowledge that programs derived from a conceptual model that has proven effective with school children, mental patients, and delinquent youths might also prove to be effective with adult felons. In light of this reluctance, the objective of the present research was to assess the applicability of applied behavior analysis procedures to a representative population of imprisoned adult male felons.

This initial effort concentrated on activities important to the operation of the institution. Meeting the day-to-day requirements inherent in the operation of a large institution, such as preparing meals and ensuring that the fundamentals of personal hygiene are observed, is a practical concern of high priority to virtually all correctional administrators. It frequently appears, however, that administrators overemphasize this aspect of institution management, devoting a disproportionate amount of their time and energies to what most would consider rather perfunctory matters. Although this apparent overemphasis may reflect some administrators' biases regarding the primary functions of their institutions, it is more likely for most a natural outcome of a realistic appraisal of basic operating requirements, the widespread reliance on inmate labor for the performance of necessary work assignments, and the lack of an effective motivational system that encourages inmate workers to complete the tasks expected of them.

The decision to deal with activities important for the operation of the institution was based on three assumptions. First, it was reasoned that correctional administrators probably will not have either the time or the inclination to turn their attention to the difficult problems involved in preparing the offender for return to the community until they can meet the basic requirements of institutional management. Second, it appeared probable that a conceptual framework that enabled administrators to deal effectively with what they considered to be practical problems would be acceptable for use in the design and operation of offender rehabilitation programs. Third, it was concluded that the objective of the experiment was in no way harmful to prospective inmate participants and would instead prove to be in their best interest. Not only did the proposed behavior modification regimen de-emphasize the use of aversive control procedures and, consequently, attack what appears to be a major factor underlying the generally debilitating effect of imprisonment (Milan and McKee, 1974), but it also offered the inmates an incentive to practise and strengthen general employability skills, such as attending to directions, following instructions, accepting constructive criticism, and working toward task completion, that would benefit them when they returned to the community.

Experiment

The objectives of this experiment were to explore the feasibility of extending the use of applied behavior analysis procedures to the day-to-day activities of adult male felons, and to probe the potential contribution of such procedures to management and rehabilitation programming efforts within a maximum security correctional institution. This investigation focused on the effects of token reinforcement procedures on the performance of activities important for the orderly and hygienic operation of all large institutions, and sought to determine the manner in which various arrangements between behaviors and token awards influenced the inmates' performance of those activities.

METHOD

Participants

Fifty-six inmates incarcerated at Draper Correctional Center, Elmore, Alabama, a maximum security state institution whose all-male population consisted primarily of younger offenders serving sentences for their first or second felony conviction, participated. The only general constraint governing consideration for participation was that inmates be eligible for either parole or unconditional release within 90 days of the project's termination date. The initial token economy cellblock population of 33 inmates was drawn at random from those who had volunteered for this study and a related Manpower Development and Training (MDT) Project. A second random drawing determined which of the initial 33 residents of the token economy cellblock would fill the 20 positions open in the MDT Project. The remaining 13 participants who resided on the token economy cellblock but were not enrolled in the MDT Project continued to perform their routine institutional work assignments.

The 23 inmates who later joined the token economy cellblock population as replacements for those who left the project were, within the guidelines of the general constraint mentioned above, selected at random from the general population of the institution. The transfer of these inmates to the token economy cellblock was treated as a routine administrative matter. However, all participants could, as a total of five did, petition to discontinue their participation in the project by submitting a standard request for a cellblock transfer to the institution's classification officer. The classification officer evaluated these petitions and, if he found them reasonable and appropriate, approved the transfer. If the inmate still desired to discontinue his participation in the cellblock token economy after the transfer was approved and space was located in another cellblock, the transfer was accomplished. The decision to discontinue participation in the project in no way altered the inmate's projected release date or diminished the general quality of his life within the institution relative to the period before his enrollment in the project. The average daily census during the course of the 420 days of the project was 22 inmates, with the 56 inmates residing on the token economy cellblock for an average of 99 days.

The mean age of the 56 inmates at the time of their inclusion in the project was 23.6 yr, with a range of 16 to 54 yr; 42 (75%) were 25 yr of age or younger. Thirty-one (55%) were white and 25 (45%) were black. Their mean grade level, as indexed by the Tests of Adult Basic Education, was 7.4 grades, with a range of 2.9 to 12.3 grades. Their mean IQ, as measured by either the Otis Test of General Ability or the Wechsler Adult Intelligence Scale, was 88.3, with a range of 64 to 112. Of the 56 inmates, 19 (34%) were sentenced from counties with populations greater than 250,000; seven (13%) from counties with populations between 100,000 and 250,000; 12 (21%) from counties with populations between 50,000 and 100,000; 14 (26%) from counties with populations between 25,000 and 50,000; and four (7%) from counties with populations less than 25,000.

Seventeen (30%) of the inmates had been previously incarcerated as adult felons, during which time they served an average of 15.0 months, with a range of 15 days to 120 months. The average length of the sentences that they were serving was 54.6 months, with a range of 12 to 300 months. The offenses for which they were serving sentences are listed in Table 1. The distribution of offenses in the token economy cellblock population reflected that of the institutional population in general. Many inmates had been convicted of multiple offenses. Crimes against property were the most common offenses, with relatively smaller numbers of inmates serving sentences for crimes against persons or for statutory or "victimless" crimes.

Setting

The inmates were housed and the project conducted in the second (top) floor of one of Draper Correctional Center's six two-story wings.

The area was a remodelled dormitory subdivided into various rooms used dormitories, classrooms, study halls, recreational areas, and staff offices. It was adequately lighted and ventilated, and provided sufficient floor space both to house the inmates and to operate the project. All support (food, clothing, medical, *etc.*), general security, and custody related services (supervision of telephone, mail, and visiting privileges, *etc.*), were provided by Draper staff. All inmates and project staff members were subject to and followed the general rules, regulations, policies, and procedures established by the Alabama Board of Corrections.

All staff members who participated in this project had a background in applied behavior analysis. Before and during the operation of the Cellblock Token Economy, 40 correctional officers received training and supervised practicum experience in applied behavior analysis (Smith, Hart, and Milan, 1972). The ages of the officers, who were representative of the correctional staff in general, ranged from 23 to 67 yr, with a mean of 49.7 yr. Their reported grade levels ranged from the seventh grade to 1 yr of college, with a mean of 11 grades. Their tested grade levels, as determined by the Tests of Adult Basic Education, ranged from 3.2 to 10.9 grades, with a mean of 6.7 grades. Approximately 90% of the officers had lived one-half or more of their lives in Alabama; 65% of these in Elmore County (the location of the correctional institution), and 35% in bordering counties that, like Elmore County, were predominantly agrarian communities. Two of the officers were black, and none was an ex-offender.

There were three sequential training cycles. The first was completed before the cellblock token economy project was begun, and officers who were assigned to the cellblock were drawn from those who had completed that first cycle of training. Additional training in the specifics of the tasks they were to perform was provided through detailed instructions and modelling expected behavior. Of the four research staff members assigned to the cellblock, two had high school diplomas and on-the-job training in applied behavior analysis, and two had baccalaureate degrees with formal course work in applied behavior analysis; two were black and a third had previously served time within the institution as a convicted murderer. The project was directed by a Ph.D. psychologist and consultation was provided by a second Ph.D. psychologist. Conflicts between the correctional and research staffs were resolved by the project director unless they involved the general policies and procedures of the institution. In such cases, conflicts were resolved jointly by the project director and the warden of the institution.

Typically, a correctional officer supervised the cellblock during each weekday morning and early afternoon while the research staff assumed responsibility for its operation the remainder of the weekday and evening, as well as the entire day on weekends and holidays. However, a research staff member frequently worked with and observed the correctional officer as he supervised the cellblock, and a correctional officer occasionally assisted a research staff member with the operation of the cellblock. Hereafter, the term "staff member" is applied interchangeably to members of the correctional and research staffs; whether the term refers specifically to a correctional officer or a member of the research staff is usually, but not always, dictated by the time of day and the day of the week under consideration.

The Tokens

Tokens consisted of "points" that were acquired and expended through a simulated checkbook banking system. Each inmate was provided with an individualized book of standard checks. The use of the simulated banking system and the individualized accounts precluded the exchange of tokens among inmates, thereby reducing the ease with which the backup reinforcers could be acquired without engaging in the target behaviors. The token reinforcement system was in effect for approximately 7 hr each weekday (from 5:30 to 7:30 a.m., and from 4:30 to 9:30 p.m.) and for 16 hr during weekends and holidays (5:30 a.m. to 9:30 p.m.). The hours of exclusion represent those times during which inmates typically left the cellblock to work or to participate in vocational training.

Backup Reinforcers and Exchange Procedures

The backup reinforcers were items and activities that could be dispensed and monitored on the token economy cellblock. They consisted of access to various reinforcing event areas (a lounge, television viewing room, and poolroom), as well as time in the institution at large (areas other than the token economy cellblock) and, by means of this procedure, access to a wide variety of potential backup reinforcers (*e.g.*, relatives and acquaintances who were in the institution but not residing on the token economy cellblock, weekend movies, club meetings, and recreational activities available in the remainder of the institution). In addition, small commodities, such as cigarettes, soft drinks, snacks, etc., could be purchased in a token economy canteen operated by the project.

TABLE 1

Offenses Committed by Residents of Token Economy Cellblock

Offenses	Number[a]	Per Cent
Crimes against property	*55*	*69.6*
Grand larceny	27	34.2
Burglary	17	21.5
Second-degree burglary	6	7.6
Buying, receiving, or concealing stolen property	4	5.1
Attempted burglary	1	1.3
Crimes against person	*13*	*16.5*
Robbery	8	10.1
Assault with intent to murder	2	2.5
Child molestation	1	1.3
First-degree manslaughter	1	1.3
Second-degree murder	1	1.3
Statutory or victimless crimes	*11*	*14.0*
Escape	2	2.5
Possession of marijuana	2	2.5
Forgery	1	1.3
Perjury	1	1.3
Possession of barbiturates	1	1.3
Possession of LSD	1	1.3
Sale of marijuana	1	1.3
Violation of probation	1	1.3
Violation of state narcotics law	1	1.3

[a] The total number of offenses is greater than the number of residents of the token economy cellblock because 18 of the residents were serving sentences for two or more offenses.

Finally, Sears' and Penney's catalogs were available for examination from the token economy canteen, and inmates wishing special items not regularly carried by the canteen could order them if they appeared in either of the two catalogs.

If the inmate wished to enter a reinforcing event area, he first wrote a check for the required amount and deposited it in a collection box at the door. An additional check was required at the beginning of each successive clock hour (*e.g.*, from 5:30 p.m. to 6:30 p.m., *etc.*). Inmates could leave and re-enter the reinforcing event area any number of times during each clock hour, the only requirement being that they had written a check for that clock hour and deposited it in the appropriate box. Time spent in the remainder of the institution during the hours the token economy was in operation was recorded on time cards that inmates punched on a time clock as they left from and returned to the cellblock. These times were then totalled and paid for at the end of each day. A staff member made periodic rounds of the cellblock throughout the day to collect all checks near the end of each hour, to prepare the deposit boxes for the next hour's expenditures, and to check for unauthorized access to the reinforcing event areas on the cellblock and unauthorized departures from the cellblock to the remainder of the institution.

The token economy canteen was open one-half hour every evening and one additional half hour in the late morning on weekends and holidays. To obtain items from the canteen, inmates wrote checks in the exact amount of the to-be-purchased commodity and exchanged the check with the storekeeper for that item. In order to purchase items from the Sears' and Penny's catalogs, an inmate deposited the point cost of the desired item in a special order account. The canteen then ordered the item from the catalog sales department of the company. Inmates were prohibited from withdrawing points from the special order account or from changing their order.

Three response-cost (fine) procedures were employed to reduce unauthorized access to the back-up reinforcers of the token economy. The objective of the first was to discourage inmates from purchasing more back-up reinforcers than they were entitled to by their earning. To accomplish this, an inmate who had overdrawn his account was charged interest, at the rate of 10% of the overdrawn amount, each day his account remained overdrawn. The second procedure dealt specifically with reducing unauthorized access to the reinforcing event areas on the cellblock. An inmate who entered a reinforcing event area without first placing the required check in the deposit box was fined the hourly cost of the area and given the choice of either then depositing the required check and staying on, or leaving. The third procedure was instituted to discourage unauthorized access to the potential back-up reinforcers available in the remainder of the institution. An inmate who left the cellblock without punching out on the timeclock was considered to have been off the facility since the staff last had evidence he was present (usually the time of the previous routine check) and was charged for the time between then and his return to the cellblock.

Early each morning a point record was completed and posted. On it was an itemized accounting of each resident's earnings and expenditures on the previous day and the resultant balance carried forward to the present day. To prevent the long-term accumulation of points and a possible decline in the reinforcing value of each day's potential earnings, the number of points inmates could carry forward from each Sunday to the following Monday was limited to 600, excluding points that were being saved in special order accounts for catalog purchases. Those with overdrawn accounts were not permitted to purchase commodities from the token economy canteen, to enter the various reinforcing event areas on the token economy cellblock, or to leave the cellblock routinely for the remainder of the institution during the hours the token economy was in operation. These restrictions were lifted when a posted point record indicated that they had overcome their point deficits and that their accounts were no longer overdrawn.

Inmates with overdrawn accounts were, however, permitted unlimited access to the two dormitories of the token economy cellblock, to the hallways and lavatory, and to a "free room" containing wooden tables and chairs. In addition, they could leave the cellblock at no cost to obtain meals, to tend to health needs and legal matters, to conduct institutional business, to mail letters, and to place telephone calls and receive visitors as further regulated by general institutional policies. Finally, all inmates were allowed to leave the cellblock at no cost either to perform their institutional job or participate in vocational training and, if they wished, exercise outside at the noon-time break during the weekday hours when operation of the token economy was suspended.

Target Behaviors and Token Award Procedures

The target behaviors were termed "morning activities" and consisted of (1) arising at a determined hour, (2) making the bed, (3) cleaning the area in the general proximity of the bed, and (4) maintaining a neat and well-groomed personal appearance. Typical payoff and cost values of representative target behaviors and backup reinforcers are presented in Table 2. These values were subject to change to answer experimental questions or to maintain balance in the token reinforcement system. Changes in payoff values, which typically involved experimental operations, were announced the day before they took effect, while changes in cost values, which were typically undertaken to maintain balance within the token economy, were announced three to five days before they were introduced.

The scoring of the four morning activities was on an all-or-none basis. Each inmate was briefed on the scoring criteria when he entered the project, and the criteria themselves were posted on a bulletin board. The criterion for arising at the appointed hour had to be met and scored between 5:30 and 7 a.m. weekdays or between 5:30 and 9 a.m.

TABLE 2

Point Values of Representative Target Behaviors and Backup Reinforcers

Target Behaviors	Points Awarded
Morning activities	
Arising on time	60
Bed made	60
Living area neat and clean	60
Personal appearance	60
Educational activities[a]	
Student performance	two per min (estimated)
Tutor performance	two per min (estimated)
Assigned maintenance tasks[b]	
Sweep main hall (back half)	60
Empty trash cans in recreation room	60
Mop front steps and landing	120
Dust and arrange furniture in television room	120

Backup Reinforcers	Points Charged
Activities available on the token economy cellblock	
Access to television room	60 per hr
Access to pool room	60 per hr
Access to lounge	60 per hr
Canteen items available[c]	
Cup of coffee	50
Can of soft drink	150
Ham and cheese sandwich	300
Pack of cigarettes	450
Leisure time away from token economy cellblock	one per min

a Students were paid on a performance- rather than time-contingent basis. Point values for units of academic material were based on an empirically derived estimated study time per unit and awarded when unit tests were passed.

b Although only four are presented here, there was a sufficient number of maintenance tasks to ensure that all residents had the potential of earning 120 points by completing their assignments. Additionally, residents could volunteer for supplementary maintenance tasks to increase their daily point earnings.

c Although only four are listed here, a large variety of items was available in the token economy canteen.

weekends and holidays. The cutoff time for the remaining three morning activities was extended one-half hour, to 7:30 a.m. weekdays and 9:30 a.m. weekends and holidays. Within these time constraints, the scoring criteria for the four morning activities were:

1. *Arising at the appointed hour.* An inmate was scored as arising on time when he was observed not in physical contact with any part of his or any other bed.

2. *Bed made.* An inmate was credited with having made his bed if the

bottom sheet, top sheet and first blanket (when present) were tightly tucked all around under the mattress; if the second blanket (when present) was folded and placed at the foot of the bed and on top of the top sheet or the first blanket, and if the pillow was smoothed, flattened, and placed at the head of the bed on top of the top sheet or the first blanket.

3. *Clean living area.* Different criteria were established for inmates assigned to top and bottom bunks. If a bunk bed was occupied by only one inmate, that inmate was scored on the basis of the requirements for the occupants of both the top and bottom bunks.

Top bunk. An inmate sleeping in a top bunk was scored as having cleaned his living area if both the top of and the floor below the adjacent dresser were free of dust (to the touch) and trash (bits of paper, burnt matches, cigarette butts, *etc.*) and if these areas and the inmate's bunk were free of personal articles (clothing, towels, shoes, *etc.*).

Bottom bunk. An inmate with a bottom bunk was credited with having cleaned his living area if the floor beneath the bunk was free of trash and if that area and the inmate's bunk were free of personal articles (shoes were permitted below the bed if lined up beginning at the wall).

4. *Neat and well-groomed personal appearance.* An inmate was credited with presenting a neat and well-groomed personal appearance if he were clean-shaven (either after a visual inspection or, if the visual inspection was inconclusive and permission had been asked of and given by the inmate, to the touch), if his hair was combed, if his t-shirt and/or shirt was tucked into his pants, if his pants were zipped and/or buttoned, if his belt (when present) was buckled, and if his shoelaces (when present) were laced and tied.

The lights in each of the two dormitories of the token economy cellblock were turned on at 5:30 a.m. weekdays and at 7:30 a.m. weekends and holidays. Beginning then and for the following 2 hr, a staff member continuously circulated through the two dormitories as the inmates arose and performed the morning activities. As he moved through the dormitories, the staff member greeted each inmate in an informal and friendly manner, rated each inmate's performance of the four morning activities, and provided feedback concerning whether or not the performances met the established criteria.

When an inmate's performance of an activity did not meet the criteria, the inmate was praised for those portions fo his performance that did meet criterion, informed of deficiencies, and given the opportunity to correct his performance. If, for example, an evaluation of an inmate's personal appearance revealed it was acceptable except for untied shoe laces, the staff member would typically have said something like: "Your personal appearance is generally acceptable. Your shave looks good and your clothes are fine, but you haven't tied your shoe laces yet. You know you are expected to do that too. I'll be around again in a few minutes to check again if you want."

When an inmate's performance of a morning activity met the established criteria, either when first examined or after a deficiency had been noted and corrected, the inmate was so informed and praised for his good performance. At this same time during those conditions of the token economy under which points were awarded contingent on the satisfactory performance of morning activities, the inmate was also instructed to add the number of points his performance represented to the point balance of his checking account. This latter procedure constituted the token reinforcement operation.

The staff member then recorded the points earned on a master data sheet. This sheet was then used to determine the percentage of morning activities completed and, during the token reinfrocement conditions of the token economy, the number of points earned for the completion of morning activities by each inmate that day. The data reported thus represented the inmate's final level of performance, either when the performance of activities met the criteria when first examined or after deficiencies had been noticed and inmates had been afforded the opportunity to make corrections. When such a procedure is employed, it is critical that special care be taken to ensure that the resultant data reflect the direct effect of the contingencies explored, rather than correlated changes in staff behavior. In this instance, for example, it was possible that the staff might provide more corrective feedback and encouragement to inmates to improve their performance under conditions in which the award of points was contingent on successful completion of morning activities than during the comparison conditions. To minimize this possibility, the staff members who collected the data in question were well-practiced in the formalized routine described above, and adhered to it strictly through all experimental conditions.

Experimental Conditions

The experiment consisted of 13 experimental conditions: (1) Baseline$_1$, (2) Officer Commands, (3) Baseline$_2$, (4) 60 Points Noncontingent$_1$, (5) 60 Points Contingent$_1$, (6) 90 Points Contingent, (7) 60 Points Contingent$_2$, (8) 60 Points Noncontingent$_2$, (9) Zero Points,

(10) 60 Points Noncontingent$_3$, (11) 60 Points Contingent$_3$, (12) Announce Baseline$_3$, and (13) Baseline$_3$. Data collection was restricted to weekdays during the first three experimental conditions. It was expanded to include weekends when the token economy was introduced in the fourth experimental condition and continued daily for the remainder of the 420 days of the project.

1. *Baseline$_1$*. This and the following two conditions preceded implementation of the token economy. In preparation for this condition, the scoring criteria for the four morning activities were explained to each inmate and posted on the token economy cellblock bulletin board. The inmates were informed that they were expected to complete each activity each day and that their performance would be recorded. During this condition, a correctional officer toured the token economy cellblock on weekdays between 5:30 and 7:30 a.m. and openly recorded the activities completed by each inmate.

During this and all subsequent conditions, inmates were informed whether or not their performance of the morning activities met the scoring criteria. If an activity met its performance criterion, the officer acknowledged this and praised the performance. If an activity did not, the officer informed inmates of their deficiencies and offered them the opportunity to correct their performance. At the same time, the officer refrained from employing the various coercive techniques typically employed to motivate performance in correctional institutions.

2. *Officer Commands*. Throughout the *Baseline$_1$* condition, the correctional officer assigned to the token economy cellblock during the morning shift insisted that he could improve the inmates' performance of the morning activities if only he were given the opportunity to do so. During this condition, the officer supplemented the procedures of the *Baseline$_1$* condition with whatever tactics he deemed necessary and appropriate to motivate inmate performance. As he saw fit, he stood by and provided direct supervision and harassment as inmates completed the activities, assigned extra work on the cellblock to those who failed to complete activities, or threatened to write disciplinary reports on the inmates with the lowest levels of performance. No disciplinary reports were written for nonperformance of the morning activities, however, for the officer had previously entered into an agreement, which was enforced throughout the experiment, that disciplinary reports would not be written for minor infractions such as these because they frequently resulted in an inmate's transfer to another cellblock within the institution or to another institution within the system. This restriction pre-

cluded the possibility that the officer would use the *Officer Commands* condition to "select-out" the inmates he considered troublesome or not deserving of inclusion in the project. This condition cannot, therefore, be interpreted as a test of the control procedures practised in the remainder of the institution. Moreover, the officer employed the tactics that were available to him in an unsystematic and unquantifiable manner. Despite these two limitations, the condition was deemed worthy of examination, for it represents the officer's "best efforts" in motivating the inmates' performance of the morning activities.

3. *Baseline$_2$*. Identical to the *Baseline$_1$* condition.

4. *60 Points Noncontingent$_1$*. This condition was employed (1) to determine the effects of general changes in the operation of the token economy cellblock that occurred when the token economy was introduced (limited access to the backup reinforcers; the availability of commodities, such as cigarettes and snacks, not previously available, *etc.*) on the performance of the morning activities and (2) to separate these from the specific effect of the contingent relationship between the performance of these activities and the award of points, which was explored in the following conditions. Throughout this condition, 60 points were awarded on a noncontingent basis (*i.e.*, independent of whether or not performance met the established criteria) for each of the four morning activities. The operation of the project was expanded to include weekends and holidays as well as weekdays. Points were awarded from the first day of this condition. Beginning on the second day, inmates were required to exchange points in order to partake of the backup reinforcers of the token economy.

5. *60 Points Contingent$_1$*. During this condition, 60 points were awarded on a contingent basis (*i.e.*, only when performance met the established criteria) for each of the four morning activities either when first rated or after deficiencies had been noted and inmates afforded the opportunity to improve their performance. Unless the contrary is indicated, these general procedures were followed throughout the remainder of the token economy.

6. *90 Points Contingent*. During this condition, the number of points awarded for each completed activity was increased by 50% to (90 points), thereby raising the potential number of points that could be earned for the four morning activities by 120 points from 240 to 360 points.

7. *60 Points Contingent$_2$*. The procedures were identical to those followed during the *60 Points Contingent$_1$* condition.

8. *60 Points Noncontingent*$_2$. The procedures were identical to those followed during the *60 Points Noncontingent*$_1$ condition.

9. *Zero Points.* This condition was similar to the *Baseline* conditions in that no points were awarded for completion of the morning activities. It differed from the *Baseline* conditions in that the token economy remained in operation, other behaviors continued to earn tokens, and access to the back-up reinforcers was contingent on the exchange of tokens. To maintain token availability at approximately the same level as the preceding conditions, the 240 points per inmate that were no longer available for completion of the morning activities were distributed among the remaining target behaviors during this condition alone.

10. *60 Points Noncontingent*$_3$. Identical to the *60 Points Contingent*$_2$ condition.

12. *Announce Baseline*$_3$. The procedures followed during this condition, which began one week before the final return-to-baseline condition of the experiment, were identical to those of the *60 Points Contingent*$_3$ condition. This condition differed from the preceding condition in that when it was instated, all inmates were informed of the day the token economy would end, and a notice to that effect was placed on the cellblock bulletin board. The one-week warning allowed residents of the cellblock to expend the points they had accumulated.

13. *Baseline*$_3$. Procedures were identical to those in effect during the *Baseline*$_1$ and *Baseline*$_2$ conditions.

Results

Reliability of Measurement

To obtain estimates of interobserver agreement on the performance of the four morning activities, the staff member on duty was accompanied by a second staff member as he rated and recorded inmate's performance. Each staff member independently scored each inmate's performance before the staff member in charge informed the inmate of the quality of his performance. There was a total of 28 of these sessions, occurring on weekday mornings distributed evenly throughout the experiment. The percentage of agreement for each day was calculated by dividing the number of agreements on the occurrence of the target behaviors by the number of agreements plus the number of disagreements and multiplying by 100. Agreements on the nonoccurrence of the target behaviors were disregarded. The percentages of agreement ranged from 54% to 100%. The average agreement for arising at the appointed time was 95.7%; for bed made, 95.2%; for cleaning the living area, 94.9%; and for presenting a neat and well-groomed appearance, 95.0%. The overall agreement averaged 95.2%.

Findings

The following analysis of the effects of experimental conditions deals primarily with data summarizing the daily performnce of the four morning activities and then secondarily with one or more of the activities alone when those data deviate from the summarized data to a sufficient degree to so warrant. The daily percentage of the four morning activities completed by all inmates of the token economy cellblock throughout the 420 days of the experiment are presented in Figure 1.

The mean percentage of morning activities that met the performance criterion during the 11 days of the *Baseline*$_1$ condition was 66.4%. During the nine days of the *Officer Commands* condition, when the correctional officer on duty exerted his "best efforts" to motivate the performance of the morning activities, the mean percentage of morning activities meeting criteria was 63.7%. The mean percentage of morning activities meeting the performance criteria during the five-day *Baseline*$_2$ condition was 68.6%. The data from these first three experimental conditions reveal that correctional officer's aversive control-oriented "best efforts" during the *Officer Commands* condition had no demonstrable effect upon the inmates' performance of the four morning activities.

The mean percentage of morning activities completed during the 35 days of the *60 Points Noncontingent*$_1$ condition rose to 74.7%. Examination of the data suggests, however, that the improvement in performance after the token economy was introduced was transitory, and that performance during the latter half of the condition was lower than during the first half and comparable to that of pretoken economy *Baseline* periods. The mean percentage of morning activities meeting the performance criteria during the first half of this period (82.0%) was markedly higher than during the second half (66.9%), while the mean precentage of activities completed during the second half was not different from that of the pretoken economy *Baselines*. It appears, then, that introduction of the token economy *per se* facilitated performance of the four morning activities, but that this improvement was short-lived, with the level of performance gradually returning to that observed before the token economy's introduction.

During the 28 days of the *60 Points Contingent*$_1$ condition, a mean of 86.0% of the morning activities met criteria. This was higher than that observed during the *60 Points Noncontingent*$_1$ condition. Moreover, performance of the activities improved over the course of this condition, with the mean percentage completed during the second half (93.3%) higher than that of the first half (78.6%). The *90 Points Contingent* condition sought to assess the effect of a moderate (50%) increase in token reward on the performance of the to-be-reinforced behavior. During the 16 days of this condition, the mean percentage of activities scored as completed was 89.6%, not different from the terminal level of performance under the *60 Points Contingent*$_1$ condition.

A mean of 93.6% of the morning activities was completed during the 19 days of the *60 Points Contingent*$_2$ condition. This was not different from either the level of performance observed during the *90 Points Contingent* condition or the terminal level of performance under the *60 Points Contingent*$_1$ condition. It must be concluded, therefore, that in this instance the 50% increase in token reward explored in the *90 Points Contingent* condition did not facilitate performance. This, however, might be the result of a ceiling effect, for performance levels were already markedly high when the condition was introduced.

During the 28 days of the *60 Points Noncontingent*$_2$ condition, a mean of 78.1% of the morning activities were completed. This was not different from the terminal level of performance under the *60 Points Noncontingent*$_1$, but was lower than both the terminal level of performance during the *60 Points Contingent*$_1$ condition and the level of performance under the *60 Points Contingent*$_2$ condition. These data indicate that the response-contingent award of tokens precipitated a clear improvement in performance with approximately 90% or more of the morning activities completed each day, a higher level of performance than under any other condition.

The *Zero Points* condition allows a comparison of the effects of the noncontingent award of tokens and the absence of token award. During the 12 days of this condition, a mean of 65.0% of the morning activities was completed, not different from the level of performance under the *60 Points Noncontingent*$_2$ condition. A mean of 67.4% of the activities was completed during the 12 days of the *60 Points Noncontingent*$_3$ condition. This level of performance was not different from the levels of performance observed under either the *Zero Points* condition or the *60 Points Noncontingent*$_2$ condition, indicating that the use of the noncontingent "incentives" is no more effective in motivating performance than is contingent praise in the absence of any such incentives which, in turn, is markedly less effective than contingent token reinforcement.

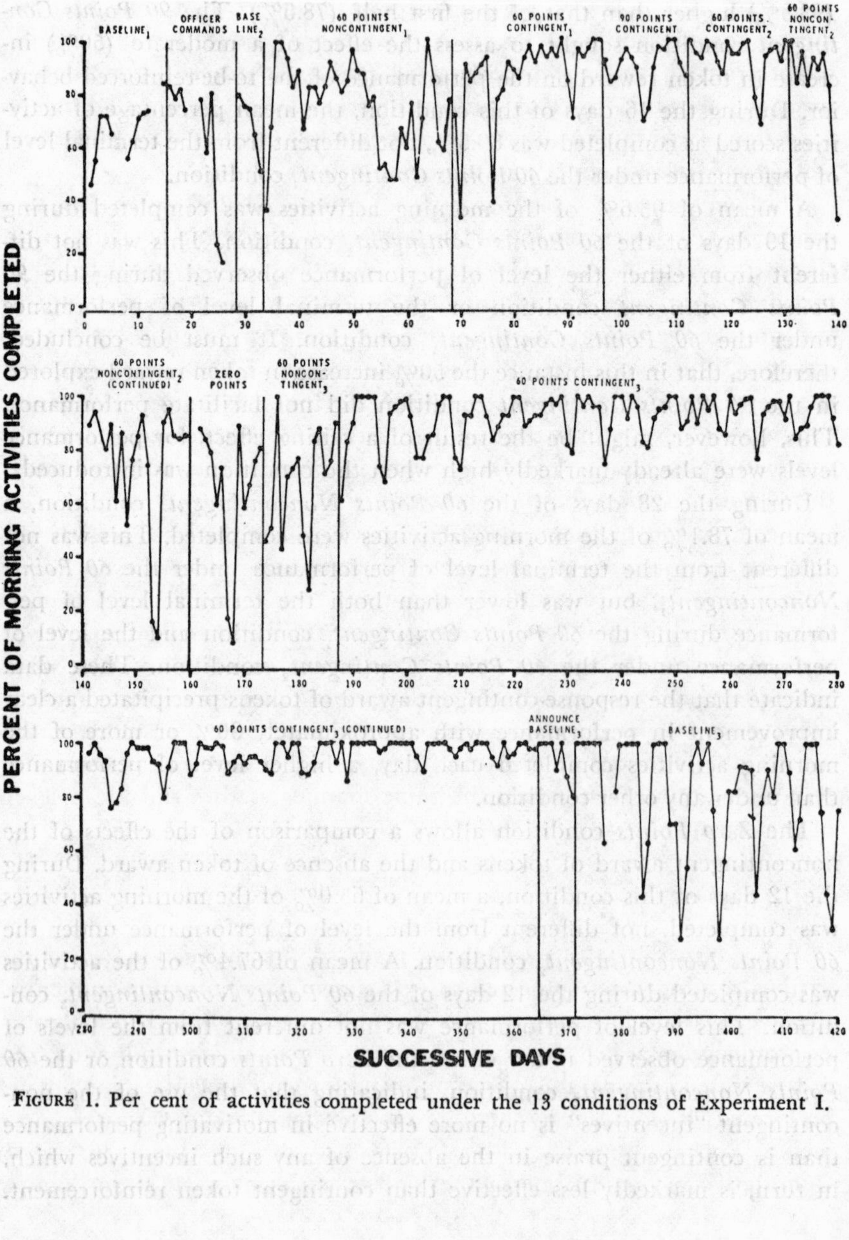

FIGURE 1. Per cent of activities completed under the 13 conditions of Experiment I.

The *60 Points Contingent*$_3$ condition was in effect for the remainder of the token economy. During the 177 days of this condition, a mean of 94.1% fo the morning activities was performed satisfactorily. As would be predicted, this level of performance was higher than that observed during the preceding *60 Points Noncontingent*$_3$ condition but not different from that of the preceding *60 Points Contingent*$_2$ condition or from the terminal level of performance of the *60 Points Contingent*$_1$ condition. Performance of the four morning activities during the one-week *Announce Baseline*$_3$ condition averaged 93.7%.

The percentage of morning activities completed during the *Baseline*$_3$ condition was lower (81.3%) than during the preceding *60 Points Contingent*$_3$ condition. Contrary to that which would be predicted, performance during this condition was superior to that observed during the pretoken economy *Baseline* periods. However, Figure 1 reveals a steady decline in performance over the course of this condition, with the percentage of activities completed during the second half of the condition (76.5%), only slightly higher than the percentage of activities completed during the pretoken economy *Baseline* periods and under the *60 Points Noncontingent* conditions.

A comparison of those conditions in which token award was contingent on performance of the morning activities with those in which tokens were either unavailable or awarded on a noncontingent basis reveals striking differences in response variability as well as in over-all response levels. It appears that introduction of token reinforcement procedures not only raised the general level of performance but also reduced day-to-day variations in response probability, and that subsequent manipulations in the contingencies of reinforcement controlled response variability in much the same manner as they did mean levels of performance.

Individual Performance Records

The group data discussed above revealed the manner in which the various contingencies subjected to experimental examination influenced the averaged performance of the token economy cellblock population. As would be expected, however, a review of the inmates' individual records revealed considerable variation in performance levels. Some inmates performed at consistently high levels throughout the various experimental conditions, while others performed at only moderate levels. Cumulative records of one of the highest performers (J.C.) and one of

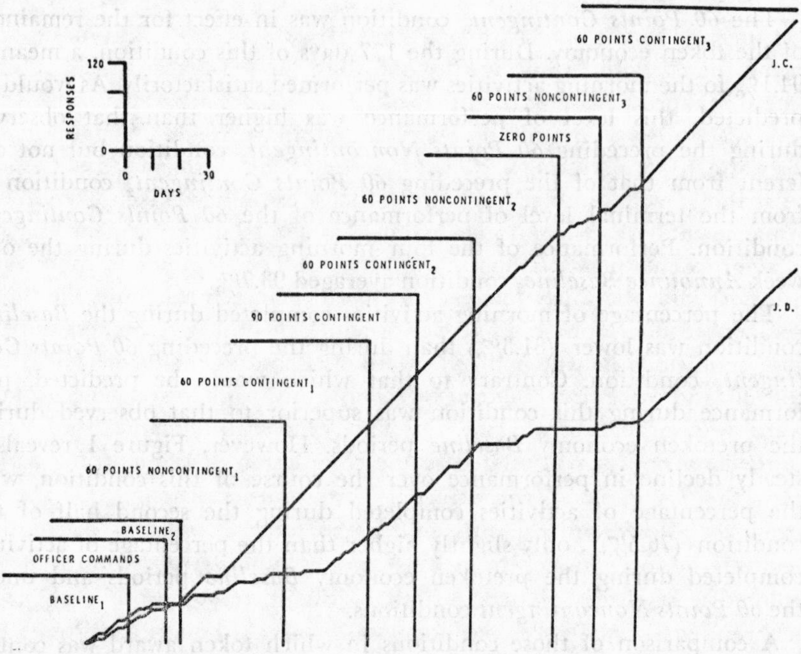

FIGURE 2. Individual cumulative records for two inmates of the completion of the four morning activities under the first 10 conditions and first portion of the eleventh condition of Experiment I.

the lowest performers (J.D.) for the four morning activities throughout the first third of the experiment are shown in Figure 2.

The performances of J.C. and J.D. approximate an "envelope" that roughly contains the performances of the remaining inmates of the token economy cellblock. J.D. appears to have had the higher level of performance of the two during the three pretoken economy phases. The performance of J.C. increased radically after the token economy was introduced, however, while the performance of J.D. continued relatively unchanged during the *60 Points Noncontingent*$_1$ condition. J.D.'s performance then improved markedly during the *60 Points Contingent*$_1$ condition and continued at a moderately high level during the *90 Points Contingent* and *60 Points Contingent*$_2$ conditions, while J.C.'s performance continued relatively unchanged. J.D.'s performance showed only some disruption during the *60 Points Noncontingent*$_2$ condition and continued at a low level throughout the *Zero Points* and *60 Points*

Contingent$_3$ conditions. Although the performance of both improved during the *60 Points Contingent*$_3$ condition, the performance of J.C. was somewhat more consistent than that of J.D.

As would be predicted, however, the similarities in the patterns of J.C.'s and J.D.'s performances in response to the contingencies examined are striking, with the various contingencies examined affecting the performance fo both in the same manner, albeit to differing degrees: the behavior of neither was affected by the *Officer Commands* condition, with both showing fairly low levels of performance throughout the three pretoken economy phases. The performance of both was highest during those conditions in which token award was contingent on performance (the *60* and *90 Points Contingent* conditions) and lowest when token award was either absent (the *Baseline, Officer Commands,* and *Zero Points* conditions) or unrelated to the completion of the morning activities (the *60 Points Noncontingent* conditions), although J.C.'s performance faltered only slightly under the latter conditions. Including even this minor variance from the expected, the various contingencies explored were clearly related to similar shifts in response probability for each resident of the token economy cellblock. Although consistency of performance and magnitude of change differed from inmate to inmate, direction of change from contingency to contingency was replicated for each inmate.

DISCUSSION

This experiment examined the effectiveness of various token economy procedures in motivating the performance of adult male felons institutionalized in a maximum security correctional institution. Performance-contingent token reinforcement was shown to be a considerably more effective motivator of inmate performance than the praise of the *Baseline* phases, the coercive procedures of the *Officer Commands* phase, and the noncontingent incentives of the *60 Points Noncontingent* phases which, in turn, did not differ among themselves. It should not be concluded, however, that praise alone had no effect, for no attempt was made to evaluate inmate performance in the absence of both praise and token reinforcement. It is possible that elimination of praise for performance of the morning activities would have resulted in a drop in performance below that observed in the *Baseline* conditions of this experiment. It may be concluded, however, that performance-contingent token reinforcement in conjunction with praise was a considerably more effective motivator of inmate performance than was praise alone.

Similarly, it should not be concluded that the superiority of token reinforcement to the procedure employed by the correctional officer during the *Officer Commands* condition demonstrates that the token economy is a more effective motivator of inmate performance than are the aversive control procedures typically employed within the correctional institution, for the correctional officer was prohibited from employing the full range of negative sanctions that he could normally bring to bear to ensure the performance of these four activities. The aversive control procedures that have been developed and refined over the years are probably as effective as or more effective than the token procedures employed here in motivating inmate performance. The token economy is, however, a considerably more effective motivator than is the correctional officer's "best effort" without recourse to the full range of aversive control procedures that would normally be available to him. Additionally, the consistently high levels of performance and reduced day-to-day variability generated by contingent token reinforcement demonstrate that the token economy is indeed a viable alternative to such aversive control procedures.

Finally, the deterioration of performance after the token economy was terminated at the end of the experiment is to be expected. Indeed, it would be surprising if the performance of the inmates had continued unchanged, for the power and importance of the contingent relationship between completion of the morning activities and token reinforcement in maintaining performance had been previously demonstrated by the deteriorations of performance observed during those phases of the token economy in which tokens were either awarded on a noncontingent basis or were not awarded at all. The objective of this experiment was to explore alternatives to existing inmate management procedures, not to develop a regimen wherein the behavior of inmates was changed in a manner that would permit the correctional officer then to maintain the performance of the morning activities in the absence of token reinforcement. This general objective would be warranted in a comprehensive rehabilitative effort for those activities that can be fostered within the institution and that have meaning for the inmate when he is released and/or have impact on the probability that the offender will succeed in the community to which he returns. This demonstration of the effectiveness of applied behavior analysis procedures with adult felons does, however, indicate that such procedures have the potential of playing a central role in the design and operation of comprehensive rehabilitative programs as the criminal justice system expands its offender rehabilitation efforts.

The cost of operating the token economy canteen was computed by totalling the census of the token economy cellblock for all days the canteen was in operation and dividing the resulting figure into the total cost of items stocked in the canteen and ordered from catalogs. The average cost of operating the canteen, which was in competition with the institution store, where the Board of Corrections sold (for "real" money) similar items, was 61 cents per man per day. Although the per-man cost for operating the token economy canteen was relatively low, even this could be reduced if potential reinforcers in the institution were incorporated into the token economy. If such things as *extra* recreation, telephone, and visiting privileges, for example, were added to the reinforcing event menu, it is quite probable that they could effectively compete with the offerings of the canteen. Not only would such extras reduce canteen expenditures, they would also increase the reinforcing properties of the tokens and, thereby, the probability that to-be-reinforced activities would be completed.

Ideally, however, the institution would abolish the practice of selling goods for profit through its store and instead operate it in the same manner that the token economy economy canteen was operated. Some inmates receive an abundant supply of funds from their family and friends, while others receive only the small amount (50 cents every two weeks) provided by the institution. Those with extensive funds can purchase virtually anything they wish, while those with no funds must turn to prison rackets and homosexual prostitution to get whatever money they can. If the institution store were employed as an adjunct to management and rehabilitation programs, the cost of stocking and operating it could be justifiably assumed by the Board of Corrections. Such a procedure would serve two equally important functions: first, it would provide the administration with powerful incentives with which to motivate performance of institutional assignments and participation in rehabilitative programs. Second, it would ensure that all inmates had the potential of equal access to the items offered in the store and, by so doing, move toward the elimination of the unequal distribution of wealth in the institution and the regressive effects of this on the inmate population.

Experiment II

The emphasis of Experiment I was on the manner in which various arrangements between inmate activities and potential reinforcers influenced the inmates' performance of those activities. The results clearly demonstrated higher levels of sustained performance under conditions in which a contingent relationship existed between behavior and reinforcer than under alternative possible arrangements. The data generated in that demonstration do not, however, reveal to what extent, if any, the token economy and the contingencies involved therein altered other aspects of the inmates' day-to-day existence in the institution. The objective was a reasonable parity between what was expected of the inmates (the morning activities and assigned maintenance tasks that the correctional center administration routinely demanded of all inmates, and the rehabilitation-oriented involvement in the leisure-time remedial education program as a student and/or tutor that the project staff sought to foster in the token economy participants) and what the inmates could expect in return (television viewing, recreation, and other activities available to inmates within the correctional center, as well as the tangible commodities dispensed by the token economy canteen). The purpose of Experiment II was to determine whether or not the token economy in Experiment I exerted on participants undue hardship in the form of increased deprivation of social intercourse and/or recreational activities.

Method

Response Definitions

A checklist consisting of classes of activities in which inmates of the correctional center might engage was constructed to enable a topographical analysis of the daily activities of the participants of the cellblock token economy project. In developing the checklist, research staff, correctional center administrator, and inmates generated lists of activities in which inmates of the institution could engage. These lists were combined and the items refined, with closely related or overlapping activities united and unobservable or inferred activities operationally defined or deleted. The composite list was then further refined during a tryout period before collection of the data reported.

The resultant Behavior Observation Checklist (BOC) consisted of 58 operationally defined classes of activities, such as *Eating, Listening to Radio/Sports, Lying Down/Awake, Reading/Book, Standing, Talking with Others/Religion, Student, etc.* In the administration of the BOC, raters were instructed to choose the more interactive, more informative categories in preference to their less interactive, less informative alternatives. For example, if an inmate was lying down, eyes open, and a radio adjacent to his bed was broadcasting a clearly audible baseball game, he was rated as *Listening to Radio/Sports* instead of *Lying Down/Awake*. Similarly, if an inmate was observed sitting at a desk in the remedial education area of the cellblock, textbook before him, and his head and eyes oriented towards the book's open pages, he was rated as *Student* in preference to either *Reading/Book* or *Sitting*. Each inmate was rated in only one category, with every inmate on the cellblock census rated during each administration of the checklist. A copy of the 58-item BOC is available on request.

Data Collection Procedures

The BOC was administered at 45-min intervals, beginning at 5:00 p.m. and terminating at 9:30 p.m. on weekdays, and beginning at 6:30 a.m. and terminating at 9:30 p.m. on Saturdays, Sundays, and holidays. Thus, the BOC was administered seven times each weekday and 21 times each Saturday, Sunday, and holiday. Each administration of the BOC required approximately 5 min. The staff member responsible for the token economy cellblock at the time of the scheduled observation toured the cellblock and rated the activities of all inmates on the cellblock census.

The resulting data were supplemented in part by the inmates' recording, by means of time clocks and punch cards as described in Experiment I, their departing and returning to the token economy cellblock. These recording procedures were an integral part of the token economy. They were, however, begun approximately one month before the token economy was introduced and were continued for approximately one month after the token economy was terminated.

Experimental Conditions

This experiment consisted of three data collection phases: (1) *Baseline*$_1$, (2) *Token Economy,* and (3) *Baseline*$_2$. The observations reported were conducted during the Thursdays and Saturdays of each condition.

Baseline$_1$. This condition consisted of observations made during the five consecutive weeks preceding the *Officer Commands* condition of Experiment I. The general procedures followed on the token economy cellblock were those described for the *Baseline*$_1$ condition of Experiment I.

Token economy. The observations occurred during the five consecutive weeks at the mid-point of the token economy of Experiment I, at which time the *60 Points Contingents* condition was in effect.

Baseline$_2$. This condition consisted of the five consecutive weeks following termination of the token economy of Experiment I.

The BOC was administered seven times each Thursday and 21 times each Saturday during each week of the three five-week periods, resulting in a total of 140 administrations under each of the three experimental conditions.

RESULTS

Reliability of Measurement

Reliability estimates were obtained in approximately one of every six administrations of the BOC. For each, a second staff member toured the token economy cellblock with the primary observer and independently rated the activities in which the residents of the cellblock were engaged. An overall percentage of agreement based on frequency data across all categories was computed for each reliability check by dividing the number of agreed-upon observations by the total number of observations made and multiplying the resulting figure by 100. Sixty-nine reliability estimates were obtained throughout the three conditions. The mean percentage of agreement was 90.5%.

Data Reduction

For each category, the frequency data generated during each BOC administration were summed across the 140 administrations performed during each of the three conditions of the experiment. Closely related categories were then grouped together, and low-frequency activities (not more than one occurrence per 100 individual ratings during any of the three conditions), which were unrelated to either the larger categories or to the remaining alternative low-frequency categories, were themselves grouped together in a *Miscellaneous* category. Eight major categories plus the residual *Miscellaneous* category emerged from this process.

1. *Not Present on Cellblock*: number of inmates residing on the token economy cellblock who were not physically present at the times of the observations. It was derived by subtracting the number of entries during census at the time of the rating.

2. *Noninteractive*: a combination of the specific categories that indexed inmates as present on the token economy cellblock but not engaged

in any discernible or significant activity. Represented here are such BOC categories as *Asleep, Sitting,* and *Walking.*

3. *Recreation/Entertainment*: this groups together activities such as *Games and Puzzles/Group, Listening to Radio/Music,* and *Watching Television/Education; News.*

4. *Conservation*: primary activity of an inmate talking to or listening to another inmate or a staff member. It excludes such activities as talking with other inmates in the course of a pool game (which would be rated *Games and Puzzles/Group*) and listening to a teacher lecture in the remedial education classroom (which would be rated *Student*).

5. *Reading*: a combination of more specific categories, such as *Reading/Book, Reading/Letter,* and *Reading/Magazine,* indexing the reading of specific types of materials.

6. *Eating/Grooming*: this category groups such related BOC activities as *Drinking* and *Eating, Grooming,* and *Urinating/Defecating.*

7. *Housekeeping*: inmate activities involved in both the cleaning and general upkeep of areas around bunks (*Maintenance/House*) and in the performance of the assigned maintenance tasks necessary for the upkeep of the cellblock in general (*Maintenance/Unit*).

8. *Education*: all forms of inmate participation in the remedial education program as either a student or a tutor of students.

9. *Miscellaneous*: this category consists of low-frequency, residual BOC activities, such as *Exercising, Fighting, Horseplaying, Participating in Hobby, and Writing/Letter.*

Findings

A preliminary examination of the data generated by representative inmates as they recorded, by means of time clocks and punch cards, the times they left and returned to the token economy cellblock indicated that introduction of the token economy had little, if any, impact upon either the inmates' movement within the institution or their involvement in leisure-time recreation activities. Although there was some day-to-day variability under each condition of the experiment, those inmates who spent the bulk of their time away from the cellblock during the *Baseline* conditions continued to do so during the *Token Economy* conditions. Similarly, those inmates who only rarely either left the token economy cellblock to participate in recreational activities during the *Baseline* conditions continued to refrain from doing so during the *Token Economy* conditions.

These findings are complemented by the data resulting from the administrations of the BOC as summarized in Table 3, which depicts the percentage of ratings falling within each of the nine summary categories under the three conditions of this experiment. The most commonly rated category of the BOC during each of the three experimental conditions was *Not Present on Cellblock*. On average, one-third of the inmates were absent from the cellblock during the observations performed under the *Baseline*$_1$ condition, and this figure changed virtually not at all during the *Token Economy* condition and the following *Baseline*$_2$ condition. The percentage of inmates engaged in *Recreation/Entertainment* activities dropped slightly, from approximately 18% to 14%, after the token economy was introduced, and then increased to 31% after the token economy was terminated.

The percentages of inmates rated in the *Conversation, Eating/Grooming, Education,* and *Noninteractive* categories exhibited a similar pattern. All were relatively low during the *Baseline*$_1$ period, increased somewhat under the *Token Economy* condition, and then declined during *Baseline*$_2$. Excepting the *Conservation* category, each was lower during *Baseline*$_1$. The percentages of inmates observed either *Reading* or *Housekeeping* decreased both during the token economy and after it terminated. The percentage of inmate activities in the *Miscellaneous* category decreased after the token economy was introduced and then increased only slightly after it ended.

DISCUSSION

The results of this comparison of the day-to-day activities of token economy participants during the token economy with those both before its implementation and after it terminated indicate that the improvements in behavior observed in Experiment I were achieved without curtailing the leisure-time recreational activities of the inmates involved. The *Baseline* data suggested that the opportunity to spend leisure time in the remainder of the institution was a potentially powerful backup reinforcer for the token economy, and this opportunity was included as such when the token economy was implemented. However, the contingencies employed do not appear to have restricted the movement of the inmates to and from the remainder of the institution, since about the same percentage of inmates were not present on the cellblock during the token economy as during the baseline periods preceding and following it. It may be concluded, then, than the utilization of time away from the cellblock as a backup reinforcer in the token economy did not in any way interfere with the participants' interaction with acquaintances not

TABLE 3

Percent of Ratings of Inmate Activities on the Behavior Observation Checklist Falling Within Nine Summary Categories Under the Conditions of Experiment II

Summary Category	$Baseline_1$	Token Economy	$Baseline_2$
Not present on cellblock	33.3	32.7	33.9
Non-Interactive	24.8	31.5	20.0
Recreation/Entertainment	17.8	13.5	30.6
Conversation	4.5	6.0	4.6
Reading	4.2	3.3	2.2
Eating/Grooming	3.8	4.0	2.5
Housekeeping	3.6	3.0	2.3
Education	0.0	2.7	0.0
Miscellaneous	8.0	3.3	3.9

residing on the token economy cellblock, nor with the opportunity to attend the weekend movies, club meetings, and other recreational activities available in the remainder of the institution.

The token economy appears to have occasioned a slight increase in the proportion of time participants were not engaged in any important activities or in any discernible interactions. However, this increase is not reflected in a comparable drop in the degree to which participants engaged in recreational and entertainment activities, such as playing pool and watching television, for participation in these activities does not appear to have been significantly influenced by introduction of the token economy. After the token economy was terminated, however, inmate participation in recreational and entertainment activities increased to a level nearly twice that observed before the token economy was introduced. This increase is difficult to explain. It might be a result of the introduction of additional recreational equipment throughout the token economy or to changes in the inmates' patterns of behavior during the token economy. Alternatively, it might reflect the turnover in the cellblock population during the latter stages of the token economy and a consequent shift in the interests of participants. In any case, the *Baseline*$_1$ and *Token Economy* data are in general agreement and support the general observation that introduction of the token economy did not curtail either the participants' social intercourse or their participation in recreational or entertainment activities.

Also of interest is the amount of time inmates devoted to housekeeping and educational activities. Although the target behaviors of Experiment I were members of the *Housekeeping* category, this experiment reveals that the procedures involved in the token conomy did not force participants to spend a disproportionate amount of time involved in these routine institutional activities. Indeed, if the token economy had any effect on the amount of time inmates spent performing these tasks, it appears that it was to lower it, for the percentage of inmates observed engaged in housekeeping activities was lower during the token economy than preceding it. On the other hand, the token economy did encourage inmates to devote some of their leisure time to the rehabilitation-oriented remedial education program, for the percentage of inmates observed participating in the education program was higher during the token economy than either before or following it. It certainly cannot be claimed that the cellblock token economy encouraged regimentation or institutionalization at the expense of the inmates' participation in rehabilitation-oriented endeavors. Indeed, the data presented here suggest the opposite.

GENERAL DISCUSSION

This research demonstrates the applicability of token reinforcement procedures to a representative population of imprisoned adult felons. Moreover, it also demonstrates that token reinforcement procedures may be successfully deployed within the correctional institution without subjecting the inmate to increased hardship or deprivation. However, as the criminal justice system becomes more research-oriented in its quest for effective methods of offender rehabilitation, it increases the possibility that it will sanction poorly conceived and poorly executed experimental projects. Such research may have the potential of not only harming the offender but also outraging the public to such a degree that subsequent research endeavors and the potential benefit they offer the offender are blocked. The criminal justice system must take decisive steps to guard against this possibility, and every effort must be made to protect the physical and psychological well-being of the inmate.

To ensure the protection of the offender, the criminal justice system should insist that its professional staff routinely submit their experimental projects to the review of their peers throughout the professional community. By so doing, the criminal justice system will further guarantee that these programs are of the highest quality and in the best interests of all concerned. A formal peer review policy not only ensures that the professionals within the criminal justice system are abreast with the most advanced thinking in the field but also that their experimental endeavors receive the scrutiny and constructive criticism essential to program refinement.

Although the combination of a thoroughly qualified professional staff and a formal policy of peer review would be expected effectively to ensure the offender's safety and well-being, it is desirable that the criminal justice system also open its experimental programs to public view and inspection. An informed public contributes to the safeguarding of the offender, for it better ensures the speedy elimination of those projects that either exert an undue hardship upon the offender while under the care of the criminal justice system or have a detrimental effect on his adjustment once he returns to the community.

In addition, the potential contribution of the offender, both to experimentation within the criminal justice system and to the safeguarding of himself and his fellow offenders, should not be underestimated. The offender, by dint of his intimate knowledge of the interworkings of the criminal justice system and the inmate subculture, can provide the professional staff information through advice and counsel that it would otherwise take them years to acquire. The research staff that includes ex-offenders will undoubtedly recognize and take into consideration a number of important variables that it otherwise would be slow to identify or would overlook altogether. Similarly, the research staff that makes provisions both to listen to the suggestions and complaints of its client population—the offenders—and then to give weight to these when questions concerning the operation of its project are debated, will probably devise more efficient and effective procedures than it would otherwise be capable of developing.

Finally, the criminal justice system must avoid the coerced participation of offenders in experimental projects that seek to research as yet unexamined practices or unvalidated procedures. It is especially difficult, however, to specify the defining characteristics of "voluntary participation" within the context of the operational policies of a correctional institution, for it is quite likely that an inmate's participation in an experimental project—or, for that matter, in any project—is easily influenced by the promise, be it explicit, implicit, or inferred, that his decision to participate will favorably influence the time of his release from the institution (e.g., positive decision by the parole board, the award of additional "good time," etc.).

It appears, therefore, that the voluntary nature of an experimental program within a correctional institution is best guaranteed when it is made explicit that the refusal to participate, participation itself, and the decision to terminate participation in no way influence an inmate's date of release from the institution. This is not to imply that demonstrable changes in behavior occurring within the program should not be considered when decisions are made concerning inmates' eligibility for release. If this is done, however, the voluntary nature of the program may be guaranteed only by taking care to ensure that comparable changes in the behavior of non-participants are given equal consideration when decisions concerning their status are made.

The program reported here incorporated the safeguards outlined above. Early in the operation of the cellblock token economy, a five-member review panel composed of prominant psychologists and sociologists visited on-site at Draper Correctional Center and reported their findings to the project's funding agency. In addition, the project was reported on and discussed at a number of professional meetings. Many of the suggestions made by the members of the review panel and by peers at professional meetings were incorporated in the project. The project itself was under constant public scrutiny. The Board of Directors of the Rehabilitation Research Foundation, which oversaw the project research, consisted of respected professionals and civic leaders. Moreover, throughout its duration, the project was visited by a steady stream of concerned citizens, civic groups, college and university classes, and media representatives.

The project staff included an ex-offender, and regular group meetings were scheduled with the residents of the token economy cellblock for the express purpose of airing their grievances and soliciting their opinions and suggestions, and these played an important part in the staff decision-making process. Participation in the project was voluntary as defined above: not only did participation in the project not influence an inmate's date of release from the institution, but an inmate could, as slightly less than 10% of the participants did, petition to eliminate himself from the project by following routine institutional procedures, and the decision to terminate participation did not influence either the inmate's date of release or the quality of his life within the institution relative to his condition before enrollment in the project.

As the criminal justice system develops both a research orientation and a research capability, it will, as the mental health field has, begin identifying shortcomings and validating effective strategies. Experimental projects are of little value, however, unless the criminal justice system makes use of their findings in its dealings, with the offender. Those shortcomings that experimental projects reveal should be eliminated from the system. Similarly, strategies and procedures of general applicability and benefit that have been validated in experimental programs should be implemented throughout the system.

Clearly, the nature of some strategies will demand that they continue to be offered on a voluntary basis alone. For example, the effectiveness of aversion therapy in the treatment of alcoholism, drug addiction, and sexual deviancy has been repeatedly demonstrated in the medical and mental health fields (e.g., Rachman and Teasdale, 1969), and these findings undoubtedly would be replicated by careful experimental research in the criminal justice field. Such a demonstration would certainly justify a move on the part of the criminal justice system to make aversion therapy available to those who requested it. Most would agree, however, that any form of coerced participation in such a program would be both unethical and unjust.

Conversely, the nature of some other strategies will demand that they be incorporated within the criminal justice system as standard operating procedures, and, as such, be applied equally with all those with whom the system has contact. The heavy reliance of corrections on punishment and aversive control procedures in its dealings with the inmate population probably contributes to both the unrest in correctional institutions and to the dyssocializing influence a period of imprisonment appears to have on the offender. The present research indicates that it is both more effective and more humane to schedule and award the incentives available in the criminal justice system systematically to encourage productive behavior than it is to threaten and withdraw or withhold them in an attempt to discourage undesirable behavior. Moreover, there is every reason to believe that the routine deployment of these alternative procedures throughout the criminal justice system will contribute to a reduction of the debilitating impact of imprisonment and its regressive effect on the released offender's adjustment in the community.

REFERENCE NOTE

1. FILIPCZAK, J., & COHEN, H. L. *The CASE II Contingency System and Where It Is Going.* Paper presented at the 80th Annual Convention of the American Psychological Association, Honolulu, 1972.

REFERENCES

BOREN, J. J., & COLMAN, A. D. Some experiments on reinforcement principles within a psychiatric ward for delinquent soldiers. *Journal of the Experimental Analysis of Behavior,* 22:29-38, 1968.

CLEMENTS, C. B., & MCKEE, J. M. Programmed instruction for institutionalized offenders: Contingency management and performance contracts. *Psychological Reports,* 22:957-964, 1968.

COHEN, H. L., & FILIPCZAK, J. *A New Learning Environment.* San Francisco: Jossey-Bass, 1971.

COHEN, H. L., & FILIPCZAK, J., & BIS, J. *CASE I: An Initial Study of Contingencies Applicable to Special Education.* Silver Spring, Maryland: Educational Facility Press—IBR, 1967.

COLMAN, A. D., & BAKER, S. L. Utilization of an operant conditioning model for the treatment of character and behavior disorders in a military setting. *American Journal of Psychiatry,* 125:101-109, 1969.

COLMAN, A. D., & BOBEN, J. J. An information system for measuring patient behavior and its use by staff. *Journal of Applied Behavior Analysis,* 2:207-214, 1969.

MCKEE, J. M., & CLEMENTS, C. B. A behavioral approach to learning: The Draper model. In H. C. Rickard (Ed.), *Behavioral Intervention in Human Problems.* New York: Pergamon Press, 1971, pp. 201-222.

MILAN, M. A., & MCKEE, J. M. Behavior modification: Principles and applications in corrections. In D. Glaser (Ed.), *Handbook of Criminology.* Chicago: Rand McNally, 1974, pp. 745-776.

National Advisory Commission on Criminal Justice Standards and Goals. *Report on Corrections.* Washington, D.C.: U.S. Government Printing Office, 1973.

RACHMAN, S., & TEASDALE, J. *Aversion Therapy and Behavior Disorder: An Analysis.* Coral Gables, Florida: University of Miami Press, 1969.

SMITH, R. R., HART, L. A., & MILAN, M. A. Correctional officer training in behavior modification: An interim report. *Proceedings of the 101st Annual Congress of Correction.* College Park, Maryland: American Correctional Association, 1972, 123-132.

21

A COMPARATIVE EVALUATION OF TWO DAY HOSPITALS

Goal Attainment Scaling of Behavior Therapy vs. Milieu Therapy

Nancy K. Austin, Robert P. Liberman, Larry W. King and William J. DeRisi

Program in Clinical Research, Camarillo-Neuropsychiatric Institute (UCLA) Research Center, California

Previous attempts at program evaluation of partial hospitalization programs have consisted largely of descriptive and anecdotal reports of programs and patient characteristics. There have been no comparative or experimental studies of the effectiveness of differing day treatment programs. In the current study, Goal Attainment Scaling, a

Reprinted with permission from the *Journal of Nervous and Mental Disease,* Vol. 163, No. 4, 253-262.

The research reported in this article was supported by Grant MH26207 from the Mental Health Services Research and Development Branch of the National Institute of Mental Health. The authors acknowledge the support and encouragement provided by Drs. Howard Davis, Frank Ochberg, Marie MacNabola, and Mr. James Cumiskey of the NIMH; and by Drs. Rafael Canton and Sarah Miller (past and present Directors of the Ventura County Mental Health Services); Dr. Louis Jolyon West (Medical Director of the UCLA Neuropsychiatric Institute); and the clinical team from the Oxnard Day Treatment Center. The opinions stated in this article are those of the authors and do not represent the official policy of the NIMH, the Regents of the University of California, or the Ventura County Health Services Agency.

goal-oriented program evaluation system, was used with 56 randomly selected partial hospitalization patients who attended two day hospitals: one program was based on behavioral-educational methods, and the other was an eclectic program based on the concepts of a therapeutic community. Patients attending the behavioral-educational program showed greater attainment of their therapeutic goals than did the patients involved in the eclectic program. The greater effectiveness of the behavioral-educational day program increased from the 3-month follow-up to the 2-year follow-up.

The day hospital approach to the treatment of psychiatric patients has been a prominent part in the optimistic wave of new services advanced by the community mental health movement. According to a survey conducted by the Joint Information Service of the American Psychiatric Association and the National Association for Mental Health, there were 139 day care programs in operation in 1968 (8). Statistical reports from the National Institute of Mental Health indicate that in 1972, there were 37,117 new patients treated with partial hospitalization in federally funded community mental health centers (1). This figure constitutes 7 percent of all new cases in 1972 vs. 16 percent of new patients treated in inpatient facilities.

However, just as the initial enthusiasm for the effectiveness of the community mental health movement has waned (4, 17), the early promise of the day care approach as a widespread alternative to hospitalization has also foundered. The realities and experiences of day care programs which have matured over the past 10 years (7) have revealed underutilization and continued referrals of patients to inpatient services. Evaluation of day care programs has demonstrated that although their patients have no higher recidivism rates than those treated as inpatients, the day hospitals tend to be highly selective in accepting patients and are able to provide exclusive and complete treatment for less than 40 percent of those who are initially accepted into the programs (8). These previous attempts at program evaluation have consisted of descriptive and anecdotal reports of programs, information about the characteristics of the patients accepted or rejected by day care centers, accounts of the treatment process, and data on rehospitalization rates. Although these reports provide a valuable baseline of descriptive and process information, they cast little light on the immediate treatment outcomes and clinical effectiveness of day care programs. The literature provides some information on the functions of day treatment with respect to other service units in a community-based mental health system, but there is a paucity of information on the direct effects of day treatment on individual patients.

Rehospitalization rates can be poor indicators of the effectiveness of day care since the events and circumstances which often precipitate rehospitalization may be distant from the treatment process in time and unconnected with the specific, previous goals of treatment. The literature on program evaluation of psychiatric services is replete with evidence that the community adjustment of former patients correlates poorly with clinical status at the time of discharge, particularly when the follow-up assessments are carried out 6 months or longer after hospitalization ends (6). From a wide variety of clinical and research sources, evidence has accumulated which points to the situational determinants of social, symptomatic, and behavioral functioning (15, 19). The implications of these data for evaluating the effectiveness of treatment in day care programs are clear: clinical outcomes should be measured within 6 months of completion of treatment, and should be conceptually and empirically related to the particular goals of the treatment program. This evaluation strategy will reflect fairly upon the efforts of the clinical personnel as well as minimize the possible confounding of the results of specific treatment by subsequently occurring, intervening life events.

There have been no comparative or experimental studies of the effectiveness of differing day treatment programs in the literature. During the past 15 years, alternative models have developed for the conduct of a day care program. These include traditional, individual and group therapies, multimodel group therapy, paraprofessional and volunteer involvement, storefront operations, therapeutic community, and behavioral-educational, structured programs. It is timely to carry out comparison of the differential effectiveness of alternative programs. The current report presents the results of a comparative outcome study of randomly selected patients who attended a day care program based on behavioral-educational methods and those who attended a program which was eclectic and based more on the concepts of a therapeutic community. The comparisons were done on 56 patients at 3, 6, and 24 months after they began the day hospital programs using a system of program evaluation called Goal Attainment Scaling (10).

Goal Attainment Scaling (GAS) allows objective measurement of the extent to which treatment goals, negotiated and agreed upon at the time of intake, are achieved. Highly individualized goals may be set for each patient using this system. The current study is distinctive because it provides a goal-oriented, clinical measurement approach which has functional value in mental health clinics, and because it is one of the first comparative studies of treatment outcome carried out in community mental health centers.

METHODS

Settings. The Oxnard Community Mental Health Center offers outpatient, day care, emergency, aftercare, and consultation and education services. The Center is located in the commercial heart of Oxnard, a city of 80,000 located in Ventura County, 50 miles north of Los Angeles. The Mental Health Center has a total catchment area which includes three cities and a population of 140,000 of which 20 percent are Mexican-American. The Center is one of three regional programs, each of which covers separate geographical areas and is administered semiautonomously by a central, county-wide directorate. The community is supported largely by agriculture, but there are many light industries, a large state hospital, and two large naval bases in the area. The Oxnard Day Treatment Center has a staff of 10, including two occupational therapists, three psychiatric nurses, three psychiatric technicians, and a psychiatrist and psychologist who both work half-time. The Oxnard Day Treatment Center (DTC) consists of two home-like and comfortably furnished lounges or group rooms, a dining room and kitchen, an occupational therapy shop, and two offices for staff. The Oxnard DTC has a behaviorally based, structured program with daily educational workshops (e.g., consumerism and personal finance, use of public agencies) in which patients learn coping skills for community adaptation. Thrice weekly therapy groups for training in social skills, individual patient sessions and conferences, a weekly staff-patient planning meeting, recreational outings and field trips, and individualized and focused occupational therapy comprise the day treatment program. The day treatment program uses a token economy system based on credit cards. More complete descriptions of the program are available in other publications (12-14). A research and demonstration project, funded by the NIMH, spearheaded programmatic changes in the Oxnard DTC leading to the behaviorally based, structured services.

Day Treatment Center II is located in an adjacent city of 65,000 and is responsible for a catchment area of 120,000. This facility is a large, modern structure of recent construction, incorporating many of the latest design concepts for the physical environment of a community mental health center (3). Built around an open courtyard are three staff offices, a kitchen and dining room, an occupational therapy shop, a recreation room, a lounge and beauty parlor, a conference room, and two lounges or group rooms. The 10 staff members of Day Treatment Center II (DTC II) include a clinical psychologist, two psychiatric social workers, two psychiatric nurses, two psychiatric technicians, two occupational therapists, and a part time psychiatrist. DTC II itself is part of a comprehensive county mental health complex, housing a psychiatric inpatient unit, outpatient department, aftercare services, emergency service, and substance abuse programs. The DTC II program has an eclectic, milieu therapy approach. Regularly scheduled are large therapeutic community meetings, group and individual therapy, occupational therapy, recreational activities, and patient-staff planning meetings. Relaxation training, music, and exercise groups are also offered.

Patients. Patients participating in each day treatment center's program served as subjects in this study. Both centers serve psychotic clients recently released from the nearby state hospital and the county's psychiatric inpatient facility, patients facing life crises or suffering severe depression and anxiety who require more attention and structure than outpatient therapy can provide them, and decompensating patients with supportive families who receive day care as an alternative to hospitalization.

Summarized in Table 1 are characteristics of the patients from both day treatment centers whose outcomes were evaluated by Goal Attainment Scaling.

An Impairment Quotient has been developed by Glaser (7) for comparing the degree of psychiatric impairment in different clinical populations. The Quotient is based on: a) a percent of patients in the population currently diagnosed as psychotic; b) percent of patients in the population ever previously hospitalized for mental illness; and c) percent of patients in the population who are not currently married. The patients from the Oxnard DTC and DTC II had Impairment Quotients of 54 and 58, respectively, which are approximately the same as day care programs described elsewhere and slightly lower than the quotients described for patients at a state hospital (7).

Table 2 classifies the presenting clinical problems for patients at each center which were the sources for the Goal Attainment Scaling. Socialization, inappropriate behaviors and speech, and anxiety/depression problems were the three most frequently occurring types of problems in the Oxnard DTC's sample, accounting for 48 percent of problems identified. For DTC II patients, the same three problems areas occurred most

TABLE 1

Background Characteristics of Patients at Oxnard DTC and DTC II Who Were Evaluated by Goal Attainment Scaling

Characteristics	Oxnard DTC ($N = 30$)	DTC II ($N = 26$)
Diagnosis[a]	%	%
Schizophrenic	40.00	34.6
Manic-depressive	13.3	7.7
Neurotic (anxiety and depression)	36.7	46.2
Personality disorder	10.0	3.8
Substance abuse	0	7.7
Sex		
Male	43.3	46.2
Female	56.7	53.8
Education		
College	30.0	23.0
High school graduate	36.7	46.2
Some high school	26.7	23.1
No high school	6.6	7.7
Age		
16-30	53.3	61.5
31-40	16.7	15.5
41 and above	30.0	23.0
Marital status		
Single	53.3	57.7
Married	36.7	23.1
Divorced & separated	6.6	11.5
Widowed	3.4	7.7
Income		
Dependent (gvt. support, family support)	86.7	80.8
Self-supporting	13.3	19.2
Previous hospitalization		
Yes	53.3	73.0
No	46.7	27.0
Median attendance		
Days in day treatment program	39.0	27.5

[a] Diagnoses were made by the clinical staff at the time of intake.

often, comprising 38 percent of all problems identified. The table indicates that problems bringing patients to day treatment varied and that both centers dealt with comparable problems.

Procedure for Goal Attainment Scaling. Goals were selected for scaling by consensus among the patient, a significant other (family members, friends, employers), and the therapist during an evaluation interview that took place 1 week after the patient's admission to the DTC. The goals were tailored for each individual on an *ad hoc* basis and were scaled and finalized only after patient, significant other, and therapist all agreed to their relevance and reasonableness.

Using Goal Attainment Scaling (GAS), each specific goal is represented on a separate scale having a continuum of five possible treatment outcomes, each with a numerical value, ranging from "Most Favorable" (+2) to "Least Favorable Outcome Thought Likely" (—2). The midpoint on the scale represents the "Expected Level of Treatment Success" (0 level), and the two intermediate outcome levels, "Less Than Expected" (—1) and "Better Than Expected" (+1), complete the range of potential treatment outcomes on the GAS guide. Goals were scaled with 6 months from the intake interview as the outcome point. There is an assumption of equal intervals between these five scale points. In Table 3 is shown a sample GAS scale. At both DTCs, the modal number of goals formulated per patient was three.

The status of each patient with regard to his/her goals was indicated at intake and at follow-up by the rater checking the scale level which best represented the patient's current functioning. The significant other supplied external validation of the patient's goals and progress at follow-up. Future projections of less and least favorable outcomes were most often marked as the starting points or status at intake for patients who, it was felt, would reach the expected level of treatment success or better. Treatment outcome is measured by movement from one scale level to another and by converting the scale levels reached at follow-up to a standardized Goal Attainment T-score (10).*

Every third patient admitted to the Oxnard DTC and DTC II was designated a GAS patient. Thirty patients from the Oxnard DTC and 26 from DTC II underwent GAS during a 14-month period. Therapists were given copies of the completed GAS guides for their patients. GAS follow-up interviews were conducted at 3-month and 6-month intervals

* More detailed information regarding the methodology, statistical assumptions, and applications of the GAS technique can be obtained from the Program Evaluation Resource Center, Park Avenue South, Minneapolis, Minn.

TABLE 2

Classification of Treatment Goals Used in GAS of Patients at the Oxnard DTC and DTC II

Classification	Oxnard DTC (% of all scales)	DTC II (% of all scales)
Alcohol/drug abuse	0.8	3.6
Anxiety/depression	12.4	12.2
Education	6.2	3.6
Employment	10.8	7.9
Inappropriate and bizarre behaviors; delusional, hallucinatory speech	13.2	10.8
Interpersonal relationships	10.8	9.4
Living arrangements	3.1	2.2
Personal appearance	4.7	2.9
Physical complaints	1.6	2.9
Relationship with therapist, day treatment participation	2.3	4.3
Self-assertion	3.9	7.2
Self-image	3.1	8.6
Socialization	22.5	15.1
Suicide attempts and thoughts	2.3	4.3
Miscellaneous	2.3	5.0
	100.0%	100.0%

following the initial GAS interview. The therapist, patient, significant other, and GAS rater were present at each follow-up. Phone call follow-ups were made 2 years after intake.

Inter-rater reliability measures were taken on 68 of the follow-ups by raters who scored the GAS guides independently after each interview. Inter-rater agreement was calculated using the Spearman rank order (rho) statistic. For each scale, outcome levels as marked by each rater were ranked. A rank of 1 was assigned to the highest outcome level (1 = +2), a rank of 2 to the next highest outcome level (2 = +1), and so on, until all scales were ranked. Separate rhos were calculated for each scale.

To control for possible systematic differences between the therapists from the two day treatment centers in their predictions for the outcome levels on a Goal Attainment Scaling guide, a panel of nine independent, "blind" clinical psychologists were asked to rate the degree of therapeutic optimism for each scale. The guides were not identifiable by center, patient, or therapist. Each guide was accompanied by a brief, clinical description of the patient's characteristics to assist the raters in assessing the reasonableness of the goal predictions. Provided in this description were the patient's age, sex, diagnosis, educational level, source of income,

TABLE 3

Sample Goal Attainment Scale

Scale Attainment Levels	Scale 1: Education
(—2) Most unfavorable treatment outcome thought likely	Patient has made no effort to enroll in high school program.
(—1) Less than expected success with treatment	Has enrolled in high school, attended less than 1 month, dropped out.
(0) Expected level of treatment success	Enrolled in high school or equivalent program; attendance sporadic.
(+1) More than expected success with treatment	In high school; attends consistently.
(+2) Most favorable treatment outcome thought likely	Consistently attending high school program with a stated career goal.

and previous treatment. Given this information, the clinicians rated each scale on a five-point basis, as shown below: 1 = very pessimistic expectations for treatment; 2 = moderately pessimistic expectations for treatment; 3 = about right degree of optimism; 4 = moderately high optimism; 5 = very high therapeutic optimism.

Each scale was assigned a rating from 1 to 5, and the overall guide rating was obtained by calculating the mean value of the sum of the scale ratings. Each guide was rated twice by different raters.

RESULTS

Inter-rater agreement was high for both Oxnard DTC and DTC II GAS follow-ups. Oxnard DTC rho coefficients ranged from .55 to 1.0 with a mean of .93; DTC II rho coefficients ranged from .49 to 1.0 with a mean of .95. Several patients from each center were unavailable for follow-up at either the 3-month or 6-month interval. All 56 patients had follow-up measures taken during at least one of the follow-up periods.

In Table 4 is summarized the standardized Goal Attainment T-scores and percentile ranks for the Oxnard DTC and for DTC II at the 3-month, 6-month, and 2-year follow-ups. Any single goal attainment score can be translated into a position on a normal curve derived from a large population of patients who have undergone GAS (10). This position can be used to derive a percentile rank, indicating the proportion of the cumulative universe of goal attainment scores that is below the particular Goal Attainment T-score being analyzed. At the 3-month follow-up point, the Oxnard DTC mean Goal Attainment score translates to a percentile rank of 86; the DTC II percentile rank is 79. At the 6-month follow-up point, the Oxnard percentile rank is 93, and the DTC II rank remains at 79. Although the results indicate better outcome scores for the patients from the Oxnard DTC, these differences were not statistically significant using a *t*-test.

Two years after intake, phone call contacts were made with 18 of the Oxnard DTC patients and 12 of the DTC II patients. The other patients had moved from the area and could not be located even after intensive searches. Psychiatric hospitalizations occurred for two patients from each day hospital cohort. There was one definite suicide and a questionable suicide in the DTC II group, but no death among the patients followed up at 2 years after their treatment at the Oxnard DTC. The difference in GAS scores at the 2-year follow-up approached statistical significance ($.05 < p < .10$, *t*-test).

In addition to the GAS T-scores, changes in scale levels were calculated for each patient by finding the difference between a patient's behavioral status at intake and at the 6-month follow-up point for each scale. For example, if a patient had a —2 intake level on a particular scale and had attained the ± 1 level at the 6-month follow-up, the change score for this scale would be ± 3. This procedure was followed for each scale, and a mean change score was calculated for each patient. These data are summarized in Table 5. Although 30 percent more of the patients attending the Oxnard DTC made substantial gains of two levels or more in their average change scores than their counterparts at DTC II, this difference did not reach statistical significance (χ^2).

A finer grain interpretation of the GAS results was performed when it was discovered, at the end of the study, that one therapist at DTC II used behavior therapies extensively, including assertive training, systematic desensitization, and contingency management. This therapist, a social worker, was a close friend of a behavioral psychologist and had taken professional training in behavior therapy through workshops during the course of this study. This therapist's cases were removed from the sample for the purposes of a secondary analysis. Change scores were then calculated for the remaining GAS patients in DTC II at the 3- and 6-month follow-up points. A comparison between the centers revealed that the scores of patients from the Oxnard DTC were significantly higher than the residual DTC II patients at the 6-, but not at the 3-month follow-up point ($p < .05$, χ^2). The data are shown in Table 6. To give examples of the kinds of changes actually made by patients as reflected in their GAS scores, a listing of some patients' goals with their starting

TABLE 4

Mean Goal Attainment Scores for Oxnard DTC and DTC II Patients at Intake, 3-Month, 6-Month, and 24-Month Follow-Up Points

	Intake Level	3-Month Follow-Up	6-Month Follow-Up	24-Month Follow-Up
Oxnard DTC				
T-score	25.60	60.92	64.49	66.43
Percentile rank	0.6	86.00	93.00	94.50
Standard deviation		12.43	10.85	13.45
$N=$	30	28	27	18
DTC II				
T-score	25.29	57.88	58.12	55.82
Percentile rank	0.4	79.00	79.00	73.00
Standard deviation		13.70	18.38	23.22
$N=$	26	19	23	12

points at intake and attainment levels at 3-and 6-month follow-up are given in Table 7.

The duration of day treatment program attendance in both day treatment centers for individual patients was statistically correlated with their 6-month GAS outcome scores. The Pearson product-moment correlation calculated for the Oxnard DTC was —.51 ($p < .005$, one-tailed test). For DTC II, the Pearson product-moment correlation was —.22 ($p < .05$). These results indicate that for the Oxnard DTC, there is a significant inverse relationship between GAS outcome scores and length of treatment. Patients achieving the highest GAS outcome scores participated in the day treatment program the shortest length of time. Thus, the possibility that Oxnard DTC patients achieved higher GAS outcome scores because of longer duration of treatment can be discounted.

The GAS guide therapeutic optimism ratings were summed for each center, and a group mean value was obtained. For both the Oxnard DTC and DTC II guides, therapeutic optimism was judged to reflect "about the right degree of optimism," with the mean rating for Oxnard DTC being 3.05, and the mean rating for DTC II being 2.98. The average therapeutic optimism scores arrived at by pairs of independent raters agreed within 0.5 scale points for 80 percent of the patients from the two day treatment centers.

GAS outcome scores for the six Mexican-American patients in the Oxnard DTC were analyzed separately. The mean outcome score for Mexican-American patients at the 3-month follow-up point (59.34) equals

TABLE 5

Mean GAS Change Scores at the 6-Month Follow-Up Point for Oxnard DTC and DTC II Patients

6-Month Mean Change Score	Oxnard DTC Patients	DTC II Patients	Total
2.0 and above	22 (81%)	14 (61%)	36
1.9 and below	5 (19%)	9 (39%)	14
Total	27 (100%)	23 (100%)	50

TABLE 6

Mean GAS Change at the 6-Month Follow-Up for Oxnard DTC Patients and Subset of DTC II Patients

6-Month Mean Change Score	Oxnard DTC Patients	DTC II Patients	Total
2.0 and above	22 (81%)	9 (53%)	31
1.9 and below	5 (19%)	8 (47%)	13
Total	27 (100%)	17 (100%)	44

that of all other Oxnard DTC patients (59.70), and at 6 months, somewhat surpasses the mean follow-up score for all other patients (68.56 to 62.97, respectively). These differences are not statistically significant. All other patients in the Oxnard DTC sample were whites, with the exception of one black and one oriental patient. Most of the Mexican-American patients were treated by Mexican-American therapists at the Oxnard DTC. The number of Mexican-American clients at DTC II ($N = 3$) was too small to carry out a similar analysis. The type of goals chosen for the Mexican-American patients did not differ from those selected for white, black, or oriental patients.

DISCUSSION

Goal Attainment Scaling, as used in this study, provides the clinician with cues and feedback on treatment decisions and outcome as well as providing the evaluator and administrator with information on the comparative effectiveness of alternative approaches to day care. As a part of routine treatment planning and evaluation, the goal attainment strategy has the advantages of being: a) adaptable to various types of patients; b) an aid in organizing and recording the process of therapy; c) relevant to the specific and sometimes changing needs of individual patients over

TABLE 7

Typical Behavioral Goals for GAS Patients, Shown at Intake, 3-Month, and 6-Month Attainment Levels

Intake	3-Month	6-Month
Complains of and is very preoccupied with tension, nervousness; complains of sleeplessness daily.	Complains of tension or anxiety every week; can sleep approximately 6 hours/night.	Complains of tension and inability to relax every other week; can sleep more than 6 hours/night.
Entirely avoids contact with friends; does not attend church.	Has one social contact a month; has attended church twice in last month.	Attends church 3 of 4 weekends; initiates social contacts twice a month.
Workshop employment program does not accept patient due to inactivity and isolated behavior.	Patient accepted to program conditionally.	Patient accepted to program, working in desired area.
Patient reports violent or self-destructive behaviors occur every month when he feels depressed.	Violent or self-destructive behavior occurs every 2 months.	Patient reports no violent or self-destructive behavior in last 8 weeks.
Speech appropriate 50% of the time; no references to bodily symptoms, "actor" talk.	Speech appropriate 60% of the time.	Speech appropriate 85% of the time.

time; and d) useful to supervisors and program managers in determining the strengths and weaknesses of clinicians as matched with patients. At the Oxnard Mental Health Center, a goal attainment format for regular clinical record keeping has been implemented for outpatients and day care patients. A one-page form provides cues and feedback for staff and patients alike for setting and evaluating weekly and monthly therapeutic goals and the treatment methods used to attain them. This goal-oriented, behavioral progress record was adapted from the GAS methods used in this study and is compatible with the problem-oriented record (14). The results of this study also shed light on the relative effectiveness of a new therapeutic approach—behavior therapy—when compared with a more traditional milieu therapy approach to day care.

At 3, 6, and 24 months after admission into the day treatment centers, the patients from the Oxnard DTC who participated in a behavioral-educational program showed greater attainment of their therapeutic goals than patients who were involved in the DTC II where a more eclectic approach was used. The differences between the groups were more noticeable at the 6- and 24-month follow-up points, substantiating the findings of Paul (16), who found that clients who received behavior therapy for public speaking anxiety continued to improve on a variety of social and personal indices more than clients who received insight-oriented therapy at a 1-year follow-up evaluation. Several outcome studies of traditional psychotherapy have demonstrated the opposite; that is, minimal treatment or waiting list controls narrowed the gap with patients who had received psychotherapy when 1- to 5-year follow-ups were made (2, 11, 18). The fact that Mexican-American patients did as well as or better than their Anglo counterparts in the Oxnard DTC's behavioral program should allay the concerns of some that behavior therapy does not fit the needs of minority, racial, or cultural groups.

The differences between the outcomes reached by patients in the behavioral program vs. the eclectic program were statistically significant only when the patients treated by a behaviorally oriented social worker at DTC II were removed from the analysis. In the present study, no attempt was made to standardize the therapeutic activities of the staff of DTC II; indeed, they would not have tolerated any such attempt at control. At the time the study was designed, it was assumed that these staff members would not use behavior therapy methods since no formal training program was being offered to them. However, there are always a certain number of professionals who actively seek out innovative methods and incorporate them into their armamentarium (5). Retrospective analysis of the therapy records of patients in DTC II revealed that the above mentioned social worker had made extensive use of behavior techniques with her clients. She had attended workshops and obtained clinical supervision from a behavioral psychologist. Thus, although she worked in the eclectic day program, her actual practice was very behavioral. In fact, she later coauthored a book on assertion training for women. The therapeutic "deviance" of this social worker from DTC II presented a problem in the analysis and interpretation of the data. Since her patients showed greater progress than the patients of any of the other DTC II therapists, when her records were omitted, the differences in mean Goal Attainment scores favored the Oxnard DTC by a statistically significant degree at the 6-month follow-up point.

In another publication, direct observational data are presented from these same two DTCs which indicate that the behavioral-educational program at the Oxnard DTC is associated with a statistically significant greater amount of social participation and staff-patient interaction than at the eclectic program at DTC II (12). These process data, based on time-sampled observations of the DTC's social milieu, provide concurrent validation for the more individualized differences in GAS outcome described in this report. Although these strands of evidence support the greater effectiveness of a behavioral-educational model for day care, any conclusions must remain tentative.

Replication is needed with greater control over the type of treatment offered by behavioral and eclectic programs and careful monitoring of therapists' behavior to insure that the stated or expected treatment matches the actual treatment. It should be noted, however, that control over therapists' professional activity may be a next to impossible feat. One group of investigators who were conducting research on comparative therapy outcomes found that although therapists were explicitly instructed and trained to carry out designated procedures, there was, in fact, great variation in the actual behavior of the therapists. The therapist used a wide spectrum of methods despite attempts at standardization (9).

Some comment should be made on the overall high rates of goal attainment at both day treatment centers. The percentile ranks of 79 to 93 based on standard T-scores compare very favorably with previously reported GAS data. A combination of factors may help to explain these excellent results with a sample of markedly impaired patients. Day care programs, at their finest, are sites for intensive and prolonged treatment. The patients in both DTCs studies in this research overaged 32 days of treatment during which they received individual and group therapy, family counseling, and an infusion of assistance with social services. The high staff to patient ratios at both DTCs—approximately 1:2 to 1:4 depending upon the daily census—permitted the partial hospitalization services to offer massive amounts of needed services to individuals for periods of 4 to 12 weeks. Finally, the clinicians' awareness that their work was being evaluated may have produced added motivation to them for reaching the goals they formulated with their patients. In other words, GAS is a treatment intervention by itself since it stimulates therapist and patient alike to set concrete, realistic goals and to monitor their progress toward them.

REFERENCES

1. *Alcohol, Drug Abuse, and Mental Health Administration. State and Regional Data, Federally Funded Community Mental Health Centers.* Survey and Reports Branch, Division of Biometry, National Institute of Mental Health, Bethesda, Md., June, 1974.
2. Brill, N. Q. Results of psychotherapy. *Calif. Med.,* 104:249-253, 1966.

3. CANTON, R. The community mental health center team. In A. Beigel, & A. I. Levenson (Eds.), *The Community Mental Health Center: Strategies and Programs*. New York: Basic Books, 1972.
4. CHU, F. D., & TROTTER, S. *The Mental Health Complex, Part I: Community Mental Health Centers*. Washington, D.C.: Center for Study of Responsive Law, 1972.
5. DAVIS, H. A. *Planning for Creative Changes in Mental Health Services: A Manual on Research Utilization*. Publication No. (HSM) 73-9147, Department of Health, Education, and Welfare, Washington, D.C., 1973.
6. ELLSWORTH, R. B., & MARONEY, R. Characteristics of psychiatric programs and their effects on patients' adjustment. *J. Consult. Clin. Psychol.*, 39:436-447, 1972.
7. GLASER, F. B. The uses of the day program. In H. H. Barten, & Bellak, L. (Eds.), *Progress in Community Mental Health*, Vol. II. New York: Grune & Stratton, 1972, pp. 221-248.
8. GLASSCOTE, R. M., KRAFT, A. M., GLASSMAN, S. M., & JEPSON, W. W. *Partial Hospitalization for the Mentally Ill: A Study of Programs and Problems*. Washington, D.C.: The Joint Information Service of the American Psychiatric Association and the National Association for Mental Health, 1969.
9. JAYARATNE, S., STUART, R. B., & TRIPODI, T. Methodological issues and problems in evaluating treatment outcomes in the family and school consultation project. In P. O. Davidson, F. W. Clark, & L. A. Hamerlynck (Eds.), *Evaluation of Behavioral Programs in Community, Residential, and School Settings*. Champaign, Ill.: Research Press, 1974, pp. 141-174.
10. KIRESUK, T., & SHERMAN, R. Goal Attainment Scaling: A general method for evaluating comprehensive mental health programs. *Community Ment. Health J.*, 4: 443-453, 1968.
11. LIBERMAN, B., FRANK, J. D., HOEHN-SARIC, R., et al. Patterns of change in treated psychoneurotic patients: A five-year follow-up investigation of the systematic preparation of patients for psychotherapy. *J. Consult. Clin. Psychol.*, 38:36-41, 1972.
12. LIBERMAN, R. P., DERISI, W. J., KING, L. W., et al. Behavioral measurement in a community mental health center. In P. O. Davidson, F. W. Clark, and L. A. Hamerlynck (Eds.), *Evaluating Behavioral Programs in Community, Residential and School Settings: Procedures of the Fifth International Banff Conference on Behavior Modification*. Champaign, Ill.: Research Press, 1974, pp. 103-139.
13. LIBERMAN, R. P., KING, L. W., & DERISI, W. J. Behavior analysis and therapy in community mental health. In H. Leitenberg (Ed.), *Handbook of Behavior Modification and Therapy*. Englewood Cliffs, N.J.: Prentice-Hall, 1976.
14. LIBERMAN, R. P., KING, L. W., & DERISI, W. J. Building a behavioral bridge to span continuity of care. *exChange*, 1:22-27, 1972.
15. LUNDIN, R. W. *Personality: A Behavioral Analysis*. New York: Macmillan, 1969.
16. PAUL, G. L. Insight vs. desensitization in psychotherapy two years after termination. *J. Consult. Psychol.*, 31:333-348, 1967.
17. SCHWARTZ, D. A. Community mental health in 1972: An assessment. In H. H. Barten, & L. Bellak (Eds.), *Progress in Community Mental Health*, Vol. II. New York: Grune & Stratton, 1972.
18. STONE, A. R., FRANK, J., NASH, E. H., & IMBER, S. D. An intensive five-year follow-up study of treated psychiatric outpatients. *J. Nerv. Ment. Dis.*, 133:410-422, 1961.
19. ULLMANN, L. P., & KRASNER, L. *A Psychological Approach to Abnormal Behavior*. Englewood Cliffs, N.J.: Prentice-Hall, 1969.

Section IX

BEHAVIOR MODIFICATION AND THE EXTENDED SOCIETY: INDUSTRY AND COMMUNITY

Commentary

BUSINESS AND INDUSTRY

The decision not to reprint any article dealing directly with the application of behavioral modification methods in industry does not imply a dearth of activity. Several key books have already appeared (e.g., Brown & Presbie, 1976; Nord, 1976) and at least one forthcoming journal is scheduled exclusively to "bridging the gap between behavioral research and the manager in business, industry and government" (*Journal of Organizational Behavior Management*).

Despite increasing interest among managers, supervisory personnel and executives in business, industry and government, behavior modification principles are still viewed with suspicion by many. The situation today in business and industry is somewhat reminiscent of the helping professions a decade or so ago when a combination of lack of information and misinformation served to reinforce the apprehensions of the majority. To meet this deficit, Brown and Presbie (1976) have put together a timely *Behavior Modification Resource Guide for Business, Industry and Government,* strategically noting along the way that behavioral procedures are meant to supplement present managerial styles rather than supplant what successful managers are already doing. The monthly magazine, *Work Performance,* also helps to close the still wide gap between behavior modification principles and their acceptance in business and industry.

Hamner and Hamner (1976) spell out the procedures for setting up a positive reinforcement program in industry. While the biggest, and probably the first, success story is that of Emery Air Freight, a variety of companies also claim improvements as a result of initiating similar programs. However, most of the claims are testimonial in nature and the length of experience—little more than four years, from 1969 to 1973—is too short for meaningful evaluation. With this limitation in mind, Hamner and Hamner surveyed 10 major organizations, all of which are currently using some form of behavior modification approach. Specifically, they were interested in knowing how many employees were covered, the kinds of employees covered, the specific goals, the frequency of self-feedback, the kinds of reinforcers used, the results of the program, the successes and failures which the managers attributed to the use of behavior modification techniques, and whether management viewed behavior modification as a fad or as a legitimate managerial strategy for improving both productivity and quality of work-life for their employees.

A systematic approach seems to yield best results. First, a program audit is conducted to determine what performance is desired and to measure the current level of that performance. Then, specific and reasonable goals are set for each worker and each employee instructed to keep a record of his or her own work. Finally, mutually agreed positive aspects of performance are reinforced. Thus, the employee has two chances of being successful: to exceed his previous level of performance and/or to exceed his or her personal goal. Also, negative feedback routinely comes only from the employee (since the employee is the only one to know when self-set objectives are not met), whereas positive feedback can come from both employee and supervisor.

Some of the points of concern and potential shortcomings noted by the Hamners include the following: Many managers feel that it is not easy to teach reinforcement principles to lower level managers. Poorly designed reward systems can sometimes interfere with the development of spontaneity and creativity; reinforcement systems that—even inadvertently—are deceptive and manipulative are both insulting to employees and disastrous to the long-term welfare of the project. Positive reinforcement programs based solely on praise can be deceptive and even manipulative when wages fail to effect productivity increases. Back in 1969, Skinner himself warned managers that a poorly designed monetary reward system could actually reduce performance. Just as a satisfactory contract has to be established with the patient in the helping professions, so the employee has to be a willing party in industry. Skinner also warned that a feedback system alone is not enough; making the work intrinsically reinforcing may be as important as getting things done.

It is now almost a quarter of a century since Drucker (1954) first described management by objectives (MBO) and it has received considerable attention and wide-spread usage. MBO as defined by Hollmann (1976a) refers to the process whereby each manager establishes and works towards achieving specific objectives in key areas of his job responsibility. A variety of basic steps are then set up for working towards these goals within a specified time period. The necessary steps involve identification of key areas and responsibilities, establishing specific objectives in these areas, periodic review of progress, and end-of-period evaluation of managerial performance in the attainment of these objectives.

Hollmann suggests that the continual dissatisfaction with MBO programs is attributable to something called the organizational climate. But first it is necessary to reach agreement as to what is meant by his nebulous term, whether this phrase refers to organizational attributes or characteristics of people, to perceptual or to objective measures of climate. And the relationship between climate, however, defined, and job satisfaction is less than certain. All in all, there is little agreement with respect either to the construct itself or its measurement. Be this as it may, Hollmann adopts the following definition of organizational climate: "Organizational climate refers to a set of measurable properties of the work environment, perceived directly or indirectly by the people who work and live in this environment and assumed influence on their motivation and behavior."

In an attempt to survey organizational climate, as so defined, and its possible relationship to successful management by objectives, Hollmann polled 111 managers in a large utility firm. He found significant positive relationships between supportiveness of the organizational climate in the managers' immediate work-groups and their assessment of MBO effectiveness. Regardless of organizational level, relevant variables included the managers' needs for independence and the types of work performed. Any device for reaffirming company commitment to MBO serves a constructive purpose. However, perhaps most important in the day-to-day operational commitment among managers using MBO is that they believe it is helping them do their jobs more effectively. Managers are far more likely to have such positive attitudes if they are using MBO in a supportive organizational climate and it is to the establishment of such a climate that research needs to be directed.

MBO programs may call for specifying a standard minimal acceptable performance and a goal for superior performance above this minimum. London and Oldham (1976) are among those who are carrying out objective studies of goal-setting by systematically varying externally imposed goals for high performance and minimal acceptable performance. Their results may be of less importance than the fact that they are thinking in these terms. Future studies will need to explore the joint effects of different types of goals on the behavior of both labor and management. Performance can suffer when an individual accepts a minimal level which is far below or far above capabilities (see also Hollmann, 1976b).

The controversy initiated primarily by Deci (see Franks & Wilson, 1976, Section VIII) remains unresolved. It will be recalled that Deci distinguishes between two classes of motivation: intrinsic and extrinsic. An intrinsically motivated person performs the activity for the rewards inherent in the activity itself. Extrinsic motivation refers to the performance of the activity because it leads to external rewards (Deci, 1972a). According to Deci, differential increases or decreases in intrinsic motivation occur as a function of the type of reward given for an activity. Thus, monetary payment could conceivably lead to an intrinsically motivated activity becoming less so. And social approval could lead to the intrinsic enhancement of a primarily extrinsically motivated activity.

Many contemporary theories of work motivation stress the assumed independent, additive natures of the effects of extrinsic and intrinsic rewards when both are applied. It follows from this assumption that workers should be rewarded materially but contingently for doing well but that this same activity should be so structured, if at all possible, to generate intrinsic motivation. However, as noted last year, whereas Deci (1972b) concluded from his data that intrinsic and extrinsic motivations are not additive, other investigators arrive at an opposite conclusion (see Notz, 1975, for a scholarly review of these and related controversies).

A well designed study by Turnage and Muchinsky (1976), limited primarily by its artificial nature, raises a number of potentially significant possibilities which await further exploration under less contrived conditions. As one might expect, the relative and interactive effects of external and internal rewards—including worker involvement in the managerial process—are job and situation related. When the job is interesting, noncontingent payment coupled with employee participation in the decision-making process seems to increase motivation. However, paying workers contingently and allowing them no participation also appears to increase motivation, and at the same time has the additional advantage of increasing productivity. Thus, when the job is basically interesting, there is some flexibility with respect to decision-making strategies and payment systems. However, when the job is boring and routine, intrinsic controls do not have comparable effects on either performance or intrinsic motivation.

While concurring with Turnage and Muchinsky's conclusion that the available data prohibit any glib or premature generalization, there does seem to be little doubt that intrinsic and extrinsic motivations do have interactive rather than additive effects. An even more recent study by Pritchard, Campbell and Campbell (1977) provides further confirmation for the Deci hypothesis that contingent and financial rewards can reduce intrinsic motivation under certain circumstances. However, like that of Turnage and Muchinsky, their study was carried out with students involved in an artificially constructed task.

A factorially designed laboratory study conducted by Farr (1976) demonstrates the importance of task characteristics. He found no support for the hypothesis that contingent pay leads to decreased intrinsic task motivation and suggests that a combination of a job designed to be high on the four core dimensions of Hackman and Lawler (1971) (variety, autonomy, task identity and feedback) with a reward system objectively linking high performance and high external reward is likely to increase both intrinsic and extrinsic motivation towards the task. "Real-life" confirmation of this interesting hypothesis is awaited. The observation made last year still seems to apply: field studies in the natural environment are required rather than more analogue investigations using college students.

Anything that can contribute towards job enrichment merits investigation. Job enrichment has its advocates and its skeptics (see Korman, Greenhaus, & Badin, 1977). While it cannot be assumed that an enriched job is desired by a majority of American blue-collar workers, favorable overall results of job enrichment programs continue to be reported (e.g. Horn, 1975; Katzell, Yakelovich, Fein, Oornati & Nash, 1975). Ever since Thorndike promulgated the Law of Effect, it has been argued that increased performance is directly and positively related to contingent rewards. But this is at variance with the experimental psychologist's conclusion that performance is higher under conditions of partial reinforcement. Despite numerous investigations and a variety of studies specifically comparing fixed ratios and various combinations (e.g., Pritchard, Leonard, Von Bergen & Kirk, 1976), the precise parameters of the complex relationships between performance and contingent rewards remain unresolved (see also Locke, 1975).

We know relatively little about the manner in which people in general interpret behavior contingent rewards, and even less about employee reactions to leader reward behavior. Keller and Szilagyi (1976) investigated the relationships between perceived leader reward behavior and subordinate perceptions of role requirements, expectancies and satisfaction. As noted last year, Jablonsky and DeVries (1972) see positive and negative reinforcements as directly affecting the individual's perception of his work environment. Based on this model, Keller and Szilagyi examined the relationships between perceived positive or punitive leader rewards, on the one hand, and role conflict and ambiguity (expectations about performance by superiors and peers), on the other. The subjects were 192 managerial, engineering and supervisory employees of a large manufacturing company. Role dynamics, expectancies and job satisfactions were substantially related to the nature of the rewards perceived to be utilized by the leader. Regardless of occupational level, positive leader rewards appeared to be more potent in accounting for employee behavior than punitive leader rewards. This finding is highly consistent with that of Sims and Szilagyi (1975) who collected data from paramedical and support personnel at a major university medical center employing some 1600 individuals. Positive rather than negative leader rewards determine organizational behavior in both industrial and helping profession settings.

Relationships are important for the practicing manager and for leadership training. Positive leader rewards are effective in influencing employee satisfaction as well as behavior. Punitive rewards are influential, but to a much lower extent. Keller and Szilagyi suggest that supervisors be encouraged to tell their employees exactly what they should do to get rewarded, thereby increasing performance to reward expectancy. And furthermore, supervisors should be encouraged to reward deserving behavior systematically. As yet, these conclusions are based on correlational data only.

Attempts are being made to apply behavioral principles to management training. For example, Byham and Robinson (1976) have developed what they call interactional modeling. Instead of teaching theory, the supervisor is provided with direct and specific steps for handling each situation. Positive models of behavior are presented and on-the-job application is stressed. Modeling, role-playing, social reinforcement and transfer of training are all involved. The training begins with the learning of new behavior which, hopefully, will lead to changes in attitudes and eventually to a cognitive understanding of the basis for the new behavior's effectiveness. While no control data are offered, the field experiences reported by Byham and Robinson are encouraging. Hopefully, future supervisory training programs will evaluate this type of interactional modeling in a more systematic fashion (cf. Goldstein & Sorcher, 1973).

As part of a recent symposium dealing specifically with this topic (Kraut, 1976), Burnaska (1976) reports the effects of behavior model training upon managers' behaviors and upon employees' perceptions of these behaviors. Some 62 randomly selected experienced middle-level managers took part in a behavior modeling course designed to teach improved interpersonal skills to managers of professional employees. Objective measurements, including a four-month follow-up, indicated that managerial interpersonal skills had improved significantly. However, employee perceptions of their manager's overall behavior showed only slight improvement—perhaps because four months is an insufficient time for the manager to use his skills most effectively with each of his employees and change their perceptions. Clearly, a more extensive study using adequate controls and long-term follow-up is indicated.

As part of this symposium, Smith (1976) reports the effects of behavior modeling training on employee morale, customer satisfaction and sales in IBM branch offices. Modeling training was effective in improving effectiveness of survey feedback meetings, employee opinion survey results, managers' communication skills, and even sales performance. In addition, managers who showed greater improvement in communication skills showed higher customer satisfaction in their branch offices. Thus, both managers' communication behavior and employees' perception of managers' communication skills improved measurably.

Job involvement or commitment is obviously related to many of the above parameters. Unfortunately, as with "organizational climate," it is difficult to establish a clear behavioral definition of this concept. Rabinowitz and Hall (1977) review the pertinent literature in terms of three theoretical perspectives: job involvement as an individual characteristic, job involvement as a situationally determined variable, and job involvement as a product of person to situation interactions. Clearly, the findings will depend upon which definition is adopted and investigated. No one of these three classes of variable shows a demonstrably stronger relationship to job involvement than any other. Nevertheless, it is Rabinowitz and Hall's conclusion that job involvement is quite stable, even though it is correlated with variables that are themselves changeable. No study of job enrichment to date has demonstrated that even major job redesigns can increase job involvement. While much of the variance in job involvement appears unexplained, job involvement seems to be a "feedback variable," a cause and an effect of job behavior. Involvement increases as a consequence of satisfying job experiences and this, in its turn, has the effect of increasing the effort the employee will exert on the job. Situation variables seem to have more effect on the attitudes of low job-involved persons than on highly job-involved persons, a conclusion (admittedly based on limited evidence) contrary to expectation.

Rabinowitz and Hall suggest for the future, multivariate studies to help isolate possibly spurious relationships, longitudinal projects to learn more about whether and how involvements change, and field experiments aimed at increasing job involvement and the use of job involvement as a predictor. They also draw attention to the neglected dangers of too much involvement. Finally, they point out that most of the work in this field has been static research and that little is known about the *process* of becoming involved in a job.

At present, there are few objective scales for the measurement of job involvement, however this term is defined. Noting this deficiency, Wiener and Gechman (1977) attempted to develop an objective measure of work commitment (defined as socially accepted work behavior that exceeds formal and/or normative expectation) in 54 female elementary school teachers. Teachers were selected as subjects because their working days were structured and, in addition, presented opportunities for voluntary efforts beyond the normal day's obligations. While the findings demonstrate the feasibility and usefulness of a behaviorally oriented scale to measure job involvement, the somewhat atypical nature of the sample—as far as the average industrial scene is concerned—makes it difficult to generalize from their findings. Furthermore, their use of a diary to measure behavioral commitment is cumbersome and not very practical.

A helpful precursor to job involvement is to become involved from the very start with the sort of occupation that is likely to be satisfying. One of the few individuals to develop a social learning theory analysis of career decision making is Krumboltz (cf. Krumboltz, Mitchell & Jones, 1976). Career counseling is more than a matching of existing personality and job characteristics. It is a process of opening up new learning experiences and motivating the client to initiate career relevant exploratory activity. Viewed in this fashion, it becomes the responsibility of the behaviorally oriented career counselor to help the client learn a rational sequence of career decision-making skills, to help him or her arrange an appropriate sequence of career-relevant exploratory learning behaviors and to teach this client how to evaluate the personal consequences of these learning experiences. But, as Thoresen and Ewart (1976) point out, first we need to know much more about how this is to be carried out. While Krumboltz's model is enticing, as yet the necessary supportive data are lacking. Longitudinal studies and direct intervention programs—to the extent that these are possible—are indicated.

The economics of our society being as they are, there is going to be—at least for the foreseeable future—a hard-core of unemployed, untrained individuals. Over the past decade there has been increasing pressure for firms to hire such individuals. Large federal subsidies and cash outlays by the industries involved have been used to develop training and counseling programs. However, few empirical studies have examined the effects of these programs and there is relatively little evidence to affirm the positive impact of these training and counseling programs as far as employee retention is concerned. Until recently, no one had made any systematic attempt to separate out the effects of training the hard-core unemployed in the tasks they had to do as compared with counseling them. To remedy this deficiency, Salipante and Goodman (1976) examined some 130 programs in 114 firms. Their results clearly indicate that it is the content of training, the actual job-skills training, that is the critical variable. Job-skills training is positively related to job retention. Somewhat surprisingly, attitudinal training (as measured by the use of role-playing) is negatively related to retention. Personal counseling activities that help the trainee adjust to the organization are related to job retention. But it is the job skills content *per se* that is important rather than any attempt to change the attitudes of these workers so that they will be more easily assimilated into the organization.

A particular type of hard-core unemployed—but not necessarily unemployable—are those who suffer from some form of physical or psychiatric handicap. The use of industrial therapy units in mental hospitals is widespread but there is little evidence that this has much effect on the numbers of patients who return to employment. As Watts (1976) points out, behavior modification methods would be particularly appropriate if geared specifically towards remedying the inappropriate behaviors of such individuals. As yet, the systematic application of these methods in such settings has been virtually overlooked.

While behavioral techniques are used very extensively in large-scale business settings, there is a paucity of empirically demonstrated applications of behavioral principles in the world of the small businessman. Employee theft is likely to be particularly devastating for the small businessman. Response cost (the removal of a reinforcer following the undesired response) is clearly inapplicable in cases of theft or inaccurate change-making because the employer can rarely identify the employee concerned. To overcome this dilemma, response costs could be applied to employees as a group. Marholin and Gray (1976) combined both group contingency procedures and individual response-cost procedures in an attempt to reduce cash shortages in a small business setting. When cash shortages in a small family-style restaurant equalled or exceeded a certain agreed percentage of the day's sales receipts, the total shortage divided by the number of cashiers working for that day was subtracted from each person's salary for the day. This procedure was effective in reducing losses, even though the response-cost contingency was used only three times throughout their study.

A number of authors (e.g. Goldiamond, 1974; Martin, 1975) have expressed specific concerns with respect to the infringement of such program contingencies upon human rights, issues which are especially pertinent when groups of individuals have to suffer the consequences of deviant behavior by only one or two of their members. It is therefore suggested by Marholin and Gray that future attempts to use these procedures include prior discussion and input from employees as well as periodic formally solicited and anonymous opinions concerning any contemplated or actually used procedures. Marholin and Gray also make the telling point that a group contingency, publically and clearly stated as part of a job description, is much more ethical and humane than the alternatives of surveillance or the use of lie detectors. However, as they caution, any possible union violations must be resolved beforehand.

The small businessman is particularly susceptible to the hazards of disaster and less able to cope with its consequences—both because of more limited financial resources and because of a more personal involvement in a self-owned business. According to the much-cited Yerkes-Dodson Law, performance under stress follows an inverted-U shape function. This relationship between stress and performance has been repeatedly demonstrated in a variety of psychological laboratories. However, up to now its verification in the natural environment has been primarily anecdotal or a matter of extrapolation. The purposes of a recent study by Anderson (1976) were twofold: To demonstrate the applicability of the Yerkes-Dodson Law in a field organizational setting and to apply these findings constructively to the problems involved in assisting the small businessman to cope with disaster. Relationships among stress, coping behaviors and performance were examined in 93 owner-managers of small businesses damaged by hurricane floods. Businesses were objectively rated on a variety of criteria to determine their relative conditions as a result of recovery efforts. Perceived stress in the owner-managers was measured by a Subjective Stress Scale. Subjects were interviewed regarding their handling of critical incidents under stress and types of recovery efforts following the flood.

Perceived stress and organizational performance displayed curvilinear, inverted-U relationship. Actual financial loss or actual stress level did not account for performance differences. Most significantly, problem-solving coping behaviors revealed the inverted-U relationship of perceived stress whereas emotional coping behaviors displayed a positive linear relationship. Owner-managers of organizations who perceived high stress exhibited substantially different coping patterns to managers perceiving even moderate or low stress. If replicated in other settings, it might eventually be possible to develop techniques for the reduction of perceived stress level to the optimum zone for that individual by showing him or her how to acquire objective coping responses for dealing with selected specific situations.

ENVIRONMENT AND COMMUNITY

Behavioral Approaches to Community Psychology by Nietzel, Winett, MacDonald, and Davidson (1977), critically reviews the developments in the complex interface between behavior therapy and the community. In his perceptive Foreword, Ullmann (1977) points out that, despite a widespread recognition of behavioral specificity as opposed to an organization across situations in terms of dimensions or traits, the tendency to forget that the focus should be upon behavior-in-reaction-to-situations rather than to responses as such remains. People react to social systems and there is no such mystical entity as the organizational establishment other than that embodied in people. The organization cannot be depersonalized, for there are always specific individuals with specific occupations and backgrounds who function in specific and complex fashions at specific times and under specific conditions. Thus, economic and social policy become major concerns; if we cannot change persons at large, we can attempt to train the individual concerned to deal with the situation. The core of behavioral community psychology is the delivery system and the people delivering the services, but not so much in terms of who delivers as what is delivered, how it is delivered and with what measurable results. Thus, argues Ullmann, the future of behavioral community psychology lies in the behavioral analysis of the influencer and his or her interactions with the people served. Such endeavors will draw heavily upon sociology and industrial psychology in general, and organizational patterns and systems of analysis in particular.

If behavioral community psychology is an interface discipline, it is important for behavioral psychologists to expand their horizons drastically. Fortunately, this is happening at a rapid rate. Journals with titles such as *Environmental Psychology and Nonverbal Behavior* are beginning to appear, and systems analysis is beginning to play an important role in the study of organizational structure and design (cf. Filley, House & Kerr, 1976).

When Von Bertalanffy evolved his "organismic" theory of life in the early 20s, it was the inauguration of a scientific approach to viewing man in terms of systems theory rather than individuals. His general systems theory is a mathematical discipline devoted to the logic of systems study and integration (see Von Bertalanffy, 1968, 1969; J. G. Miller, 1976). At the same time, it was a bitter attack against stimulus-response theories and it is only recently that behavioral scientists are beginning to incorporate behavioral principles within the rubric of general systems theory (see Dockens, 1975; Franks & Wilson, 1976). It is Dockens' thesis that a general systems approach can be successfully integrated with that of the behavior modifier and that such a combination can be combined with other systems so as to cover the area traditionally conceded to ecology.

According to Dockens, this sort of integration permits the application of operant principles to the design of cultures, a process begun with the pioneering studies of Tharp and Wetzel (1969) and leading now to the new discipline of behavioral ecology and the study of the relationships between the behavior of the organism and the environment.

Traditional ecological psychology has tended to neglect both personality factors and basic psychological processes such as perception, cognition and social learning theory. Environmental psychology, whose concern is with the impact of the environment on individual and group behavior, is similar to ecological psychology. Both stress naturalistic, longitudinal research into the interchange between man and his milieu. But it is Binder, Stokols and Catalano's (1976) contention that environmental psychology, through its consideration of individual psychological processes, offers a more comprehensive analysis of the total interrelationship between the person and his complex environment.

Social psychology differs from both ecological and environmental psychology in that it places considerable emphasis upon natural in addition to man-made environments. It devotes more attention to the construction of environmental taxonomies organized around the psychosocial dimensions of diverse settings. As noted last year, one of the most significant methodological contributions to research in this area has been the development by Moos of standardized scales to measure the psychosocial attributes of different environments (cf. Moos, 1974, 1975, 1976a).

As Binder et al. point out, ecological psychology, environmental psychology and social psychology all have specific and interrelated implications for architecture and urban design, and it is to this end that Michelson (1970) has developed his intriguing notion of "intersystem congruence" as a guide to environmental design. The physical and social characteristics of an environment have to be congruent with the personal needs and cultural values of its inhabitants. Moos himself (1976b) is well aware of the interrelationships between social environmental stimuli, the physical characteristics of the environment, and the health and general well-being of the individual.

Environments which facilitate work pressure appear to be associated with high rates of coronary disease. Variables pertaining to autonomy, responsibility and time urgency are all related to physiological arousal and psychological dysfunction. And sometimes, when these variables are subjected to experimental investigation, the results are not always as expected. For example, Wohlwill, Nasar, DeJoy and Foruzani (1976) compared the effects of noise and active task involvement as opposed to passive exposure. Contrary to expectation but consistent with many previous findings, performance on a dial-monitoring task was unaffected by noise. Individuals can engage in complex tasks, coping effectively with considerable demands for attention and efficient information processing even under conditions of intense auditory distraction. Nevertheless, the experience does exact a toll. Wohlwill et al.'s subjects evidenced considerably lowered frustration tolerance even though actual task performance was apparently not disrupted by noise. In other words, after-effects are present and, perhaps even more important, not dependent on the power of the noise to disrupt the performance. This has obvious implications which warrant further intensive investigation.

In Moos' functional-reinforcement approach, the environment is viewed as an instrument for obtaining valued goals or reinforcers. Rossman and Ulehla (1977) view a wilderness environment as an instrument for gaining such reinforcers as solitude or contact with nature. Unfortunately, if understandably, using a questionnaire rather than a behavioral approach, these authors explored the reinforcing values to wilderness users of various rewards to be found only in such natural settings. For some of us, there are apparently valued rewards which are to be obtained only from natural settings, the more remote the better. Such findings can be of relevance for such programs as Outward Bound, developed to provide inner-city youth with wilderness experience and channel their adventure and competency needs into socially acceptable directions rather than less satisfactory and more antisocial alternative behaviors.

In one sense, the converse side of the coin is presented by Edny and his associates in their concern with the parameters of human territoriality and privacy. The behavior of the organism on home ground is different from behavior elsewhere and the parameters involved are, as yet, but little understood (Edney, 1976a; Edney, 1976b; Edney & Buda, 1976). Explanation of such activities in the animal world in terms of instinctual drives has been made popular by the speculations of such writers as Ardrey (1966). But the sometimes encountered theriomorphic extension of such a point of view to human beings—the illogical assumption that what is a valid explanatory concept for animals is equally valid for man, a kind of reverse anthropomorphism—would be unacceptable to the behavioral scientist without substantiating data even if it could be demonstrated for animals. We would opt for systematic study of the parameters of human territoriality and privacy in terms of some extension of social learning theory in combination with social, ecological and environmental psychology. Edney's survey of the little that is known, together with his own data-based investigations, marks a starting point in this largely unexplored domain. (See our somewhat related discussion of E. Wilson's [1975] sociobiology in Section VIII of Franks & Wilson [1976]).

Slovic, Fischoff and Lichtenstein's (1977) comprehensive review of behavioral decision theory points to several trends of relevance here. Decision theory is being studied from diverse vantage points, ranging from medicine, geography and psychology, to engineering and management science. But, increasingly, research emphasis is upon the psychological underpinnings of observed behavior as these relate to the decision-making process. For example, Trigg, Perlman, Perry and Janisse (1976) studied antipollution behavior in terms of perceived outcome and locus of control. Internal versus external locus of control refers to the manner in which individuals believe that reinforcers and other environmental occurrences are contingent upon their own behavior rather than luck, change or powerful others. While their study, conducted as part of an attitudes survey, suffers from limitations common to most questionnaire surveys of behavior, their findings are not without interest. Internals rather than externals have the more accurate information about environmental pollution. More important, only when people have favorable expectations about future levels of pollution is internal locus of control associated with greater involvement in conventional forms of social action. This could be of considerable relevance in any attempt to develop antipollution activists.

In the first paper reprinted in this Section, Holahan makes the important point that assumptions concerning relationships between urban design and human behavior are very different, depending on whether they are promulgated by an urban design specialist or a behavioral scientist. The modern designer favors a visually simple environment and the behavioral scientist is interested in a functionally complex environment. This can lead to sharply different conceptions of what is desirable. The physical design of high-rise apartment buildings is very much a case in point, as such buildings may have aesthetic advantages but are functionally likely to block off many of those avenues of social exchange which characterize the ghetto. To date, much of the discussion in this area has been based upon speculation or anecdotal evidence and it is for this reason, among others, that Holahan's data-based study is of importance. As predicted, an old neighborhood and an innovative project yielded higher levels of social behavior than traditional housing projects. But socializing was greatest in the innovative project. While generalization of these conclusions to other settings without further data is clearly unwarranted, Holahan's study serves well to remind us that effective urban design requires evaluation at functional as well as purely aesthetic levels.

Hopefully, when individuals such as Wodarski (1976) set forth procedural steps in the implementation of behavioral modification programs in open settings, they will take such considerations into account. It is well that Wodarsky advocates assessment of the organizational environment, involvement with staff concerns, staff training, interpretation of the program to the agency staff, collaboration with other agencies, public relations, explication of terms, monitoring and execution of the program. But this may not be sufficient.

Similar arguments apply to the sophisticated studies of work-sharing systems and experimental living groups documented by Miller and his associates (Feallock & Willer, 1976; Miller, Lies, Petersen & Feallock, 1976). Feallock and Miller demonstrate an effective device for reducing one of the major causes of the high-failure rate in experimental group-living arrangements—failure to share household chores. But it may well be that the actual physical arrangements generate at least as important reinforcement contingencies as those advocated by Feallock and Miller. Fountains and benches within scalloped gardens can be reinforcing alternatives to sterile waiting rooms. In many a mental care service delivery system, the physical structures are neither reinforcing to use nor to work in for either staff or patients. Young (1976) advocates a new approach to design which is based on client needs as well as the more traditional budgetary and directly functional considerations. Whether it is possible to create a warm and comfortable atmosphere which is both functional and respectful of clients and workers as human beings without excessive additional expense remains to be seen.

Social control theories which take into account social learning models but fail to incorporate modern ecology theory are likely to be limited in their effectiveness. For example, while the systematic use of behavioral procedures with delinquent groups is increasing, the neglect of sophisticated ecological and environmental influences is less than heartening. The lack of concern with socio-political issues is equally disheartening. Nietzel et al. go so far as to characterize behavioral investigation in this area as "technical, methodological and theoretical stagnation."

Stressing ethical and political responsibilities, Nietzel et al. offer specific steps for working with juveniles which guarantee their rights while continuing the therapeutic or correctional process. Conger's (1976) remedy involves a synthesis of two by now more or less traditional models of delinquent behavior based upon social control and learning theory, respectively. According to Conger, a combination of the social "bonding" of control theory with the principles of social learning theory could lay the groundwork for a more comprehensive theory of behavior than either perspective alone. However, in their more pristine forms both these theories tend to ignore ecological and extra-psychological influences.

In Nietzel et al.'s opinion, behavior modification with adult offenders is equally circumscribed. Most behavior modification procedures for identified criminals have been conducted in penal institutions. The more outstanding locations include the Draper Correctional Center in Alabama; the notorious and now defunct START tier program at the Medical Center for Federal Prisoners in Springfield County, Missouri; the LEAA-funded Contingency Management Program (CMP) in Virginia, also defunct; and the much criticized aversion therapy programs at Atascadero State Hospital (see Franks & Wilson, 1976) and the Vacaville Rehabilitation Center, both in California. Regardless of other limitations, most of these programs disregard or pay no more than lip-service to ecological or socio-political considerations.

Socio-political, ethical and legal issues in behavior modification are closely interwoven. Nowhere is this more apparent than in the field of correction and in human rights to treatment or no treatment (see Commentary, Section I; also Shapiro, 1974). As Nietzel et al. point out, the issues involved are more complex than the rhetoric on either side allows. Ultimately, as we have endeavored to stress in previous volumes in this Series, it boils down to the nature of the image of man espoused by the individuals concerned rather than a matter of allegiance to any principle of learning. It is perhaps with this in mind that Nietzel et al. take issue with Bornstein, Bugge and Davo's (1975) contention that the task for behaviorists is "formulating an intervention program to increase governmental and public acceptability regarding the practice of and extent in behavior modification" (p. 65). In Nietzel et al.'s own words: "One's doubts about the ethics of systematic behavioral control are unlikely to be mitigated by professionals who attempt to reinforce the 'right values.' "

As far as specific ecological problems are concerned, behavior modifiers have evolved a variety of ingenious strategies for coping with modern day environmental hazards. Environmental pollution seems to be a problem of which most individuals are aware, but to which few relate themselves as possible contributors. Tuso and Geller (1976) review some 32 post-1970 studies directed towards the improvement of man-environment relations. All were relatively successful in changing the probability of an ecology-related response, all utilized basic methodologies applicable to large-scale community programs, most were conducted in field settings. Almost half were designed to influence behavior related to litter and most were preventive or remedial in nature. Preventive measures tended to emphasize response priming or prompting, corrective measures, or some form of positive reinforcement.

Robinson's (1976) review of investigations into littering behavior in public places leads him to the conclusion that even greater emphasis needs to be placed on environmental influences in which the new unit of study is the behavior-environment relationship rather than the behavior in contextual isolation. Whether this is called social ecology, ecological psychology, or environmental psychology is of little importance—it all amounts to much the same thing. The analysis and prediction of littering control draw strength from a variety of disciplines: social psychology, perception, learning, behavior modification, industrial psychology, sociology, ecology and town and country planning. Regardless of orientation or discipline, most investigators view the environment and behavior as intertwined to the point of being inseparable. As Robinson points out, this involves much more than the trite dictum "environment effects behavior." It also implies that behavior cannot be appreciated fully apart from its intrinsic relationship to the physical environment, and that the definition of behavior must be with an environmental context.

Geller, Witner and Orebaugh (1976) investigated the effects of various written measures upon trash-depositing behavior. Three separate experiments conducted in two large grocery stores compared the effects of different prompt conditions upon paper-disposal behavior. A second study, reported in the same article, looked at the effects of a prompt requesting an antisocial behavior. On four consecutive days, the message "Please Litter—Dispose of on Floor" was printed on the bottom of all distributed handbills. This particular behavior was selected because scrutiny of previous data showed that very few handbills were dropped on the floor. Their Litter Prompt did indeed increase the proportion of the handbills very effectively, demonstrating that a written prompting technique could produce appropriate antisocial as well as more constructive behaviors. As the authors point out, the present study adds to the abundance of research demonstrating that people obey instrucions even when this compliance results in antisocial behavior. But here again, this is an oversimplification. Would the results have been different had the instructions been to litter banana skins rather than message-carrying fliers?

Crump, Nunes, and Crossman (1977) are concerned with a somewhat related problem—what are the effects of litter on littering behavior? Since most behaviors are emitted in the presence of only certain selected stimuli, it is argued that it would be valuable to identify those stimuli which set the occasion for littering. Hopefully, an effective antilittering program could then be initiated by removing such stimuli from the environment and replacing them with stimuli more conducive to antilittering. One such controlling stimulus may be the litter already present—clean areas tend to stay clean. Working within the Unita National Forest in northern Utah, Crump et al. studied a variety of individuals using a picnic complex over an extended period. In the already littered areas, people tended not to discard additional litter, a finding directly at variance with previous reports. While the authors advance a number of more or less plausible suggestions to account for this discrepancy, the main conclusion we draw is that much further investigation is necessary before any meaningful conclusion can be generated. It may well be that the findings are specific to the environment under study—previous investigations focused on urban settings.

Recycling could be one effective and socio-economically constructive solution to the problem of litter disposal. In 1975, Geller, Chaffee and Ingram gave residents of university dormitories a raffle coupon for delivering at least one sheet of paper to a designated collection room. For a contest condition, two dormitories were paired and the residents who collected the most paper won $15. The amounts of paper collected during the raffle and contest contingencies were equivalent and both were markedly greater than that collected during baseline conditions. The value of these findings is limited by the fact that a relatively small proportion of residents participated in the project under any condition.

In 1976, Witmer and Geller conducted a somewhat improved replication of the above study. This time, while prompt conditions led to only small increases in returned paper, both the contest contingency and a modified raffle condition were much more effective in promoting paper recycling. Unfortunately, participation was still limited to less than 15% of the dormitory residents. Nevertheless, the technique itself is of interest and, at least in principle, applicable to a variety of other commodities as the demand for recycled material waxes and wanes.

In an unpublished study cited by Neitzel et al., Luyben and Bailey (1975) compared a simple reward procedure in a mobile home park with a proximity condition. In the reward system, children who turned in newspapers at a designated time and place could choose a toy whose value varied in accordance with the amount of newspaper returned. In the proximity condition, seven containers were placed in the park. Each procedure had its advantages and disadvantages. Luyben and Bailey suggest that the proximity procedure might work best in a retirement community and the reward system in neighborhoods with many young children. More recently, Reid, Luyben, Rawers and Bailey (1976) attempted to increase newspaper recycling in apartment complexes. Personal prompts (given as part of door-to-door interviews) and the placement of additional containers resulted in 50% to 100% more newspapers being placed in the containers than in a baseline condition in which only one container was available.

Prompting and distributing recycling containers in close physical proximity to common activities contribute effectively to increasing the amount of newspapers recycled. As suggested, future research might well compare prompting with proximity as independent variables. Both methods of investigating littering and recycling offer certain advantages in that they focus on procedures that are simple, inexpensive and readily applicable at community and neighborhood levels. Whether a large scale intervention program could be implemented and supported by the community remains to be seen.

A somewhat related problem which can produce equally unaesthetic results is that of lawn-walking. Hayes and Cone (in press, b) studied the behavioral effects of three types of intervention: manipulating a response more or less incompatible with the undesirable response, forcing pathway usage and prompting appropriate behaviors by labeling the areas apart. Appropriate response behaviors were manipulated by storing benches on the grass and, where pathways had been worn by lawn-walking behavior, by obstructing the walkways with chains and so forth. To initiate pathway usage, a fence was installed around the grass area, forcing entry on to the more accessible pathway route. Benches located around the peripheral served to locate the area as a park, with written identification as a minipark and requests not to trample the grass. The study, an ABA design, lasted three weeks, with each of the above conditions in effect for one day. The environmental change most effective in reducing lawn-walking was the strategic placement of park benches. Contrary to expectations, obstructing the pathways with chains also reduced lawn-walking. Locating benches on the rock pathways actually increased walking on the grass islands—a procedure originally proposed by the University's professional planners as a solution to the lawn-walking problem! Both the fence and the peripheral benches decreased inappropriate lawn-walking only slightly; the sign prompt produced the most decreases.

Most strategies for litter reduction, paper recycling and so forth produce desirable effects that are only temporary. Arbuthnot, Tedeschi, Wagner, Turner, Kressel and Rush (1975) suggest that, in the long run, procedures to change the individual's cognitions towards ecology might be more valuable than behavior modification procedures alone. To this end, they implemented what they called a "foot-in-the-door" technique to produce such cognitive changes. The assumption is that, if subjects first perform a simple task similar to the final desired task, they will then more readily perform the desired task. The subjects were permanent residents of a small community and three request treatments were devised—a Survey, an Appeal, and a Letter. Half of the letters were "emotional" and half were "rational" in tone. All were accompanied by a postcard to be mailed to the city council in support of a community recycling program. The number of subjects who actually mailed the postcards and the number of subjects who began using the community recycling center was closely and positively related to the number of treatments received (Survey, Appeal and/or Letter). The nature of the letter did not produce differential results. Unfortunately, as Tuso and Geller point out, this study suffers from a number of confounding limitations.

With the problem of energy conservation assuming increasing prominence in recent years, a behavioral approach to energy consumption assumes greater significance. There are some half-dozen relatively recent studies whose concerns have been with changing either the magnitude or pattern of energy use. Winett and Nietzel (1975) made money incentives contingent upon reduced energy (electricity and natural gas used by residential consumers given information on reduction procedures). One group received information packets and forms to record the energy use, another received the same information and, in addition, were placed on a monetary incentive plan. The results, not surprisingly, indicated a highly significant effect of monetary incentive upon electricity conservation. However, somewhat surprisingly, the data with respect to natural gas did not show any difference between the groups.

Hayes and Cone (in press, a) extended this work, separating the confounding effects of monetary payment from utility bill savings for reduced energy use and examining the effects of feedback alone. Their results clearly show that information by itself or with a payment scheme has little effect, that feedback has only minor temporary effect and that a 100% payment scheme produces immediate and stable reductions.

One difficulty in modulating energy consumption is that consumers tend to use large amounts of electrical energy for short periods during the day, a phenomenon known as peaking, which results in inefficient use of existing power plants. The second paper to be reprinted in this Section, by Kohlenberg, Phillips and Proctor, is, to the best of our knowledge, the only behavioral study on this topic so far available. It is also important because of certain methodological innovations such as the introduction of in-home meters. Peaking, unlike a straightforward reduction in energy use, would aid the utility company in the modulation of their available resources without bringing about any significant reduction in income. But effective peaking shaping would presumably be closely related to complex changes in the lifestyles of the individuals concerned, such as staggered working hours and modified transport systems. Once again, it seems an inescapable conclusion that a systems and total environmental-ecological approach is most likely to produce lasting and generalizable effects.

An unusual paper by Winett (1976) documents experiences encountered in attempting to gain monetary support for a research program involving the effects of incentives in promoting residential energy conservation. A five-stage, carefully delineated, research program was outlined for modifying residential energy usage by means of a variety of contingency or incentive systems. Two projects successfully completed in 1974 and 1975, respectively, indicated a number of areas in which subsequent research could be directed. Before conducting the first demonstration project in the fall of 1973, Winett and his associate contacted a local electric and gas company. After much discussion, the company felt that it could not be involved with incentive programs but that it would probably "deal with conservation programs by continually raising prices." Meanwhile, the university refused to support the first project because the grant reviewers felt that it was not expedient to become involved in "politically unwise incentive programs." Thus, the demonstration survey studies had to be financed by the investigators themselves. Following positive local newspaper and radio publicity, they contacted an agency in the state government and a very large regional power company. The state agency was not geared towards the larger efforts needed and the power company, "philosophically" opposed to the use of incentives, advocated instead a strategy of escalating prices. More interest was shown in home insulation programs than in anything else and the proposal was turned down.

But all was not lost for, from these disheartening experiences, Winett derived a number of strategic principles for future campaigns. He reports surprise (we wonder why) at the frequent reactions encountered, involving such words as "carrot," "bribery," "conditioning," "philosophically wrong." It is always necessary to be aware of this resistance and to outline a number of strategies for coping with it. Apparently to their surprise—but not to ours—psychologists were found to have little credibility outside their own circumscribed areas of professional intervention. If this is so, then this, too, may well be an area for behavioral modification—we must be doing something wrong! Some of the problem, suggests Winnett, lies in the inflexibility of psychologists in approaching the various agencies. As part of the need to reappraise the mode of entry into systems such as power companies, the already noted "foot-in-the-door" tactic is advocated. This is, in essence, a shaping strategy for gaining initial entry into the system by making minimal demands and even offering some service rather than asking the organization for funds to promote what is, from the agency's point of view, a drastic shift in energy consumption practices. Finally, there is the matter of timing and the need to monitor closely the social shifting climate if proposals are to be properly and opportunely presented.

Transportation, architecture and population change all come within the view of the behavioral community psychologist. Parsons (1976) draws attention to the need for the introduction of the principles of engineering psychology (human factors) into the armamentarium of the community behavioral psychologist. For example, if people drove more cautiously, there might be fewer accidents. Any strategy for introducing cautious behavior into driving is to be commended. Parsons suggests that the "precautionary pause" based on a longer response latency and reduced force be conditioned into drivers as avoidance behavior. Accidents and near-accidents can be viewed as aversive consequences that generate driver avoidance behavior (including the precaution response). As yet, the real-life driving environment, including motivational designs to bring about this process, remains largely unexplored despite the accumulation of much laboratory data to indicate the feasibility of such an approach.

Another area of environment pollution is that of noise abatement. Meyers, Artz, and Craighead (1976) developed a reinforcement system utilizing instructions, modeling, feedback and group reinforcement in an attempt to reduce disruptive noise in three university residents' halls. The fourth hall received the same treatment program without the reinforcement component. Unfortunately, while generally effective in reducing disruptive noise, there was no generalization of behavior change to nontreatment conditions. According to Kazdin and Bootzin (1972), programming of the natural environment could be the most effective technique for increasing generalization (see also Kazdin, 1975; Kazdin, 1977). By programming, they mean the institution of permanent reinforcement contingencies designed to produce the requisite behavior change. Another approach might be the development of self-control programs.

Reiss, Piotrowski and Bailey (1976) compared the effectiveness and cost-efficiency of three different techniques designed to encourage low-income rural parents to seek dental care for their children. The families of 51 children in need of immediate dental care were allocated to one of three matched groups: the one-prompt group (typed note only); the three-prompt group; (note, telephone contact and home visit) and a one-prompt plus $5 incentive program. The most effective strategy, both with respect to dental and follow-up visits, was that of the one-prompt plus $5 incentive. Furthermore, the cost-effectiveness analysis showed this incentive condition to be less costly than the three-prompt condition encouraging initial dental visits. We do not think this finding surprising and it is certainly consistent with studies in related areas such as energy reduction.

A group much neglected in the teaching of adaptive community skills is that of the mentally handicapped. In a recent study reported by Page, Iwata and Neef (1976), five retarded male students were taught basic pedestrian skills in a classroom. Training was conducted on a simulated city traffic model, each subject being taught five specific skills involved in street-crossing. Not only could pedestrian skills be successfully taught to retarded persons in the classroom setting, in addition these skills generalized to the natural environment with little or no training. This study is of importance because it represents one of the few successful attempts to teach adaptive behaviors in a situation removed from the environment in which the behaviors usually take place. The program further possesses a number of compelling practical advantages. It is simple to administer, it can be readily taught by classroom aides, it requires little time for completion and it encourages increased independence on the part of the individuals who learn these skills. There are even some indications that the learning generalizes to performance in skills as yet untrained. The authors offer one note of caution: The teaching of these skills may not always be welcomed by parents or guardians because, with increased mobility, comes increased traffic and other hazards.

The final paper reprinted in this section, by McNess, Egli, Marshall, Schnelle and Risley, is concerned with one of the most frequent crimes in the United States, shoplifting. Identification by signs and stars of merchandise likely to be stolen seems to be the most effective device, more effective than publicity campaigns or warning signs. In the absence of truly educational systems geared towards cognitive restructuring of values, the procedures outlined by McNess et al. may be of considerable practical utility. As the authors note, it remains the task of future research to address the issue of comparative effectiveness of the procedures described in their report.

As noted in our Commentary to Section I, a cross-cultural perspective introduces a host of additional parameters into the world of behavior modification. For example, Bauermeister and Jemail (1976) contrast the findings with respect to parents or teachers acting as behavior therapists in natural environments in the United States with their counterparts in Puerto Rico. And Schultz and Sherman (1976) question the assumption that tangible reinforcers are the most effective ones for lower-class as contrasted with middle-class children—an assumption made either implicitly or explicitly by researchers and practitioners alike. It is their considered opinion, based on the analysis of some 60 studies conducted within the past decade, that social class differences and reinforcer effectiveness cannot be assumed and with this we certainly concur. However, the tendency is still to believe that children from lower-class environments favor material reinforcements whereas those from the middle class respond most favorably to intangible reinforcements. Perhaps the wide dissemination of this paper will serve as a correction, or at least as a need for re-examination, of this notion.

In similar fashion, Gardner (1976) points out that one cannot assume the facile transportation from one culture to another of behavior modification procedures even when the cultures—in this context, America and Australia—seem superficially not dissimilar. And the growing science of behavioral economics (see Franks & Wilson, 1976, Winkler, 1976) has to involve more than a systematic study of the economics of a token economy considered in isolation. No token economy operates within a vacuum and the cultural setting of the larger society within which the token economy is carried out would seem likely to effect what goes on within the token economy per se.

Finally, we draw attention to the important relationships pertaining between behavior and malnutrition, what has been described as the ecology of malnutrition, the behavior patterns of mothers and children towards one another which influence both mental and physical development. For example, of 56 young children tested in a Phillipine mountain village by Guthrie, Masangkay and Guthrie (1976), 16 were too sick to respond to the testing situation and an additional 15 with histories of severe malnutrition obtained very low scores on the Bailey scale of mental development. The poor performance of these malnourished children seems to be part of a larger pattern in which vigorous efforts were made to keep children from crying by giving them heavily sugared food, by carrying them most of the time, and by the provision of little verbal stimulation. The links between reinforcement, physical malnutrition, poor sanitation, general health, social behavior, and mental development are both complex and pervasive. There are important feedback relationships among malnutrition, infections due to sanitation deficiencies and the social behavior of the child and its caretakers. In many ways, the malnourished child and his family behave in manners which compound the difficulties and lead to further adverse effects on cognitive development. In his or her misery, the malnourished and physically ill child is not able to participate in opportunities to learn. By whimpering when stimulated and by refusing to eat appropriate food when offered, the child inadvertently cuts himself off from what is needed for cognitive or physical growth and so a vicious cycle is perpetuated. Hopefully, this is an area of investigation which will be included in the domain of the behavioral community and cultural psychologist and psychiatrist.

To achieve what Sarason (1974) terms the psychological sense of community, behavior modifiers will have to expand their horizons drastically and transcend that focus upon the individual from whence much of the original therapeutic impetus was generated. The many encouraging developments noted in this Commentary notwithstanding, the tendency to avoid the articulation of environmentally and socially meaningful theoretical rationales remains (Goodwin & Tu, 1975; Rappaport, Davidson, Wilson & Mitchell, 1975). Texts such as that of Nietzel et al. and innovative behaviorally based community psychology programs such as those offered by Seidman and Rappaport (1974) and Krasner (1975) mark steps in an appropriate direction.

SECTION IX: BEHAVIOR THERAPY AND THE EXTENDED SOCIETY: INDUSTRY AND COMMUNITY

22

ENVIRONMENTAL EFFECTS ON OUTDOOR SOCIAL BEHAVIOR IN A LOW-INCOME URBAN NEIGHBORHOOD: A NATURALISTIC INVESTIGATION

Charles J. Holahan

The University of Texas at Austin

Outdoor behavior was measured and compared using a behavioral mapping procedure across three contrasting environments in a low-income urban neighborhood. The environments were an old ghetto neighborhood of low-rise tenement houses, a traditional high-rise housing project, and an innovative high-rise housing project, where a creative outdoor design had been added to encourage outdoor use. As predicted, the old neighborhood and the innovative project showed higher levels of outdoor socializing than did the traditional project. Unexpectedly, the old neighborhood showed the highest level of task-oriented activity relative to recreation and leisure. Several propositions concerning the relationship between behavior and urban environment are considered, and a number of implications for urban design are advanced.

Reprinted with permission from *Journal of Applied Social Psychology*, 6, 1, 48-63, 1976.

The data in this study were collected while the author was a post-doctoral fellow in the Environmental Psychology Program at the City University of New York.

The author wishes to thank Arlene Gehring for her assistance in conducting the study, and Walter Stephan and Robert Helmreich for their comments on the manuscript.

The physical transformation of the central city presents one of the most challenging social psychological issues in contemporary society. Gradually, the old tenement neighborhood boasting a robust social life is being replaced by high-rise housing projects distinguished instead by social isolation. The vivid contrast between the social vitality of the ghetto and the barrenness of the new high-rise projects has been eloquently described by Jacobs (1961). In a systematic investigation in Puerto Rico, Hollingshead & Rogler (1963) found that while over 60% of slum dwellers liked living in the slum, over three-quarters of residents relocated in a new housing project were dissatisfied with their living conditions. The Pruitt-Igoe houses in St. Louis, which were hailed as a modern design achievement, have become notorious for their almost total failure to function effectively at a social psychological level (Rainwater, 1968; Yancy, 1971). Newman (1973) has recently documented the consistent relationship between low social cohesion and high crime level typical in high-rise public housing.

At issue are contrasting basic assumptions concerning the relationship between urban design and human behavior. Typically, modern designers have favored a visually simple environment, while behavioral scientists interested in design problems have preferred a functionally complex environment. While both favor order in the urban environment, conceptions of what type of order is needed differ sharply. The designer, for example, strives to create order on a purely visual scale. Such visually oriented designs tend to spatially separate diverse types of behavior. Jacobs (1961) has sternly criticized this approach to urban design.

> To approach a city, or even a city neighborhood, as if it were a larger architectural problem, capable of being given order by converting it into a disciplined work of art, is to make the mistake of attempting to substitute art for life.

The behavioral scientist, in contrast, envisions order emerging at a functional level. He tends to favor mixing diverse types of behavior, allowing them to function in complimentary and mutually supportive ways.

Critics of modern urban design contend that the emphasis on simplicity of form has neglected the important social function played by the outdoor environment in the urban neighborhood. Design strategies which emphasize screening off diversified activities from one another in the name of visual aesthetics impede the rich informal social exchange characteristic of the low-income neighborhood. Fried and Gleicher (1970) describe the urban ghetto as a region in which an immense and interrelated set of social networks is localized. Fried (1963) has reported the grief reaction experienced by residents of an urban ghetto who were relocated by urban renewal. The grief, which showed most of the features of mourning for a lost person, was interpreted as directly related to the disruption of the ghetto's social network. Social functions, such as communication and group support in low-income neighborhoods, are met through informal and largely accidental social contact between people pursuing diversified tasks in public open spaces. Hartman (1963) has written:

> . . . In most working class communities which have been reported in the literature, there was considerable interaction with the surrounding physical and social environment, an interaction which formed an integral part of the lives of the people. . . . Among a population for whom sitting on stoops, congregating on street corners, hanging out of windows, talking with shopkeepers, and strolling in the local area formed a critical part of the *modus vivendi,* the concept of personal living space must certainly be expanded to include outdoor as well as indoor space.

The physical design of high-rise apartment buildings, in particular, blocks many of the avenues of social exchange characteristic of the ghetto. For example, in the ghetto, windows of tenement houses offer a rich medium through which ghetto residents can hail passers-by or converse casually with neighbors in adjacent buildings. Also, because local stores are typically scattered throughout the ghetto neighborhood, residents are brought naturally within range of the doors and windows of many other neighbors while pursuing daily errands (Gans, 1962). High-rise housing, in contrast, is characterized by a minimum of semi-public space between apartments, and tends to exert an atomizing effect on informal relationships. Yancy (1971) has noted that families living in Pruitt-Igoe retreated to the interior of their apartments, losing the social support and neighborly protection found in other lower and working class neighborhoods. Hollingshead and Rogler (1963) concluded that the central reason residents of the housing project in their study disliked their housing was that it lacked the comfortable and informal social exchange with neighbors typical of the ghetto.

To date, with the exception of a small body of survey research, almost all of the argument in this area has been highly speculative. In fact, there have been no empirical data to support the basic contention that high-rise housing projects are characterized by a less scoial and active outdoor life than is the old ghetto neighborhood. The purpose of this study was to afford such an empirical test. Specifically, the study was designed to (1) measure and compare the level of outdoor socializing across three contrasting urban environments—an old ghetto neighborhood, a traditional high-rise housing project, and a housing project where an innovative design solution was intended to encourage and support street activity; and (2) develop a behavioral portrait of each of these environments, including both the range of activities which occur in public spaces and some of the environmental features which support street activity. On the basis of previous speculations concerning the relationship between behavior and urban design (Fried & Gleicher, 1970; Gans, 1962; Hartman, 1963; Jacobs, 1961), it was predicted that the old neighborhood and the innovative project would be characterized by higher levels of outdoor social behavior than would the traditional project. It was further anticipated that the old neighborhood and the innovative project would demonstrate outdoor behavioral profiles typified by higher frequencies of recreational and leisure behavior relative to functional or task-oriented activity than would the traditional project.

METHOD

Design

Three adjacent sites within a low-income, inner-city neighborhood were selected for comparison—an old neighborhood of low-rise tenement houses, a traditional high-rise housing project, and an innovatively designed high-rise housing project. The two projects were comparable in age, project size, and building height. Residents of the three sites were similar in socio-economic level and racial background. Behavioral measures were collected in each site on three Saturday afternoons during the summer. Measures were of two types: (1) a 5 min time-sample of the social behavior of a random sample of 15% of individuals outdoors in each site, and (2) a profile of the range of activities of all individuals outdoors in each site based on a single observation of each individual.

Environmental Settings

The area selected for study was a neighborhood in New York City's lower east side, which was low-income, predominantly Puerto Rican and Black, and slowly being redeveloped by the city. The old neighborhood site consisted of 5 different blocks randomly selected from the 36-block neighborhood adjacent to the two projects. The old neighborhood was characterized by 3- to 5-story tenements, built in a row, flush with the sidewalk. Eighty-five percent of buildings in the neighborhood were completed before 1940. While the neighborhood was predominately residential, occasional commercial establishments (such as grocery stores, candy stores, and cleaners) were mixed in at the street level. Physically, the neighborhood met the description of an urban slum. Housing quality varied, but tended toward poor condition, with some badly deteriorated buildings, and an occasional boarded-up site. Density in the old neighborhood, as in both projects, ranged from 350 to 400 persons per acre. Median montly rent in the old neighborhood was $76, compared to $82 in both projects.

The two housing projects were built along the eastern boundary of the old neighborhood and were adjacent to both the old neighborhood and to one another. Both projects were completed in 1949, and were similar in the physical design of project buildings. Each had 16 to 18 buildings of up to 14 floors. Amount of outdoor space was comparable for both projects and was of a "super-block" nature, i.e., a number of city blocks were included in the project grounds and closed to automobile traffic. The two projects differed markedly, however, in the design of outdoor space. The traditional project, which was typical of most public housing projects, consisted chiefly of grassy areas which were fenced off to prohibit tenant use, a few playgrounds with minimal and badly deteriorated playground equipment, and row benches along the asphalt entrance ways. The innovative project boasted a modernistic and aesthetically pleasing outdoor environment which had been added to the project in 1965 specifically to encourage and support outdoor activity.* The innovative design was restricted to the large central project area, and stood in contrast to the standard row benches along the peripheral entrance ways. The new design features were of three types: (1) a modernistic adventure playground and wading area, which included creatively designed concrete and timber playground equipment, replaced the old central playground; (2) a red brick-surfaced pedestrian mall surrounded by small groupings of benches and tables was built over the previously closed-off grassy areas; and (3) a large sunken amphitheater was added as a forum for public events. Figure 1 shows a schematic representation of the three environmental settings.

* The innovative outdoor environment was designed by architect M. Paul Friedberg.

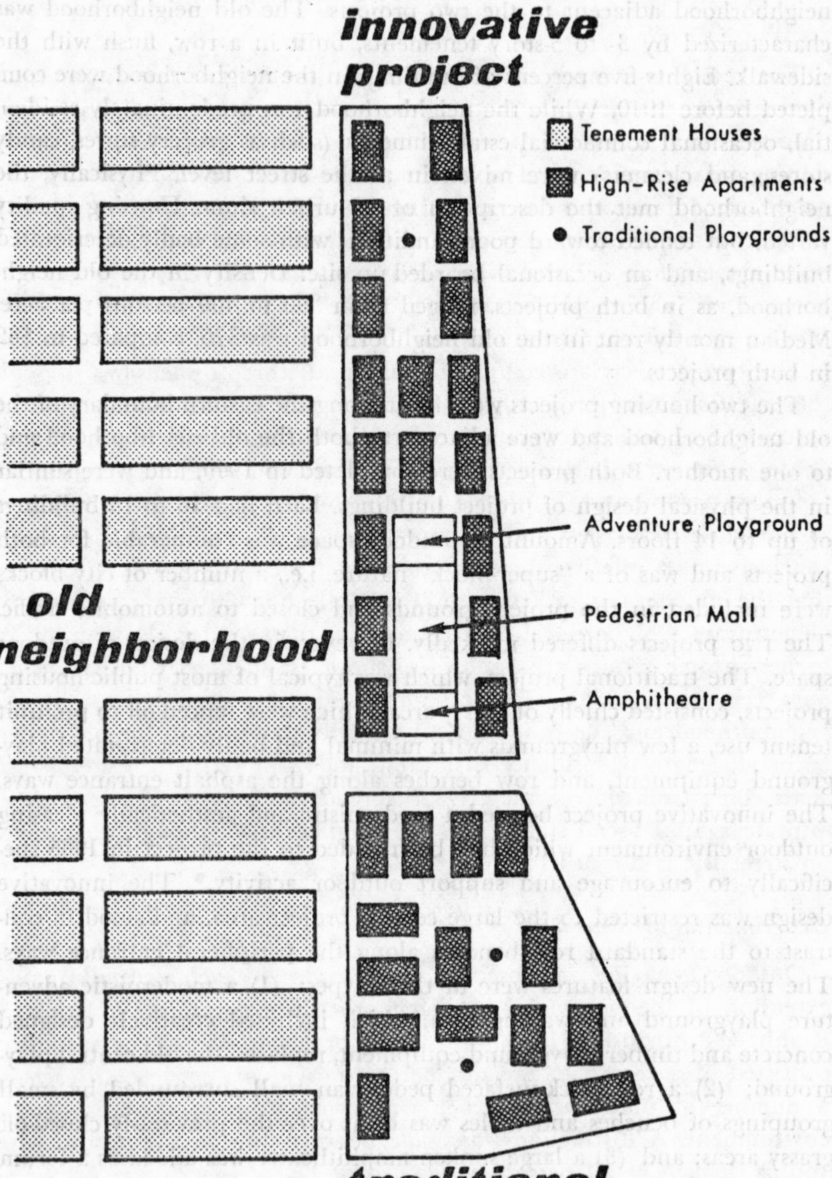

FIG. 1. Schematic representation of the three environmental settings.

Sample Selection

The residents in each environmental setting did not constitute a random assignment of subjects to experimental conditions. Self-selection processes may be assumed to have been of some importance in determining area of residence. The best source of information concerning any systematic differences between settings in resident characteristics is the U.S. Census of 1970, since census tracts correspond almost exactly to the three areas studied. Three types of information are relevant: race, economic level, and mobility patterns. Table 1 summarizes this information for each environmental setting.

The two projects are comparable along all three dimensions, though the traditional project is slightly higher than the innovative project in percentage of whites to nonwhites, median income, and length of residence. Differences between the old neighborhood and the two projects are more pronounced. In the old neighborhood, the percentage of whites to nonwhites is highest and economic level is lowest. While there is no conclusive data relating these variables to street activity, indications are that the influence is probably mixed. While nonwhites are believed to demonstrate a higher level of street activity than whites (Brower, 1973), higher income groups are assumed to show less such activity than lower ones (Hartman, 1963). The most important difference between the old neighborhood and the projects is in mobility patterns. In the old neighborhood, length of residence is shortest, and a higher percentage of residents come from out of the city or abroad .Both these factors tend to militate against social stability in the neighborhood, though their effect on street life is difficult to predict.

Experimental Measures

Outdoor behavior was observed and recorded in each setting using an extension of the behavioral mapping procedure developed by Ittelson, Rivlin, & Proshansky (1970). The behavioral map of each environment consisted of a record of the number of individuals engaged in each of a number of predetermined behavior types in each sub-area of the environment. A distinction was made between youths and adults, with youths defined as all persons judged to be below age 20, and adults as all persons age 20 and above. Through initial observation sessions in an adjoining area, a list of behavior categories was selected which covered most of the behavioral variance for the settings studied. In addition to scoring type of behavior, each subject's specific location in the environ-

TABLE 1

PERCENTAGE OF RESIDENTS IN EACH ENVIRONMENTAL SETTING BY RESIDENT CHARACTERISTICS*

Characteristic	Environmental setting		
	Old neighborhood	Traditional project	Innovative project
Race			
White	35	21	16
Black	16	29	24
Spanish (mother tongue)	49	49	60
Economic level			
Median income	$5,128	$5,774	$5,399
Unemployment (% for 16 years and above)	36	32	33
Families below poverty level	30	25	26
Mobility patterns			
Length of residence			
1965–70	62	34	41
1960–64	18	27	36
1959 or earlier	20	39	23
Previous residence			
N.Y. (central city)	73	86	88
N.Y. (outside central city)	2	2	.5
Outside N.Y.	9	3	2.5
Abroad	16	9	9

*Based on U.S. Census of 1970.

ment was recorded at each observation interval. Observations involved complete coverage of all physical spaces in the selected environments on a time-sampling basis. Observations were recorded on data sheets designed for quick and easy use by observers.

Two specific types of behavioral maps were collected: (1) *Individual Social Records* (ISR) and (2) *Activity Maps* (AM). The ISR procedure was designed to compare the *level* of social behavior over environmental settings. A random number table was used to randomly select 15% of the persons in each site for observation. Then, in a time-sampling procedure, a recording of each subject's behavior was performed at 30-sec intervals for a period of up to ten intervals. Each subject was given a score indicating the percent of his behavior which fell into each of the three following behavior categories.

(1) *Verbal interaction*—social interaction between two or more persons which included conversation.

(2) *Nonverbal interaction*—social interaction between two or more persons which did not include conversation. Social behavior included such activities as ball playing, repairing an automobile, sitting in a group, and walking together when these activities clearly involved two or more people in a social grouping. The distinction between verbal and nonverbal was determined by whether or not the individual selected for observation was engaged in conversation (speaking or listening) at the instant his behavior was recorded.

(3) *Isolation*—any activity performed by an individual in isolation, i.e., sitting alone or walking alone.

The AM procedure was designed to compare the *distribution* of a range of activities over environmental settings. It involved an instantaneous recording of the behavior of all subjects in each site, based on a single observation of each individual. Each subject was given a score indicating which of the three following activity categories his behavior fell into.

(1) *Active recreation*—ball playing, using playground equipment, bike riding.

(2) *Leisure*—sitting, standing, and casual activity, such as listening to a radio.

(3) *Functional*—task-related activity, such as shopping, child care, and repairing an automobile. Previous research has shown the behavioral mapping procedure to have high inter-observer and split-halt reliability (Ittleson et al., 1970). After training in the specific behavioral scoring procedures used here, inter-rater reliability was determined for the two observers. Agreement exceeded 90% on all measures.

Procedure

The timing of observations was determined by the desire to compare the three settings during peak outdoor use. Observations were conducted by two trainees from CUNY's Environmental Psychology Program on three Saturday afternoons from 1:00 to 5:30 during the months of June and July. All observations were conducted in good weather where the temperature ranged between 75 and 95 degrees. In order to minimize accidentally repeating observations of the same subject, while at the same time permitting a sampling of the three settings over time, the following observation procedure was developed. Each environment was divided into three equal physical sub-areas, and each sub-area was observed only once, with a different sub-area being observed each Saturday. Thus, on the first Saturday of observations, one sub-area was observed from each of the three environments. On the following Saturday, one of the remaining sub-areas was observed in each environment, and so on. The particular sub-area to be observed on a given Saturday and the sequence of observations across environments were determined randomly. Each observer spent 1½ hours in each of the three sites during each observation period, resulting in a total of 4½ hours of observation in each site over the course of the study. The two observers walked together, proceeding through each sub-area by a preselected route. While one observer employed the ISR procedure, the other used the AM procedure. Observers carried a stopwatch and behavior score sheets attached to a clipboard. They were dressed casually (as were neighborhood residents), and attempted to neither attract attention nor to interact with residents.

RESULTS

Individual Social Records

The total number of subjects observed under the ISR procedure in the old neighborhood, the traditional project, and the innovative project was 48, 48, and 29 respectively. Table 2 shows the percent of behavior in each social behavior category across the three environmental settings for all subjects and for youths and adults separately, along with the results of the one-way analyses of variance. Let us look first at the data for all subjects. The difference between the three settings was statistically significant at the .01 level for verbal interaction. The Scheffé (1959) multiple-comparison procedure was used to test differences between specific environmental settings. This procedure indicated that there was significantly more verbal interaction in the average of the old neighborhood and innovative project compared to the traditional project, as predicted ($F = 7.14$, $df = 2/122$, $p < .05$). Individual comparisons showed that the difference between the innovative and traditional projects was statistically significant ($F = 9.14$, $df = 2/122$, $p < .025$), while the differences between the old neighborhood and either the traditional or the innovative

TABLE 2

PERCENT OF BEHAVIOR IN EACH SOCIAL BEHAVIOR CATEGORY BY AGE GROUP ACROSS THE THREE ENVIRONMENTAL SETTINGS

Age group	Social behavior category	Environmental setting			ANOVA		
		Old neighborhood	Traditional project	Innovative project	F	df	p
All subjects	Verbal	63	52	80	4.57	2/122	.01*
	Nonverbal	23	23	6	3.36	2/122	.04*
	Isolated	14	25	14	1.33	2/122	.27
Youths	Verbal	62	53	91	7.10	2/66	.002*
	Nonverbal	32	26	8	3.00	2/66	.06
	Isolated	6	21	1	3.79	2/66	.03*
Adults	Verbal	64	50	61	.58	2/56	.57
	Nonverbal	16	18	4	.95	2/56	.39
	Isolated	20	32	35	.75	2/56	.48

*Significant with $\alpha = .05$.

projects were not statistically significant. The Scheffé procedure indicated that there was significantly less nonverbal interaction in the innovative project than in the average of the old neighborhood and the traditional project ($F = 6.71$, $df = 2/122$, $p < .05$), the old neighborhood alone ($F = 5.25$, $df = 2/122$, $p < .10$), or the traditional project alone ($F = 5.64$, $df = 2/122$, $p < .10$). [Sheffé recommends an alpha level of .10 in using his multiple comparison procedure.] The traditional project showed the highest level of isolated behavior, though this was not statistically significant.

It is revealing to further analyze the ISR data in terms of age. For youths, the differences between the three sites were particularly strong, while for adults there were no statistically significant differences over settings. For youths, the differences between settings were statistically significant at the .002 level for verbal interaction, the .03 level for isolation, and approached significance for nonverbal interaction ($p < .06$). The Scheffé multiple comparison procedure indicated that there was significantly more verbal interaction in the average of the old neighborhood and the innovative project than in the traditional project ($F = 7.72$,

TABLE 3

COMPARISON OF OBSERVED AND EXPECTED PERCENT OF SUBJECTS IN EACH AGE GROUP ACROSS THE THREE ENVIRONMENTAL SETTINGS*

Environmental setting	Old neighborhood		Traditional project		Innovative project	
Age group	Youths	Adults	Youths	Adults	Youths	Adults
Observed %	35	65	50	50	65	35
Expected %	38	62	48	52	50	50

*Expected figure is based on U.S. Census of 1970.

$df = 2/66$, $p < .05$). Individual comparisons showed more verbal interaction in the innovative project than in either the old neighborhood ($F = 6.99$, $df = 2/66$, $p < .05$) or the traditional project ($F = 13.84$, $df = 2/66$, $p < .01$). Nonverbal interaction was again lowest in the innovative project. Isolated behavior for youths was highest in the traditional project and lowest in the innovative project (only 1%). The Scheffé procedure indicated that there was significantly more isolated behavior in the traditional project than in the average of the old neighborhood and the innovative project ($F = 6.64$, $df = 2/66$, $p < .05$).

Activity Maps

The total number of subjects observed under the AM procedure in the old neighborhood, the traditional project, and the innovative project was 287, 280, and 178 respectively. An analysis of subjects by age group in the three environmental settings itself reflects an interesting difference between sites. Table 3 shows the percent of subjects observed outdoors during this study and the actual percentage of residents in each setting as reflected in the 1970 census. The census data showed that both projects had approximately equal numbers of youths and adults, while the old neighborhood had approximately a 6 to 4 ratio of adults to youths. The observed frequencies closely conformed to the actual frequencies in the old neighborhood and the traditional project. In the innovative project, however, the observed frequencies reflected a stronger preference for using the outdoor environment on the part of youths relative to adults. The difference between observed and expected frequencies

TABLE 4

PERCENT OF BEHAVIOR IN EACH ACTIVITY CATEGORY BY AGE GROUP ACROSS THE THREE ENVIRONMENTAL SETTINGS

Age group	Activity behavior category	Environmental setting		
		Old neighborhood	Traditional project	Innovative project
All subjects	Active recreation	6	15	26
	Leisure	53	51	51
	Functional	41	34	22
Youths	Active recreation	11	28	36
	Leisure	39	41	47
	Functional	50	31	17
Adults	Active recreation	4	2	10
	Leisure	60	61	60
	Functional	36	37	30

of youths and adults in the innovative project was statistically significant by the Chi Square test ($\chi^2 = 16.38$, $df = 1$, $p < .001$).*

Table 4 shows the percent of behavior in each activity category across the three environmental settings for all subjects and for youths and adults separately. Let us examine first the data for all subjects. In all settings, leisure activity represented approximately 50% of outdoor behavior. Differences between settings occurred in the relative distribution of active recreation and functional behavior. Active recreation was least in the old nieghborhood, somewhat higher in the traditional project, and highest in the innovative project. Functional activity showed exactly the opposite pattern. These differences between settings were statistically significant at the .001 level ($\chi^2 = 43.3$, $df = 4$). For youths, the differences between settings were statistically significant ($\chi^2 = 32.9$, $df = 4$, $p < .001$), while for adults the differences were not significant. The activity distributions for the two age groups considered separately were generally similar to

* All χ^2 tests on the AM data were performed on the actual frequency of subjects in each cell. To facilitate interpretation, the tables reflect the percent of subjects in each cell.

that for all subjects. However, for youths the level of active recreation was relatively higher, and the level of leisure activity relatively lower, than for adults.

It is interesting to note the relationship of activity level to specific physical features of the outdoor environment. Table 5 shows the distribution of behavior in each setting across physical features of the environment. While the small cell totals preclude statistical comparison, some key contrasts between settings warrant comment. In the old neighborhood, 90% of outdoor behavior occurred along the sidewalk, much of it in the vicinity of entrances to residential or commercial establishments. In both projects, the most used environmental feature was benches. Surprisingly, in the innovative project the adventure playground was little used. In the traditional project, as expected, the large grassy areas were almost totally vacant.

DISCUSSION

As predicted, the old neighborhood and the innovative project were characterized by higher levels of social behavior than was the traditional project. Interestingly, though, socializing was actually greater in the innovative project than in either of the other sites. This latter finding seemed due particularly to the successful functioning of the innovative project environment as a recreational space for youths. Concerning the relative frequency of behavior types, the old neighborhood unexpectedly showed the highest level of functional activities relative to recreation and leisure. Apparently, the street life of the old neighborhood was based less on its directly meeting recreational and leisure needs than on its providing opportunities for residents to casually interact while pursuing a range of diverse tasks.

Generalizability of these findings is limited by the fact that the study's design involves an in-depth analysis of particular urban settings rather than a random sampling across such environments. Nevertheless, several important propositions concerning the relationship between behavior and urban design in the settings studied do emerge from the study's findings.

(1) Effective urban design requires evaluation at a functional, in addition to an aesthetic, level.

(2) Public open space provides an important avenue for social contact in the low-income neighborhood.

(3) Much of the social function in the low-income neighborhood is

TABLE 5

PERCENT OF BEHAVIOR IN EACH OBSERVATION SITE DISTRIBUTED OVER MICRO-FEATURES OF THE ENVIRONMENT

Micro-feature	Environmental setting		
	Old neighborhood	Traditional project	Innovative project
Sidewalk	64	29	34
Building entrance	25	3	8
Grassy area	0	3	0
Playground	0	27	8
Bench	6	35	46
Other	5	3	4

played by "informal" social spaces, i.e., spaces designed for one function, which in practice support a range of social activities not anticipated by the original designer.

These propositions are consistent with, and lend empirical support to, the viewpoints concerning design and behavior which have emerged from previous speculations (Fried & Gleicher, 1970; Gans, 1962; Hartman, 1963; Jacobs, 1961) concerning low-income urban neighborhoods. Let us consider each of these issues more fully.

The pattern of bench use in the project environments reflected clearly the intimate relationship between design and function. The most used benches in both projects were those along the major entranceways to the projects, which overlooked both the streets of the old neighborhood and the entrances to many of the project buildings. This was especially interesting in the innovative project, where benches which afforded good viewing of many people engaged in daily activities were greatly preferred over the more creatively designed benches in the interior of the project. The differential use of the innovative project environment across age groups can also be explained in functional terms. The innovative project proved a remarkably successful social setting for youths, but not for adults. Adults were also less inclined than youths to use the outdoor spaces in the innovative project. While the innovative design met the recreational demands of youths, it did not provide for the many functional needs that attract adults outdoors. The old neighborhood was probably attractive to adults precisely because it met a wide range of functional needs in addition to recreation and leisure.

These findings convincingly demonstrate that outdoor public space is an important medium for social exchange in the low-income neighborhood. Over three-quarters of outdoor behavior across all environmental sites was social in nature. Of particular interest is the role played by "informal" public spaces in supporting the casual social behavior so typical of the low-income neighborhood. For example, in the old neighborhood, 90% of outdoor behavior occurred along the sidewalk, near entranceways, on stoops, and along the curb. People tended to meet one another while engaged in different though complementary activities, and used such opportunities for informal and casual social exchange. In addition, the grassy areas in the traditional project, which designers have pointed to proudly as evidence of new-found open urban space, were almost never used because they were fenced off for an aesthetic rather than a functional impact. The creativily designed adventure playground in the innovative project was also little used. In fact, most of the active recreation in both projects was ball playing. The children we observed clearly preferred open spaces for ball playing rather than more playground equipment. In the innovative project, the adventure playground equipment went almost unused, while children usurped any available space for ball playing, including the observation area around the playground, the main access to the pedestrian mall, and even the floor of the amphitheatre.

Finally, the study lends some implications concerning the design of "street furniture," such as benches. The effective design of street furniture includes not only its form but also its location relative to other street furniture and to adjacent activity patterns. Unfortunately, the benches along the entranceways of both projects, which were well situated for viewing behavior, were poorly designed as physical props or supports for socializing. Arranged in a straight row, they forced individuals to sit shoulder-to-shoulder, and inhibited rather than supported active social contact. Also, since the benches were situated in the flow of pedestrian traffic, a passerby stopping to talk to a seated person became a hindrance to the free flow of traffic. The design of stoops in the old neighborhood, in contrast, allowed face-to-face conversation, while also permitting an interested passerby to comfortably join the conversation by stepping out of the line of traffic.

In summary, it appears that the lower level of socializing in the traditional project relative to the older low-income neighborhood was due to two factors. First, the faults seems to lie more in badly designed outdoor space than in high-rise living per se. The innovatively designed project environment proved more supportive of active socializing between youths than did the environment of the old neighborhood. Second, an aesthetically designed environment without the potential to support a range of functional activities is not sufficient to attract outdoor socializing among adults. A better solution would be a project integrated with the commercial and adult recreational attractions of the old neighborhood. The ideal situation would encourage mixed functional uses—recreational, leisure, consumer, task-oriented—in order to attract individuals to use available open space. Then, innovative design features—nooks, benches, tables—might be added to facilitate and support the informal social contact likely to occur between persons who meet accidentally while pursuing diversified tasks in such multi-functional space.

REFERENCES

BROWER, S. Outdoor recreation as a function of the urban housing environment. *5th Annual Meeting of the Environmental Design Research Association,* Childhood-City Workshop, Virginia Polytechnic Institute, 1973.

FRIED, M. Grieving for a lost home. In L. J. Duhl (Ed.), *The Urban Condition: People and Policy in the Metropolis.* New York: Basic Books, 1963.

FRIED, M., & GLEICHER, P. Some sources of residential satisfaction in an urban slum. In H. M. Proshansky, W. H. Ittelson, & L. G. Rivlin (Eds.), *Environmental Psychology: Man and His Physical Setting.* New York: Holt, Rinehart & Winston, 1970.

GANS, H. J. Social and physical planning for the elimination of poverty. Paper presented at the Conference of the American Institute of Planners, Washington, D.C., 1962.

HARTMAN, C. The limitations of public housing: Relocation choices in a working-class community. *Journal of the American Institute of Planners,* 24:283-296, 1963.

HOLLINGSHEAD, A. B., & ROGLER, L. H. Attitudes toward slums and public housing in Puerto Rico. In L. J. Duhl (Ed.), *The Urban Condition: People and Policy in the Metropolis.* New York: Basic Books, 1963.

ITTELSON, W. H., RIVLIN, L. G., & PROSHANSKY, H. M. The use of behavioral maps in environmental psychology. In H. M. Proshansky, W. H. Ittelson, & L. G. Rivlin (Eds.), *Environmental Psychology: Man and His Physical Setting.* New York: Holt, Rinehart & Winston, 1970.

JACOBS, J. *The Death and Life of Great American Cities.* New York: Vintage Book, 1961.

NEWMAN, O. *Defensible Space.* New York: Collier Books, 1973.

RAINWATER, L. Fear and the house-as-haven in the lower class. In B. J. Frieden & R. Morris (Eds.), *Urban Planning and Social Policy.* New York: Basic Books, 1968.

SCHEFFÉ, H. *The Analysis of Variance.* New York: Wiley, 1959.

YANCY, W. L. Architecture, interaction and social control. *Environment and Behavior,* 3 (1):3-21, 1971.

SECTION IX: BEHAVIOR THERAPY AND THE EXTENDED SOCIETY: INDUSTRY AND COMMUNITY

23

A BEHAVIORAL ANALYSIS OF PEAKING IN RESIDENTIAL ELECTRICAL-ENERGY CONSUMERS

Robert Kohlenberg, Thomas Phillips and William Proctor

University of Washington

This study was concerned with "peaking", which is the tendency for electrical-energy users to consume at high rates for brief periods during the day. Peaking results in the inefficient use of generating facilities, which may lead to unfavorable effects on the environment, such as the construction of new energy producing facilities or the activation of older, less safe, generating units. A continuous data collection system to monitor consumption of electrical energy was installed in the homes of three volunteer families. Information, feedback, and incentives were evaluated for their effects on peak energy consumption. A combination of feedback plus incentives was most effective and reduced peaking about 50%. Removal of experimental treatments resulted in a return to pre-treatment patterns of consumption.

DESCRIPTORS: energy conservation, electrical energy conservation, peaking.

Reprinted with permission from the *Journal of Applied Behavior Analysis,* 9, 13-18, No. 1 (Spring 1976).

This research was conducted in collaboration with Seattle City Light.

The shape of the demand curve for energy over each 24-hr day for residential consumers contributes, in part, to the electrical-energy crisis. In the morning and afternoon, energy consumption peaks at more than three times the daily average (Seattle City Light, 1973). In the Seattle area, where residential consumption accounts for 40% of the total, the morning peak begins at 8:00 a.m. and ends at 1:00 p.m.; the afternoon peak occurs between 6:00 and 8:00 p.m. Although most electrical energy is consumed by industrial and commercial users, the peaking problem is most pronounced in residential consumers (Seattle City Light, 1973). When the nature of the electrical-energy supply is considered, these peaks have ramifications relevant to the energy crisis and the quality of the environment.

Electrical energy must be produced at the precise moment it is needed. It is not generated at one time and stored for later use. The supplier for such energy must therefore design and build a facility that can meet maximum demand, however short in duration that demand might be. Since there are peaks in demand, generating facilities are used at full capacity for only brief periods of time. Much of the time, some generating facilities are not used. Thus, the increased need for electrical-energy generating facilities is a function of increased demand and of the temporal patterning of that demand.

In areas where fossil-fuel energy sources are used, peaking necessitates construction of new plants and consequent environmental impact. Demand peaks also result in activation of older, less efficient, and less environmentally safe facilities. In the Seattle area, where hydroelectric energy sources are used, peaking adds to the requirement for construction and raising of dams and, at times, the activation of older fossil-fuel facilities. At present, a local controversy surrounds the utilities' plan to raise a dam and consequently flood some 8000 acres of land in the U.S. and Canada.

In response to the peaking problem, two solutions are commonly proposed. The primary approach, a technological solution, is to increase the capability to supply more power. Thus, new sources of electrical power (thermonuclear, geothermal, solar) would be developed, and, while needed research and development was going on, more of the present type of power-generating facilities would be constructed.

The second approach, a behavioral solution, is to change the consuming behavior of people such that present electrical energy sources are used more efficiently. The present study was conducted to provide information on variables influencing the consuming behavior of people so that peak demand would be decreased.

The electrical-energy consuming behavior of three families was studied over a three-month period. Twenty-four-hour chart recorders were installed in each residence to monitor total electrical energy consumed in each 15-min interval. The main variables tested were (1) information, that is, subjects were told about peaking and its relationship to the local environment, and the wattage ratings of appliances in their home; (2) feedback, a signal triggered by peaking in the household; and (3) feedback plus a monetary incentive. The effects of these variables were assessed by changes in the peak rate of energy consumption.

METHOD

Subjects

Three middle-class families, living in individual homes, had as primary wage-earners, an engineer, a lawyer, and a businessman. The primary occupation of the wives in all three families was housewife. There were two children, the oldest of which was 11 yr, in each residence. None of the residences was electrically heated, but each had an electric stove, a dryer, a dishwasher, and an electric water heater. Subjects were solicited through a notice in a local conservation club newsleteer. In addition to requesting that families volunteer to participate in an environmentally related research study on electric-energy consumption, the notice also stated that devices would be installed in their homes to record energy consumption. The notice resulted in calls to the experimenter by 12 families; all expressed an interest in participating. The criteria for selecting subjects were (1) that they lived in the local utility district, (2) had at least two children at home, and (3) did not use electrical power for home heating.

Procedure

The research spanned three-months from early January through March, divided into six consecutive two-week phases. Each phase was preceded by a visit to the home during which the experimenters gave instructions. The only other interaction between subjects and experimenters occurred when data were collected. Weekly data collection consisted of an experimenter visiting a home and removing the data recorded for the preceding week. Although the experimenters were cordial, they did not supply any information to families while collecting data. The data were automatically recorded on the device described below, and data records were not visible to the subjects.

The sequence of events was as follows:

1. Initial instructions, installation of recording device, beginning of the first two-week phase (Baseline I).

2. Information instructions, beginning of second two-week phase (Information).

3. Feedback instructions, installation of feedback device, begin third two-week phase (Feedback).

4. Baseline II instructions, removal of feedback device, begin fourth two-week phase (Baseline II).

5. Incentive instructions, re-install feedback device, begin fifth two-week phase (Incentive plus Feedback).

6. Baseline III instructions, removal of feedback device, begin final two-week phase. (Baseline III).

In some cases, up to four days elapsed between the two-week phases for which data were obtained. This was particularly true for those phases that involved installation and adjustment of apparatus. As pointed out later, only 13 days of data were obtained in a few conditions because some data were lost during the change, over from one phase to the next.

Initial Instructions

Subjects were informed that a device was to be installed to record normal power use. Subjects were also informed that the researchers would make weekly visits to the home to collect the data and check for malfunctions in the recorder. Finally, they were told that additional instructions would be given later in the experiment. An appointment calendar was given to each family with the request that they record vacations, trips, and meals not taken at home.

Information. The peaking problem and its relationship to the raising of Ross Dam, a subject of local controversy, was presented. The subjects were asked to avoid the use of too much power at any one time, and to try to reduce peaking. They were given a list of 100-W light-bulb equivalents for the power ratings of the electrical appliances they had in their home. For example, a color TV is equivalent to three 100-W light bulbs. If the experimenter was asked, subjects were told that they would be given information as to how they did after the study was completed.

Feedback. A current-sensitive relay was installed on the main service to the home. The trigger level was adjusted such that current levels exceeding 90% of the peak levels recorded in the previous two weeks would close a relay. The relay was in turn connected to a 40-W light bulb installed in the witchen or immediately outside the witchen window facing the kitchen counter and sink. The information given during the previous phase was reviewed, along with an explanation of the signal light and how it might be used as an aid to reducing peak consumption.

Baseline II

Subjects were told that the feedback device (signal light) would be disconnected, and if they were engaging in behaviors that reduced peaking, they should feel free to continue such behaviors if they so desired. It was pointed out, however, that during this phase, no particular demands or requests were being made.

Incentive and feedback. Subjects were informed that ehe feedback condition did reduce peaking behavior, but not markedly. They were asked to make special efforts to demonstrate that it is possible to reduce peaking with highly motivated families. As an additional incentive, they were given the opportunity to earn twice the amount of their power bill. Double the prorated amount of the electricity bill for the coming two-week period of time was to be rebated if they could reduce peaking 100%, compared to baseline amounts. One hundred percent of the two-week electricity bill was to be paid for a 50% reduction in peaking. Payments of 200% and 50% of the bill were to be made for 75% and 25% reductions in peaking, respectively. In addition to the monetary incentive, the feedback light was reconnected and subjects were instructed how to compute peaking reductions from the chart recorder installed in their home. They were also told to feel free to inspect the chart at any time, and the silver paper covering the chart recorder window was removed.

Baseline III

During this final phase, the feedback light was removed, subjects were told that they were no longer on the incentive system, and that they were free to engage in a pattern of power consumption comfortable for them, and that would be representative of their future habits.

Apparatus and Data Format

Recording equipment consisted of Esterline-Angus, 15-min power recorders. Each 15 min, the recording pen reset to zero. The raw data thus consisted of a long strip chart of vertical lines of varying height; the height of each line represented the relative energy consumed for that 15-min interval. In addition to the Esterline-Angus recorders, current-sensitive relays were utilized as described above.

RESULTS AND DISCUSSION

The cumulative number of energy units above the criterion for peaking for each family is given in Figure 1. The figure shows that information did not seem to affect behavior resulting in peaks in power consumption. However, it does appear that feedback, to some extent, and the incentive and feedback condition, to a larger extent, did reduce peaking in each family.

Although most of the data in Figure 1 are presented in 14-day blocks, there are three instances in which one day's data were lost. The cumulative records shown in Figure 1 for Family A, Baseline II and Baseline III, and Family B, Feedback, represent 13-day blocks. In the case of Family A, the missing data would enhance the apparent experimental effects shown in the figure. In the case of the Feedback condition for Family B, however, the missing day's data would reduce the overall level of the cumulative record for that condition, and hence reduce slightly the apparent effect shown in Figure 1.

Figure 1 reveals little carryover from an experimental condition to the following baseline period. Although the Baseline III period for each of the three families shows the smallest cumulative number of energy units consumed above peak level, note that this research spanned a period from early January through March. During these months, total power consumption in this area decreases slightly, due to an increasing number of daylight hours and a decreasing use of heating equipment for ignition or forced air.

The information condition had little effect for all three families, consistent with results reported by Herbelein (1974), who attempted to influence consumption of electrical energy by apartment dwellers. There are several interpretations of this finding. The first might be that the nature of the information intervention, which consisted of a brief meeting with the family, was not sufficient to produce changes in the basic pattern of living and lifestyle of the family. The reductions in peaking observed in the feedback and incentive-feedback conditions did require such changes. The times at which dishes were washed, showers taken, and clothes dried were said to be quite inconvenient by each of the

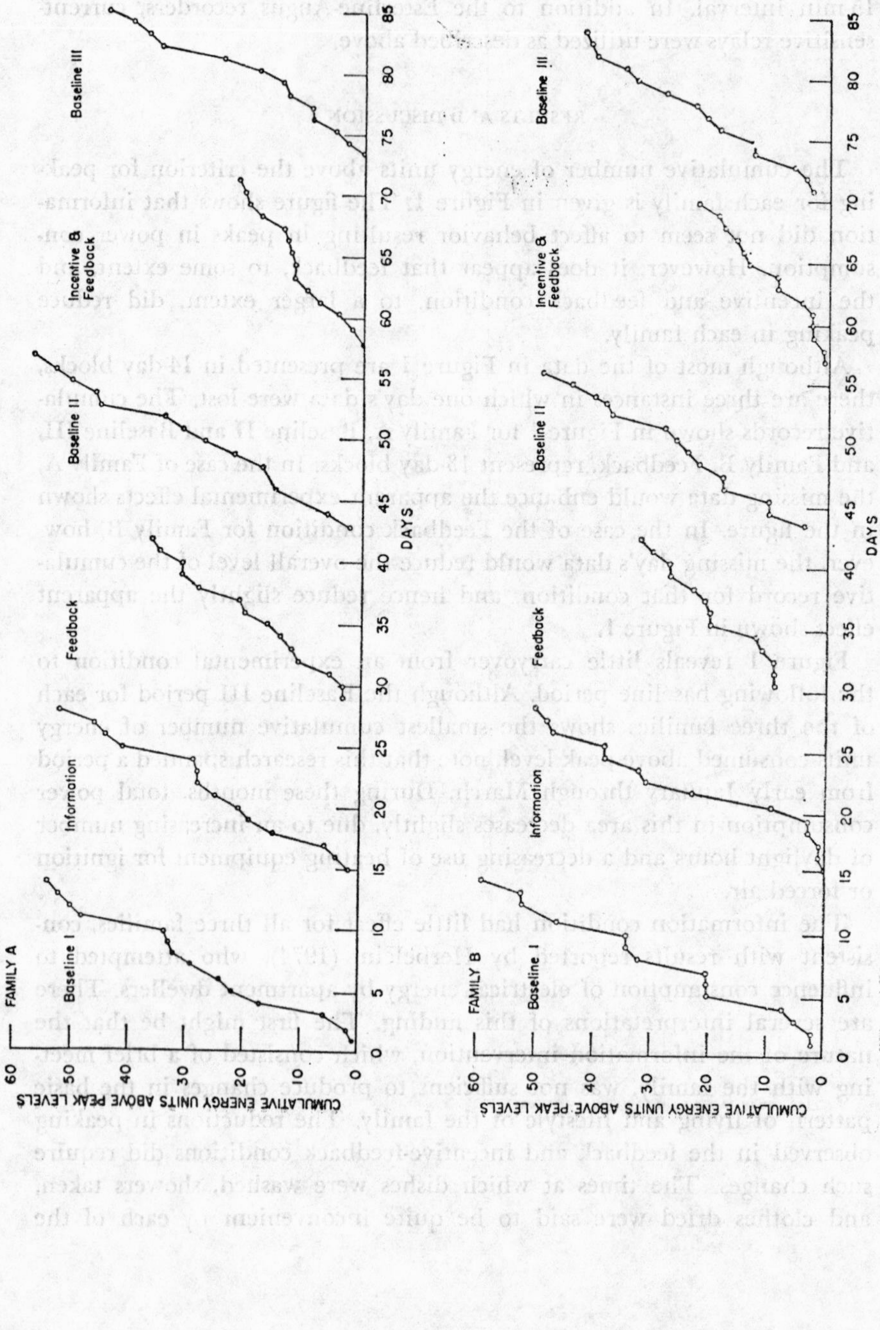

FAMILY A
Baseline I
Information
Feedback
Baseline II
Incentive & Feedback
Baseline III
DAYS
CUMULATIVE ENERGY UNITS ABOVE PEAK LEVELS
FAMILY B
Baseline I
Information
Feedback
Baseline II
Incentive & Feedback
Baseline III
DAYS
CUMULATIVE ENERGY UNITS ABOVE PEAK LEVELS

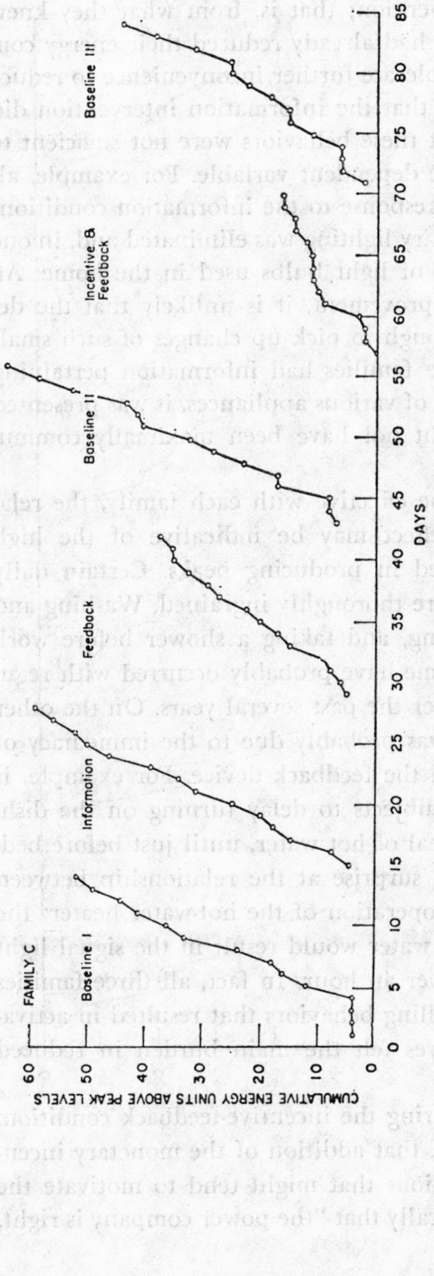

Fig. 1. Cumulative energy units above criterion peak level for each experimental condition and for each family.

families. Second, it is possible that since the present subjects were already concerned with the environment, they had made their maximal response to the information type of intervention; that is, from what they knew of the energy crisis, these families had already reduced their energy consumption and were unwilling to tolerate further inconvenience to reduce peaking. A final interpretation is that the information intervention did result in changes in behavior, but these behaviors were not sufficient to produce significant changes in the dependent variable. For example, all families reported that their main response to the information conditions was to make sure that all unnecessary lighting was eliminated and, in one case, to reduce the power ratings of light bulbs used in the home. Although such behaviors are an improvement, it is unlikely that the dependent variable was sensitive enough to pick up changes of such small magnitude. Also, even though the families had information pertaining to the relative power consumption of various appliances, it was presented in a quantitative form that might not have been maximally communicative.

Although feedback seemed to be effective with each family, the relatively small magnitude of this effect may be indicative of the high strength of the behaviors involved in producing peaks. Certain daily patterns of running a household are thoroughly ingrained. Washing and drying clothes on Monday morning, and taking a shower before work or cooking hot meals at dinner time have probably occurred with regularity for each of these families over the past several years. On the other hand, the effect that was shown was probably due to the immediacy of the information provided through the feedback device. For example, it may not have occurred to some subjects to delay turning on the dishwasher, which consumes a great deal of hot water, until just before bedtime. All three families indicated surprise at the relationship between activation of the signal light and operation of the hot-water heater; the use of moderate quantities of hot water would result in the signal light going on and remaining on for over an hour. In fact, all three families reported the most difficulty controlling behaviors that resulted in activation of the hot-water heater. Wives felt the main burden in reduced peaking.

The largest effect was shown during the incentive-feedback condition. It should be pointed out, however, that addition of the monetary incentive was confounded with instructions that might tend to motivate the subjects more. They were told basically that "the power company is right, people can't change. We will have to raise Ross Dam." During this condition, families were also given instructions in reading and interpreting the chart produced by the chart recorder. Thus, a great deal of additional information was provided, *e.g.*, a family could easily see at what hours peaks occurred and how they performed compared to the previous day. The difficulty in reducing peaking behavior was clearly illustrated in this condition. Highly motivating instructions, signal-light feedback, monetary incentive, and recorder-chart feedback reduced but did not eliminate peaking.

The generality of the present results is of course limited by the sample size and nature of the families participating. On the one hand, employing subjects already "concerned about the environment" could be interpreted as using a highly motivated group of subjects; thus, the effects observed might be the maximum effects possible with these variables. On the other hand, it can be argued that such concerned subjects have already taken steps to reduce energy consumption and that the magnitude of the effects observed here are diminished by this former effect. On the basis of the present data, one cannot determine how much each of these possibilities might have contributed to the obtained effects. However, the results do indicate that there is a limit to the inconvenience families are willing to tolerate to reduce peaking. That is, if the data obtained during Baseline III conditions are representative of the future peak energy consumption of these families, they do not appear much different from that shown before experimental interventions were introduced (*i.e.*, Baseline I).

Voltage reductions that would dim the lights, or an easily readable watt-hour meter in the home are two of the many possibilities for providing feedback devices that might influence consumption. Although little more than an educated guess, a cost-effective procedure for changing energy consumption might use TV and radio to provide immediate feedback about the consuming behavior of large groups of people. It would seem fairly simple to add this type of information to pleas for changes in energy consumption that are often heard on radio and TV. Best of all, of course, would be a study in which the media were used to provide information both with and without feedback in order to assess experimentally the effect of this variable.

Although this study indicated that it was difficult to change consuming behavior, the data did show that feedback was important in producing the behavior changes observed.

REFERENCES

HEBERLEIN, T. *Conservation Information, the Energy Crisis and Electricity Consumption in an Apartment Complex.* Unpublished manuscript. University of Wisconsin, Madison, Wisconsin, 1974.

Seattle City Light. *Report on Energy Consumption and Components of System Load.* Rate department, 1973, Seattle, Washington.

SECTION IX: BEHAVIOR THERAPY AND THE EXTENDED SOCIETY: INDUSTRY AND COMMUNITY

24

SHOPLIFTING PREVENTION: PROVIDING INFORMATION THROUGH SIGNS

M. Patrick McNees, Daniel S. Egli, Rebecca S. Marshall, John F. Schnelle, and Todd R. Risley

Luton Community Mental Health Center, Middle Tennessee State University, and the University of Kansas

Shoplifting is one of the most frequent crimes in the United States, yet there is no agreement about effective prevention procedures. Since most prevention strategies are aimed at either increasing public awareness of the severity of the consequences or increasing the threat of detection, procedures that contain these elements were evaluated. Posting signs around a department of a department store pointing out that shoplifting is a crime, etc., partially reduced shoplifting rates. When merchandise that was frequently taken was identified by signs and stars, shoplifting decreased to near zero. Publicity campaigns to inform the public of consequences for shoplifting may produce desirable results,

---

Reprinted with permission from the *Journal of Applied Behavior Analysis,* 9, 399-405, No. 4 (Winter 1976).

The authors wish to express their sincere appreciation to Paul Grimes of Harvey's Department Store and Phillip Allen of Big-K Department Store, Murfreesboro, Tennessee. Portions of the study were presented at the American Psychological Association, Chicago, 1975, and at the Association for the Advancement of Behavior Therapy, San Francisco, 1975.

but identifying likely shoplifting targets, which may increase the likelihood of detection, effectively reduces shoplifting rates.

Descriptors: shoplifting, prevention techniques, information systems, multiple baseline, community psychology, crime control, recording and measurement techniques.

Applied behavior analysts have focused on a number of community problems, including litter control (Burgess, Clark & Hendee, 1971; Chapman and Risley, 1974; Geller, Farris & Post, 1973; Kohlenberg & Phillips, 1973; Powers, Osborne & Anderson, 1973), bus ridership (Everett, Haywood & Meyers, 1974), an urban recreation center's operations (Pierce & Risley, 1974), and training a community board to solve problems (Briscoe, Hoffman & Bailey, 1975). In business-related problems, Hermann, Montes, Dominguez, Montes & Hopkins (1973) found that bonuses effectively increased the punctuality of industrial workers. Jones & Azrin (1973) focused on the problem of job finding.

However, one of the most pervasive community and business problems has been virtually ignored. Shoplifting has increased from $2.5 billion in 1969 ("Holiday Shoplifting Heads for a Record," 1973) to an estimated $4.8 billion or approximately $13 million per day in 1974 ("To Catch a Thief," 1974). It has been said that if all incidents of shoplifting were reported, it would be the largest single crime in the United States (Weinstein, 1974). Even though shoplifting is the major profit-killer in retail stores (Humphries, 1975), every citizen in the community also suffers a loss. In 1973 it was estimated that each American family pays $150 per year in hidden costs due to shoplifting ("Christmas is Coming," 1973).

While no empirically documented shoplifting-prevention procedures are apparent in the literature, at least two different methods have been used to control stealing. Azrin & Wesolowski (1974) reduced stealing by retarded persons with an over-correction procedure. Switzer, Real, & Bailey (in press) found that stealing in a second-grade classroom was reduced when a group contingency was applied. For an over-correction procedure to be an effective shoplifting prevention strategy, it would seem that shoplifters would have to be consistently detected. However, it is estimated that an extremely small number of individuals who take merchandise are detected. Additionally, the application of a direct group consequence is probably not feasible in normal business.

The most common current approaches to the shoplifting problem are usually aimed at either increasing the public's awareness of the consequences of shoplifting, or increasing the threat of detecting shoplifters.

Campaigns designed to increase public awareness take a variety of forms, ranging from city-wide campaigns, such as Philadelphia's STEM (Shoplifters Take Everybody's Money) campaign (Philadelphia's Way of Stopping the Shoplifter," 1972), to educational programs in schools, to posters in stores. Commonly used procedures to increase the likelihood of detection range from the use of store detectives to electronic devices that signal when merchandise has passed through the door without being deactivated by the cashier.

Although many procedures have been employed to prevent shoplifting, all have been limited by inadequate measurement systems, thus making it impossible to determine the effectiveness of the procedures (Curtis, 1969; "Holiday Shoplifting Heads for a Record," 1973). Infrequent stock inventories appear to be one reason for the difficulty in determining the effectiveness of prevention strategies. Changes in apprehension rates, another "measure" of shoplifting, have not been demonstrated to parallel changes in shoplifting rate.

Since most current shoplifting-prevention strategies are designed to increase either public awareness or the threat of detection, procedures containing these elements were evaluated. The first study evaluated the effects of general antishoplifting signs (stating that shoplifting is a crime and that it increases the cost of merchandise); the second study investigated the effect of signs and symbols that specifically identified merchandise found to be frequently missing. Thus, the two studies represent evaluations of not only a procedure that defines some of the consequences of shoplifting, but also a procedure that increases the threat of being detected.

STUDY I

METHOD

Setting

The study was conducted in a department store in Murfreesboro, Tennessee (population 25,000). The manager of the department store indicated that he had a shoplifting problem, particularly in the young women's clothing department. This department was shielded from view from the remaining portion of the store except for two entrances. The department contained three dressing rooms, and was located some 18 m from the nearest cash register. Typically, except during busy periods, sales personnel were not assigned specifically to this area. In all cases, merchandise was displayed on hanging racks about 1.8 m long and at eye, chest, and waist levels. Throughout the study, a uniformed security guard moved about the store; no other shoplifting-prevention procedures were in use.

Measurement System

Before the study commenced, approximately 25 items from each type of merchandise in the department were randomly selected as "key" items. A yellow tag was then stapled to the back of the portion of the price tag that the cashier removed and kept for restocking purposes. A code letter was marked on each yellow tag to identify the type of merchandise (i.e., "B" indicated jeans). Cashiers were instructed to remove the yellow tag when the restocking tag was removed and place it in a box below the cash register.

To determine the number of missing items, an observer made inventory checks in the department each morning before the store opened. All tagged merchandise was counted and recorded according to the code letters. The manager of the store then supplied the observer with the tags from merchandise that had been sold. Thus, to calculate the number of missing items in each category, the number of items counted in stock for that category was added to the number sold for the category and this sum was subtracted from the number of originally tagged items. For example, suppose 10 pairs of jeans were coded "B" on Day 1. On Day 2, the observer would count the number of coded jeans remaining in stock, say seven. Then the observer would count the number of "B" tags that had been removed from merchandise that had been sold; for example, two. Thus, the number of missing items would be $10 - (7 + 2) = 1$.

Each day, the observer tagged new items of each type of merchandise to replace those items that had been sold or taken. In this way, the total number of items tagged each day for each type of merchandise remained constant.

The sampling procedure allowed a quick determination of the types of merchandise that were frequently missing; in this department, pants and youth tops were frequently missing. These items were thus selected as dependent measures for this investigation. The cost of the target merchandise ranged from $3.98 (one type of top) to $16.95 (a two-piece top combination). No systematic price reduction occurred for the target merchandise during the study.

The same basic procedure used to identify the merchandise that was frequently missing was used in the formal investigation. Before baseline, all tags were removed from the merchandise, then 100 of the most frequently taken tops and 100 pants were randomly selected, tagged, and coded. This represented approximately 10% of all pants and tops in the department. The recordings were done as described previously.

On 76% of the days, a second recorder made independent counts with the primary observer. "First-count" reliability was calculated by dividing the higher of the two totals into the lower for each category. Overall reliability averaged over 0.99.

When both observers had finished the count, the primary observer compared the two sets of records. If there was not total agreement, without giving specific feedback, the primary observer instructed the secondary observer to recount the merchandise. The primary observer also recounted the same merchandise. This procedure was followed until total agreement was reached. Total agreement data are presented in this study.

To reduce the probability of overlooking tags in the cashier's box, an individual who sorted the tags for restocking purposes later in the day put the yellow tags aside and returned them to the observer the following morning. On the two occasions that tags were overlooked, the data were corrected for the error. To ensure that the cashiers were taking the yellow tag from purchased merchandise, individuals who were not known to be associated with the project "bought" coded merchandise and took it through the checkout procedure. On the three occasions per experimental phase that the checks were made, the cashier always removed the coded tag.

To deal with the problem of merchandise being taken from the department and placed in other parts of the store by customers or store personnel, the employees were asked to remove any yellow tags from stock that they were moving to other parts of the store. Similarly, employees were asked to remove tags from any coded items that were seen outside the target department and to return them to a special box, which was checked daily by the observer.

Baseline I

The number of items sold and missing were measured for 26 days. Due to different (and shorter) store hours, no observations were made on Sunday. Therefore, Saturday, and Sunday appear as one data point, which results in 23 instead of 26 baseline data points. During this period, the store continued the same activities as before measurement was begun.

Departmental Antishoplifting Signs

Before opening for business on observation day 24, five antishoplifting signs containing four messages were placed in the department. The signs were 30 by 47 cm and had 2.5-cm high letters. The signs included the points: (1) Shoplifting is stealing; (2) Shoplifting is a crime; (3) Shoplifting is not uplifting; (4) Shoplifting is stealing; and (5) Shoplifting helps inflation. The signs remained in the department for 20 days (17 observation days).

Baseline II

During this phase, the signs were taken down for five observation days.

RESULTS

Placing of antishoplifting signs appeared to reduce, but not eliminate shoplifting. Figure 1 shows the cumulative shoplifting and sales rates before the signs were placed in the department, while the signs were there, and after the signs were removed.

The mean number of items missing per day during Baseline I is 1.30, and sales averaged 1.04. During the intervention, the number of missing items per day fell to 0.88; sales remained at approximately the same level (1.00). When the signs were removed, the number of missing items rose to 1.4 per day and sales to 2.0 per day.

Thus, it appears that the placement of antishoplifting signs in the department may have produced a decrease in shoplifting without affecting sales rates. If similar changes were present with a larger sample the procedure would probably be recommended as being both inexpensive and useful.

STUDY II

METHOD

Setting

The setting was identical to that in Study I. No new shoplifting-prevention procedure was begun during this investigation.

Measurement-System

The data-recording procedure employed in this study was similar to that for Study I. However, the following changes were made: (a) Colored

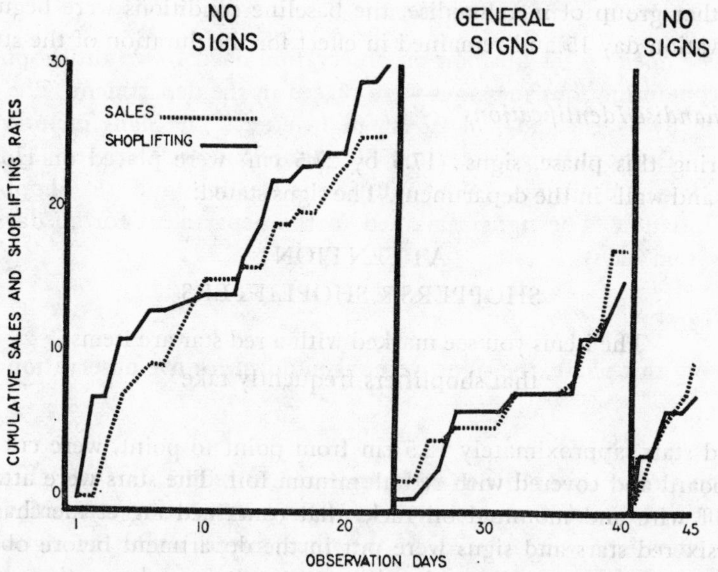

Fig. 1. Cumulative rates of sales (broken line) and shoplifting (solid line) before, during, and after general antishoplifting signs were placed in the department.

instead of letter-coded tags were used to distinguish types of merchandise; (b) small pieces of yellow tape were wrapped around the top of clothes hangers to allow easier tracking of target merchandise (the cashier removed the tape when a target item was sold); (c) three groups of merchandise were targeted instead of two (the same two groups as in Study I, with the addition of 100 items that had not been identified as frequently stolen during the original sampling procedure). Reliability was recorded for over 76% of the days in a fashion identical to that in Study I.

Baseline

The number of items sold and missing each day (Saturday and Sunday were counted as one day) were measured for each of three groups of merchandise: one group of young ladies' tops, one group of young ladies' pants, and one group that consisted of a random selection of other merchandise in the same department. The baseline condition lasted for 33 observation days for the pants and 47 observation days for the tops, thus constituting a multiple baseline across two groups of merchandise. For the other group of merchandise, the baseline conditions were begun on observation day 15 and remained in effect for the duration of the study.

Merchandise Identifications

During this phase, signs (17.5 by 27.5 cm) were placed on clothing racks and walls in the department. The signs stated:

ATTENTION

SHOPPERS & SHOPLIFTERS

The items you see marked with a red star are items
that shoplifters frequently take

Red stars, approximately 12.5 cm from point to point, were cut from cardboard and covered with red aluminum foil. The stars were attached to stiff wire and mounted on racks that contained target merchandise. The six red stars and signs were put in the department before observation day 34 and were directed only at pants. Before observation day 48, six more stars were added in the department to designate frequently taken tops. This condition remained in effect for the duration of the study.

RESULTS

Figure 2 reflects the cumulative rates of missing merchandise and sales before the merchandise was publicly identified as being frequently taken, and after signs and stars were used to identify each type of merchandise.

There was a dramatic reduction in missing target merchandise when the merchandise was specified as being frequently taken by shoplifters (baseline $x = 0.66$ versus intervention mean $= 0.06$ tops taken per day; and baseline $x = 0.50$ versus intervention $x = 0.03$ pants taken per day). There was no systematic change in sales after identifying the merchandise.

Cumulative shoplifting rates for comparison merchandise are presented in Figure 3. Points at which pants and tops were publicly identified as being frequently taken are denoted by arrows. There appears to be no change in shoplifting rates for the comparison merchandise, thus reducing the probability that shoplifters merely switched from the target merchandise to nontargeted merchandise.

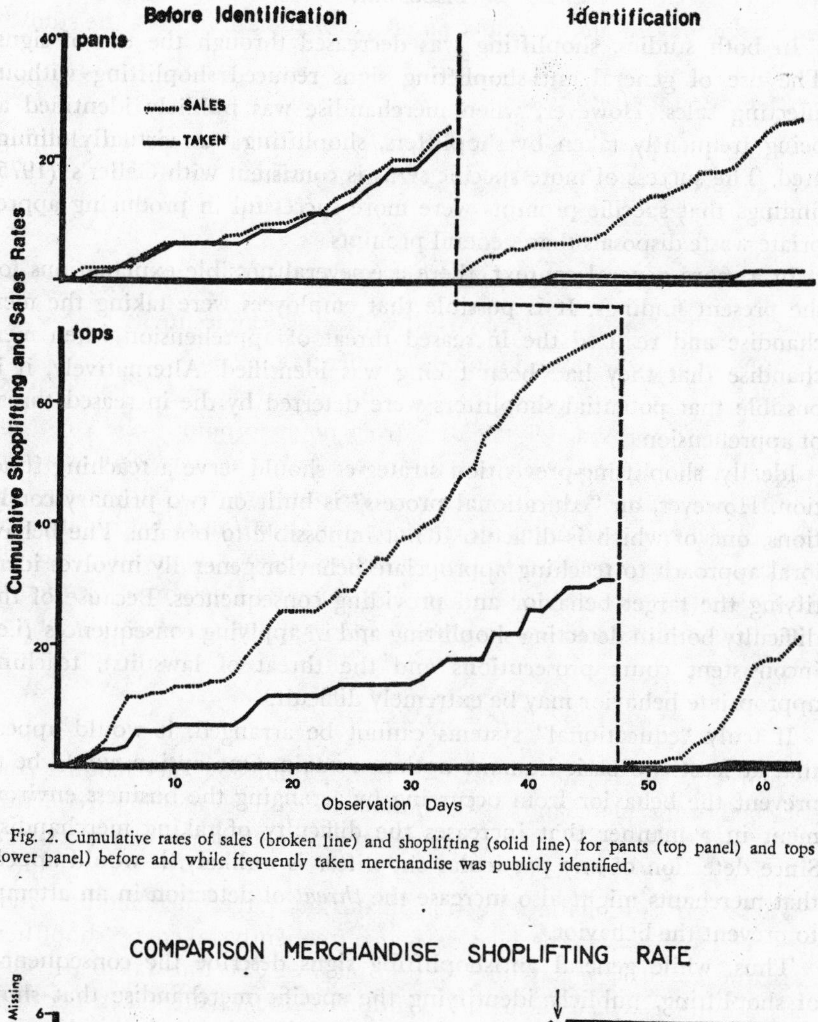

Fig. 2. Cumulative rates of sales (broken line) and shoplifting (solid line) for pants (top panel) and tops (lower panel) before and while frequently taken merchandise was publicly identified.

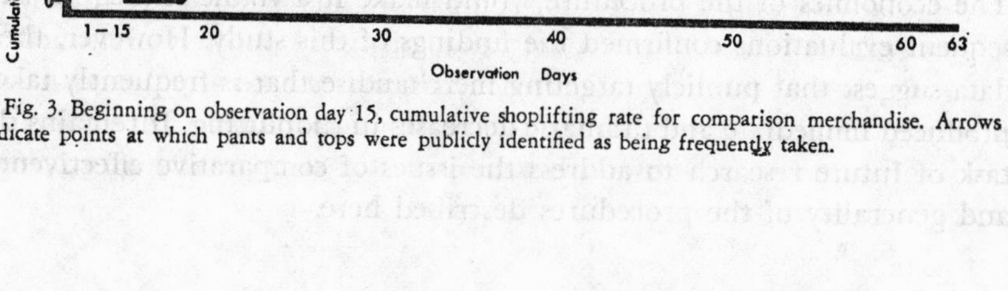

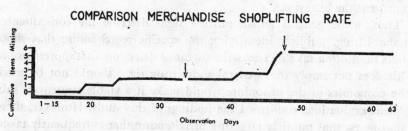

Fig. 3. Beginning on observation day 15, cumulative shoplifting rate for comparison merchandise. Arrows indicate points at which pants and tops were publicly identified as being frequently taken.

DISCUSSION

In both studies, shoplifting was decreased through the use of signs. The use of general anti-shoplifting signs reduced shoplifting without affecting sales. However, when merchandise was publicly identified as being frequently taken by shoplifters, shoplifting was virtually eliminated. The success of more specific signs is consistent with Geller's (1975) findings that specific prompts were more successful in producing appropriate waste disposals than general prompts.

In a more general context, there are several possible explanations for the present findings. It is possible that employees were taking the merchandise and realized the increased threat of apprehension when merchandise that they had been taking was identified. Alternatively, it is possible that potential shoplifters were deterred by the increased threat of apprehension.

Ideally, shoplifting-prevention strategies should serve a teaching function. However, an "educational process" is built on two primary conditions, one of which is difficult, if not impossible to obtain. The behavioral approach to teaching appropriate behavior generally involves identifying the target behavior and providing consequences. Because of the difficulty both in detecting shoplifting and in applying consequences (i.e., inconsistent court prosecutions and the threat of lawsuits), teaching appropriate behavior may be extremely difficult.

If truly "educational" systems cannot be arranged, it would appear that at least two basic humane options remain. One option would be to prevent the behavior from occurring by arranging the business environment in a manner that increases the difficulty of taking merchandise. Since detection of any particular shoplifter is unlikely, it would appear that merchants might also increase the *threat* of detection in an attempt to prevent the behavior.

Thus, while general antishoplifting signs describe the consequences of shoplifting, publicly identifying the specific merchandise that shoplifters most often take increases the threat of detection and apprehension. This does not imply that general shoplifting signs should not be used. The economics of the procedure would make it a viable strategy if subsequent evaluations confirmed the findings of this study. However, these data suggest that publicly targeting merchandise that is frequently taken produced immediate and dramatic decreases in shoplifting. It remains the task of future research to address the issues of comparative effectiveness and generality of the procedures described here.

REFERENCES

AZRIN, N. H., & WESLOWSKI, M. D. Theft reversal: An overcorrection procedure for eliminating stealing by retarded persons. *Journal of Applied Behavior Analysis,* 7:577-581, 1974.

BRISCOE, R. V., HOFFMAN, O. B., & BAILEY, J. S. Behavioral community psychology: Training a community board to problem solve. *Journal of Applied Behavior Analysis,* 8:157-168, 1975.

BURGESS, R. L., CLARK, R. N., & HENDEE, J. C. An experimental analysis of anti-litter procedures. *Journal of Applied Behavior Analysis,* 4:71-75, 1971.

To catch a thief. *Newsweek,* Sept. 23, 1974, pp. 79-80.

CHAPMAN, C., & RISLEY, T. R. Anti-litter procedures in an urban high-density area. *Journal of Applied Behavior Analysis,* 7:377-383, 1974.

Christmas is coming. *Nation,* 1973, p. 614.

CURTIS, B. Security: a challenge to shoplifters. *Publishers Weekly,* 169:40-42, 1969.

EVERETT, P. B., HAYWOOD, S. C., & MEYERS, A. W. The effects of a token reinforcement procedure on bus ridership. *Journal of Applied Behavior Analysis,* 7:1-9, 1974.

GELLER, E. S. Increasing desired waste disposals with instructions. *Man-Environment Systems,* 5:1-4, 1975.

GELLER, E. S., FARRIS, J. C., & POST, D. S. Prompting a consumer behavior for pollution control. *Journal of Applied Behavior Analysis,* 6:367-376, 1973.

HERMANN, J., MONTES, A. I., DOMINGUEZ, B., MONTES, F., & HOPKINS, B. L. Effects of bonuses for punctuality on tardiness of industrial workers. *Journal of Applied Behavior Analysis,* 6:563-570, 1973.

Holiday shoplifting heads for a record. *U.S. News and World Report,* December 10, 1973, p. 47.

HUMPHRIES, R. J. *Stealing is Big Business.* Hollywood, Florida: Distribution Advisors International, 1975.

JONES, R. J., & AZRIN, N. H. An experimental application of a social reinforcement approach to the problem of job-finding. *Journal of Applied Behavior Analysis,* 6: 345-353, 1973.

KOHLENBERG, R. & PHILLIPS, T. Reinforcement and the rate of litter depositing. *Journal of Applied Behavior Analysis,* 6:391-396, 1973.

Philadelphia's way of stopping the shoplifter. *Business Week,* May 6, 1972, pp. 57-59.

PIERCE, C., & RISLEY, T. R. Recreation as a reinforcer: Increasing membership and decreasing disruptions in an urban recreation center. *Journal of Applied Behavior Analysis,* 7:403-411, 1974.

POWERS, R. B., OSBORNE, J. G., & ANDERSON, E. G. Positive reinforcement of litter removal in the natural environment. *Journal of Applied Behavior Analysis,* 6:579-586, 1973.

SWITZER, E. B., REAL, T. E., & BAILEY, J. S. The reduction of stealing behavior in second graders using a group contingency. *Journal of Applied Behavior Analysis* (in press).

WEINSTEIN, G. W. The truth about teenage shoplifting. *Parents Magazine,* April, 1974, pp. 42-43, 60-61.

Section X

THERAPEUTIC STRATEGIES, CASE STUDIES AND CLINICAL EXTENSIONS

Commentary

We begin this Section with a discussion of therapeutic strategies and the increasing acceptance of self-help programs. This is followed by a selective review of progress in seven clinical areas, including the burgeoning new field of behavioral medicine.

NON-PRESCRIPTION BEHAVIOR THERAPY

Throughout this Series, we have maintained the position that behavior therapy is an approach rather than a series of techniques. The behavior therapist must be both a sensitive clinician and an expert in behavioral science. This contrasts sharply with the position of such individuals as London (1972) for whom behavior therapists are little more than skilled technicians. It is in the light of these two contrasting points of view that we now consider the rise of what Rosen (1976a) refers to as "non-prescription" behavior therapies.

Bibliotherapy, in the sense of the use of any literary work in the treatment of physical or emotional problems, has long been with us. The advent of self-help treatment programs which offer specific sets of therapeutic procedures is a newer but rapidly growing innovation. Glasgow and Rosen (in press) divide these programs into three categories: self-administered—in which a written program constitutes the sole basis of treatment, with clients administering material to themselves with no therapist contact whatsoever; minimal contact—in which there is some contact with the therapist, but the clients relies primarily on a written program; therapist-administered programs—in which the clients have regular meetings with the therapist to clarify or elaborate the information presented in the self-help manual. To this we would add another dimension which cuts across all three categories, namely the nature of the pathology involved. For example, the tolerance limits for evaluating a self-help program for alcoholism or pedophilia must surely be different to those for a program geared towards the instigation of general well-being or the reduction of interpersonal feelings of minor inadequacy.

In principle, effective self-help programs could be of inestimable value. Treatment would become available to more people and at a minimal cost, allowing professionals to focus on individuals for whom such programs are insufficient. If Valins and Nisbet's (1972) attribution theory model of emotional disorders is correct, self-attributed behavior change has more chances of being maintained than behavior change initiated from without. Recent research suggests that self-determined behavior change requirements are more effective in eliciting behavior than requirements imposed by an external agent (Bandura, 1977a; Brownell, Colleti, Ersner-Hershfield, Hershfield & Wilson, 1977). While it is not true that all individuals fare better under self-directed programs than external ministrations—the precise parameters involved require delineation—it would seem that self-administered behavioral programs are likely to be more acceptable to the public.

In their comprehensive review of some 150 self-help procedures, Glasgow and Rosen (in press) conclude that the great majority lack any meaningful validation. Studies such as that of Rosen, Glasgow and Barrera, reprinted in Section II, are rare. Even the better self-help programs fail to present adequate validating data, the 1976 revision by Wenrich, Dawley, and General of an earlier manual offering step-by-step instructions for dealing with learned fears or phobias through systematic desensitization with minimal or no therapist intervention being a case in point.

Marshall, Presse and Andrews (1976) report a controlled evaluation of their self-administered desensitization manual for public speaking anxiety (Marshall & Andrews, 1972). The use of the manual under both self-administered and minimal contact conditions was compared with therapist-directed desensitization and various control groups. While all treatment groups self-reported greater reduction in anxiety than the various controls, none of the treatment procedures had any significant effect on behaviorally manifest anxiety during a public speaking session.

In what is probably the only tested fear-reduction program which does not rely on desensitization, Mathews, Teasdale, Munby, Johnston and Shaw (in press) report upon a manual for the treatment of agoraphobia.

Techniques involved include *in vivo* practice, recommended tranquilizers and spouse participation. The results of an intensive study of 12 married agoraphobic women are most encouraging.

The weight-reduction literature—a topic discussed more extensively in Section VI—is more encouraging. Despite the relatively unimpressive long-term results for most weight reduction programs, self-help weight control programs appear to offer promise, especially when some minimal professional contact in maintained (see Stunkard & Mahoney, 1976). This success may be due, in part, to the variety of procedures comprising the typical self-program, including nutritional guidance.

Hagen (1974) was the first to report any evaluation of a self-administered weight-reduction program. The value of this study, which yielded generally favorable results, is limited by his choice of subjects, highly motivated female undergraduates. This makes generalization to other client-types unwarranted. Fernan (see Stunkard & Mahoney, 1976) also evaluated this manual, again with encouraging findings. A manual developed by Hanson has recently been evaluated by Hanson, Borden, Hall, and Hall (1976) with generally favorable results. At the end of a 10-week treatment program, minimal contact and therapist directed groups were superior to the various placebo controls. Although between-group differences were not statistically significant at the one-year follow-up, the minimal contact condition had led to the greatest weight reduction. Barrios and Christensen (in press) obtained strikingly similar findings.

Perhaps the most extensive research into the use of self-help manuals for obese individuals has been carried out by Bellack and his associates (see Bellack, 1976; Bellack, Glanz & Simon, in press; Polly, Turner & Sherman, 1976; Schwartz, 1976). The general conclusion from these studies seems to be that minimal contact or therapist-administered conditions are much more effective than entirely self-administered programs —a finding which is not surprising.

Recent years have seen an emphasis on self-help treatment programs for sexual dysfunction. Programs have been developed for the treatment of female orgasmic dysfunction (Heiman, LoPiccolo & LoPiccolo, 1976), general sexual dysfunction (Raley, 1976) and premature ejaculation (Lowe & Mikulas, 1975; Zeiss, in press). With the possible exception of programs for premature ejaculation, current self-help sex therapies do not seem to have been evaluated in any systematic fashion.

It is unfortunate that self-help sex therapy books have not been adequately assessed since this is an area where the potential for harm is great. Individuals with serious disorders requiring skilled intervention could be misled into the belief that such a manual is all that is needed. And for some individuals, the advice offered could be traumatic. For example, Barbach (1975) and Heiman, LoPiccolo and LoPiccolo (1976) instruct women to masturbate while being viewed by a partner, to use vibrators for self-stimulation and to role play orgasm (see Commentary, Section VII).

It is not as if leaders in the field are not aware of the limitations of their programs. For example, Mahoney and Mahoney (1976b) state: "We remain a long way from any semblance of justification of complacency in weight regulation; significant poundage losses are still in the minority and long-term maintenance has remained unexamined" (p. 30). Yet, in the same year these very same authors published a book entitled *Permanent Weight Control: A Total Solution for the Dieter's Dilemma* (Mahoney & Mahoney, 1976a).

Rosen (1976a) highlights the clinical implications of non-prescription treatments and the need for validation. Adequately developed self-administered programs should serve as a minimum standard against which professional practice could be assessed. Programs administered by private therapists should be at least as effective as empirically validated self-administered treatment. Otherwise, neither the additional costs nor the clinician's time are justified. What then, asks Rosen, are the responsibilities of a clinician once adequate self-help programs exist? Should therapists only employ techniques that have been demonstrated to be more effective for particular behavior problems than readily available non-prescription programs? Or should therapists be free to employ whatever techniques are deemed appropriate? And finally, if therapists can give treatments without restraint, should they be expected to inform their clients of evidence with respect to alternative treatment possibilities?

Rosen's putative solution for his dilemma is to establish a committee within the American Psychological Association (it could just as well be the American Psychiatric Association) to begin a dialogue on strategies and procedures for encouraging and perhaps even monitoring the adequate development of self-help programs. Goldiamond (1976b) takes strong issues with this unfortunate singling out of behavioral treatments for professional overseeing, suggesting that some problems are best left to the independent judgment of the public. While sympathizing with Goldiamond's objections, Rosen (1977) reaffirms the need for at least some informed consideration of these issues under the aegis of some appropriate professional organization. We concur. As Brownell, Heckerman and Westlake (1976) suggest, it may be healthier to have no weight reduction program than one which obtains only short-term effects. And if mental health professionals fail to recognize the issues involved, it seems difficult to see how the public at large can be expected to do so, let alone make the informed judgments that Goldiamond expects of them.

As noted, the tolerance limits may well be deliberately adjusted according to the nature of the program. For example, one of us (Franks, 1977) had recently to review Miller and Muñoz' (1976) somewhat ambitiously titled book *How to Control Your Drinking*. As self-help books go, this is a clear and well-written presentation of more or less established behavioral techniques in a form that can be readily assimilated by the average layperson. At the same time, it is sufficiently comprehensive to provide a precise guide for the beginning professional. Unfortunately, it is just this combination of characteristics which could make this book a potential hazard for the less than wary reader. Whether the goal be abstinence or controlled drinking, do-it-yourself programs for problem drinkers must be critically evaluated *prior* to public dissemination. What is not warranted at this stage, in our opinion, is the public launching of a self-help manual with the deceptive title *How to Control Your Drinking*. Data are one hallmark of good behavior therapy and data are required before the appearance of a book of this nature on the open market (see Commentary, Section IV). This is especially so when the goal is controlled drinking, a subject of considerable complexity and controversy. Had this been a self-help manual in some more innocuous (and less clinical) area such as the promotion of general well-being, then we might not have as much concern over its premature appearance.

Self-help manuals are proliferating and here to stay, as witnessed by the number of such publications which come across our editorial desk. We are apparently not the only ones who feel concerned by the appearance of these books and the inconsistent nature of the reviews they receive. Rosen (in press) addresses himself to the review of such manuals in the pages of *Behavior Therapy*. While recognizing the possibility of debate with respect to the development and control of these non-prescription behavior therapies, there is little doubt that we all agree upon one point—that professional evaluation of the clinical efficacy of do-it-yourself books must be based on data rather than on opinion or heresay. Unfortunately, as Rosen points out, most self-help book reviews in *Behavior Therapy* are not data-based. Thus, an assertion training book is said to be "one of the better ones in a soggy field" (Sufrin, 1977) and a popular weight-loss program is praised as "the best book yet available for the obese person who wishes to try to lose weight without professional help" (Stunkard, 1977). Neither of these books has been systematically compared with their competitors. Subjective comments about readability, content and literary style need to be separated from statements about validity.

MULTIMODAL APPROACHES

Techniques in themselves are far from new and it is a relatively easy task to devise an indefinite number of techniques at the notional level. It is less easy to validate them. Consider, for example, the technique of thought stopping. Thought stopping ("the art of controlling one's thoughts") was first reported by Lewis in 1875, and rediscovered by Bain in 1928 (see Rosen & Ornstein, 1976). The technique is widely advocated as part of the behavior therapist's armamentarium, but there are few data pertaining to its validity. Until recently (Olin, 1976), even less appeared in the literature concerning the possible clinical dangers of the technique, let alone its validity. Yet, thought stopping continues to be advocated as a method of choice in many instances. It is important both to avoid the Scylla of arid, mechanistic and impersonal stimulus response intervention and the Charybdis of failure to be answerable to the data, of being less than willing to give up entirely or in part any suggestion that is found wanting in the light of controlled research.

Of the new books which have appeared this year purporting to avoid both of these potential disaster areas, the two most important are probably those of Goldfried and Davison (1976), entitled *Clinical Behavior Therapy*, and Lazarus and his associates (1976), entitled *Multimodal Behavior Therapy*. By implication, the title of the first book carries with it the message that this is neither just another training manual explicating the well known technology of behavior therapy nor one more tiresome voice in what some consider to be the behavioral wilderness crying out for a touch of humanity. Rather, it is a positive statement about what the authors believe behavior therapy to be all about, the calculated integration of man and methodology. The second book is the latest venture of an experienced clinician whose influence upon the field is profound. Multimodal behavior therapy has been the subject of many a discussion throughout this series, including the present volume. Taken together, the BASIC ID and the multimodal approach constitute one of the most comprehensive non-psychodynamic systems of assessment and therapy so far available (Franks, 1976).

Whether this system does or does not fall under the rubric of "behavior therapy" is probably far less important than its submission to rigorous, documented and controlled investigation at every phase. There are many deficiencies at the present time. For example, it is not always clear into which modality any particular treatment technique falls. Furthermore, if a system is to be viewed as behavioral—interpreting this term in the broadest possible sense—both assessment and outcome claims must be directly referrable to events which are observable, verifiable and empirically validated. By these criteria, despite its promise, much of multimodal therapy must be credited with the old Scottish version of not proven.

In his review of this book, Beck (1977) delineates a number of assumptions which could profitably be subject to further discussion and exploration. For example, it cannot be assumed that the categories of the BASIC ID are independent and of equal significance. We also note that journal articles which extoll the application of multimodal therapy need to be supplemented by substantive data *before* rather than after publication. The facile phrase "empirical research seems indicated to test the efficacy of the multimodal behavioral approach formally" (Popler, 1977) at the end of an anecdotal report can no longer be used as an excuse for postponing controlled investigation.

MARITAL BEHAVIOR THERAPY

The term marital behavior therapy (MBT), a topic already discussed in our Commentary to Section VII, is used in diverse ways: to refer sometimes to behavioral techniques with one partner of a dyad, sometimes to systematic training programs based on the reciprocity hypothesis; sometimes to social exchange theory; sometimes to the coercion hypothesis; and sometimes to mutual contracting strategies involving spouses and other individuals. Many of the concepts and even the strategies deployed predate the recent history of MBT. For example, MBT cannot even claim exclusive rights to contracting. A decade ago, two systems analysts wrote lucidly about reciprocity as the key to marital success, discussing "quid pro quo" contracts and how to go about implementing them (Lederer & Jackson, 1968). And even neo-Freudians such as Sager, Kaplan, Gundlach, Kremer, Lenz and Royce (1971) discuss marital discord as "the failure of one or the other spouse to fulfill these unconscious contractual expectations."

While much sound advice is offered, this advice is all too often based on clinical experience—not always a bad thing in itself—rather than data. For example, Ellis (1976) endorses Mace's (1976) recommendations for dissipating anger in marriage. A rational emotive theory of anger is used to derive a number of clinically, if not empirically, validated cognitive behavioral methods for minimizing anger between marital partners. So far so good—but where are the data? In similar vein, Martin (1976) points to the disadvantages of quid pro quo negotiation in behavior therapy but, again, with no data to bolster his argument. A list of reasons why mates would not be willing to engage in some form of rational negotiation is not sufficient in itself. Questions such as which therapeutic components are responsible for change, what selection criteria should be used, and what the psychological and social processes are that underlie change have received little serious attention (cf. Mayadas & Duehn, 1977; Wright & Fitchen, 1976).

Clinicians tend to fall into two categories in this respect: those whose primary goals are to change overt behavior and those whose main objectives are to effect changes in cognitive dimensions (Glick & Gross, 1975). Personal predilection rather than the problem area itself often decides the sort of research that is to be investigated.

The behavior exchange model is supposed to be specific, amenable to experimental manipulation and to offer considerable face validity (Saxon, 1976). But once again, an ounce of empirical investigation is worth a pound of fiat. For example, Gottman, Notarius, Markman, Bank, Yoppi, and Rubin (1976) compared two hypotheses about conflict resolution in distressed and nondistressed marriages. According to the behavior exchange hypothesis, nondistressed couples are more likely to produce observer-coded positive behavior than couples who are under stress (confirmed to some extent by Birchler, Weiss, and Vincent, 1975). According to the second hypothesis, there is a greater reciprocity of positive exchange in non-distressed than in distressed marriages (Azrin, Naster & Jones, 1973; Weiss, Hops & Patterson, 1973).

To evaluate these two hypotheses, Gottman et al. developed an innovative "talk table" device, in which only one person could speak at a time. After speaking, the speaker codes the "intended impact" of his or her message. Before speaking, the listener codes the "actual" impact of the message. This relatively inexpensive and simple way of studying behavior exchange in marriage seems to elicit different patterns of exchange in different kinds of couples. Its elegant simplicity lends itself to objective investigation at least as readily as other procedures requiring elaborate coding strategies.

In a thoughtful article appropriately subtitled "Has practice tuned out theory?" Glisson (1976) argues for two major points: that deficiencies exist in the theoretical frameworks upon which strategies of marital behavior counseling are predicated; and that sufficient empirical support does not exist to validate these techniques and hence the underlying theory (see also our Commentary to Section VII).

The concept of reinforcement, focal to much of MBT, is open to serious debate. Studies by Premack (e.g. 1971) are typically cited in support of the notion that, at least for the short-term, predictions regarding reinforcement can be made. In his penetrating appraisal of the clinical applications of the Premack principle, Danaher (1974) points out that, while the principle provides a method of empirical prediction of reinforcements, certain constraints must be adhered to in measuring possibilities and responses. One requirement is that the assessment be limited to "intrinsically maintained responses in the free-operant environment." Other constraints pertain to the use of average probability data and the fact that the stimuli must be self-administered by the subjects. Premack's experiments most commonly involve laboratory animals and self-administered primary reinforcers. More complex interactions of the marital dyad involve the use of secondary reinforcers administered by the spouse.

The emphasis on treatment strategy is at the expense of theory testing and development. And even as far as treatment is concerned, the pertinent parameters of the various techniques have not as yet been adequately delineated. There is a need for multiple baseline designs, in which different behaviors and different components of the treatment package are systematically explored, with larger samples and more replication. And, few data exist with respect to the spontaneous remission rates of recovery in distressed marital relationships (Glisson, 1976; Gurman, 1973).

The first paper in this Section, by Scheiderer and Bernstein, outlines a useful strategy for those situations in which only unilateral marital counseling (working with one partner) is possible. It is, of course, only successful to the extent that the cooperative spouse is intelligent and able to work with the marital partner as directed. Although this study offers no control data or any form of single-subject design, it serves as a guideline for future controlled research. It is also of interest that a nonprofessional therapist is employed in the marital situation.

OBSESSIONAL DISORDERS

The next paper, by Rachman, deals with the modification of obsessions. Rachman argues persuasively for a new approach in the behavioral modification of obsessions. Neutralizing rituals (attempts to "put things right") are given their appropriate significance and construed as being functionally equivalent to other kinds of compulsive rituals. The affected person should therefore be asked to initiate the obsessional thoughts, impulses and images and then to refrain from putting matters right, i.e., to refrain from carrying out any internal or external neutralizing activities. Traditional methods of treating obsessional ruminations—such as thought stopping—are not very effective and we can afford to overlook no method of promise (see Broadhurst, 1976).

According to the anxiety-reduction hypothesis, when people experience anxiety they engage in activities that reduce their discomfort. Those responses that successfully reduce anxiety are strengthened. It is argued that the compulsive rituals of the obsessive-compulsive persist because of their anxiety-reducing effects. Yet, curiously enough, this hypothesis had never been put to a direct test until the advent of Rachman and his group (Hodgson & Rochman, 1972; Röper, Rachman & Hodgson, 1973). Their findings that ritualistic acts and compulsive checking rituals both tend to reduce discomfort and/or anxiety were somewhat inconclusive and a more recent study was carried out in which 12 obsessive-compulsive checkers carried out a provoking act followed by a compulsive checking ritual, in the natural situation and under two conditions, with the experimenter present and with the experimenter absent (Röper & Rachman, 1976).

The provoking act produced subjective discomfort, tension and anxiety, feelings which were reduced after the completion of the checking ritual. Both the increases and post-ritual decreases in discomfort were more pronounced in the spontaneous occurrence condition with the experimenter absent. These results are consistent with the hypothesis that compulsive rituals serve to reduce discomfort. Unlike previous studies, treatment occurred in the patient's home rather than the laboratory. It is important to note that, contrary to the direction of the distortion suggested by Beech and Liddell (1974), the anxiety reducing effects of the rituals were *more* pronounced when the patient was alone at home. The increasing discomfort from a provocative action and the decrease in discomfort after completion of the checking ritual is much more pronounced when the patient is alone.

According to Alban and Nay (1976), ritual rechecking can be effectively treated by imposing increasingly lengthy scheduled duration of relaxation just prior to ritual performance (the "delay therapy" of Mayer, 1973—see Franks & Wilson, 1974). While Alban and Nay report on only one uncontrolled case study of a 27-year-old male with a life-long history of ritual re-checking, the fact that the rechecking behavior was completely extinguished over the course of 12 therapy weeks and did not recur in 28 weeks of follow-up is encouraging.

INSOMNIA

While insomnia is an everyday—or perhaps we should say every night—occurrence, it can also be one of the primary features of serious psychiatric disorders such as depression. And yet, until recently, it has been the subject of very few systematic behavioral investigations. Attempts to devise an effective diagnostic system for insomnia have been less than fruitful. A number of different classification systems are available, often mutually inconsistent and rarely operationally defined.

Behavior therapists tend to employ different kinds of methods in assessing insomnia: self-report, self-rating and physiological. Behavior therapy for insomnia has primarily taken the form of some kind of relaxation training or stimulus control technique. A few papers suggest biofeedback (Birk, 1973), response cost (Maultsby, 1972) or a metronome technique (Rothman, 1969) as additional procedures. Appropriate controls have been rare, no one has compared single-item desensitization with systematic desensitization, autogenic training with single-item or systematic desensitization, nor has hypnotic relaxation been compared with single-item or systematic desensitization. None of these techniques has been contrasted with similar control procedures and no one has compared behavioral techniques with pharmacological or other psychotherapeutic methods (Knapp, Downs & Alperson, 1976).

Knapp et al. are equally pessimistic when it comes to an evaluation of outcome. None of the experimental studies reviewed by these authors yielded significant differences between any of the treatments employed. Much more may be required than relaxation and stimulus control. Nay (1977) suggests the infusion of cognitive components and a multiprocess point of view.

It is possible that relaxation training in the treatment of insomnia is effective primarily because of its placebo value and numerous studies have addressed themselves to this matter (see Section II). To shed further light on this unresolved issue, Lick and Heffler (1977) compared the effectiveness of progressive relaxation training with and without a supplementary relaxation recording (to be played at home), and an attention placebo program carefully scheduled to maintain a high level of expectancy. Both relaxation training procedures were significantly more effective than either placebo or no-treatment controls not only in the direct reduction of the insomnia but also in the reduction of sleep-inducing medication and self-report measures of trait anxiety. Interestingly enough in view of the various theories concerning the mechanisms involved in the role of relaxation in the induction of sleep, multisystem physiological data gathered during the last treatment sessions showed no demonstrable relationship between reduction in arousal during relaxation training and improvement in sleeping behavior.

Mitchell and White (1977) applied their successful behavioral self-management program for coping with migraine headaches to the problem of predormital insomnia in which the onset of sleep is delayed. Working with college students and young staff, it was shown that a combination of training in progressive muscle relaxation, mental relaxation, and cognitive control procedures effectively reduced both pre-sleep tension and pre-sleep intrusive cognitions, with a concomitant improvement in latency of sleep onset and overall sleep satisfaction. These benefits were maintained at four month follow-up. Three subjects were trained only in the cognitive control procedures. While muscle relaxation reduced pre-sleep tension, there was no evidence that this, in itself, decreased pre-sleep intrusive cognitions, for which the addition of mental relaxation training seems necessary. But, as these authors note, further study is needed to confirm the existence of separate effects for muscle and mental relaxation, and to unravel the probably complex relationships between changes in pre-sleep tension, pre-sleep intrusive cognitions and latency to sleep onset.

Woolfolk, Carr-Kaffashan, and McNulty (1976) suggest a set of attention-focusing techniques derived from methods of meditation. Only recently has Western science begun to study the effects of meditation separated from the mystical religions of the East. Zen and Yoga meditation have been found to reduce cortical excitation, a finding of particular significance in view of the data adduced by Monroe (1967) to the effect that insomniacs manifest higher levels of arousal before and during sleep than a matched set of controls. Analysis of data for 24 recruited insomniacs show both meditation and progressive relaxation to be superior to most treatments in reducing the latency of sleep onset. These treatments did not differ in effectiveness. At six-month follow-up both meditation and relaxation groups showed significant improvement over pretreatment levels whereas pretreatment and follow-up means for the control group did not differ.

Speculation concerning the induction of sleep by the relaxation method centers on two possible mechanisms: reduction of physiological arousal and interruption of cognitive activity incompatible with sleep. According to Woolfolk (1975), the assumption that the attention-focusing components of relaxation techniques function to produce sleep onset only via the second mechanism is unwarranted. Most sleep studies using attention-focusing procedures employ independent checks on arousal reduction. Woolfolk (1975) suggests that focusing on monotonous or repetitive stimuli can be associated with substantial reductions in physiological arousal.

While the Woolfolk et al. study does not really elucidate the mechanism involved, it does demonstrate the effectiveness of an attention-focusing method for reducing the latency of sleep onset. Their brand of meditation possesses certain advantages: it is quickly learned, it involves no apparatus or special conditions, it can be readily combined with other components in a comprehensive sleep program, and (like most behavioral methods of treating insomnia) it is much safer than the use of hypnotic drugs.

Ribordy and Denney (1977) have also recently completed a critical review of the behavioral treatment of insomnia. Desensitization does seem to be an effective treatment for insomnia. However, only one of the studies reviewed employed an adequate control group and desensitization appears to be no more effective than the relatively simpler procedure of applied relaxation. Two components are involved in applied relaxation: training in deep relaxation by such induction techniques as progressive relaxation, autogenic training, self-hypnotic induction or biofeedback; and instructions regarding the application of this training upon retiring for the night. Ribordy and Denney's conclusion is that applied relaxation procedures are both more effective and easier to carry out than systematic desensitization. It is suggested, once again, that insomniacs have higher levels of autonomic arousal immediately prior to enduring sleep (Monroe, 1967). Applied relaxation presumably results in a lowering of pre-sleep arousal levels. But without physiological measures this remains in the realm of speculation.

Attribution theory, reviewed next by Ribordy and Denney, deals with the individuals' perceptions with respect to the causes for the psychological effects observed within themselves. In 1970, Storms and Nisbett recruited a college sample of "light sleepers" under the guise of a dream-research project. Subjects were assigned to three conditions—pill arousal, pill relaxation and no pill. Subjects in the first two groups were told that the study concerned the effects of body activity on dreams and were instructed to take a pill prior to going to bed. Those in the pill arousal group were told that the pill would increase their level of arousal, those in the pill relaxation group were told that the pill would decrease their level of arousal and relax them. As predicted, it was found that subjects in the pill-arousal groups were able to re-attribute pre-sleep arousal to a non-emotional external source, experience less emotionality and therefore fell asleep in less time than was normally required. Those in the pill-relaxation group experienced pre-sleep arousal, in spite of the pill, and a heightened emotional state and this compounded the insomnia problem, keeping them awake longer than usual.

In a more recent replication, Lowery, Denney and Storms (1976)—cited by Ribordy and Denney—found that subjects in the pill-arousal condition reported no change in their sleep onset latencies, even though they rated their difficulties in falling asleep as being less following the source reattribution manipulation. Neither study shows changes in both behavioral and subjective measures, and both are required if source attribution procedures are to be considered effective. Self-reports need to be supplemented by direct behavioral and physiological measures. Ribordy and Denney also suggest the use of deception as a research strategy, disguising the purpose of the study. As they point out, the vulnerability of self-report measures to demand characteristics is substantially lessened when subjects are unaware that the study in which they are participating is a treatment study, or even a study concerned with insomnia.

Finally, they suggest the use of counterdemand manipulations in conjunction with placebo treatment and active treatment groups to provide further control over the operation of demand characteristics. The criteria to be met in deciding whether a subject is an insomniac or not (Borkovec, Steinmark & Nau, 1973) are insufficiently rigorous. Subjects with only moderate levels of insomnia can meet these criteria and there is some evidence that the exclusive use of moderate insomniacs may produce distorted findings concerning the effectiveness of various treatment procedures. Moderate and severe insomniacs may also differ quantitatively as well as qualitatively. For example, severe insomniacs may have a greater familiarity with their symptoms, with the effects of hypnotic drugs upon these symptoms and with various treatment processes.

HEADACHES

Headaches are at least as common as insomnia. Virtually every adult has experienced some form of headache at some time or another. Of the 15 classes of headaches identified by the ad hoc committee on classification of headaches (Ad Hoc Committee on Classification of Headache,

1962) tension headache, also referred to as muscle-contraction, psychogenic or nervous headache, is the most frequent. Gradual in onset, characterized by persistent sensation of band-like pain or tightness in the head, it may last for hours, weeks or even months. While the etiology remains unclear, the consensus seems to be that tension headache is an individual response to psychological stress and that it may develop from sustained contraction of skeletal muscles about the face, scalp, neck and shoulders (see Holroyd, Andrasik & Westbrook, in press).

Despite the generally recognized belief that tension headaches result from failure to cope with psychological stress, there have been few attempts to evaluate cognitive treatment approaches which directly attempt to improve the sufferer's ability to cope with stress. Holroyd et al. assigned 31 headache sufferers to one of three groups: stress-coping training; biofeedback training; or a waiting control group. The stress-coping training program employed cognitive oriented therapy procedures (e.g. Beck, 1976) to teach individuals to identify their reactions to stress and then to employ cognitive stress coping skills. Biofeedback and relaxation procedures focused on teaching individuals to counter psychological stress by evoking a learned relaxation response (Stoyva, 1976). Both treatments were administered with counter-demand instructions (see Steinmark & Borkovec, reprinted in Franks & Wilson, 1975) to minimize the inference of implicit demands for improved performance. The subjects were 31 recruited individuals (27 females and 4 males) with a mean duration headache problem of six years and no demonstrable organic basis.

The stress-coping technique, which focused on providing general coping skills rather than being tailored specifically for tension headaches, turned out to be an effective treatment, both immediately after the conclusion of treatment and at 30 weeks follow up. What is most surprising, in view of the literature, is the relatively poorer showing of the biofeedback training procedure. The biofeedback training group showed reductions in frontalis electromyographic activity, but only the stress-coping training group showed substantial improvement in daily recordings of headaches.

The importance of general stress factors in both the understanding and control of headaches is underscored by Norton and Nielson (1977) who direct attention to consequent events: What are the factors maintaining the headache? Is the headache produced by factors antecedent to the headache? This approach is obviously consonant with that of Fordyce's (1976a, 1976b) discussion of pain (see Commentary, Section

X, Franks & Wilson, 1976). According to Norton and Nielson, the problem of treating headaches with biofeedback or relaxation methods is not that the headache pain might not be reduced, but rather that, since the individual concerned has not developed other, more appropriate ways of interacting with the environment, the headaches will recur. In other words, biofeedback and relaxation procedures may decrease pain behaviors but not increase "well behaviors."

To assess the relative effectiveness of verbal and EMG relaxation, Hutchings and Reinking (1976) randomly assigned 18 medically documented tension headache sufferers to one of three conditions: a taped combination of the procedures of Jacobson, Wolpe, Lazarus, Schultz and Luthe (!); EMG feedback relaxation training; or EMG relaxation training combined with the verbal relaxation melange. The two EMG assisted groups showed significantly better results in terms of reduction of headache activity and the rate at which reduction took place than the verbal relaxation group alone.

Since tension headaches result from states of heightened muscle contraction in the scalp area, relaxation procedures should emphasize muscle relaxation. As Hutchings and Reinking's data testify, verbal relaxation methods are effective, but not as effective as EMG assisted procedures. However, these results do not support the contention that EMG feedback training combined with relaxation is superior to any other treatment condition. Combining EMG biofeedback with other procedures seems to add little.

When Chesney and Shelton (1976) examined the separate and combined effects of muscle relaxation and biofeedback in the treatment of tension headaches, the findings were somewhat different. A muscle relaxation treatment alone and a combined muscle relaxation/biofeedback treatment were equally more effective than either a biofeedback treatment alone or a no-treatment control method in reducing headache frequency. Furthermore, both the muscle relaxation treatment and the combined muscle relaxation and biofeedback treatment were significantly more effective in reducing headache duration than the biofeedback treatment. It is their conclusion that, while frontalis EMG may be a helpful adjunct for relaxation training, relaxation training and practice, rather than biofeedback, are essential.

Biofeedback as a treatment for migraine originated at the Menninger Foundation in the early 1970s (Sargent, Green & Walters, 1972, 1973, 1973a). Briefly, the procedure consists of training patients to increase finger temperature, assisted by visual feedback and the repetition of autogenic phrases such as "My hands are warm." In a more systematic study, unfortunately of only two subjects, Wickramasekera (1973) successfully treated two individuals suffering from migraine with biofeedback temperature training which omitted the autogenic phrases. (See Blanchard and Young, 1974 for an extensive review in this area; see also Commentary, Section III.)

In Section III we reprint a paper by Friar and Beatty on the management of migraine by trained control of vaso-constriction. In this Section we reprint next an article by Reeves which stresses the cognitive skills-training components of tension headache reduction and, once again, underscores the importance of cognitive factors in the treatment of tension headache. Mitchell and White (1976) likewise attribute the success of their semi-automated training procedure for chronic tension headache sufferers to the provision of skills for the identification and modification of both the sources of stress in the environment and the reactions to these stresses. Symptom-oriented intervention not only fails to account for individual response variability to tensions in the environment, it also ignores the accumulative and harmful interactive effects of environmental, situational and antecedent stresses critical to the production of tension headaches. To focus on the last link in the behavioral chain that perceives pain, the muscle tension and the headache symptoms, is less than sufficient if the headache sufferer is not provided with alternative behaviors for coping with the stressful features of his environment.

The next paper to be reprinted, by Blanchard and Abel, is also concerned with the application of biofeedback principles. Unlike early attempts to obtain biofeedback control over episodic sinus tachycardia, Blanchard and Abel include adequate baseline and control phases. And whereas many have achieved feedback-assisted control of heart rate, this is one of the few to demonstrate control of heart rate in the absence of feedback.

SPEECH DISORDERS

At least four books and numerous articles concerned in part with the behavioral treatment of speech disorders have appeared this year: Harris (1976); Ince (1976a); Lovaas (1977); and Ritvo (1976). Ten years ago, when Lovaas began, comparatively little was known about how to build a language in anybody let alone the autistic child which is the subject of the Lovaas book. Now this project possesses generality far beyond the original intent. The techniques developed are being applied to retarded children and even in the teaching of language to subhumans. But perhaps more important, their book is directed towards those who work with children on a day-to-day basis, in particular parents. What emerges throughout their book, as with that of Harris (1976), is the necessity for painstaking attention to small detail, with the promise of minute increments of reward. If ever the behavioral maxim of "think small" is relevant, it is in this setting.

Speech refers to the noncontent aspects of verbal behavior, such as rate, volume, pitch, and the functions of the peripheral speech mechanisms. Language refers to the content variables of verbal communication. Ince directs his attention to disabilities in both of these areas. These include speech intelligibility, due to physical deformity, dysarthria, usually the result of a stroke, and a variety of language deficits such as aphasia. (Note that our concern here is not with the behavioral treatment of *functional* speech disorders such as hysterical mutism or the suppression of psychotic speech.)

Persistent anterograde amnesia following insult to the brain is a common occurrence which can readily result in a variety of language disturbances, of which one of the most common is a lack of spontaneous or narrative speech. Individuals exhibiting this deficit cannot engage in spontaneous conversation. Typically, they respond to any verbal prompt with some habitual, stereotypic expression and all attempts to restore spontaneous speech have been unsuccessful. McMordie (1976) reports an attempt to eliminate this deviant speech pattern by means of relaxation and verbal suggestion. The subject was a 29-year-old male about to enter college, who sustained massive brain damage, blindness in his right eye, and permanent damage to his right leg and arm as a result of an automobile accident. The uniqueness of the situation was accentuated by his not remembering having been blinded and maimed. Consequently, he was repeatedly finding out that his right eye was blind and talking about death after each realization. At the time of the study he had been hospitalized for three years, with no change and a poor prognosis. Spontaneous speech was nonexistent, even though the patient could converse fairly intelligently if given frequent and continual prompting. For 25 days—excluding baseline and reversal periods—he was treated with a combination of relaxation and verbal suggestion. Inappropriate speech, including death wishes, declined dramatically, the key factor apparently being the avoidance of any new activity which might claim the patient's attention during the relaxation process. To bring about such change in a man who was believed to be incapable of change is impressive!

Stuttering is an area of speech pathology which lends itself to a behavioral approach (e.g. Shames & Egolf, 1976). An important maladaptive behavior in stuttering is excessive muscle tension in the jaws, mouth and areas directly related to speech production, and behaviorally oriented speech therapists have long utilized a variety of techniques to decrease muscle tension in the speech area. Lanyon, Barrington and Newman (1976) now report the preliminary development of an EMG biofeedback technique appropriate for use with stutterers. Subjects can be trained to relax their masseter muscles, thereby affecting a major reduction in the level and nature of their stuttering. All eight of their subjects, recruited through newspaper advertisements, were able to learn masseter relaxation in a laboratory setting. Stuttering was greatly reduced or absent under these controlled laboratory conditions, and when feedback was removed generalization occurred, the subjects progressing successfully through increasingly complex units of speech. However, for clinical or social utility, any method must be generalizable to the natural environment. The limited generalization reported by Lanyon et al. under conditions of no feedback is not really comparable to the real-life situation.

The essential difference between the relatively successful metronome technique developed by Brady (1971) and Lanyon et al.'s EMG biofeedback procedure seems to be that the latter modifies the physiological link that is hypothesized to be maintaining the stuttering behavior. Its modification should bring about a direct reduction in stuttering without further instruction. In developing this technique, the authors have set for themselves the task of programming generalization, i.e. the systematic introduction of new interpersonal stimuli into the speaking situation while the subject keeps his or her masseter muscle tension at an appropriate low level. Their stated future plans also include emphasis upon spontaneous speech rather than reading, together with the utility of auditory rather than visual feedback for teaching muscle relaxation skills. Of perhaps equal importance might be a determination of whether or not the treatment-induced reduction in muscle tension in the masseter muscles generalizes to no feedback conditions.

Although subject to certain difficulties (see Adams & Hotchkiss, 1973; Silverman & Trotter, 1973), investigations into metronome-conditioned speech training (MCSR) still continue. For example, Öst, Götestam and Melin (1976) compared the effectiveness of MCSR with shadowing and a waiting-list control group. Five subjects in each group received 20 sessions of individual therapy over a three-month period. Assessment of nonfluency and a number of words per minute during spontaneous speech and reading aloud were made before, after, and at 14-month follow-up. Subjects treated with MCSR significantly reduced their degree of nonfluency during spontaneous speech, whereas the shadowing subjects increased their rates of speech during the reading aloud. Thus, MCSR would seem to be superior to shadowing with respect to spontaneous speech but not with respect to reading. Some combination of both procedures may be maximally effective. As always, the critical factors in the treatment of stuttering are transfer and maintenance of the treatment program and it is possible that such a combination may be more effective than either carried out separately.

One problem that most stutterers find particularly difficult is answer-the telephone, presumably because the conversants are not visible to one another. Lee, McGough and Peins (1976) adapted the tape recorder method used in language teaching to the resolution of this problem. Teaching material recorded on one tape elicits student responses which are then recorded. Later, the student listens to this recording and compares it with the voice of the teacher. Acting as his own critic, he then uses daily practice sessions to improve his speaking skill.

All three of the cases reported by Lee et al. had received at least six months of tape-recorded therapy before undergoing the automated desensitization which was the subject of their present report. A 15-minute instructional tape was prepared which asked for 15 seconds of muscle relaxation, followed by 15 seconds of pleasant scene-imagining, followed by appropriate vocal response. Beginning at the third step in the ascending 9-step hierarchy of vocal responses, which ranged from uttering a sound to listening to a rude caller suggesting that someone else be fetched to the phone to speak, the subject was required to pick up a real disconnected telephone as he made his replies.

If anxiety plays an integral component in most forms of stuttering, attention must be given to antecedent factors (Florin, 1976). It has long been known that instructions, external conditions and various antecedent conditions produce changes in the speech and speech associated behaviors of people who stutter. But much of the ensuing data are difficult to interpret because the majority of investigators have adopted a molar definition of stuttering. If behaviors are not specified separately, it is not possible to determine which speech and/or speech associated behaviors decreased or the extent of the decrement for each behavior. Thus, Oelschlaeger and Brutten (1976) make the important point that the first step in any investigation of stuttering is to define the behavioral measures molecularly. For example, in a recent study reported by these authors, frequency of measured repetitions and interjections responded differentially to instructional stimuli. This observation might well have been masked had a molar definition of behavioral measures been employed.

EPILEPSY AND SEIZURE CONTROL

The final paper in this section, by Balaschak, is concerned with the behavioral modification of organically based epilepsy. Epilepsy is an example of a problem that is usually treated from a medical standpoint despite the fact that it is really a complex and varied syndrome, and despite the fact that, in many cases, the physician is unable to achieve satisfactory control of the patient's seizures through medication alone. The study reported by Balaschak is of interest because she offers a well-thought-out example of an attempt to treat a child with organic seizures behaviorally within the school environment. It is most unfortunate that the teacher was unable to cooperate further in this project. However, it is apparent that neither medication alone nor medication plus traditional psychotherapy was effective in eliminating Joan's potentially injurious seizures, whereas behavior therapy produced a demonstrably dramatic lessening in the frequence of her seizures.

In another paper, Balaschak (1976) reports the successful treatment of three children with seizure disorders resistant to medication. By a combination of reward and time-out procedures implemented by parents, teachers and hospital staff under the direction of a behaviorally oriented psychologist, not only did the seizure rate decrease, but there were added benefits such as the reduction of medication. Balaschak stresses the importance of a multidisciplinary approach to the diagnosis and treatment of refractory epilepsy, a point which is taken up by a variety of other investigators.

Ince (1976b) reports the case of a 12-year-old boy who experienced numerous daily seizures in school over four years and was consequently fearful and reluctant to attend school. Following systematic desensitization for anxiety associated with recurrent seizures, a combination of relaxation and association of a cue word with a calm body state was employed to eliminate the seizures. Following relaxation, the child was instructed to repeat the cue word several times and, after repeated pairings, to verbalize the cue word to himself whenever he felt the aura of an approaching seizure. This resulted in avoidance of the onset of seizures and total elimination of both grand and petit mal seizures. Long-term follow-up showed no recurrence of the seizures. What would have been interesting in this particular case, as Ince himself intimates, would have been to determine precisely what roles the parents played in the maintenance of his seizures.

Grand mal epilepsy has also been treated by covert conditioning techniques (Daniels, 1975). Here, again, the point is made that it is necessary to use these techniques in conjunction with manipulation of the environment to develop a more total therapeutic program. Daniels reports an interesting case study of initially successful seizure control in a 22-year-old girl. Subsequent recurrence of seizures was associated with unfavorable changes in her external environment which caused her to become depressed and cease utilizing previously effective self-control strategies.

Many severely retarded or profoundly disturbed individuals present problems in seizure control. Most behavioral techniques are inappropriate or too difficult to apply and, regardless of their proven value and safety, strict guidelines with respect to the rights of patients usually preclude the use of noxious stimulation. It then becomes a matter of innovation and ingenuity to devise procedures that are likely to be effective, appropriate and acceptable to all concerned. Iwata and Lorentzson (1976) report a study of a 41-year-old nonambulatory retarded male living in a state residential facility who began to exhibit seizure-like activity approximately one month prior to institutionalization some 10 years earlier. The program specifically devised for this individual involved increased daily activities, differential reinforcement of other behavior and time-out procedures. The marked decreases in seizures activity obtained during the treatment phases of the study were maintained during subsequent fading of the activities and the differential reinforcement of other behavior.

In reflex epilepsy, the paroxysmal electroactivity is evoked by some particular stimulus or stimulus complex. The evoking stimulus is most often limited to one sensory modality but numerous cross-modal stimulus complex cases have been reported. Although the wide variety of stimuli that can become elicited cues in reflex epilepsy might seem to support the notion that the disorder is learned, Adams (1977) reminds us that, in fact, a conditioning based etiology has not yet been demonstrated in humans.

The techniques used in the behavioral treatment of reflex epilepsy involve, in the main, increasing stimulus tolerance. The epileptogenic stimulus is introduced at an innocuous level and increased in intensity and/or duration as the seizures fail to occur. What is most important, as Adams points out, is the need for careful stimulus presentation. Errors in technique may well resensitize the patient. Competing responses have also been used in the treatment of reflex epilepsy. For example, a patient who had seizures after reading any material for over one minute was instructed to tap his knee with his hand whenever selected words occur in the text, thus providing a competing action (Forster, Paulsen, & Baughman, 1969). Such a strategy may well be useful in treating reflex epilepsy even when the seizures have no demonstrable learned basis.

BEHAVIORAL MEDICINE

Fabrega (1975a, b, 1976a, b) highlights in detail the inadequacies of the biomedical model in accounting for the psychosocial problems related to health care and rightly draws attention to the need for an expanded model that accounts for both biomedical and psychosocial concerns. His solution takes the form of a proposed new subdiscipline which he terms ethnomedical science based upon the concept of "generic disease." Generic disease refers to phenomena that involve "a person-centered, harmful and undesirable deviation or discontinuity in the value of one or any number of different measures that can characterize an individual through time, all of which are associated with impairment or discomfort; and the condition so described is not desired, which means that it gives rise to a need for corrective action." Ethnomedicine is the study of generic disease and its implications for psychosocial problems as they relate to medical practice (Fabrega, 1975b).

Wilson (1977b) takes the position that, no matter how reformulated, adumbrating a basic disease model of psycho-social maladaption is counterproductive, and prevailing trends in such socially relevant areas as homosexuality, alcoholism and schizophrenia serve to reaffirm this contention. An alternative model, dealing with the application of social learning principles to medically related problems, is that of "behavioral medicine" (Williams & Gentry, 1977). Behavioral medicine is enjoying increasingly empirical support and would seem to offer a logical and viable development as behavior modification extends into the growing field of general health care (Blanchard, 1977). In this respect, we note the forthcoming appearance of a journal of the same name.

In a brief but informative overview of behavioral medicine, Epstein and Martin (1977) point out that behavioral principles can be used in three ways in the health care system: for disease and disability prevention; for disease and disability treatment; and for improvement of medical health care delivery. For example, Patel (1976) demonstrates the reduction of serum cholesterol and blood pressure in hypertensive patients after relaxation training. Pomerleau, Bass and Crown (1975) go so far as to suggest that application of behavior modification principles in preventative medicine may prove to be as important a contribution as the development of antibacterial agents in the first half of the century. While this may be a somewhat premature conclusion, there is no doubt that it is one of the more significant contributions that behavior modification can make at this time.

Epstein and Martin divide prevention into secondary and primary components. Secondary prevention involves attempting to change health and prevent disability after an important risk factor has been identified; primary prevention presents the procedures for decreasing the possibility of developing a risk factor. There is also a somewhat different dichotomy in terms of managerial prevention, which refers to changes in risk factors by environmental management, and personal prevention, which involves changes in behavior that may directly affect health.

Behavioral procedures have been used in primary prevention, such as the reduction of the probability of high-school age children beginning to smoke. But the majority of applications of behavioral procedures, according to Epstein and Martin, have been in personal secondary prevention, using behavioral techniques to change health factors. However, behavioral techniques may be used in primary and secondary prevention. For example, seat belts in motor cars may not be sufficiently effective unless regularly used: At a recent symposium on behavioral medicine, Christopherson (cited by Epstein & Martin, 1977) reported a procedure to increase parental use of seat belts for their children (see also Commentary, Section IX).

Personal secondary prevention involves screening programs to identify high risk individuals, treatment of these individuals and finally methods of modifying the risk factors. Epstein and Martin highlight some of the more interesting and effective ways of implementing behavioral techniques at all three levels. The modification of obesity, and the reduction of smoking, serum cholesterol, blood pressure, and electrocyte levels are all examples of the application of behavioral techniques in the treatment of high risk factors among the general population. Increasingly, behavioral principles are being applied in general medical areas. For example, Suinn (1977) reports the application of behavioral methods in increasing the efficiency and well-being of the U.S. Nordic Ski Team during the XII Olympiad in Innsbruck; LeBow (1973, 1976) has written extensively upon the application of behavioral modification principles in nursing practice, and Cautela (1977) has developed a Pavlovian theory of cancer.

Last year in this Section we focused upon Fordyce's strategy for investigating and modifying chronic pain (Fordyce, 1976a, 1976b). In his generally positive review of Fordyce's work, Abel (1977) drawn attention to a few shortcomings of what is, by and large, an excellent contribution to the burgeoning area of behavioral medicine. For example, in Abel's experience as a practicing psychiatrist, antidepressants should be deployed only with patients manifesting unequivocal depressive symptomatology (and then at therapeutic levels and durations in excess of those advocated by Fordyce) and never routinely.

Ritchie (1976) describes a treatment program for changing controlling behavior in the chronic pain patients that combines operant techniques with the use of tokens. The goal of the program was to help patients give up attempting to control their environment through pain responses. A token economy was applied to modify the activity level of 22 patients with chronic pain syndromes. The patients were assigned either to a treatment group in which tokens were given for changing activity level, to a control group or to an activity management schedule. There was a significant but temporary difference between treatment and control group activity levels when compared during the treatment manipulation period. The differences in pain levels between the two groups was not significant. These findings do not suggest that operant conditioning eliminates pathogenic factors, but do support the view that specific pain problems are correctable through proper training. Furthermore, these data suggest that a token economy system may improve pain patients' abilities to respond in a manner suited both to themselves and their environment.

Anorexia nervosa is another physical disorder that lends itself to treatment by behavioral means. Brady and Rieger (1975) report an ongoing program with 16 anorexia nervosa patients treated at the psychiatric inpatient service at the hospital of the University of Pennsylvania over the past five years. All 16 patients were successfully treated by an operant reinforcement paradigm in which successive powerful reinforcers were made contingent upon achieving a minimum daily weight. All patients gained weight both during the short-term and a follow-up period extending from 4 to 59 months after discharge. An interesting by-product was the development of other adaptive behaviors in addition to the weight gain.

In stark contrast, Williams (1976) reports a behavior modification program for six anorexic patients which he describes as a "resounding failure." The treatment package involved relaxation, desensitization, aversion and token procedures, self-monitoring, thought stopping, assertion training and a variety of individualized techniques to help with sexual problems. At six months follow-up, two patients were clearly worse, two were no different but discouraged and two were only marginally improved. No patient gained weight. As possible explanation, Williams advances the traditional psychodynamic argument that the secondary gains accrued from the anorexic symptomatology (attention from significant others and relief from the responsibilities of adult sexuality) exceeded the disadvantages. However, it is not necessary to invoke a psychodynamic model to examine this process objectively. For example, in a paper also referred to in our Commentary to Section I, Blanchard and Hersen (1976) conceptualize secondary gain in terms of the external social reinforcers that the patient receives contingent upon evidencing his or her particular symptoms. Goldblatt and Munitz (1976) likewise employ what may be termed behavioral secondary gain theory to account for certain conversion hysteric symptomatology.

From their experience with weight restoration by operant reinforcement procedures, several general principles or guidelines are offered. These may be summarized as follows: 1) from the start, it is essential to obtain and record reliable daily weight under standardized conditions; 2) the patients should be observed for three or four days to obtain baseline weight data and knowledge of their daily habits; 3) once a reinforcer is selected, the contingency should be applied unequivocally to all concerned; 4) if a patient gains weight consistently, the contingency should be continued until the weight is in the normal range. If he or she does not, a more potent reinforcer must be selected and tried in the same manner; 5) confrontation and interaction with the patient over issues of food, eating or weight gain should be restricted to carrying out the contingencies as delineated; 6) in general, the contingency should not involve the direct reinforcement of eating behavior. It is better to allow the patient to choose what is eaten, when it is eaten and how it is eaten. The only requirement is that the patient gains weight, thus allowing maximum choice and freedom to work out the issues of autonomy and independence. 7) As discharge from the hospital draws near, outpatient therapy, usually behavioral oriented family therapy, should be arranged.

Despite the success noted by Brady and Rieger, we concur with their conclusion that more controlled clinical research on behavioral treatment of anorexia nervosa is needed, particularly of the single use experimental design variety to verify unequivocally that therapeutic environmental contingencies actually do control eating behavior. In addition, there is a need for controlled clinical comparisons of short- versus long-term efficacies of operant reinforcement approaches as contrasted with more traditional medical and psychiatric regimes.

Davis, Mitchell and Marks (1976) describe a behavior modification program for the treatment of encopresis which can be adapted for use by parents in the home. They, too, stress the need for a follow-up program to ensure that the parents continue to handle the child consistently. In similar fashion, Barnes (1976) reports the use of token economy control of fluid overload in a renal patient undergoing hemodialysis. Dietary indiscretions in fluid overload are continuing problems for such individuals and frequently cause self-dialysis patients to return to hospitals. Careful analysis of dietary noncompliance usually reveals a number of specific responses which can be easily measured and then modified through the use of appropriate reinforcers deemed medically more desirable (e.g. fluid intake and salt consumption, protein intake). An agreement was made with the patient to engage in a token economy program whereby, for observing diet restrictions, he could gain a specific number of points which could be exchanged for water or liquid, not to exceed 800 cc per day. Diet restrictions specified no water with meals, no extra salt with meals and no snack between meals. The patient, a 43-year-old male with renal failure secondary to malignant hypertension, presented symptoms which could not be controlled by medication. At six month follow-up of the above regime, he was continuing to self-dialyze at home, remain normotensive, emotionally stable and physically active. The emotional stability was particularly important since depressive reactions are relatively frequent occurrences in such situations.

Patients undergoing hemodialysis can lose a serious degree of control over the contingencies sustaining premorbid behavior. Reinforcements typically accompanying good health are curtailed or even discontinued, at which time primary reinforcers, such as food or water, assume increased importance, often to the detriment of the patient's health. Restriction of fluid intake in these patients can make available a primary reinforcer for behavior change. When used within a token economy paradigm, contingencies may be rearranged to teach the patient to reinforce his own responses, thus achieving some measure of self-control and paving the way for generalization to the extra-therapy situation.

Finally, we draw attention to the increasing use of behavior modification in rehabilitation medicine (cf. Sanders, 1975; Ince, 1976a). As Peck (1976) points out, operant conditioning techniques can be used as ancillary to standard rehabilitation procedures, as rehabilitation procedures themselves and as guidelines for the general management of sick people, both in institutions and in the home. However, Peck rightly points to the lack of attention to experimental design which still pervades this new field. It is not always easy to engage in a reversal design when dealing with physically handicapped individuals. Many of the problems dealt with are chronic and have proved so resistant to previous intervention that to demonstrate a change, even with a simple A-B design, is convincing enough. Furthermore, many of the behaviors (such as the building up of muscular strength) are obviously not amenable to any form of reversal design. Nevertheless, whenever possible, considerable attention should be given to the improvement of the design itself.

SECTION X: THERAPEUTIC STRATEGIES, CASE STUDIES AND CLINICAL EXTENSIONS

25

A CASE OF CHRONIC BACK PAIN AND THE "UNILATERAL" TREATMENT OF MARITAL PROBLEMS

Edwin G. Scheiderer

College of Medicine and Dentistry of New Jersey

and

Douglas T. Bernstein

Western Washington State College

Summary—When a client's problems are deeply rooted in his or her marriage, a therapist should usually work with both husband and wife. However, when either spouse refuses cooperation, unilateral marriage counseling, in which the client identifies problem areas in the marriage and becomes a behavioral engineer (with the therapist as a consultant), can be employed. This procedure is illustrated in the case of a 52-yr-old woman who reported numerous marital problems accompanied by chronic back pain.

The ideal course of action in most marital problems is to have both husband and wife involved in the treatment program. Unfortunately, this cannot always be accomplished since spouses often not only refuse to admit to any problem but decline even to visit a therapist. In such cases, therapeutic goals may still be decided upon and treatment pro-

Reprinted with permission from *Journal of Behaviour Therapy and Experimental Psychiatry*, 1976, Vol. 7, 47-50.

grams set up in which the husband or wife becomes a behavioral engineer for the marriage (Tharp & Wetzel, 1969). This means that the husband or wife who initially sought professional help acts both as client and mediator between therapist and spouse. Assuming that a client has described his or her marriage in reasonably accurate terms, and that the desired marital changes are appropriate, realistic, and ethically permissible, unilateral marriage counseling can be a viable treatment approach.

CASE HISTORY

Mrs. X was a 52-yr-old woman who came to a psychological clinic complaining of a chronic, low back pain that had occurred daily since she was 15, becoming progressively worse from midday until bedtime. Repeated medical investigation had failed to provide a physiological basis for the pain. Neither a series of eight electroshock treatments nor a brief participation in a sensitivity-type group experience had alleviated it. Although Mrs. X was able to maintain her job as a secretary, the pain hampered her freedom of movement on the job; and also her ability to fall asleep.

Mrs. X's marriage was unsatisfactory. Her husband spent all of his time either at work or engaged in his hobbies. Conversation was minimal and meals were often eaten separately. She had a close relationship with both of her college-age daughters, and several friends; yet she found it difficult to view herself as a competent, worthwhile person. She was perfectionistic and constantly afraid of criticism from those around her.

TREATMENT

It appeared that Mrs. X's pain was related to tension due to her negative self-evaluation in the marriage and in social interactions and that changes in both areas would be necessary to insure positive changes in her back condition. Mr. X refused repeated invitations to visit the clinic for discussion of the marital situation, and so, since Mrs. X was an intelligent woman, it was hypothesized that she could learn to implement agreed-upon programs unilaterally. A set of overlapping programs was developed in this way and is described in relation to specified treatment targets.

Back Pain

Mrs. X was trained in progressive relaxation (Bernstein & Borkovec, 1973; Jacobson, 1938; Wolpe, 1958). Emphasis was given to the muscles of the lower back, which was tensed by arching the back.

Self-evaluation

A major area of concern was Mr. X's indifference to Mrs. X which was related, in part, to her own low self-evaluation. It was emphasized that by utilizing cognitive restructuring procedures, Mrs. X could gain self-control over her own evaluative thoughts (cf. Cautela, 1969; Kanfer & Phillips, 1970; Ellis, 1962; Goldfried, Decenteceo & Weinberg, 1974).

The first step was to have Mrs. X keep an anecdotal record of all interpersonal interactions lasting more than 5 minutes. She was briefly to summarize the antecedents, her overt verbal behavior and covert thoughts, and finally the consequences. During ongoing verbal interactions, it became apparent that her thoughts and overt verbal responses were heavily intertwined. This procedure made Mrs. X more aware of how she was allowing her own internal evaluative thoughts to supercede the actual feedback she was getting from other people.

The second step consisted of Mrs. X composing a list of ten positive "self-evaluative/assertion" statements which she could periodically read over and subvocalize until they began to occur more spontaneously. These statements included, "I'm just as important a person as my husband" and "most people will respect me and listen to my opinions and feelings." Mrs. X was asked to subvocally repeat any of the statements which would be appropriate while engaged in a specific verbal interaction.

As a third step, Mrs. X was asked to make a list of positive things she could do for and say to other people as well as herself. In addition, she was to record examples of others' positive actions and comments toward her. The list included compliments, "favors," and the like. In this manner, Mrs. X was maximizing her opportunities positively to reinforce her own "self-evaluative/assertion" statements.

Weight Reduction Program

Related to her low self-opinion was Mrs. X's overweight. The weight reduction plan of Stuart & Davis (1972) was introduced with minor changes.

Communication and Interaction with Husband

It was suggested that Mrs. X spend more time talking to her husband, even if this meant turning off the television set or following him around the house. Conversations began around topics of mutual interest, such as the day's activities, reactions to current events, or information related by a friend, and provided a context in which serious discussions of topics relating to marital complaints could later be brought up. It was pointed out that Mrs. X's previous habit of waiting for the proper time to discuss things usually resulted in such topics never being discussed.

Mrs. X consulted with the therapist in defining problem areas of the marriage and was advised on how to deal with such problems—e.g., she was given an explanation of the principles of reinforcement and extinction, and shown how to apply them to specific problems. One goal was to have her husband speak in a more positive and complimentary way both about things she had done exceptionally well and also about jobs done routinely (cooking, house cleaning, errands, and the like). She was also made aware of the need to model behavior she desired from her husband, and to reinforce his appropriate responses. If he was unjustifiably critical, she was to ignore his criticism and tell herself that she hadn't done anything to justify it. In addition, she was to try to change the negative tone of the conversation in any way possible, even if it meant changing the topic.

Wherever her husband's behavior needed to be modified, Mrs. X was carefully to apply or withhold reinforcement. Reinforcers consisted of positive comments and/or non-verbal responses. Mrs. X constructed a "menu" of reinforcers for her husband (offering him a sandwich or a dish of ice cream, running an errand for him, buying him a record or a necktie) and, in each case, she was to informally verbalize the specific contingency, e.g. "I just wanted to make a pot of coffee for you to show you that I really appreciated your starting the car for me this morning."

Along with her relative inexperience in freely disclosing positive thoughts and feelings to her husband, Mrs. X also found it difficult to make routine requests. She was therefore instructed to define 12 assertive responses she wanted to be able to make and to rank them in self-defined order of difficulty. A new response was assigned each week following successful completion of the preceding response. These responses ranged from asking Mr. X to stop off at a store on the way home to informing him that she would go on vacation with him only if he agreed to visit her out-of-town relatives. Additional responses were later elicited in regard to Mrs. X's work situation and inability to be assertive with her boss.

Social Activity

Mrs. X expressed a great desire to get out and engage in more social activity, especially with her husband. Her previous attempts to initiate such activity had usually resulted in failure and sequential feelings of rejection, anger, guilt, and intensified back pain. She had almost given up social activities, except for visits to a few close friends. This self-imposed social deprivation not only reduced her pleasure in life but also reinforced her attitude that she was unworthy and undeserving. She was asked to list 20 preferred activities (e.g., shopping, movies, going out to dinner) and each week to select at least one activity to enjoy alone or with a friend *and* at least one activity in which she would ask her husband to participate. She was free to add new activities to the list and substitutions were allowed for previously agreed upon activities. The goals here were to allow her husband continued opportunities for spending more time with Mrs. X and to help her learn that she could go out without him. He was free to refuse an invitation, but these occasions provided Mrs. X with experience in accepting a refusal without self-criticism and in selecting an alternative activity.

RESPONSE TO TREATMENT

Mrs. X was seen for a total of 20 sessions over a period of 7 months. The frequency and intensity of the back pain gradually decreased until she had no pain whatever during the last one and one-half months of therapy. Written contact 6 months after termination revealed no further back problems.

There were major changes in the marital situation. Mr. and Mrs. X spent every evening meal together as well as a period of at least 30 min discussing the day's events, problem solving, or listening to music. Once a week, they went to a social function, e.g., a dog show, the movies, a restaurant, or an office party. Mrs. X described the changes as a return to "courting days" and the changes were best illustrated by their decision to resume sexual intercourse (usually once a week) after several years' abstinence. Her weight had decreased from 220 lb to 175 lb.

Mrs. X also became more at ease in social activities whether alone or with a friend. She joined a history club and the U.S.O., and was able to develop two new close friendships. She reported feeling more comfortable with other people in public and could state her opinion without fear of criticism. She engaged in one social activity per week alone, with a friend, or in conjunction with a social organization.

As a result of her experience as a behavioral engineer, Mrs. X was much more aware of how other people's behavior interacted in a complex way with her own. Thus she no longer labelled herself the sole cause of her problems. It was suggested that because she had learned many specific skills which could be helpful to other people, she might consider joining some type of volunteer organization (e.g., a "hotline" for distressed people or "mental hospital companion") and thus utilize her listening skills. She was aware of her limitations as a "therapist," but felt very self-confident in her interactions with other people, and proud that the therapist had made this suggestion.

DISCUSSION

Unilateral marriage counseling is an aspect of individual therapy, in which the client is not seen as the main focus of attention, but the interaction between husband and wife. The client soon realizes he is changing a system and not just his own attitudes or feelings.

There are four major assignments for the client-mediator. First, he must have a reasonably accurate assessment of the problem areas, including a conception of what behaviors are not desirable and can be changed. The second task is to formulate, with the therapist, a treatment program for the client and the spouse. It is, of course, important that the therapist and client weigh the probable consequences of each change. Next, the client must implement the suggested treatment program. At this point, the client assumes a great deal of responsibility since the therapist is not present during the interactions between client and spouse. The client must realize that change is two-sided and avoid the temptation to justify any action as being sanctioned by the therapist. The final stage is reassessment. The client reports to the therapist what changes have occurred. Such changes may be in the area of verbal interaction, work routines, leisure activities, sexual behavior and related behavior.

REFERENCES

BERNSTEIN, D. A. & BORKOVEC, T. D. *Progressive Relaxation Training: A Manual for Therapists*. Champaign, Ill.: Research Press, 1973.

CAUTELA, J. R. Behavior therapy and self-control: Techniques and implications. In C. M. Franks (Ed.), *Behavior Therapy: Appraisal and Status*. New York: McGraw-Hill, 1969.

ELLIS, A. *Reason and Emotion in Psychotherapy*. New York: Lyle Stuart, 1962.

GOLDFRIED, M. R., DECENTECEO, E. T., & WEINBERG, L. Systematic rational restructuring as a self-control technique. *Behav. Therapy*, 5:247-254, 1974.

JACOBSON, E. *Progressive Relaxation*. Chicago: University of Chicago Press, 1938.

KANFER, F. H. & PHILLIPS, U. S. *Learning Foundations of Behavior Therapy*. New York: Wiley, 1970.

STUART, R. B. & DAVIS, B. *Slim Chance in a Fat World: Behavioral Control of Obesity*. Champaign, Ill.: Research Press, 1972.

THARP, R. & WETZEL, R. *Behavior Modification in the Natural Environment*. New York: Academic Press, 1969.

WOLPE, J. *Psychotherapy by Reciprocal Inhibition*. Stanford, Calif.: Stanford University Press, 1958.

SECTION X: THERAPEUTIC STRATEGIES, CASE STUDIES AND CLINICAL EXTENSIONS

26

THE MODIFICATION OF OBSESSIONS: A NEW FORMULATION

S. Rachman

Institute of Psychiatry, London

Summary—Following the theoretical analysis proposed in 1971, it is suggested that obsessions produce both discomfort and attempts to "put matters right." These attempts are construed as being functionally equivalent to compulsive rituals. A two-part approach to treatment is described. It consists of satiation training and/or the prevention of internal and external neutralizing rituals (i.e., attempts to "put matters right" are prevented). The present analysis is proposed as part of a move towards an integrated, consistent approach to the practice and theory of behavior modification in dealing with obsessional and compulsive problems.

The purpose of this paper is to formulate a revised approach to the modification of obsessions. The central proposal is a paradox; for reasons to be given, it is proposed that instead of teaching obsessional patients to curtail their ruminations, we should encourage them to produce the thoughts to request.

It will be admitted that the modification of obsessional ruminations remains a problem. The most commonly used modification technique is *thought-stopping,* which despite its obvious appeal, has not received the necessary buttressing evidence. Acting on a suggestion made by J. G.

Reprinted with permission from *Behaviour Research and Therapy,* 1976, Vol. 14, 437-443.

Taylor, Wolpe (1958) introduced thought-stopping into behavior therapy. While it is true that there are some persuasive case-illustrations of its value (Wolpe, 1958, 1970; Yamagami, 1971; Kumar & Wilkinson, 1971; Stern, 1970), the only published trial on ruminations (Stern, Lipsedge & Marks, 1973), failed to produce evidence of its clinical effectiveness. Only four out of the eleven patients treated showed useful improvements and it is by no means certain that their gains can be attributed to the thought-stopping technique. In view of the claims of success in individual case studies however, it would be premature to abandon the experimental investigation of thought-stopping on the grounds of this trial, particularly as a limited amount of treatment was provided and that was confined to tape-recorded instructions. The report by Kumar and Wilkinson (1971) was more favorable but none of their four cases were suffering from obsessional ruminations: their thoughts consisted of fears of illness and death and were diagnosed as "phobias." The most encouraging results so far, were obtained by Hackman and McClean (1975) who found thought-stopping to be as effective as exposure in the treatment of a group of mixed obsessional compulsive patients. It is not possible to determine from their results whether thought-stopping was more or less effective in dealing with ruminations. Moreover, it is possible that a significant part of the therapeutic effect was attributable to non-specific factors. The specific value of thought-stopping has yet to be determined. Other methods of treatment which have been attempted include aversive shock conditioning, aversion relief, desensitization, conditioned inhibition (Broadhurst, 1976).

As a counter to ruminations, the method of paradoxical intention is intuitively appealing and the clinical descriptions of Gertz (1976) and others carry conviction, even if the rationale is unsatisfactory. Solýom and his colleagues (1972) carried out a pilot study on ten ruminators and reported an improvement rate of 50%. The specificity of the therapeutic effect is especially interesting. With one exception, when the target thought changed, the control thought remained unaltered. This line of research seems worth pursuing, for the reasons given and because the method has some features in common with a *satiation method* that has shown promise in our own clinical research. In the satiation method our patients are asked to obtain and hold the obsession for prolonged periods of up to fifteen minutes or more per trial. With successive trials they experience difficulties in obtaining and/or retaining the thought or image. Solyom et al. (1972) describe their *paradoxical intention method* in this way: ". . . instead of trying to push the intruding, frightening, or useless thought out of his mind, he was to dwell deliberately on the thought, indeed to elaborate and exaggerate it and convince himself of its validity," (p. 293). The attempt to exaggerate or elaborate the thought plays no part in the satiation method. So far from accepting the validity of the obsession, our satiation patients are told that most people experience unwanted, unacceptable, intrusive thoughts but that they rarely attach significance to these useless ideas and therefore can dismiss them easily. The patients are encouraged to regard their obsessions as alien and useless and then taught how to *de-toxify* them by the satiation method. The relative merits of paradoxical intention and satiation will be examined experimentally in due course.

It is perhaps worth making the point that one or more of the methods referred to here may prove to be of therapeutic value. It is not the case that they have been tested and found wanting; none of them has yet been evaluated adequately.

Even if thought-stopping is finally shown to be an effective technique there will be grounds for uneasiness. It is theoretically awkward to absorb thought-stopping into the bag of currently used techniques for dealing with obsessional compulsive problems. It is an *ad hoc* technique that rests on its empirical strength. As Broadhurst (1976) observed, it "has little in the way of psychological rationale to recommend it," (p. 176). It is hoped that the present proposals will allow a closer fit between theory and treatment and also conform more closely with prevailing modification techniques used in managing obsessional and compulsive disorders (Rachman, Hodgson & Marks, 1971; Hodgson, Rachman & Marks, 1972; Rachman, Hodgson & Marks, 1973; Marks, Hodgson & Rachman, 1975; Hodgson & Rachman, 1976).

Before setting out the theoretical and practical proposals in full, it is necessary briefly to recapitulate the underlying theoretical stand-point. "Obsessional ruminations are repetitive, intrusive and unacceptable thoughts. They may be distasteful, shameful, worrying or abhorrent or a combination of all these characteristics. In content they generally comprise thoughts of harming others, causing accidents to occur, swearing or distasteful sexual or religious ideas. Those patients who repeatedly worry about the possibility that they may have injured someone (or may do so in the future) frequently engage in avoidance behavior which they feel will reduce the probability of harming other people," (Rachman, 1971, p. 229). In extreme cases the avoidance behavior results in the patient becoming housebound. While obsessional ruminations most often occur in conjunction with compulsive activities, each activity can occur and persist independently. There is a frequent association between obsessions and depression (see Rachman, 1971, 1973).

Obsessions are similar to noxious stimuli and both are resistant to habituation (p. 231). During a normal mood state unacceptable thoughts produce little disturbance and can be absorbed. In the presence of a disturbance of mood however, most commonly agitated depression, people who have had a strict training will be considerably disturbed by the appearance of worrying or distasteful thoughts. By a process of sensitization, the disturbances produced by the thoughts increase the person's responsiveness to them. This sensitization will be experienced as a deterioration in mood (perhaps an increase in agitation) and an elevation in the amount of disturbance produced by the occurrence of the thoughts. The discomfort produced by the thoughts causes the person to seek reassurance. The temporary relief achieved by reassurance positively reinforces the occurrence and expression of the disturbing thoughts. In the new formulation the patient's attempts to make amends, to put matters right (internally and/or externally), is introduced as a key concept (see below). Broadly speaking, the patient's inability to habituate to ruminative stimuli can be overcome by presenting the noxious stimulation under conditions which favor habituation, and/or by effecting a direct improvement in mood state (Rachman, 1971, p. 234).

Clinically this treatment approach might take the form of providing anti-depressant or tranquilizing drugs, followed by habituation training. Increasing toleration of the ruminations (habituation) may then be expected to contribute to an improvement and stabilization of mood. "During the early stages of habituation treatment, a temporary increase in the disturbance caused by the ruminations may occur," (p. 232).

It was suggested that "under calm conditions, long exposures to ruminative thoughts well result in quicker habituation than short exposures," (p. 234). Although it has not been the subject of a formal trial, recent clinical experiences indicate that a development of this approach to treatment, here referred to as *the satiation method,* may prove fruitful. In clinical practice, the responses of patients suggest that the satiation technique helps to drain the unpleasantness from the repetitive idea, image or impulse. It is like a process of *de-toxification.* When the obsession loses its disturbing intensity, habituation can proceed. (Teasdale's clinical impression is that satiation fails to reduce the intensity or duration of ruminations if the person is too depressed*—personal communication. If this is confirmed, the case for supplementary medication will be strengthened). Although the satiation technique appears in a number of cases to have been of some help, in certain instances it was insufficient to produce an adequate clinical outcome.

The present proposals are: (a) in addition to satiation treatment, we should (b) place great emphasis on training the ruminators to refrain from "putting right" the effects of their ruminations.

In my earlier paper it was hypothesized that "ruminative thoughts are accompanied by psychophysiological and subjective disturbances." This proposition, which has since received some experimental support from the research of Stern, Lipsedge & Marks (1973), is the starting point for the new proposal. The unpleasantness that accompanies a rumination leads to attempts to reduce the discomfort. These attempts may include overt avoidance behavior or more commonly attempts to "put matters right" internally. By this I mean that the patient tries to neutralize or make amends for the unacceptable thought, image or impulse. It is not uncommon for the person to feel that the unacceptable thought, image or impulse may, if left unaltered, cause some actual harm to other people. While in their calmer moments they usually are able to recognize the irrationality of this belief, such recognition does not strip the rumination of its power to disturb. Attempts at "putting right" may take many forms. They may be amendatory, neutralizing, reparative, corrective, preventive or restorative, but as the word *neutralize* appears to cover most cases, it will be used to signify the attempt at "putting right." Sometimes the patient has to form a satisfactory counter-thought, or a counter-image, or utter words or numbers of special significance, or form an image of the people who feature in the rumination now back in a state of safety, or form a virtuous thought, or utter an incantation, or have a "releasing" thought or image. It is contended that these methods of putting matters right (neutralizing behavior) are equivalents of compulsive checking rituals or repetitive requests for reassurance. If this view is correct, it follows that the method for treating ruminations should be patterned on the successful methods of treating other forms of compulsive rituals. The ritual equivalent should be subjected to a period of response prevention or response blocking in the same way that a patient with compulsive checking rituals is first exposed to the provoking situa-

* It is implied in the original version of the theory and in the present elaboration, that satiation (or detoxification) is unlikely to be effective when the person is unduly agitated; prior relaxation may be essential.

tion and then instructed to refrain from carrying out the pertinent checking ritual (Hodgson & Rachman, 1976). So the ruminators should be exposed to the provoking trigger (i.e., the disturbing thought, image or impulse) and then instructed to refrain from carrying out the checking ritual (i.e., refrain from putting things right). If one agrees to construe the problem in this way, then it follows that a treatment technique comprising exposure to the disturbing rumination, followed by instructions to refrain from carrying out neutralizing rituals, should prove to be substantially more effective than thought-stopping and slightly more effective than the satiation treatment. It is predicted that a combination of satiation and the type of response prevention procedure described here, will make a robust therapeutic combination. The question of when to use satiation or response prevention, or a combination of both of these methods, is taken up later in the article.

To recapitulate, the combined method of treatment would consist of two steps: (a) Provocation of the urge to carry out the neutralizing behavior—the urge is produced by instructing the person to obtain the disturbing image or thought or impulse. (b) The person is then instructed to refrain from all attempts (internal or external), at neutralizing the effect of the image or thought or impulse.

The technique can be illustrated by reference to a few cases. In the first, a conscientious prosecuting attorney was seriously troubled by obsessional doubts about whether or not he had, or might in the future, inadvertently write a compromising note to a criminal whom he had prosecuted. As a result of these obsessional doubts, he went to great lengths to avoid writing paper, post-boxes, and indeed any activity involving writing. He had to carry out hundreds of multiple checks of his clothing, drawers, cupboards, etc., each day. In his case the connection between the rumination and the ritual of putting things right was evident in his external and internal behavior. He checked his clothing and drawers for compromising evidence (external) and had to recall in minute detail the events of each day (internal). He also put matters right by another internal method; if he was troubled by the image of a piece of paper containing writing, he could gain some peace by forming a counter-image of the same piece of paper absolutely clean. A well-focused image of a blank piece of paper might take an hour to attain, but it brought relief. During treatment he was asked to form and hold the ruminations for five to fifteen minutes per trial, and to refrain from "putting matters right." He was also told to refrain from carrying out any overt checking rituals, such as repeatedly searching his clothes for pieces of paper. The clinical outcome was successful. The frequency of ruminations and of associated rituals, both declined steeply.

In the second case, a young married woman who suffered from ruminations about harm coming to her close relatives, was unable to carry on with her everyday activities unless and until she cancelled out the effects of these distressing thoughts by carrying out overt touching rituals, a double eye-blink, a "good thought" or a ritualistic phrase that would "release her," e.g., she had some relief from repeating the phrase "God is good," subvocally ten times. A part of her successful treatment (significantly reduced rituals and ruminations) involved the deliberate formation of the obsessions and the voluntary inhibition of all neutralizing rituals, internal and external. The third case, another young married woman, suffered from repetitive and intrusive images of an abhorrent nature. One of her most distressing images consisted of four people lying dead in open coffins in an open grave. Once this image intruded, she was unable to continue with her normal activities unless and until she put matters right by having one or more images in which she saw the same four people standing and walking about seemingly healthy. The main part of her initially successful treatment (greatly reduced ruminations and rituals) consisted of requesting her to obtain this and related thoughts and images, and then to refrain from carrying out any neutralizing rituals. It remains to be seen if her improvement endures.

In addition to its therapeutic possibilities, this revised formulation offers the advantage of congruity with other, successful treatments for obsessional and compulsive problems. Like the prevailing treatment mode for obsessional-compulsive cleaners and checkers, it comprises deliberate exposure to the provoking experience followed by prevention of the execution of the relevant compulsive ritual (see Hodgson & Rachman, 1976). If it is correct, the formulation helps to tidy up some loose ends in the theory and practice of behavior modification for obsessional and compulsive problems.

The formulation also fits more comfortably into the theory of obsessional ruminations put forward by Rachman in 1971. If we continue to regard the rumination as a noxious stimulus which gives rise to distress and consequent attempts at avoidance, then habituation training (in this context referred to as the satiation method), followed by the prevention of the avoidance reaction, fits tidily into the theory.

The formulation may add to our comprehension of the nature of obsessions, and of their relation to compulsions. It is suggested that we can assume a functional equivalence, in most cases, between compulsive checking rituals, cleaning rituals, requests for reassurance, and neutralizing rituals (i.e., attempts at putting right). In most cases these forms of behavior achieve a degree of anxiety/discomfort reduction, and it can be assumed that this partial success is responsible for the reinforcing effect of the ritualistic behavior. It is hypothesized that attempts at putting right, like other ritualistic equivalents, are subject to modification by the process of response prevention. It is predicted that the urges associated with these neutralizing rituals follow the same pattern of spontaneous decay that has been observed to occur in the urges associated with compulsive checking rituals (see Rachman, de Silva & Roper, 1976) .The predictions made earlier (Rachman, 1971) about the conditions that are likely to facilitate habituation to ruminative thoughts and images, remain unaltered.

Incidentally, it would follow from the present analysis that thought-stopping might well succeed in truncating the duration of ruminations without necessarily reducing the associated discomfort.

Treatment

The patient is given full therapeutic instructions before the actual treatment begins. He is told that many people experience unpleasant, unwanted and unacceptable thoughts, or images or impulses. It is explained that under normal mood conditions most people can dismiss these unwelcome ideas without difficulty. However, when they are associated with depressed mood or agitation it proves to be rather difficult to eliminate the unwanted thoughts. The treatment technique is then explained to them and they are told that they will be required deliberately to form the unwanted thoughts and retain them for prolonged periods. The concept of response prevention is explained and they are told that they have to refrain from carrying out any neutralizing activities, internal or external. At the same time they are warned that the formation of the unpleasant thoughts and the exercise of response prevention will be accompanied by some discomfort, especially in the early stages of treatment. Throughout the explanation and the conduct of the treatment program itself, great emphasis is laid upon the necessity for self-management. Patients are told that we are attempting to teach them a technique for dealing with the unwanted and unacceptable ideas and that like any successful training they should carry their new skill with them when they leave the clinic. The need for accurate and regular recording of the pertinent aspects of the behavior is stressed and they are given some examples to follow. They are also warned that even after they have succeeded in modifying their ruminations, the recurrence of serious disturbances of mood might herald a return of obsessions, but that they can then reapply the control techniques which form the most important part of the treatment program.

The treatment program itself begins with the collection of baseline data. The patient is required to record the occurrence of each rumination—its content, duration, associated disturbance and the strength of any accompanying urge to carry out neutralizing rituals. Once an adequate baseline has been established, the most troublesome obsessions are subjected to satiation treatment, i.e., repeated prolonged presentations of the obsession. The therapist records the latency to acquire the obsession and the number of times it fades during each trial period. When good progress is being made, the latency will increase and the obsession will show an increase in tendency to fade during the trial period.

Once the satiation treatment is under way, the response prevention procedures are introduced. The person is urged to avoid carrying out any neutralizing activities. Throughout each session and between sessions recording of relevant data must be continued. Once good progress is evident in both aspects of the treatment, the therapist should fade out. The patient is instructed to continue practicing the two techniques even in the absence of the therapist. Depending on the needs of the particular case, the therapist may decide to place great emphasis on the satiation part of the modification program or the response prevention part. In some cases only one of the two elements of the retraining program may be needed.

This brings us to a consideration of the selection of suitable cases for this type of treatment approach. First and foremost, it seems to be appropriate for those patients whose ruminations are associated with or followed by strong urges to put matters right. In the assessment which always precedes satisfactory behavioral treatment, special attention should be paid to this aspect of the person's complaint. It is essential to get the person to describe in the greatest possible detail the exact nature and content of the ruminations and their effects. One of the key questions is, "How do you attempt to deal with the discomfort you experience during and after ruminations?" Useful follow-up questions include the following: "How do you bring the rumination to an end?" "How long does the rumination last?" "What helps to shorten the duration of the rumination?" If it turns out that the person frequently engages in neutralizing behavior, then it is quite likely that he will respond to the modification program described here. If on the other hand, he neither engages in internal or external neutralizing rituals, repeated prolonged presentations of the ruminative content are likely to be sufficient. This possibility is dealt with by the prediction made in the earlier theoretical analysis: "Under calm conditions, long exposures to ruminative thoughts would result in quicker habituation than short exposures" (Rachman, 1971, p. 234). When the ruminations are followed by overt compulsive rituals such as repetitive checking or requests for reassurance, these are simply put on a response prevention regime.

As with other behavioral modification programs of this sort, it is to be expected that some patients well find the program distressing, especially in the early stages. If such distress occurs it is best dealt with by providing encouragement, comfort and powerful social reinforcement for persisting under uncomfortable conditions. Patients can be reassured that the discomfort produced by the provoking ruminative experience is likely to dissipate within a reasonably short time. At the end of one hour, well over half of the discomfort is likely to have dissipated and by the end of two hours, there should be little trace of it (see Rachman, de Silva & Roper, 1976). It is likely that recovery from the distress provoked by the ruminative experience can be facilitated by congenial and supportive company, strongly distracting tasks and the other measures described in the paper referred to.

It is important for the person to take an active part in the planning, recording and execution of the treatment as soon as possible. Once he has acquired the rudiments of the treatment and is carrying out the program satisfactorily in the presence of the therapist, he should be encouraged to undertake increasing amounts of *practice on his own*. This is particularly important because obsessions almost certainly occur more frequently and disturbingly when a person is alone. Even more than in other behavior modification programs, full and accurate recording of the interventions and their effects are of great importance. This is because the major treatment instruction and manipulation are not immediately accessible to the therapist. In order to assess the effects of the intervention, it is essential that therapists have access to detailed, day-by-day records compiled by the patient. After the provocation of discomfort by the instructed ruminations, the therapist should request the patient to record his discomfort and urges at fifteen-minute intervals, for up to two hours. In this way it is possible to determine whether the decay of compulsive urges and discomfort is following the predicted pattern.

To conclude, it is proposed that the modification of obsessions should follow a new approach—one which conforms with the methods that have proved to be moderately successful in the modification of other forms of obsessional and compulsive problems. It is argued that this can best be achieved by recognizing the significance of neutralizing rituals and by construing them as being functionally equivalent to other kinds of compulsive ritual. The practical consequences of this view are that we should request the affected person to obtain the obsessional thoughts, impulses or images and then to refrain from putting matters right (i.e., refrain from carrying out any internal or external neutralizing activities).

ACKNOWLEDGEMENTS

I wish to thank P. de Silva and H. Shackleton for their assistance.

REFERENCES

BROADHURST, A. It's never too late to learn: An application of conditioned inhibition to obsessional ruminations in an elderly patient. In H. J. Eysenck (Ed.), *Case Studies in Behaviour Therapy*. London: Routledge and Kegan Paul, 1976.

GERTZ, H. Experience with the logotherapeutic technique of paradoxical intention in the treatment of phobic and obsessive-compulsive patients. *Am. J. Psychiat.*, 123: 548-558, 1967.

HACKMAN, A. & MCLEAN, C. A comparison of flooding and thought-stopping. *Behav. Res. and Therapy*, 13:263-270, 1975.

HODGSON, R. & RACHMAN, S. The modification of compulsive behaviour. In H. J. Eysenck (Ed.), *Case Studies in Behaviour Therapy*. London: Routledge and Kegan Paul, 1976.

HODGSON, R., RACHMAN, S., & MARKS, I. The treatment of obsessive-compulsive neurosis: Follow-up and further findings. *Behav. Res. and Therapy*, 10:181-189, 1972.

KUMAR, K. & WILKINSON, J. Thought stopping: A useful treatment in phobias of "internal stimuli." *Br. J. Psychiat.*, 119:305-307, 1971.

MARKS, I., HODGSON, R., & RACHMAN, S. Treatment of chronic obsessive-compulsive neurosis by *in vivo* exposure. *Br. J. Psychiat.*, 127:349-364, 1975.

RACHMAN, S. Obsessional ruminations. *Behav. Res. and Therapy*, 9:229-235, 1971.

RACHMAN, S. Some similarities and differences between obsessional ruminations and morbid preoccupations. *Can. Psychiat. Ass. J.*, 18:71-74, 1973.

RACHMAN, S., DE SILVA, P., & ROPER, G. The spontaneous decay of compulsive urges. *Behav. Res. and Therapy*, 14:445-453, 1976.

RACHMAN, S., DE SILVA, P., & SELIGMAN, M. Prepared phobias and obsessions: Clinical outcome. *Behav. Res. and Therapy*, in press.

RACHMAN, S., HODGSON, R., & MARKS, I. The treatment of chronic obsessive compulsive neurosis. *Behav. Res. and Therapy*, 9:237-247, 1971.

RACHMAN, S., MARKS, I., & HODGSON, R. The treatment of obsessive-compulsive neurotics by modelling and flooding. *Behav. Res. and Therapy*, 11:463-471, 1973.

SOLYOM, L., GARZA-PEREZ, J., LEDWIDGE, B., & SOLYOM, C. Paradoxical intention in the treatment of obsessive thoughts: A pilot study. *Compreh. Psychiat.*, 13:291-297, 1972.

STERN, R. Treatment of a case of obsessional neurosis using a thought-stopping technique. *Br. J. Psychiat.*, 117:441-442, 1970.

STERN, R., LIPSEDGE, M., & MARKS, I. Obsessive ruminations: A controlled trial of a thought-stopping technique. *Behav. Res. and Therapy*, 11:659-662, 1973.

WOLPE, J. *Psychotherapy by Reciprocal Inhibition*. Stanford: Stanford University Press, 1957.

WOLPE, J. *The Practice of Behavior Therapy*. Oxford: Pergamon Press, 1970.

YAMAGAMI, T. The treatment of an obsession by thought-stopping. *J. Behav. Ther. Exp. Psychiat.*, 2:135, 1971.

SECTION X: THERAPEUTIC STRATEGIES, CASE STUDIES AND CLINICAL EXTENSIONS

27

EMG-BIOFEEDBACK REDUCTION OF TENSION HEADACHE

A Cognitive Skills-Training Approach

John L. Reeves
Dalhousie University

The biofeedback literature affirms the therapeutic efficacy of EMG-biofeedback-assisted relaxation for the treatment of tension headache. However, this form of therapy has failed to focus on the role of cognitive variables in the control and perception of tension headache. The present case study provides a prototype treatment combining cognitive behavior—modification procedures with EMG-biofeedback training to treat a subject with chronic tension headache. Phase I, baseline, involved collecting mean EMG and daily headache activity, emphasizing specification of environmental stressors. Phase II, cognitive skills—training, focused on: (1) identifying negative self-statements (cognitions) related to stressors, and (2) training the subject to replace negative self-statements with coping self-instructions. This treatment resulted in a 33% headache reduction over baseline, with no concomitant changes in frontalis EMG. Phase III, EMG-biofeedback training, resulted in a 38% reduction in mean EMG level and a 66% reduction in mean headache activity when compared to baseline. The results suggest the importance of attending to cognitive factors in the treatment of tension headache.

Reprinted with permission from *Biofeedback and Self-Regulation,* Vol. 1, No. 2, 1976.
This paper was presented at the 6th annual meeting of the Biofeedback Research Society, Monterey, California, 1975.

Laboratory research provides evidence that stress reactions can vary as a function of cognitive variables, though the nature of the threatening event remains constant (Langer, Janis & Wolfer, 1974). Tolerance to aversive events has been increased by the availabiiity of an externally (Kanfer & Goldfoot, 1966) or internally (Barber & Cooper, 1972) produced distractor, perceived control over the aversive event (Averill, 1973; Glass & Singer, 1972), and providing information regarding the stressor (Janis, 1971; Johnson & Leventhal, 1974; Lazarus & Alfert, 1964). The effectiveness of these procedures has been shown to be enhanced by providing subjects with an opportunity to rehearse in the presence of milder stressors (Janis, 1971; Meichenbaum, Turk & Burstein, 1974). From such laboratory research, guidelines emerge for training clinically useful coping strategies.

Meichenbaum and Cameron (1973) have incorporated these mechanisms into a procedure referred to as *stress inoculation training.* Essentially, highly anxious subjects were shown the degree to which attention to and negative cognitions (self-statements) about an aversive event determine the amount of stress experienced. Subjects were then taught to identify and substitute such anxiety-engendering self-statements with positive coping self-instructions and relaxation. Finally, the subjects were given the opportunity to rehearse and implement these cognitive coping skills under a variety of laboratory-induced stressors. Stress inoculation provided the most efficacious treatment modality, relative even to such successful treatment procedures as systematic desensitization.

Recently Langer et al. (1974) employed a variation of this procedure to reduce pre- and postoperative stress reactions in hospitalized patients. Patients who received instructions regarding the "cognitive reappraisal of anxiety-provoking events, and calming self-talk" showed immediate positive change in ability to cope with discomfort and anxiety when compared to other treatment modalities not incorporating coping instructions. Thus, in keeping with the experimental literature, the coping self-instructions may be viewed as acting to distract the subjects from the negative aspects of the stressful situation(s), as well as providing them with a perceived control of the situation—the subject knows that he can initiate coping self-instruction in any situation.

These studies highlight that cognitive reappraisal, in the form of coping self-statements, can be clinically employed to reduce stress reactions. The present case study proposed to extend the applicability of cognitive reappraisal, in the form of a modified stress inoculation—training procedure, to treat a severe case of chronic tension headache. Since recently developed EMG-biofeedback techniques have proved successful in treating tension headache (Budzynski, Stoyva, Adler & Mullaney, 1973), little attention has been given the potential role of cognitive variables in determining and controlling the perception of headache. Such data may provide useful information regarding the etiology of tension headache, since "psychological components" have been generally regarded to be a necessary condition for the onset or exacerbation of tension headache (Bakal, 1975; Tasto & Hinkle, 1973).

METHOD

Subject

The subject was a 20-year-old single female student referred from the University Health Service for treatment of chronic tension headache. Medical and neurological examination failed to disclose contributing causes. The headaches began approximately 5 years prior to the initiation of treatment, and were refractory to the typical array of medications, i.e., Fiorinal and Valium. She appeared to be functioning normally regarding most interpersonal areas.

Recording Procedure

The subject sat in a comfortable reclining chair in a sound-attenuated, shielded room adjoining the recording room. Frontalis EMG was recorded using a Biofeedback Technology 401 Feedback Myograph (bandpass = 30-1000 Hz) and Hewlett-Packard silver/silver chloride electrodes with a Redux paste medium. The electrodes were placed 1 inch above each eyebrow directly above the center of the eye, with the reference electrode in the center of the forehead, using an elastic headband.

The average EMG in microvolts (rms) was recorded for 20 1-min blocks, using a variable time period integrator described by Mader, Marble & Reeves (1974).

Self-Recording of Headache

Self-recordings of headache activity were collected on $3 \times 5''$ index cards divided into 24 1-hr intervals (Budzynski, Stoyva & Adler, 1970). A 5-point headache pain-intensity scale was used, with *1* indicating "a very low-level headache that enters awareness only at times when attention is devoted to it," and *5* indicating "intense incapacitating headache." Headaches were recorded on an hourly basis throughout the duration of the project. Mean intensity ratings were calculated each day following the procedure of Budzynski et al. (1973).

Procedure

Phase I: Baseline. The first session involved collecting historical information from the subject, followed by a brief overview of the program. The procedure for self-recording of headache activity was described in detail. Then followed a discussion designed to provide the subject with preparatory information (Janis, 1971) regarding the "nature" of stress reactions, emphasizing tension headache. This discussion focused on the "heavy situational" components involved in most stress disorders. She was told that often her headache was more severe than it could have been because she failed to identify the situation as stressful early enough. It was explained that successful treatment required accurate pinpointing of situations that precipitated headaches. This would involve keeping a "headache diary" along with the self-recording charts. Examples were provided from the self-reports of other patients.

Following this discussion, the subject was introduced to the EMG device. She was told that the device would allow the experimenter to monitor those muscles involved in a tension headache, thus providing information as to the progress of treatment. A 20-min recording session was then conducted, and questions answered concerning the recording procedures. All subsequent baseline sessions (3/week for 2 weeks) were structured first to elicit and pinpoint situations that precipitated headaches, followed by a 20-min EMG-recording session. The subject's daily headache charts were collected. She was also told to sit comfortably for 15 min each day and pinpoint and list situations in which headaches were likely to occur.

The most frequent general "headache" situations were found to be:

1. Situations in which a more assertive response would have been appropriate.
2. Crowded shopping situations (particularly when tired).
3. Academic/evaluative situations.
4. Situations in which a time limit is externally imposed.

Phase II: Cognitive Skills Training. The second phase of treatment, a modified stress inoculation procedure (Meichenbaum et al., 1974), was designed to teach the subject cognitive coping skills, and provide her with an opportunity to rehearse them. The initial discussion focused on the inconsistencies and variability in headache activity across similar stressful circumstances. Following the procedure of Langer et al. (1974) with surgical patients, it was explained that it was rarely situations themselves that caused headaches; rather, it was the cognitions or thoughts people have regarding them and the attention they give these thoughts. Since examination situations frequently elicited headache, examples of how negative cognitions mediated such reactions were provided. For example, it was suggested that much of her time prior to and during an examination was spent catastrophizing about how miserably she was going to do, and being preoccupied with feelings of inadequacy, anticipation of punishment, and loss of status or esteem. The discussion focused on the idea that one's thoughts or self-statements could actually control the amount of distress experienced. The experimenter elicited negative self-statements from the subject regarding a variety of stressful situations. The experimenter then went on to suggest that the subject, by changing her self-statements regarding stressful situations, could "short-circuit" the headache response. Examples were given, and elicited, of "coping self-instructions," e.g., "Don't worry, worrying won't help anything"; "Control yourself, just think about what I have to do"; "I am in control." Following Meichenbaum et al. (1974), the subject was instructed to imagine herself in stressful situations, identify the negative self-statements, and then instruct herself to cope, first aloud (with the experimenter providing feedback and reinforcement), and then covertly. The experimenter explained that whenever the subject "heard herself" thinking negative self-statements, that behavior should immediately act as a "cue" or "reminder" to produce "positive-coping" self-instructions. She was also told to mentally rehearse instructing herself to cope in stressful situations for 15 min, during which the subject was instructed to mentally rehearse coping with stressors. All subsequent cognitive skills-training sessions (3/week for 2 weeks) began by discussing how she had employed coping self-instructions in vivo, followed by a 20-min recording session. The subject's daily headache charts were then collected.

Phase III: EMG-Biofeedback Training. The third phase of training involved EMG-biofeedback training (Budzynski et al., 1973). Discussion focused on the idea that much of the pain experienced was a result of sustained contraction of the head and neck muscles, and that a powerful adjunct to treatment would involve learning to relax the affected muscles. The theory and technique of biofedback were then presented to the subject. An overview of the biofeedback control of tension-headache research was presented. The technique, described in detail by Budzynski et al. (1973), consisted of providing a feedback tone proportional in frequency to the level of EMG activity through Nova stereophones placed on a table next to her. A shaping procedure was used whereby she was instructed to keep the feedback tone as low as possible by relaxing. The amplifier gain was gradually increased, thus requiring her to produce lower level of frontalis muscle potential in order to maintain the lower frequency tone. Following the "stress-management procedures" of Budzynski (1973), the subject was also instructed to again covertly rehearse her coping self-instructions while maintaining low levels of the feedback tone and experiencing feelings of relaxation.

The biofeedback training phase lasted 6 weeks (3/week), with each session beginning with a brief discussion of how the subject had employed her "newly acquired coping skills," followed by a 20-min-recording session. She was also instructed to practice "stress management" for 15 min each day. Her daily headache charts were collected. During the final week of training, the analog feedback was gradually faded out by progressively lowering the volume of the tone.

Phase IV: Follow-up. A follow-up was conducted 6 months after the final session of Phase III. During the follow-up phase, the subject was requested to again record headache activity for 2 weeks, and scheduled for 2 more no-feedback recording sessions (1/week). A follow-up questionnaire designed to evaluate deleterious "spin-off" effects (i.e., symptom substitution) similar to that used by Budzynski et al. (1973) was also administered on the final session of this phase.

RESULTS AND DISCUSSION

Janis (1971) has posited that providing information regarding a stressful event increases stress tolerance. The information is said to result in the "work of worrying," or cognitive rehearsal of the impending threats that allows the subject to develop realistic, self-delivered reassurances, minimizing the emotional impact of the stressor, when confronted. The results of the present case report (Figure 1), however, suggest that cognitive rehearsal alone is not enough to produce changes in self-reported headache activity or EMG. As can be seen in Figure 1, during the baseline phase, headache and EMG levels remained constant, even though the subject engaged in the "work of worrying" in the form of instructions

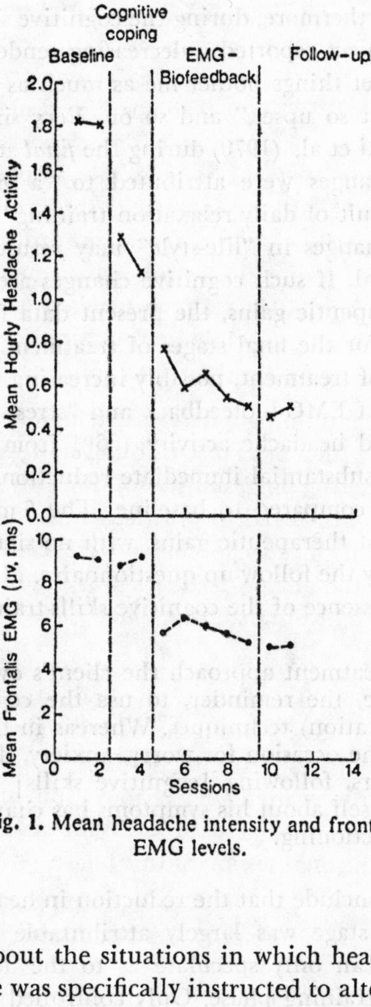

Fig. 1. Mean headache intensity and frontalis EMG levels.

to list and think about the situations in which headaches were likely to occur. Not until she was specifically instructed to alter cognitive appraisal or self-statements of stress situations did reductions in self-reports of headache occur, e.g., a 33% reduction from baseline. Moreover, these headache reductions were not accompanied by comparable decreases in frontalis EMG, in part precluding a somatic explanation.

These results corroborate the findings of Langer et al. (1974) with surgical patients. They found that only patients specifically instructed in cognitive reappraisal skills showed significant drops in pre- and post-operative stress reactions with no corresponding physiological reductions, when compared to patients receiving information only (work of worrying) and controls. Furthermore, during the cognitive skills-training phases of this study, the subject reported a decreasing tendency to overreact to stress; e.g., "I don't let things bother me as much as they used to"; "It's silly to let myself get so upset," and so on. Very similar changes were reported by Budzynski et al. (1970) during the *final* stages of biofeedback treatment. Those changes were attributed to "a general lowering of arousal level, as a result of daily relaxation training." The present study suggests that such changes in "life-style" may result in the absence of lower levels of arousal. If such cognitive changes are important for the maintenance of therapeutic gains, the present data further suggest that rather than waiting for the final stages of treatment, these skills can be learned at the onset of treatment, possibly increasing therapeutic efficacy.

The introduction of EMG-biofeedback and "stress management training" further decreased headache activity (66% from baseline), and was closely paralleled by substantial immediate reductions in frontalis EMG levels of 38%, when compared to baseline. The 6-month follow-up affirmed maintenance of therapeutic gains, with no signs of symptom substitution as assessed by the follow-up questionnaire. Meichenbaum (1974) has summarized the essence of the cognitive skills-training approach:

> . . . In such a treatment approach the client's own maladaptive behavior is the cue, the reminder, to use the cognitive coping and behavioral (relaxation) techniques. Whereas in the past the client's symptoms were the occasion for worry, anxiety, depression and maladaptive behaviors, following [cognitive skills] training, what the client says to himself about his symptoms has changed to more adaptive modes of functioning.

While one might conclude that the reduction in headache activity during the biofeedback stage was largely attributable to lower levels of frontalis EMG, one can only speculate as to the active component(s) during the cognitive training phase. Only controlled research can ascertain whether these headache reductions reflected distraction, information, perceived control, preexposure to milder stressors, rehearsal, a lowering in an unrecorded index of arousal, or some combination of these. By experimentally varying these factors, one might elucidate information regarding the cognitive conditions that produce tension headaches.

To the extent that conclusive inferences can be drawn from a single case design, the present study suggests promising extension and integration of cognitive modification procedures with biofeedback technology for the control and treatment of tension headache.

REFERENCES

AVERILL, J. Personal control over aversive stimuli and its relationship to stress. *Psychological Bulletin,* 80:286-303, 1973.

BAKAL, D. A. Headache: A biopsychological perspective. *Psychological Bulletin,* 8: 369-382, 1975.

BARBER, T. X., & COOPER, B. J. Effects on pain of experimentally induced and spontaneous distraction. *Psychological Reports,* 31:647-651, 1972.

BUDZYNSKI, T. H. Biofeedback procedures in the clinic. *Seminars in Psychiatry,* 5:537-547, 1973.

BUDZYNSKI, T. H., STOYVA, J. M., & ADLER, C. Feedback-induced muscle relaxation: Application to tension headaches. *Journal of Behavior Therapy and Experimental Psychiatry,* 1:205-211, 1970.

BUDZYNSKI, T. H., STOYVA, J. M., ADLER, C. S., & MULLANEY, D. J. EMG biofeedback and tension headache: A controlled outcome study. *Psychosomatic Medicine,* 35: 484-496, 1973.

GLASS, D., & SINGER, J. *Urban Stress: Experiments in Noise and Social Stressors.* New York: Academic Press, 1972.

JANIS, I. L. *Stress and Frustration.* New York: Harcourt, Brace, Jovanovich, 1971.

JOHNSON, J. E., & LEVENTHAL, H. Effects of accurate expectations and behavioral instructions on reactions during a noxious medical examination. *Journal of Personality and Social Psychology,* 29:710-718, 1974.

KANFER, F. H., & GOLDFOOT, D. A. Self-control and tolerance of noxious stimulation. *Psychological Reports,* 18:79-85, 1966.

LANGER, E. J., JANIS, I. L., & WOLFER, J. A. Reduction of psychological stress in surgical patients. Unpublished manuscript, Yale University, 1974.

LAZARUS, R. S., & ALFERT, E. Short-circuiting of threat by experimentally altering cognitive appraisal. *Journal of Abnormal and Social Psychology,* 69:195-205, 1964.

MADER, D. J., MARBLE, A. E., & REEVES, J. L. An inexpensive variable time period integrator for electromyographic signals. *Behavior Research Methods Instrumentation,* 6:411-415, 1974.

MEICHENBAUM, D. Self-instructional methods. In A. Goldstein & F. Kanfer (Eds.), *Helping People Change: Methods and Materials.* New York: Pergamon Press, 1974.

MEICHENBAUM, D., & CAMERON, R. Stress inoculation: A skills training approach to anxiety management. Unpublished manuscript, University of Waterloo, 1973.

MEICHENBAUM, D., TURK, D., & BURSTEIN, S. The nature of coping with stress. Paper presented at the NATO-sponsored conference on Dimensions of Anxiety and Stress, Athens, Greece, September 1974.

TASTO, D. L., & HINKLE, J. E. Muscle relaxation treatment for tension headache. *Behaviour Research and Therapy,* 11:347-349, 1973.

SECTION X: THERAPEUTIC STRATEGIES, CASE STUDIES AND CLINICAL EXTENSIONS

28

AN EXPERIMENTAL CASE STUDY OF THE BIOFEEDBACK TREATMENT OF RAPE-INDUCED PSYCHOPHYSIOLOGICAL CARDIOVASCULAR DISORDER

Edward B. Blanchard and Gene G. Abel

University of Mississippi Medical Center

A patient with a 15-year history of a rape-induced psychophysiologic cardiovascular disorder, episodic sinus tachycardia, and subsequent "blackout spells," was treated using a biofeedback procedure. The patient was taught to control her heart rate in the presence of audio tape descriptions of rape which earlier had instigated tachycardia episodes. Appropriate control phases in the treatment procedure helped to isolate the biofeedback training as responsible for the improvement.

Reports describing the treatment of cardiac arrhythmias through biofeedback (Weiss & Engel, 1971; Scott, Blanchard, Edmunson & Young, 1973; Engel & Bleecker, 1974) hold out much promise. But problems in experimental design limit the inferences and conclusions which may be drawn (Blanchard & Young, 1974).

Reprinted with permission from *Behavior Therapy*, 7, 113-119, 1976.

This research was supported by National Heart and Lung Institute Grant, IROHL 14906.

The present report describes the biofeedback treatment of a patient with a rape-induced psychophysiologic cardiovascular disorder, namely a sinus tachycardia triggered by certain sexual cues. Care was taken to conduct the treatment of this case with appropriate control conditions (Barlow & Hersen, 1973) so as to isolate the therapeutic conditions.

The idea of teaching a patient to control his heart rate through biofeedback training as a means of dealing with stressful situations is not new: Prigatano & Johnson (1972) and Sirota, Schwartz & Shapiro (1974) have conducted analogue studies along these lines. However, in addition to not involving clinical patients, the latter two studies suffer from other problems: Prigatano and Johnson's subjects did not learn to control heart rate variability and showed no behavioral difference in comparison to an untreated group of spider-fearful subjects. In the study of Sirato et al., subjects were trained to increase or decrease heart rate while undergoing mildly aversive electrical shocks. While the evidence for the subjects' having learned to decrease their heart rate is somewhat questionable, due primarily to not having allowed for the decrease in heart rate because of adaptation, this group of subjects did rate the shocks as less painful than subjects who were trying to increase heart rate.

CASE HISTORY

The patient, a 30-year-old, married female with a history of "spells" since age 14, at which age she was raped by her sister's boyfriend. Repulsed by this event and feeling guilty, she concealed it from her family. The "spells" began shortly thereafter and, although having some variability, they generally were associated with a feeling of nausea and vomiting, a choking sensation with the onset of tachycardia, and a numbness of the extremities. The patient reported a vague sense of altered state of consciousness, had lost control of her bladder on one occasion, but had never lost control of bowels during a "spell." She reported no loss of consciousness, that is, she was able to hear what was occurring around her, but she was simply unresponsive for a minute or two. A number of months following the rape, the patient became aware that she was pregnant and concealed this from her parents until her seventh month of gestation. Great turmoil developed within the home, eventually leading to the patient's leaving town during the latter stages of pregnancy, delivering the child and giving it up for adoption. On returning to her home town, the patient perceived that others began thinking of her as the town slut. Her thoughts of guilt about the rape continued unabated, as did the spells.

Her history from the age of 20 to her initial psychiatric contact with the experimenters was an endless repetition of numerous organic evaluations. She was followed for approximately 15 years as having a possible convulsive disorder. Four EEGs, numerous skull series, lumbar punctures, and pneumoencephalograms were all within normal limits, and the frequency of the patient's spells was unaffected by anticonvulsant drugs (Mensatoin, Dilantin, phenobarbital). Her final neurological evaluation 2 years prior to initially being seen led to the conclusion that the patient's spells were psychogenic. Cardiovascular evaluations were likewise extensive with numerous possible diagnoses being entertained, but physical evaluations plus electrocardiograms (including a 10-hr, MoHetz II type) failed to confirm any specific cardiac disorder.

The subject's extensive medical evaluations (running $3-4,000 per year) eventually led to her psychiatric referral. During the sessions which followed, she was able to identify the antecedents of her symptoms as thoughts and ruminations about having been raped, and more importantly, how individuals in her natural environment (especially her home town) might perceive her. Thoughts of returning home frequently preceded episodes of tachycardia. In the last 10 years, her fears were aggravated when she was propositioned by men in her home town, events she interpreted as directly resulting from her having been raped at age 14.

The patient's therapy initially involved group therapy to increase her verbalization regarding chronic marital problems and her marked passivity regarding her symptomatology. In the course of therapy, the specific stimuli that elicited her spells became more apparent. Since they were rather easily circumscribed to the sexual area, and since the patient focused so strongly on her somatic problems, particularly the tachycardia episodes, a biofeedback treatment designed specifically to help the patient in this area was instituted. Throughout this treatment, the patient continued in group therapy and was stabilized on Dilantin, 100 mg twice per day.

METHOD

Apparatus

The apparatus has been described in detail elsewhere (Scott et al., 1973). Briefly, it consisted of a polygraph and various electronic counters and timers by which (1) the patient's heart rate could be measured and printed out on a minute-to-minute basis, and (2) the patient could be given binary visual feedback of heart rate on a beat-by-beat basis as to whether it was above or below a criterion level.

All treatment sessions were conducted in an air conditioned, sound attenuated room. The patient sat in a recliner during sessions and was visually monitored via television.

*Procedure**

All sessions lasted 40 min. Each one was divided into four parts: The first 15 min was devoted to adaptation of the patient to the laboratory situation; during the next 5 min the session, baseline heart rate was determined; and finally, two consecutive 10-min experimental trials were conducted. During the latter two trials, various experimental procedures, to be described, were introduced.

Audio tapes. The patient's tachycardia episodes were instigated primarily by thoughts or other external cues related to sexual topics, especially rape. In the absence of these internal or external cues, her heart rate was usually in the normal range. To instigate the symptomatic behavior so that it could be treated, we played audio tape descriptions of scenes involving rape to the patient. The use of audio tape descriptions of sexual behavior for generating sexual arousal in patients has been described and demonstrated previously (Abel, Levis & Clancy, 1970; Abel, Barlow & Blanchard, Note 1).

Three different 10-min audio tape descriptions were developed, relying on the patient's history to determine which stimuli might provoke her episodes of tachycardia. The first description (Rape 1) was an explicit and detailed account of the actual rape episode. On listening to it, the patient later reported that although the description recounted the events of the actual rape, it failed to cause her emotional distress because the actual rape was less provocative than the attitudes of those in her environment who might know about the rape. The second and third descriptions (Rape 2 and Rape 3) subsequently were an elaboration of scenes in the patient's home town where she cencountered the attitudes and opinions that she feared most, such as scenes of men calling her on the telephone to proposition her, neighbors talking about her illicit sexual activities when she was younger, etc. Two 10-min audio tape descriptions of neutral scenes were also developed, scenes that were not emotionally charged for the patient, such as her fixing meals or going for a ride.

* The authors acknowledge the assistance of Mary R. Haynes in conducting the sessions.

These tapes were played to the patient during the experimental trials in a manner described below.

Baseline 1. In the first four baseline sessions, no audio tapes were played and the patient continued to sit quietly. These sessions were designed to adapt the patient to the laboratory and to determine the degree of change in heart rate produced by continued adaptation within the session.

Baseline 2. In the next two baseline sessions, tapes Rape 1 and Neutral were played in counterbalanced order for the experimental trials. When Rape 1 proved relatively ineffective in generating the symptomatic cardiac responses, Rape 2 was introduced. Rape 2 and Neutral were then presented for four sessions, with the order of presentation within a session counterbalanced across sessions.

Feedback training. Next, the patient was taught to lower her heart rate, using the feedback and shaping procedure described in detail by Scott et al. (1973). Briefly, it consists of giving the patient binary feedback of heart rate on a beat-by-beat basis by means of a running time meter. The patient is instructed to try to lower her heart rate, and that when she is making the correct response, the meter is running. The criterion for feedback is changed according to a predetermined shaping schedule designed to keep the patient in fairly close contact with the criterion.

In this phase of the treatment, the patient first received 10 min of training with feedback only. This was followed by a second 10 min in which she received feedback plus the neutral audio tape so that she could learn to gain control of her heart rate while listening to an audio description. This phase of treatment was continued for eight sessions, until the patient was showing consistently good control of heart rate lowering.

Feedback plus rape 2. Next, the patient was given an opportunity to apply her newly acquired ability in heart rate control. For the first 10 min she received only feedback of heart rate control. For the next 10 min she was instructed to listen to Rape 2, become involved in it, but still try to lower her heart rate using the feedback. This procedure was continued for 25 sessions until the patient had four consecutive sessions in which heart rate was lowered by at least two beats per minute (BPM).

Baseline 2. The degree to which the patient had learned self-control of heart rate was assessed in the next phase by returning to baseline condi-

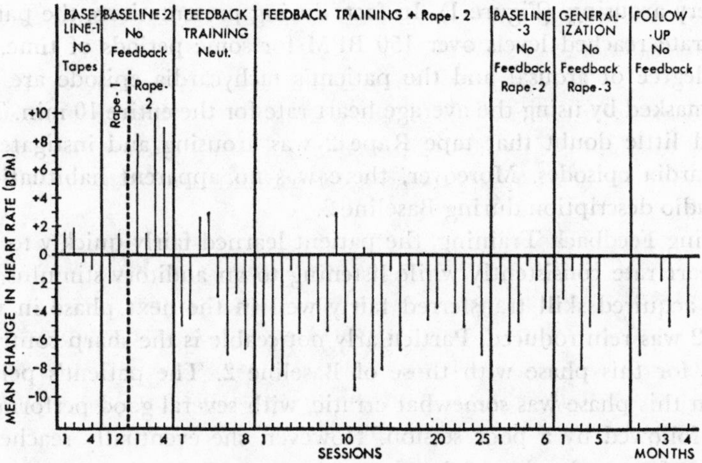

FIG. 1. Change in patient's average heart rate from session-baseline to experimental trial on a session by session basis for all phases of treatment.

tions. The patient again listened to tapes Rape 2 and Neutral in counterbalanced order, and controlled her heart rate without the assistance of feedback.

Generalization. The final phase involved a test of generalization. An entirely new rape description, Rape 3, was introduced into the no-feedback trials in order to see how the patient could maintain control of heart rate, and continue to lower it, while listening to a novel stimulus.

During the first four phases, sessions were usually held three or four times per week. During the last two phases, sessions were held only twice per week.

RESULTS

The values plotted in Figure 1 were determined by subtracting the average heart rate for the 5-min session baseline from the average heart rate for the entire 10-min trial during which a rape audio tape was presented. During the Feedback Training phase, in which no rape descriptions were presented, heart rate from the trial during the Neutral tape was used. These difference values are presented as changes in heart rate, either an increase indicating arousal or a decrease indicating control.

In Baseline 2, tape Rape 1 produced little arousal, whereas Rape 2 was very arousing (Figure 1). In fact, during presentations, the patient's heart rate reached levels over 150 BPM for some periods of time. This high degree of arousal and the patient's tachycardia episode are somewhat masked by using the average heart rate for the entire 10 min. There seemed little doubt that tape Rape 2 was arousing and instigated the tachycardia episodes. Moreover, there was no apparent habituation of this audio description during Baseline 2.

During Feedback Training, the patient learned fairly quickly to lower her heart rate consistently while listening to an auditory stimulus. This newly acquired skill transferred fairly well in the next phase in which Rape 2 was reintroduced. Particularly noticeable is the sharp contrast in results for this phase with those of Baseline 2. The patient's performance in this phase was somewhat erratic, with several good performances being followed by a poor session. However, she eventually reached the criterion for termination of the phase.

In the final experimental control phase, Baseline 3 and Generalization, the patient continued to show good control of heart rate *in the absence of feedback*. The failure to find a reversal in the heart rate data when feedback was withdrawn, while weakening the experimental analysis, was the desired clinical effect, and demonstrated the patient's ability to control heart rate in the absence of feedback.

Follow-up sessions during which the patient received no feedback while listening to either Rape 2 or Rape 3 were held at 1, 3, and 4 months. The patient continued to maintain good heart rate control during these sessions.

Clinical Course

During the presentation of Rape 1, the patient reported minimal anxiety. During the presentation of Rape 2, however, concomitant with her sinus tachycardia in excess of 150 BPM, the patient reported marked anxiety to the cues presented in the tape. Following completion of such trials, the patient would frequently remain in the laboratory for 15 to 20 min crying excessively and discussing her guilt. During such episodes, she was allowed to ventilate, but the therapist was cautious to provide no more than minimal support. Her clinical course during feedback training using the neutral tapes was unremarkable. Feedback training with tape Rape 2 initially elicited some subjective discomfort, but as treatment progressed, the patient reported sustained reduction of anxiety while listening to it. The patient was most impressed during the generalization sessions. She spontaneously reported that this tape (Rape 3) was especially effective at eliciting those exact thoughts which, antecedent to treatment, had usually precipitated her tachycardia. She was surprised that her usual tachycardia was not elicited.

The patient continued to have episodes of sinus tachycardia and other aspects of her "spells" on about a once per week basis into the Feedback plus Rape 2 phase. During this phase the "spells" began to disappear. By the end of treatment the tachycardia episodes and "blackout spells" had virtually disappeared.

During follow-up, 4 weeks after termination of the generalization sessions, the patient actually returned to her home town, and saw some of the men who had propositioned her in the past. Prior to treatment, such occurrences had always led to the development of her tachycardia and "spells." Further clinical support for the effectiveness of her treatment occurred when she was forced (due to some social obligations) to go into the home of one of the men who had propositioned her in the past. During the social encounter, she met and talked with one of the men, contact with whom, in the past, had routinely precipitated her spells. The patient was very pleased when no spell followed the social engagement.

One element of her psychological symptoms was not altered by the treatment: depressive symptomatology and loss of appetite following conflicts with her husband. This symptomatology, which had always been present in her history, continued even following biofeedback training.

DISCUSSION

This case has several novel features: First, it represents a case of episodic sinus tachycardia treated by a biofeedback approach in which adequate baseline and control phases were included. A previous case reported by Engel and Bleecker (1974) showed a definite clinical effect; however, as noted by Blanchard and Young (1974), the experimental design of the latter study was such as to limit its scientific value. Secondly, it represents a wedding in a clinical case of biofeedback training with the use of audio tapes to generate arousal.

With this particular patient, several alternative behavior therapy approaches were considered: both systematic desensitization (Wolpe, 1958) and flooding (Marks, 1972). These two were ruled out here for two reasons: The patient showed a great preoccupation with somatic complaints, particularly as related to her heart; and her episodic sinus tachycardia was, in and of itself, a decided problem. Thus, the decision was made to attack the problem behavior directly.

It is possible that direct relaxation training could have been equally as effective as the biofeedback training in this case, or that the biofeedback procedure itself was only an elaborate means of teaching relaxation. Blanchard & Young (1974) have speculated that many of the clinical effects of biofeedback treatment, particularly with cardiovascular disorders, may be due to teaching the patient how to relax. Thus, it is not possible to rule out an explanation of present results based on relaxation; however, the design used does enable us to say that the total biofeedback training package, whatever its ultimate mode of action, was responsible for the observed changes.

Finally, this study demonstrates control of heart rate in the absence of feedback. Many studies in the biofeedback area have demonstrated feedback-assisted control of heart rate, but only a few have assessed the degree of maintenance of this control in the absence of feedback. Such control is necessary for any biofeedback training to have utility for the patient in the natural environment.

REFERENCE NOTE

1. ABEL, G. G., BARLOW, D. H., & BLANCHARD, E. B. *Developing Heterosexual Arousal by Altering Masturbatory Fantasies: A Controlled Study.* Paper presented to Annual Meeting of Association for Advancement of Behavior Therapy, Miami Beach, Florida, December 1973.

REFERENCES

ABEL, G. G., LEVIS, D., & CLANCY, J. Aversion therapy applied to taped sequences of deviant behavior in exhibitionism and other sexual deviations: A preliminary report. *Journal of Behavior Therapy and Experimental Psychiatry,* 1:58-66, 1970.

BARLOW, D. H., & HERSEN, M. Single case experimental designs: Uses in applied clinical research. *Archives of General Psychiatry,* 29:319-325, 1975.

BLANCHARD, E. B., & YOUNG, L. D. Clinical applications of biofeedback training: A review of evidence. *Archives of General Psychiatry,* 30:573-589, 1974.

ENGEL, B. T., & BLEECKER, E. R. Application of operant conditioning techniques to the control of the cardiac arrhythmias. In P. Obrist, A. H. Black, J. Brener, & L. V. DiCara (Eds.), *Contemporary Trends in Cardiovascular Psychophysiology.* Chicago: Aldine-Atherton, 1974.

MARKS, I. M. Flooding (Implosion) and allied treatments. In W. S. Agras (Ed.), *Behavior Modification: Principles and Clinical Applications.* Boston: Little Brown & Co., 1972.

PRIGATANO, G. P., & JOHNSON, H. J. Biofeedback control or heart rate variability to phobic stimuli: A new approach to treating spider phobia. *Proceedings of Annual*

Convention, APA. Washington, D.C., American Psychological Association, 1972, pp. 403-404.

SCOTT, R. W., BLANCHARD, E. B., EDMUNSON, E. D., & YOUNG, L. D. A shaping procedure for heart rate control in chronic tachycardia. *Perceptual and Motor Skills, 37*: 327-338, 1973.

SIROTA, A. D., SCHWARTZ, G. E., & SHAPIRO, D. Voluntary control of human heart rate: Effect of reaction to aversive stimulation. *Journal of Abnormal Psychology*, 83:261-267, 1974.

WEISS, T., & ENGEL, B. T. Operant conditioning of heart rate patients with premature ventricular contractions. *Psychosomatic Medicine*, 33:301-321, 1971.

WOLPE, J. *Psychotherapy by Reciprocal Inhibition*. Stanford, Ca.: Stanford University Press. 1958.

SECTION X: THERAPEUTIC STRATEGIES, CASE STUDIES AND CLINICAL EXTENSIONS

29

TEACHER-IMPLEMENTED BEHAVIOR MODIFICATION IN A CASE OF ORGANICALLY BASED EPILEPSY

Barbara A. Balaschak

Miami University, Oxford, Ohio

Significant reduction of seizures in an 11-year-old epileptic girl was achieved through a contingency management program implemented by her classroom teacher. The program was designed to shift the focus from her actual seizures to her seizure-free time periods. A chart of "good times" was kept by the teacher, and rewards of candy and verbal praise were given at the completion of a totally seizure-free week at school. Seizures diminished from an estimated average of three per week to one per week over the total treatment period. The program was discontinued due to the teacher's unwillingness to reinstate it following the child's lengthy absenteeism and changes in her medication. Seizures then returned to the baseline rate through the remainder of the school year. Lack of adequate controls made it impossible to attribute success directly and entirely to the behavioral intervention. However, it is unlikely that such dramatic change could be solely attributed to mere chance, the continuation of her medication, or her continued traditional psychotherapy. The results suggest the need for more

---

Reprinted with permission from *Journal of Consulting and Clinical Psychology,* 44, 2, 218-223, 1976.

heuristic case studies of seizure disorders treated as an operant chain and the need for subsequent tightly controlled research.

In the early history of behavior modification its use often seemed restricted to "last ditch efforts" on "back ward" cases. Over the past 15 years there has been a wide dissemination of information on the implementation and successes of a variety of behavioral techniques in a wide range of cases (Morrow, 1971). Many people who were previously apprehensive of and opposed to the use of behavioral approaches seem to be more open to their application. As a result, therapists have been allowed a freer hand in creatively applying behavioral principles in unique ways and in non-back-ward settings.

Paralleling advances in behavior modification and changes in attitude on the part of both professionals and nonprofessionals are a number of discoveries about a person's apparent ability to affect his own body experience. Included in these advances are techniques in autonomic nervous system conditioning (Kimmel, 1974; Miller, 1969) and in control of pain (Davison & Valins, 1969; Fordyce, Fowler, & DeLateur, 1968). Researchers in biofeedback are continuously developing innovative applications of biofeedback to the solution of medical problems (Johnson & Meyer, 1974).

Epilepsy is an example of a medical problem that is treated almost exclusively from a medical standpoint. In many cases the source of the seizure activity can be diagnosed by electroencephalograms (EEGs) and other means as being organically based, and the seizures are treated by standard pharmacological agents. Epilepsy, however, is a complex and varied syndrome, and in some cases the physician is unable to achieve satisfactory control of the patient's seizures through medication alone. Though psychological factors are often considered to affect the seizure activity, few patients are referred for psychotherapy as an alternative for seizure control, particularly if their seizures began at an early age and are thought to be organically based. Those who are referred for psychotherapy tend to be those people who evidence "false seizures" or who appear to be hysterical personality types (Freedman & Kaplan, 1967).

There have been indications in the literature that seizure activity can be reduced by procedures other than purely medical ones. In the 1800s there were reports anecdotally of "dynamic therapy" successes. Efron's two articles (1956, 1957) about the treatment of a woman with uncinate fits are among the earliest complete descriptions of behaviorally oriented approaches to a seizure disorder.

Since these earlier articles, several other successful applications of behavior modification techniques with seizure disorders have been reported. There is only one published account of behavioral treatment of psychogenic seizures in a child. Gardner (1967) instructed the parents of a 10-year-old girl with psychogenic seizures to ignore her inappropriate behaviors such as seizures or tantrums while rewarding her appropriate behaviors with attention. Within 2 weeks the child's seizures dropped to zero, tantrums increased to about three per week (but did not rise to the prehospitalization level of five or six per week), then dropped out altogether within the month. Thus the parents were primarily responsible for carrying out the prescribed behavioral treatment, which combined time out from reinforcements for undesirable behavior with reward for desired behavior.

Reinforcement was also the primary behavioral technique used by Flannery and Cautela (1973), who treated a 22-year-old retarded male patient with epilepsy of encephalic origin. His seizures had never been amenable to chemotherapy, and the drugs had reached near toxic levels. They set up a reward system in which he received social praise and candy if he was seizure free for that day. In a period of 28 weeks (including 3 weeks of vacation), 19 were comprised of one or less seizures (13 weeks were totally seizure free)—compared with the baseline of about three seizures per week. In another example of contingency manipulation in an institutional environment, Richardson (Note 1) reported marked deceleration of seizure-related symptoms in two female patients (ages 22 and 34) suffering from grand mal epilepsy. Rewards such as transfer to an open ward, parole, and visits from a boyfriend were made contingent on the absence of seizure symptoms. Medication continued without change.

The role of relaxation training in diminishing seizure activity in a 28-year-old female patient was emphasized by Mostofsky and Vick (Note 2). They also suggested that subtle reinforcements during the training sessions (e.g., praising the client for her ability to stop a seizure) may also have been beneficial. Johnson and Meyer (1974) utilized relaxation and biofeedback (electromyogram and EEG feedback training) with an 18-year-old female patient who had had severe grand mal seizures since age 8 and was allergic to Dilantin. Her baseline was three seizures per month. During the 6½-month period of treatment, the patient had only four seizures, an average of .62 per month. Three of these four seizures occurred at the end of a 3-week nontreatment period. Relaxation was also a part of the systematic desensitization used by Parrino (1971). He reduced seizure activity in a 36-year-old male patient by pinpointing the stimuli he believed to be triggering the emotional antecedents of the seizures and then utilizing systematic desensitization.

Mostofsky (1972) believes that imaginative interventions to control seizures are a real possibility. Though neither epilepsy nor the control of seizures is fully understood, he suggests that behavior therapy need not sit idly by until conclusive evidence or localization and etiology can be specified. He suggested that a first step might be to have epilepsy recognized as a psychosomatic illness and to proceed to treat the observable symptom syndrome. It was this philosophy that was observed in the present case study in which reduction of the frequency of observable seizures was the goal.

Most case studies reported in the literature are concerned with teenage or adult patients. In addition, many of these people are either temporarily hospitalized or are long-term institutionalized patients. Why there are so few studies with children and so few studies that take place in more natural environments is unclear. The following case study offers one example of an attempt to treat a child's seizures behaviorally within a normal school environment.

CASE STUDY

Joan is an 11-year-old girl who attends a regular fourth-grade class for the majority of her school day and some classes for retarded children (i.e., for particular subjects such as math and reading) in a suburban public school system. At the age of 18 months she was diagnosed as having organically based epilepsy. One of her parents and two of her siblings also have seizure disorders, but their conditions have been adequately controlled by medication. At the age of 6 years 10 months Joan achieved a Wechsler Intelligence Scale for Children (WISC) Full Scale score of 90 (average range). At age 8 a diagnosis of diffuse cerebral dysfunction was made, based on various test scores indicating increased impairment of intellectual functioning. Two years later (8 years 10 months) she attained a WISC Full Scale score of 83, thus placing her in the dull normal range. Joan's psychological problems included a severe inability to function independently, general immaturity, lack of friends, and a tendency toward denial of her seizures.

Joan was referred by her neurologist to a local mental health center for further diagnostic evaluation at age 9 following the development of "atypical" seizures. These were described as very lengthy seizures (as long as 1 hour in duration) and were judged to be "hysterical" and to require further psychological evaluation. She has been seen on a once-a-week basis in traditional individual treatment at the mental health center since the diagnostic evaluation. Psychotherapy was recommended to help understand the causes of the hysterical seizures and diminish their frequency. Other goals over the past 2 years of therapy have included helping Joan to express her feelings and to increase her self-esteem. Even though the unusually lengthy seizures are no longer occurring, the total number of Joan's seizures does not seem to have diminished either as a result of therapy or various combinations of medication. At the beginning of the school year Joan was having seizures daily for about the first 2 weeks. They then diminished to an average of three per week (as estimated by her teacher from her own recollection and nurse's records). Joan's mother reported that on weekday evenings and on weekends she often had one or more seizures per day.

Joan has been seen regularly by both her pediatrician and her neurologist. At the beginning of the school year Joan was receiving 50 mg of Dilantin three times a day and 15 mg of Phenobarbital four times a day. The severity of her seizures was varied. Sometimes she was able to maintain her position in her chair at her desk while her head fell to the side or forward. These seizures were about a minute or two in duration. Other seizures involved falls, usually backward. Movement in her left arm and leg were sometimes observed during these seizures. She could completely recover in about 5 minutes with no apparent after effects. When she had a seizure, Joan seemed not to take any precautions such as sitting down. She would claim that she could not tell when they were coming. However, from direct observation of Joan both her teacher and I found that at times she did have some awareness of an impending seizure and demonstrated this by taking some precautions regarding breakable objects she was carrying just prior to a seizure.

Joan was referred to me by her regular classroom teacher, who was concerned about the frequency of her seizures. She had observed that the seizures sometimes coincided with Joan's having to deal with a new or anxiety-provoking situation. Perceived rejection (by one of her classmates) and criticism (e.g., receiving a poor grade on a test) are examples of observed stimuli for seizure activity. When I spoke with Joan's mother about the possibility that certain emotional situations might act as triggers for Joan's seizures, she agreed that this might be the case for some of the seizures. In fact, she offered several examples of situations occurring at home in which she felt that some of Joan's seizures were expressions of frustration and anger when she did not get her own way (e.g., was not allowed to go to the movies).

Joan's teacher noted various inappropriate behaviors that were reflective of lack of self-confidence. In contrast to her fourth-grade classmates, Joan seemed incapable of making the simplest decisions. An example of the extreme degree of this behavior was being unable to decide what color crayon to use in a drawing. She would always ask for directions from her teacher in any free-choice situation. She often asked permission to do an activity that she knew was appropriate and was a part of her standard daily routine (e.g., leaving the classroom to go to her math session). There is a long history of dependency. Due to Joan's presumed inability to perceive the onset of any of her seizures and her concomitant lack of precautions for them, physical injuries sometimes occurred during falls. Because of the unpredictability of both the seizures and subsequent injuries, her mother seldom allowed her to go anywhere alone or accompanied only by her peers. Joan also took no responsibility for her medication. She was dependent on her parents, teacher, and even her classmates to be reminded to take her medication at the appropriate times.

Procedure

Based on the information obtained from Joan's teacher and mother, it was hypothesized that some of Joan's seizure activity was precipitated by emotion-laden situations and was operantly controlled, causing her a great deal of attention and concern. With the permission of her mother and the cooperation of her teacher, a behavioral program was designed in which attention (in the form of verbal praise) and a reward were to be given to Joan if she attained a certain number of seizure-free time periods during the school day. (I later learned that the procedure was similar to the paradigm used by Flannery and Cautela, 1973.)

First a conference was held with Joan's mother to obtain additional information about Joan's seizures, medical history, and psychotherapy and to discuss the proposed treatment procedure and the rationale behind it. Joan's mother indicated that the frequency of her daughter's seizures and her subsequent falls were a source of great concern. Potential head injury was also a concern of her neurologist, who had been considering requiring Joan to wear a helmet as a precautionary measure. Joan's mother decided to allow school personnel to try a new approach since others had failed. She was especially interested in the notion of emphasizing the positive—the seizure-free time periods. During this conference no home-based treatment plan was arranged. However, it was later learned that Joan's mother began applying a similar type of treatment plan at home in an informal way. For example, she would promise to allow Joan to attend an activity away from home with a friend if she had no seizures for a day.

Joan's teacher was instructed to pay as little attention as possible to Joan's seizure activity. Her teacher was given a simple chart dividing each school day into three time periods: morning, lunch, and afternoon. This chart was called Joan's "good times chart." The teacher discussed the purpose of the chart with Joan, indicating that she would receive one check mark for each seizure-free time period. The chart was kept at the teacher's desk. Joan was told that if she was able to achieve a certain number of check marks she would receive a prize (a candy bar of her choice) at the end of the week. No other directions were given to Joan as to how she was expected to prevent or stop a seizure. However, her teacher was advised to urge Joan to talk with her about anything that made her anxious or upset. The purpose of this was to provide Joan with an alternate behavior for the seizures. The procedure was presented much as one might present a contract, in a matter-of-fact manner. It is of interest that Joan neither questioned nor protested the program; she seemed to enjoy the challenge of it.

Unfortunately, the teacher did not fully understand the directions with regard to setting the criterion for the weekly reward. Rather than setting an easily achievable goal such as 7 check marks out of the possible 15 for one week, she made the criterion 15 out of 15. When this error was discovered, the teacher was urged to make the criterion easier. However, when she attempted to do this, Joan objected, preferring to have as her goal a completely seizure-free week at school.

The chart was kept secret from the rest of the children. The teacher kept it at her desk and was responsible for filling it in, although Joan was asked to report to the teacher any seizure that she experienced when the teacher was not present to observe it. In addition to keeping this chart, the teacher encouraged Joan to come to her if she felt nervous or upset for any reason.

Concurrent with the keeping of the good times chart was the marking of a chart on Joan's assertive or self-initiated behaviors (such as beginning an assignment independently). However, no reward system was devised relating to this behavior. The teacher discontinued the use of this chart after a few weeks because she felt that the behavior had increased so rapidly that there would be no future need to develop a separate treatment program to increase it. However, she did try to remain aware of improvements in the area of self-initiated, independent behaviors and to praise them.

The primary treatment goal was to reduce the number of seizures. The secondary goal was to increase self-initiated, independent behaviors. The teacher was asked to note the time and circumstances of any seizure so that other precipitating stimuli might be discovered. It was suggested that she discuss with Joan the necessity of trying to recognize the imminent onset of her seizures and take appropriate precautions. For example, she assured Joan that it was better for her to sit on the floor and minimize the danger to herself than to try to completely deny that the seizure was about to occur. In addition to helping Joan deal with these issues, the teacher also worked with the entire class. A cartoon-type film about epilepsy was shown to the entire class, and an open discussion was held afterward in which Joan was able to answer the questions of her classmates about her seizures.

The behavioral program began in mid-November. Joan's medication remained the same as it had been since the beginning of school and for some time previous to that. On the third day prior to Christmas vacation, her medication was changed. The Dilantin dose remained the same (50 mg three times a day), but her Phenobarbital was increased from 15 mg four times a day to 30 mg three times a day. The treatment procedure continued through January and February despite at least one more change in medication and the introduction of the wearing of a protective helmet (in late January). In March and April Joan was ill with mononucleosis and could not attend school. When she returned to school at the end of April, the behavioral program was not continued.

I assumed that upon Joan's return to school her teacher would reinstitute the behavioral program as it had been prior to Joan's illness. I was a 1-day-a-week consultant to Joan's school and was not aware of her return to classes until her fourth day back. I was also unaware that the teacher had arbitrarily decided to discontinue the behavioral program. When questioned about her rationale for not reinstituting the already demonstrated successful procedure, the teacher explained that she wanted Joan to catch up on a great deal of missed schoolwork and that she felt that reinstituting the behavioral program might be an added pressure on Joan. The teacher felt that at this point in the school year it was more important to emphasize academics, and she wanted Joan to gradually reacquaint herself with the daily academic routines and tasks. She also felt that changes of medication related to Joan's illness and her general psychological state might make it too difficult for Joan to achieve the weekly reward.

Despite my urgings to continue the reward program, the teacher refused to do so. She did, however, agree to continue to chart the number of the child's seizures from this point (end of April) through the close of school in late June. I felt that continued monitoring of seizure activity was essential. It was my intent to again urge that the behavioral program be used if there were a dramatic increase in the child's seizure rate. Why the teacher was so reluctant to continue the program is unclear. It seemed as though she believed that Joan was expending a great deal of "mental energy" to accomplish seizure control and that the mental activity was somehow being taken away from application to her studies. Various other analyses, including overprotectiveness, are also possible to account for the teacher's behavior. However, since I was initially called into this case by the teacher as a consultant, I did not have a strong therapeutic contract. Rather than being the primary therapist in this case, my role was relegated to that of a consultant to the teacher—the person who had full responsibility for the child during the school day and who was under no obligation to follow my suggestions.

RESULTS

During the first 3 days of the treatment program, Joan had no seizures. Since it was the end of the week, her teacher rewarded her. On Monday of the first full week of the program, Joan had one seizure. She told her teacher that she did not feel the seizure coming on. At home during this same week and a half, her mother reported that Joan had had only two seizures compared to the earlier, preexperimental baseline of averaging at least one per day at home. Both Joan and her mother were pleased with Joan's progrss. Joan was clearly attributing some of the success to herself when, on the seventh day of the program, she spontaneously remarked to her teacher, "I think I've got this under control now."

An approximate baseline of three seizures per week for the first 50 school days (10 weeks) was established from teachers' reports and the nurse's records. With the exception of 1 week in February for which the teacher misplaced her chart, Joan's seizure activity for the remainder of the school year is documented by the teacher's daily charts. The data are presented in naturally occurring time periods: (a) pretreatment, September through mid-November; (b) Treatment Phase 1, mid-November until December vacation and change in medication; (c) Treatment Phase 2, January and February; and (d) no treatment. The data are presented in percentages (seizures/days of school; see Table 1).

Joan's seizure activity diminished dramatically during Phase 1 and con-

TABLE 1

Comparison of Number of Seizures to Days of School

Cumulative school days (177)		No. seizures/no. school days
Pretreatment		30/50 (60)
Phase 1		4/24 (16.7)
Phase 2		7/28 (25)
No treatment		
March-April	(absent)	—
April-June		25/40 (62.5)

Note: Numbers in parentheses are percentages.

tinued at a relatively low level in Phase 2 despite changes in medication and the additional requirement of wearing the helmet (which was a source of embarrassment to Joan). Even though seizures were diminishing at school in the early weeks of treatment, the seizures continued to occur at home until Joan's mother instituted her own informal contingency management program described earlier.

During the treatment period (Phase 1), Joan's mother reported two instances of excessive frequency of seizure activity at home. Joan had 15 seizures the weekend of her birthday (which might be attributable to generalized excitement) and 7 seizures one afternoon and evening following a phone call to her home from her physician. At school, during the treatment period, the teacher noted that the situations in which seizures occurred were departures from the normal school routine. For example, more than once a seizure occurred when a new lunch mother (monitor) was introduced and in a novel situation (e.g., attending a special school play).

During the no-treatment phase from late April to the end of June, Joan's seizure rate returned to its pretreatment level of three per week. Several factors related to dependency may have contributed to this rise in seizure rate. In January she began to wear the prescribed protective helmet, which was an emotionally traumatic event for her. In order to help her deal with wearing the helmet, her psychotherapist and her mother kept emphasizing to her that she could "only be helped by taking her medication and wearing her helmet." Such emphasis on external control devices may have made Joan doubt the efficacy of her previous efforts at self-control of her seizures.

DISCUSSION

Despite the number of uncontrolled variables in this case study, the dramatic lessening in the frequency of Joan's seizure activity in school seems to suggest something stronger than mere chance. If one accepts the notion that the behavioral program was responsible for some of the improvement, it is still impossible to know the precise features that contributed to the change. One might hypothesize that the positive relationship between Joan and her teacher, fostered by the seizure-free behavior, was an important rewarding variable. The charting of the behavior itself may have been influential. Increased self-esteem based on attribution of improvement to the self rather than to the medication alone may have been a viable force. This latter hypothesis is in keeping with the findings of Davison and Valins (1969). The increased assertiveness and independence evidenced by Joan early in the treatment program may indicate that these behaviors were competing responses that eliminated the need for her to respond to a situation with seizure activity.

It seems apparent that neither medication alone nor medication plus traditional psychotherapy was sufficiently effective in completely eliminating Joan's potentially injurious seizures (although her hysterical seizures were eliminated). However, further conclusions cannot be drawn because of the lack of adequate controls. Lack of continued cooperation from Joan's teacher eliminated the possibility of further study of her ability to control her seizures.

With the increasing number of case studies using various behavioral techniques to reduce seizure activity in epileptics, it is becoming more important to develop research that might help determine which type of therapy works best with which types of cases, particularly in more normative settings such as home, classroom, or outpatient clinic. Though many of these case studies show significant improvement, it must be remembered that seizures are difficult to classify. It is therefore difficult to generalize the results that the respective procedures find. This is why broader and more long-term research should be undertaken to determine the usefulness of behavior modification techniques (e.g., reward, punishment, charting, biofeedback, relaxation, desensitization, etc.) in the treatment of general seizure activity.

REFERENCE NOTES

1. Richardson, R. A. *Environmental Contingencies in Seizure Disorders.* Paper presented at the meeting of the Association for Advancement of Behavior Therapy, New York, October 1972.

2. MOSTOFSKY, D. I., & VICK, S. H. *The Therapeutic Value of Muscle Relaxation in Seizure Control: A Case Study.* Mimeo, Boston University, 1973.

REFERENCES

DAVISON, G. C., & VALINS, S. Maintenance of self-attributed and drug-attributed behavior change. *Journal of Personality and Social Psychology,* 11:25-33, 1969.

EFRON, R. The effect of olfactory stimuli in arresting uncinate fits. *Brain,* 79:267-277, 1956.

EFRON, R. The conditioned inhibition of uncinate fits. *Brain,* 80:251-261, 1957.

FLANNERY, R. B., & CAUTELA, J. R. Seizures: Controlling the uncontrollable. *Journal of Rehabilitation,* 39:34-36, 1973.

FORDYCE, W. E., FOWLER, R. S., DELATEUR, B. An application of behavior modification technique to a problem of chronic pain. *Behavior Research and Therapy,* 6:105-107, 1968.

FREEDMAN, A. M., & KAPLAN, H. I. (Eds.). *Comprehensive Textbook of Psychiatry.* Baltimore: Williams & Wilkins, 1967.

GARDNER, J. E. Behavior therapy treatment approach to a psychogenic seizure case. *Journal of Consulting Psychology,* 31:209-212, 1967.

JOHNSON, R. K., & MEYER, R. G. Phased biofeedback approach for epileptic seizure control. *Journal of Behavior Therapy and Experimental Psychiatry,* 5:185-187, 1974.

KIMMEL, H. D. Instrumental conditioning of automatically mediated responses in human beings. *American Psychologist,* 29:325-335, 1974.

MILLER, N. Learning of visceral and glandular responses. *Science,* 163:434-445, 1969.

MORROW, W. R. *Behavior Therapy Bibliography, 1950-1969. University of Missouri Studies* (Vol. 54). Columbia: University of Missouri Press, 1971.

MOSTOFSKY, D. I. Behavior modification and the psychosomatic aspects of epilepsy. In D. Upper & D. S. Goodenough (Eds.), *Behavior Modification with the Individual Patient.* Nutley, N.J.: Roche Laboratories, 1972.

PARRINO, J. J. Reduction of seizures by desensitization. *Journal of Behavior Therapy and Experimental Psychiatry,* 2:215-218, 1971.

REFERENCES TO EDITORS' COMMENTARIES

ABEL, G. G. Review of A. A. Lazarus, Multimodal behavior therapy. *American Journal of Psychiatry*, 1977, 134:221-222.

ABEL, G. G. Review of W. E. Fordyce, Behavioral methods for chronic pain and illness. *Behavior Therapy*, 1977, 8.

ABEL, G. G., BARLOW, D. H., BLANCHARD, E. D., & GUILD, D. The components of rapists' sexual arousal. *Archives of General Psychiatry*, 1977, 34:895-903.

ABRAMS, D. & WILSON, G. T. Self-monitoring and smoking behavior. Unpublished manuscript, Rutgers University, 1977.

ADAMS, K. M. Behavioral treatment of reflex or sensory-evoked seizures. *Journal of Behavior Therapy and Experimental Psychiatry*, 1977, 7:123-127.

ADAMS, M. R. & HOTCHKISS, J. Some reactions and responses of stutterers to miniaturized metronome and metronome-conditioning therapy: Three case reports. *Behavior Therapy*, 1973, 4:565-569.

AD HOC COMMITTEE ON CLASSIFICATION OF HEADACHE. *Journal of the American Medical Association*, 1962, 179:717-718.

ALBAN, L. S. & NAY, N. R. Reduction of ritual checking by a relaxation-delay treatment. *Journal of Behavior Therapy and Experimental Psychiatry*, 1976, 7:151-154.

ALEXANDER, J. F. & PARSONS, B. V. Short-term behavioral intervention with delinquent families: Impact on family process and recidivism. *Journal of Abnormal Psychology*, 1973, 81:219-225.

AMERICAN PSYCHIATRIC ASSOCIATION TASK FORCE ON BEHAVIOR THERAPY. Report No. 5: *Behavior Therapy in Psychiatry*. Washington, D.C.: American Psychiatric Association, 1973.

ANDERSON, C. R. Coping behaviors as intervening mechanisms in the inverted-V stress-performance relationship. *Journal of Applied Psychology*, 1976, 61:30-34.

ANDERSON, L., FODOR, I., & ALPERT, M. A comparison of methods for training self-control. *Behavior Therapy*, 1976, 7:649-658.

ANDRASIK, F., KLARE, G. R., & MURPHY, W. D. Readability and behavior modification texts: Cross-cultural comparisons and comments. *Behavior Therapy*, 1976, 7:539-543.

APPELBAUM, A. S. Rathus Assertiveness Schedule: Sex differences and correlation with social desirability. *Behavior Therapy*, 1976, 7:699.

ARBUTHNOT, J., TEDESCHI, R., WAGNER, M., TURNER. J., KRESSEL, S., & RUSH, R. Introduction of pro-environmental behavior: The foot-in-the-door technique applied to recycling, 1975. Unpublished manuscript cited by Tyse and Geller.

ARDREY, R. *The Territorial Imperative*. New York: Dell, 1966.

ARKELL, R. N., KUBO, H. R. & MEUNIER, C. P. Readability and parental behavior modification literature. *Behavior Therapy*, 1976, 7:242-244.

ARKOWITZ, H. A., LEVINE, A., GROSSCUP, S., O'NEIL, A., YOUNGREN, M., ROYCE, W. S., & LARGAY, D. Clinical applications of social skill training: Issues and limitations in generalization from analogue studies Paper presented at the 10th Annual Convention of the Association for Advancement of Behavior Therapy. New York, December, 1976.

ARMSTRONG, H. E. & BAKKER, C. B. Behavioral self-analysis in the medical curriculum. *Journal of Medical Education,* 1976, 51:758-762.

AVELLAR, J. & KAGAN, S. Development of competitive behaviors in Anglo-American and Mexican-American children. *Psychological Reports,* 1976, 39:191-198.

AXELROD, S., BRANDER, M., COLE, B., DOUGHERTY, P., CRYSTAL, J. & HAMMER, T. Use of behavior modification procedures in marital situations by non-professionals. Unpublished manuscript, 1977.

AYLLON, T., LAYMAN, D., & KANDEL, H. J. A behavioral-educational alternative to drug control of hyperactive children. *Journal of Applied Behavior Analysis,* 1975, 8:137-146.

AZRIN, N. A strategy for applied research: Learning based but outcome oriented. *American Psychologist,* 1977, 32:140-149.

AZRIN, N. H., NASTER, B. J., & JONES, R. Reciprocity counseling: A rapid learning-based procedure for marital counseling. *Behaviour Research and Therapy,* 1973, 11:365-382.

BACHMAN, J. A. Self-injurious behavior: A behavioral analysis. *Journal of Abnormal Psychology,* 1972, 80:211-224.

BAIN, J. A. *Thought Control in Everyday Life.* New York: Funk & Wagnalls, 1928.

BALASCHAK, B. A. Behavior modification with epileptic children: Preliminary case reports. Paper presented at the American Psychological Association Convention, Washington, D.C., 1976.

BALCH, P. & BALCH, K. Establishing a campus-wide behavioral weight reduction program through the university student health service: The use and training of health service personnel as behavioral weight therapists. *Journal of the American College Health Association,* 1976, 25:148-152.

BALTES, M. M. & ZERBE, M. B. Independence training in nursing-home residents. *The Gerontologist,* 1976, 16:428-432.

BANCROFT, J. H. J. The application of psychophysiological measures to the assessment and modification of sexual behavior. *Behaviour Research and Therapy,* 1971, 9:119-130.

BANCROFT, J. H. *Deviant Sexual Behaviour.* Oxford: Oxford University Press, 1974.

BANCROFT, J. Comments on Silverstein's review of "Deviant Sexual Behavior." *Behavior Therapy,* 1976, 7:693-694.

BANDURA, A. *Principles of Behavior Modification.* New York: Holt, Rinehart & Winston, 1969.

BANDURA, A. Behavior therapy and the models of man. *American Psychologist,* 1974, 29:859-869.

BANDURA, A. Self-efficacy: Toward a unifying theory of behavioral change. *Psychological Review,* 1977 (a), 84:191-215.

BANDURA, A. *Social Learning Theory.* Englewood Cliffs, N.J.: Prentice-Hall, 1977 (b).

BANDURA, A., BLANCHARD, E. B., & RITTER, B. The relative efficacy of desensitization and modeling approaches for inducing behavioral, affective, and cognitive changes. *Journal of Personality and Social Psychology,* 1969, 13:173-199.

BANDURA, A., JEFFERY, R. W., & GAJDOS, E. Generalizing change through participant modeling with self-directed mastery. *Behaviour Research and Therapy,* 1975, 13:141-152.

BARBACH, L. G. Group treatment of preorgasmic women. *Journal of Sex and Marital Therapy,* 1974, 1:139-145.

BARBACH, L. G. *For Yourself: The Fulfillment of Female Sexuality.* New York: Doubleday, 1975.

BARLOW, D. H. Assessment of sexual behavior. In A. R. Ciminero, K. S. Calhoun, &

H. E. Adams (Eds.), *Handbook of Behavioral Assessment*. New York: Wiley, 1977.

BARNES, M. R. Token economy control of fluid overload in a patient receiving hemodialysis. *Journal of Behavior Therapy and Experimental Psychiatry*, 1976, 7:305-306.

BARRERA, M. & GLASGOW, R. E. Design and evaluation of a personalized instruction course in behavioral self-control. *Teaching of Psychology*, 1976, 2:81-83.

BARRIOS, E. & CHRISTENSEN, A. C. A comparison of self-control procedures, financial payoff contingent on weight loss and the use of weight reduction partners as a means of losing weight. Cited in Glasgow and Rosen, in press.

BAUERMEISTER, J. J. & JEMAIL, J. A. Teachers as experimenters and behavioral engineers: An extension and cross-cultural replication. *InterAmerican Journal of Psychology*, 1976, 10:41-45.

BECK, A. T. *Depression: Clinical, Experimental and Theoretical Aspects*. New York: Hoeber, 1967.

BECK, A. T. *Cognitive Therapy and the Emotional Disorders*. New York: International Universities Press, 1976.

BECK, A. T. Review of A. A. Lazarus' Multimodal behavior therapy. *Behavior Therapy*, 1977, 8:292-294.

BECKER, I. M. & ROSENFELD, J. G. Rational emotive therapy—A study of initial therapy sessions of Albert Ellis. *Journal of Clinical Psychology*, 1976, 32:872-876.

BEECH, R. H. & LIDDELL, A. Decision-making, mood states and ritualistic behaviour. In R. H. Beech (Ed.), *Obsessional States*. London: Methuen, 1974.

BEGELMAN, D. A. Homosexuality and the ethics of behavioral intervention. *Journal of Homosexuality*, 1977, 2:213-219.

Behaviourism: A framework for common sense therapy. Editorial. *British Medical Journal*, October 2, 1976, 776-777.

BELLACK, A. S. A comparison of self-reinforcement and self-monitoring in a weight reduction program. *Behavior Therapy*, 1976, 7:66-75.

BELLACK, A. S., GLANZ, L., & SIMON, R. Covert imagery and individual differenecs in self-reinforcement style in the treatment of obesity. *Journal of Consulting and Clinical Psychology*, in press.

BELLACK, A. S. & HERSEN, M. Self-report inventories in behavioral assessment. In J. D. Cone & R. P. Hawkins (Eds.), *Behavioral Assessment: New Directions in Clinical Psychology*. New York: Brunner/Mazel, 1977.

BELLACK, A. S., HERSEN, M., & TURNER, S. M. Generalization effects of social skills training in chronic schizophrenics: An experimental analysis. *Behaviour Research and Therapy*, 1976, 14:391-398.

BELLACK, A. S., HERSEN, M., & TURNER, S. M. Role-play tests for assessing social skills: Are they valid? *Behavior Therapy*, in press.

BELLACK, A. S. & SCHWARTZ, J. S. Assessment for self-control programs. In M. Hersen & A. S. Bellack (Eds.), *Behavioral Assessment: A Practical Handbook*. New York: Pergamon, 1976.

BENSON, J. S. & KENNELLY, K. J. Learned helplessness: The result of uncontrollable reinforcements or uncontrollable aversive stimuli? *Journal of Personality and Social Psychology*, 1976, 34:138-145.

BERECZ, J. Treatment of smoking with cognitive conditioning therapy: A self-administered aversion technique. *Behavior Therapy*, 1976, 7:641-648.

BERGIN, A. E. The evaluation of outcomes. In A. E. Bergin, & S. L. Garfield (Eds.), *Handbook of Psychotherapy and Behavior Change*. New York: Wiley, 1971.

BERGIN, A. E. & STRUPP, H. H. New directions in psychotherapy research. *Journal of Abnormal Psychology*, 1970, 76:113-126.

BERMAN, J. S. & KENNY, D. A. Correlational bias in observer ratings. *Journal of Personality and Social Psychology*, 1976, 34:263-273.

BERNSTEIN, D. A. & MCALISTER, A. The modification of smoking behavior: Progress and problems. *Addictive Behaviors,* 1976, 1:89-102.

BERTALANFFY, L., VON. *Organismic Psychology and Systems Theory.* Worcester, Ma.: Clark University Press, 1968.

BERTALANFFY, L., VON. *General System Theory: Foundations, Development, Applications.* New York: Braziller, 1969.

BETTELHEIM, B. *The Empty Fortress: Infantile Autism and the Birth of the Self.* New York: The Free Press, 1967.

BIGLAN, A. & KASS, D. J. The empirical nature of behavior therapies. *Behaviorism,* 1977, 5:1-15.

BIJOU, S. W. & GRIMM, J. A. Behavioral diagnosis and assessment in teaching young handicapped children. In T. Thompson & W. S. Dockens (Eds.), *Applications of Behavior Modification.* New York: Academic Press, 1975.

BIKLEN, D. P. Behavior modification in a state mental hospital: A participant-observer's critique. *American Journal of Orthopsychiatry,* 1976, 46:53-61.

BINDER, A., STOKOLS, D., & CATALANO, R. Social ecology: An emerging discipline. *The Journal of Environmental Education,* 1976, 8:32-43.

BIRCHLER, G. R., WEISS, R. L., & VINCENT, J. P. Multimethod analysis of social reinforcement exchange between maritally distressed and nondistressed spouse and stranger dyads. *Journal of Personality and Social Psychology,* 1975, 31:349-360.

BIRK, L. Biofeedback: Behavioral medicine. *Seminars in Psychiatry,* 1973, 5:361-370.

BIXENSTINE, V. E. On the logic of logical form: A criticism of Tryon's models of behavior disorder. *American Psychologist,* 1977, 32:572-575.

BLACKWELL, B. Treatment adherence. *British Journal of Psychiatry,* 1976, 129:513-531.

BLANCHARD, E. B. Behavioral medicine: A perspective. In R. B. Williams & W. D. Gentry (Eds.), *Behavioral Approaches to Medical Treatment.* Cambridge, Mass.: Ballinger, 1977.

BLANCHARD, E. B. & HERSEN, M. Behavioral treatment of hysterical neurosis: Symptom substitution and symptom return. *Psychiatry,* 1976, 39:118-129.

BLANCHARD, E. B. & YOUNG, L. D. Clinical applications of biofeedback training: A review of evidence. *Archives of General Psychiatry,* 1974, 30:573-589.

BOERSMA, K., DEN HENGST, S., DEKKER, J., & EMMELKAMP, P. M. G. Exposure and response prevention in the natural environment: A comparison with obsessive-compulsive patients. *Behaviour Research and Therapy,* 1976, 14:19-24.

BORKOVEC, T. D. Investigations of fear and sleep disturbance: Methodological measurement, and theoretical issues in therapy outcome research. In G. E. Schwartz & D. Shapiro (Eds.), *Conscious and Self-regulation: Advances in Research.* New York: Plenum, 1977.

BORKOVEC, T. D., KALOUPEK, D. G., & SLAMA, K. The facilitative effect of muscle tension-release in the relaxation treatment of sleep disturbance. *Behavior Therapy,* 1975, 6:301-309.

BORKOVEC, T. D., STEINMARK, S., & NAU, S. Relaxation training and single-item desensitization in the group treatment of insomnia. *Journal of Behavior Therapy and Experimental Psychiatry,* 1973, 4:401-403.

BORKOVEC, T. D., STONE, N. M., O'BRIEN, G. T., & KALOUPEK, D. G. Evaluation of a clinically relevant target behavior for an analog outcome research. *Behavior Therapy,* 1974, 5:503-513.

BORKOVEC, T. D., WEERTS, T. C., & BERNSTEIN, D. A. Assessment of anxiety. In A. R. Ciminero, K. S. Calhoun, & H. E. Adams (Eds.), *Handbook of Behavioral Assessment.* New York: Wiley, 1977.

BORNSTEIN, P., BUGGE, L., & DAVOL, G. Good principle, wrong target—an extension of "token economies come of age." *Behavior Therapy,* 1975, 6:63-67.

BORNSTEIN, P. H. & QUEVILLON, R. P. The effects of a self-instructional package on overactive preschool boys. *Journal of Applied Behavior Analysis,* 1976, 9:179-188.

BOWLES, P. E., JR. & NELSON, R. O. Training teachers as mediators: Efficacy of a workshop versus the bug-in-the-ear technique. *Journal of School Psychology,* 1976, 14: 15-26.

BRADY, J. P. Metronome conditioned speech retraining for stuttering. *Behavior Therapy,* 1971, 2:129-150.

BRADY, J. P. An unfair indictment of behavior therapies? *American Journal of Psychiatry,* 1976, 113:852.

BRADY, J. P. Behavior therapy and sex therapy. *American Journal of Psychiatry,* 1976, 33:896-899 (a).

BRADY, J. P. & RIEGER, W. Behavioral treatment of anorexia nervosa. In T. Thompson & W. Dockens (Eds.), *Applications of Behavior Modification.* New York: Academic Press, 1975.

BRAFF, D. L., RASKIN, M. R., & GEISINGER, D. Management of interpersonal issues in systematic desensitization. *American Journal of Psychiatry,* 1976, 133:791-794.

BRIGHTWELL, D. R. One-year follow-up of obese subjects treated with behavior therapy. *Diseases of the Nervous System,* 1977 (in press).

BRIGHTWELL, D. R. & CLANCY, J. Self-training of new eating behavior for weight reduction. *Diseases of the Nervous System,* 1976, 37:85-89.

BROADHURST, A. It's never too late to learn: An application of conditioned inhibition to obsessional ruminations in an elderly patient. In H. J. Eysenck (Ed.), *Case Studies in Behaviour Therapy.* London: Routledge & Kegan Paul, 1976.

BROWN, B. B. *New Mind, New Body: Biofeedback—New Directions for the Mind.* New York: Harper and Row, 1974.

BROWN, P. L. & PRESBIE, R. J. *Behavior Modification in Business, Industry and Government.* New Paltz, N.Y.: Behavior Improvement Associates, 1976.

BROWNELL, K. D. & BARLOW, D. H. Measurement and treatment of two sexual deviations in one person. *Journal of Behavior Therapy and Experimental Psychiatry,* 1976, 7:349-354.

BROWNELL, K. D., COLETTI, G., ERSNER-HERSHFIELD, R., HERSHFIELD, S. M., & WILSON, G. T. Self-control in school children: Stringency and leniency in self-determined and externally imposed performance standards. *Behavior Therapy,* 1977, 8:442-455.

BROWNELL, K. D., HECKERMAN, C. L., & WESTLAKE, R. M. Therapist and group contact as variables in the behavioral treatment of obesity. Paper presented at the Annual Meeting of the Association for Advancement of Behavior Therapy, New York, 1976.

BRUNER, J. S. & TAGIURI, R. The perception of people. In G. Lindzey (Ed.), *Handbook of Social Psychology* (Vol. 2). Cambridge, Mass.: Addison-Wesley, 1954.

BRUNI, E. Psychotherapists as sex therapists. *Psychotherapy: Theory, Research and Therapy,* 1974, 11:277-281.

BUDD, K. S. The intersection of behavior modification and the law: A conflict of principles. Paper presented at the 82nd Annual Convention of the American Psychological Association, New Orleans, 1974.

BUDD, K. S. & BAER, D. M. Behavior modification and the law: Implications of recent judicial decisions. *The Journal of Psychiatry and Law,* 1976, 4:171-244.

BURNASKA, R. F. The effects of behavior modeling training upon managers' behavior and employees' perceptions. *Personnel Psychology,* 1976, 29:329-335.

BURTON, A. *What Makes Behavior Change Possible?* New York: Brunner/Mazel, 1976.

BUTTERFIELD, W. H. & SCHWITZGEBEL, R. K. Psychology under legislative control—medical devices bill: Implications of the medical devices amendments of 1976. *Behavioral Engineering,* 1976, 3:103-104.

BYHAM, W. & ROBINSON, J. Interaction modeling: A new concept in supervisory training. *Training and Development Journal,* 1976, 2:46-49.

CADDY, G. R. & LOVIBOND, S. H. Self-regulation and discriminated aversive conditioning in the modification of alcoholics' drinking behavior. *Behavior Therapy,* 1976, 7:223-230.

CALLNER, D. A. Behavioral treatment approaches to drug abuse: A critical review of the research. *Psychological Bulletin,* 1975, 82:143-164.

CALLNER, D. A. & ROSS, S. M. The reliability and validity of three measures of assertion in a drug addict population. *Behavior Therapy,* 1976, 7:659-667.

CAMPBELL, D. T. & FISKE, D. W. Convergent and discriminant validation by the multitrait-multimethod matrix. *Psychological Bulletin,* 1959, 56:81-105.

CATANIA, A. C. The myth of self-reinforcement. *Behaviorism,* 1975, 3:192-199.

CATANIA, A. C. Self-reinforcement revisited. *Behaviorism,* 1976, 4:157-162.

CAULFIELD, J. B. & MARTIN, R. B. Establishment of praise as a reinforcer in chronic schizophrenics. *Journal of Consulting and Clinical Psychology,* 1976, 44:61-67.

CAUTELA, J. R. *Behavior Analysis Forms for Clinical Intervention.* Champaign, Ill.: Research Press, 1977.

CAUTELA, J. Toward a Pavlovian Theory of Cancer. *Scandinavian Journal of Behaviour Therapy,* 1977 (in press).

CAUTELA, J. R. & UPPER, D. Behavioral analysis, assessment and diagnosis. In D. Upper (Ed.), *Perspectives in Behavior Therapy.* Kalamazoo, Mich.: Behaviordelia, 1977.

CHANDRA, S. Repression, dreaming and primary process thinking: Skinnerian formulations of some Freudian facts. *Behaviorism,* 1976, 4:53-75.

CHEFFERS, J. T. F., LOWE, B., & HARROLD, R. D. Sports spectator behavior assessment by techniques of behavior analysis. *International Journal of Sports Psychology,* 1976, 7:1-13.

CHESNEY, M. A. & SHELTON, J. L. A comparison of muscle relaxation and electromyogram biofeedback treatments for muscle contraction headache. *Journal of Behavior Therapy and Experimental Psychiatry,* 1976, 7:221-225.

CHESSER, E. S. Behaviour therapy: Recent trends and current practice. *British Journal of Psychiatry,* 1976, 129:289-307.

CHRISTENSEN, D. E. Effects of combining methylphenidate and a classroom token system in modifying hyperactive behavior. *American Journal of Mental Deficiency,* 1975, 80:266-276.

CHRISTOPHERSON, E. R. Behavioral pediatrics (cited by Epstein & Martin, 1977).

CIMINERO, A. R. Behavioral assessment: An overview. In A. R. Ciminero, K. S. Calhoun & Adams (Eds.), *Handbook of Behavioral Assessment.* New York: Wiley, 1977.

CIMINERO, A. R., CALHOUN, K. S., & ADAMS, H. E. (Eds.), *Handbook of Behavioral Assessment.* New York: Wiley, 1977.

CIMINERO, A. R., NELSON, R. O., & LIPINSKI, D. P. Self-monitoring procedures. In A. R. Ciminero, K. S. Calhoun, & H. E. Adams (Eds.), *Handbook of Behavioral Assessment.* New York: Wiley, 1977.

CLAESON, L. & MALM, U. Social training in chronic schizophrenia: A comparative study of treatment with and without a token economy system. *European Journal of Behavioural Analysis and Modification,* 1976, 3:169-175.

CLARK, W. B. & CALAHAN, D. Changes in problem drinking over a four-year span. *Addictive Behaviors,* 1976, 1:251-260.

COCHRANE, R. & SOBOL, M. P. Myth and methodology in behaviour therapy research. In M. P. Feldman & A. Broadhurst (Eds.), *Theoretical and Experimental Bases of the Behaviour Therapies.* New York: Wiley, 1976.

COLE, C. & MORROW, W. R. Refractory parent behaviors in behavior modification training groups. *Psychotherapy: Theory, Research and Practice,* 1976, 13:162-169.

CONE, J. D. The relevance of reliability and validity for behavioral assessment. *Behavior Therapy,* 1977, 8:411-426.

CONGER, R. D. Social control and social learning models of delinquent behavior: A synthesis. *Criminology,* 1976, 14:17-39.

CONRAD, S. R. & WINCZE, J. P. Orgasmic reconditioning: A controlled study of its effects upon the sexual arousal and behavior of adult male homosexuals. *Behavior Therapy,* 1976, 7:155-166.

COYNE, J. C. Depression and the response of others. *Journal of Abnormal Psychology,* 1976, 85:186-193 (a).

COYNE, J. C. Toward an interactional description of depression. *Psychiatry,* 1976, 39: 23-40 (b).

CREER, T. L., RENNE, C. M., & CHRISTIAN, W. P. Behavioral contributions to rehabilitation and childhood asthma. *Rehabilitation Literature,* 1976, 37:226-233.

CROWE, M. J., MARKS, I. M., AGRAS, W. S., & LEITENBERG, H. Time-limited desensitization, implosion and shaping for phobic patients: A crossover study. *Behaviour Research and Therapy,* 1972, 10:319-328.

CRUMP, S. L., NUNES, D. L., & CROSSMAN, E. K. The effects of litter on littering behavior in a forest environment. *Environment and Behavior,* 1977, 9:137-146.

CSILLAG, E. R. Modification of penile erectile response. *Journal of Behavior Therapy and Experimental Psychiatry,* 1976, 7:27-29.

CURRAN, J. & GILBERT, F. A test of the relative effectiveness of a systematic desensitization program and an interpersonal skills training program with date anxious subjects. *Behavior Therapy,* 1975, 6:510-521.

CURRAN, J. P., GILBERT, F. S., & LITTLE, L. M. A comparison between behavioral replication training and sensitivity training approaches to heterosexual dating anxiety. *Journal of Consulting and Clinical Psychology,* 1976, 23:190-196.

DANAHER, B. G. Theoretical foundations and clinical applications of the Premack principle: Review and critique. *Behavior Therapy,* 1974, 5:307-324.

DANIELS, L. K. Treatment of grand mal epilepsy by covert and operant conditioning techniques. *Psychosomatics,* 1975, 16:65-67.

DAVIDSON, P. O. (Ed.). *The Behavioral Management of Anxiety, Depression and Pain.* New York: Brunner/Mazel, 1976.

DAVIS, H., MITCHELL, W. S., & MARKS, F. A behavioural programme for the modification of encopresis. *Child Care, Health and Development,* 1976, 2:273-282.

DAVISON, G. Elimination of a sadistic fantasy by a client-controlled counter conditioning technique: A case study. *Journal of Abnormal Psychology,* 1968, 73:84-90.

DAVISON, G. C. Behavior modification techniques in institutional settings. In C. M. Franks (Ed.), *Behavior Therapy: Appraisal and Status.* New York: McGraw-Hill, 1969.

DAVISON, G. C. Homosexuality: The ethical challenge. *Journal of Homosexuality,* 1977, 2:195-204.

DECI, E. L. Intrinsic motivation, extrinsic reinforcement and inequity. *Journal of Personality and Social Psychology,* 1972, 22:113-120 (a).

DECI, E. L. The effects of contingent and noncontingent rewards and controls on intrinsic motivation. *Organizational Behavior and Human Performance,* 1972, 8: 217-229 (b).

DEFFENBACHER, J. L. Group desensitization of dissimilar anxieties. *Community Mental Health Journal,* 1976, 12:263-266.

DENNEY, D. R. & SULLIVAN, B. J. Desensitization and modeling treatments of spider fear using two types of scenes. *Journal of Consulting and Clinical Psychology,* 1976, 44:573-579.

DILORETO, A. *Comparative Psychotherapy.* New York: Aldine-Atherton, 1971.

DOCKENS, W. S. Operant conditioning: A general systems approach. In T. Thompson & W. S. Dockens, *Applications of Behavior Modification.* New York: Academic Press, 1975.

DORR, D. Some practical suggestions on behavioral consulting with teachers. *Professional Psychology*, 1977, 11:95-102.

DOUGLAS, V. I., PARRY, P., MARTON, P., & GARSON, C. Assessment of a cognitive training program for hyperactive children. *Journal of Abnormal Child Psychology*, 1976, 4:389-410.

DRUCKER, P. F. *The Practice of Management*. New York: Harper, 1954.

DUKER, P. C. Remotely applied punishment versus avoidance conditioning in the treatment of self-injurious behaviors. *European Journal of Behavioural Analysis and Modification*, 1976, 3:179-185 (a).

DUKER, P. C. Remotely applied punishment versus avoidance conditioning in the treatment of self-injurious behaviours. *European Journal of Behavioural Analysis and Modification*, 1976, 3:188 (b).

DUNLAP, J. T. & LIEBERMAN, L. R. On "The end of ideology in behavior modification." *American Psychologist*, 1973, 28:936-938.

D'ZURILLA, T., WILSON, G. T., & NELSON, R. A preliminary study of the effectiveness of graduated prolonged exposure in the treatment of irrational fear. *Behavior Therapy*, 1973, 4:672-685.

D'ZURILLA, T. J. & GOLDFRIED, M. R. Problem solving and behavior modification. *Journal of Abnormal Psychology*, 1971, 78:107-126.

EDNEY, J. J. Human territories: Comment on functional properties. *Environment and Behavior*, 1976, 8:31-47 (a).

EDNEY, J. J. The psychological role of property rights in human behavior. *Environment and Planning*, 1976, 8:811-822 (b).

EDNEY, J. J. & BUDA, M. A. Distinguishing territoriality and privacy: Two studies. *Human Ecology*, 1976, 4:283-296.

EISLER, R. M. The behavioral assessment of social skills. In M. Hersen, & A. J. Bellack, *Behavioral Assessment: A Practical Handbook*. New York: Pergamon, 1976.

ELLIS, A. *Reason and Emotion in Psychotherapy*. New York: Stuart, 1962.

ELLIS, A. *The Essence of Rational Psychotherapy: A Comprehensive Approach to Treatment*. New York: Institute for Rational Living, 1970.

ELLIS, A. Techniques of handling anger in marriage. *Journal of Marriage and Family Counseling*, 1976, 2:305-316.

ELLIS, A. Review of A. T. Beck "Cognitive therapy and the emotional disorders." *Behavior Therapy*, 1977, 8:295-296.

EMMELKAMP, P. M. G. & WESSELS, H. Flooding in imagination vs. flooding *in vivo*: A comparison with agoraphobics. *Behaviour Research and Therapy*, 1975, 13:7-15.

EMMELKAMP, P. M. G. & STRAATMAN, H. A psychoanalytic reinterpretation of the effectiveness of systematic desensitization: Fact or fiction? *Behaviour Research and Therapy*, 1976, 14:245-249.

EMRICK, C. D. A review of psychologically oriented treatment of alcoholism: I. The use and interrelationships of outcome criteria and drinking behavior following treatment. *Quarterly Journal of Studies on Alcohol*, 1974, 35:523-549.

EPSTEIN, L. H. & MARTIN, J. E. Behavioral medicine. *Newsletter of the Association for Advancement of Behavior Therapy*, 1977, 4 (3):5-6.

EPSTEIN, L. H., MILLER, P. M., & WEBSTER, J. S. The effects of reinforcing concurrent behavior on self-monitoring. *Behavior Therapy*, 1976, 7:89-95.

EPSTEIN, L. H., PARKER, F. C., & JENKINS, C. C. A multiple baseline analysis of treatment for heroin addiction. *Addictive Behaviors*, 1976, 1:327-330.

EVANS, D. R. A systematized introduction to behavior therapy training. *Journal of Behavior Therapy and Experimental Psychiatry*, 1976, 7:23-26.

EWING, J. A. & ROUSE, B. A. Failure of an experimental treatment program to inculcate controlled drinking in alcoholics. *British Journal of Addiction*, 1976, 71:123-134.

EYSENCK, H. J. The effects of psychotherapy. *Journal of Consulting Psychology,* 1952, 16:319-324.

EYSENCK, H. J. The learning theory model of neurosis—A new approach. *Behaviour Research and Therapy,* 1976, 14:251-268 (a).

EYSENCK, H. J. Behaviour therapy—dogma or applied science? In P. Feldman & A. Broadhurst (Eds.), *The Experimental Basis of Behavior Therapy.* New York: Wiley, 1976 (b).

FABBRI, R., JR. Hypnosis and behavior therapy: A coordinated approach to the treatment of sexual disorders. *The American Journal of Clinical Hypnosis,* 1976, 19: 4:7.

FABREGA, H. The need for an ethnomedical science. *Science,* 1975, 189:969-975 (a).

FABREGA, H. The position of psychiatry in the understanding of human disease. *Archives of General Psychiatry,* 1975, 32:1500-1512 (b).

FABREGA, H. Toward a theory of human disease. *The Journal of Nervous and Mental Disease,* 1976, 162:299-312 (a).

FABREGA, H. The function of medical-care systems: A logical analysis. *Perspectives in Biology and Medicine,* 1976, 20:108-119 (b).

FALK, J. L. The nature and determinants of adjunctive behaviour. In R. M. Gilbert & J. D. Keehn (Eds.), *Schedule Effects: Drugs, Drinking, and Aggression.* Toronto: University of Toronto Press, 1972, pp. 148-173.

FARR, J. L. Task characteristics, reward contingency, and intrinsic motivation. *Organizational Behavior and Human Performance,* 1976, 16:294-307.

FEALLOCK, R. & MILLER, K. L. The design and evaluation of a worksharing system for experimental group living. *Journal of Applied Behavior Analysis,* 1976, 9:277-288.

FEATHER, B. W. & RHOADS, J. M. Psychodynamic behavior therapy: Theory and rationale. *International Journal of Psychiatry,* 1973, 11:135-153.

FELDMAN, M. P. & MACCULLOCH, M. J. *Homosexual Behaviour: Therapy and Assessment.* New York: Pergamon Press, 1971.

FELDMAN, P. Helping homosexuals with problems: A commentary and a personal view. *Journal of Homosexuality,* 1977, 2:241-249.

FESHBACH, S. The use of behavior modification procedures: A comment on Stolz et al. *American Psychologist,* 1976, 31:538-541.

FILLEY, A. C., HOUSE, R. J., & KERR, S. *Managerial Process and Organizational Behavior,* 2nd Edition. Glenview, Ill.: Scott, Foresman and Co., 1976.

FLANDERS, N. A. *Teacher Influence, Pupil Attitudes and Achievement,* USHEW, Office of Education Co-operative Research Project No. 397, University of Minnesota, Minneapolis, 1960.

FLAXMAN, J. Quitting smoking. In E. Craighead, A. E. Kazdin, & M. J. Mahoney (Eds.), *Behavior Modification: Principles, Issues, and Applications.* Boston, Mass.: Houghton Mifflin Company, 1976.

FLORIN, I. Stuttering: Theoretical approaches, experimental research results, suggestions for therapy. *European Journal of Behavioural Analysis and Modification,* 1976, 3: 189-200.

FOA, E. B. The referral and self-referral practices of behavior therapists: A comparative study. *Journal of Behavior Therapy and Experimental Psychiatry,* 1976, 7:331-334.

FORDYCE, W. E. *Behavioral Methods for Chronic Pain and Illness.* St. Louis, Mo.: C. V. Mosby, 1976 (a).

FORDYCE, W. E. Behavioral concepts in chronic pain and illness. In P. O. Davidson (Ed.), *The Behavioral Management of Anxiety, Depression and Pain.* New York: Brunner/Mazel, 1976 (b).

FORGIONE, A. G. The use of mannequins in the behavioral assessment of child molesters: Two case studies. *Behavior Therapy,* 1976, 7:678-685.

FORSTER, F., PAULSEN, W., & BAUGHMAN, F. Clinical therapeutic conditioning in reading epilepsy. *Neurology*, 1969, 19:71-77.

FOY, D. W., MILLER, P. M., EISLER, R. M., & O'TOOLE, D. H. Social-skills training to teach alcoholics to refuse drinks effectively. *Journal of Studies on Alcohol*, 1976, 37:1340-1345.

FRANKEL, F. & SIMMONS, J. Q. Self-injurious behavior in schizophrenic and retarded children. *American Journal of Mental Deficiency*, 1976, 80:512-522.

FRANKS, C. M. Behavior therapy and its Pavlovian origins. In C. M. Franks (Ed.), *Behavior Therapy: Appraisal and Status*. New York: McGraw-Hill, 1969.

FRANKS, C. M. Foreword. In A. A. Lazarus, *Multimodal Behavior Therapy*. New York: Springer, 1976.

FRANKS, C. M. Clockwork orange revisited: Travesty and truth about aversive conditioning. In O. L. McCabe (Ed.), *Changing Human Behavior: Psychotherapy and Behavior Change*. New York: Grune & Stratton, 1977 (b).

FRANKS, C. M. The case for controlled drinking. Review of W. R. Miller & R. C. Muñoz, *How to Control Your Drinking*. *Contemporary Psychology*, 1977, 22:668-669.

FRANKS, C. M. & BIEN, N. Z. Review of the American Psychiatric Association Task Force Report No. 5: Behavior Therapy in Psychiatry. *Behavior Therapy*, 1974, 5:718-720.

FRANKS, C. M. & WILSON, G. T. *Annual Review of Behavior Therapy: Theory and Practice*, Vol. I. New York: Brunner/Mazel, 1973.

FRANKS, C. M. & WILSON, G. T. *Annual Review of Behavior Therapy: Theory and Practice*, Vol. II. New York: Brunner/Mazel, 1974.

FRANKS, C. M. & WILSON, G. T. *Annual Review of Behavior Therapy: Theory and Practice*, Vol. III. New York: Brunner/Mazel, 1975.

FRANKS, C. M. & WILSON, G. T. *Annual Review of Behavior Therapy: Theory and Practice*, Vol. IV. New York: Brunner/Mazel, 1976.

FREDERIKSEN, L. W. Single-case designs in the modification of smoking. *Addictive Behaviors*, 1976, 1:311-320.

FREDERIKSEN, L. W., JENKINS, J. O., & CARR, C. R. Indirect modification of adolescent drug abuse using contingency contracting. *Journal of Behavior Therapy and Experimental Psychiatry*, 1976, 7:377-378.

FREDERIKSEN, L. W., JENKINS, K. O., FOY, D. W., & EISLER, R. M. Social-skills training to modify abusive verbal outbursts in adults. *Journal of Applied Behavior Analysis*, 1976, 9:117-126.

FREDERIKSEN, L. W., PETERSON, G. L., & MURPHY, W. D. Controlled smoking: Development and maintenance. *Addictive Behaviors*, 1976, 1:193-196.

FREEMAN, W. & MEYER, R. G. A behavioral alteration of sexual preferences in the human male. *Behavior Therapy*, 1975, 6:202-212.

FREUND, K. Should homosexuality arouse therapeutic concern? *Journal of Homosexuality*, 1977, 2:235-240.

FRIEDMAN, P. H. *The Effects of Modeling and Role Playing on Assertive Behavior*. Unpublished doctoral dissertation. University of Wisconsin, 1968.

GAGNON, J. H. & DAVISON, G. C. Asylums, the token economy, and the metrics of mental life. *Behavior Therapy*, 1976, 7:528-534.

GALASSI, J. P., HOLLANDSWORTH, J. G., RADECKI, J. C., GAY, M. L., HOWE, M. R., & EVANS, C. L. Behavioral performance in the validation of an assertiveness scale. *Behavior Therapy*, 1976, 7:447-452.

GALASSI, M. D. & GALASSI, J. P. The effects of role playing variation on the assessment of assertive behavior. *Behavior Therapy*, 1976, 7:343-347.

GALE, E. N. & CARLSSON, S. Look carefully: A short note on symptom substitution. *Behaviour Research and Therapy*, 1976, 14:77.

GAMBRILL, E. D. The use of behavioral methods in a short-term detention setting. *Criminal Justice and Behavior,* 1976, 3:53-66.

GARDNER, J. M. Cross-cultural diffusion of behaviour modification. In P. W. Sheehan & K. D. White (Eds.), *Behaviour Modification in Australia.* Parkville, Victoria: Australian Psychological Society, 1976.

GARFIELD, S. L. & KURTZ, R. Clinical psychologists in the 1970s. *American Psychologist,* 1976, 31:1-9.

GATCHEL, R. J. & PROCTOR, J. D. Effectiveness of voluntary heart rate control in reducing speech anxiety. *Journal of Consulting and Clinical Psychology,* 1976, 44: 381-389.

GATHERCOLE, C. E. Remotely applied punishment versus avoidance conditioning in the treatment of self-injurious behaviours. *European Journal of Behavioural Analysis and Modification,* 1976, 3:186-187.

GELDER, M. G., BANCROFT, J. H. J., GATH, D., JOHNSTON, D. W., MATHEWS, A. M., & SHAW, P. M. Specific and non-specific factors in behavior therapy. *British Journal of Psychiatry,* 1973, 123:445-462.

GELFAND, D. M. & HARTMANN, D. P. *Child Behavior Analysis and Therapy.* New York: Pergamon, 1975.

GELLER, E. S. Increasing desired waste disposals with instructions. *Man-Environment Systems,* 1975, 5:125-128.

GELLER, E. S., CHAFFEE, J. L., & FARRIS, J. C. Research in modifying lecturer behavior with continuing student feedback. *Educational Technology,* 1975, 15:31-35.

GELLER, E. S., CHAFFEE, J. L., & INGRAM, R. E. Promoting paper recycling on a university campus. *Journal of Environmental Systems,* 1975, 5:39-57.

GELLER, E. S., WITMER, J. F., & OREBAUGH, A. L. Instructions as a determinant of paper-disposal behaviors. *Environment and Behavior,* 1976, 8:417-439.

GILBERT, R. M. Drug abuse as excessive behavior. *Canadian Psychological Review,* 1976, 17:231-240.

GIRODO, M. & HENRY, D. R. Cognitive, physiological and behavioural components of anxiety in flooding. *Canadian Journal of Behavioral Science/Review,* 1976, 8:224-231.

GITTELMAN-KLEIN, R., KLEIN, D. F., ABIKOFF, H., KATZ, S., GLOISTEN, A. C. & KATES, W. Relative efficacy of methylphenidate and behavior modification in hyperkinetic children. An interim report. *Journal of Abnormal Child Psychology,* 1976, 4:361-379.

GLASS, G. V. & SMITH, M. L. *Meta-analysis of Psychotherapy Outcome Studies.* Unpublished manuscript, University of Colorado, 1976.

GLASGOW, R. E. & ROSEN, S. M. Behavioral bibliotherapy: A review of self-help behavior therapy manuals. *Psychological Bulletin* (in press).

GLICK, B. R. & GROSS, S. G. Marital interaction and marital conflict: A critical evaluation of current research strategies. *Journal of Marriage and the Family,* 1975, 37: 505-512.

GLISSON, D. H. A review of behavioral marital counseling: Has practice tuned out theory? *The Psychological Record,* 1976, 36:95-104.

GLOGOWER, F. & SLOOP, E. W. Two strategies of group training of parents as effective behavior modifiers. *Behavior Therapy,* 1976, 7:117-184.

GLOVER, J. H. & MCCUE, P. A. Electrical aversion therapy with alcoholics: A comparative follow-up study. *British Journal of Psychiatry,* 1977, 130:279-286.

GOLDBLATT, M. & MUNITZ, H. Behavioral treatment of hysterical leg paralysis. *Journal of Behavior Therapy and Experimental Psychiatry,* 1976, 7:259-263.

GOLDFRIED, M. R. Systematic desensitization as training in self-control. *Journal of Consulting and Clinical Psychology,* 1971, 37:228-234.

GOLDFRIED, M. Behavioral assessment. In I. B. Weiner (Ed.), *Clinical Methods in Psychology.* New York: Wiley, 1976.

GOLDFRIED, M. R. & DAVISON, S. C. *Clinical Behavior Therapy*. New York: Holt, Rinehart & Winston, 1976.

GOLDFRIED, M. R. & LINEHAN, M. M. Basic issues in behavioral assessment. In A. R. Ciminero, K. S. Calhoun, & H. E. Adams (Eds.), *Handbook of Behavioral Assessment*. New York: Wiley, 1977.

GOLDFRIED, M. R. & SPRAFKIN, J. N. *Behavioral Personality Assessment.* Morristown, N.J.: General Learning Press, 1974.

GOLDIAMOND, I. Toward a constructional approach to social problems. *Behaviorism,* 1974, 2:1-84.

GOLDIAMOND, I. Fables, armadyllics, and self-reinforcement. *Journal of Applied Behavior Analysis,* 1976, 9:521-525 (a).

GOLDIAMOND, I. Singling out self-administered behavior therapies for professional overview. *American Psychologist,* 1976, 31:142-147 (b).

GOLDMAN, H., KLEINMAN, K. M., SNOW, M. Y., BIDUS, D. R., & KOROL, B. Relationship between essential hypertension and cognitive functioning: Effects of biofeedback. *Psychophysiology,* 1975, 12:569-573.

GOLDSMITH, J. B. & MCFALL, R. M. Development and evaluation of an interpersonal skill-training program for psychiatric inpatients. *Journal of Abnormal Psychology,* 1975, 84:51-58.

GOLDSTEIN, A. P. & SORCHER, M. *Changing Supervisor Behavior*. New York: Pergamon, 1973.

GOODWIN, L. & TU, J. The social psychological basis for public acceptance of the social security system: The role for social research in public policy formation. *American Psychologist,* 1975, 30:875-883.

GÖTESTAM, K. G., MELIN, L., & ÖST, L. Behavioral techniques in the treatment of drug abuse: An evaluation review. *Addictive Behaviors,* 1976, 1:205-226.

GOTTMAN, J., NOTARIUS, C., MARKMAN, H., BANK, S., YOPPI, B., & RUBIN, M. E. Behavior exchange theory and marital decision making. *Journal of Personality and Social Psychology* 1976, 34:14-23.

GRANT, R. L. & MALETSKY, B. M. Application of the Weed system to psychiatric records. *Psychiatry in Medicine,* 1972, 3:119-129.

GREEN, L. The temporal and stimulus dimensions of self-monitoring in the behavioral treatment of obesity. Unpublished doctoral dissertation, Rutgers University, 1976.

GREER, S. E. & D'ZURILLA, T. J. Behavioral approaches to marital discord and conflict. *Journal of Marriage and Family Counseling,* October, 1975, 299-315.

GREINER, J. M. & KAROLY, P. Effects of self-control training on study activity and academic performance: An analysis of self-monitoring, self-reward, and systematic-planning components. *Journal of Counseling Psychiatry,* 1976, 23:495-502.

GORMAN, A. S. & KNISKERN, D. P. Research on marital and family therapy: Progress, perspective and prospect. In S. L. Garfield & A. E. Bergin (Eds.), *Handbook of Psychotherapy and Behavior Change: An Empirical Analysis* (Second Edition). New York: Wiley, in press.

GRONLUND, N. E. *Preparing Criterion-referenced Tests for Classroom Instruction*. New York: Macmillan, 1973.

GURMAN, A. S. The effects and effectiveness of marital therapy: A review of outcome research. *Family Progress,* 1973, 12:145-170.

GURMAN, A. S. Contemporary marital therapies: A critique and comparative analysis of psychodynamic, systems and behavioral approaches. In T. Paolino, & B. McGrady (Eds.), *Marriage and Marital Therapy from Three Perspectives*. New York: Brunner/Mazel, in press.

GURMAN, A. S. & KNISKERN, D. P. Enriching research on marital enrichment programs. *Journal of Marriage and Family Counseling,* 1977, 3:3-11.

GUTHRIE, G. M., MASANGKAY, Z., & GUTHRIE, H. A. Behavior, malnutrition, and mental development. *Journal of Cross-Cultural Psychology,* 1976, 7:169-180.

HACKMAN, J. R. & LAWLER, E. E. Employee reactions to job characteristics. *Journal of Applied Psychology Monograph,* 1971, 55:259-286.

HAFNER, R. J. Fresh symptom emergence after intensive behaviour therapy. *British Journal of Psychiatry,* 1976, 129:378-383.

HAFNER, J. Letter to the editor. *British Journal of Psychiatry,* 1977, 130:419-420.

HAGEN, R. L. Group therapy vs. bibliotherapy in weight reduction. *Behavior Therapy,* 1974, 5:222-234.

HAGEN, R. L., FOREYT, J. P., & DURHAM, T. W. The dropout problem: Reducing attrition in obesity research. *Behavior Therapy,* 1976, 7:463-471.

HALL, J. N. Comment on L. Claeson & U. Malm, Social training in chronic schizophrenia. *European Journal of Behavioral Analysis and Modification,* 1976, 3:176-177.

HALL, S. M. & HALL, R. G. Outcome and methodological considerations in behavioral treatment of obesity. *Behavior Therapy,* 1974, 5:352-364.

HAMBURG, S. Behavior therapy in alcoholism: A critical review of broad-spectrum approaches. *Journal of Studies on Alcohol,* 1975, 36:69-87.

HAMNER, W. C. & HAMNER, C. P. Behavior modification on the bottom line. *Organizational Dynamics,* 1976, Spring, 3-21.

HANSON, R. W., BORDEN, B. L., HALL, S. M., & HALL, R. G. Use of programmed instruction in teaching self-management skills to overweight adults. *Behavior Therapy,* 1976, 7:366-373.

HARE, R. D. *Psychopathy: Theory and Research.* New York: Wiley, 1970.

HARRIS, S. L. *Teaching Speech to a Non-verbal Child.* Lawrence, Ks.: H. & H. Enterprises, 1976.

HARTMAN, W. & FITHIAN, M. A. *Treatment of Sexual Dysfunction.* California: Center for Marital and Sexual Studies, 1972.

HARTSOOK, J. E., OLCH, D. R., & DE WOLF, V. A. Personality characteristics of women's assertiveness training group participants. *Journal of Counseling Psychology,* 1976, 23:322-326.

HASTINGS, D. W. Sexual potency disorders of the male. In A. M. Freedman & H. I. Kaplan (Eds.), *Comprehensive Textbook of Psychiatry.* Baltimore: Williams & Wilkins, 1967.

HAYES, L. A. The use of group contingencies for behavioral control: A review. *Psychological Bulletin,* 1976, 83:628-648.

HAYES, S. C. & CONE, J. D. Reducing residential electrical energy use: Payment, information, and feedback. *Journal of Applied Behavior Analysis* (in press, a).

HAYES, S. C. & CONE, J. D. Decelerating environmentally destructive lawn-walking behavior. *Environment and Behavior* (in press, b).

HEDQUIST, F. J. & WEINHOLD, B. K. Behavioral group counseling with socially anxious and unassertive college students. *Journal of Counseling Psychology,* 1970, 17:237-242.

HERENDEEN, D. L., DEMSTER, B., & WIMER, P. Evaluation in an applied setting: Assessment of intervention using a modified multiple baseline design (in press).

HEIMAN, J., LOPICCOLO, L., & LOPICCOLO, J. *Becoming Orgasmic: A Sexual Growth Program for Women.* Englewood Cliffs, N.J.: Prentice-Hall, 1976.

HELM, D. Psychodynamic and behavior modification approaches to the treatment of infantile autism empirical similarities. *Journal of Autism and Childhood Schizophrenia,* 1976, 5:27-41.

HERSEN, M. Token economies in institutional settings. *Journal of Nervous and Mental Disease,* 1976, 162:206-211.

HERSEN, M. & BARLOW, D. *Single Case Experimental Designs: Strategies for Studying Behavior Change.* New York: Pergamon, 1976.

HERSEN, M. & BELLACK, A. S. (Eds.), *Behavioral Assessment: A Practical Handbook.* New York: Pergamon, 1976.

HERSEN, M. & BELLACK, A. S. A multiple-baseline analysis of social-skills training in chronic schizophrenics. *Journal of Applied Behavior Analysis,* 1976, 9:239-245 (a).

HERSEN, M. & BELLACK, A. S. Social skills training for chronic psychiatric patients: Rationale, research findings, and future directions. *Comprehensive Psychiatry,* 1976, 17:559-580 (b).

HERSEN, H. & BELLACK, A. S. Assessment of social skills. In A. R. Ciminero, K. S. Calhoun, & H. E. Adams (Eds.), *Handbook of Behavioral Assessment.* New York: Wiley, 1977.

HERSEN, M., EISLER, R. M., & MILLER, P. M. An experimental analysis of generalization in assertive training. *Behaviour Research and Therapy,* 1974, 12:295-310.

HESCHELES, D. & KAVANAGH, T. Technical eclecticism and open-case consultation: A psychotherapeutic training model. *Psychological Reports,* 1976, 39:1043-1046.

HODGSON, R. & RACHMAN, S. The effects of contamination and washing in obsessional patients. *Behaviour Research and Therapy,* 1972, 10:111-117.

HOLLAND, J. Ethical considerations in behavior modification. *Journal of Humanistic Psychology,* 1976, 16:71-78.

HOLLMANN, R. W. Supportive organizational climate and managerial assessment of MBO effectiveness. *Academy of Management Journal,* 1976, 19:560-576 (a).

HOLLMANN, R. W. Applying MBO research to practice. *Human Resources Management,* 1976, Winter, 28-36 (b).

HOLROYD, K. A. Cognition and desensitization in the group treatment of test anxiety. *Journal of Consulting and Clinical Psychology,* 1976, 44:991-1001.

HOLROYD, K. A., ANDRASIK, F., & WESTBROOK, T. Cognitive control of tension headache.

HORN, P. Work involvement pays off. *Psychology Today,* 1975, 9:89.

HUNT, G. H. & AZRIN, N. H. The community-reinforcement approach to alcoholism. *Behaviour Research and Therapy,* 1973, 11:91-104.

HUTCHINGS, D. F. & REINKING, R. H. Tension headaches. What form of therapy is most effective? *Biofeedback and Self-Regulation,* 1976, 1:183-190.

INCE, L. *Behavior Modification in Rehabilitation Medicine.* Springfield, Ill.: C. C Thomas, 1976 (a).

INCE, L. P. The use of relaxation training and a conditioned stimulus in the elimination of epileptic seizures in a child: A case study. *Journal of Behavior Therapy and Experimental Psychiatry,* 1976, 7:39-42 (b).

INGLIS, J., CAMPBELL, D., & DONALD, M. W. Electromyographic biofeedback and neuromuscular rehabilitation. *Canadian Journal of Behavioral Science/Review of Canadian Science Comp.,* 1976, 8:299-323.

IWATA, B. A., BAILEY, J. S., BROWN, K. M. FOSHEE, T. J., & ALPERN, M. A performance-based lottery to improve residential care and training by institutional staff. *Journal of Applied Behavior Analysis,* 1976, 9:417-431.

IWATA, B. A. & LORENTZSON, A. M. Operant control of seizure-like behavior in an institutionalized retarded adult. *Behavior Therapy,* 1976, 7:247-251.

JABLONSKY, S. F. & DEVRIES, D. L. Operant conditioning principles extrapolated to the theory of management. *Organizational Behavior and Human Performance,* 1972, 7:340-358.

JACOBSON, N. S. & MARTIN, B. Behavioral marriage therapy: Current status. *Psychological Bulletin,* 1976, 83:540-556.

JAFFE, P. G. & CARLSON, P. M. Relative efficacy of modeling and instructions in eliciting social behavior from chronic psychiatric patients. *Journal of Consulting and Clinical Psychology,* 1976, 44:200-207.

JEGER, A. M. & GOLDFRIED, M. R. A comparison of situation tests of speech anxiety. *Behavior Therapy*, 1976, 7:252-255.

JENSEN, R. E. A behavior modification program to remediate child abuse. *Journal of Clinical Child Psychology*, 1976, 5:30-32.

JOHNSTON, D. W., LANCASHIRE, M., MATHEWS, A. M., MUNBY, M., SHAW, P. M., & GELDER, M. G. Imaginal flooding and exposure to real phobic situations: Changes during treatment. *British Journal of Psychiatry*, 1976, 129:372-377.

JONES, F. W. & HOLMES, D. S. Alcoholism, alpha production, and biofeedback. *Journal of Consulting and Clinical Psychology*, 1976, 44:224-228.

KAGAN, S. & CARLSON, H. Development of adaptive assertiveness in Mexican and United States children. *Developmental Psychology*, 1975, 11:71-78.

KAGEL, J. H., BATTALIO, R. C., WINKLER, R. C., & WINETT, R. A. Energy conservation strategies: An evaluation of the effectiveness of price changes and information on household demand for electricity. Unpublished manuscript, Texas A and M University, 1970 (cited by Nietzel et al., 1977).

KALLMAN, W. M. & FEUERSTEIN, M. Psychophysiological procedures. In A. R. Ciminero, K. S. Calhoun & H. E. Adams (Eds.), *Handbook of Behavioral Assessment*. New York: Wiley, 1977.

KANDEL, H. J., AYLLON, T., & ROBERTS, M. D. Rapid educational rehabilitation for prison inmates. *Behaviour Research and Therapy*, 1976, 14:323-331.

KANFER, F. Self-monitoring: Methodological limitations and clinical applications. *Journal of Consulting and Clinical Psychology*, 1970, 35:148-152.

KANFER, F. H. & SASLOW, G. Behavioral diagnosis. In C. M. Franks (Ed.), *Behavior Therapy: Appraisal and Status*. New York: McGraw-Hill, 1969.

KANTOR, J. R. Behaviorism, behavior analysis, and the career of psychology. *The Psychological Record*, 1976, 26:305-312.

KAPLAN, H. *The New Sex Therapy*. New York: Brunner/Mazel, 1974.

KAPLAN, H. S., KOHL, R. N., POMEROY, W. B., OFFIT, A. K., & HOGAN, B. Group treatment of premature ejaculation. *Archives of Sexual Behavior*, 1974, 3:443-452.

KAPLAN, R. M. & LITROWNIK, A. J. Some statistical methods for the assessment of multiple outcome criteria in behavioral research. *Behavior Therapy*, 1977, 8:383-392.

KATZ, R. C., THOMAS, S. L., & WILLIAMSON, P. Effects of self-monitoring as a function of its expected benefits and incompatible response training. *The Psychological Record*, 1976, 26:533-540.

KATZ, R. C. & WOOLLEY, F. R. Improving patient records through problem orientation. *Behavior Therapy*, 1975, 119-124.

KATZELL, R. A., YANKELOVICH, D., FEIN, M., OORNATI, O. A., & NASH, A. *Work, Productivity and Job Satisfaction*. New York: Psychological Corporation, 1975.

KAYE, S., TRICKETT, E. J., & QUINLAN, D. M. Alternative methods for environmental assessment: An example. *American Journal of Community Psychology*, 1976, 4: 367-377.

KAZDIN, A. E. Effects of covert modeling and modeling reinforcement on assertive behavior. *Journal of Abnormal Psychology*, 1974, 83:240-252 (a).

KAZDIN, A. E. Reactive self-monitoring: The effects of response desirability, goal setting, and feedback. *Journal of Consulting and Clinical Psychology*, 1974, 42:704-716 (b).

KAZDIN, A. E. *Behavior Modification in Applied Settings*. Homewood, Ill.: Dorsey Press, 1975 (a).

KAZDIN, A. E. Covert modeling, imagery assessment, and assertive behavior. *Journal of Consulting and Clinical Psychology*, 1975, 43:716-724 (b).

KAZDIN, A. E. Effects of covert modeling, multiple models, and model reinforcement on assertive behavior. *Behavior Therapy*, 1976, 7:211-222.

KAZDIN, A. *The Token Economy*. New York: Plenum, 1977.

KAZDIN, A. & BOOTZIN, R. The token economy: An evaluative review. *Journal of Applied Behavior Analysis,* 1972, 5:343-372.

KAZDIN, A. E. & WILCOXON, L. A. Systematic desensitization and nonspecific treatment effects: A methodological evaluation. *Psychological Bulletin,* 1976, 83:729-758.

KAZDIN, A. E. & WILSON, G. T. Criteria for evaluating psychotherapy. Unpublished manuscript, Center for Advanced Study in the Behavioral Sciences, Stanford, California, 1977.

KAZDIN, A. E. & WILSON, G. T. *Evaluation of Behavior Therapy: Issues, Evidence, and Research Strategies.* Cambridge, Mass.: Ballinger, in press.

KEELEY, S. M., SHEMBERG, K. M., & CARBONELL, J. Operant clinical intervention: Behavior management or beyond? Where are the data? *Behavior Therapy,* 1976, 7: 292-305.

KELLER, R. T. & SZILAGYI, A. D. Employee reactions to leader reward behavior. *Academy of Management Journal,* 1976, 19:619-626.

KENDALL, P. C., FINCH, A. J., & GILLEN, B. Readability and human interest scores as objective aids in behavior therapy text selection. *Behavior Therapy,* 1976, 7:535-538.

KENT, R. N. & FOSTER, S. L. Direct observational procedures: Methodological issues in naturalistic settings. In A. R. Ciminero, K. S. Calhoun, & H. E. Adams (Eds.), *Handbook of Behavioral Assessment.* New York: Wiley, 1977.

KENT, R. N. & O'LEARY, K. D. Treatment of conduct problem children: BA and/or PhD Therapists. *Behavior Therapy,* 1977, 8:653-658.

KIRSCHNER, N. M. Generalization of behaviorally oriented assertive training. *The Psychological Record,* 1976, 26:117-125.

KLAUS, D., HERSEN, M., & BELLACK, A. S. Survey of dating habits of male and female college students: A necessary precursor to measurement and modification. *Journal of Clinical Psychology,* 1977, 33:369-375.

KLEIN, D. C. & SELIGMAN, M. E. P. Cited by Seligman, M. E. P., Klein, D. C., & Miller, W. R. Depression. In H. Leitenberg (Ed.), *Handbook of Behavior Modification and Therapy.* Englewood Cliffs: Prentice-Hall, 1976.

KLERMAN, S. L. Behavior control and the limits of reform. Hastings Center Report, August, 1975, 40-46.

KNAPP, T. J., DOWNS, D. L., & ALPERSON, J. R. Behavior therapy for insomnia: A review. *Behavior Therapy,* 1976, 7:614-625.

KOCKOTT, G., DITTMAR, F., & NUSSELT, L. Systematic desensitization of erectile impotence: A controlled study. *Archives of Sexual Behavior,* 1975, 4:493-500.

KOOCHER, G. P. Civil liberties and aversive conditioning for children. *American Psychologist,* 1976, 31:94-95.

KORMAN, A. K., GREENHAUS, J. H., & BADIN, I. J. Personnel attitudes and motivation. *Annual Review of Psychology,* 1977, 28:175-196.

KOULACK, D., LEBOW, M. D., & CHURCH, M. The effect of desensitization on the sleep and dreams of a phobic subject. *Canadian Journal of Behavioral Science,* 1976, 8:418-421.

KRASNER, L. On the death of behavior modification: Some comments from a mourner. *American Psychologist,* 1976, 31:387-388.

KRASNER, L. The classroom as a planned environment. Presented at the annual meeting of the American Educational Research Association, Washington, D.C., 1975.

KRAUT, A. J. Developing managerial skills via modeling techniques: Some positive research findings—a symposium. *Personnel Psychology,* 1976, 29:325-328.

KREITLER, S., SHAHAR, A., & KREITLER, H. Cognitive orientation, type of smoker and behavior therapy of smoking. *British Journal of Medical Psychology,* 1976, 49: 167-175.

KRUMBOLTZ, J. D., MITCHELL, A. M., & JONES, G. B. A social learning theory of selection. *The Counseling Psychologist,* 1976, 6:71-81.

KUHN, T. S. *The Structure of Scientific Revolutions.* Chicago: Chicago University Press, 1962.

KWITEROVICH, D. K. & HORAN, J. J. Solomon evaluation of a commercial assertiveness program for women. *Behavior Therapy,* 1977, 8:501-502.

LANDO, H. A. Self-pacing in eliminating chronic smoking: Serendipity revisited? *Behavior Therapy,* 1976, 7:634-640.

LANG, A. R., YOECKNER, D. J., ADESSO, V. J., & MARLATT, G. A. Effects of alcohol on aggression in male social drinkers. *Journal of Abnormal Psychology,* 1975, 84:508-518.

LANG, P. J. The mechanics of desensitization and the laboratory study of fear. In C. M. Franks (Eds.), *Behavior Therapy: Appraisal and Status.* New York: McGraw-Hill, 1969.

LANG, P. J. & LAZOVIK, A. D. Experimental desensitization of a phobia. *Journal of Abnormal and Social Psychology,* 1963, 66:519-525.

LANGER, E. J. & RODIN, J. The effects of choice and enhanced personal responsibility for the aged: A field experiment in an institutional setting. *Journal of Personality and Social Psychology,* 1976, 34:191-198.

LANYON, R. I., BARRINGTON, C. C., & NEWMAN, A. C. Modification of stuttering through EMG biofeedback: A preliminary study. *Behavior Therapy,* 1976, 7:96-103.

LAWS, D. R. & RUBIN, H. B. Instructional control of an autonomic sexual response. *Journal of Applied Behavior Analysis,* 1969, 2:93-99.

LAWSON, D. M., WILSON, G. T., BRIDDELL, D. W., & IVES, C. C. Assessment and modification of alcoholics' drinking behavior in controlled laboratory settings: A cautionary note. *Addictive Behaviors,* 1976, 1:299-303.

LAYNE, C. C., RICKARD, H. C., JONES, M. T., & LYMAN, R. D. Accuracy of self-monitoring on a variable ratio schedule of observer cerification. *Behavior Therapy,* 1976, 7:481-488.

LAZARUS, A. A. Learning theory and the treatment of depression. *Behaviour Research and Therapy,* 1968, 6:83-89.

LAZARUS, A. A. *Behavior Therapy and Beyond.* New York: McGraw-Hill, 1971 (a).

LAZARUS, A. A. Where do behavior therapists take their troubles? *Psychological Reports,* 1971, 28:349-350 (b).

LAZARUS, A. A. Women in behavior therapy. In V. Franks & V. Burtle (Eds.), *Women in Therapy: New Psychotherapies for a Changing Society.* New York: Brunner/Mazel, 1974.

LAZARUS, A. A. *Multimodal Behavior Therapy.* New York: Springer, 1976.

LAZARUS, A. A. Has behavior therapy outlived its usefulness? *American Psychologist,* 1977, 32:550-554.

LAZARUS, A. A. & WILSON, G. T. Behavior modification: Clinical and experimental perspectives. In R. B. Wolman (Ed.), *The Therapist's Handbook.* New York: Van Nostrand Reinhold, 1976.

LAZARUS, R. S. A cognitively oriented psychologist looks at biofeedback. *American Psychologist,* 1975, 30:553-561.

LEBOW, M. D. Behavior modification: A significant method in nursing practice. Englewood Cliffs, N.J.: Prentice-Hall, 1973.

LEBOW, M. Applications of behavior modification in nursing practice. In M. Hersen, R. M. Eisler, & P. M. Miller (Eds.), *Progress in Behavior Modification,* Volume 2, 1976. New York: Academic.

LEBOW, M. D. *Approaches to Modifying Patient Behavior.* New York: Appleton-Century-Crofts, 1976.

LEDERER, W. J. & JACKSON, D. D. *The Mirages of Marriage.* New York: Norton, 1968.

LEE, B. S., MCGOUGH, W. E., & PEINS, M. Automated desensitization of stutterers to use of the telephone. *Behavior Therapy,* 1976, 7:110-112.

LEIBLUM, S. R., ROSEN, R. C., & PIERCE, D. Group treatment format: Mixed sexual dysfunctions. *Archives of Sexual Behavior,* 1976, 5:313-322.

LEITENBERG, H. Behavioral approaches to treatment of neuroses. In H. Leitenberg (Ed.), *Handbook of Behavior Modification and Behavior Therapy.* Englewood Cliffs, N.J.: Prentice-Hall, 1976 (a).

LEITENBERG, H. (Ed.). *Handbook of Behavior Modification and Behavior Therapy.* Englewood Cliffs, N.J.: Prentice-Hall, 1976 (b).

LEMERE, F. & VOEGTLIN, W. L. An evaluation of the aversion treatment of alcoholism. *Quarterly Journal of Studies on Alcohol,* 1950, 11:199-204.

LEON, G. R. Current directions in the treatment of obesity. *Psychological Bulletin,* 1976, 83:557-578.

LEON, G. R. Review of S. Yen and R. W. McIntire "Teaching behavior modification." *Behavior Therapy,* 1977, 8:300-302.

LETOURNEAU, J. E. Application of biofeedback and behavior modification techniques in visual training. *Journal of Optometry and Physiological Optics,* 1976, 53:187-190.

LEVINE, F. M. & FASNACHT, G. Token rewards may lead to token learning. *American Psychologist,* 1974, 29:816-820.

LEVIS, D. J. Learned helplessness: A reply and an alternative S-R interpretation. *Journal of Experimental Psychology: General,* 1976, 105:47-65.

LEVIS, D. *Chastity; or Our Secret Sins.* Philadelphia: Maclean, 1875.

LEWINSOHN, P. M. A behavioral approach to depression. In R. J. Friedman & M. M. Katz (Eds.), *The Psychology of Depression: Contemporary Theory and Research.* New York: Wiley, 1974.

LIBERMAN, R. P., MCCANN, M. J., & WALLACE, C. J. Generalization of behaviour therapy with psychotics. *British Journal of Psychiatry,* 1976, 129:490-496.

LIBERMAN, R. P., WHEELER, E., & SANDERS, N. Behavioral therapy for marital disharmony: An educational approach. *Journal of Marriage and Family Counseling,* 1976, 2:383-395.

LICHTENSTEIN, E., HARRIS, D. E., BIRCHLER, G. R., WAHL, J. H. & SCHMAHL, D. P. Comparison of rapid smoking, warm smoky air, and attention placebo in the modification of smoking behavior. *Journal of Consulting and Clinical Psychology,* 1973, 40:92-98.

LICHSTEIN, K. L. & SCHREIBMAN, L. Employing electric shock with autistic children. *Journal of Autism and Childhood Schizophrenia,* 1976, 6:163-173.

LICK, J. & BOOTZIN, R. Expectancy factors in the treatment of fear: Methodological and theoretical issues. *Psychological Bulletin,* 1975, 82:917-931.

LICK, J. R. & HEFFLER, D. Relaxation training and attention placebo in the treatment of severe insomnia. *Journal of Consulting and Clinical Psychology,* 1977, 45:153-161.

LINDSEY, D. Behavioral technology and human subjectivity. *Corrective and Social Psychiatry and Journal of Behavior Technology Methods and Therapy,* 1975, 21:17-18.

LINDSLEY, O. R. Direct measurement and prothesis of retarded behavior. *Journal of Education,* 1966, 9:27-36.

LITMAN, G. K. Behavioral modification techniques in the treatment of alcoholism: A review and critique. In R. J. Gibbins, Y. Israel, H. Kalant, R. E. Popham, W. Schmidt, & R. G. Smart (Eds.), *Research Advances in Alcohol and Drug Problems,* Vol. III. New York: Wiley, 1976.

LLOYD, R. W. & SALZBERG, H. C. Controlled social drinking: An alternative to abstinence as a treatment goal for some alcohol abusers. *Psychological Bulletin,* 1975, 82:815-842.

LOCKE, E. A. Personnel attitudes and motivation. *Annual Review of Psychology,* 1975, 26:457-480.

LOCURTO, C. M. & WALSH, J. Reinforcement and self-reinforcement: Their effects on originality. *American Journal of Psychology,* 1976, 89:281-291.

LONDON, M. & OLDHAM, S. R. Effects of varying goal types and incentive systems on performance and satisfaction. *Academy of Management Journal,* 1976, 19:537-546.

LONDON, P. The end of ideology in behavior modification. *American Psychologist,* 1972, 27:913-320.

LOVAAS, O. I. *The Autistic Child: Language Development through Behavior Modification.* New York: Irvington, 1977.

LOVIBOND, S. H. & CADDY, G. Discriminated aversive control in the moderation of alcoholics' drinking behavior. *Behavior Therapy,* 1970, 1:437-444.

LOWE, J. C. & MIKULAS, W. L. Use of written material in learning self-control of premature ejaculation. *Psychological Reports,* 1975, 37:295-298.

LOWERY, C. R., DENNEY, D. R. & STORMS, M. D. *Insomnia: A Comparison of the Effects of Placebo Pill Attributions and Nonpejorative Self-attribution.* Unpublished manuscript, University of Kansas, 1976.

LUBER, R. F. & HERSEN, M. A systematic behavioral approach to partial hospitalization programming: Implications and applications. *Corrective and Social Psychiatry and Journal of Behavior Technology Methods and Therapy,* 1976, October, 22:33-37.

LUBORSKY, L., SINGER, B., & LUBORSKY, L. Comparative studies of psychotherapies: Is it true that everyone has won and all must have prizes? *Archives of General Psychiatry,* 1975, 32:995-1008.

LUYBEN, P. D. & BAILEY, J. S. Newspaper recycling behavior: The effects of reinforcement versus proximity of containers. Unpublished manuscript, Florida State University, 1975 (cited by Nietzel et al., 1977).

MACE, D. R. Martial intimacy and the deadly love-anger cycle. *Journal of Marriage and Family Counseling,* 1976, 2:131-132.

MAHONEY, M. J. *Cognition and Behavior Modification.* Combridge, Mass.: Ballinger, 1974.

MAHONEY, M. J. Terminal terminology: A self-regulated response to Goldiamond. *Journal of Applied Behavior Analysis,* 1976, 9:515-517.

MAHONEY, M. J. Reflections on the cognitive-learning trend in psychotherapy. *American Psychologist,* 1977, 32:5-13 (a).

MAHONEY, M. J. Personal science: A cognitive learning therapy. In A. Ellis (Ed.), *Handbook of Rational-Emotive Therapy.* New York: Springer, 1977 (b).

MAHONEY, M. J. & ARNKOFF, D. Cognitive and self-control therapies. In S. L. Garfield & A. E. Bergin (Eds.), *Handbook of Psychotherapy and Behavior Change,* 2nd Ed. New York: Wiley, in press.

MAHONEY, M. J., KAZDIN, A. E. & LESSWING, N. J. Behavior modification: Delusion or deliverance. In C. M. Franks & G. T. Wilson (Eds.), *Annual Review of Behavior Therapy: Theory and Practice,* Vol. 2. New York: Brunner/Mazel, 1974.

MAHONEY, M. J. & MAHONEY, K. *Permanent Weight Control.* New York: W. W. Norton, 1976 (a).

MAHONEY, M. J. & MAHONEY, K. Treatment of obesity: A clinical exploration. In B. J. Williams, S. Martin, & J. Foreyt (Eds.), *Obesity: Behavioral Approaches to Dietary Management.* New York: Brunner/Mazel, 1976 (b).

MARBURG, C. C., HOUSTON, B. K., & HOLMES, D. S. Influence of multiple models on the behavior of institutionalized retarded children: Increased generalization to other models and other behaviors. *Journal of Consulting and Clinical Psychology,* 1976, 44:514-519.

MARCUS, N. & LEVIN, G. Clinical applications of biofeedback: Implications for psychiatry. *Hospital and Community Psychiatry,* 1977, 28:21-25.

MARHOLIN, D. & BIJOU, S. A behavioral approach to assessment of children's behavioral disorders. *Child Welfare*, 1977, 56:93-106.

MARHOLIN, D. & GRAY, D. Effects of group response-cost procedures on cash shortages in a small business. *Journal of Applied Behavior Analysis*, 1976, 9:25-30.

MARINNACCI, A. A. & HORANDE, M. Electromyogram in neuromuscular re-education. *Bulletin of the Los Angeles Neurological Society*. 1960, 25:57-71.

MARKS, I. M. Management of sexual disorders. In H. Leitenberg (Ed.), *Handbook of Behavior Modification and Behavior Therapy*. Entlewood Cliffs, N.J.: Prentice-Hall, 1976 (a).

MARKS, I. M. The current status of behavioral psychotherapy: Theory and practice. *American Journal of Psychiatry*, 1976, 133:253-261 (b).

MARKS, I. M., BOULOUGOURIS, J. C., & MARSET, P. Flooding versus desensitization in the treatment of phobic patients: A crossover study. *British Journal of Psychiatry*, 1971, 119:353-375.

MARKS, I. & GELDER, M. Transvestism and fetishism: Clinical and psychological changes during faradic aversion. *British Journal of Psychiatry*, 1967, 113:711-739.

MARKS, I. M., HALLAM, R. S., CONNOLLY, J., & PHILPOTT, R. *Nursing in Behavioural Therapy*. London: The Royal College of Nursing of the United Kingdom, 1977.

MARKS, I., RACHMAN, S., & HODGSON, R. Treatment of chronic obsessive-compulsive neurosis by in-vivo exposure. *British Journal of Psychiatry*, 1975, 127:349-364.

MARLATT, G. A. A comparison of aversive conditioning procedures in the treatment of alcoholism. Presented at the annual meeting of the Western Psychological Association, April 1973.

MARLATT, G. A. The drinking profile: A questionnaire for the behavioral assessment of alcoholism. In E. J. Mash & L. G. Terdal (Eds.), *Behavior Therapy Assessment: Diagnosis, Design, and Evaluation*. New York: Springer, 1976.

MARLATT, G. A. Craving for alcohol, loss of control and relapse: A cognitive-behavioral analysis. Paper presented at NATO International Conference on Behavioral Approaches to Alcoholism, Bergen, Norway, August, 1977.

MARSHALL, W. L. & ANDREWS, W. R. *A Manual for the Self-Management of Public Speaking Anxiety*. Kingston, Ontario: McCarthur College Press, 1972.

MARSHALL, W. L., PRESSE, L., & ANDREWS, W. R. A self-administered program for public speaking anxiety. *Behaviour Research and Therapy*, 1976, 14:33-39.

MARTIN, P. *A Marital Therapy Manual*. New York: Brunner/Mazel, 1976.

MARTIN, R. *Law and Behavior Change: Limits on Psychology in Schools, Prisons and Mental Health*. Champaign, Ill.: Research Press, 1975.

MARTIN, R. Ethical and legal implications of behavior modification in the classroom. Paper presented at the First Annual Conference in School Psychology, Temple University, Philadelphia, Pa., June, 1972.

MARZILLIER, J. S., LAMBERT, C., & KELLETT, J. A controlled evaluation of systematic desensitization and social skills training for socially inadequate psychiatric patients. *Behaviour Research and Therapy*, 1976, 14:225-238.

MASH, E. J. & TERDAL, L. G. (Eds.). *Behavior Therapy Assessment: Diagnosis, Design, and Evaluation*. New York: Springer, 1976.

MASTERS, W. H. & JOHNSON, V. E. *Human Sexual Inadequacy*. Boston: Little, Brown, 1970.

MASTRIA, M. A. & HOSFORD, R. L. Assertive training as a rape prevention measure. Paper presented at the 10th Annual Convention of the Association for Advancement of Behavior Therapy, New York, December 1976.

MATHEWS, A. M., JOHNSTON, D. W., LANCASHIRE, M., MUNBY, M., SHAW, P. M., & GELDER, M. G. Imaginal flooding and exposure to real phobic situations: Treatment outcome with agoraphobic patients. *British Journal of Psychiatry*, 1976, 129:362-371.

MATHEWS, A., TEASDALE, J., MUNBY, M., JOHNSTON, D., & SHAW, P. A home based treatment program for agoraphobia. *Behavior Therapy,* in press.

MATSON, F. W. Comment on Holland's article. *Journal of Humanistic Psychology,* 1976, 16:79-80.

MAULTSBY, M. C. A behavioral approach to irrational anxiety and insomnia: Decreasing prescription suicides. *Journal of the American Medical Women's Association,* 1972, 27:416-419.

MAYADAS, N. S. & DUEHN, W. D. Stimulus-modeling (SM) videotape for marital counseling: Method and application. *Journal of Marriage and Family Counseling,* 1977, 3:35-42.

MCCONAGHY, N. Is a homosexual orientation irreversible? *British Journal of Psychiatry,* 1976, 129:556-563.

MCCUTCHEON, B. A. & ADAMS, H. E. The physiological basis of implosive therapy. *Behaviour Research and Therapy,* 1975, 13:93-100.

MCFALL, R. M. & LILLESAND, D. B. Behavior rehearsal with modelling and coaching in assertion training. *Journal of Abnormal Psychology,* 1971, 77:313-323.

MCFALL, R. M. & MARSTON, A. R. An experimental investigation of behavior rehearsal in assertive training. *Journal of Abnormal Psychology,* 1970, 76:295-303.

MCGLYNN, F. D. & MCCLAREN, H. A. Components of desensitization in modification of fear among genuinely fearful subjects. *Psychological Reports,* 1975, 37:959-969.

MCGOVERN, K. B., STEWART, R. C., & LOPICCOLO, J. Secondary orgasmic dysfunction, 1. Analysis and strategies for treatment. *Archives of Sexual Behavior,* 1975, 4:265-275.

MCGRATH, M. J. & HALL, S. M. Self-management treatment of smoking behavior. *Addictive Behaviors,* 1976, 1:287-292.

MCKEACHIE, W. J. Psychology in America's bicentennial year. *American Psychologist,* 1976, 31:819-833.

MCMORDIE, W. R. Reduction of perseverative inappropriate speech in a young male with persistent anterograde amnesia. *Journal of Behavior Therapy and Experimental Psychology,* 1976, 7:67-69.

MCREYNOLDS, W. T., BARNES, A. R., BROOKS, S., & REHAGEN, N. J. The role of attention-placebo influences in the efficacy of systematic desensitization. *Journal of Consulting and Clinical Psychology,* 1973, 41:86-92.

MCREYNOLDS, W. T. & PAULSEN, B. K. Stimulus control as the behavioral basis of weight loss procedures. In G. J. Williams, S. Martin, & J. Foreyt (Eds.), *Obesity: Behavioral Approaches to Dietary Management.* New York: Brunner/Mazel, 1976.

MEICHENBAUM, D. Cognitive modification of test anxious college students. *Journal of Consulting and Clinical Psychology,* 1972, 39:370-380.

MEICHENBAUM, D. Self-instructional methods. In F. H. Kanfer & A. P. Goldstein (Eds.), *Helping People Change.* New York: Pergamon, 1975.

MEICHENBAUM, D. Behavior therapy: The state of the art. Review of Franks and Wilson: Annual Review of Behavior Therapy: Theory & Practice. *Contemporary Psychology,* 1976, 21:707-708.

MEICHENBAUM, D. A cognitive-behavior modification approach to assessment. In M. Hersen & A. S. Bellack (Eds.), *Behavior Assessment: A Practical Handbook.* New York: Pergamon, 1976.

MEICHENBAUM, D. Cognitive factors in biofeedback therapy. *Biofeedback and Self-Regulation,* 1976, 1:201-215.

MEICHENBAUM, D. *Cognitive Behavior Modification.* New York: Plenum, 1977.

MEICHENBAUM, D., GILMORE, J., & FEDORAVICIUS, A. Group insight versus group desensitization in treating speech anxiety. *Journal of Clinical and Consulting Psychology,* 1971, 36:410-421.

MELIN, L., ANDERSSON, B. E., & GÖTESTAM, K. G. Contingency management in a methadone maintenance treatment program. *Addictive Behaviors,* 1976, 1:151-158.

MENDELSON, J. H. & MELLO, N. K. Experimental analysis of drinking behavior of chronic alcoholics. *Proceedings of the New York Academy of Science,* 1966, 133: 828-845.

MEYER, R. G. Delay therapy: Two case reports. *Behavior Therapy,* 1973, 4:709-711.

MEYER, R. E., MCNAMEE, H. B., MIRIN, S. M., & ALTMAN, J. L. Analysis and modification of opiate reinforcement. *The International Journal of the Addictions,* 1976, 11:467-484.

MEYER, V. & REICH, B. Letter to the Editor. *British Journal of Psychiatry,* 1977, 130: 418-419.

MEYERS, A. W., ARTZ, L. M., & CRAIGHEAD, W. E. The effects of instruction, incentive and feedback on a community problem: Dormitory noise. *Journal of Applied Behavior Analysis,* 1976, 9:445-457.

MICHELSON, W. *Man and His Urban Environment: A Sociological Approach.* Reading, Ma.: Addison-Wesley, 1970.

MILLER, J. G. Second annual Ludwig von Bertalanffy memorial lecture. *Behavioral Science,* 1976, 21:219-227.

MILLER, K. K. & MILLER, O. L. Maintaining attendance of welfare recipients in self-help prgorams by supplementary reinforcement. Paper presented at the Annual Convention of the American Psychological Association, Washington, D.C., 1969.

MILLER, L. C. Method factors associated with assessment of child behavior: Fact or artifact. *Journal of Abnormal Child Psychology,* 1976, 4:209-219.

MILLER, L. K., LIES, A., PETERSEN, D. L., & FEALLOCK, R. The positive community: A strategy for applying behavioral engineering to the redesign of family and community. In E. R. Mash, L. A. Hamerlynck, & L. C. Handy (Eds.), *Behavior Modification and Families.* New York: Brunner/Mazel, 1976.

MILLER, N. E. Learning of visceral and glandular responses. *Science,* 1969, 163:434-445.

MILLER, P. M. Assessment of addictive behaviors. In A. R. Ciminero, K. S. Calhoun, & H. E. Adams (Eds.), *Handbook of Behavioral Assessment.* New York: Wiley, 1977.

MILLER, W. R. Alcoholism scales and objective assessment methods: A review. *Psychological Bulletin,* 1976. 83:649-674.

MILLER, W. R. & MUÑOZ, R. S. *How to Control Your Drinking.* Englewood Cliffs, N.J.: Prentice-Hall, 1976.

MISCHEL, W. Processes in the delay of gratification. In L. Berkowitz (Ed.), *Advances in Experimental Social Psychology,* Vol. 7. New York: Academic Press, 1974.

MITCHELL, K. R. & WHITE, R. G. Self-management of tension headaches: A case study. *Journal of Behavior Therapy and Experimental Psychiatry,* 1976, 7:387-389.

MITCHELL, K. R. & WHITE, R. G. Self-management of severe predormital insomnia. *Journal of Behavior Therapy and Experimental Psychiatry,* 1977, 8:57-63.

MONEY, J. Bisexual, homosexual and heterosexual: Society, law and medicine. *Journal of Homosexuality,* 1977, 2:229-233.

MONROE, L. J. Psychological and physiological differences between good and poor sleepers. *Journal of Abnormal Psychology,* 1967, 72:255-264.

MOORE, B., MISCHEL, W., & ZEISS, A. Comparative effects of the reward stimulus and its cognitive representation in voluntary delay. *Journal of Personality and Social Psychology,* 1976, 34:419-424.

MOOS, R. H. *Evaluating Treatment Environment: A Social Ecological Approach.* New York: Wiley, 1974.

MOOS, R. H. *Evaluating Correctional and Community Settings.* New York: Wiley, 1975.

MOOS, R. H. *The Human Context: Environmental Determinants of Behavior.* New York: Wiley, 1976 (a).

MOOS, R. H. Evaluating and changing community settings. *American Journal of Community Psychology,* 1976, 4:313-326 (b).

MOWRER, O. H. *Learning Theory and Personality Dynamics.* New York: Arnold Press, 1950.

MUNJACK, D., CRISTOL, A., GOLDSTEIN, A., PHILLIPS, D., GOLDBERG, A., WHIPPLE, K., STAPLES, F., & KANNO, P. Behavioural treatment of orgasmic dysfunction: A controlled study. *British Journal of Psychiatry,* 1976, 129:497-502.

MUSANTE, G. J. The dietary rehabilitation clinic: Evaluative report of a behavioral and dietary treatment of obesity. *Behavior Therapy,* 1976, 7:198-204.

NASH, J. Curbing dropout from treatment for obesity. Paper presented at the Tenth Annual Convention of the Association for Advancement of Behavior Therapy, New York, December, 1976.

NATHAN, P. E. & BRIDDELL, D. W. Behavioral assessment and treatment of alcoholism. In B. Kissin & H. G. Beglieter (Eds.), *The Biology of Alcoholism,* Vol. 5. New York: Plenum Press, 1977.

NATHAN, P. E. & O'BRIEN, J. S. An experimental analysis of the behavior of alcoholics and nonalcoholics during prolonged experimental drinking. *Behavior Therapy,* 1971, 2:455-476.

NAY, W. R. Analogue measures. In A. R. Ciminero, K. S. Calhoun, & H. E. Adams (Eds.), *Handbook of Behavioral Measurement.* New York: Wiley, 1977.

NELSON, R. O., LIPINSKI, D. P., & BLACK, J. L. The effects of expectancy on the reactivity of self-recording. *Behavior Therapy,* 1975, 6:337-349.

NELSON, R. O., LIPINSKI, D. P., & BLACK, J. L. The reactivity of adult retardates' self-monitoring: A comparison among behaviors of different valences, and a comparison with token reinforcement. *The Psychological Record,* 1976, 26:189-201 (a).

NELSON, R. O., LIPINSKI, D. P., & BLACK, J. L. The relative reactivity of external observations and self-monitoring. *Behavior Therapy,* 1976, 7:314-321 (b).

NELSON, R. O., RUDIN-HAY, L., & HAY, W. M. Comments on Cone's "The relevance of reliability and validity for behavioral assessment." *Behavior Therapy,* 1977, 8: 427-430.

NIETZEL, M. T., WINETT, R. A., MACDONALD, M. L., & DAVIDSON, S. W. *Behavioral Approaches to Community Psychology.* New York: Pergamon Press, 1977.

NORD, W. R. (Ed.). *Concepts and Controversy in Organizational Behavior,* 2nd Ed. Santa Monica, Cal.: Good Year Publishing Co., 1976.

NOTZ, W. W. Work motivation and the negative effects of intrinsic rewards: A review of implications for theory and practice. *American Psychologist,* 1975, 30:884-890.

NORTON, G. R. & NIELSON, W. R. Headaches: The importance of consequent events. *Behavior Therapy,* 1977, 8:504-506.

NOVACO, R. W. Treatment of chronic anger through cognitive and relaxation controls. *Journal of Consulting and Clinical Psychology,* 1976, 44:681.

OBLER, M. Systematic desensitization in sexual disorders. *Journal of Behavior Therapy and Experimental Psychiatry,* 1973, 4:93-101.

OBSERVER. Concerning cognitive reversionism in psychology. *The Psychological Record,* 1977, 2:351-354.

OELSCHLAEGER, M. L. & BRUTTEN, G. J. The effect of instructional stimulation on the frequency of repetitions, interjections, and words spoken during the spontaneous speech of four stutterers. *Behavior Therapy,* 1976, 7:37-48.

O'LEARY, D. E., O'LEARY, M. R., & DONOVAN, D. M. Social skill acquisition and psychosocial development of alcoholics: A review. *Addictive Behaviors,* 1976, 1:111-120.

O'LEARY, S. G. & O'LEARY, K. D. Behavior modification in the school. In H. Leitenberg (Ed.), *Handbook of Behavior Modification.* Englewood Cliffs, N.J.: Prentice-Hall, 1976. Pp. 475-515.

O'LEARY, K. D., PELHAM, W. E., ROSENBAUM, A., & PRICE, G. H. Behavioral treatment of hyperkinetic children. *Clinical Pediatrics,* 1976, 15:510-515.

O'Leary, K. D. & Wilson, G. T. *Behavior Therapy: Application and Outcome.* Englewood Cliffs, N.J.: Prentice-Hall, 1975.

Olin, R. J. Thoughtstopping: Some cautionary observations. *Behavior Therapy*, 1976, 7:706-707.

Öst, L., Götestam, K. G., & Melin, L. A controlled study of two behavioral methods in the treatment of stuttering. *Behavior Therapy*, 1976, 7:587-592.

Page, M. M. Demand characteristics and the verbal operant conditioning experiment. *Journal of Personality and Social Psychology*, 1972, 23:372-378.

Page, S., Caron, P., & Yates, E. Behavior modification methods and institutional psychology. *Professional Psychology*, 1975, 9:175-181.

Page, T. J., Iwata, B. A., & Neef, N. A. Teaching pedestrian skills to retarded persons: Generalization from the classroom to the natural envidonment. *Journal of Applied Behavior Analysis*, 1976, 9:433-444.

Parsons, H. M. Caution behavior and its conditioning in driving. *Human Factors*, 1976, 18:397-408.

Patel, C. Reduction of serum cholesterol and blood pressure in hypertensive patients by behavior modification. *Journal of the Royal College of General Practitioners*, 1976, 26:211-215.

Patterson, E. L., Griffin, J. C., & Panyan, M. C. Incentive maintenance of self-help skill training programs for non-professional personnel. *Journal of Behavior Therapy and Experimental Psychiatry*, 1976, 7:249-253.

Patterson, G. R., Hops, H., & Weiss, R. Interpersonal skills training for couples in the early stages of conflict. *Journal of Marriage and the Family*, 1975, May 1975, 295-303.

Patterson, G. R., Weiss, R. L., & Hops, H. Training of marital skills: Some problems and concepts. In H. Leitenberg (Ed.), *Handbook of Behavior Modification and Behavior Therapy*. Englewood Cliffs, N.J.: Prentice-Hall, 1976.

Pattison, E. M. A conceptual approach to alcoholism treatment goals. *Addictive Behaviors*, 1976, 1:177-192 (a).

Pattison, E. M. Nonabstinent drinking goals in the treatment of alcoholics. In R. J. Gibbins, Y. Israel, H. Kalant, R. E. Popham, W. Schmidt, & R. G. Smart (Eds.), *Research Advances in Alcohol and Drug Problems*, Vol. III. New York: Wiley, 1976 (b).

Paul, G. L. *Insight Versus Desensitization in Psychotherapy*. Stanford: Stanford University Press, 1966.

Paul, G. & Bernstein, D. *Anxiety and Clinical Problems: Systematic Desensitization and Related Techniques*. Morristown, N.J.: General Learning Press, 1973.

Pearlman, J., Coburn, K., & Jakubowski-Spector, P. *Assertive Training for Women: A Stimulus Film*. American Personnel and Guidance Associations, 1973.

Peck, D. F. Operant conditioning and physical rehabilitation. *European Journal of Behavioral Analysis and Modification*, 1976, 3:158-164.

Peters, M. Aversive conditioning and alcoholism: A nineteenth century case report. *Canadian Psychological Review Psychologie Canadienne*, 1976, 17:61.

Peterson, D. R. *The Clinical Study of Social Behavior*. New York: Appleton-Century-Crofts, 1968.

Phillips, D., Fischer, S. C., Groves, G. A., & Singh, R. Alternative behavioral approaches to the treatment of homosexuality. *Archives of Sexual Behavior*, 1976, 5: 223-228.

Polly, S., Turner, R. D., & Sherman, A. R. A self-control program for the treatment of obesity. In J. D. Krumboltz & C. E. Thoresen (Eds.), *Counseling Methods*. New York: Holt, Rinehart & Winston, 1976.

Pomerleau, O., Bass, F., & Crown, V. Role of behavior modification in preventive medicine. *New England Journal of Medicine*, 1975, 292:1277-1282.

POMERLEAU, O., PERTSCHUK, M., & STINNET, J. A critical examination of some current assumptions in the treatment of alcoholism. *Journal of Studies on Alcohol*, 1976, 37:849-867 (a).

POMERLEAU, O. F., PERTSCHUK, M., ADKINS, D., & BRADY, J. P. *Comparison of Behavioral and Traditional Treatment for Problem Drinking.* Paper presented at the Annual Meeting of the Association for Advancement of Behavior Therapy, New York, December, 1976 (b).

POPLER, K. Agoraphobia: Indications for the application of the multimodal behavioral conceptualization. *The Journal of Nervous and Mental Disease*, 1977, 164:97-101.

PREMACK, D. Catching up with common sense on two sides of a generalization: Reinforcement and punishment. In R. Glaser (Ed.), *The Nature of Reinforcement.* New York: Academic Press, 1971.

PRITCHARD, R. D., CAMPBELL, K. M., & CAMPBELL, D. J. Effects of extrinsic financial rewards on intrinsic motivation. *Journal of Applied Psychology*, 1977, 62:9-15.

PRITCHARD, R. D., LEONARD, D. W., VON BERGEN, C. W., & KIRK, R. J. The effects of varying schedules of reinforcement on human task performance. *Organizational Behavior and Human Performance*, 1976, 16:205-230.

QUEIROZ, L. O. S., GUILHARDI, H. J., & MARTIN, G. L. A university program in Brazil to develop psychologists with specialization in behavior modification. *The Psychological Record*, 1976, 26:181-188.

QUINSEY, V. L. & BERGERSEN, S. G. Instructional control of penile circumference in assessments of sexual preference. *Behavior Therapy*, 1976, 7:489-493.

QUINSEY, C. L. & HARRIS, G. A comparison of two methods of scoring the penile circumference response: Magnitude and area. *Behavior Therapy*, 1976, 7:702-704.

QUINSEY, V. L., STEINMAN, C. M., BERGESEN, S. G., & HOLMES, R. G. Penile circumference, skin conductance, and ranking responses of child molesters and "normals" to sexual and nonsexual visual stimuli. *Behavior Therapy*, 1975, 6:213-219.

RABINOWITZ, S. & HALL, D. T. Organizational research on job involvement. *Psychological Bulletin*, 1977, 84:265-288.

RACHLIN, H. Self control. *Behaviorism*, 1974, 2:94-107.

RACHMAN, S. *The Effects of Psychotherapy*. New York: Pergamon Press, 1971.

RACHMAN, S. Observational learning and therapeutic modeling. In M. P. Feldman & A. Broadhurst (Eds.), *Theoretical and Experimental Bases of the Behaviour Therapies*. New York: Wiley, 1976 (a).

RACHMAN, S. The passing of the two-stage theory of fear and avoidance: Fresh possibilities. *Behaviour Research and Therapy*, 1976, 125-131 (b).

RACHMAN, S. & HODGSON, R. Synchrony and desynchrony in fear and avoidance: I. *Behaviour Research and Therapy*, 1974, 12:311-318.

RALEY, P. *Making Love*. New York: Dial Press, 1976.

RAPAVILAS, A. D., BOULOUGOURIS, J. C., & STEFANIS, C. Compulsive checking diminished when over-checking instructions were disobeyed. *Journal of Behavior Therapy and Experimental Psychiatry*, 1977, 8:111-112.

RAPPAPORT, J., DAVIDSON, W., WILSON, M., & MITCHELL, A. Alternatives to blaming the victim or the environment: Our places to stand have not moved the earth. *American Psychologist*, 1975, 30:525-528.

RATHUS, S. A. A 30-item schedule for assessing assertive behavior. *Behavior Therapy*, 1973, 4:398-406.

RATHUS, S. A. & NEVID, J. S. Concurrent validity of the 30-item Assertiveness Schedule with a psychiatric population. *Behavior Therapy*, 1977, 8:393-397.

RAW, M. Persuading people to stop smoking. *Behaviour Research and Therapy*, 1976, 14:97-101.

REDD, W. H. & SLEATOR, W. *Take Charge: A Personal Guide to Behavior Modification.* New York: Random House, 1976.

REEDER, C. W. & KUNCE, J. T. Modeling techniques, drug-abstinence behavior, and heroin addicts: A pilot study. *Journal of Counseling Psychology,* 1976, 23:560-562.

REID, D. H., LUYBEN, P. L., RAWERS, R. J., & BAILEY, J. S. The effects of prompting and proximity of containers on newspaper recycling behavior. *Environment and Behavior,* 1976, 8:471-482.

REISINGER, J. J., ORA, J. P., & FRANGIA, G. W. Parents as change agents for their children: A review. *Journal of Community Psychology,* 1976, 4:103-123.

REISS, M. L., PIOTROWSKI, W. D., & BAILEY, J. S. Behavioral community psychology: Encouraging low-income parents to seek dental care for their children. *Journal of Applied Behavior Analysis,* 1976, 9:387-397.

REKERS, G. A. Stimulus control over sex-typed play in cross-gender identified boys. *Journal of Experimental Child Psychology,* 1975, 20:136-148.

REKERS, G. A. & YATES, C. E. Sex-typed play in feminoid boys versus normal boys and girls. *Journal of Abnormal Child Psychology,* 1976, 4:1-8.

REKERS, G. A., YATES, C. E., WILLIS, T. J., ROSEN, A. C., & TAUBMAN, M. Childhood gender identity change: Operant control over sex-typed play and mannerisms. *Journal of Behavior Therapy and Experimental Psychiatry,* 1976, 7:51-57.

RENNE, C. M. & CREER, T. L. Training children with asthma to use inhalation therapy equipment. *Journal of Applied Behavior Analysis,* 1976, 9:1-11.

RESNICK, L. B. & LEINHARDT, G. Commentary on Stallings' Implementation and child effects of teaching practices in Follow Through classrooms. *Monographs of the Society for Research in Child Development,* 1975, 40:123-133.

RHOADS, J. M. & FEATHER, B. W. The application of psychodynamics to behavior therapy. *American Journal of Psychology,* 1974, 131:17-20.

RIBORDY, S. C. & DENNEY, D. R. The behavioral treatment of insomnia: An alternative to drug therapy. *Behaviour Research and Therapy,* 1977, 15:39-50.

RICH, A. R. & SCHROEDER, H. E. Research issues in assertiveness training. *Psychological Bulletin,* 1976, 83:1081-1096.

RICHARDS, D. S. Improving study behaviors through self-control techniques. In J. Krumboltz & C. E. Thoresen (Eds.), *Counseling Methods.* New York: Holt, Rinehart & Winston, 1976.

RIMLAND, B. *Infantile Autism.* New York: Appleton-Century-Crofts, 1964.

RIMM, D. C., SNYDER, J. J., DEPUE, R. A., HAANSTAD, M. J., & ARMSTRONG, D. P. Assertive training versus rehearsal and the importance of making an assertive response. *Behaviour Research and Therapy,* 1976, 14:315-321.

RITCHIE, R. J. A token economy system for changing controlling behavior in the chronic pain patient. *Journal of Behavior Therapy and Experimental Psychiatry,* 1976, 7:341-343.

RITVO, E. R. (Ed.). *Autism: Diagnosis, Current Research and Management.* New York: Spectrum, 1976.

ROBINSON, S. N. Littering behavior in public places. *Environment and Behavior,* 1976, 8:363-384.

ROLLINS, H. A., MCCANDLESS, B. R., THOMPSON, M. & BRASSELL, W. R. Project success environment: An extended application of contingency management in inner-city schools. *Journal of Educational Psychology,* 1974, 66:167-178.

ROMANCZYK, R. G. & GOREN, E. R. Severe self-injurious behavior: The problem of clinical control. *Journal of Consulting and Clinical Psychology,* 1975, 43:730-739.

ROMANCZYK, R. G., TRACEY, D. A., WILSON, G. T., & THORPE, G. L. Behavioral techniques in the treatment of obesity: A comparative analysis. *Behaviour Research and Therapy,* 1973, 11:629-640.

RÖPER, G. & RACHMAN, S. Obsessional-compulsive checking: Experimental replication and development. *Behaviour Research and Therapy,* 1976, 14:25-32.

Röper, G., Rachman, S., & Hodgson, R. An experiment on obsessional checking. *Behaviour Research and Therapy*, 1973, 11:271-277.

Rosen, G. *Don't Be Afraid: A Program for Overcoming Your Fears and Phobias.* Englewood Cliffs, N.J.: Prentice-Hall, 1976 (a).

Rosen, G. M. Subjects' initial therapeutic expectancies and subjects' awareness of therapeutic goals in systematic desensitization: A review. *Behavior Therapy*, 1976, 7:14-27 (b).

Rosen, G. M. The development and use of nonprescription behavior therapies. *American Psychologist*, 1976, 31:139-141 (c).

Rosen, G. M. *Non*prescription behavior therapies and other self-help treatments: A reply to Goldiamond. *American Psychologist*, 1977, 32:178-179.

Rosen, G. M., Glasgow, R. E., & Barrera, M. A two-year follow-up on systematic desensitization with data pertaining to the external validity of laboratory fear assessment. *Journal of Consulting and Clinical Psychology*, 1977, in press.

Rosen, G. M. & Ornstein, H. A historical note on thought stopping. *Journal of Consulting and Clinical Psychology*, 1976, 44:1016-1017.

Rosen, G. M. Suggestion for an editorial policy on the review of self-help treatment books. *Behavior Therapy*, in press.

Rosen, R. C. Suppression of penile tumescence by instrumental conditioning. *Psychosomatic Medicine*, 1973, 35:509-514.

Rosenthal, T. L. Modeling therapies. In M. Hersen, P. Miller, & R. Eisler (Eds.), *Progress in Behavior Modification*, Vol. 2. New York: Academic Press, 1976.

Rosenfield, S. & Houtz, J. Evaluation of behavior modification studies using criterion referenced measurement principles. *The Psychological Record*, 1976, 26:269-278.

Rosenthal, R. & Jacobson, L. *Pygmalion in the Classroom*. New York: Holt, Rinehart & Winston, 1968.

Rosenthal, T. L. & Reese, S. L. The effects of covert and overt modeling on assertive behavior. *Behaviour Research and Therapy*, 1976, 14:463-469.

Ross, R. R. & Price, M. J. Behavior modification in corrections: Autopsy before mortification. *International Journal of Criminology and Penology*, 1976, 4:305-315.

Ross, S. & Zimiles, H. The differentiated child behavior observational system. *Instructional Science*, 1976, 5:325-342.

Rossman, B. B. & Ulehla, Z. J. Psychological reward values associated with wilderness use: A functional reinforcement approach. *Environment and Behavior*, 1977, 9:41-66.

Rothman, I. Practice rhythmic desensitization for stuttering, insomnia, and anxiety. *Journal of the American Osteopathic Association*, 1969, 68:573-577.

Rozensky, R. H. & Bellack, A. S. Individual differences in self-reinforcement style and performance in self- and therapist-controlled weight reduction programs. *Behaviour Research and Therapy*, 1976, 14:347-364.

Rugh, J. D. & Schwitzgebel, R. L. Instrumentation for behavioral assessment. In A. R. Ciminero, K. S. Calhoun, & H. E. Adams, *Handbook of Behavioral Assessment*. New York: Wiley, 1977.

Rush, A. J., Beck, A. T., Kovacs, M., & Hollon, S. Comparative efficacy of cognitive therapy and pharmacotherapy in the treatment of depressed out-patients. *Cognitive Therapy and Research*, 1977, 1:17-37.

Russell, M. A. H., Armstrong, E., & Patel, U. A. Temporal contiguity in electric aversion therapy for cigarette smoking. *Behaviour Research and Therapy*, 1976, 14:103-123.

Ryan, V. L., Krall, C. A., & Hodges, W. F. Self-concept change in behavior modification. *Journal of Consulting and Clinical Psychology*, 1976, 44:638-645.

Sadler, O. W., Seyden, T., Howe, B., & Kaminsky, T. An evaluation of "groups for parents": A standardized format encompassing both behavior modification and humanistic methods. *Journal of Community Psychology,* 1976, 4:157-163.

Sager, C. J., Kaplan, H. S., Gundlach, R. H., Kremer, M., Lenz, R., & Royce, J. R. The marriage contract. *Family Process,* 1971, 10:311-326.

Salipante, P. & Goodman, P. Training, counseling, and retention of the hard-core unemployed. *Journal of Applied Psychology,* 1976, 61:1-11.

Sanders, R. M. *Behavior Modification in a Rehabilitation Facility.* Carbondale and Edwardsville, Ill.: Southern Illinois University Press, 1975.

Sanson-Fisher, R. W., Seymour, F. W., & Baer, D. M. Training institutional staff to alter delinquents' conversation. *Journal of Behavior Therapy and Experimental Psychiatry,* 1976, 7:243-247.

Sarason, S. B. *The Psychosocial Sense of Community: Prospects for a Community Psychology,* San Francisco: Jossey-Bass, 1974.

Sargent, J. D., Green, E. E., & Walters, E. D. The use of autogenic training in a pilot study of migraine and tension headaches. *Headache,* 1972, 120-124.

Sargent, J. D., Green, E. E., & Walters, E. D. Preliminary report on the use of autogenic feedback techniques in the treatment of migraine and tension headaches. *Psychosomatic Medicine,* 1973, 35:129-135.

Sargent, J. D., Walters, E. D., & Green, E. E. Psychosomatic self-regulation of migraine headache. *Seminars in Psychiatry,* 1973, 5:415-428 (a).

Saxon, W. A. The behavioral exchange model of marital treatment. *Social Casework,* 1976, 57:33-40.

Scaver, W. B. & Patterson, A. H. Decreasing fuel oil consumption through feedback and social commendation. Unpublished manuscript. The Pennsylvania State University, 1975. (Cited by Nietzel et al., 1977).

Schaefer, H. H., Tregerthan, G. J., & Colgan, A. H. Measured and self-estimated penile erection. *Behavior Therapy,* 1976, 7:1-7.

Schmahl, D. P., Lichtenstein, E., & Harris, D. E. Successful treatment of habitual smokers with warm, smoky air and rapid smoking. *Journal of Consulting and Clinical Psychology,* 1972, 28:105-111.

Schneidman, B. & McGuire, L. Group therapy for nonorgasmic women: Two age levels. *Archives of Sexual Behavior,* 1976, 5:239-247.

Schroeder, H. E. & Rich, A. R. The process of fear reduction through systematic desensitization. *Journal of Consulting and Clinical Psychology,* 1976, 44:191-199.

Schultz, C. B. & Sherman, R. H. Social class, developments, and differences in reinforcer effectiveness. *Review of Educational Research,* 1976, 46:25-59.

Schwartz, J. S. An evaluation of the contribution of a variety of self-reinforcement techniques and a behavioral contracting procedure to a therapeutic weight loss program. *Dissertation Abstracts International,* 1976, 36 (7-B), 3625. (Abst.)

Scott, J. W. & McLaughlin, T. F. The use of peers in classroom behavior change. *Contemporary Psychology,* 1976, 1:384-392.

Seidman, E. & Rappaport, J. The educational pyramid: A paradigm for training, research, and manpower utilization in community psychology. *American Journal of Community Psychology,* 1974, 2:119-130.

Seligman, M. E. P., Klein, D. C., & Miller, W. R. Depression. In H. Leitenberg (Ed.), *Handbook of Behavior Modification and Behavior Therapy.* Englewood Cliffs, N.J.: Prentice-Hall, 1976.

Shames, G. H. & Egolf, D. B. *Operant Conditioning and the Management of Stuttering: A Book for Clinicians.* Englewood Cliffs, N.J.: Prentice-Hall, 1976.

Shapiro, A. K. The behavior therapies: Therapeutic breakthrough or latest fad? *American Journal of Psychiatry,* 1976, 133:154-159 (a).

Shapiro, A. K. Reply to Brady. *American Journal of Psychiatry,* 1976, 133:852 (b).

Shapiro, D. & Surwit, R. S. Learned control of psychological function and disease. In

H. Leitenberg (Ed.), *Handbook of Behavior Modification and Behavior Therapy.* Englewood Cliffs, N.J.: Prentice-Hall, 1976.

SHAPIRO, M. Legislating the control of behavior control: Autonomy and the coercive use of organic therapies. *Southern California Law Review,* 1974, 47:337-356.

SHERMAN, A. R., MULAC, A., & MCCANN, M. S. Synergistic effect of self-relaxation and rehearsal feedback in the treatment of subjective and behavioral dimensions of speech anxiety. *Journal of Consulting and Clinical Psychology,* 1974, 42:819-827.

SHIMP, C. P. Organization in memory and behavior. *Journal of the Experimental Analysis of Behavior,* 1976, 26:113-130.

SHIVERICK, D. D. The ethics of conformity and behavior modification: A reply to Lindsey's stereotype of behavioral technology. *Corrective and Social Psychiatry and Journal of Behavior Technology Methods and Therapy,* 1976, 22:16-17.

SIDMAN, M. *Tactics of Scientific Research: Evaluating Experimental Data in Psychology.* New York: Basic Books, 1960.

SIECK, W. A. & MCFALL, R. M. Some determinants of self-monitoring effects. *Journal of Consulting and Clinical Psychology,* 1976, 44:958-965.

SIEGEL, L. J., DRAGOVICH, S. L., & MARHOLIN, D. The effects of biasing information on behavioral observations and rating scales. *Journal of Abnormal Child Psychology,* 1976, 4:221-233.

SILVERMAN, F. H. & TROTTER, W. D. Impact of pacing speech with a miniature electronic metronome upon the manner in which a stutterer is perceived. *Behavior Therapy,* 1973, 4:414-419.

SILVERMAN, L. H., FRANK, S. G., & DACHINGER, P. A psychoanalytic reinterpretation of the effectiveness of systematic desensitization. Experimental data bearing on the role of merging fantasies. *Journal of Abnormal Psychology,* 1974, 83:313-318.

SIMS, H. P. & SZILAGYI, A. D. Leader reward behavior and subordinate satisfaction and performance. *Organizational Behavior and Human Performance,* 1975, 16:426-438.

SKINNER, B. F. *Contingencies of Reinforcement.* New York: Appleton-Century-Crofts, 1969.

SKINNER, B. F. *Beyond Freedom and Dignity.* New York: Alfred A. Knopf, 1971.

SKOPEC, H. M. & CASSIDY, A. Sometimes our plans go awry. In M. D. LeBow (Ed.), *Approaches to Modifying Patient Behavior.* New York: Appleton-Century-Crofts, 1976.

SLOANE, R. B., STAPLES, F. R., CRISTOL, A. H., YORKSTON, N. J., & WHIPPLE, K. *Psychotherapy Versus Behavior Therapy.* Cambridge, Mass.: Harvard University Press, 1975.

SLOANE, R. B., STAPLES, F. R., WHIPPLE, K., & CRISTOL, A. H. Patients' attitudes toward behavior therapy and psychotherapy. *American Journal of Psychiatry,* 1977, 133: 134-137.

SLOVIC, P., FISCHOFF, B., & LICHTENSTEIN, S. Behavioral decision theory. *Annual Review of Psychology,* 1977, 28:1-34.

SMITH, L. C., HAWLEY, C. J., & GRANT, R. L. Questions frequently asked about the problem-oriented record in psychiatry. *Hospital and Community Psychiatry,* 1974, 24:17-22.

SMITH, P. E. Management modeling training to improve morale and customer satisfaction. *Personnel Psychology,* 1976, 29:351-359.

SMITH, R. R., MILAN, M. A., WOOD, L. F., & MCKEE, J. M. The correctional officer as a behavioral technician. *Criminal Justice and Behavior,* 1976, 3:345-359.

SOBELL, L. C. & SOBELL, M. B. Outpatient alcoholics give valid self-reports. *Journal of Nervous and Mental Disease,* 1975, 161:32-42.

SOBELL, M. B. & SOBELL, L. C. Individualized behavior therapy for alcoholics. *Behavior Therapy,* 1973, 4:49-72 (a).

SOBELL, M. B. & SOBELL, L. C. Alcoholics treated by individualized behavior therapy: One year treatment outcome. *Behaviour Research and Therapy*, 1973, 11:599-618 (b).

SOBELL, M. B., & SOBELL, L. C. Second year treatment outcome of alcoholics treated by individualized behavior therapy: Results. *Behaviour Research and Therapy*, 1976, 14:195-216.

SOBELL, L. C., SOBELL, M. B., & VANDERSPEK, R. Three independent comparisons between clinical judgment, self-report, and physiological measures of blood alcohol concentrations. Presented at the annual meeting of the Southeastern Psychological Association, New Orleans, March, 1976.

SPIEGLER, M. D., COOLEY, E. J., MARSHALL, G. J., PRINCE, H. T., PUCKETT, S. P., & SKENAZY, J. A. A self-control versus a counterconditioning paradigm for systematic desensitization: An experimental comparison. *Journal of Counseling Psychology*, 1976, 26:83-86.

SPIELBERGER, C. D. & DENIKE, L. D. Descriptive behaviorism versus cognitive theory in verbal operant conditioning. *Psychological Review*, 1966, 73:306-326.

SPIVAK, S., PLATT, J. J., & SHURE, M. D. *The Problem-Solving Approach to Adjustment.* San Francisco: Jossey-Boss, 1976.

STALLINGS, J. Implementation and child effects of teaching practices in follow through classrooms. *Monographs of the Society for Research in Child Development*, 1975, 40 (7-8, Serial No. 163).

STEERS, R. M. & BRAUNSTEIN, D. N. A behaviorally-based measure of manifest needs in work settings. *Journal of Vocational Behavior*, 1976, 9:251-266.

STEINBERG, E. P. & SCHWARTZ, G. E. Biofeedback and electrodermal self-regulation in psychopathy. *Journal of Abnormal Psychology*, 1976, 85:408-415.

STEINMARK, S. W. & BORKOVEC, T. D. Active and placebo treatment effects on moderate insomnia under counterdemand and positive demand instructions. *Journal of Abnormal Psychology*, 1974, 83:157-163.

STERN, R. Letter to the Editor. *British Journal of Psychiatry*, 1977, 130:418.

STERN, R. & MARKS, I. Brief and prolonged flooding. *Archives of General Psychiatry*, 1973, 28:270-276.

STOLZ, S. B., WIENCKOWSKI, L. A., & BROWN, B. S. Behavior modification: A perspective on critical issues. *American Psychologist*, 1975, 30:1027-1048.

STONE, N. M. & BORKOVEC, T. D. The paradoxical effect of brief CS exposure on analogue phobic subjects. *Behaviour Research and Therapy*, 1975, 13:51-54.

STORMS, M. D. & NISBETT, R. E. Insomnia and the attribution process. *Journal of Personality and Social Psychology*, 1970, 16:319-328.

STOYVA, J. Self-regulation and the stress related disorders: A perspective on biofeedback. In D. Mostofsky (Ed.), *Behavior Control and Modification of Physiological Activity*. Englewood Cliffs, N.J.: Prentice-Hall, 1976.

STRUPP, H. H. *Psychotherapy: Clinical, Research, and Theoretical Issues.* New York: Jason Aronson, 1973.

STRUPP, H. H. & HADLEY, S. W. A tripartite model of mental health and therapeutic outcomes: With special reference to negative effects in psychotherapy. *American Psychologist*, 1977, 32:187-196.

STUART, R. B. Behavioral control of overeating. *Behaviour Research and Therapy*, 1967, 5:357-365.

STUART, R. B. Operant interpersonal treatment for marital discord. *Journal of Consulting and Clinical Psychology*, 1969, 33:675-682.

STUART, R. B. A three-dimensional program for the treatment of obesity. *Behaviour Research and Therapy*, 1971, 9:177-186.

STUART, R. B. & DAVIS, B. *Slim Chance in a Fat World.* Champaign, Ill.: Research Press, 1972.

STUART, R. B. & LOTT, L. A. Behavioral contracting with delinquents: A cautionary note. *Journal of Behavior Therapy and Experimental Psychiatry,* 1972, 3:161-169.

STUART, R. B., TRIPODI, T., JAYARATNE, S., & CAMBURN, D. An experiment in social engineering in serving the families of predelinquents. *Journal of Abnormal Child Psychology,* 1976, 4:243-261.

STUMPHAUZER, J. S. Elimination of stealing by self-reinforcement of alternative behavior and family contracting. *Journal of Behavior Therapy and Experimental Psychiatry,* 1976, 7:265-268.

STUMPHAUZER, J. S. Modifying delinquent behavior: Beginnings and current practices. *Adolescence,* 1976, 41:13-28.

STUNKARD, A. J. Obesity and the social environment: Current status, future prospects. Paper presented at the Bicentennial Conference on Food and Nutrition in Health and Disease, Philadelphia, Pennsylvania, December 3, 1976 (a).

STUNKARD, A. J. *The Pain of Obesity.* Palo Alto, Ca.: Bull Publishing Co., 1976 (b).

STUNKARD, A. J. & MAHONEY, M. J. Behavioral treatment of the eating disorders. In H. Leitenberg (Ed.), *Handbook of Behavior Modification and Behavior Therapy.* New York: Appleton-Century-Crofts, 1976.

STUNKARD, A. J. Review of Mahoney and Mahoney's "Permanent weight control: A total solution to the dieter's dilemma." *Behavior Therapy,* 1977, 8:297-298.

SUEDFELD, P. & IKARD, F. F. Use of sensory deprivation in facilitating the reduction of cigarette smoking. *Journal of Consulting and Clinical Psychology,* 1974, 42:888-895.

SUFRIN, M. Review of Fensterheim and Baer's "Don't say yes when you want to say no." *Behavior Therapy,* 1977, 8:290-291.

SUINN, R. M. Behavioral methods at the Winter Olympic Games. *Behavior Therapy,* 1977, 8:152-153.

SUINN, R. M. & RICHARDSON, F. Anxiety management training: A nonspecific behavior therapy program for anxiety control. *Behavior Therapy,* 1971, 2:498-510.

TARLOW, G., ALEVIZOS, P. N., & CALLAHAN, E. J. Assessing the conversational behaviour of psychiatric patients: Reliability and validity of the Verbal Report Form (VRF). *Canadian Journal of Behavioral Science,* 1976, 8:334-346.

TASTO, D. L. Self-report schedules and inventories. In A. R. Ciminero, K. S. Calhoun, & H. E. Adams (Eds.), *Handbook of Behavioral Assessment.* New York: Wiley, 1977.

TAYLOR, C. B., FARQUHAR, J. W., NELSON, E., & AGRAS, S. The effects of relaxation therapy upon high blood pressure. *Archives of General Psychiatry,* 1977, 34:339-345.

THARP, R. G. & WETZEL, R. J. *Behavior Modification in the Natural Environment.* New York: Academic Press, 1969.

THASE, R. G. & MOSS, M. K. The relative efficacy of covert modeling procedures and guided participant modeling on the reduction of avoidance behavior. *Journal of Behavior Therapy and Experimental Psychiatry,* 1976, 7:7-12.

THORESEN, C. E. & EWART, C. K. Behavioral self-control and career development. *The Counseling Psychologist,* 1976, 6:29-42.

THORESEN, C. E. & MAHONEY, M. J. *Behavioral Self-control.* New York: Holt, Rinehart & Winston, 1974.

THORESEN, C. E. & WILBUR, C. S. Some encouraging thoughts about self-reinforcement. *Journal of Applied Behavior Analysis,* 1976, 9:518-520.

THORPE, G. L. Desensitization, behavior rehearsal, self-instructional training and placebo effects on assertive-refusal behavior. *European Journal of Behavioural Analysis and Modification,* 1975, 1:30-44.

THORPE, G. L., AMATU, H. I., BLAKEY, R. S., & BURNS, L. E. Contributions of overt instructional rehearsal and "specific insight" to the effectiveness of self-instructional training: A preliminary study. *Behavior Therapy,* 1976, 7:505-511.

TITTLER, B. I., ANCHOR, K. N., & WEITZ, L. J. Measuring change in openness: Behavtioral assessment techniques and the problem of the examiner. *Journal of Counseling Psychology,* 1976, 23:473-478.

TRACEY, D., KARLIN, R., & NATHAN, P. E. Behavioral analysis of chronic alcoholism in four women. *Journal of Consulting and Clinical Psychology,* 1976, 44:832-842.

TRICKETT, E. J. & MOOS, R. H. Personal correlates of contrasting environments: Student satisfactions in high school classrooms. *American Journal of Community Psychology,* 1974, 2:1-12.

TRIGG, L. J., PERLMAN, D., PERRY, R. P., & JANISSE, M. P. Anti-pollution behavior: A function of perceived outcome and locus of control. *Environment and Behavior,* 1976, 8:307-313.

TRYON, W. W. A system of behavioral diagnosis. *Professional Psychology,* 1976, 7:495-506.

TRYON, W. W. Models of behavior disorder: A formal analysis based on Wood's taxonomy of instrumental conditioning. *American Psychologist,* 1976, 31:509-518 (a).

TRYON, W. W. Behavior modification therapy and the law. *Professional Psychology,* 1976, 7:468-474 (b).

TRYON, W. W. Another example of a paradigm class: A reply to Bixenstine's "Criticisms." *American Psychologist,* 1977, 32:525-577.

TSOI-HOSHMAND, L. Behavioral competence training: A model of rehabilitation. *The International Journal of the Addictions,* 1976, 11:709-718.

TURIN, A. & JOHNSON, W. G. Biofeedback therapy for migraine headaches. *Archives of General Psychiatry,* April 1976, 33:517-519.

TURKEWITZ, H., O'LEARY, K. D., & IRONSMITH, M. Generalization and maintenance of appropriate behavior through self-control. *Journal of Consulting and Clinical Psychology,* 1975, 43:577-583.

TURNAGE, J. L. & MUCHINSKY, P. M. The effects of reward contingency and participative decision making on intrinsically and extrinsically motivating tasks. *Academy of Management Journal,* 1976, 19:482-489.

TURNER, R. D., POLLY, S., & SHERMAN, A. R. A behavioral approach to individualized exercise programming. In J. D. Krumboltz & C. E. Thoresen (Eds.), *Counseling Methods.* New York: Holt, Rineholt, & Winston, 1976.

TUSO, M. A. & GELLER, E. S. Behavior analysis applied to environmental/ecological problems: A review. *Journal of Applied Behavior Analysis,* 1976, 9:526.

ULLMANN, L. P. Foreword to M. T. Nietzel, R. A. Winett, M. L. MacDonald, & W. S. Davidson, *Behavioral Approaches to Community Psychology.* New York: Pergamon, 1977.

VALINS, S. & NISBETT, R. E. Attribution processes in the development and treatment of emotional disorders. In E. E. Jones, D. E. Kanouse, H. H. Henley, R. E. Nisbett, S. Valins, & B. Weiner (Eds.), *Attribution: Perceiving the Causes of Behavior.* Morristown, N.J.: General Learning Press, 1972.

VARGAS, E. A. Rights: A behavioristic analysis. *Behaviorism,* 1975, 3:178-190.

WACHTEL, P. L. *Psychoanalysis and Behavior Therapy: Towards an Integration.* New York: Basic Books, 1977.

WAHLER, R. G., HOUSE, A. E., & STENBAUGH, E. E. *Ecological Assessments of Child Problem Behavior.* New York: Pergamon, 1976.

WALKER, H. M. & HOPS, H. Use of normative peer data as a standard for evaluating classroom treatment effects. *Journal of Applied Behavior Analysis,* 1976, 9:159-168.

WATTS, F. N. Modification of the employment handicaps of psychiatric patients by behavioral methods. *The American Journal of Occupational Therapy,* 1976, 30: 487-490.

WEED, L. L. *Medical Records, Medical Education, and Patient Care.* Cleveland, Ohio: Case Western Reserve University Press, 1969.

WEIN, K. S., NELSON, R. O., & ODOM, J. V. The relative contributions of reattribution and verbal extinction to the effectiveness of cognitive restructuring. *Behavior Therapy,* 1975, 6:459-474.

WEINMAN, B., GELBART, P., WALLACE, M., & POST, M. Inducing assertive behavior in chronic schizophrenics: A comparison of socioenvironmental, desensitization, and relaxation therapies. *Journal of Consulting and Clinical Psychology,* 1972, 39:246-252.

WEISS, R. L., HOPS, H., & PATTERSON, G. R. A framework for conceptualizing marital conflict: A technology for altering it, some data for evaluating it. In L. A. Hamerlynck, L. C. Handy & E. J. Mash (Eds.), *Behavior Change: The Fourth Banff Conference on Behavior Modification.* Champaign, Ill.: Research Press, 1973.

WEITZMAN, B. Behavior therapy and psychotherapy. *Psychological Review,* 1967, 74:300-317.

WENRICH, W. W., DAWLEY, H. H., & GENERAL, D. A. *Self-Directed Desensitization: A Guide for the Student, Client and Therapist.* Kalamazoo, Mich.: Behaviordelia, 1976.

WERRY, J. S. & SPRAGUE, R. L. Hyperactivity. In C. G. Costello (Ed.), *Symptoms of Psychopathology.* New York: Wiley, 1970.

WEXLER, D. Token and taboo: Behavior modification, token economies and the law. *California Law Review,* 1973, 61:81-109.

WHITLEY, M. P. & POULSEN, S. B. Assertiveness and sexual satisfaction in employed professional women. *Journal of Marriage and the Family,* August, 1975, 573-581.

WICKRAMASEKERA, I. Aversive behavior rehearsal for sexual exhibitionism. *Behavior Therapy,* 1976, 7:167-176.

WIENER, Y. & GECHMAN, A. S. Commitment: A behavioral approach to job involvement. *Journal of Vocational Behavior,* 1977, 10:47-52.

WIENS, A. N. Pharmacologic aversive counterconditioning to alcohol in a private hospital: Some follow-up data. Paper presented at the Annual Meeting of the Alcohol and Drug Problems Association of North America, New Orleans, La., September, 1976.

WIENS, A. N., MONTAGUE, J. R., MANAUGH, T. S., & ENGLISH, C. J. Pharmacological aversive counterconditioning to alcohol in a private hospital: One-year follow-up. *Journal of Studies on Alcohol,* 1976, 37:1320-1324.

WILLIAMS, B. J., MARTIN, S., & FOREYT, J. P. *Obesity: Behavioral Approaches to Dietary Management.* New York: Brunner/Mazel, 1976.

WILLIAMS, R. B. & GENTRY, W. D. (Eds.). *Behavioral Approaches to Medical Treatment.* Cambridge, Mass.: Ballinger, 1977.

WILLIAMS, W. A comprehensive behaviour modification programme for the treatment of anorexia nervosa: Results in six cases. *Australian and New Zealand Journal of Psychiatry,* 1976, 10:321-324.

WILSON, E. O. *Sociobiology: The New Synthesis.* Cambridge, Mass.: Harvard University Press, 1975.

WILSON, G. T. Effects of false feedback on avoidance behavior: "Cognitive" desensitization revisited. *Journal of Personality and Social Psychology,* 1973, 28:115-122.

WILSON, G. T. Behavioral treatment of obsessive-compulsive disorders. In C. M. Franks (Ed.), *Behavior Therapy: Techniques, Principles and Patient Aids,* Vol. 2. New York: A BMA Audio Cassette Publication, 1976.

WILSON, G. T. Behavioral medicine as an alternative to ethnomedical science: A response to Fabrega. Paper presented at the National Academy of Science Conference on Substance Abuse, March, 1977 (a).

WILSON, G. T. Booze, beliefs, and behavior: Cognitive factors in alcohol use and abuse. Paper presented at NATO International Conference on Behavioral Approaches to Alcoholism, Bergen, Norway, August, 1977 (b).

WILSON, G. T. Training the behavior therapist: Models and methodology. Unpublished manuscript. Center for Advanced Study in the Behavioral Sciences, 1977 (c).

WILSON, G. T. Toward specifying the "nonspecifics" in behavior therapy. A social learning analysis. Unpublished manuscript, 1977 (d).

WILSON, G. T. Alcohol and human sexual behavior. *Behaviour Research and Therapy,* in press (a).

WILSON, G. T. Aversion therapy for alcoholism: Issues, ethics, and evidence. In G. A. Marlatt & P. E. Nathan (Eds.), *Behavioral Assessment and Treatment of Alcoholism.* New Brunswick, N.J.: Center for Alcohol Studies, in press (b).

WILSON, G. T. Cognitive behavior therapy: Paradigm shift or passing phase? In J. P. Foreyt & D. Rathjen (Eds.), *Cognitive Behavior Therapy: Research and Application.* New York: Plenum. In press (c).

WILSON, G. T. Toward specifying the "nonspecifics" in behavior therapy: A social learning analysis. In A. Burton (Ed.), *Pivotal Issues in Behavior Change.* San Francisco: Jossey-Bass, in press (d).

WILSON, G. T. On the much discussed nature of the term "behavior therapy." *Behavior Therapy,* in press (e).

WILSON, G. T. & DAVISON, G. C. Behavior therapy and homosexuality: A critical perspective. *Behavior Therapy,* 1974, 5:16-28.

WILSON, G. T. & EVANS, I. M. Adult behavior therapy and the therapist-client relationship. In C. M. Franks & G. T. Wilson (Eds.), *Annual Review of Behavior Therapy: Theory and Practice,* Vol. IV. New York: Brunner/Mazel, 1976.

WILSON, G. T. & EVANS, I. M. The therapist-client relationship in behavior therapy. In R. S. Gurman & A. M. Razin (Eds.), *The Therapist's Contribution to Effective Psychotherapy: An Empirical Approach.* New York: Pergamon, in press, 1977.

WILSON, G. T. & LAWSON, D. M. Expectancies, alcohol, and sexual arousal in male social drinkers. *Journal of Abnormal Psychology,* 1976, 85:587-594 (a).

WILSON, G. T. & LAWSON, D. M. The effects of alcohol on sexual arousal in woman. *Journal of Abnormal Psychology,* 1976, 85:489-497 (b).

WILSON, G. T. & LAWSON, D. M. Expectancies, alcohol, and sexual arousal in women. Unpublished manuscript, Rutgers University, 1977.

WILSON, G. T., LEAF, R. C., & NATHAN, P. E. The aversive control of excessive alcohol consumption by chronic alcoholics in the laboratory setting. *Journal of Applied Behavior Analysis,* 1975, 8:13-26.

WILSON, G. T. & TRACEY, D. A. An experimental analysis of aversive imagery versus electrical aversive conditioning in the treatment of chronic alcoholics. *Behaviour Research and Therapy,* 1976, 14:41-51.

WINCZE, J. P. & CAIRD, W. K. The effects of systematic desensitization and video desensitization in the treatment of essential sexual dysfunction in women. *Behavior Therapy,* 1976, 7:335-342.

WINE, J. Test anxiety and direction of attention. *Psychological Bulletin,* 1971, 76:92-104.

WINETT, R. A. Disseminating a behavioral approach to energy conservation. *Professional Psychology,* 1976, 7:222-228.

WINETT, R. A. & NIETZEL, M. T. Behavioral ecology: Contingency management of consumer energy use. *American Journal of Community Psychology,* 1975, 3:123-133.

WINKLER, R. C. New directions for behaviour modification in homosexuality, open education and behavioural economics. In P. W. Sheehan & K. D. White (Eds.), *Behaviour Modification in Australia.* Parkville, Victoria: Australian Psychological Society, 1976.

WINSHIP, B. J. & KELLEY, J. D. A verbal response model of assertiveness. *Journal of Counseling Psychology,* 1976 23:215-220.

WITMER, J. F. & GELLER, E. Facilitating paper recycling: Effects of prompts, raffles and contests. *Journal of Applied Behavior Analysis,* 1976, 9:315-322.

WODARSKI, J. S. Procedural steps in the implementation of behavior modification programs in open settings. *Journal of Behavior Therapy and Experimental Psychiatry,* 1976, 7:133-136.

WOHLWILL, J. F., NASAR, J. L., DEJOY, D. M., & FORUZANI, H. H. Behavioral effects of a noisy environment: Task involvement versus passive exposure. *Journal of Applied Psychology,* 1976, 61:67-74.

WOLFF, E. & EPSTEIN, L. H. A procedure for implementing the problem-oriented medical record in open settings. *Behavior Therapy,* 1977, 8:506-507.

WOLFF, W. T. & MERRENS, M. R. Behavioral assessment: A review of clinical methods. *Journal of Personality Assessment,* 1974, 38:3-16.

WOLLERSHEIM, J. P. Effectiveness of group therapy based upon learning principles in the treatment of overweight women. *Journal of Abnormal Psychology,* 1970, 76: 462-474.

WOLPE, J. *Psychotherapy by Reciprocal Inhibition.* Stanford: Stanford University Press, 1958.

WOLPE, J. Behavior therapy and its malcontents, I. Denial of its bases and psychodynamic fusionism. *Journal of Behavior Therapy and Experimental Psychiatry,* 1976, 7:1-5 (a).

WOLPE, J. Behavior therapy and its malcontents II. Multimodal eclecticism, cognitive exclusivism and "exposure" empiricism. *Journal of Behavior Therapy and Experimental Psychiatry,* 1976, 7:109-116 (b).

WOLPE, J. Conditioning is the basis of all psychotherapeutic change. In A. Burton (Ed.), *What Makes Behavior Change Possible?* New York: Brunner/Mazel, 1976 (c).

WOLPE, J. *Theme and Variations: A Behavior Therapy Casework.* New York: Pergamon, 1976 (d).

WOLPE, J. Behaviourism. *British Medical Journal,* February 12, 1977, 441 (a).

WOLPE, J. Inadequate behavior analysis: The Achilles heel of outcome research in behavior therapy. *Journal of Behavior Therapy and Experimental Psychiatry,* 1977, 8:1-3 (b).

WOOLFOLK, A. E., WOOLFOLK, R. L., & WILSON, G. T. A rose by any other name. . . . Labeling bias and attitudes toward behavior modification. *Journal of Consulting and Clinical Psychology,* 1977, 45:184-192.

WOOLFOLK, R. L. Psychophysiological correlates of meditation. *Archives of General Psychiatry,* 1975, 32:1326-333.

WOOLFOLK, R. L., CARR-KAFFASHAN, L., & MCNULTY, T. F. Meditation training as a treatment for insomnia. *Behavior Therapy,* 1976, 7:359-365.

WRIGHT, J. C. A comparison of systematic desensitization and social skill acquisition in the modification of a social fear. *Behavior Therapy,* 1976, 7:205-210.

WRIGHT, J. & FITCHEN, C. Denial of responsibility, videotape feedback and attribution theory: Relevance for behavioral marital theory. *Canadian Psychological Review,* 1976, 17:219-230.

YEN, S. & MCINTIRE, R. W. (Eds.). *Teaching Behavior Modification.* Kalamazoo, Mi.: Behaviordelia, 1976.

YOUNG, L. D., LANGFORD, H. G., & BLANCHARD, E. G. Effect of operant conditioning of heart rate on plasma renin activity. *Psychosomatic Medicine,* 1976, 38:278-281.

YOUNG, L. G. A model for reinforcing mental health facilities: A student's view. *Community Mental Health Journal,* 1976, 12:422-431.

YULIS, S. Generalization of therapeutic gain in the treatment of premature ejaculation. *Behavior Therapy,* 1976, 7:355-358.

ZEISS, R. A. Self-directed treatment for premature ejaculation: Preliminary case reports. *Journal of Behavior Therapy and Experimental Psychiatry,* in press.

ZIMMERMAN, J. & ZIMMERMAN, E. H. Towards humanizing education: Classroom behavior management revisited. *The Psychological Record,* 1976, 26:387-397.

ZUSMAN, J. Can program evaluation be saved from its enthusiasts? *American Journal of Psychiatry,* 1976, 133:1300-1304.